S0-AFY-887

Studies in Emotion and Social Interaction

Paul Ekman
University of California, San Francisco

Klaus R. Scherer
Justus-Liebig-Universität Giessen

General Editors

Handbook of Methods in Nonverbal Behavior Research

Studies in Emotion and Social Interaction

This series is jointly published by the Cambridge University Press and the Editions de la Maison des Sciences de l'Homme, as part of the joint publishing agreement established in 1977 between the Fondation de la Maison des Sciences de l'Homme and the Syndics of the Cambridge University Press.

Cette collection est publiée en co-édition par Cambridge University Press et les Editions de la Maison des Sciences de l'Homme. Elle s'intègre dans le programme de co-édition etabli en 1977 par la Fondation de la Maison des Sciences de l'Homme et les Syndics de Cambridge University Press.

Handbook of Methods in Nonverbal Behavior Research

Edited by Klaus R. Scherer *and* Paul Ekman

Cambridge University Press

Cambridge
London New York New Rochelle
Melbourne Sydney

Editions de la Maison des Sciences de l'Homme

Paris

152.384
H191

Published by the Press Syndicate of the University of Cambridge
The Pitt Building, Trumpington Street, Cambridge CB2 1RP
32 East 57th Street, New York, NY 10022, USA
296 Beaconsfield Parade, Middle Park, Melbourne 2306, Australia
and
Editions de la Maison des Sciences de l'Homme
54 Boulevard Raspail, 75270 Paris Cedex 06

© Maison des Sciences de l'Homme and Cambridge University Press 1982

First published 1982

Printed in the United States of America

Library of Congress Cataloging in Publication Data

Main entry under title:

Handbook of methods in nonverbal behavior research.

(Studies in emotion and social interaction)

Includes index.
1. Nonverbal communication (psychology)–Research.
2. Psychological research–Methodology.
I. Scherer, Klaus Rainer.
II. Ekman, Paul. III. Series.
BF637.C45H29 152.3'84 81-9940 AACR2

ISBN 0 521 23614 2 hard covers
ISBN 0 521 28072 9 paperback

Contents

Contributors

Klaus R. Scherer
Department of Psychology
Justus-Liebig-Universität Giessen

Paul Ekman
Human Interaction Laboratory
Department of Psychiatry
University of California, San Francisco

Ralph V. Exline
Department of Psychology
University of Delaware

B. J. Fehr
Department of Psychology
University of Delaware

Adam Kendon
Department of Anthropology
Connecticut College

Howard M. Rosenfeld
Department of Psychology
University of Kansas

Robert Rosenthal
Department of Psychology and Social Relations
Harvard University

J. A. R. A. M. van Hooff
Vakgroep Vergelijkende Fysiologie
Rijks Universiteit, Utrecht

Harald G. Wallbott
Department of Psychology
Justus-Liebig-Universität Giessen

Candace West
Department of Sociology
University of California, Santa Cruz

Don H. Zimmerman
Department of Sociology
University of California, Santa Barbara

Editorial preface

In the last 20 years social and behavioral scientists have focused increasingly on nonverbal behaviors such as facial and vocal expression, gaze, and body movement, often in a context of research on communication and face-to-face interaction. Although no coherent body of knowledge or theory has emerged, specialized research methods have been developed that are useful to investigators other than those who consider themselves specialists in nonverbal behavior. Mother–infant interaction, patterning of emotional behavior, sign languages among the deaf, and interpersonal sensitivity are just a few of the research areas to which these methods are relevant. This handbook addresses both specialists in "nonverbal communication" and researchers interested in nonverbal behavior as but one aspect of their research topics. Anyone concerned with measuring what a person does in addition to and/or while speaking will find pertinent information about the relevant methods here.

This information has not been widely available heretofore, even to those who specialize in the study of nonverbal behavior. Not the province of any one discipline, not tied to any single set of theoretical issues, reports are scattered across many journals, many of them with limited circulation. The methods employed are rarely described in detail and almost never presented in comparison to alternative approaches.

This handbook provides authoritative critical reviews of each of a number of separate research methods relevant to nonverbal behavior. Each chapter provides an in-depth critical evaluation of the paradigms and techniques available for measuring and analyzing a particular aspect of nonverbal behavior. We sought as authors individuals who not only were experts in the use of particular methods but also were willing to undertake, critically and evenhandedly, reviews evaluating the alternative methods and options available.

The first chapter introduces the handbook by providing some idea of the historical development of empirical research on nonverbal behavior, noting the contribution of some of the pivotal figures or research traditions. The choices that underlie different methods and approaches are discussed, and the decisions faced in undertaking this type of research are made explicit. The next four chapters deal with the measurement of distinct behavioral elements produced by different types of motor activity in different parts of the body: facial movement, eye movement or gaze, vocalization, and body movement.

In Chapter 2, Paul Ekman reviews the role of the face as a signal system, contrasts and critically compares several procedures for facial movement, and gives a detailed account of his own measurement system.

Ralph Exline and Barbara Fehr, in Chapter 3, systematically describe the variables that can be used to measure gaze in social interaction and review the various methodological decisions that are relevant for conducting such studies.

In Chapter 4, Klaus Scherer outlines the functions of vocalizations, reviews appropriate research designs, and describes the relevant parameters and assessment procedures for acoustic analysis and auditory evaluation of vocalizations.

In Chapter 5, Howard Rosenfeld explores the dimensions that can be used to characterize body movement and orientation and describes instruments and coding schemes that have been designed to measure gestures and body motion.

In Chapter 6, Robert Rosenthal deals with research designs and methods suitable to investigating the inferences observers draw from different nonverbal behaviors in judgment studies, systematically discussing such matters as judge sampling and stimulus presentation, as well as various statistical analysis techniques.

Going beyond the measurement of behavior elements in Chapter 7, Jan van Hooff brings an ethological perspective to the question how the sequential and hierarchial organization of these types of nonverbal behavior can be categorized and analyzed.

In Chapter 8, Adam Kendon is concerned with research strategies for the study of the organization of behavior, verbal and nonverbal, in interaction systems. After reviewing the antecedents and the history of what has been termed the structural approach, he presents a detailed outline, using the study of greetings as an example, of the development of an appropriate, theoretically based, strategy of investigation.

In Chapter 9, Candace West and Don Zimmerman deal with the study of conversation as a communication system, outlining the paradigms and procedures recently developed in the research tradition of conversational analysis.

An increasing number of studies of nonverbal behavior use film, videotape, or audiotape records for analysis. An appendix deals with these practical issues. Harald Wallbott reviews the advantages and disadvantages of different recording systems and provides some advice for recording procedures and troubleshooting.

The chapters, taken together, offer both an overview of the questions being asked about the assessment of nonverbal behavior and a detailed survey of the methods available for systematic description and analysis of particular types of behavior, their advantages, and their disadvantages. The authors not only provide a "state of the art" report but, further, point new directions for further research.

Preliminary versions of the chapters in this handbook served as the basis for lecture and workshop presentations at a NATO Advanced Study Institute, "Methods of Research in Nonverbal Communication," held at Birkbeck College, London, from September 5 through 15, 1979. In many cases, the chapters benefited from critical feedback and advice from the faculty members of the Institute – including, in addition to the authors of the chapters, Mario von Cranach, Heiner Ellgring, Pierre Garrigues, Erving Goffman, Rolf Kuschel, Hubert Montagner, Harriet Oster, and Pio Ricci-Bitti – and also from the 120 participants from 15 countries.

We are grateful to the NATO Scientific Affairs Division for supporting the organization of the conference that provided the basis for this handbook. We are grateful also to Angela Summerfield and her associates at London University for providing a most hospitable and stimulating locale for the conference.

We appreciate the interest and help of our editor at Cambridge University Press, Susan Milmoe.

Paul Ekman's work as an editor of this volume was supported in part by a Research Scientist Award from the National Institute of Mental Health, MH 06092, and a grant from the Harry Frank Guggenheim Foundation. Klaus Scherer's work as an editor was supported by the Justus-Liebig-Universität Giessen.

KLAUS R. SCHERER
PAUL EKMAN

1. Methodological issues in studying nonverbal behavior

KLAUS R. SCHERER AND PAUL EKMAN

1.1. A selective historical sketch of methodological development in nonverbal behavior research

Interest in the actions of the voice, the face, and the body can be traced back to the writings of the earliest philosophers. The expression of emotion and intention and the role of nonverbal behavior in rhetoric have occupied some of the major thinkers over the centuries (see Key, 1977; Laver, 1980). Much of the relevant writing, however, is characterized by speculation and introspection. In some cases, a primitive type of systematic observation constituted the basis for inference (Bell, 1806; Duchenne, 1862; Piderit, 1867). Yet, despite some systematic experimental work on expression by anatomists and physiologists during the eighteenth and early nineteenth centuries, the history of the empirical study of nonverbal behavior begins with Charles Darwin and his monumental study, "The expression of the emotions in man and animals" (1872/1965). In this seminal book, Darwin not only introduced some of the major substantive and theoretical issues that still guide much of the research in this area, but also pioneered some of the methods of research.

Two theoretical issues posed by Darwin are at the root of much of the recent controversy in the field. The first issue, central to Darwin's interest in evolution, concerns the issue of the innateness versus the social learning of nonverbal behavior. Although Darwin did not deny that culture and social structure strongly affect nonverbal behavior, he was convinced that facial expressions are biologically determined and, furthermore, that there is phylogenetic continuity in their evolution. This central notion of biological determinism has strongly affected the choice of methods used in collecting evidence for its support. An important aspect of Darwin's methods is the comparative approach, that is, comparing expressive behavior in many animal species, including man. The basis for such comparison is systematic observation in the form of repeated, close scrutiny of the behavior of an organism in different states and the detailed and careful description of even minute observable changes in action and appearance.

Darwin meticulously observed expressive behavior patterns and in many cases used drawings and photographs to obtain a permanent iconic image of the behavior under study. As objects of study he used naturally occurring expressions as well as experimentally induced ones and expressions posed by actors. He also drew extensively on anecdotal reports in the literature, on the visual arts, and on reports by acquaintances and fellow scientists, particularly about facial expression in different cultures. Although Darwin was impressed on the voyage of the *Beagle* with his ability to understand the facial expressions of individuals from many countries, he obtained more systematic data later. From England he sent a list of questions to 36 people living or working in other countries; he asked, for example, "Is astonishment expressed by the eyes and mouth being raised?" (Darwin, 1872/1965, p. 15).

The second theoretical issue, which is closely related to the first, is the communicative use of expressive signs. In many ways, Darwin pioneered the functional analysis of behavior that characterizes modern ethology. Most of his theoretical efforts consisted of attempts to derive the underlying functional significance of the observable expressive behavior. Darwin clearly acknowledged the fact that some nonverbal behaviors, specifically symbolic gestures, serve primarily communicative functions, and that these are used "voluntarily and consciously" in a culturally shared code, although he was convinced that all of these movements had "some natural and independent origin" (Darwin, 1872/1965, p. 355). Although conventional gestures that varied across cultures might have as their main function communication, Darwin maintained that the innate facial expressions did not originate in a need to communicate, although they provided important information to others.

Darwin was the first to study observers' judgments of facial expression, noting that observers who did not know the context in which an expression occurred still agreed about the emotion shown. The judgment method has become one of the most commonly used in studies of nonverbal behavior (see Rosenthal, Chapter 6). Darwin also experimented, often with his own children, to observe reactions to a variety of sounds, gestures, and facial expressions. Clearly, modern methodologists would have many objections to details of Darwin's procedures; these would reflect the nascent state of most methods during the last half of the nineteenth century. Yet, at the same time, Darwin's approach compares very favorably with that taken in modern single-shot studies, so far as comprehensiveness, appropriateness of the methods, and detail of observation are concerned.

Darwin's contemporaries in other disciplines, particularly the early German anthropological psychologists (see Allport, 1968, pp. 48–50), also showed much interest in nonverbal behavior. In the process of examining differences and similarities between different races and cultures, they paid much attention to communication systems such as language, gestures, and facial expression (Kleinpaul, 1888/1972; Wundt, 1900–1920). However, their writings, which were mostly compilations of reports from ethnographic studies and of anecdotes, did not spawn much of a research tradition. Such a tradition was established at the beginning of the twentieth century, when the psychology of expression (*Ausdruckspsychologie*) attained a dominant position in German psychology and quickly spread to other countries (without, however, achieving a similar importance). The basic tenet of this tradition was the assumption that individual differences between persons manifest themselves in a particular style of expressive movement, which homomorphically affects all aspects of motor activity, such as facial and bodily movement, handwriting, vocalization, and so on. Whereas many of the representatives of this approach were given to nonempirical pursuits like introspection and phenomenology, others did use more empirical, quantitative methods. In many cases they produced fairly precise observations and descriptions of nonverbal phenomena, often using induction methods (e.g., producing an emotion by imagination or by exposing subjects to arousing stimuli). Furthermore, they introduced systematic behavior sampling methods, obtaining as a result different behavior samples, from several persons, sometimes at several points in time (e.g., Allport & Vernon, 1933; Bühler, 1933; Pear, 1931; Wolff, 1943). In this tradition we also find the first consistent attempts to use quantitative measurement and statistical analysis.

Under the influence of Nazism, segments of German psychology degenerated into an ideology of racial determinism. Some German psychologists attempted to show that the superiority of the Aryan races was manifest even in expressive behavior patterns. In an attempt to procure evidence that would prove these claims wrong, a young social scientist at Columbia University, David Efron, conducted a classic study, published in book form in 1941, which is still counted among the best studies in the field of nonverbal behavior, both in theoretical rigor and in development of appropriate methodology (Efron, 1941/1972).

Efron used both naturalistic observation and some experimental induction in his study of the gestures of Jewish and Italian immigrants in New York. He was one of the first to use film extensively to document sequences of nonverbal behavior (see also Bateson & Mead, 1942), and he made much use of the frame-by-frame analysis methods that have become one of the hallmarks of nonverbal behavior analysis. In addition, Efron used drawings to code iconically the most important aspects of the movement patterns, thus developing a rudimentary transcription system. He also recognized that the functional classification of movement patterns is an important part of an analysis of bodily movement as an element of expression and communication systems. His distinction of types of hand movements was adopted and further developed in later studies (Ekman & Friesen, 1969, 1975; see Rosenfeld, Section 5.7). Finally, Efron used observers to determine how particular gestures would be decoded, in order to assess their role in a nonverbal signaling system. Interestingly, Efron ignored the face almost entirely, focusing his efforts primarily on body movement. Many of the classes of behavior he noted for the body, such as speech emphasis, can also be seen in facial actions (see Ekman, 1979). It is difficult to overestimate the important role of David Efron as a pioneer for both conceptual and methodological development in the field (see also Rosenfeld, Chapter 5). Unfortunately, many researchers have remained ignorant of his work or have not acknowledged its influence; often methods used by Efron were "rediscovered" many years later.

Another pioneer who has had much influence on the field both conceptually and methodologically, although his work has generated curiously little empirical research, is Ray Birdwhistell. An anthropologist by training, Birdwhistell was heavily influenced by structural linguistics (particularly the work of Harris, Bloomfield, Trager, and Smith) and introduced this way of thinking and its methodology to the analysis of movement behavior. Proceeding from the assumption that human movement is organized in a code with a design similar to that of language (see Hockett, 1960), Birdwhistell (1952) attempted to create a science of "kinesics" in analogy to phonetics. Accordingly, he attempted to define movement units within a hierarchically organized code, which he believes to be almost entirely determined by cultural convention and learning. Birdwhistell, along with other researchers, advocated the heavy use of cinematic techniques and the microanalysis of the filmed behavior, with slow motion and frame-by-frame analysis (as Efron had recommended 10 years earlier); Birdwhistell also developed a transcription system that was one of the first instances of an attempt at exhaustive symbolic transcription of nonverbal behavior (apart from attempts at dance notation; see Hutchinson, 1970). Though this system has not ever been used extensively, only for illustrative purposes on very short behavior samples, it has had a strong impact on discussion about the transcription and analysis of nonverbal behavior. Kendon provides a detailed description of Birdwhistell's approach and an appreciation of his role in Section 8.2. Critical evaluations of the system can be found in Ekman (1957, p. 146; Section 2.2) and Rosenfeld (Section 5.7).

One of the most notable developments of the fifties and sixties was the strengthened concern of psychiatrists and clinical psychologists with nonverbal behavior, a concern resulting in the establishment of many new approaches and methods. Even though most of these researchers were concerned with mental patients, the rationales for studying nonverbal behavior and the approaches used differed widely, depending on the goals of the inquiry – evaluating the diagnostic value of nonverbal behavior, tracing the etiology of the illness in patterns of social communication, or studying the process of clinical interviews – as well as on the theoretical persuasion of the clinician – psychoanalysis, transactional analysis, behavior therapy, and so on. It would be most interesting to trace the development of interests and the mutual influences of the major researchers in this period in detail. Here only some of the major strands of research can be taken into account.

One distinctive approach, sometimes referred to as the *natural history* approach (reviewed in detail by Kendon in Section 8.2), represents the confluence of ideas from anthropology, structural linguistics, information theory, and psychiatry and is associated with the names of Bateson, Birdwhistell, Brosin, Fromm-Reichmann, Hockett, and McQuown. This group was particularly concerned with a structural analysis of the communication patterns between patients and therapists, using phonetic, paralinguistic, and "kinesic" transcription techniques. One of the problems that has plagued this approach is that it is never quite clear what rules control the identification of structural units and hierarchical organization. More recently, Scheflen (1966, 1973) and Kendon (1970, 1973, Chapter 8) have attempted to indicate with greater specificity how to proceed in order to identify the structural organization of behavior.

Another approach to the analysis of nonverbal behavior stemming from clinical concerns is the psychoanalytic approach. Freud and some of his contemporaries commented on the fact that nonverbal behavior might reveal unconscious processes that are repressed and consequently not verbalized (Ferenczi, 1926; Freud, 1904; Reich, 1949). Psychiatrists in this tradition have looked at both body motion and vocalization, and mostly have used clinical observation, filmed records, microanalysis, and functional behavior classification to assess the diagnostic value of nonverbal behavior for nonverbalized affect. A number of conceptual–methodological distinctions were contributed, some of which continue to be used today. Krout (1931) distinguished autistic movements from gestures, Mahl (1968) showed the usefulness of distinguishing movements that are directed at the self and communicative movements, and Ekman and Friesen (1969) and Freedman (1972) both elaborated these distinctions in dealing with hand movements. Ekman (1965) also contrasted the information available from the face and body, as Dittmann (1962) had done and as many others have done since then. Mahl and Schulze (1964) worked with vocalization patterns, such as *ah* and non-*ah* speech disturbance types, which have paved the way for more detailed analysis of vocal behavior.

In the area of voice analysis, clinicians have been pragmatically interested in the diagnostic use of vocal characteristics for signs of particular syndromes and for changes over time. Among the methodological contributions that have been made in this area are the identification of categories for the auditory evaluation of voice quality characteristics (e.g., Moses, 1954) and the use of acoustic analysis techniques for the assessment of nonlinguistic aspects of vocalizations (Ostwald, 1963).

Yet another approach linked to the practice of psychiatry and clinical psychology and centered mainly around the analysis of interview processes is the *interaction chronography* approach pioneered by Chapple (1948/49) and subsequently utilized by Matarazzo and Wiens and their co-workers (Matarazzo & Wiens, 1972) and Jaffe and Feldstein and their collaborators (Feldstein & Welkowitz, 1978; Jaffe & Feldstein, 1970). The methodological innovation introduced by this tradition is the objective and sometimes automatic measurement of time-based parameters of conversation sequences (see Scherer, Section 4.6).

Although also coming to the field with clinical interests, Paul Ekman, trained as a psychologist, turned toward the investigation of some of the more basic issues concerning nonverbal behavior, such as the nature of emotional expression and the semiotic aspects of nonverbal behavior (resurrecting the questions studied by Darwin and Efron, and influenced also by Tomkins and contemporary ethologists). Ekman developed a theoretical classification of five types of nonverbal behavior, based on differences in origins, usage, and coding. In addition, he attempted to make full use of the methodological canon of psychology in the analysis of nonverbal behavior, including the measurement of frequency and rate of behavioral phenomena, systematic sampling procedures, the construction of category and coding systems with known reliability, and the use of statistical analysis. Together with Wallace Friesen, he invested much research effort in the development of measurement systems for body motion (particularly speech illustrator movements and symbolic gestures) and the more recent development of an anatomical system for measuring the face (Ekman, 1957; Ekman & Friesen, 1969, 1976, 1978). Ekman and Friesen's methods and conceptual framework have been used by many other investigators.

A research tradition with increasing impact on the study of human nonverbal behavior is ethology and, more recently, the special branch of human ethology. Because all animal behavior is nonverbal, animal ethologists have had to develop methods of observation and analysis suitable to uncovering the organization underlying the observable behavior patterns (Eibl-Eibesfeldt, 1970; Hinde, 1972). Among the important contributions made within this tradition is the development of sophisticated techniques for the analysis of sequences and clusters of behavior (see van Hooff, Chapter 7). This approach has had a very strong influence on the recent surge of interest in the study of human development and mother–infant interaction, where these techniques are used and further refined (Blurton Jones, 1971).

Finally, methodological impulses come from the research tradition of conversational analysis as developed in microsociology and ethnomethodology (Garfinkel, 1967; Goffman, 1963, 1971; Schegloff, 1968; Schegloff & Sacks, 1973). The particular contributions of this tradition are strategies to uncover the rule systems that govern much of our interaction with others and the role that verbal and nonverbal behaviors play in these systems (see West and Zimmerman, Chapter 9).

After this short review of some of the major historical developments that have influenced the methodology presently available to study nonverbal behavior, we now turn toward a more systematic discussion of the aspects or features that characterize particular approaches or methods and the choices facing a researcher intent on investigating nonverbal behavior empirically.

1.2. Basic issues in studying nonverbal behavior

The study of nonverbal behavior is characterized by two major focuses of interest: the study of the individual and the study of the interaction. In a very fundamental sense, these different focuses also represent major philosophical traditions, as reflected in the different disciplinary affiliations of the researchers and the rather different strategies and methods of research employed. Biological and psychological researchers tend to be most interested in the determinants and processes of nonverbal behavior on the individual level. These researchers often endorse the belief that it is necessary to understand the factors governing the behavior of the individual better before studying the complex patterns of social interaction between individuals. Many sociologists and anthropologists, on the other hand, believe that it is more important to focus attention on the nature of social interaction and the social and cultural factors that determine the complex interrelationships and interaction processes occurring between social actors. In this tradition, it is often held that individual behavior is strongly governed by social forces and the dynamics of the interaction situation; according to this view, then, studies of the behavior of isolated individuals are rather useless.

Apart from the different focuses of interest and the underlying epistemological traditions, specific research approaches have dominated in each of these research traditions. Researchers interested in the individual have tended to use experimental methods that allow quantitative analysis of individual behavior and aggregation over individuals and situations. Researchers focusing on the interaction, on the other hand, have preferred the observation of naturally occurring behavior in social interaction, and have often used qualitative techniques to describe moment-to-moment changes in behavior, and structural rather than quantitative description for very short segments of an interaction. However, although such a methodological specialization may have developed to some extent in past research, it is by no means obligatory, nor is it found universally. There are, for example, quite a few researchers interested in the individual who use qualitative moment-to-moment description of naturally occurring behavior, and there are researchers who study interaction processes by way of experimental and quantitative methodology. Just as there is no logical necessity for choosing a particular method given a particular focus of research interest, there is no logical necessity for keeping these two focuses of research interest apart or, worse, for considering them as antithetical. Clearly, both are legitimate and important, and it is hardly possible to make a reasonable judgment about the greater urgency or validity of either one of them.

In this section, we attempt to characterize these different research interests in somewhat more detail, trying to show that they complement rather than contradict each other. In order to understand human social interaction, the biological and psychological determinants of behavior, as well as the cultural and situational norms and rules affecting interaction processes, have to be taken into account. Unfortunately, the focuses of research on the individual or on the interaction have in the past sometimes been associated with the issue of innate or biologically determined versus learned or culturally determined behavior. There is no necessary link here: human behavior is jointly determined by biological and cultural factors, and it is an empirical issue to determine the nature and strength of the respective influences. The effect of social factors can be studied with the individual as the focus of study, as in the investigation of culturally mediated stereotypical inferences from nonverbal cues. Similarly, biological issues can be studied with the interaction as a major focus, as in the study of mother–infant bonding.

Let us now turn to a more detailed discussion of the main questions that have been asked within the focus on the individual and within the focus on interaction, trying to relate these to the historical research traditions that they grow out of or draw from.

Researchers focusing on the behavior of the individual have generally been interested in three major issues: (1) externalization or expression of traits and states, (2) inferences from nonverbal cues, and (3) intraindividual organization of behavior.

As pointed out previously, the investigation of the externalization or expression of personality, action tendencies, or emotion was one of the earliest research issues in studying nonverbal behavior. This issue has been of both theoretical and practical interest. On the theoretical level, investigations have concerned, in psychology, expressive styles of personality and the expression of emotion and, in ethology, intention signals. On the practical or applied level, the diagnostic value of nonverbal behavior for personality and affect disturbances has been explored. The research strategy employed in these studies has generally consisted of searching for correlations between states and traits, as induced or assessed by some kind of external criterion, and measuring particular types of nonverbal behavior.

The study of inferences from nonverbal behavior cues (attributing traits, states, and intentions to the actor) belongs squarely in the area of person perception and impression formation in social psychology. Unfortunately, much of the person perception research has moved away from the person. Researchers in this field have been preoccupied for decades with studying verbal labels rather than behavioral cues, generating quite a bit of evidence on semantic processing but almost none on impression formation and cue utilization (K. R. Scherer & Scherer, 1981). Most of the relevant research has been conducted recently under the heading of nonverbal communication research. Here the research strategy consists of exposing observers to stimulus persons displaying various kinds of nonverbal behaviors (often posed) and assessing the inferences observers make from these, sometimes checking the accuracy of the inferences against some kind of external criterion. Unfortunately, this research approach has often not taken advantage of the methodological sophistication – in such areas as deciding what kinds of scales to use, the problem of artifacts, judgment conditions, and so on – that has been attained within the field of person perception (see Rosenthal, Chapter 6).

A third approach with the individual as a focus of research, one that has appeared only recently, is the study of the intraindividual organization of action, including nonverbal behavior. Here an attempt is made to investigate the hierarchical structure in the organization of behavior, including the execution of plans and strategies on different levels and the synchronization of different types of simultaneously occurring motor activities (see von Cranach & Harré, in press).

Studies in which the interaction process is the focus of interest can also be subdivided into three fairly distinct approaches: (1) the nature of the cultural communication code, (2) the coordination of behavior in social interaction, and (3) the study of interpersonal relationships.

The first approach, studying the nature of the cultural communication code, is most closely associated with the work of Birdwhistell. As described in the preceding section, Birdwhistell assumed that nonverbal signals are organized in a culturally shared code similar to the language code. This assumption points toward a research strategy making use of techniques developed for linguistic inquiry. The major aspect of such a research strategy is reliance on a few illustrative cases for investigation of the nature of the code, the assumption being that the elements of the code and their relationships are discrete and invariant and that the analysis of a few instances of usage of the code will be sufficient to unravel its structure (just as ancient languages have been deciphered from the inscriptions on a single tombstone).

The second approach, strongly based on the work of Birdwhistell, is concerned with the microexamination of the moment-to-moment structure of the process of interaction. Here researchers study the way in which interaction partners manage to coordinate their behavior in a complex dancelike pattern. Examples of studies using this approach are Duncan's (1972) work on turn-taking, Condon and Ogston's (1967) study of interactional synchrony, and Kendon's study of greetings (see his detailed discussion in Chapter 8).

The third approach is quite different in that it represents the more typically psychological approach to the study of interaction. Studies of this kind, which often proceed by manipulating the behavior of one person in the interaction, look for signs that indicate the nature of the relationship of the interaction partners or their respective status. This approach is concerned with the nonverbal marking of relationships, rather than with the nature of the code or the complex coordination of behavior. Examples of this approach are found in many studies on eye contact (Argyle & Dean, 1965; Ellsworth & Ludwig, 1972; Exline & Fehr, Chapter 3) and in work on posture and positions (Mehrabian, 1969, 1972).

To summarize, the distinction between approaches with the individual as focus and those with the interaction as focus is based on differences in scientific interest and perceived research priorities. Some researchers, partly because of their disciplinary origins, are more interested in studying the individual and the factors that determine his or her behavior and consider it important to start studying social behavior by considering the contributions made by the individuals. Others are more interested in social and cultural phenomena and consider the interaction of individuals a more logical place to start studying human behavior. Only very extreme adherents of either approach, however, would question the validity of the other perspective, although there are of course some differences of opinion concerning the usefulness of certain concepts and research approaches.

Thus, clearly, these two focuses of research are complementary rather than contradictory. It is only the complexity of the appropriate research design and the amount of time and expertise needed that deter researchers from studying the individual and the interaction at the same time. It would seem possible, for example, to study how introverts and extroverts coordinate their behavior in different types of social interactions.

Indeed, there have been some attempts to combine the study of the individual and of the interaction in a single research project. Paul Ekman and his collaborators have studied the effect of stress on the communicative behavior of Japanese and American students, both individually and in social interactions, to assess the effect of social rules and situational determinants on communicative behavior (Ekman, 1972). Duncan and Fiske (1977) have looked at variables defining the individual in a context of studying turn-taking behavior and the rules that govern this type of interaction regulation. K. R. Scherer and his collaborators have looked at individual variables and social situational variables that determine the behavior of public officials in dealing with clients, trying to assess both the effect on individual behavior and the effect on the nature of the interaction as a whole (U. Scherer & Scherer, 1980). Exline and his collaborators have studied Machiavellianism in its effect on nonverbal behavior in deception (see Exline & Fehr, Chapter 3). It is to be expected that future research using either the individual or the interaction as a focus will make increasing use of the findings of the other approach, and it is to be hoped that integrative studies trying to combine the two focuses of interest will increase in number.

It is particularly important to stress that the choice of a particular research focus does not necessarily determine the methodological approach to be used. Though there has been a tendency for the two approaches to prefer different research techniques, as already noted, this is more a historical accident than a logical necessity. On the whole, it may be very detrimental to equate research interest, conceptual preferences, and choice of particular research methodologies with possibly exclusive types of approaches. Unfortunately, this seems to have been the effect of the widely cited distinction between *structural* and *external variable* studies introduced by Duncan in 1969 in an attempt to review the literature on nonverbal communication at that time.

This distinction reified two types of research, which, as we have been trying to show, cannot really be consistently differentiated on any set of dimensions. The distinction between *structural* and *external variable* implies differences in scientific interest, conceptual schemes, disciplinary orientation, fundamental unit of inquiry, preferred methodology, and research priorities. Fundamentally, a researcher's decisions on any of these dimensions are independent of one another. If, as has been the case, there is a clustering of some of these decisions in particular historical research approaches, this may be of interest for a historian of science, but it should not limit the choice of options for research.

It is the purpose of this chapter to consider these methodological options in somewhat more detail. Clearly, the points that will be made cover only a small part of the large number of issues relevant for empirical research in nonverbal behavior (see Weick, 1968). However, many methodological issues are relevant to any kind of empirical study in the social and behavioral sciences and are adequately treated in many existing sources on research methodology in this domain. Here we are selecting for discussion either those issues concerning which there are chronic deficiencies or no established standards in the nonverbal literature or those which are unique to a particular approach or have more than general importance.

For the selection of the appropriate method to be used and as a safeguard against possible artifacts, the nature of the phenomenon to be studied has to be carefully considered. In many studies on nonverbal behavior the phenomenon to be studied consists in the relationship of some nonverbal behavior as a sign to an underlying referent or external variable, that is, in the *coding* of nonverbal signs. The first detailed discussion of the issue of coding of nonverbal behavior was provided by Ekman and Friesen (1969).

Because there are important implications for methodological decisions, we will briefly review the nature of nonverbal coding. The nature of coding, that is, the kind of relationship between sign and referent, can be described by three major dimensions: (1) discrete versus continuous/graded, (2) probabilistic versus invariant, and (3) iconic versus arbitrary (Ekman & Friesen, 1969; Giles, Scherer, & Taylor, 1979; K. R. Scherer, 1977). Verbal signs are generally coded discretely, invariantly, and arbitrarily; that is, a particular word does or does not mean a particular thing, the word always and for everybody means this thing, and the nature of the word does not bear any relationship to the nature of the thing.

Although some nonverbal signs are coded in the same way, others are coded continuously, probabilistically, and iconically. In other words, a nonverbal sign may change with changes in the extent or strength of a referent (e.g., loudness of voice with degree of emphasis); it may mean a particular thing only for certain persons or certain situations (e.g., high voice pitch may indicate stress for some speakers but not for others, and thus there is only a certain probability that it signals stress in any one case); and it is often part of the thing or a homomorphic representation of the thing it signals (as blushing is part of the arousal state it signifies).

Thus the coding of nonverbal behaviors varies from, on the one extreme, languagelike coding to, on the other, very loose probabilistic associations between behaviors and external referents that semiotic purists would refuse to call coding. For example, gestural emblems, movements with precise meanings (see Ekman, 1976; Johnson, Ekman, & Friesen, 1975), are close to language coding in many respects because, although they often are iconically coded, their signification of external referents is invariant and generally discrete. That loudness of the voice is a sign of extroversion only for some speakers in some cultures (see K. R. Scherer, 1979a) indicates, on the other hand, a probabilistic relationship, and voice level may vary continuously with the strength of the extroversion disposition. It is thus debatable whether we can talk of a code at all in this domain (although it can be argued that this vocal behavior might be used like other elements of communication codes in self-presentation and interaction regulation; see K. R. Scherer, 1979a, pp. 197–201), or only of a statistical correlation.

We do not, at this point, want to discuss the nature of code systems and the requirements under which behaviors qualify as code elements. The preceding discussion was intended to show that nonverbal behaviors differ in their relationships to external referents of which they might be signs. Depending on the nature of this relationship, different research procedures are required for study of the characteristics of the signs and their usage. Obviously, the extent to which nonverbal behaviors are coded like language determines the extent to which classical linguistic techniques, such as the contrastive analysis of consensually defined discrete units in fairly small samples, can be used in their investigation. For example, the intersubjective agreement on the denotative meaning of most words is so high (invariant coding or very high probability of consensual use) that significance testing is superfluous. Of course, this does not mean that statistical methods cannot be used in studying messages that are discretely and invariantly coded. Although the coding may be evident, the *use* of the respective signal (i.e., when shown and by whom) needs to be studied empirically, using statistical techniques. However, the more the coding resembles a statistical association, the more indication there is for standard psychological techniques, relying on operationalized measurement procedures with known reliability and statistical analysis of fairly sizable samples.

Unfortunately, we do not yet well understand the coding characteristics for many nonverbal behaviors, and we are thus faced with the dilemma of having to make choices about research procedures without knowing very much about their appropriateness for the research object. All too often, this dilemma is solved by having recourse to one's theoretical predilections. Thus researchers trained in anthropology or linguistics tend to presuppose that most of the nonverbal behaviors they are dealing with are coded in a languagelike manner and that structural linguistic techniques are appropriate. If the assumption is incorrect, the research results may not be valid. For example, if a researcher isolates what seem to be consensually valid units of nonverbal behavior with a particular signification, without checking on the reliability with which such a distinction can be made, the conclusions of the study will be in error if the behavior is in fact probabilistically coded and the signification varies with sign encoders and decoders or the situation or setting in which it occurs.

Psychologically trained researchers, on the other hand, tend to lean toward the assumption that there are probabilistic relationships between behaviors and external referents and attempt to determine the nature of the relationship by statistical analysis of a number of cases, often trying to isolate variables by controlling or manipulating factors in experiments. The danger of an unreflective use of this approach consists in the strong possibility of missing important structural relationships between nonverbal behaviors in relation to external referents, because often only one-to-one correlations are studied and other variables or behaviors are controlled by manipulation or exclusion. However, appropriate research designs using multivariate procedures and configurational analyses may alleviate this danger to some extent.

We do not want to imply by these two examples that there is a linguistic and a psychological methodology and that one has to choose between them in studying nonverbal behavior. This is not the case. The options available and the choices to be made are of course much more complex. Apart from different assumptions about the nature of the code and their subsequent effects on choice of research methodology, there are different views in various disciplines of the social and behavioral sciences on the nature of scientific activity and on what constitutes proof for the description and explanation of a phenomenon.

One can distinguish among at least three kinds of research activities: (1) discovery, (2) proof, and (3) illustration. The role of these three is seen very differently in different areas of the social and behavioral sciences. There are those who believe that the work ends with discovery or with illustration. There are others who believe that these are just the first steps and that very different and more demanding activities are required to establish proof. Most researchers subscribing to an empirical, experimental approach believe that discovery is the first step, which has to be followed by proof and eventually by illustration for the dissemination of the findings. Another way to view the difference between traditions is that what is considered proof for some is for others considered only the discovery of a hypothesis still needing proof, or the illustration of a claim not proven. And proof, which is seen as the sine qua non by some, is considered pedestrian reiteration of the already obvious by others.

The methodology and techniques that are most appropriate for discovery, illustration, and proof are rather diverse, and it would seem reasonable to make the appropriate choice of methodology on the basis of the purpose of the research approach.

1.3. Sampling nonverbal behavior

Scientific research, including the study of nonverbal behavior, always requires sampling of the object to be studied. Only a limited number of people can be studied in a limited number of settings, and we can observe only a small part of their behavior. Thus the researcher has to make a large number of decisions about the sampling of the behavior that he intends to study, such as *where* to study the behavior (for example, in the field or the laboratory), *which behavior* to study (i.e., natural or arranged behavior), *who* ought to be observed (that is, which persons and how many of them), *how* the observation is to be conducted (for example, direct observation or recording of the behavior), for *how long* these persons will be observed, and finally *which aspects* of the behavior are to be noted. In this section we shall consider some of the issues involved in making these decisions.

Field versus laboratory

The term *field* is used by social scientists to refer to the typical settings of human behavior, such as living rooms, schools, public places, and a myriad of other social settings in which our daily behavior is situated. The field is any setting that is not a laboratory. Although it is possible to simulate some of the major aspects of social settings in the laboratory, these re-creations never completely approximate real-life settings. Thus, if there is no need to observe in the laboratory, one should study nonverbal behavior in the field. In many cases, however, it is necessary to use the laboratory. Whenever the coding characteristics of the nonverbal behavior studies are probabilistic and continuous, and statistical analysis techniques are required, a certain degree of control of the relevant variables and of comparability of the conditions under which the behavior unfolds is desirable. Furthermore, if film or video records are required for microscopic measurement or if very high quality audio records have to be made for acoustic analysis, the technical facilities available only in laboratories need to be employed (particularly when several cameras are to be used, recorders synchronized, separate audio records made, etc.; see Wallbott, Technical Appendix). Similarly, the laboratory approach has to be used for studies in which instruments for the direct measurement of particular aspects of nonverbal behavior (such as transducers, floor switches, etc.; see Rosenfeld, Chapter 5) are to be used (although it is sometimes possible to use sophisticated recording instrumentation in the field, too).

Whether behavior is to be sampled in the field or the laboratory depends on the issue and the type of nonverbal behavior to be studied as well as the nature of the data desired. Both offer advantages and disadvantages (see Exline & Fehr, Section 3.2). If little is known about the nonverbal behavior of interest, it is advisable to start a research project with field observations to obtain a feeling for the characteristics of the behavior and the factors that might influence it. After such information has been obtained, it is more easily possible to devise a representative research design for behavior sampling in the laboratory.

Clearly, not all settings, situations, or interaction patterns can be simulated in the laboratory. Political rallies, religious ceremonies, and weddings, among many other cases, have to be observed in the field. Again, the choice between laboratory and field depends on the interest of the researcher and the nature of the question to be asked. Given the constraints of both settings, concessions and compromises have to be made for usefulness and appropriateness.

Naturally occurring versus arranged behavior

Unfortunately, the choice between field and laboratory is often confused with the distinction between natural and artificial behavior. This is misleading. Nobody wishes to study the artificial, and it goes without saying that researchers studying behavior in the laboratory do not agree that their object of study is artificial behavior. Artificiality is always a problem in behavioral research and is just as likely to be found in the field as in the laboratory.

In a laboratory, people do not behave as they would in their living rooms, but then, they do not behave in their living rooms as they would in a bus, a church, or an office. Many behavior patterns and interactions between strangers are as natural in a laboratory as in any other unfamiliar formal setting. The only exception would be a situation in which subjects tend to be suspicious of everything and everyone around them out of fear of deception and nonacceptance of the roles in which others present themselves. This is often the case with psychology students, who have a long history of participation in complicated experiments in which things never were what they seemed. Fortunately, this is not true for all people whose behavior can be studied in a laboratory.

One precondition for the occurrence of "natural" behavior is that the task characteristics and the situational demands be such that natural behavior, in the sense of being appropriate to these demands, is functional in that context. If a person is required to do things that seem foolish or irrelevant to that person's life, unnatural behavior will result. If the task characteristics and the demands made are highly realistic and involving, as in simulated jury discussions, for example, or if subjects are required to perform an activity that they are engaged in day after day, as in simulating client contacts with civil service officials (U. Scherer & Scherer, 1980), the resulting behavior will be natural both in comparability with real-life behavior patterns and in affective involvement. Thus the distinction is not between natural and artificial behavior but between naturally occurring and arranged behavior, by which we mean behavior in the occurrence and possibly in the unfolding of which the researcher has had a hand.

One source of artificiality in many studies in which the interaction is arranged is that the situation is totally ahistorical. Typically there is no shared past experience between the participants in an arranged interaction, and there is little likelihood of any future interaction once the experiment is over. It is possible, however, to arrange an interaction in a laboratory that eliminates these problems. For example, friends or couples may be studied, or even people previously unacquainted if they can be expected to interact with each other. Another source of artificiality in many arranged situations is that they have little relevance to the subject, quite apart from the participants' unfamiliarity with one another. Again, a laboratory experiment may be arranged so that it is relevant to the career, values, or goals of the participant.

One of the problems with the sampling of naturally occurring behavior is the difficulty of obtaining repeated instances of the same type of behavior in a comparable context. Another problem is the lack of control over the factors determining the occurrence and the particular characteristics of particular behavior, such as aspects of the physical environment, the identity and behavior of significant others, and so on. Unfortunately, both of these aspects of behavior sampling are essential for the systematic study of particular issues, as, for example, the correspondence between a wide range of parameter values in the behavioral signs and differences in degree or strength of underlying external referents (e.g., emotional states) or the nature of the inference processes based on different types of nonverbal cues. In many such research situations, sampling of arranged behavior has to be used to obtain the appropriate evidence.

The study of behavior that has in some way been arranged by the observer has many advantages. Not only does it allow study of samples of behavior that may only rarely occur naturally, but the researcher can also arrange the behavior repeatedly to obtain replications of the findings. In addition, the observation or recording conditions of the behavior can be better controlled, and the researcher can attempt to guard against observer bias. Furthermore, it is often feasible to manipulate specific aspects of the setting and thus obtain a better idea of how different factors interact with each other in determining the behavior of the persons studied. One must always be careful to avoid artificiality and to question whether the results can be generalized. However, the same cautions often apply equally to those studies of naturally occurring behavior in which the person or persons observed realize that they are being scrutinized. Similarly, it is not usually possible to generalize from one piece of behavior observed under "natural" conditions to other behaviors of the same person or other persons even in the same situation, unless one has sampled very many such behaviors.

The literature on nonverbal behavior abounds with examples of different techniques for arranging behavior: role playing, the showing of films, the administration of electroshocks, the manipulation of the behavior of interaction partners (confederates), the use of professional or amateur actors, and many others.

Behavior patterns can be induced by the researcher through a wide variety of means. He or she can, for example, ask the subject to perform a certain task, such as wrapping a perambulator, solving arithmetic problems, describing a dirty movie, or occupying a table in the library. The behavioral reactions to each of these tasks enjoin a number of nonverbal behaviors, which may include those of interest to the researcher. Furthermore, the researcher can produce in the subjects a certain state, such as a particular emotion (e.g., via stimuli, insults, etc.) or a particular motivation (e.g., by food deprivation, exposure to a flirtatious member of the other sex, etc.), and observe the resulting behavioral reactions. In many cases these induced behaviors are "natural"; they are just not "naturally occurring." These methods are among the most powerful techniques available for behavior sampling. They allow the researcher control over the persons to be observed, many of the factors that determine the behavior, and often, the context in which the action takes place. As long as the tasks set for the subjects or the methods used to induce states of various sorts are realistic and part of the subjects' repertoire, there is little reason to expect that the behavior will be artificial.

Any kind of observation of behavior will lead to changes in that behavior; in many cases even the possibility of observation will produce such changes. Even field observation of naturally occurring behavior, with the naked eye or a camera (see Wallbott, Section A.6), can have an intrusive effect on the persons observed and often will change their behavior. There are a number of studies showing that behavior differs if the subject knows that he or she is being observed (see the studies reviewed in Ekman & Oster, 1979). Increased concern with the ethics of observing or recording behavior without the consent of the observed brings with it the risk that only self-conscious behavior will be studied. This is always a problem in arranged behavior sampling, because subjects know that they are in a contrived situation; but asking for consent to record may make it worse. In naturally occurring behavior in familiar surroundings, observation or even recording generally would be very unusual, and asking for consent could be even more intrusive than in a laboratory. In many cases institutions concerned with human subjects' rights will accept a procedure in which observation or recording occurs without knowledge of the observed and consent is obtained afterwards (with records destroyed if agreement is denied). At the very least, the recording instruments should be concealed to reduce their salience, even if their presence is revealed to those observed.

There are two major dimensions involved in arranging behavior: the requests made of the person whose behavior is to be studied and the manipulation of the situation by the researcher. The researcher can, in making requests, explicitly specify a role for the person studied, that is, either emphasize one of the person's roles out of his or her role repertoire, for example, that of a husband or wife, or ask the subject to play a role that is not a normal one, for example, that of a police officer. Alternatively, the researcher can leave the role implicit, assuming that the person studied will adopt a role appropriate to the situation. Secondly, the researcher can explicitly specify a specific task, such as solving a puzzle, playing a game, or posing a specific affect; or the task can be left implicit, defined by the situation, such as waiting for an experiment to begin or a partner to arrive.

As far as the manipulation of the situation goes, a researcher can administer a specific external stimulus, such as showing a film, administering electroshocks, or manipulating the temperature in a room. Secondly, the context or setting in which the behavior is to take place can be changed. This often involves the suggestion of a particular definition of the situation; for example, it may be implied that a person is competing with another person or group, that his or her behavior is being monitored by experts, or something similar. Thirdly, in situations involving an interaction, the researcher can manipulate the nature of the subject's behavior by using a stooge or a confederate who has been briefed about the behavior to adopt in the interaction. Situations in which this manipulation is used vary from the use of interviewers with prearranged interview schedules to the use of confederates whose task it is to anger the subject under observation.

We cannot consider all the techniques that have been used to arrange behavior in research on nonverbal behavior. We will concentrate here on some particularly important ones, discussing issues relevant to reducing artificiality.

One of the most frequent techniques of arranging behavior is the use in an interaction of a confederate or collaborator of the researcher. This technique has been a frequent one in experimental investigations of nonverbal behavior in which researchers have attempted to induce a certain behavior or to observe the reaction of the subject in response to the preprogrammed behavior of the confederate. In this case it is not possible to study interactive effects as they might actually occur. Even if one is exclusively interested in the behavior of the subject, one cannot exclude the possibility of artifacts. For example, the subject's behavior may be unusual in part because he is responding to someone who follows a fixed schedule. In looking at standardized interviews with psychiatric patients one is impressed by how often the patients' reactions are determined by the need to switch topics abruptly, because that is what the schedule calls for. Thus standardized interviews may distort the picture of psychopathological syndromes and not even represent the usual clinical interview.

Although the interaction in this case is not "natural," in the sense that the behavioral choices of one participant are preplanned and at least partly independent of the actions of his partner, there is no reason to assume that the behavior of the person studied is always "unnatural," unless one has reason to suspect that that person is aware of the manipulation. In some cases, the subject can even be told that he is dealing with a confederate in a simulation, as long as the task requirements are such that the subject is forced to react in an appropriate, serious manner. For example, U. Scherer and Scherer (1980) used lay actors as "standard clients" (allowing the manipulation of social class and aggressive vs. submissive behavior) in interactions with public officials. The behavioral reactions (and the subjective evaluation) of the subjects showed that the demands of the task and the situation generally were such that they had to use their standard behavioral repertoire for that situation in order to appear competent.

Such experimental simulations should not be confused with role playing. In role playing nothing is at stake and subjects are generally asked just to portray a particular person or role. In experimental simulations, the person plays himself, and if the situation is properly arranged, his competence and his self-esteem are at stake; he cannot afford not to treat this as a real situation and make use of all his skills to establish his competence as an actor in the interaction. Again, we do not want to claim that such experimental simulations are exactly like naturally occurring behavior in all aspects. There may indeed be differences in the nature or strength of the behavioral reactions, but as noted before, such effects can never be excluded when the person observed is aware of the observation. On the other hand, using confederates in experimental simulations provides the researcher with a very powerful technique for repeatedly producing particular types of behavior in response to situational factors controlled within an experimental design. Many studies on nonverbal communication are almost impossible to conduct without using this technique (see Exline & Fehr, Section 3.3).

Another type of arranged behavior that has been frequently used is posing and playacting. This technique is generally used in studies of inference processes from nonverbal cues, where the researcher needs some control over and some range of parameters or cues – a control and range that are impossible to obtain from the recording of naturally occurring behavior. This has been a particular problem in the area of emotional expression. The open expression of emotion is regulated by culturally determined display rules (Ekman, 1972), and most societies do not allow the expression of very strong emotions in public (quite apart from the ethical problem involved in recording such expressions). Therefore, posing by professional or lay actors has often been used in the study of the recognition of emotion from nonverbal cues. For a more detailed discussion of the advantages and disadvantages of this approach see Ekman, Friesen, and Ellsworth (1972, pp. 35–38) and K. R. Scherer (1981). These discussions show that there are research issues that cannot be studied appropriately without the use of posing. However, as with the use of confederates, there are more or less sophisticated ways of using this technique. In posing, greater artificiality is to be expected if actors are simply asked to "show fear" than if they are asked to act out a small scenario in which they can identify with particular persons and particular affects. In some cases, depending on the research issue, posers can be given very precise instructions, based on findings from naturally occurring behavior, about the behavioral cues they are supposed to produce. For example, the Facial Action Coding System (see Ekman, Chapter 2) can be used to specify the facial actions to be produced for a study of emotion inference from systematically varied facial cues.

Unfortunately, researchers often choose a particular technique without carefully considering its pros and cons. The issues raised here may help to render the basic decisions involved in the choice of a particular technique more salient. In very many procedures the requests made of the person whose behavior is arranged are left implicit. Though this procedure has the advantage that behavior is less constrained by the investigator's demands, it has the disadvantage that different persons may construct or perceive their roles and tasks very differently. Obviously, this will render a comparison of the behavior observed very difficult. If roles and tasks are left unspecified, it is necessary to ask the person observed, after the observation, how he or she defined the situation and which reference or standard was used in deciding on a specific role or task perception. Furthermore, it is essential to establish the extent to which explicit roles or tasks specified are comparable and compatible with roles or tasks normally encountered by the person observed. Clearly, it would be very important for the evaluation of the behavior observed if the role that has been requested is one which the confederate has never played before and with which he or she may have had very little experience.

Sampling persons

In the best of all possible worlds in which to investigate research questions, one would like to be able to look at as many people as possible in as many settings as possible, to examine as many different aspects of the nonverbal behavior as possible, and to look at as many of these behaviors as occur within the setting. However, practical constraints usually require that we compromise on many aspects of the sampling issue. The nature of the compromise, that is, the decision about which requirements have to be sacrificed to the limited time and resources available, should depend upon at least two considerations: (1) the question being asked and (2) the generalization being sought. For example, is one trying to answer a question for all persons or just for a particular type of person? Is one trying to answer a question that is independent of settings or one that varies with types of settings? Is one trying to answer a question that cuts across several modalities of behavior, concerning, for example, the organization of different nonverbal behaviors, or is the question specific to a particular type of nonverbal behavior?

A further consideration in sampling concerns the purpose of a particular research project. Sampling considerations will be very different if one is concerned with discovery from what they will be if one attempts to provide proof for a phenomenon discovered in just a small sample. If one is interested in discovery, one is often willing to economize on the number of subjects and often even on the number of settings in order to look at as many modalities of behavior as possible and to observe as much behavior as possible within a particular setting or interaction. Thus the various aspects of sampling are clearly interrelated and dependent upon the purpose of the research project. This interdependence should be kept in mind during our discussion of the particular dimensions. We will first deal with the choice of the type of person to be studied.

In some cases, for example, if one is interested in discovering the basic rules of nonverbal communication, one has little basis for specifying which persons ought to be observed. At the opposite extreme, one can have questions so precise that it is quite easy to specify very narrowly which persons ought to be observed. For example, if the nonverbal behavior of babies of a particular age is to be studied, the group of persons constituting the population for sampling is quite well defined. Thus the choice of the persons to be studied is often inherent in the research issue – a study of mother–infant interaction or kindergarten play, for example, or the diagnosis of depression. In such cases, the major problem usually is to obtain access to the group of persons one is interested in observing. In some cases, however, problems may occur because the group to be studied is not well defined or is less homogeneous than one thought. For example, much of the research on the nonverbal behavior of schizophrenics suffers from the fact that this diagnosis covers an enormous number of different psychopathological syndromes (as well as etiological factors), a situation that vitiates any attempt to treat "schizophrenics" as a homogeneous group and dashes hopes to find consistent nonverbal behavior patterns (K. R. Scherer, 1979b). Thus, if the research issue demands a particular type of actors, one has to be very careful to assure that the group studied does indeed exhibit the characteristics that are theoretically important.

There are two kinds of generalization issues involved here. First, one needs to have reasonable certainty that one is in fact looking at the population that is to be studied. In this case, the question is whether one can generalize from the persons sampled to that particular subgroup of persons. In many cases this is not automatically the case. Though the example of psychopathological patients is a particularly difficult one, given the many problems in defining diagnostic groups, the issue is equally problematic with other groups of persons that cannot be easily defined on the basis of objective characteristics such as age or sex. It is quite difficult, for example, to generalize from a small sample of persons observed to social class, occupational group, or some other socially defined type.

The second generalization issue concerns generalizing from the sample observed to the population as a whole. Although many researchers acknowledge that they are studying a specific group of persons, they often seem to assume implicitly that generalization to the population as a whole is possible. For example, in the history of nonverbal communication research the clinical interview has played a major role. Often interactions between therapists and psychologically disturbed patients have been studied with the implication that the findings can be generalized to the general population. It is possible, however, that the clinical interview is a very specific kind of interaction with rules of its own and that it is not possible to generalize from the nonverbal behavior of disturbed persons to the nonverbal behavior of "normals." If one is interested in applying one's results to the general population to illustrate basic patterns of nonverbal behavior, it seems to be necessary to sample at least two different subgroups.

If the type of nonverbal behavior under study can be profitably investigated with any kind of person, the issue of easy availability and easy access becomes central. Often, the natural choice for researchers in university settings is college students, particularly if they have to serve as subjects to obtain course credit. Although college students constitute a somewhat limited population, this would not in itself present a problem, were it not for the fact that many students, particularly in psychology, are often experiment-wise and more prone than others to be affected by demand characteristics (Orne, 1962) or experimenter expectancy (Rosenthal, 1966) in unpredictable ways. Thus researchers have to be unusually careful to avoid such artifacts when dealing with students, although the wide distribution of popular body language books may present a severe problem for demand characteristics with any type of subject population, if the purpose of the investigation is known.

An investigator who takes advantage of the easy availability of college students should try to study at least one population of nonstudents, even if it is only a very small subset, to check on the possibility of artifacts and/or sample specificity. The choice of this second sample is determined by many different considerations. Obviously, if one does not want to generalize to the population as a whole, but only to young people, one would be content with a second group of young persons who happen not to be enrolled in a university. However, if one wants to generalize to the population at large, it might be advisable to choose a second sample that is extremely different, for example, middle-aged convicts.

Obviously, the more one believes that the phenomenon under study is a very basic one that should not be affected by many social and individual factors, the more extreme should be the comparison samples. In some cases, it is necessary to choose a very highly specialized group to make this point. For example, in attempting to show that many of the basic processes in the facial expression of emotion are innate, Ekman and his collaborators had to study isolated New Guineans to make the point (Ekman, Sorensen, & Friesen, 1969). Thus the type of phenomenon to be demonstrated and the kind of generalization that the researcher attempts to make have a very strong impact on the decisions concerning sampling. Of course, given the many different types of groups in any society, it is never safe to generalize to the entire population, even if several groups have been observed. However, a sample of two groups is a vast improvement over a sample of one.

Apart from the type of person to be studied, it is important to decide on the number of persons whose behavior is to be observed. Given that the analysis of human behavior is a very time-consuming task, many researchers in the area of nonverbal communication have been content with rather few cases, in some studies with a single case. This is very problematical, however, because, particularly in a single case, there is no way to determine to what extent the behavior patterns found are a function of the characteristics of that particular person. The assumption that behavior patterns that follow well-defined social or cultural rules can be observed even in a single case is valid only if the existence of such strong cultural patterns has been established before. For most phenomena this is not the case. Consequently, a minimum of two persons should be studied, even if the researcher is convinced that he or she is dealing with very universal phenomena, to check the extent to which the behavior is determined by the individual characteristics of a particular person.

Similarly, if one attempts to determine differences between types of persons observed, such as differences between males and females, one needs at least two cases of each type to see whether there are smaller variations within types than between types. It would be desirable to have many more subjects for statistical analysis, in which the sources of variation could be determined more precisely. This may be impossible in cases where a particular type of interaction or a particular type of individual is difficult to observe in great numbers or in which the analysis is so time-consuming that it cannot be conducted for a large number of persons. But though it is only rarely acceptable to use single case studies for any kind of generalization, they may be very valuable in initial approaches to particular phenomena and in an attempt to develop hypotheses to be tested later. Furthermore, it is extremely useful to observe a single individual frequently and over a long period of time, to get a more complete sampling of the behavior in context than is normally possible in studies employing a large number of subjects. Yet a single case study is not sufficient to establish the existence of a particular phenomenon or relationship. Unfortunately, many of the phenomena studied in nonverbal behavior research have shown rather large individual differences; not very many have been robust enough to survive the sampling variation produced by individual differences.

Obviously, the more probabilistic the coding of the nonverbal behavior, the more important it is to observe a fairly large number of encoders. Here it is advisable to use a group of encoders with fairly homogeneous characteristics, as otherwise it is impossible to determine, in the case of negative results, whether there is no relationship or whether it is dependent on the type of person. Even if the results are positive, they may be dependent on the particular encoder. Just how homogeneous such groups of encoders should be is difficult to say. Often the researcher has to use prior knowledge or intuition about individual differences to make the decision. For example, if there is good evidence for strong sex differences in a particular nonverbal behavior, it is advisable to limit the study to members of one sex or, if feasible, to include several members of each sex. If the researcher is unable to keep a group of subjects nicely balanced in essential characteristics, he or she should at least attempt, through questionnaires, to assess some of the major characteristics, such as age, education, geographical origin, social class, and, possibly, personality, to be able to check in at least a rudimentary way whether these factors may have made a difference. At times, the outcome of such checks allows a better understanding of the pattern of findings (or lack thereof) and suggests hypotheses for further study (see K. R. Scherer, 1972).

Although more difficult, it is not impossible to find fairly homogeneous groups of persons that can be studied outside colleges. Possibilities include the use of church and community groups, participants in adult education centers, and members of organizations and institutions.

The nature of behavior sampling

On the pages to follow we will deal with a number of decisions concerning particular aspects of sampling behavior and the procedures used in securing such behavior samples out of a stream of behavior over time in social contexts.

Sampling the individual versus the interaction. Obviously, if the individual is studied in a situation where he or she is alone, only the behavior of that individual person can be sampled. Similarly, when the purpose of the research is to study patterns of interaction, two or more individuals will have to be sampled. However, if the focus of interest is the individual and the factors that determine his or her behavior in an interaction, it becomes crucial to decide whether the behavior of that individual alone ought to be sampled or whether it is necessary also to sample the behavior of an interaction partner.

Clearly, this problem can be decided only on the basis of the specific question asked. If the effects of factors totally independent of the interaction partner or the interaction situation as a whole are to be assessed (e.g., the effects of drugs on behavior), it would seem to be sufficient to focus just on the behavior of the individual. However, in most cases, it is difficult to exclude the effect of the behavior of the interaction partner or partners when assessing the determinants of an individual's behavior. Consequently, in most cases where interactive behavior is observed, it is necessary to sample the behavior of all the persons interacting, even if the focus of interest is on one individual. If confederates are used, it is advisable to employ more than one, to be certain that the results are not specific to the effect of one particular person. In some cases, the reason for this is simply to check on the success of a particular manipulation in the experiment. For example, often a confederate or interviewer has been programmed by the investigator to behave in a certain way. In these cases, it is necessary to sample the behavior of the confederate to establish whether the instructions are being followed, as well as to check how the behavior of the subject affects the behavior of the confederate.

Technical problems become almost insurmountable if more than two persons are to be observed or recorded simultaneously, if many modalities are to be investigated, or if close-up recordings are required. Most studies in which the behavior of more than one person was sampled have been conducted with dyads. Clearly, in studies in which the interaction is the focus of research, it is essential that all participants of the interaction be included in the behavior sampling. If exact temporal correspondence between the behavior patterns of two or more actors is to be investigated, fairly elaborate precautions have to be taken to make sure that the behavioral records and possibly the audiovisual recordings are well synchronized. This question becomes particularly important if audiovisual recording is used to sample behavior (see Wallbott, Technical Appendix).

Direct observation versus audiovisual recording. This choice is of major importance for research design and procedure, because a decision to record often has many implications for the approach to be taken. As mentioned earlier, the technical requirements for adequate recording (see Wallbott, Technical Appendix) are fairly obtrusive, and unless at least some aspects of the recording procedure can be hidden from the subject's view, the researcher has to count on some change in the behavior observed, owing to the subject's reaction to being recorded. Furthermore, both the physical setting and the temporal structure of an interaction have to be accommodated to the technical constraints of the recording. Last, though not least, recording is expensive, both in the equipment required and in the tape and/or film material used.

Despite these disadvantages, audiovisual recording of behavior is becoming more and more frequent in the analysis of nonverbal behavior. There are many important advantages: the possibility of replaying and observing a sequence of behavior over and over, of viewing the behavior in slow motion, of doing microscopic frame-by-frame analysis, of using the material for judgment studies, and many others. Another advantage of obtaining a permanent record is that it is possible to measure, through repeated passes, many more aspects of behavior than can possibly be measured in the one real-time pass possible when no record is obtained.

Because of these advantages of recording behavior, direct observation is preferable only if recording is too costly, if it would be too obtrusive in a natural setting, or if the features or categories of behavior to be observed are very simple and are unlikely to be changed in the course of the research. There are such situations, and in them researchers should forgo recordings. They should realize, however, that in direct observation much more stringent demands need to be made on careful reliability checks of the coders or observers, because the scores cannot be checked again later.

In this chapter, the issue of direct observation versus audiovisual recording can be discussed only very briefly. Given the importance of the issue, the reader is referred to the literature on observational methods (Sackett, 1978; Weick, 1968), as well as to the discussion of specific problems in observation and recording in the individual chapters of this volume (Ekman, Chapter 2; Exline & Fehr, Chapter 3; Kendon, Chapter 8; Rosenfeld, Chapter 5; Scherer, Chapter 4; Wallbott, Technical Appendix).

Single versus repeated sampling. In almost all of the existing studies of nonverbal behavior, encoders have been observed on only one occasion and in only one situational context, the assumption being that the use of nonverbal signals will not differ depending on situational characteristics or the identity of the interaction partners. This assumption may be quite wrong, of course. We do know that even speech patterns change rather noticeably depending on situational context (Brown & Fraser, 1979), and it would be quite surprising if this were not the case for the much less stringently coded nonverbal signals. It seems reasonable to assume that the more probabilistic the relationship between a nonverbal behavior and an external referent is, the more situation dependent it might be. In the civil servant study mentioned earlier (U. Scherer & Scherer, 1980), the officials had to deal with two different cases (differing in the amount of power the official could wield) involving two different clients. Results showed different relationships between personality and attitudes and nonverbal behavior for each of the cases, indicating that personality dispositions and attitudes may differentially determine the nonverbal behavior patterns shown under different situational constraints.

Clearly, it would be most desirable to sample behavior repeatedly from the same person, both in similar situations and in different situations, with the same interaction partners at different times and with different partners. Such behavior sampling procedures are both more complex and more demanding of time and money than the single case studies that dominate the field. Yet it is difficult to see how one can confidently assume that the coding and usage patterns found in a single behavioral sample are indeed independent of the situation and the interaction partner.

Single-culture studies versus cross-cultural comparison. Most of the studies in the field have been conducted not only on single cases, but also in a single culture. Although most of these studies have been conducted only in the United States, the authors of textbooks and review chapters usually do not bother to note that the results reported may be culture-specific and that the relationships between nonverbal behavior and external referents might be very different in other cultures. If all or even most nonverbal behavior were to be strongly biologically determined, as the basis for the expression of emotion seems to be (Ekman, 1972), this might not be of great consequence. But even in emotional expression, strong cultural differences in display rules have been found (Ekman, 1972), which render generalizations of findings across cultures rather dubious. In some of the studies that have included cross-cultural comparison, very different patterns of results have emerged for the cultures investigated (see Key, 1977, pp. 138–139). A more extensive discussion of this issue cannot be offered at this point. However, we feel strongly that it is necessary to devote more effort to cross-cultural comparison in order to understand better the effect of cultural factors on nonverbal behavior and the significance of such behavior in communication.

Whereas the importance of cross-cultural assessment of nonverbal behavior is only rarely alluded to in studies on nonverbal behavior, there is more frequent concern with the importance of ethnic group or race and gender (see Harper, Wiens, & Matarazzo, 1978; Key, 1977). Clearly, there are other intracultural factors that urgently require more systematic study, such as differences between social classes, ages, or occupations. It is to be expected that our knowledge of nonverbal behavior would be greatly advanced if researchers would turn toward a more complete sampling of the social and cultural contexts in which to observe nonverbal behavior. Similarly, anthropological and ethnographical studies should be considered more frequently in planning research on nonverbal behavior. Finally, apart from the comparison of different social and cultural settings for human behavior, a comparative approach studying similarities and differences in the nonverbal behavior patterns in animals and humans may also highlight the functions of nonverbal behavior revealingly (K. R. Scherer, 1981).

Exhaustive versus selective sampling. One can either observe or record an entire interaction or select certain excerpts. Very often this decision depends on the length as well as on the nature of the behavior being sampled. If out of a lengthy behavior sequence only one particular time frame is important for the analysis – for example, the verdict in a jury trial – it is obviously sufficient to record just this segment of the interaction. The situations in which the behavior sequences of interest are so clearly identifiable are very rare, however. Often a researcher may be able to decide only after many repeated viewings of the behavior sequence which parts of that sequence are relevant for his or her question.

If it is impossible to record the total interaction or behavior sequence because of practical considerations, selective samples are drawn. The two most frequently used techniques are (1) the sampling of representative segments of the interaction (e.g., taking 5-minute sequences from the beginning, middle, and end), and (2) fixed-interval sampling (e.g., observing or recording a minute of behavior at 5-minute intervals). Both the choice of appropriate sampling procedures and the decisions on sampling intervals and observation periods depend on a large number of theoretical and practical issues, such as the frequency of occurrence of the behaviors studied, their duration, and so on (see detailed discussion in Fagen & Young, 1978; Sackett, 1978). Such selective samples are often drawn for the analysis, even if the entire interaction has been recorded, because an analysis of very lengthy behavior samples is too costly and time-consuming if elaborate microscopic analysis procedures are used.

One of the basic issues is the decision whether to pick naturally defined units like openings and closings, greetings, departures, interruptions, and the like or to use arbitrary time samples, such as every fifth minute of the interaction. If arbitrary time samples are used, there is little or no ambiguity about the selection procedure or the definition of the units, because they are defined by the objective parameter time. With this procedure, however, natural social units of behavior are in danger of being fragmented; the researcher is prevented from following a complete pattern of behavioral events and hence from understanding the relationships between different behavior patterns over time. The use of naturally occurring units has the advantage of avoiding such fragmentation but the disadvantage of having to reach agreement on the operation for determining beginning and ending of these natural events, which may be difficult to attain. Furthermore, the length of the samples may differ sizably across interactions.

Both of these procedures have the problem of comparability, that is, of establishing whether one is looking at the same or at different types of time periods or units across persons and interactions. Great care has to be taken in defining such units to make sure that there is reason to believe that the behavior patterns under study will reliably occur within sampling units chosen across individuals and across different settings.

Complete versus partial behavior sampling. Sometimes researchers are interested only in one aspect of the total nonverbal behavior pattern, such as gaze, facial expressions, or vocal behavior. They then have the option of observing or recording only this particular aspect of the nonverbal behavior. In many cases the decision to restrict sampling to a particular behavior pattern or modality has been simply a matter of convenience resulting from restrictions of apparatus, technique, or time. The problem of isolating particular aspects of behavior or modalities of behavior out of an integrative whole has only rarely been considered. This is unfortunate, because such isolation precludes an analysis of the relationships between different aspects of nonverbal behavior. On the other hand, if audiovisual recording is used, it is often very difficult to record adequately all the different aspects of nonverbal behavior with as much detail as the analysis requires (e.g., obtaining close-ups of the face, adjusting the camera angle to allow determination of gaze, etc.). Yet it may be desirable to record behavior as completely as possible (within reason), even if it is unclear at the time of the recording whether all aspects sampled can be analyzed later.

If one decides to divide up behavior, either because only some behaviors will be measured, or because observers will be used to compare judgments based on different sources, how should one proceed? Usually the choice has fallen on the end organs involved in producing the behavior, for example, hands, legs, body, face, or speech. Alternatives would be to focus on the central mechanisms that produce the end-organ behavior, or the mechanisms involved in the perceiver. Take two examples: one, judgment; the other, measurement. If one is interested in measuring emphasis movements, why study just the hands? The head, the voice, the facial muscles can all similarly produce emphasis. In all likelihood the same central neural mechanism sends out emphasis signals to various end organs. If one is interested in studying how observers process verbal and nonverbal behavior, one might divide channels according to whether the right or the left hemisphere of the brain handles the information, rather than concentrate on the verbal–face–body interaction, because within both the verbal domain and the face there are probably highly symbolic left-hemisphere-processed items and analogic right-hemisphere-processed items.

1.4. Measuring nonverbal behavior

After the researcher has decided how to sample the behavior, he or she has to decide which aspects of the nonverbal behavior are to be measured and which measurement procedures are to be used. In the case of direct observation, observers have to be given checklists that they can use to record the occurrence of specific behavior patterns, or instruments (such as event recorders) to codify the occurrence and duration of various behavior patterns. If nonverbal behavior has been recorded on film or magnetic tape, a larger set of options for measurement procedures is available, because measurements of various types can be performed during repeated passes through the material and because there is the possibility of slow motion and frame-by-frame analysis of visual records and acoustic analysis of auditory records. This section describes some of the basic options for measurement procedures; details and examples are discussed in subsequent chapters.

The choice of particular measurement procedures mainly depends on the phenomena to be investigated. In some cases, these may be difficult to observe because they are internal to the organism; examples are anatomic, chemical, or electrical phenomena (e.g., movement of a muscle). In such cases, measurement procedures must either directly assess these internal phenomena, as through physiological recordings, or utilize outward indicators of them. In most cases, however, researchers are interested in the consequences of such underlying phenomena for the visible or audible behavior of the person. The nature of the measurement systems to be used to isolate and measure the respective variables describing the nonverbal behavior under study are hotly debated in nonverbal behavior research. Some of the options available for study and analysis of nonverbal behavior are discussed here.

The major distinction is between descriptive approaches and inferential approaches (allowing for a mixed category that contains some elements of both). What we mean by descriptive approaches are attempts to capture particular aspects of behavior patterns by using transcription or category systems that describe the spatiotemporal characteristics of particular movements. Inferential approaches, on the other hand, go beyond the description of behavior patterns in time and space by using functional or motivational criteria to provide a categorization or typification of particular behavior patterns. Thus descriptive approaches attempt to use very objective techniques that do not require an observer's inference about the function and purpose of a particular behavior pattern, in terms either of the actor's intention or of the social function of a behavior (see also Ekman, Section 2.5).

Furthermore, the techniques available for the measurement of nonverbal behavior are differentiated by whether they are (1) highly microscopic, precise, and highly differentiated – that is, capable of making very fine distinctions between various aspects of the behavior observed and looking at very fine grained changes in the behavior – or (2) more macroscopic or global, identifying only fairly large-scale phenomena. Clearly, the use of a microscopic differentiated system has the advantage of providing a very fine resolution and allowing an empirical basis for the later procedure of collapsing categories into more integrative ones. It has the disadvantage, however, of being very cumbersome, and it presents the danger of losing particular phenomena because of too atomistic an approach. A more macroscopic system has the advantage of being more economical and providing a better relationship between the signal and the function of a behavior pattern, but it presents the problem that important clues might be missed, and it is virtually impossible (except for a reanalysis at very high cost) to decompose macroscopic categories into more fine grained items.

Finally, measurement systems can be differentiated according to their comprehensiveness or selectivity. It is claimed that some measurement systems will accommodate any kind of behavior that occurs within the general stream of behavior. In other systems, coverage is restricted to just some items or patterns of behavior, selected out of the stream of behavior for recording. In many cases, it is problematic to postulate that a system is comprehensive unless all anatomic possibilities for motor behavior are taken into account (see Rosenfeld, Chapter 5). Selective systems, on the other hand, have the disadvantage that often the selection may be not a reasoned one but one based on opportunism or convenience. As we go on now to consider the advantages and disadvantages of some particular measurement techniques illustrating these dimensions, it should be kept in mind that machines and observers always operate jointly, because almost all machines still need human operators and observers, at least for interpretation of the data.

Judges and coders versus instruments and apparatus

At present, perceptual units can only be identified and categorized by human judges, because even the most advanced computers still lack the pattern-recognition ability required for this task. Physical characteristics, however, can be measured both by machine and by human judges. Obviously, in those cases where machines can be used without recourse to human judges, more objective and reliable data can be expected. For example, although listeners hear fundamental frequency of voice as pitch, their judgment of the physical value is not nearly as good as is electroacoustic measurement, both because of the nature of the auditory system and because of the listeners' lack of appropriate scaling ability (see Scherer, Section 4.6).

In many cases, however, machine analysis must be supplemented by human observers, generally in order to perform pattern-analysis tasks that are beyond the capability of even sophisticated instruments. For example, if spatial coordinates for the movement of the hand are to be entered into a computer to allow objective measurement of speed and acceleration of movement, human observers have to be used to mark a fixed part of the hand (e.g., the middle finger knuckle) with a light pen or another computer-access device (see Rosenfeld, Section 5.5). As the examples in many of the chapters in this volume will show, in general, a combination of human judges or operators and machines has to be used for the analysis of physical characteristics. In some cases, movement patterns are so complex that highly trained coders must be used to identify the physical components of an action, as for example in the Facial Action Coding System developed by Ekman and Friesen (see Ekman, Chapter 2).

The use of judges or coders in behavioral research is a highly complex research procedure, the dangers of which are underestimated by many researchers. Many published studies in this area suffer from serious problems concerning judge selection, judgment procedure, and most often, insufficient checks on the reliability of the judgments. A comprehensive discussion of the issues to be considered in conducting judgment or decoding studies is found in Rosenthal (Chapter 6; see also Ekman, Section 2.1).

Persons doing the observation can be naive or trained. Naive observers will usually mix description with inference or evaluation. Trained observers can operate at different levels, varying from the strictly descriptive to the inferential. In descriptive approaches the observer frequently utilizes iconic or digital transcription systems or classifications. Inferences made by observers can be termed judgments and may refer to intent, motive, affect, conversational function, and so on. In most cases, the inferences do not specify the sign vehicles upon which they are based. Intermediate but closer to description are behavioral rating systems, which are usually more gross than transcription or classification systems. Closer to inference, on the other hand, are functionally based ratings or classifications.

The terminology in this area is very confusing. Various terms are used – often interchangeably – to describe the persons engaged in ratings or classifications. The most general term seems to be *observer*, that is, a person who does nonverbal measurement; the specific type of measurement is not specified. *Coder*, *scorer*, or *transcriber* is used if description but not inference is the major type of measurement to be done by the observer. In the case of a *coder*, the major task seems to be the recording of data from machine analyses. The term *scorer* is used in those cases where observers are to classify behaviors into different typologies or classes or categories. A *transcriber* is usually involved in transforming or notating behavior into a behavioral record of some written form. The term *judge*, on the other hand, is used in those cases in which the observers are mainly asked for inference rather than description, that is, cases where the major interest of the researcher is in assessing the judge's interpretation of the behavior. Finally, the more neutral term *rater* is used for global assessment on adjective or attribute scales in which either inferential or behavioral characteristics are being evaluated.

Some issues in transcription and classification

Transcription by symbolic notation is very much influenced by the phonetic–linguistic tradition, which assumes that every portion of speech consists of a meaningful unit. Adherents of the transcription method for nonverbal behavior assume that the same is true for behavior generally and that it is therefore essential to provide an exhaustive transcription of all aspects of behavior. A large number of transcription systems for nonverbal behavior have been developed or adapted from areas such as dance notation (see Birdwhistell, 1970; Hutchinson, 1970; Kendon, Chapter 8; Rosenfeld, Chapter 5; Scherer, Chapter 4). Some of the advantages and disadvantages of using the transcription method are discussed in later chapters. In general, however, it seems fair to state that the usefulness of a thorough transcription of nonverbal behavior as a way of providing evidence for any of the major research issues in the field has not yet come forth. Most of these transcription systems are exhausting to use, but there is no evidence that they are exhaustive. In fact, one of their key problems is that usually there is no explicit statement about how the investigator decided what to include, and the user is led to believe that a transcription is complete just because it is long and cumbersome. Furthermore, many of these transcription systems have been developed in a way that makes them difficult to use in statistical analyses, though there is no necessary reason for this to be the case.

As mentioned before, coding or category systems are selective, in that only a certain number of predefined units are analyzed. There seem to be three major types of such coding schemes: (1) natural language labels, (2) categories of physical characteristics, and (3) functional categories.

Natural language-label categories make use of the segmentation and categorization potential inherent in culturally shared language labels. Thus categories such as *smile, laughter, frown, pout, giggle,* and the like are presumed to be used in a comparable fashion by judges and thus to be usable as coding schemes (possibly on the basis of a checklist of labels of this sort). The use of such categories is not infrequently reported in the literature, particularly in human ethology, sociolinguistics, and social psychology. Although this procedure is quick, it may also be rather dirty. Unfortunately, researchers using this method often do not bother to establish whether their judges really do all mean the same facial movements by *smile* or all agree on the sound quality of a *giggle.* Because there may be regional and interindividual differences in language-label use, the comparability of results obtained with different judges cannot be established. Furthermore, many natural language labels contain evaluative connotations. For example, the label *gloomy voice* contains not only a voice quality description but also a characterization of the state of the speaker. Thus it is difficult to know to what extent judges using natural language labels use their inferences and attributions about psychological states and interpersonal processes in assigning labels to behaviors.

Category systems using physical characteristics as criteria can be more objectively defined. For example, a scorer could categorize as "right head lean" all head movements where the head is tilted to the right to at least a particular angle (see Rosenfeld, Chapter 5). Or the scorer could determine fundamental frequency (pitch) contours and categorize them as going up or down or up-and-down (see Scherer, Section 4.6; Stern & Wasserman, 1979). As long as coders can be expected to be reasonably precise about the interpretation of physical measurements, a high reliability of such categorizations will result. One possible drawback is the fact that classification on the basis of particular physical features cannot be guaranteed to result in valid or meaningful categories.

The third approach to coding attempts ensures that valid categories do result by basing them on functional considerations, that is, classifying behaviors on the basis of their role in communication or individual coping. The best example of such functional coding schemes is a number of hand movement coding systems differentiating self-manipulatory movements such as scratching or stroking, with presumed individual adaptation functions, from "illustrating" or "object-focused" movements, with an information-transmission or interaction-regulation function (Ekman & Friesen, 1969; K. R. Scherer, Wallbott, & Scherer, 1979; see also Rosenfeld, Section 5.5). Possible problems with this kind of measurement system include the necessity of making a priori judgments about the functions of certain behaviors, the danger that coders will make inferences concerning the intentions of actors in categorizing movements by function, and the difficulty of differentiating movements that have similar functions but that could be profitably distinguished on other grounds.

1.5. Some comments on data analysis

The possibilities for the analysis of the data obtained through the measurement procedures just discussed do not differ dramatically from the choices researchers usually face in analyzing their data. Depending on the purpose of the study, different types of analysis techniques can be used: exploration vs. testing hypotheses, quantitative vs. qualitative analysis, statistical vs. illustrative approaches, and so on. Many examples of these different possibilities will be found in the individual chapters in this volume, and comprehensive coverage of the various aspects of these data-analytic procedures can be found in most surveys of data analysis in the social and behavioral sciences.

One serious deficiency of much of the research in nonverbal behavior is that in general only central tendencies in the data are reported. Very rarely is each individual or each record examined individually and in detail. If one is trying to characterize general nonverbal behavior for a specific type of person, let alone the species, then one cannot be content with simply describing the mean or reporting a correlation. An attempt must be made to inspect individual records and behavior patterns and to report the number of instances that fit the general trend indicated in the statistical coefficients. One should try to explain the reason why behavior patterns for some individuals do not conform to the central tendencies. In many cases, this is an important possibility for the improvement of a theory or hypothesis.

For example, in a study of stress and deception among nurses (Ekman, Friesen, & Scherer, 1976), a number of phenomena were apparent on the group level, such as increase of fundamental frequency from baseline to stress. However, looking at each of the individual subjects made it readily apparent that there were moderator variables, mostly personality characteristics, that could serve to separate the subjects into two groups characterized by very different types of nonverbal reactions (K. R. Scherer, 1979b).

Very frequently, researchers tend to look not at raw data but only at the output generated by statistical analysis packages. This may be quite misleading in cases where the distribution of various behavioral categories is very important for the question being asked. It is thus advisable to look more frequently at the distributions and the scatterplots between variables, and not just at the means and the variances. In many cases, the data should be transformed before statistical analyses are performed, because changes in the mean might be associated with change in the variance.

Among data-analytic methods that are very relevant for nonverbal behavior research and that are not well established in the social and behavioral sciences are the qualitative analyses of the structure of interactive behavior (see Kendon, Chapter 8; West & Zimmerman, Chapter 9), as well as the sequence and cluster analysis methods designed to study sequences and changes rather than aggregates (see van Hooff, Chapter 7).

Given that most of the research and the analyses on nonverbal behavior are exploratory, the use of statistical procedures without consideration of individual behavior patterns and raw data is not really justified. It is only after a phenomenon and its characteristics have been fairly well established that we can use high-powered data analysis techniques. Also, given our very restricted knowledge about nonverbal behavior, we should not stick to single cases, as pointed out previously. When we are dealing with measurement techniques that are imprecise, in areas which are not yet well explored and in which we do not have much conceptual guidance, it is all the more problematical to be content with a single case.

1.6. Conclusions

This chapter has been an attempt to survey some of the major methodological issues facing students of nonverbal behavior. Although our review has shown that behavior sampling and measurement procedures are closely linked to research issues and theoretical assumptions, there is no inherent dichotomy between qualitative, structural, and interactional approaches, on the one hand, and experimental, quantitative, and psychological studies, on the other. Although this distinction may have some basis in the historical development of the field, and although it was sharpened by early reviews of the literature, it can and it must be overcome if the nature and function of nonverbal behavior are to be studied comprehensively. Nonverbal behavior expresses both traits and states of individuals and serves as a culturally shared and structured signaling system. What is more, it performs both of these functions at the same time and often through the very same movements. Thus studies focused on the individual and studies focused on interaction and communication have to complement each other. Researchers leaning toward a particular focus and raised in a particular theoretical tradition need to take cognizance of the wide variety of methodological approaches available for the empirical study of nonverbal behavior, and need to base their choices on appropriateness rather than prejudice. We hope that this handbook will help them to do so.

References

Allport, G. W. The historical background of modern social psychology. In G. Lindzey & E. Aronson (Eds.), *The handbook of social psychology* (2nd ed., Vol. 1). Reading, Mass.: Addison-Wesley, 1968.

Allport, G. W., & Vernon, P. E. *Studies in expressive movement*. New York: Macmillan, 1933.

Argyle, M., & Dean, J. Eye-contact, distance and affiliation. *Sociometry*, 1965, *28*, 289–304.

Bateson, G., & Mead, M. *Balinese character: A photographic analysis* (Vol. 2). New York: Special Publications of the New York Academy of Sciences, 1942.

Bell, C. *Essays on the anatomy and philosophy of expression: As connected with the fine arts*. London, 1806.

Birdwhistell, R. *Introduction to kinesics*. Washington, D.C.: Foreign Service Institute; Louisville: University of Louisville Press, 1952. Now available in microfilm only from University Microfilms, Inc., 313 N. First St., Ann Arbor, Mich. Partly reprinted as an appendix to R. Birdwhistell, *Kinesics and context*. Philadelphia: University of Pennsylvania Press, 1970.

Birdwhistell, R. L. *Kinesics and context*. Philadelphia: University of Pennsylvania Press, 1970.

Blurton Jones, N. G. Criteria for use in describing facial expressions. *Human Biology*, 1971, *43*, 365–413.

Brown, P., & Fraser, C. Speech as a marker of situation. In K. R. Scherer & H. Giles (Eds.), *Social markers in speech*. Cambridge: Cambridge University Press, 1979.

Bühler, K. *Ausdruckstheorie*. Jena: Fischer, 1933.

Chapple, E. D. The interaction chronograph: Its evolution and present application. *Personnel*, 1948/49, *25*, 295–307.

Condon, W. S., & Ogston, W. D. A segmentation of behavior. *Journal of Psychiatric Research*, 1967, *5*, 221–235.

Darwin, C. *The expression of the emotions in man and animals*. Chicago: University of Chicago Press, 1965. (Originally published, London: John Murray, 1872.)

Dittman, A. T. The relationship between body movements and moods in interviews. *Journal of Consulting Psychology*, 1962, *26*, 480.

Duchenne, B. *Mécanisme de la physionomie humaine; ou, Analyse electrophysiologique de l'expression des passions*. Paris: Baillière, 1862.

Duncan, S. D., Jr. Nonverbal communication. *Psychological Bulletin*, 1969, *72*, 118–137.

Duncan, S. D., Jr. Some signals and rules for taking speaking turns in conversations. *Journal of Personality and Social Psychology*, 1972, *23*, 283–292.

Duncan, S. D., Jr., & Fiske, D. W. *Face-to-face interaction*. Hillsdale, N.J.: Erlbaum, 1977.

Efron, D. *Gesture, race, and culture*. The Hague: Mouton, 1972. (Originally published, 1941.)

Eibl-Eibesfeldt, I. *Ethology: The biology of behavior*. New York: Holt, Rinehart & Winston, 1970.

Ekman, P. A methodological discussion of nonverbal behavior. *Journal of Psychology*, 1957, *43*, 141–149.

Ekman, P. Differential communication of affect by head and body cues. *Journal of Personality and Social Psychology*, 1965, *2*, 726–735.

Ekman, P. Universal and cultural differences in facial expression of emotion. In J. R. Cole (Ed.), *Nebraska Symposium on Motivation* (Vol. 19). Lincoln: University of Nebraska Press, 1972.

Ekman, P. Movements with precise meanings. *Journal of Communication*, 1976, *26*, 14–26.

Ekman, P. About brows: Emotional and conversational signals. In M. von Cranach, K. Foppa, W. Lepenies, & D. Ploog (Eds.), *Human ethology*. Cambridge: Cambridge University Press, 1979.

Ekman, P., & Friesen, W. V. The repertoire of nonverbal behavior: Categories, origins, usage, and coding. *Semiotica*, 1969, *1*, 49–98.

Ekman, P., & Friesen, W. V. *Unmasking the face*. Englewood Cliffs, N.J.: Prentice-Hall, 1975.

Ekman, P., & Friesen, W. V. Measuring facial movement. *Environmental Psychology and Nonverbal Behavior*, 1976, *1*, 56–75.

Ekman, P., & Friesen, W. V. *Manual for the Facial Action Coding System*. Palo Alto, Calif.: Consulting Psychologists Press, 1978.

Ekman, P., Friesen, W. V., & Ellsworth, P. C. *Emotion in the human face: Guidelines for research and an integration of findings*. New York: Pergamon Press, 1972 (2nd rev. ed., P. Ekman, Ed., Cambridge University Press, in press).

Ekman, P., Friesen, W. V., & Scherer, K. R. Body movement and voice pitch in deceptive interaction. *Semiotica*, 1976, *16*, 23–27.

Ekman, P., & Oster, H. Facial expressions of emotion. *Annual Review of Psychology*, 1979, *30*, 527–554.

Ekman, P., Sorenson, E. R., & Friesen, W. V. Pan-cultural elements in facial displays of emotion. *Science*, 1969, *164*, 86–88.

Ellsworth, P. C., & Ludwig, L. M. Visual behavior in social interaction. *Journal of Communication*, 1972, *22*, 375–403.

Fagen, R. M., & Young, D. Y. Temporal patterns of behavior: Durations, intervals, latencies, and sequences. In P. W. Colgan (Ed.), *Quantitative ethology*. New York: Wiley, 1978.

Feldstein, S., & Welkowitz, J. A chronography of conversation: In defense of an objective approach. In A. W. Siegman & S. Feldstein (Eds.), *Nonverbal behavior and communication*. Hillsdale, N.J.: Erlbaum, 1978.

Ferenczi, S. Embarrassed hands. Thinking and muscle innervation. In S. Ferenczi, *Further contributions to the technique and theory of psychoanalysis*. London: Hogarth Press, 1926.

Freedman, N. The analysis of movement behavior during the clinical interview. In A. Siegman & B. Pope (Eds.), *Studies in dyadic communication*. New York: Pergamon Press, 1972.

Freud, S. *Die Psychopathologie des Alltagslebens*. London: Imago, 1904.

Garfinkel, H. *Studies in ethnomethodology*. Englewood Cliffs, N.J.: Prentice-Hall, 1967.
Giles, H., Scherer, K. R., & Taylor, D. M. Speech markers in social interaction. In K. R. Scherer & H. Giles (Eds.), *Social markers in speech*. Cambridge: Cambridge University Press, 1979.
Goffman, E. *Behavior in public places*. London: Collier-Macmillan, 1963.
Goffman, E. *Relations in public: Microstudies of the public order*. New York: Harper & Row, Colophon Books, 1971.
Harper, R. G., Wiens, A. N., & Matarazzo, J. D. *Nonverbal communication: The state of the art*. New York: Wiley, 1978.
Hinde, R. A. (Ed.). *Non-verbal communication*. Cambridge: Cambridge University Press, 1972.
Hockett, C. F. Logical considerations in the study of animal communication. In W. E. Lanyon & W. N. Tavolga (Eds.), *Animal sounds and communication*. Washington, D.C.: American Institute of Biological Sciences, 1960.
Hutchinson, A. *Labanotation: The system for recording movement* (Rev. ed.). New York: Theatre Art Books, 1970.
Jaffe, J., & Feldstein, S. *Rhythms of dialogue*. New York: Academic Press, 1970.
Johnson, H. G., Ekman, P., & Friesen, W. V. Communicative body movements: American emblems. *Semiotica*, 1975, *15*, 335–353.
Kendon, A. Movement coordination in social interaction: Some examples described. *Acta Psychologica*, 1970, *32*, 100–125.
Kendon, A. The role of visible behavior in the organization of social interaction. In M. von Cranach & I. Vine (Eds.), *Social communication and movement: Studies of interaction and expression in man and chimpanzee*. London: Academic Press, 1973.
Key, M. R. *Nonverbal communication: A research guide and bibliography*. Metuchen, N.J.: Scarecrow Press, 1977.
Kleinpaul, R. *Sprache ohne Worte: Idee einer allgemeinen Wissenschaft der Sprache*. The Hague: Mouton, 1972. (Originally published, Leipzig: Friedrich, 1888.)
Krout, M. H. Symbolic gestures in the clinical study of personality. *Transactions of the Illinois State Academy of Science*, 1931, *24*, 519–523.
Laver, J. *The phonetic description of voice quality*. Cambridge: Cambridge University Press, 1980.
Mahl, G. F. Gestures and body movements in interviews. In J. Shlien (Ed.), *Research in psychotherapy* (Vol. 3). Washington, D.C.: American Psychological Association, 1968.
Mahl, G. F., & Schulze, G. Psychological research in the extralinguistic area. In T. Sebeok, A. S. Hayes, & M. C. Bateson (Eds.), *Approaches to semiotics*. The Hague: Mouton, 1964.
Matarazzo, J. D., & Wiens, A. N. *The interview: Research on its anatomy and structure*. Chicago: Aldine-Atherton, 1972.
Mehrabian, A. Significance of posture and position in the communication of attitude and status relationships. *Psychological Bulletin*, 1969, *71*, 359–372.
Mehrabian, A. *Nonverbal communication*. Chicago: Aldine-Atherton, 1972.
Moses, P. J. *The voice of neurosis*. New York: Grune & Stratton, 1954.
Orne, M. T. On the social psychology of the psychological experiment. *American Psychologist*, 1962, *17*, 776–783.
Ostwald, P. F. *Soundmaking: The acoustic communication of emotion*. Springfield: Charles C. Thomas, 1963.
Pear, T. H. *Voice and personality*. London: Chapman & Hall, 1931.
Piderit, T. *Mimik und Physiognomik*. Detmold, 1867.

Reich, W. *Character-Analysis* (3rd ed.). New York: Farrar, Straus & Giroux, 1949.

Rosenthal, R. *Experimenter effects in behavioral research.* New York: Appleton-Century-Crofts, 1966.

Sackett, G. P. (Ed.). *Observing behavior* (Vols. 1–2). Baltimore: University Park Press, 1978.

Scheflen, A. E. Natural history method in psychotherapy: Communicational research. In L. A. Gottschalk & A. H. Auerbach (Eds.), *Methods of research in psychotherapy.* New York: Appleton-Century-Crofts, 1966.

Scheflen, A. E. *Communicational structure: Analysis of a psychotherapy transaction.* Bloomington: Indiana University Press, 1973.

Schegloff, E. A. Sequencing in conversational openings. *American Anthropologist,* 1968, *70,* 1075–1095.

Schegloff, E. A., & Sacks, H. Opening up closings. *Semiotica,* 1973, *8,* 289–327.

Scherer, K. R. Judging personality from voice: A cross-cultural approach to an old issue in interpersonal perception. *Journal of Personality,* 1972, *40,* 191–210.

Scherer, K. R. Affektlaute und vokale Embleme. In R. Posner & H. P. Reinecke (Eds.), *Zeichenprozesse: Semiotische Forschung in den Einzelwissenschaften.* Wiesbaden: Athenaion, 1977.

Scherer, K. R. Personality markers in speech. In K. R. Scherer & H. Giles (Eds.), *Social markers in speech.* Cambridge: Cambridge University Press, 1979. (a)

Scherer, K. R. Nonlinguistic vocal indicators of emotion and psychopathology. In C. E. Izard (Ed.), *Emotions in personality and psychopathology.* New York: Plenum, 1979. (b)

Scherer, K. R. Speech and emotional states. In J. Darby (Ed.), *The evaluation of speech in psychiatry.* New York: Grune & Stratton, 1981.

Scherer, K. R., & Scherer, U. *Nonverbal behavior and impression formation in naturalistic situations.* In H. Hiebsch, H. Brandstätter, & H. H. Kelley (Eds.), *Proceedings of the XIInd International Congress of Psychology, Leipzig (GDR), Social Psychology.* Berlin/Amsterdam: VEB Deutscher Verlag der Wissenschaften and North Holland, 1981.

Scherer, K. R., Wallbott, H. G., & Scherer, U. Methoden zur Klassifikation von Bewegungsverhalten: Ein funktionaler Ansatz. *Zeitschrift für Semiotik,* 1979, *1,* 187–202.

Scherer, U., & Scherer, K. R. Psychological factors in bureaucratic encounters: Determinants and effects of interactions between officials and clients. In W. T. Singleton, P. Spurgeon, & R. B. Stammers (Eds.), *The analysis of social skill.* New York: Plenum, 1980.

Stern, D. N., & Wasserman, G. A. *Intonation contours as units of information in maternal speech to pre-linguistic infants.* Paper presented at the meeting of the Society for Research on Child Development, San Francisco, 1979.

von Cranach, M., & Harré, R. (Eds.). *Goal-directed action.* Cambridge: Cambridge University Press, in press.

Weick, K. E. Systematic observational methods. In G. Lindzey & E. Aronson (Eds.), *The handbook of social psychology* (2nd ed. Vol. 2). Reading, Mass.: Addison-Wesley, 1968.

Wolff, W. *The expression of personality.* New York: Harper, 1943.

Wundt., W. *Völkerpsychologie* (Vols. 1–10). Leipzig: Engelmann, 1900–1920.

2. Methods for measuring facial action

PAUL EKMAN

2.1. Introduction

Of all the nonverbal behaviors – body movements, posture, gaze, proxemics, voice – the face is probably the most commanding and complicated, and perhaps the most confusing. In part, the face is commanding because it is always visible, always providing some information. There is no facial equivalent to the concealment maneuver of putting one's hands in one's pockets. Whereas sounds and the body movements that illustrate speech are intermittent, the face even in repose may provide information about some emotion or mood state. Many nonverbal behaviors simply do not occur when a person is alone, or at least do so very rarely. For example, it would be unusual for someone to shrug or gesture hello when totally alone. Yet facial expressions of emotion may be quite intense even when a person is alone. They are not occasioned only by the presence of others. In fact, social situations can dampen facial expression of emotion (Ekman, 1972; Ekman & Friesen, 1975, chap. 11).

The face is commanding also because it is the location for the senses of smell, taste, sight, and hearing. It is the site of the intake organs for inputs of air, water, and food necessary to life. It is the output source for speech, and what we hear in part is determined by the lip movements we see with the speech (McGurk & MacDonald, 1976). It commands attention because it is the symbol of the self. The faces of those we care about are hung on walls, displayed on desks, carried in wallets.

Multimessage–multisignal system

This commanding focus of attention is quite complex. The face can be considered as a multimessage, multisignal semiotic system (Ekman, 1978). The face conveys not only the message of individual identity, but also messages about gender and race. Certain changes in the face reveal, more or less truthfully, age. There are standards for beautiful and ugly, smart and stupid, strong and weak faces. And apart from stereotypes, there have been claims for accurate information about personality traits, psychopathology, and intelligence from facial behavior.

These different messages (identity, gender, beauty, traits, etc.) have as their source one of four types of facial signal systems: static, slow, artificial, and rapid. *Static* signs include the size, shape, and relative locations of the features and the contours produced by the underlying bony structure. These static signs are the likely vehicles for transmitting information about identity and beauty. Examples of *slow* sign vehicles would be the accumulation of wrinkles, pouches, and bags, which occur with and convey information about age. *Artificial* signs, such as cosmetics and plastic surgery, attempt to disguise these slow age signs. The *rapid* signs include the actions produced by the muscles (typically called expressions), as well as changes in muscle tonus, blood flow, skin temperature, and coloring.

Most research on the face has focused just upon these rapid signs, in particular, the momentary movements of the face and the muscle tonus changes as sign vehicles for information about emotion and mood. Rapid signs may also be relevant sources for other messages, for correct or incorrect information about traits, attitudes, personality, and so on.[1] Our focus in this chapter is upon the methods for measuring momentary facial movement (expressions). Later such methods will be compared with electromyographic measures of muscular activity.

Two methodological approaches

Ekman and Friesen (Ekman, 1964, 1965; Ekman & Friesen, 1968, 1969; Ekman, in press) distinguished two methodological approaches for studying nonverbal behavior, namely, measuring judgments about one or another message and measuring the sign vehicles that convey the message.[2] Often either method can be used to answer a question. Take, for example, the question whether facial expressions vary with psychopathology. Suppose a sample was available of facial behavior during interviews with patients who had a diagnosis of schizophrenia or depression, and with a control group who had no psychiatric problems. To utilize the *message judgment* approach, the facial movements in these interviews would be shown to a group of observers, who would be asked whether each person they viewed was normal, schizophrenic, or depressive. If the judgments were accurate, this would answer the question, showing that facial expressions do convey messages about psychopathology. To utilize the *measurement of sign vehicles* approach, some or all of the facial movements would be classified or counted in some fashion. If the findings showed, for example, that depressives raised the inner corners of their eyebrows more than the other two groups, whereas schizophrenics showed facial movements that very slowly faded off the face, this would also answer the question affirmatively.

Although both approaches can answer the same question, each provides different information. The message judgment approach would show that people can tell from viewing a face whether a person is schizophrenic, depressive, or normal. That cannot be learned from the other approach, which does not determine whether observers can accurately judge this message. But by measuring the sign vehicles it is possible to find out exactly what differs in the faces of the two groups: Is it the timing or the particular movements, or both, that show whether a person is depressive or schizophrenic? That cannot be learned from the first approach, which never determines exactly what the observers respond to when making their judgments.

Let us turn now to some of the other relationships between the outcomes of these two approaches. Consider these cases:

1. Negative findings with message judgment and positive findings with sign vehicle measurement. This suggests that people (at least those used in the study) do not know what to look for or cannot see the differences in facial behavior. Careful measurement of the facial sign vehicles might have revealed hitherto unknown differences. Once known, these clues to psychopathology might make it possible for observers to make judgments accurately. Or perhaps the clues are such that people will never be able to make this judgment accurately when viewing the behavior at real time. The differences in facial behavior might be too subtle to be seen without repeated or slowed viewing and precise measurement.

2. Positive findings with message judgment and negative findings with sign vehicle measurement. The positive results show that there must be some difference in the facial sign vehicles, for how else would the observers achieve accuracy in their judgment? This outcome shows that something must be faulty in the measurement of the sign vehicles. Either the measurement was not reliable or it was selective rather than comprehensive, and there was bad luck in selecting just those facial movements that did not differ.

3. Negative findings with message judgment and negative findings with sign vehicle measurement. This all-too-frequent outcome may occur because the face simply does not provide information about the topic being studied. Or something may have been faulty in the sampling. For example, there may not have been sufficient care in obtaining high agreement among experts about the diagnosis of the patients. Or perhaps the patients were receiving medications that suppressed some behavioral differences. Also, this outcome does not eliminate the possibility that there were differences in facial movement related to psychopathology that the observers did not know about or could not see (thus the message judgment approach failed), and that were missed by a faulty technique for measuring the facial sign vehicle. Was the measurement of sign vehicles comprehensive rather than selective? If it was selective, the possibility always remains that movements unrelated to psychopathology were measured.

The difference between these two approaches – message judgment and the measurement of sign vehicle – has sometimes been confusing, because both may involve observers (Rosenthal, for example, concluded there is little difference between the two; see Section 6.1). It is what the observers do that matters. In message judgment they make *inferences* about something underlying the behavior – emotion, mood, traits, attitudes, personality, and the like. In measuring sign vehicles the observers *describe* the surface of behavior; they count how many times the face moves, or how long a movement lasts, or whether it was a movement of the frontalis or corrugator muscle. (Describing which muscle produced a movement may require an inference, but it is an inference about a physical characteristic, not about underlying psychological phenomena.) Observers who describe behavior are supposed to function like machines, and indeed might someday be replaced by an optical scanner. Techniques for measuring sign vehicles that fail to remove inferences about meaning from the description of behavior will be faulted in the evaluation that follows.

It is not accident that in message judgment studies observers typically are shown a sample of facial behavior at real time, because the purpose usually is to generalize to more natural interpersonal perception. (An exception is the use of still photographs in message judgment studies. These experiments cannot claim any relevance to usual life circumstances.) In sign vehicle measurement there is usually repeated and slowed-motion viewing, because the object is precise description, not observation under natural circumstances.

Though the two approaches can both answer the same questions, they can also answer different questions, for they focus on different phenomena. Message judgment research is not typically focused on the face. The face is but an input, although there may be study of different types of faces, as in the psychopathology example. In message judgment studies the focus is instead on the person observing the face and/or on the message obtained. Questions have to do with whether a difference is detectable or accurate; there are individual differences among observers, reflecting skill, gender, personality, and the like; messages obtained are best represented as dimensions or categories; and so on.

Facial sign vehicles are measured when the focus is upon unearthing something fairly specific about facial behavior itself, not about the perception of the face. It is the only method that can be used to answer such questions as:

1. To what extent is the facial activity shown by newborns and young infants systematic, not random, and which particular actions first show such systematic organization? To answer this question, facial behavior shown during samples taken at different developmental points or in different situational contexts can be measured. Then the probabilities of particular co-occurrences and sequential patterns of facial actions can be evaluated (see Oster & Ekman, 1978).
2. Which particular facial actions are employed to signal emphasis in conversation? Facial actions that co-occur with verbal or vocal emphasis must be measured to determine if there are any actions that consistently accompany any emphasis (see Ekman, 1980).
3. Is there a difference in the smile during enjoyment as compared to a discomfort smile? The particular facial actions evident in smiling movements must be measured when persons are known, by means other than the face, to be experiencing positive and negative affect (see Ekman, Friesen, & Ancoli, 1980).
4. Are there differences in heart rate that accompany nose wrinkling and upper lip raising versus opening the eyes and raising the brows? Facial behavior must be measured to identify the moments when these particular facial configurations occur in order to examine coincident heart rate activity (see Ancoli, Kamiya, & Ekman, 1980; Malmstrom, Ekman, & Friesen, 1972).

These examples are not intended to convey the full range of issues that can be addressed only by measuring facial sign vehicles. They should, however, serve to illustrate the variety of questions requiring this approach. One might expect the measurement of sign vehicles approach to have been followed often, as it is required for study of many different problems. But there have been only a few such studies compared to the many that have measured the messages judged when viewing the face. It is much easier to perform the latter sort of study. The investigator need not tamper with the face itself, other than by picking some sample to show. Data are obtained quickly: One can measure observers' judgments much more quickly than one can describe reliably the flow and variety of facial movement.

Perhaps the most important obstacle to research measuring sign vehicles has been the lack of any accepted, standard, ready-for-use technique for measuring facial movement. Each investigator who has measured facial movement has invented his technique in large part de novo, rarely making use of the work of his predecessors. Some have seemed to be uninformed by the previous literature. Even the more scholarly have found it difficult to build upon the methods previously reported, because descriptions of facial activity are often vaguer than they appear upon first reading. A facial action may seem to be described in sufficient detail and exactness until an attempt is made to apply that description to the flow of facial behavior.

Coverage

The 14 techniques for measuring facial actions reviewed in this chapter cover a span of 55 years, from Landis's 1924 report to the study by Izard that became available from the author in late 1979. Five were not presented by the authors as methods that could be used by others, but were reported in the course of describing substantive results. They have been included for various reasons. Landis is included because he was among the first to build a measurement system based on the anatomy of muscle action, and his negative findings were influential for the next forty years. Frois-Wittmann (1930) and Fulcher (1942) were both innovative for their times, but their methods and findings have been largely forgotten by the current generation of researchers. McGrew's (1972) behavioral checklist has influenced those studying children from an ethological viewpoint. Nystrom (1974) has been included because there is much interest today in measuring facial action in infants. The other 9 techniques reviewed represent all of the systems for measuring facial movement that have been proposed, some of which have attracted considerable interest and research activity.

A few reports describing facial actions in detail have been omitted. Discussions of facial behavior that did not report a procedure for measurement – such as Hjorstjo (1970), Lightoller (1925), and Seaford (1976), all of which provided very enlightening discussions of the anatomical basis of facial movement – are not included. Depictions of facial expressions primarily designed to train observers to recognize emotion, rather than measure facial movement (Ekman & Friesen, 1975, are excluded even though some investigators have used them to measure the face (Hiatt, Campos, & Emde, 1977). Izard's Affex (previously called FESM) has also been excluded because observers are required to judge emotion rather than describe the appearance of facial movement. Unlike most message judgment approaches to the measurement of the face, Izard's Affex provides the observers with training about the various clues believed to signal each emotion. There is no way to know, of course, what clues the observers actually rely upon when they make their emotion judgments, because all the investigator obtains is the end point in the observers' inferences. Though the aim of Affex is to provide quick data about emotions, it cannot allow investigation of what indeed are the facial clues to each emotion. Other techniques designed to provide economical measures of emotion (Ekman & Friesen's EMFACS and Izard's MAX) are considered in this chapter because they involve describing facial appearance rather than making direct inferences about underlying states. Reports that used but did not add new methodological features to one of the techniques here reviewed are excluded. Also omitted (except for a later discussion of electromyography [EMG]) are techniques that intrude by attaching something to the subject's face, marking the subject's face, or moving the subject around in front of a camera (Rubenstein, 1969).

The measurement techniques that are reviewed share the features of being unobtrusive; requiring a permanent visual record (video or cinema) that allows slowed or multiple viewing, rather than being applicable to behavior as it occurs; and relying upon an observer who scores or codes behavior according to a set of predetermined categories or items.

This chapter cannot teach the reader how to measure facial actions. Nor does it fully describe most of the measurement techniques, many of which would require a whole chapter, and some an entire book. (Exceptions are the techniques of Birdwhistell, Landis, and Nystrom, each of whom provided little more detail than what is reported here.) Instead, the emphasis is upon the criteria to be considered in evaluating any measurement technique, either one of those available or one that the reader might devise. The strengths and weaknesses of each technique will be made evident, so that the reader is better able to choose which might be best for a particular research problem. Already (Scherer & Ekman, Section 1.4) some mention has been made of the need for reliability and the virtues of a comprehensive measurement system. We

will begin, however, with a different criterion, one that is at the heart of each system: How was it discovered? What basis did the investigator have for proposing his or her technique?

2.2. The basis for deriving units

Each of the 14 measurement techniques contains a list of facial actions such as a brow raise, nose wrinkle, lip corners down, and so on. Measurement includes noting whether any action (or, with some techniques, combination of actions) is present. Later we will consider how each technique describes actions and differentiates one action from another, but here we are concerned with the question how the author decided upon his or her particular list. The lists vary in number of items from a low of 22 to a high of 77. Some actions appear in all techniques, other actions in only some techniques, and still others in just one technique. Sometimes behavior that is treated as a single action by one technique appears subdivided as two distinct actions by others. For example, raising the eyebrows is treated as one behavioral unit by some techniques, but appears as three separate units – inner brow raise, outer brow raise, and the combination of inner and outer brow raise – in other techniques. Most authors did not explain what they considered when they included or excluded a facial action, what basis they had for subdividing a unit another researcher had treated as a single action, or why they found it wise to collapse a distinction drawn by another investigator. In fact, most did not acknowledge the work of their predecessors, but instead acted as if they had invented their system and had no knowledge of differences between it and the systems of their earlier or contemporary colleagues.[3]

Investigators – often failing to specify the sample, setting, or persons viewed – usually said only that they looked at behavior and that their list of facial actions was simply the product of what they saw. Something more is needed, however, to account for the differences among these techniques, even allowing for the fact that each investigator observed a different behavior sample. What stood out, which attributes were noticed when an action occurred, how the flow of behavior was segmented by the investigator probably depended upon theoretical commitments. Only a few were explicit.

Birdwhistell (1952) tried to organize units and select behavior to construct a system paralleling linguistic units.[4] Grant (1969) advocated the selection and organization of measurement units according to function. This puts the cart before the horse, because the measurement technique so constructed was to be used to discover the function of those very behaviors. Among ethologists, Blurton Jones (1971) was most explicit in considering the anatomical basis for facial actions, although he did not say that this was the final or even the major basis for his decisions about what to include, and he did not specify how he arrived at his list of minimal units of behavior.

Ekman, Friesen, and Tomkins (1971), in contrast to the aforementioned investigators, derived their list of facial actions from explicit theory about the facial actions relevant to emotion, rather than from observation of some sample of behavior. The cart-before-horse criticism applies to them also. Although they could find out whether the actions proposed for one emotion do or do not accurately reflect that emotion, they could not discover signals for emotion that they did not know about in advance. Izard, eight years later, also used theory about emotion signals as the basis for selecting actions to score in his measurement technique MAX. His decisions were based on inspection of still photographs of posed emotions that had yielded high agreement among observers who made global judgments about emotion.[5]

The anatomical basis of facial action provided a third totally different basis for deriving units of behavior. The measurement units were presumably based on what the muscles allow the face to do. Because we all have the same muscles (for all practical purposes), this approach might be expected to have led the investigators who followed it to arrive at the same listings of facial actions. This is not the case. For example, Landis had 22 actions and Frois-Wittmann 28, and yet they both claimed to have based their measurement units on the anatomy of facial action. In part, the discrepancies occurred because of explicit decisions to select only certain actions. Most standard anatomy texts list many, usually not all, facial muscles with rather simple, only partially correct, and usually quite incomplete accounts of how each muscle changes appearance. Most investigators who based their technique on anatomy selected only some muscles, and usually did not explain the basis for their selection. Ekman and Friesen (1976, 1978) and Ermiane and Gergerian (1978) were exceptions, each attempting to determine all the actions the anatomy allows. Both studies attempted to determine this by systematically exploring the activity of each single muscle; Ekman and Friesen also resurrected Duchenne's (1862) technique of determining how muscles change appearance by inserting a needle into and electrically stimulating muscles.

The discrepancies among the most recent techniques (Ekman & Friesen; Ermiane & Gergerian; Izard's MAX) are due to differences in purpose and in procedure for obtaining reliability. Both Ekman and Friesen and Ermiane and Gergerian attempted to include in their lists changes in appearance that are independent of each other. If a muscle contraction would produce two or three changes in appearance, these were gathered together as multiple indexes of the activity of one unit or muscle. For example, when the entire frontalis muscle acts, it will (1) raise the eyebrows; (2) produce horizontal furrows running across the forehead (except in infants, who have a fatty pad in the forehead blocking such wrinkles); and (3) expose more of the eye cover fold (the skin between the upper eyelid and the eyebrow). Both Ekman and Friesen and Ermiane and Gergerian listed these multiple signs together as different ways of recognizing that this one action had occurred. Izard, however, treated signs (1) and (2) of frontalis muscle activity as separate measurement units, giving each equal, independent, separate status, failing to recognize that they are signs of the same action. He ignored sign (3).

Izard also differed from the others in selecting only movements that he judged relevant to emotion. Ekman and Friesen and Ermiane and Gergerian intended to include all the possible appearance changes that the muscles can produce. This sometimes meant creating more than one measurement unit, if use of different strands of a single muscle or different portions of that muscle was found to produce visibly different changes in appearance. For example, Ekman and Friesen and Ermiane and Gergerian distinguished a number of different facial action units that are based on various uses of what anatomists have termed one muscle – the orbicularis oris, which circles the lips. Izard included only some of these separate appearance changes. Strangely, Izard excluded specific actions that are said by many theorists to signal emotions and that are shown by Ekman and Friesen's data to be emotion signals. Izard and Dougherty (1981) say that actions were dropped that were not efficient, but inspection of that article and of earlier versions of Izard's scoring technique (FMCS) suggests instead that Izard never considered a number of facial actions important to differentiating among emotions.

The Ekman and Friesen technique differed from the others in another important respect. Anatomy was only part of their basis for the derivation of measurement units. They also determined whether observers could reliably distinguish all of the appearance changes resulting from the various muscles. If two appearance changes could not be reliably distinguished, they were combined, even if different muscles were involved. If Ekman and Friesen erred, it was on the side of caution, by excluding distinctions that observers with considerable training might perhaps be able to distinguish. The opposite error may have been made by Ermaine and Gergerian and by Izard. They included distinctions without reporting exploration or test of whether each and every distinction could reliably be made by those who learn their system (see Section 2.7 on reliability).

Tables 2.1, 2.2, and 2.3 and the chapter appendix compare the 14 measurement techniques on each of the criteria (arranged as columns) that are discussed. The basis for deriving units provides the order in which the 14 techniques appear: first the one system that is linguistically based; then those that are ethologically based; then one that is theoretically based; and finally those based on the anatomy of facial action.

2.3. Comprehensiveness or selectivity

Three aspects of facial movement can be measured either selectively or comprehensively. Most investigators have considered how to measure only the type of action, not its intensity or its timing. *Type* refers to whether it was a brow raise, or an inner corner brow raise, or a brow lower, or some other action. *Intensity* refers to the magnitude of the appearance change resulting from any single facial action. *Timing* refers to the duration of the movement, whether it was abrupt or gradual in onset, and so on.

Type of action

A technique for measuring the type of facial action can be selective, measuring only some of the actions that can occur, or it may claim to be comprehensive, providing a means of measuring all visible facial action. There are advantages and disadvantages in each case. If the technique is selective, it is important to know what has been excluded; and if it claims to be comprehensive, there must be some evidence to establish that this is indeed the case.

The great advantage of a selective technique is economy. Because only some of the mass of facial actions must be attended to, the work can be done more quickly. Suppose an investigator wants to measure whether fear is reduced by exposure to one set of instructions versus another. A measurement technique that allows measurement of just the occurrence of three or four fear facial expressions would be ideal, because it will not matter if the occurrence of anger, disgust, distress, or some other emotion is missed. Even if the technique does not include *all* of the fear facial expressions (and at this time there is no conclusive or even

Table 2.1. *Summary of methods for measuring facial behavior for units and comprehensiveness*

		Comprehensiveness		
	Basis for deriving units	Type of action	Intensity of action	Timing of action
Linguistically based				
Birdwhistell (1952)	Observation of interpersonal behavior; parallel linguistic units	Not claimed to be comprehensive; 53 actions	No provision	No provision
Ethologically based				
Blurton Jones (1971)	Observation of 500 still photographs of 2–5-year-old children	Measures any child's facial expressions; 52 actions	6 degrees of eye openness; 4 degrees of lip separation; 2 degrees of frowns	No provision
Brannigan & Humphries (1972)	Observation of children and adults	Not claimed to be comprehensive; 70 actions	No provision	No provision
Grant (1969)	Observation of children and adults	Not claimed to be comprehensive; 53 actions	No provision	No provision
McGrew (1972)	Observation of 3–4-year-old children	Not claimed to be comprehensive; 31 actions	No provision	No provision
Nystrom (1974)	Observation of 1-month-old infants	Not claimed to be comprehensive; 35 descriptors	No provision	No provision
Young & Decarie (1977)	Observation of 36 infants	Measures 42 facial configurations; selected only to be relevant to emotion in the last quarter of first year in six test situations	No provision	No provision

Theoretically based				
Ekman, Friesen, & Tomkins (1971)	Theory about emotion expression	Measures signs of just 6 emotions; 77 descriptors	No provision	Start–stop
Izard MAX (1979[b])	Theory about emotion signals; data from posed still photographs	Measures just actions needed to identify emotion in infants; 27 descriptors	No provision	Start–stop
Anatomically based				
Ekman & Friesen (1976, 1978)	Muscular	Measures all visible movements; 44 action units that singly or in combination can score any observed action	Four actions have 3-point rating on intensity; provision to rate intensity in other actions	Start–stop and onset–apex–offset
Frois-Wittmann (1930)	Muscular	Not claimed to be comprehensive; 28 descriptors	No provision	No provision
Fulcher (1942)	Muscular	Not claimed to be comprehensive; absence/presence of 16 muscular actions	Amount of movement in each of three facial areas rated	No provision
Ermiane & Gergerian (1978)	Muscular	Measures all visible movements; 27 muscle actions	Each action rated on 3-point intensity scale	No provision
Landis (1924)	Muscular	Not claimed to be comprehensive; 22 descriptors	Each action rated on 4-point intensity scale	No provision

definitive evidence about all the facial actions for *any* emotion), a selective technique could be useful. It might not matter that some or even most fear expressions were not scored, nor that blends of fear with other emotions were not scored; enough might be measured to show the effect. If the findings were negative, however, the investigator would not know whether the cause was an inadequate experimental treatment (in this example, the instructions might not have differed sufficiently) or failure to measure all of the fear expressions. In such an instance the investigator might want to turn to a comprehensive technique.

Some questions require a comprehensive technique and cannot be answered with a selective one. Suppose the investigator wishes to discover which facial actions signal fear, anger, sadness, and so on.[6] Or perhaps he or she wishes to discover whether different actions are employed to serve a linguistic rather than an emotive function, or to learn what people show on their faces when their heart rates show a sharp acceleration, or whether there are cultural or social class differences in facial actions during a greeting. A comprehensive technique would have to be employed. Once there was reasonably conclusive evidence on any of these issues, then such evidence could provide the basis for selective use of portions of a comprehensive system. For example, Ekman, Friesen, and Simons (in preparation), building upon the earlier research of Landis and Hunt (1939), have strong evidence about the particular combination of facial actions and the timing of those actions that index the startle reaction.[7] Once that has been replicated by other laboratories, those interested in the startle in particular could utilize just that portion of Ekman and Friesen's comprehensive scoring technique.

Only a comprehensive technique allows for discovery of actions that the investigator did not know about in advance and permits a complete test of an a priori theory about facial sign vehicles. A third advantage of a comprehensive technique is that it provides a common nomenclature for descriptions of facial behavior. If many investigators were to use the same comprehensive technique, comparison of findings would be facilitated because investigators, even those who used it selectively, would key their units to a single list of facial actions. Investigators considering selective scoring might well want first to study a comprehensive technique, in order to become acquainted with the entire array of facial actions, so that they could be explicit about what it is they are choosing not to measure.

Wedded to these advantages of comprehensive facial scoring is the disadvantage of cost. It takes more time to learn a comprehensive technique, and it takes more time to apply it, for nothing (presumably) is left out.

It is no accident that the only techniques that claim to be comprehensive – Ekman and Friesen and Ermiane and Gergerian – were anatomically based. An inductive approach would be too costly if comprehensiveness was the goal. Too large a sample of diversified behavior would have to be observed to have a reasonable likelihood of achieving completeness. By contrast, it should be possible to achieve comprehensiveness by exploring how each muscle works, because the muscles produce the actions observed. This is not as simple as it might first seem, because muscles can act in concert, not just singly. Facial expressions are rarely the consequence of the activity of a single muscle. Even the smile, which is principally the work of the single zygomatic major muscle, typically involves two or three other muscles as well, and not every smile involves the same other muscles. Moreover, what happens to appearance when muscles act in concert is not always the sum of the changes associated with each of the components. And the activity of one muscle may obscure the presence of another. It is important, therefore, that a comprehensive technique list not simply the ways of recognizing how each single facial action appears, but also the ways of scoring the occurrence of these units of facial action when they combine in simultaneous or overlapping time. Only the Ekman and Friesen technique has done so.

A last issue regarding how comprehensively a technique measures the *type* of facial action is what evidence is provided to demonstrate that the system is what it claims to be. One wants to know whether the universe of facial movement can be described by the technique, or at least what part of the universe has been omitted. If there is uncertainty about comprehensiveness it should be clear whether it is about just some or all actions. An empirical answer would be possible if either of the techniques claiming comprehensiveness (Ekman and Friesen and Ermiane and Gergerian) had scored large samples of facial actions of males and females of diverse ages, from various cultural, ethnic, and class backgrounds, in a wide variety of social and individual settings. Neither has been used this extensively.

Alternatively, comprehensiveness could be determined by experimentally generating all possible permutations of facial actions. Ekman and Friesen explored the comprehensiveness of their technique by producing voluntarily on their own faces more than 7,000 different combinations of facial muscular actions. These included all permutations of the actions in the forehead area, and for the lower face all of the possible combinations of two muscles and of three muscles. Although they believe their system is relatively comprehensive[8] only time and application to diverse samples of facial behavior will establish it to be so.

Ermiane and Gergerian did not provide any evidence of comprehensiveness. They determined only that their system would describe the actions of single muscles, and a few of the combined actions of two or three muscles.

Intensity of action

Actions vary not only in type (inner corner brow raise versus raise of the entire brow) but also in intensity. A brow raise may be weak or strong; the lift of the brow, the extent of exposure of the eye cover fold and gathering of skin on the forehead, may be very slight or great. The intensity of a facial action may be of interest for a variety of reasons. For example, Ekman et al. (1980) found that the intensity of zygomatic major muscle action was correlated with retrospective self-reports about the intensity of happiness experienced.[9]

Ermiane and Gergerian was the only one of the 13 other techniques to provide for comprehensive measurement of intensity. Nine of the techniques treated facial action as an all-or-nothing phenomenon, or as if there were evidence that variations in intensity are without significance. One (Grant) even confused intensity with type of action, listing as different action types appearance changes that are due only to variations in intensity. A few made provision for scoring the intensity of four or five actions (see Table 2.1). In recent unpublished work, Ekman and Friesen found that the logic provided in their scoring system for measuring the intensity of four actions can be extended to the other facial actions, but evidence has not yet been provided that such extensions can be made reliably for all the actions in their technique.

Timing of action

A facial action has a starting and a stopping point. It is often more difficult to ascertain the exact determination of these points than to decide which action occurred (see the discussion of timing in Section 2.6). From start to stop, other aspects of timing may be distinguished:

1. *Onset time*: the length of time from the start until the movement reaches a plateau where no further increase in muscular action can be observed
2. *Apex time*: the duration of that plateau
3. *Offset time*: the length of time from the end of the apex to the point where the muscle is no longer acting

Onsets and offsets may vary not only in duration but in smoothness; for example, an offset may decline at a steady rate, or steps may be apparent. Similarly, an apex may be steady or there may be noticeable fluctuations in intensity before the offset begins. When examined closely the separate actions that compose a facial expression do not start, reach an apex, and stop simultaneously. In even a common expression, such as surprise, the raising of the eyebrows may reach an apex while the dropping of the jaw is still in onset.

For some questions it is possible that simple counts of the occurrence of particular actions may be sufficient, without measurements of onset, apex, and offset. The investigator may want to know only how often or for how long a person raised the brow, wrinkled the nose, or depressed the lip corners. Even when interest is limited to simple summary measures of the occurrence of single actions, there is no rationale for using frequency rather than duration measures (which require stop–start determination) other than economy. A frequency count will underrepresent those actions which go on for long periods of time and overrepresent frequent brief actions.

Limiting measurement to single actions is hazardous regardless of whether frequency or duration is measured. Nose wrinkling, for example, may signify one thing when it occurs in overlapping time with a lower lip depression (disgust) and something quite different when it flashes momentarily while the lip corners are pulled upwards (an action that Ekman and Friesen suggest functions like a wink to accentuate a smile). A pulling down of the lip corners may signify sadness when it accompanies raised inner corners of the brows with drooping upper eyelids. When this same action occurs with the entire brow raised and the lower lip pushed up it may be a disbelief gesture. These interpretations, which have not all been tested, cannot be tested unless the timing of actions is measured. What evidence does exist (Ekman & Friesen, 1978) suggests that it is unwise to measure the face as if each action can be counted separately, as if each action has an invariant meaning apart from other actions that overlap in time.

Measurement of combinations of facial actions (what is usually meant by an expression) requires at least a determination that actions overlap, if not precise determination of the stopping and starting points of each action. Ekman and Friesen (1978) further suggest that it is overlap in the apex that is crucial to determining whether actions that co-occur are organized as part of the same event, signal, or expression. Their reasoning is that when one action begins (onset) while another action is fading (offset), it is not likely that they have been centrally directed as part of the same signal. Suppose, for example, that there has been an overlap in the apex of brow lowering, tightening and pressing together of the red parts of the lips, and raising the upper eyelid. Ekman and Friesen have hypothesized that these elements compose one of the anger expressions. Overlap in the apex of these actions would support their notion that an anger signal had occurred and that these actions should be so counted, and not tallied separately. Let us suppose that there was also a nose wrinkle, with an apex overlapping these anger actions. Ekman and Friesen suggest that this would be a blend of disgust with anger. If the nose wrinkling reached its apex as these anger actions were in offset, they suggest that it be characterized as a sequence of anger followed by disgust. Test of these hypotheses requires precise measurement of onset, apex, and offset.

A number of other research questions also require comprehensive measurement of the timing of facial actions. For example, does a brow raise and upper eyelid raise occur before or during an increase in loudness in speech or a deceleration in heart rate? Ekman, Friesen, and Simons (in preparation) have found that onset time is crucial in isolating from idiosyncratic facial actions those muscular actions which always occur in unanticipated startle reactions. Only actions that began within 0.1 second were evident in all unanticipated startles; offset time did not distinguish the idiosyncratic from uniform facial actions. In another situation offset time, rather than onset, may be crucial; for example, Ekman and Friesen (1975, chap. 11) hypothesized that stepped offsets occur more often in deceptive than in felt emotional expressions.

Most of the 14 techniques do not describe procedures for measuring starting and stopping points and totally ignore onset, offset and apex measurement. The data reported usually consists only of frequency counts. Ekman and Friesen's technique is the only one to describe how to measure these different aspects of timing. In a study now in progress these authors are comparing the relative validity scores of such comprehensive measurements of timing with a more economical frequency checklist version of their Facial Action Coding System (see Section 2.9).

2.4. Depicting facial measurement units

It is not as easy as it may at first seem to depict clearly what is referred to by a facial measurement unit. Some authors did not bother, because they did not expect others to try to use their methods. Regrettably, this lack of clarity also has caused some uncertainty about their substantive results. Take the example "down corners mouth," which is found in the measurement techniques of Birdwhistell, Brannigan and Humphries

(1972), Grant, and Nystrom. Does this phrase describe instances in which the mouth corners have been pulled down? Or those in which the mouth corners are down because the chin and lower lip have been pushed up in the middle? Or does it refer just to expressions in which the mouth corners are down because the center of the upper lip has been raised? Or is it all of them?

The first column in Table 2.2 describes how measurements were depicted in each of the 14 techniques. The chapter appendix lists how a particular facial action (brow raise) was depicted by each technique.

Most techniques used but a few words to describe each measurement unit. Some supplemented this description with a few still photographs. Only three techniques went beyond this step to provide more thorough illustration of each unit. Ekman and Friesen, Ermiane and Gergerian, and Izard's MAX technique all provided visual illustrations of every measurement unit. All provided some explanations of the anatomical basis of each action, Ekman and Friesen and Ermiane and Gergerian more thoroughly than Izard. Ermiane and Gergerian provided still photographs of each action and combination considered; Izard provided video, photographs, and drawings; and Ekman and Friesen provided still photographs, cinema, and video illustrations.

2.5. Separating inference from description

Although many investigators have been interested in inferring something about the signal value or function of facial actions, not all have recognized that such inferences should not be intermixed with descriptions in their measurement techniques. The measurement must be made in noninferential terms that describe the behavior, so that inferences about underlying states, antecedent events, or consequent actions can be tested by empirical evidence.

Mixing inference with description may also make the measurements quite misleading. Few single-muscle actions have an invariant meaning. Take the example of the so-called frown (lowering and drawing the brows together). This action is not always a sign of negative affect; depending upon the timing of the action, what other actions co-occur with it, and the situational context, it may signify quite different matters. It would be misleading to be identifying the occurrence of a frown when the brow lowering is signaling concentration, or conversational emphasis.

Because humans make the measurement, inferences cannot be elimi-

Table 2.2. *Summary of methods for measuring facial behavior: unit depiction, inference/description, and application*

	Way in which each unit is depicted	Use of inference or description	Types of records and persons to which measurement has been applied
Linguistically based			
Birdwhistell (1952)	Two or three words	Mixed: e.g., *pout, smile, sneer*	Not known
Ethologically based			
Blurton Jones (1971)	Verbal description of changed appearance of features, a few drawings and illustrative photos	Mostly description but a few inferential terms: e.g., *frown, pout*	Infants and children
Brannigan & Humphries (1972)	Verbal description	Mixed: e.g., *wry smile, angry frown, sad frown, threat*	Children and adults
Grant (1969)	Primarily verbal description, some photos	Mixed: *sad frown, aggressive frown, smile, sneer,* etc	Children and adults
McGrew (1972)	Verbal description; compared to Grant, Blurton Jones	Mostly description but a few inferential terms: e.g., *pout, frown, grin*	Children
Nystrom (1974)	Verbal description	Description	Neonates
Young & Decarie (1977)	Verbal description	Mixed: *fear face, sad face, shy smile,* etc.	Infants in last quarter of first year
Theoretically based			
Ekman, Friesen, & Tomkins (1971)	Photographs of descriptor	Description	Video and still photos of adults' posed and spontaneous expressions
Izard MAX (1979[b])	Verbal description, photos, drawings, and video	Description	Video of infants

Table 2.2. *(cont.)*

	Way in which each unit is depicted	Use of inference or description	Types of records and persons to which measurement has been applied
Anatomically based			
Ekman & Friesen (1976, 1978)	Verbal description, still photos, and cinema illustrations of each action and certain combinations of actions	Description	Spontaneous, deliberate, and posed video and photos of neonates, children, adults, deaf stutterers, mental patients
Frois-Wittmann (1930)	Verbal description; very brief	Only one inferential term: *frown*	Still photos of poses by one adult
Fulcher (1942)	Verbal description; very brief	Description	Films of poses by blind and sighted children
Ermiane & Gergerian (1978)	Verbal description, still photos	Description	Adult poses and patients' spontaneous photographs
Landis (1924)	Verbal description	Description	Neonates

nated, but they need not be encouraged or required. If the person scoring a face identifies the brows being lowered and/or drawn together, the scorer may still make the inference that he or she is describing a frown. But Ekman and Friesen (1978) reported that when people use a measurement technique that is solely descriptive, as time passes the scorer increasingly focuses on the behavioral discriminations and is rarely aware of the possible meaning of the behavior. Although there can be no guarantee that inferences are not being drawn, a measurement technique should neither encourage nor require inferences about meaning by the terminology or descriptions it employs.

Both Ekman and Friesen and Izard separated their hypotheses about the signal value of facial actions from the descriptive materials to be used in training a person to measure facial behavior. Ermiane and Gergerian intermixed inferences about the meaning of behavior with the information necessary to learn their descriptive system. Theirs is the only technique to contain inferences about how given facial actions are indicative of specific personality processes and types of psychopathology. Birdwhistell, Blurton Jones, Brannigan and Humphries, Grant, McGrew, Young and Decarie (1977), and Frois-Wittmann all used some inferential or emotional terms (e.g., *frown, smile, sneer, angry frown*) mixed in with descriptive terms. (This is not always evident from the chapter appendix, because not all who mixed inference with description did so for the brow raise.)

Both Ekman and Friesen and Izard listed hypotheses about the emotion signaled by particular facial actions. Ekman and Friesen were explicit about the particular combinations of units they considered as emotion signals; 1,000 such predictions were included in their published system, and more than 2,000 more are contained in a forthcoming report (Friesen & Ekman, in preparation). Izard's MAX contains only those facial actions which, he claims, distinguish among the emotions. Ekman and Friesen have evidence that Izard is wrong, that he has excluded a number of actions relevant to emotions. For example, Izard does not include levator labii superioris caput infraorbitalis, an action relevant to both disgust and anger, except when this muscle acts unilaterally. Ekman, Friesen, and Ancoli (1980) found that bilateral evidence of this muscle correlated with the subjective report of disgust. Ekman and Friesen also found that when this action is accompanied by the narrowing of the red margins of the lips (another action ignored by Izard), the signal changes from disgust to anger. These errors are the product of limited sampling: Izard chose his actions on the basis of what he observed in a set of photographs of posed emotions.

2.6. Types of records and persons to which measurement has been applied

Still or motion records

Although a number of techniques claim that they can be used with motion records, most have not dealt with the complexities in the timing of facial action that a motion record reveals. These investigators may never have been confronted with the complexity of the temporal organization of facial actions because of either the type of behavior or the type of record they examined. If only posed expressions were measured (as in the case of Ermiane & Gergerian), variations in timing might not be apparent. Posers generally try to perform all the required movements at once, in overlapping time, with similar very short onsets, long-held apexes, and abrupt short offsets. Variations would not be apparent, nor would the reason to measure them. An investigator who used his or her method only to score still photographs also might not know of these complexities in timing, because the camera shutter freezes all action. Though Izard has scored some motion records, he preselected only certain brief segments of videotape to score, segments in which the infants seemed to be emitting expressions that looked like those in posed photographs of adults. Thus he has not dealt with the complexities that a motion record reveals. Other investigators may have failed to consider the timing of facial movement because they tried to apply their systems in real time, as the behavior occurred, and even if they had videotape or film, they may not have examined the records in slowed or repeated replay.

It will be most important for investigators to make use of motion measuring the timing of facial actions whenever they want to study spontaneous behavior, taking a strictly descriptive approach; or interrelate facial activity and some other simultaneous behavior (speech, respiration, body movement, etc.); or distinguish configurations in which the temporary organization of multiple facial actions suggests that they be considered parts of the same signal or expression. (See the discussion of the research questions that require measurement of timing in Section 2.3.)

Modifications for varying age levels

Ideally, a facial measurement system should be applicable to the study of individuals of any age, by making provision for any modifications needed to measure infants or the aged. The appearance of certain facial actions is quite different in neonates and infants from what it is in young children and adults. Oster (1978; Oster & Ekman, 1978), who worked with Ekman and Friesen during the final stages in the development of their measurement system, has studied the neuroanatomical basis for these differences. She has provided (Oster & Rosenstein, in preparation) a set of transformations for utilizing the Ekman and Friesen system with neonates and infants. Izard's MAX technique is specifically limited to measuring infants, but he provides only a few overly general descriptions of potentially confusing infant–adult differences. No other investigator has attended to this problem, not even those who measured young infants and neonates.

Parallel problems may occur in measuring facial activity in quite elderly people, because age signs may necessitate some modifications in scoring rules to avoid mistakes in identifying certain actions. No one has considered this.

2.7. Reliability

The need for reliability is obvious to psychologists. To some anthropologists and sociologists the quest for reliability has seemed a peculiar madness that deflects psychologists from the real problem at hand. For example, Margaret Mead, in the last years of her life, wrote "Psychologists . . . are more interested in validity and reliability than in what they are actually studying" (1975, p. 211). Yet if a measurement system cannot be shown to be reliable, there is no way of knowing whether even the investigator who invented the system recognizes the same facial action when it twice occurs. The need to demonstrate reliability seems especially important with facial behavior. For here there is an enormous variety of behaviors that can occur, with no names for most. And those who have observed facial actions have produced very different catalogs.

Some ethologists (e.g., Young & Decarie) have argued that if the same finding is obtained in two independent studies, there is no need to demonstrate that the measurement technique was reliable. This reasoning should not be applied to the area of facial measurement, where there have been completely contradictory reports by different investigators (e.g., the argument about universality between Birdwhistell and Ekman). If we knew that Birdwhistell and Ekman had each used a reliable measurement technique (preferably the same one), at least we could be certain about what was seen, and search differences in sampling, situation, or interpretation as sources of their disagreement. When a measurement technique is intended to be usable by other investigators, it is especially important for its originator to demonstrate that he or she as well as others can use it reliably. (See also Section 2.1, where reliability was discussed in the context of the relationship between the outcomes of message judgment studies and measurement of sign vehicle studies.)

Let us consider now various aspects of reliability, for it is not a simple matter to establish. A number of requirements can be enumerated:

1. The researcher, rather than just giving an overall index of agreement, should provide data to show that high agreement can be reached about the scoring of specific facial actions. Typically, some actions are easier to recognize than others. Unless reliability data are reported for the scoring of each facial unit, it is not possible to evaluate which discriminations may be less reliable.

2. Data on reliability should be reported from the measurement of spontaneous, not just posed, behavior, and from the flow of behavior as revealed in a motion record, not just from still photographs or slices abstracted from video or cinema, which may yield higher agreement.

3. Reliability data should be provided for (*a*) infants, (*b*) children, (*c*) adults, and (*d*) aged populations, because reliability on just one group does not guarantee reliability on the others.

4. The most common source of unreliability in behavioral measurement, whether it be of face or of body, is the failure of one person to see what another scores. Usually this occurs when an action is small in size. This source of disagreement can be attenuated if the technique specifies a threshold that must be surpassed for the action to be scored. Specifying minimum thresholds alerts the persons doing the scoring to subtle signs and provides explicit bases for decisions about when a change in appearance is likely to be ambiguous. A technique that provides such threshold definitions should therefore yield higher agreement.

5. Reliability should be reported not only for the person(s) who developed the technique, but also for learners who did not previously have experience with facial measurement. Data about the range of reliabilities achieved by new learners should be provided and compared to those for experienced or expert scorers. A technique will be more generally useful if it can be learned independently, without direct instruction from the developer. This usually requires a self-instructional set of materials, practice materials with correct answers, and a final test for the learner to take.

6. Reliability should be reported for the scoring of not just (*a*) the type of action, but also (*b*) the intensity of actions and (*c*) the timing of actions.

Of the 14 measurement techniques, 5 did not report data on any aspect of reliability. The other 9 provided fairly sparse data on reliability, with the exception of Ekman and Friesen and Izard. Even these techniques did not meet all the requirements just listed. Table 2.3 lists the specific reliability requirements met by each technique.

Table 2.3. *Summary of methods for measuring facial behavior: reliability and validity*

		Validity			
	Reliability	Descriptive	Emotional	Conversational	Other
Linguistically based					
Birdwhistell (1952)	Not reported	None	None	None	None
Ethologically based					
Blurton Jones (1971)	Data reported on requirements 1, 2, 3*b*, 6*a*	None	None	None	None
Brannigan & Humphries (1972)	Not reported	None	None	None	None
Grant (1969)	Not reported	None	None	None	Predicts severity of mental illness, but no data reported
McGrew (1972)	Data reported on requirements 1, 2, 3*b*, 6*a*	None	Spontaneous	None	Predicts gender differences & relation to agonistic interaction
Nystrom (1974)	Data reported on requirements 1, 2, 3*b*, 6*a*	None	None	None	None
Young & Decarie (1977)	Not determined by authors	None	Spontaneous, but no data reported	None	Said to differentiate infants' response when mother departs and when she frustrates, but no data reported

Theoretically based					
Ekman, Friesen, & Tomkins (1971)	Data reported on requirements 2 and 3*c*	None	Posed and spontaneous: positive vs. negative, stressful vs. neutral film conditions; differentiates patterns of heart rate	None	Predicts attribution of emotion
Izard MAX (1979*b*)	Data reported on requirements 2, 3*a*–*b*, 5, 6*a*	None	Posed	None	Provides preliminary data on relations to vocalization and body movement in infants
Anatomically based					
Ekman & Friesen (1976, 1978)	Data reported on requirements 1, 2, 3*a*–*c*, 4, 5, 6*a* & *c*	Meets performed actions and EMG criteria	Posed and spontaneous; measures intensity and type of emotion; differentiates startle reaction; differentiates certain deliberate from spontaneous expressions	Measures syntactic and emphasis signals	None
Frois-Wittmann (1930)	Not reported	None	Posed	None	Predicts developmental changes; compares blind and sighted

Table 2.3. *(cont.)*

		Validity			
	Reliability	Descriptive	Emotional	Conversational	Other
Fulcher (1942)	Data reported on requirements 2, 3*b*, 6*a*	None	Posed	None	None
Ermiane & Gergerian (1978)	Data reported only on scoring photos of poses and on requirement 3*c*	None	Posed	None	None
Landis (1924)	Not reported	None	None	None	Predicts individual differences

2.8. Validity

Descriptive validity

The validity of a technique designed to measure facial movement entails questions on a number of levels. Most specifically (and concretely), validity requires evidence that the technique actually measures the behavior it claims to measure. When a technique claims to measure brow raise, are the brows actually raised, or is it just the inner corners that are raised? If the technique claims to measure the intensity of an action, such as whether the brow raise is slight, moderate, or extreme, do such measurements correspond to known differences in the intensity of such an action? The problem, of course, is how to know what facial action occurs, what criterion to utilize independently of the facial measurement technique itself. Two approaches have been taken:

1. Performed action criterion: Ekman and Friesen trained people to be able to perform various actions on request. Records of such performances were scored without knowledge of the performances requested. Ekman and Friesen's Facial Action Coding System (FACS) accurately distinguished the actions the performers had been instructed to make.

2. Electrical activity criterion: Ekman and Friesen, in collaboration with Schwartz (Ekman, Schwartz, & Friesen, in preparation), placed surface EMG leads on the faces of performers while the performers produced actions on request. Utilizing the extent of electrical activity observed from the EMG placements as the validity criterion, they found that FACS scoring of facial movement accurately distinguished the type and the intensity of the action. (This study is described in more detail in Section 2.10.)

Utility or validity

Some measurement techniques contain hypotheses about the particular facial actions that signal particular emotions (Ekman and Friesen; Ekman, Friesen, and Tomkins; Ermiane and Gergerian; Izard). For these techniques it is appropriate to ask whether the hypotheses are correct, but the answer does not pertain to the validity of the techniques, only to that of the hypotheses. Suppose the facial behaviors found to signal emotion were exactly the opposite of what had been hypothesized by the developer of the technique. Such evidence would not show that the technique was invalid, only that the hypotheses were wrong. In fact, the discovery that the hypotheses were wrong would itself require that the technique measure facial movement accurately. Suppose a study not only failed to support the investigator's hypotheses about the actions that signal emotions but found that there were no facial actions related to emotion. If one could discount the possibility that the sample did not include emotional behavior, this might suggest that the facial measurement technique was not *relevant* to emotion. It might have measured just those facial behaviors which are unrelated to emotion. Another technique applied to the same sample of facial behavior might uncover the actions related to emotion.

Two techniques (Ekman and Friesen and Ermiane and Gergerian) claim not to be specific to the measurement of any one type of message, such as emotion, but to be of general utility, suitable for the study of any question for which facial movement must be measured. Such a claim can be evaluated by evidence that the technique has obtained results when studying a number of different matters.

Posed emotions. Many techniques have been shown to be able to differentiate poses of emotion or judgments of emotion poses: Ekman and Friesen; Ekman, Friesen, and Tomkins; Ermiane and Gergerian; Frois-Wittman; Fulcher; Izard. In the studies that used a selective technique it is not possible to know whether there might have been other facial actions not included in the scoring technique that might have predicted the emotion poses or judgments just as well or better. The two comprehensive techniques – Ekman and Friesen and Ermiane and Gergerian – provided that information. They were able to show that it was the movements they specified as emotion-relevant, not other movements, that were signs of particular emotions. Ekman and Friesen's FACS also predicted not only *which* emotion was posed or judged, but the *intensity* of emotion as well.

Poses, however, by definition are artificial. Although they may resemble spontaneous facial expressions in some respects (see Ekman, in press), one difference is that they are likely to be easier to score. The onset may be more coordinated and abrupt, the apex frozen, and the scope very intense or exaggerated (see the discussion in Section 2.6). Evidence that a technique is a valid measure of emotion cannot rest just upon measurement of poses; it is necessary to determine that the measurement will be valid when it measures spontaneous emotional expression.

Spontaneous emotions. A number of studies have shown the validity of Ekman and Friesen's FACS in measuring the occurrence of spontaneous emotional expressions. Ancoli (Ancoli, 1979; Ancoli et al., 1980) studied autonomic nervous system (ANS) responses when subjects watched a pleasant or stress-inducing film. A different pattern of ANS response during the two films was found only during the times in each film-viewing period when the face registered maximal emotional response. In another study of that data, Ekman et al. (1980) found that FACS accurately predicted the subjects' retrospective reports of their emotional experience while watching the films: the intensity of happy feelings, the intensity of negative feelings, and, specifically, the intensity of the emotion disgust. Ekman, Friesen, and Simons (in preparation) differentiated the specific facial actions that signify a startle reaction from the emotional reactions subsequent to being startled. Both the type of actions and the onset time were crucial to this distinction. They also were able to differentiate a genuine from a simulated startle accurately. Ekman, Hager, and Friesen (1981) examined the differences between deliberate facial movements and spontaneous emotional expressions. Scoring the intensity of each specific facial action on each side of the face, they found that requested facial movements were asymmetrical more often than spontaneous emotional expressions: The actions usually were more intense on the left side of the face for the deliberate, but not for the spontaneous, emotional expressions. Krause (1978) utilized FACS to measure facial actions during conversations among stutterers and nonstutterers. As he predicted, the facial actions specified in FACS as relevant to anger occurred more often among the stutterers. There is little or no comparable evidence that the other facial measurement techniques listed in Table 2.3 can be used to measure spontaneous emotional expressions.

The only exception is Izard's use of his MAX technique to study infants. He found that observers scoring brief segments of videotape showing infant expressions *selected* to correspond to adult posed expressions could reliably identify the actions making up those expressions. This shows that his technique can be used to identify at least those particular expressions when they occur in spontaneous behavior. At this point, however, there is no evidence to support Izard's claim that an infant producing a particular expression is experiencing a particular emotion or blend of emotions. Because Izard has not described infants' facial behavior comprehensively, he cannot even specify how representative the selected expressions are in the behavior of infants of a given age and in a variety of situations.

Oster (1978; Oster & Ekman, 1978) has provided more complete information about the range of facial muscle activity observed in young infants and about the young infant's capacity for coordinated facial movement. Unlike Izard, she began not by looking for adult posed expressions but by analyzing the configurations and sequences of facial actions actually produced by infants in a variety of situations. Oster found that almost all of the single facial actions included in FACS are apparent early in life. Though certain combinations of facial actions common in adult facial expression can be observed in the newborn period, others have not been observed in young infants. Oster (1978; Oster & Ekman, 1978) has argued that the only way to determine the affective meaning and signal function of infants' facial expressions is by a detailed description of the expressions themselves – including their timing and sequencing – combined with a thorough functional analysis of their behavioral correlates and stimulus context. Though far from complete, Oster's work has provided evidence that complex, spontaneous facial actions observed in young infants (e.g., smiling, brow knitting, pouting) are not random but represent organized patterns and sequences of facial muscle activity that are reliably related to other aspects of the infants' behavior (e.g., looking at or away from the care giver, motor quieting or restlessness, crying). Such relationships can provide insights into the infant's affective state and cognitive processes.

Conversational signals

Ekman and Friesen's FACS has been found useful in studying facial actions that play a role as conversational rather than as emotional signals.[10] Camras (1977) found differences in the syntactic form of questions that do and do not contain facial actions functioning as "question markers." Ekman, Camras, and Friesen (in preparation) found that the semantic context predicts which of two facial actions is used to provide speech emphasis. Baker (1979) used FACS to measure the facial actions shown by deaf persons when they sign. She has isolated particular combinations of facial actions that appear to serve syntactic functions.

Stable individual characteristics

Although Ermiane and Gergerian intended their facial measurement technique to differentiate personality and psychopathology, they have not reported any validity evidence. There is no evidence that any of the other facial measurement techniques are valid measures of any stable personal characteristic.

2.9. Costs

This last criterion for evaluating measurement techniques was not included in Table 2.3 because Ekman and Friesen was the only study to provide information about time costs for learning to measure and for scoring a specified sample of behavior. It takes approximately 100 hours to learn FACS. More than half of that time is spent scoring practice materials (still photographs and cinema) included in FACS at the end of each chapter in the instructional manual. Ekman and Friesen do not know whether people will still achieve high reliability if they skip such practice; they do know that high reliability was achieved when all the instructional steps were followed.

The costs for using a measurement technique once it is learned are much more difficult to estimate. For FACS and probably any other technique, the costs depend upon how densely the facial behaviors are packed in the time sample to be scored. Consider first comprehensive scoring in which FACS is used to measure *all* visible facial activity in a 15-second period. This could take as little as 1 minute if only one or two easily distinguished actions occurred and the investigator wanted only to locate start–stop points for each action. It could take as long as 10 hours, however, if the behavior was as densely packed as it is in the facial activity of deaf persons signing, and if onset–apex–offset was scored for every action. Ekman and Friesen have not observed any other instances in which facial behavior is so densely packed over so many seconds.

If selective rather than comprehensive scoring is done, the costs are lower. Presume that the investigator wants to score only actions that are said to be indicative of disgust, and he or she selects the actions listed in the *Investigator's Guide to FACS* (in Ekman & Friesen, 1978) that are predicted to be prototypic for that emotion. A 2:1 ratio, 30 seconds of scoring time for every 15 seconds of live action, is probably a reasonable estimate.

Ekman and Friesen have recently developed a more economical system for measuring the occurrence of single emotions, based on FACS. Occurrences of actions considered to be the most common signs of anger, fear, distress and/or sadness, disgust and/or comtempt, surprise, and happiness are noted. In what they call EMFACS (EM standing for emotion), time is saved in three ways:

1. Scoring does not extend to the particular action, but only to whether a member of a group of specified actions occurred. For example, there are seven signs grouped together that Ekman and Friesen consider relevant to disgust. EMFACS does not differentiate among nose wrinkling, nose

wrinkling plus upper lip raising plus lower lip depression, nose wrinkling plus lower lip elevation, and so on. If any of these is seen, a check is made for that grouping. All actions not in one of the groupings are ignored.

2. Intensity of action is not scored, although intensity is included in the requirements for particular actions within a grouping. For example, a slight depression of the lip corners with slight pushing up of the lower lip is included in the sad grouping, but when those two actions are moderate or strong they are not included.
3. The timing of actions is not measured; only a frequency count is taken. EMFACS takes one-fifth the time of FACS, but of course it suffers from all of the problems already discussed in detail for selective as compared to comprehensive measurement techniques.

Izard's MAX technique is similar to Ekman and Friesen's EMFACS. It, too, groups actions presumed to be relevant to the same emotion, and makes no provision for scoring the timing or the intensity of action. Unlike FACS, it requires the scorer to examine different regions of the face separately, and admittedly, it includes in some regions changes in appearance that are due to actions in another region. By contrast, FACS and EMFACS alert the scorer to all the appearance changes resulting from particular muscles. Rather than inspecting an arbitrary division of the face in three regions, the scorer learns where to look in the face for those changes. Izard's MAX technique was developed by collapsing some of the distinctions he had made in his earlier FMCS technique, but FMCS was itself selective, not comprehensive.

The virtue of EMFACS compared to Izard's MAX and other selective techniques is that what has been excluded is exactly specified. Work in progress by Ekman and Friesen will compare the validity of EMFACS with FACS scoring of the same videotapes of spontaneous facial actions obtained during interviews with depressed patients. This study will show how the two techniques compare in differentiating interviews at the time of admission to a mental hospital from interviews at time of discharge, in agreement with psychiatric diagnosis and in relationship to patients' self-reports of affect and mood.

2.10. Other techniques for facial measurement

EMG

A number of recent studies (see especially the work of Schwartz, Fair, Salt, Mandel, & Klerman, 1976a, 1976b) used surface EMG to measure facial activity in relation to emotion. In this procedure, quite small electrodes, about 1 cm in diameter, are taped onto the surface of the skin, which is first prepared by a slight scraping and application of paste or solution to enhance electrical contact. Wires or leads are run from the electrodes to the recording machine. Four methodological difficulties are encountered in EMG measurement of facial activity.

First, the placement of leads on the face may itself inhibit facial activity. Movement of the head may loosen the electrodes, as may large facial muscular movements. To prevent these problems, subjects usually have been studied in isolation, or at least not when freely partaking in a conversation. Typically, subjects have been measured when trying to pose, imagine, remember, or create for themselves an emotional experience. Even in these situations, if a subject makes a large expression he will feel the tape that holds the electrode in place pull or tear. The use of surface EMG probably thus inhibits large expressions even if the experimenter does not explicitly do so by instruction or by choice of task for the subject to perform.

A second problem has to do with ambiguities about just what is being measured by surface EMG. Placing leads on the surface of the face often has the consequence, for most facial areas, of picking up activity in more than just the muscle targeted by the investigator. There is more than one muscle in most of these facial areas, and often their fibers interweave or they lie on top of each other. Although investigators using surface EMG have usually been careful to talk about a *region* rather than a muscle, their reasoning and much of their interpretation assumes success in isolating the activity of specific muscles. Ekman and Friesen, in a joint study with Schwartz (Ekman, Schwartz, & Friesen, in preparation), found that in the corrugator region the activity of many muscles other than corrugator itself was recorded by the electrode placed in this region: orbicularis oculi; levator labii superioris alaeque nasi; frontalis, pars medialis. The activity of these other muscles can be distinguished from that of corrugator, and they can be distinguished from each other, but these distinctions require more electrodes, some of which must be placed in adjacent facial regions. Another way to obtain measurement of specific muscles is to insert fine wires into a muscle, a procedure which, though not as painful as it sounds, is not practicable for many studies.

The third problem – whether EMG can provide measurement of more than just one or two emotional states – is fundamental to the complexity of facial activity. Most emotions cannot be identified by the activity of a single muscle. Happiness may be the only exception, but even here evidence (Ekman et al., 1980) suggests that the differentiation of felt from simulated happiness, of controlled from uncontrolled happiness, and of slight from extreme happiness requires measurement of more than one muscle. Disgust might be measured by the activity of two muscles, and surprise by the activity of three. To measure anger, or fear, or sadness, many muscles need to be measured. There are limits, however, to the number of leads that can be placed on a person's face – limits dictated both by the necessity of monitoring so many channels of activity and by the number of wires that an investigator can paste on someone's face without being totally outrageous. The present state of surface EMG measurement is not likely to allow more than either the gross distinction between positive and negative affect or the targeting of only one or two emotions for study. (Just such findings have been reported for imagined and posed emotions.) Surface or even fine-wire EMG does not seem a method that lends itself to the study of situations in which an investigator wants to know about the occurrence of three, four, or more emotions, especially if the investigator does not wish to miss various manifestations of each emotion and blends among them. And, of course, EMG imposes the additional constraints of intrusiveness and limitations on the potential for movement.

Davidson (in press) raised a fourth problem common to studies using EMG to measure facial behavior. There is no standard system, as there is for EEG, for specifying exactly where to place an EMG electrode in order to detect activity in a particular facial region. Though investigators know roughly where each muscle is located, there is considerable latitude about exactly where to put an electrode. Without rather precise guidelines about electrode placement, research is vulnerable to error owing to unknown variations in electrode placement within and between subjects.

Consider the use of surface EMG to measure whether there is more or less activity in the zygomatic major region on the two sides of the face. Any differences obtained might not be due to the greater involvement of the right or left hemisphere but might to an unknown extent reflect differences in placement of the EMG electrode in relation to the muscle mass on the two sides of the face. Between-subjects designs, in which, for example, a measure of zygomatic major was correlated with a personality test score, would also be vulnerable to error owing to electrode placement. These problems can be circumvented by utilizing research designs in which EMG activity is compared in two or more conditions for each subject.

When EMG is used to measure change over time, and the leads must be placed on the face more than once, variations in placement of the leads on each occasion can introduce errors. Miller (1981–1982) has solved this problem by devising a template that can be attached to a subject repeatedly to ensure that electrode placement is identical on different occasions.

Surface EMG can play an important role in certain methodological studies of facial behavior. Mention was made earlier of Ekman and

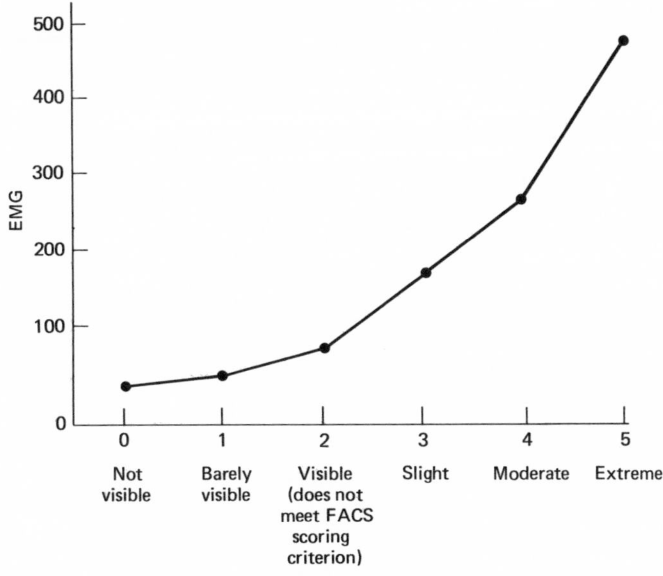

Figure 2.1. Plot of relationship between FACS and EMG measurement of performances of Action Unit 1 (frontalis, pars medialis)

Friesen's use of fine-wire EMG to stimulate and record facial movement in order to discover how the muscles work to change appearance. Surface EMG could be used to help teach people how the muscles work as part of the process of teaching them a visual measurement procedure such as FACS. Surface EMG can also be used to calibrate and investigate measurement of visible facial behavior. As mentioned earlier, Ekman and Friesen, in joint work with Schwartz (Ekman, Schwartz, and Friesen, in preparation), verified that the intensity scoring embodied in FACS is reliably related to changes in electrical activity. Persons highly skilled in the ability to activate specific muscles (Ekman and Oster) moved specific muscles on command at different intended intensity levels, while a video record was made and surface EMG was recorded. FACS scoring was later found to be highly correlated with the EMG readings (Pearson $r = 0.85$). Figure 2.1 shows an example from this data, a plot of the relationship between EMG measures of electrical activity and FACS scoring of the intensity of action for a specific muscle.

The major use for surface EMG is, however, not for such methodological studies, but for measures of phenomena that are difficult or impossible to measure with techniques based on visible movements. Ekman, Schwartz, and Friesen (in preparation) were able to show that there are reliable electrical changes associated with muscle tonus changes that are not visible. For two muscles studied systematically (corrugator and frontalis, pars medialis), there were significant changes in EMG without any visible sign of activity when the performer was instructed just to think about each muscle. This study also showed that there are visible clues to muscle tension, measurable by EMG, when there is no movement. The persons measuring the faces with FACS guessed which muscle had been tensed when they could not see any movement. Sometimes the person guessing felt that there was no basis for the guess. At other times there seemed to be evidence of very slight tightening or bulging of skin. Analyses showed that when these guesses were correct – when the scorer predicted which muscle the performer was tensing, even though no movement was visible – there was a greater increase in EMG than when the guesses were incorrect.

EMG, then, may be the only method for measuring nonvisible changes in muscular tension, and for measuring changes that, while barely visible, involve not movement but bulging of the skin and would be hard to measure with any of the techniques described in Table 2.1.

Measurement of contour

Lasko (1979) has recently developed a method for measuring changes in the contour of different facial features (lips) or areas (infraorbital triangle). The researcher places a grid over each film or video frame in order to measure angles and area changes precisely. The method is designed to study changes resulting from muscular tension, blood flow gravity changes, or swellings owing to other causes. The technique appears promising for study of changes in appearance that are too small and too gradual to be measured readily with the techniques designed to measure movement. There is little reliability or validity data yet available, however. Also, the technique may be quite limited in its application, because only frames in which the subject's head position is exactly the same can be compared.

Other possible measures

There are other visible changes in the face that have not been systematically measured, that is, perspiration, blushing, and blanching. Thermal changes also could be measured, but no one yet has done so systematically.

2.11. Conclusions

This chapter has reviewed measurement techniques for only one type of signal: rapid, not slow or static. Among these, only one kind of rapid signal – visible movement – has been considered. Most of the studies that have used one or another technique to measure visible movement were concerned with only one of the many messages rapid signs may convey: information about emotion. Presumably, future research will expand to consider other messages and to develop methods for measuring rapid signals other than movement, as well as the variety of slow and static signals.

A few techniques have become available recently – those of Ekman and Friesen, Ermiane and Gergerian, and Izard. The first two were designed to be applicable to the study of any message, not just emotion. The availability of these techniques should encourage many more studies of facial movement. Wedding such studies of facial sign vehicles to studies using the more traditional message judgment approach should allow discovery of the particular actions that form the basis for correct and incorrect inferences when people judge facial expression. These techniques may also allow discovery of particular facial actions that are not customarily known or even knowable by the usual observer, movements that are too subtle and/or complex to notice or interpret when seen once at real time.

If research is generated by these facial measurement techniques, then the techniques themselves may well not survive: As a larger empirical base develops, it should become possible to improve, modify, or replace the techniques now in use. The methodological issues discussed in this chapter, however, should endure as guidelines for what to consider in developing or evaluating any procedure for measuring facial movement.

Appendix. How the facial action brow raise *is described in each of the 14 measurement techniques*

Birdwhistell
Raised Brows

Blurton Jones
A very conspicuous movement of raising the eyebrows which can be rather difficult to judge on photographs because of the individual variations in the resting position of the brows. One or more of the following criteria could apply:

a) The height of the brow above the eye corner appears to be equal or more than the width of the open eye. (Fig. 3a measure B equal or greater than A).

b) Horizontal lines visible across the forehead above the brows.
c) There is an enlarged area between the brow and the eyelids which is often highlighted (very pale) in photographs.
d) There is a less sharp fall from the brow into the eye socket (orbit) because the brow is raised beyond the edge of the orbit which it normally covers. Therefore there is less shadow between brow and eye than usual.
e) The shape of the eyebrows change, becoming more curved when they are raised (but they are not curved when the brows are slanted or oblique as well as raised).

Brow raising is presumably a result of contraction of the frontal belly of the occipto-frontalis, which can occur simultaneously with corrugator or orbicularis occuli contraction. Thus many oblique brows were also scored as raised.

Brannigan & Humphries

One or both eyebrows are raised and are held, at least briefly, in the raised position. They are not drawn in towards the midline and are not tilted.

Grant

The eyebrows are raised and stop in the raised position for an appreciable time (see plate 10A).

Flash. A quick raising and lower of eyebrows.

These two elements are very similar in use. They seem to have an attractive function, drawing the attention of the other person to the face. They are concerned with regulation and timing of speech.

Nystrom

– horizontal wrinkles
– elevated brows

(*Note*: These are listed by Nystrom as separate scoring items in his technique.)

Young & Decarie

Brow raise stare:

Brow: the eyebrows are raised and held giving them a curved appearance and creating horizontal creases on the brow. There is no inward movement of the eyebrows and no vertical furrow.

Eyes: The eyes may be held wide open but not sparkling, wrinkling at the corners and forming of pouching under the eyes. Blinking may be decelerated, and the head is definitely held in its regular forward position. Visual fixation on a specific target is characteristic of this expression.

Mouth: as in normal face.

Other: as in normal face.

(*Note*: Young & Decarie present this as a total face score. No provision is made for scoring if the brow raise action occurs without the eye action or with some other mouth action.)

Ekman, Friesen, & Tomkins

(*Note*: Two photographs depict this scoring item. The authors' Facial Affect Scoring Technique contains only visual, not verbal, descriptions.)

Izard: MAX (Maximally Discriminative Facial Movement Coding System)

Code 20: The brows are raised in their normal shape. The forehead shows some thickening and the tissue under the eyebrows some thinning out as a result of the eyebrows being raised. The thickening or massing of tissue in the forehead gives way to long transverse furrows with increasing age. The nasal root is narrowed. The skin directly below the eyebrows is stretched upward.

Code 30: The eyes have a widened and roundish appearance. The furrow above the eyelashes of the upper lid may be visible. The widened, roundish appearance of the eyes is brought about mainly by the eyebrow raise of code 20 that lifts and stretches the tissue between the eyebrow and the eyelid. The upper eyelid is not raised. The artist's drawing for 20 also illustrates 30.
(*Note*: Izard furnishes video examples of this action in addition to the artist's drawing.)

Ekman & Friesen: FACS (Facial Action Coding System)

There is one large muscle in the forehead area which raises the eyebrows. The medial (or central) portion of this muscle (Action Unit [AU] 1) can act separately from the lateral portion of this muscle (AU 2). The photograph on the left in Figure 2-1 shows the muscular basis of AU 1 and AU 2. The photograph on the right in Figure 2-1 shows the direction in which the muscle pulls skin when it contracts. The movement of AU 1 is to pull the medial part of the brow and center of the forehead upwards. The movement of AU 2 pulls the brow and the adjacent skin in the lateral portion of the forehead upwards towards the hairline. The combination of these two actions raises the inner (Action Unit 1) and the outer corners (Action Unit 2) of the eyebrows [2] producing changes in appearance which are the product of their joint action.

Appearance Changes Due 1 + 2

(1) Pulls the entire eyebrow (medial to lateral) upwards.
(2) Produces an arched appearance to the shape of the eyebrow.
(3) Bunches the skin in the forehead so that horizontal wrinkles appear across the entire forehead. The wrinkles may not appear in infants and children.
(4) Stretches the eye cover fold so that it is more apparent.
(5) In some people (those with deeply set eyes) the stretching of the eye cover fold reveals their upper eyelid, which usually is concealed by the eye cover fold.

Compare the photograph of AU 1 + 2 with the photograph of a neutral face.

Inspect the film depiction of AU 1 + 2

How to do 1 + 2

(*Note*: Ekman & Friesen's technique teaches learners how to perform each action so that they can utilize their own facial actions to understand the mechanics and appearance of the face.)

This should be easy to do. Simply lift your eyebrows up, both ends as high as you can. Note the wrinkling in your forehead. In some people the wrinkling does not occur but the skin is still bunched up. In some people these wrinkles are permanently etched (see photographs 0 and 0w) but they deepen noticeably when 1 + 2 acts.

Minimum requirements for scoring 1+2

The minimum requirements listed earlier in the MANUAL for scoring AU 1 alone and those for AU 2 alone are altered significantly in this combination.

(1) Entire brow raised *slightly*.

If you did not see the brows move it must also meet the additional requirements:

(2) *Slight* horizontal wrinkles or muscle bunching reaching across forehead. If horizontal wrinkles are evident in the neutral face, change from the neutral appearance must be *slight*.

and (3) *Slightly* more exposure of the eye cover fold than in neutral.

or (4) If there is no wrinkling or bunching in the brow, but the brow raise and exposure of the eye cover fold is *marked*, you can score 1 + 2.

(*Note*: The extent of action required by the terms *slightly*, *marked*, *extreme*, and *maximal* is defined visually in both photographs and motion picture film examples.)

Frois-Wittmann
Brows raised.

Fulcher
Frontalis which raises the brows wrinkling the forehead transversely.

Ermiane & Gergerian
Frontalis – the eyebrow levator. Externalized emotionality.
(Raises the eyebrows).
Letting himself go to an impression.
(*Note*: A few photographic illustrations show this action.)

Landis
Frontalis. This is the vertical sheet muscle of the forehead, the contraction of which produces transverse wrinkles ("the wrinkled brow").

Acknowledgments

The preparation of this chapter was supported by a grant from the NIMH, MH 11976; a Research Scientist Development Award, MH 06092, from the NIMH; and a grant from the Harry F. Guggenheim Foundation. I am grateful to Wallace V. Friesen, Joseph C. Hager, and Maureen O'Sullivan for their many helpful suggestions and comments on earlier drafts.

Notes

1. Findings and hypotheses about the messages provided by static, slow, and rapid signals are discussed in Ekman, 1978.
2. Over the years I have proposed a number of different phrases to distinguish these two approaches. In previous discussions the *message judgment* approach has been labeled the stimulus, communicative, or judgment approach, and the *measurement of sign vehicles* approach has been labeled the response, indicative, or components approach. It is to be hoped that the present terms, taken from semiotics, allow a more lucid differentiation of these two methods.
3. Izard (personal communication, 1979) said that as part of an attempt to establish independent discovery, he deliberately did not examine Ekman & Friesen's Facial Action Coding System, even though it had already been published at the time when he was developing his measurement techniques.
4. See Kendon (Chapter 8) for a praiseworthy account of Birdwhistell, and Rosenfeld (Chapter 5) for a critique of Birdwhistell's methods.
5. Though neither of Izard's techniques (Affex or MAX) has been published as of late 1980, he has furnished information about both to those who inquire. Included are scoring manuals and illustrative material. An earlier version of MAX, FMCS (Facial Movement Coding System), is not available to others and is not discussed in this chapter.
6. Investigators studying the face of course do not agree about whether there is

definitive evidence regarding the particular facial actions that do and do not signal each emotion. Ekman and Oster (1979, p. 543), in reviewing the last decade of research on this topic, concluded that it is still a question of whether "facial expressions provide accurate information about the distinctions among several negative and positive emotions. The only evidence [indicating that] facial expressions [provide such discrete information] is for posed expressions." Izard (1979b) takes a much more positive view in describing what his measurement technique can do: "The content universe sampled by MAX consists of all the facial movements or appearance changes that signal affect" (p. 38). The evidence to support that claim is weak, however. One finding cited as evidence of validity is that scoring with MAX correlates with observers' judgments of emotion using Affex, but there is no validity evidence for Affex. The other validity evidence claimed is that infant facial expressions selected to correspond to adult poses and thus identified by MAX as representing one or another emotion are judged by observers to show those emotions. Here the limitation in evidence is threefold: (1) Judge agreement only establishes consensus; it does not demonstrate that the actions actually represent the emotions they are judged to show; (2) because the scoring technique was selective, there is no way of knowing whether other actions not scored might predict observers' message judgments just as well or better; (3) because the observers' choices were restricted, there is no way of knowing whether they would have described the infants' faces with the same emotion terms, or with any emotion terms at all, if they had been allowed free description.

7. In part because of its very uniformity, Ekman and Friesen consider the startle reaction to be not an emotion but instead a reflex. Other writers about emotion (e.g., Tomkins, 1962) disagree and classify startle with the emotion of surprise.
8. They acknowledge that for certain actions – for example, the movements of the tongue – their technique is not complete.
9. Frequency and duration measures also correlated with retrospective self-report, and the highest correlation was obtained with a score that combined intensity, frequency, and duration.
10. The distinction between emotional and conversational signals, with examples of how the same eyebrow movements can play either role, is given in Ekman, 1979.

References

Ancoli, S. *Psychophysiological response patterns of emotion*. Unpublished doctoral dissertation, University of California, San Francisco, 1979.

Ancoli, S., Kamiya, J., & Ekman, P. *Psychophysiological differentiation of positive and negative affect*. Paper presented at the annual meeting of the Biofeedback Association of America, Colorado Springs, 1980.

Baker, C. *Non-manual components of the Sign Language signal*. Paper presented at the NATO Advanced Study Institute on Sign Language and Cognition, Copenhagen, August 1979.

Birdwhistell, R. *Introduction to kinesics*. Washington, D.C.: Foreign Service Institute; Louisville: University of Louisville Press, 1952. Now available in microfilm only from University Microfilms, Inc., 313 N. First St., Ann Arbor Mich. Partly reprinted as an appendix to R. Birdwhistell, *Kinesics and context*. Philadelphia: University of Pennsylvania Press, 1970.

Blurton Jones, N. G. Criteria for use in describing facial expression in children. *Human Biology*, 1971, *41*, 365–413.

Brannigan, C. R., & Humphries, D. A. Human nonverbal behavior, a means of communication. In N. G. Blurton Jones (Ed.), *Ethological studies of child behavior*. Cambridge: Cambridge University Press 1972.

Camras, L. Facial expressions used by children in a conflict situation. *Child Development*, 1977, *48*, 1431–1435.

Davison, R. Psychophysiological studies of laterality. *Psychophysiology*, in press.

Duchenne, B. *Mechanisme de la physionomie humaine; ou, Analyse electrophysiologique de l'expression des passions*. Paris: Bailliere, 1862.

Ekman, P. Body position, facial expression and verbal behavior during interviews. *Journal of Abnormal and Social Psychology*, 1964, *68*(3), 295–301.

Ekman, P. Differential communication of affect by head and body cues. *Journal of Personality and Social Psychology*, 1965, *2*(5), 725–735.

Ekman, P. Universals and cultural differences in facial expressions of emotion. In J. Cole (Ed.), *Nebraska Symposium on Motivation* (Vol. 19). Lincoln: University of Nebraska Press, 1972.

Ekman, P. Facial signs. In T. Sebeok (Ed.), *Sight, sound and sense*. Bloomington: University of Indiana Press, 1978.

Ekman, P. About brows: Emotional and conversational signals. In M. von Cranach, K. Foppa, W. Lepenies, & D. Ploog (Eds.), *Human ethology*. Cambridge: Cambridge University Press, 1979.

Ekman, P. Facial asymmetry. *Science*, 1980, *209*, 833–834.

Ekman, P., Camras, L., & Friesen, W. V. *Facial emphasis signals*. Manuscript in preparation.

Ekman, P. & Friesen, W. V. Nonverbal behavior in psychotherapy research. In J. Shlien (Ed.), *Research in Psychotherapy* (Vol. 3). Washington, D.C.: American Psychological Association, 1968.

Ekman, P. & Friesen, W. V. The repertoire of nonverbal behavior. *Semiotica*, 1969, *1*(1), 49–98.

Ekman, P., & Friesen, W. V. *Unmasking the face: A guide to recognizing emotions from facial clues*. New Jersey: Prentice-Hall, 1975.

Ekman, P. & Friesen, W. V. Measuring facial movement. *Journal of Environmental Psychology and Nonverbal Behavior*, 1976, *1*, 56–75.

Ekman, P., & Friesen, W. V. *The Facial Action Coding System: A technique for the measurement of facial movement*. Palo Alto, Calif.: Consulting Psychologists Press, 1978.

Ekman, P., Friesen, W. V., & Ancoli, S. Facial signs of emotional experience. *Journal of Personality and Social Psychology*, 1980, *39*(6), 1125–1134.

Ekman, P., Friesen, W. V., & Ellsworth, P. *Emotion in the human face: Guidelines for research and an integration of findings*. New York: Pergamon Press, 1972 (2nd rev. ed.: P. Ekman, Ed., Cambridge University Press, in press).

Ekman, P., Friesen, W. V., & Simons, R. *Cognitive controls of the startle reaction*. Manuscript in preparation.

Ekman, P., Friesen, W. V., & Tomkins, S. S. Facial Affect Scoring Technique: A first validity study. *Semiotica*, 1971, *3*, 37–58.

Ekman, P., Hager, J. C., & Friesen, W. V. The symmetry of emotional and deliberate facial actions. *Psychophysiology*, 1981, *18*, 101–106.

Ekman, P., & Oster, H. Facial expressions of emotion. *Annual Review of Psychology*, 1979, *30*, 527–554.

Ekman, P., Schwartz, G., & Friesen, W. V. *Electrical and visible signs of facial action*. Manuscript in preparation.

Ermiane, R., & Gergerian, E. *Atlas of facial expressions; Album des expressions du visage*. Paris: La Pensee Universelle. 1978.

Friesen, W. V., & Ekman, P. (Eds.). *Analyzing facial action*. Book in preparation.

Frois-Wittmann, J. The judgment of facial expression. *Journal of Experimental Psychology*, 1930, *13*, 113–151.

Fulcher, J. S. "Voluntary" facial expression in blind and seeing children. *Archives of Psychology*, 1942, *38*(272), 1–49.

Grant, N. B. Human facial expression. *Man*, 1969, *4*, 525–536.

Hiatt, S., Campos, J., & Emde, R. *Fear, surprise, and happiness: The patterning of facial expression in infants*. Paper presented at the meeting of the Society for Research in Child Development, New Orleans, 1977.

Hjorstjo, C. H. *Man's face and mimic language*. Lund: Studentlitterature, 1970.

Izard, C. *Facial expression scoring manual*. [FMCS.] Unpublished manuscript, 1979. (a)

Izard, C. *The maximally descriminative facial movement coding system*. [MAX.] Unpublished manuscript, 1979. Available from Instructional Resources Center, University of Delaware, Newark. (b)

Izard, C. E., & Dougherty, L. M. Two complementary systems for measuring facial expressions in infants and children. In C. E. Izard (Ed.), *Measuring emotions in infants and children*. Cambridge: Cambridge University Press, 1981.

Krause, R. Nonverbales interaktives Verhalten von Stotterern. *Schweizrische Zeitschrift fur Psychologie und ihre Anwendungen*, 1978, *3*, 16–31.

Landis, C. Studies of emotional reactions: II. General behavior and facial expression. *Journal of Comparative Psychology*, 1924, *4*, 447–509.

Landis, C., & Hunt, W. A. *The startle pattern*. New York: Holt, Rinehart & Winston, 1939.

Lasko, M. *A method to measure curvature in facial expressional features: A complex mathematical description*. 1979. Unpublished manuscript.

Lightoller, G. H. S. Facial muscles: The modiolus and muscles surrounding the rima oris with some remarks about the panniculus adiposus. *Journal of Anatomy*, 1925, *60* (Pt. 1).

Malmstrom, E., Ekman, P., & Friesen, W. V. *Autonomic changes with facial displays of surprise and disgust*. Paper presented at the meeting of the Western Psychological Association, Portland, Oreg., 1972.

McGrew, W. C. *An ethological study of children's behavior*. New York: Academic Press, 1972.

McGurk, H., & MacDonald, J. Hearing lips and seeing voices. *Nature*, 1976, *26*(4), 746–748.

Mead, M. Review of *Darwin and facial expression*, ed. by P. Ekman. *Journal of Communication*, 1975, *25*(1), 209–213.

Miller, A. J. Electromyography in analysis of neuromuscular function. In E. Harvold (Ed.), *Hemifacial microsomia and other related craniofacial anomalies. Cleft Palate Journal Monograph*, 1981–1982, No. 1.

Nystrom, M. Neonatal facial-postural patterning during sleep: I. Description and reliability of observation. *Psychological Research Bulletin*, 1974, *14*(7), 1–16.

Oster, H. Facial expression and affect development. In M. Lewis & L. A. Rosenblum (Eds.), *Affect development*. New York: Plenum, 1978.

Oster, H., & Ekman, P. Facial behavior in child development. In A. Collins (Ed.), *Minnesota Symposium on Child Development* (Vol. 11). Hillsdale, N.J.: Erlbaum, 1978.

Oster, H., & Rosenstein, D. Measuring facial movement in infants. In W. V. Friesen & P. Ekman (Eds.), *Analyzing facial action*. Book in preparation.

Rubenstein, L. Facial expressions: An objective method in the quantitative evaluation of emotional change. *Behavior Research Methods and Instrumentation*, 1969, *1*, 305–306.

Schwartz, G. E., Fair, P. L., Salt, P., Mandel, M. R., & Klerman, G. L. Facial expression and imagery in depression: An electromyographic study. *Psychosomatic Medicine*, 1976, *38*, 337–347. (a)

Schwartz, G. E., Fair, P. L., Salt, P., Mandel, M. R., & Klerman, G. L. Facial muscle patterning to affective imagery in depressed and non-depressed subjects. *Science*, 1976, *192*(4238), 489–491. (b)

Seaford, H. W. *Maximizing replicability in describing facial behavior*. Paper presented at the meeting of the American Anthropological Association, Washington, D.C., 1976.

Tomkins, S. S. *Affect, imagery, consciousness*. Vol. 1: *The positive affects*. New York: Springer, 1962.

Young, G., & Decarie, T. G. An ethology-based catalogue of facial/vocal behaviors in infancy. *Animal Behavior*, 1977, *25*(1), 95–107.

3. The assessment of gaze and mutual gaze

RALPH V. EXLINE AND B. J. FEHR

Two decades of empirical research on interpersonal visual attention has demonstrated that both investigators and their subjects share an intense concern with the action of the eyes directed toward or away from others. Such action has been variously labeled. Some labels have been general, for example, *visual interaction* (Exline, 1963; Simmel, 1921), *looking behavior* (Cline, 1967; Gibson & Pick, 1963), *visual behavior* (Exline, Gray, & Schuette, 1965), *eye signals* (Ellgring & von Cranach, 1972), and, more recently, *gaze* (Argyle & Cook, 1976; Argyle & Ingham, 1972). Others have been somewhat more specific, for example, *gaze direction* (Kendon, 1967; Vine, 1971), *stare* (Ellsworth, Carlsmith, & Henson, 1972), and *direct gaze* (Ellsworth, 1975). Simultaneously exchanged looks between two persons have been referred to as the *mutual glance* (Simmel, 1921), *mutual visual interaction* (Exline, 1963), *looking into the line of regard* (Lambert & Lambert, 1964), *eye contact* (Argyle & Dean, 1965), and, again more recently, *mutual gaze* (Argyle & Cook, 1976; Argyle & Ingham, 1972).

Increased precision in the identification of the phenomena being studied was provided by von Cranach (1971), who suggested a number of differentiated definitions for the eye behavior that had been and could be studied. He pointed to the differences that characterized one-sided looks, face gazes,[1] mutual looks, eye contact, gaze avoidance, and gaze omission. Even so, Kirkland and Lewis (1976) expressed concern over the "vagueness and apparent arbitrariness" (p. 1278) of the vocabulary employed to refer to visual interaction in the research literature. In an attempt to clarify the terminology, these authors instructed a sample of English-speaking women to rank order a number of gaze-related terms to describe eye fixations of increasingly long duration. Their data suggest that for such women, at least, there is significant agreement that duration serves to differentiate such terms as *glance, look, gaze, leer,* and *stare,* in increasing order.

Although it is likely that contextual frames as well as time considerations are necessary to the ultimately valid conceptual differentiation of many gaze-related terms (e.g., compare *leer, glare,* and *stare*), Kirkland and Lewis do call attention to relevant properties of the phenomena we measure. Regardless of how we label our variable, what we actually record are eye fixations, their duration, and the point or points of fixation – time and location, such are the raw materials of our measures.

Every sighted person has the potential to observe and in crude fashion measure the presence or absence of the social visual attention exhibited by those interacted with or observed in interaction. Most of us assume that we do it well. We assume that we know when we are being looked at or avoided, and on the basis of this assumed knowledge, we speculate, hypothesize, infer, attribute; for, as Ellsworth (1975) puts it, the direct gaze of another is salient, arousing, and involving. Given the power of the gaze, it is important to verify the assumption that we know when we are the object of another's social attention – otherwise we may be inappropriately aroused and become mistakenly involved.

We suspect that most people have, at one time or another, falsely assumed that they were the focus of such attention. One such error occurred when one of us sat directly opposite a stranger at knee-to-knee distance while mutually gazing at him in a subway car. A subjective feeling of ambiguous involvement was linked to an escalating rise in emotional tension. Then a slight convergence (focusing) of the other's eyes was followed by his immediately looking away. The tension experienced was based on an erroneous assumption that stemmed from an error in measurement. It was mistakenly assumed that the other was engaging in a mutual gaze when in fact he merely stared, unfocused, into space.

Recently a colleague fell into a similar trap. Standing on one side of a narrow counter, she began to respond to a clerk who looked up at her with a smile and friendly greeting. Our colleague's answering smile froze foolishly on her face as a taller male, behind and very slightly to one side, responded to the look and greeting of his friend, the clerk.

Both of the events just reported are samples of what von Cranach (1971) has termed the *eye-gaze* (wherein only one of a pair of actors gazes at the other's eyes), though the gazer mistakenly assumes that the pair is involved in mutual *eye contact,* in which both partners look into the other's eyes, . . . and both . . . are aware of the mutual look" (p. 220). These examples demonstrate the importance of the fixation point to the definition of the gaze, as well as the care that must be taken to determine it accurately if we are not to be misled.

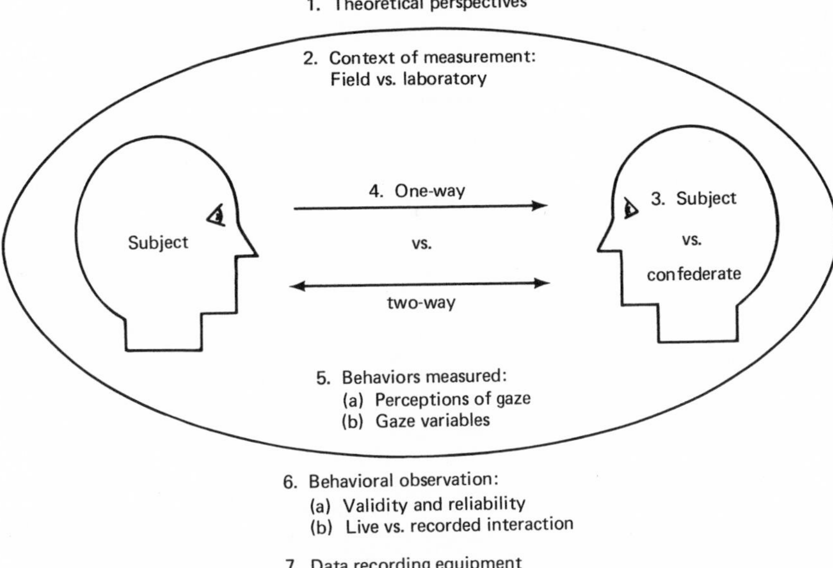

Figure 3.1. Schematic representation of measurement decisions in visual interaction research.

A number of investigators have addressed themselves to the problem of reliable and accurate measurement of the phenomena of interpersonal gaze, namely, the recording of the frequency and duration of one person's looks at and away from another person's line of regard. This work, which will be discussed later in more detail, has resulted in a better understanding of the conditions that must be met before an investigator can be comfortable in asserting that he or she has in fact measured eye contact per se. Indeed, in the interest of precision, it may be wise to accept von Cranach's suggestion that we discard the concept of *eye contact* for that of the *mutual look*. Whatever terminology is finally decided upon, we are confident that investigators will continue to study human gaze behavior and its meaning for and impact upon co-interactants in social transactions. Such studies involve many interlocking decisions that investigators of gaze phenomena must make in the process of designing and implementing their research. We intend in this chapter to call attention to these decisions, and we will attempt to clarify the considerations that investigators may wish to keep in mind as they decide among the options available to them.

Figure 3.1 provides a schematic diagram depicting the decision points involved in the conduct of research on visual interaction. It is the discussion of these decisions which constitutes the focus of this chapter. The list that follows briefly identifies the decision points illustrated in Figure 3.1; subsequent sections will develop each point thoroughly (see also Scherer & Ekman, Chapter 1).

1. One's theoretical perspective will clearly play a major role in determining the research strategy employed.
2. Measurements may be made in the context of a controlled laboratory or in a more naturalistic field setting.
3. One may observe the interaction between two naive subjects or between one subject and a trained confederate.
4. The gaze of both interactants may be recorded, or, especially when a confederate is employed, the gaze of only one person may be recorded.
5. Two gross categories of behaviors may be obtained: (*a*) the perceptions of a co-interactant's gaze may be ascertained via questionnaires and interviews; (*b*) the visual behavior of participants may be assessed.
6. The interaction may be recorded on film or videotape or observed live. Various considerations affect the choice: (*a*) there are a variety of issues relating to obtaining valid and reliable data from human observers; (*b*) film or video recording provides both assets and liabilities.
7. A variety of data-recording devices is available, from stopwatches to computers.

3.1. Influences of theoretical perspectives

Investigators have approached the study of nonverbal behavior from a variety of theoretical perspectives, each of which carries different implications for the methodology to be used in collecting data. Among broad perspectives delineated by von Cranach and Vine (1973) are: (1) the structural approach; (2) the adaptations of Mead's (1934) symbolic interactionism proposed by Goffman (1961) and Garfinkel (1967); (3) the ethological approach; and (4) the external variable approach. Each of these approaches will be discussed in terms of its implications for choice of methods in the study of interpersonal gaze.

Birdwhistell's (1970) and Scheflen's (1966) uses of the structural approach follow the model of structural linguistics. Behavior, including nonverbal behavior, is viewed as a rule-governed, holistic, hierarchically organized system. Thus "communication should be studied as a total performance in true communication situations" (von Cranach & Vine, 1973, p. 3). Structural analysis is preferred to the investigation of single variables, and interpersonal gaze is considered in relation to other variables in the context of real-life interaction situations. Scheflen (1966), for example, in the context of observing a psychotherapeutic session, has described a regularly occurring structural unit (a unit of analysis) in which gaze behavior figures. The unit, called *cigarette lighting*, has six components: the therapist (1) takes out a cigarette, (2) waits until the patient finishes a story, (3) puts the cigarette in her mouth, (4) *waits until the patient looks away*, (5) lights up (which also involves watching the patient until he diverts his eyes), and (6) discards the match. This unit "belonged to a context in which the therapist temporarily stopped conversing and began to try to interrupt the patient's story. Also, the patient began to talk more rapidly and use more single bar junctions (a linguistic activity that discourages interruption)" (p. 276).

In Scheflen's example the interest is not in measuring gaze behavior per se, but in the observation that a specific gaze behavior, for example, patient looking away, is but one element consistently occurring in a specific set of chronologically ordered behaviors, which set in turn is consistently related to a therapist's attempt to interrupt a patient. One whose theoretical perspective embraced the natural history model would thus not choose to record through observation the various points upon which a person's social visual attention appears to be fixated, its frequency and duration, and so on, but rather would choose to demonstrate that some variety of gaze behavior regularly co-occurs with other definable categories of behavior in an interaction sequence. This approach thus requires a methodology that enables the investigator to obtain a relatively permanent filmed or videotaped history of a social interaction. The investigator may utilize frame-by-frame analysis techniques to view the interaction again and again in order to determine if patterned consistencies in gaze can be fitted into a structural unit comprised of non-gaze behaviors. Another example of the approach would be Kendon's 1967 study, in which he found that a specific pattern of looking away and back as a speaker neared the end of a speech unit was associated consistently with turning the "floor" over to another speaker. Assessment and measurement of the gaze are inherent in both examples just cited. Scheflen's use of the term *looks away* in the structural unit he calls cigarette lighting implies that the patient has previously *looked at* the therapist, and Kendon's study clearly requires that the observer be able both to differentiate looking at from looking away and to determine at what precise point or points during speech these behaviors occur. Thus, although reliable and valid judgments that one person has looked at and away from another are necessary, proponents of structural analysis generally do not report such data.

A related approach favored by Goffman (1961, 1963) and Garfinkel (1967) has as its object "the description of cultural rules and roles that govern interactive behavior in a given situational context . . . [T]he methods used vary from participant observation to the analysis of biographies and histories and even to quasi-experiments in field settings" (von Cranach & Vine, 1973, p. 4). This approach requires one to collect data in the field, a choice that, for the study of interpersonal gaze, creates a very difficult measurement task.

The ethological approach emphasizing the biological roots of behavior originally utilized the study of species other than *homo sapiens* to determine the bases of our own behavior (Chance, 1967; van Hooff, 1962; Lorenz, 1937, 1950; Tinbergen, 1951). More recently, Eibl-Eibesfeldt (1970), Hutt and Hutt (1970), Blurton Jones (1972), Tinbergen (1974), and others have applied principles of animal ethology to the study of human behavior, using naturalistic observation of behavioral units in the human habitat. In this approach:

> Observation and description must form the first part of any study. This should give rise to hypotheses, which may be . . . only testable in experiments . . . An experiment normally consists of some controlled modification of the situation where the modified and unmodified situation are compared for their effects . . . whether these (experiments) are done on animals or people or indoors or outdoors is quite irrelevant. [Blurton Jones, 1972, p. 10]

The ethologically oriented investigator of gaze, then, first must choose to study the phenomena in a naturalistic interaction situation; there he or she looks for observable behaviors that "(a) [are] repeated in the same form, and (b) look as if they affect other individuals" (Blurton Jones, 1972, p. 11). An example involving gaze is described by Tinbergen and Tinbergen (1972), as they suggest a strategy for establishing an affiliative tie with a normal young child:

> One can see a great deal of the behavior of the child out of the corner of one's eye . . . usually the child will start by simply looking intently at the stranger, studying him guardedly. One may . . . judge it safe to now and then look briefly at the child and assess more accurately the state the child is in. If . . . one sees the child avert its glance, eye contact must at once be broken off. Very soon the child will stop studying one. It will approach gingerly, and it will soon reveal its strong bonding tendency by touching one . . . This is often a crucial moment: one must *not* respond by looking at the child (which may set it back considerably) but by cautiously touching the child's hand with one's own. [Pp. 29–30]

The quotation from Tinbergen and Tinbergen clearly is a prescription for strategic interaction, not a description of a procedure for collecting data in an ethological investigation. Nevertheless, it points to implications for the measurement of gaze relevant to those who choose to study the phenomena from the ethological perspective. One who observes such natural interactions must be alert to behaviors other than gaze, behaviors that nevertheless may be a function of the gaze pattern. Such complex interactions are very difficult to code in real time and, in fact, may well prove to be beyond the capacity of one or even several observers. This approach, similar to those described earlier, would seem to benefit from the production of a sound film or videotaped record that could be viewed repeatedly. Unobtrusive recording of such interactions presents major problems for the investigator.

Additional measurement problems are suggested by Tinbergen and Tinbergen's description. One studies the child "out of the corner of one's eye"; the child looks "intently" at the stranger, "studying him guardedly"; one looks "briefly at the child"; "eye contact must be broken off"; and so on. It will be shown that accurate and reliable assessment of gaze into the eyes becomes increasingly difficult the more the head is angled away from a direct orientation. Thus to know with certainty the exact target of an observed "looks out of the corner of one's eye" may reflect an act of faith rather than a statement of fact. Similarly, to establish that one looks briefly at another, or that eye contact has been broken off, requires the observer to obtain verification that the brief look did in fact focus on the other and that the broken "eye contact" was indeed preceded by the awareness of two persons that each, simultaneously, looked into the other's eye(s). Those who use the ethological method to study gaze behavior have many problems to overcome.

But have we properly posed the measurement problem for those who approach the study of social visual attention from the theoretical perspectives of structural analyses and/or ethology? Do we expect too much precision and rigor too soon in the observation and description of gaze in naturalistic settings? Neither of the two approaches precludes the use of procedures in which the measurement of social gaze can, after observation and description has led to the formation of hypotheses, be effected under more rigorous, controlled conditions. Both approaches stress the desirability of conducting controlled experiments following a natural history description. Scheflen (1966) argues that after structural units and their relations in a hierarchy of levels are determined, "we can experiment to determine more exactly their role in a system. We can find out what will happen in the larger picture if we remove a unit . . . In this sense the natural history unit ultimately uses a classical technique" (p. 284). Again, Tinbergen's (1951) work with sticklebacks clearly shows that ethologists use controlled laboratory procedures to test hypotheses derived from naturalistic observation.

Kendon's 1967 study of gaze direction in social interaction provides an example of how the removal (actually the absence) of a unit in an ongoing interaction can be used to test a hypothesis arrived at after intensive study of patterns of gaze direction in relation to the occurrences of utterances. Kendon filmed 5 minutes of conversation between seven pairs of strangers who were getting acquainted with one another. A frame-by-frame transcription of the film showed that the speaker (*P*) rather consistently looked away at the beginning of an utterance lasting 5 seconds or longer, looked back at the listener (*Q*) as the end of the utterance approached, and continued to look at *Q* after falling silent. Speculating that this pattern constituted a signal to *Q* that *P* was turning the floor over to *Q*, that is, that *P* was ready for *Q*'s response, Kendon hypothesized that *Q*, on receiving this pattern, would respond more quickly than when he received a pattern in which *P* continued to look away as he ended his utterance.

At this point, Kendon could have designed a controlled laboratory study to test the hypothesis. Instead, true to the natural history approach (see Kendon, Section 8.1), he tested it by finding two pairs whose conversations were characterized both by the usual pattern and by a large number of utterances in which *P* continued to look away during and following the ending phase of the utterance. Such utterances in effect omitted the gaze unit coordinated with turning over the floor. His data showed that 71% of utterances ending with an away look were followed either by no response or by a delayed response, whereas only 29% of utterances ending with an extended look elicited delayed or no response (pp. 36–37).

As has just been suggested, Kendon's hypotheses could have been tested in a laboratory situation. An investigator could have instructed a confederate to look at the research subject during and following the end of each utterance with one set of subjects and to withhold the end-of-utterance look at the subject with another set – a between-subjects design. Alternatively, the investigator could have tested these hypotheses in a within-subjects design by instructing the confederate to give the subject the usual end-of-utterance look for a given time period, switch to the no-look pattern for a comparable time, and revert to the original end-of-utterance look pattern for a final time period. As we have already shown, such a strategy is not incompatible with the ethological or natural history approach. Nevertheless, those utilizing such perspectives could argue that the confederate's effort to follow a program like the one just described could introduce other variables not found in natural situations, and thus reduce comparability and complicate the interpretation of resulting data.

Had programmed confederates been used as described, the study would have been representative of the approach that Duncan (1969) has called the *external variable* approach (see Scherer & Ekman, Section 1.2), a theoretical perspective in which the concern is with gaze in relation to other aspects of the looker (personality, role, proximity), or with manipulating levels or direction of gaze to study its impact upon a co-interactant. Examples of the former would be Exline's studies of *n* affiliation (1963) and Machiavellianism (Exline, Thibaut, Hickey, & Gumpert, 1970), Exline, Ellyson, and Long's study of power role behavior (1975), and Argyle and Dean's study of affiliative conflict (1965). Examples of the latter would be Ellsworth and Carlsmith's investigation of affective response (1968), Ellsworth et al.'s study of staring (1972), and Exline and Yellin's (1969) report on arousal of rhesus monkeys.

The use of laboratory settings, confederates, and controlled procedures is characteristic of this approach, which simplifies several aspects of data collection. Although most research on visual interaction stems from this perspective, results have been criticized as being based on molecular and unsystematic premises, being difficult to integrate into a systematic framework, and having been elicited in such unnatural situations as to raise doubts concerning their external validity (von Cranach & Vine, 1973).

Von Cranach and Vine (1973) recommend synthesizing general systems theory with a functional–developmental view that incorporates biological inheritance and cultural tradition in order to study social and expressive behavior (p. 14). Nevertheless, they grant that contributions still can be made by those using the external variable approach, especially if they use it as Argyle (1972) recommends, namely, to create "rigorously designed experiments, which test hypotheses, but which are carried out in realistic settings with clear meanings and conventions, and which contain all the main ingredients of social behavior" (p. 244).

Although studies representing the external variable approach are more likely to be carried out in laboratory settings, this approach has also generated a number of studies in which data were collected in naturalistic situations outside the laboratory (Ellsworth et al., 1972; LaFrance & Mayo, 1976; Snyder, Grether, & Keller, 1974). Such investigators generally choose field settings in order to demonstrate the generalizability of relationships found in the laboratory, to eliminate demand characteristics, or to replicate, extend, or refute previous findings from field studies. LaFrance and Mayo (1976), for example, attempted to measure gazes of speakers and listeners in a public place in order to discover if apparent differences in black–white gaze patterns they found in the laboratory were generalizable to more natural settings.

We have suggested in this section that a paper focused on methodological issues must recognize that theoretical concerns play a dominant role in the choice of methods (see also Scherer & Ekman, Section 1.2). As described in the schematic overview of the gaze-recording situation represented in Figure 3.1, various and specific options are available to those engaged in gaze research. Depending on their theoretical perspectives, researchers make certain choices, choices that sometimes appear to ignore what we know about the ease of the data collection, as well as about the validity and reliability of gaze recorded under various circumstances. This is not to suggest that methodological considerations should determine theoretical perspectives (though we suspect they sometimes do) but rather to stress that investigators should be aware of the pitfalls and benefits associated with different methodologies, ever attempting to improve the methods that flow from their own theoretical predilections. We will next turn to the effects of the context of measurement on the assessment of gaze.

3.2. Context of measurement: field versus laboratory

We have attempted to show that the researcher's theoretical perspective plays a major role in the decision to choose field as opposed to laboratory as the setting in which to measure gaze behavior. It is difficult in the field to ensure that it will be possible to collect reliable and valid gaze data without attracting the attention of the interactants. The major difference between field and laboratory measurement lies in the greater control over the movement of people through space that the investigator can exert in the laboratory. Because it is easier in the laboratory to fix the location of those to be measured, observers and/or recording instruments can be unobtrusively positioned at distances close enough to ease the collection of reasonably reliable and valid gaze data.

This is not to say that one cannot find public locations in which participants in an interaction are set in relatively fixed observable locations. Persons could be observed seated at a small table in an open area of a restaurant, or in a pedestrian mall that features space arrangements and physical objects permitting unobtrusive observers an unobstructed view of conversation pairs. We wish only to point out that measuring gaze in the field, as compared to the lab, poses many more and more difficult kinds of technical problems, problems that require considerable ingenuity to solve.

LaFrance and Mayo (1976), for example, employed a team of three observers who attempted to record visual interaction between conversing dyads in college cafeterias, business district fast-food outlets, and waiting rooms in hospitals and airports. In their own words, observers

> positioned themselves so as to be able to see both participants in a potentially observable dyad and yet remain relatively inconspicuous themselves. Two observers were equipped with stopwatches and the third with coding sheets to record looking times and listening times in seconds. In rotating roles, one observer was designated to determine the member of the observed dyad who was listening and to record the amount of listening time. The second observer recorded the number of seconds that the designated listener spent looking into the face of the other. At each point of speaker–listener exchange in the observed conversation, these two raters ceased observing and reported the times recorded to the third observer, who noted these amounts on the coding sheets. After 15 seconds observations were resumed for whichever participant in the conversation was in the listener role at that time. [P. 550]

Compare this rather awkward procedure, in which the investigator must be concerned with the distance, positioning, and acuity of the observers, to a laboratory situation in which more ideal observer conditions can be established, and in which data automatically recorded on instruments permit precise identification of time and event relationships.

The problems noted in connection with LaFrance and Mayo's procedures have, to some extent, been avoided by filming social interaction in the field. By this means, Kendon and Ferber (1973) and Cary (1978) produced permanent records that permitted (1) leisurely and potentially exact codings of several behaviors, rather than the one or two behaviors recorded less exactly by LaFrance and Mayo (1976), and (2) the determination of reliability coefficients. Nevertheless, filming (or videotaping) in the field poses problems of illumination, scope, and obtrusiveness. To reduce obtrusiveness and obtain a wider view of the setting, Kendon and Ferber (1973) placed a camera some 6 m from the actors. At this distance, however, it was impossible to tell specifically where a person looked. Cary (1978) solved the latter problem to some extent by using a zoom lens and 35-mm film to obtain a tight shot of high resolution. The greater clarity of detail thus obtained was so expensive, however, that in order to reduce the cost of data collection, he set his shutter to operate at 1-second intervals. This decision may have caused him to miss a number of fleeting glances toward and away from the co-interactant.

The greater difficulty of measuring gaze in the field may explain why many investigators of gaze in such settings choose to manipulate rather than to measure gaze. We have already referred to the "staring" study of Ellsworth et al. (1972). To this we can add other studies. Kleinke (1977) utilized different levels of gaze crossed with touching to determine whether men and women leaving a phone booth would react favorably to a young woman's request for a dime. Ellsworth and Langer (1976) also varied level of gaze to study helping behavior, and on our own campus we conducted an unpublished study in which male and female students seated on a bench by a wide campus walkway did or did not stare at approaching pedestrians in order to determine whether the walkers veered away more from the stare (they did) (Exline, 1971). Fehr (1968) conducted a hallway study in which she attempted to manipulate and measure gaze simultaneously. A student leaning against a wall began looking at the eye region of approaching persons when they reached a point some 4.5 m away. The confederate not only stared continuously at the other throughout the approach, but also recorded the other's return gaze by operating a pocketed push-button switch that activated an Esterline-Angus event recorder concealed in an adjacent classroom. This procedure permitted construction of a detailed profile of the others' gaze patterns as they approached – data that could not have been obtained had only stopwatches been used. The technique, however, raised not only the issue of the unusualness of the 100% gaze (to be discussed in a later section) but also a question of the effect on measurement of the dual role of the confederate – observer.

We have implied that gaze in field studies may be easier to manipulate than to measure. It should be noted, however, that to manipulate gaze does not necessarily free the researcher from the obligation to measure it. In a staring study mentioned earlier, Ellsworth et al. (1972) report that they eliminated data from several subjects who apparently were distracted by a display in a nearby store window. They were able to do so because they required their staring confederates to verify the stare induction by reporting whether or not the subject noticed the experimental stimulus. This is a measurement problem, and the validity of the conclusion that the induction "took" is only as good as the accuracy and acuity of both the confederate and the subject, who also must notice the staring confederate.

This latter point is relevant to the interpretation of the results of Snyder et al. (1974), in a study in which confederates were instructed to attempt to hitch a ride while either staring or not staring at passing motorists. Confederates were to "fixate on the driver's gaze and maintain this gaze as long as possible until the driver either stopped or drove on" (p. 167). The distance suggested by the description was such that it may have been difficult to ascertain whether the drivers noticed the look or saw instead a consistent head and face orientation that itself was interpreted as an appeal. Suppose, for example, that the confederates had looked at the top of the driver's head. Would the driver have noticed the difference?

The discussion concerning the question of subjects' awareness of the gaze induction points to yet another implication of the decision to assess gaze in the field, namely, that it is more likely in the field than in the laboratory that it will be difficult to establish subjects' awareness of the gaze behavior that is necessary for a proper test of hypotheses concerning the manipulation. A subject who, upon entering a small experimental room, is faced by a staring or nonstaring confederate is much more likely to be aware of the gaze than is a motorist driving on a highway, or waiting for a traffic signal to change. The high probability that the laboratory subject will be aware of the gaze induction, though not the manipulation, enables the investigator to test the hypotheses concerning such induction more efficiently in the laboratory setting.

The studies mentioned in this section illustrate a number of aspects of gaze assessment that pose particular problems for research on visual interaction in the field.[2] For example, the manipulation of gaze requires consideration of the subject's perception of the look, and even when observation conditions are optimal, we know that it is difficult to tell precisely where someone is looking. These difficulties cannot necessarily be resolved by asking the recipient of a glance to indicate where his or her partner is looking. Interactants are often not consciously aware of another's line of regard. Furthermore, it is difficult and often impossible in field situations to obtain such information from the target of the gaze. Contemplate, for example, the feasibility of pursuing a motorist down a busy highway to determine whether he was aware that a hitchhiker standing beside the road had attempted to establish eye contact. Observers of "live" action also require some method of recording gaze, and the methods employed range from the use of check sheets and stopwatches to work with portable, time-coded electronic systems. Note, too, that in order to avoid the unnatural situations created when small armies of observers surround the targeted subjects, it is necessary to reduce the number of gaze variables examined, and thus to scale down the scope of the analysis.[3] Finally, although recording experimental sessions on film or videotape permits one to make optimal use of the data, one must be concerned with the obtrusiveness and resolution of such recordings (see Wallbott, Technical Appendix, Section A.6).

3.3. Use of a confederate versus another naive subject

Visual interaction is studied in the context of an interaction of relationship between at least two individuals. We assume that at least one of these persons will be a "naive" subject, but it must be decided whether the other will also be naive or will be a confederate of the experimenter. The use of a confederate clearly enables us to control certain aspects of the situation, for example, the frequency, direction, and length of gaze, and also the general demeanor of one of the participants. However, accompanying the gain in control is a concomitant loss in the spontaneity that certain theoretical perspectives require. Here we consider ways in which confederates have been used, examining the advantages and disadvantages of such use.

One dimension to be discussed is the extent to which the investigator controls a confederate's behavior. Investigators can obtain a high degree of control over the stimulus gaze by producing videotapes of confederates, which are then played to subjects. LeCompte and Rosenfeld (1971) showed subjects a videotape of a confederate who, at two designated points in a script, either gazed or did not look up while reading task instructions. Subjects then rated the confederate. Marsh (1970) showed subjects videotapes of confederates who were programmed to look at or away from the audience according to design. Subjects were told that the confederate was another student with whom they were communicating via on-line television. The subject was to read a speech to the standard listener, whose visual behavior was varied in different conditions. In both of these examples, control was maximal, but in the second case spontaneity was reduced to zero. In both cases the deception lent itself to discovery, for had an inquisitive subject persisted in trying to question the "co-interactant," the unresponsivity of the other could well have aroused suspicion.

Although the use of videotaped, artificial "co-interactants" can create problems that may outweigh their value as standardized stimulus presentations, there are two research areas in which recorded presentations are very useful. First, a number of investigations have explored the impact on television audiences when nonverbal behaviors of a televised image vary in natural or controlled fashion. Second, recorded interactions between people whose gaze behavior varies, either naturally or as an experimentally controlled variable, may be shown to judges who are asked to attribute meaning to the behaviors (Kleck & Nuessle, 1968).

Providing somewhat less control but permitting more spontaneity than recorded presentations is the use of confederates trained to control their own gaze behavior while talking with another interactant. For example, Exline et al. (1965) instructed a confederate interviewer to look each subject in the eye throughout an interaction period, and then measured the incidence of the subject's returned gaze. This procedure, which has been employed by a number of researchers primarily to simplify recording, has been criticized for its artificiality (Ellsworth & Ludwig, 1972). It may be said in defense of the procedure, however, that if the confederate is primarily in the role of listener, as in an interviewing situation, the high level of gaze is not different from naturally occurring behavior. Also, the 100 percent gaze need not be a stare. The face can be relaxed and the conversation normal. Subjects by and large are unaware of such behavior, and it does not strike them as unusual. It is clearly preferable to provide more variation in confederate behavior, and currently available recording equipment makes this easily possible; nevertheless, the studies that have used the 100 percent gaze procedure do provide meaningful information.

Argyle, Lefebvre, and Cook (1974) investigated the meaning attributed to various gaze patterns by training confederates in five visual patterns: continuous gaze, looking continuously while talking and not at all while listening, looking continuously while listening and not at all while talking, normal gaze, and nearly zero gaze. This again represents a fairly simple level of confederate manipulation, and furthermore, some of the patterns are rather unusual. The investigators, however, were expressly interested in the meanings attributed to various gaze patterns, and pushing the patterns to extremes may accentuate the differences in meaning.

Although confederates find it easier to use the foregoing gaze patterns, they can be trained to vary their overall level of gaze while maintaining naturally occurring internal relationships between, for example, look–listen and look–speak behaviors. Fehr (1981) trained confederates to converse with subjects while maintaining either normal gaze or one somewhat above or below normal, depending upon the characteristic level of each confederate's gaze. Though it took several training sessions for them to adapt to an altered gaze pattern, the confederates were quite successful at this task and, without training, maintained conventional relationships between look–listen and look–

speak (the percentage of look–listen tends to be greater than the percentage of look–speak; see Exline et al., 1965) and at the same time managed shifts from happy to sad conversation content (direct gaze is greater when recounting a happy experience; see Exline, Paredes, Gottheil, & Winkelmayer, 1979).

Extremely precise control of an interacting confederate's gaze behavior was obtained by Ellyson, Dovidio, Corson, and Vinicur (1980).

> The female confederate was programmed to look into the line of regard of the subject when she felt, with her hand, a mild electrical signal sent to the underside of the chair in which she was seated. For this "electric chair" procedure, a microswitch was used to open and close a circuit allowing mild electric current to be delivered to the confederate's chair at precise intervals. This microswitch, in turn, was controlled by a moving loop of 16 mm film that was systematically perforated with holes. When a signal pen encountered a hole in the film, the microswitch closed the electrical circuit and sent the signal to the confederate's chair. When a solid portion of the film was encountered, the signal pen was deflected[,] which opened the circuit and ended the signal.
>
> The confederate's chair was modified with two exposed wires below the outer rim of the seat. By touching the two wires simultaneously the confederate completed the circuit and received the mild, but reliable, electrical signal. Thus, the visual behavior of the confederate was controlled without the subject's knowledge. The microswitch that controlled the signal was also connected to an Esterline Angus event recorder (model 190M) which recorded when the signal was activated. The variable schedule of the confederate's visual attention, therefore, was identical across all subjects and was designed to be typical of female visual behavior found in previous studies of interacting peers (Argyle & Cook, 1976) . . . Across the discussion of the three tasks, the confederate looked 48% of the time when she was speaking and 68% of the time when she was listening. [P. 330]

This procedure provides for the precise control of the overall time spent looking as well as the average duration of glances. The tactile cue is especially suited to the task. A visual cue would require the confederate to divert her line of regard away from the subject periodically to check the cue, whereas an auditory cue could, potentially, elicit a visual orienting response from the confederate; it also could be heard by the subject. Olfactory and gustatory cues would be novel and interesting, but it would be difficult to control precisely the time of onset and offset of the cue. One can imagine, however, a situation in which the gaze demanded by Ellyson et al.'s technique would be inappropriate to the ongoing interaction and would prove to be antithetical to the purpose of the research. Nevertheless, the present level of computer technology suggests that it should be possible to develop a gaze-control mechanism like Ellyson's, but one that would permit the confederate some freedom to respond spontaneously to the flow of interaction.

In line with the last suggestion, consider an experimental situation in which two people, one subject and one confederate, were talking. During the conversation four observers would determine the points at which each person spoke and/or gazed into the eyes of his or her cointeractant. This information would be coded directly into a computer, which would be programmed to inform the confederate periodically whether his or her previous level of gaze should be maintained, raised, or lowered. Such messages could be automatically transported via electric shocks to one arm of the confederate's chair (signaling "look more"), to the other arm (signaling "look less"), or to neither arm (meaning "no change necessary"). One could also employ this type of instrumentation for yoked control studies.

The use of confederates creates problems over and above that of lack of spontaneity. Confederates, even if they are explicitly unaware of the specific hypothesis associated with a study, can become aware of the various experimental conditions. This knowledge can lead to subtle confederate behaviors that systematically bias results. Also, one cannot avoid the question whether results obtained with confederates can be generalized to all interactions. Ellsworth and Ross (1975) employed subjects as "single-session 'confederates'" in an attempt to mitigate these problems. Pairs of naîve participants were scheduled together, one person performing only as a subject and one becoming a quasi-confederate of the experimenter. The "confederates" were instructed to perform one of four gaze patterns while listening to the "subject" reveal personal information:

> In the two *direct gaze* conditions, listeners were instructed to communicate a sense of personal relationship to the speaker by looking into his eyes. In the *constant gaze* condition, the listener was told to look at the speaker's eyes continuously without regard for changes in his speech or behavior. In the *contingent gaze* condition he was instructed to look up only when the speaker discussed himself in personal, open, or intimate terms, and to stop looking at the speaker "if he starts wandering off and talking about impersonal topics." The listener was also directed to "shape"

> self-revelation by reinforcing increasing intimacy on the part of reluctant or uncomfortable speakers. A few examples of personal and impersonal statements were given to the listeners; but they were encouraged to employ a flexible standard, responding to fluctuations and relative levels of intimacy within the speaker's communication. In the two gaze *avoidance conditions*, listeners were instructed to avoid embarrassing and inhibiting the talker by avoiding eye contact with him. In the *constant avoidance* condition, the listener was told to avoid eye contact during the experimental session regardless of the speaker's behavior. In the *contingent avoidance* condition, the listener was instructed to avert his gaze whenever the speaker discussed himself in personal, open, or intimate terms, and to look at the speaker during impersonal utterances. As in the contingent gaze condition, the listener was instructed to "shape" self-revelation, in this case using gaze aversion rather than direct gaze as the reinforcer. The gaze avoidance instructions exactly paralleled the direct gaze instructions, except for the specific intimacy-encouraging behavior recommended.
>
> In the control condition, listeners were given no visual behavior instructions. Instead, the experimenter merely provided a preview of the reasons for designating one speaker and one listener. [Pp. 597–598]

Although equipment failures precluded measuring the gaze behavior of all the "confederates," available information from 39 dyads indicated that the listeners were well able to follow the instructions. For situations in which it would be applicable, this procedure would appear to be a most useful adjunct to the more traditional confederate paradigms.

There is one interesting aspect of the use of confederates in visual interaction research to which we have found no reference. In our laboratory, confederates trained to provide a level of gaze different from their own almost unanimously report strong personal affective reactions that could have important implications for the research. For example, white American females, when asked to reduce their level of gaze to 50% or lower while sharing experiences with or interviewing a subject, report a fair amount of discomfort. They feel that they are rude and detached from the interaction. These feelings influence many other behaviors, including the tendency to give or withhold such social reinforcements as head nods or minimal verbal encouragement, posture, and the extent to which gesture accompanies speaking. Increased training can reduce such initial reactions and lead to standardization of the corollary nonverbal behaviors. Nevertheless, investigators should be aware of the possibility that instructing confederates to utilize nonconventional levels of visual attention could affect other aspects of their behaviors in unanticipated ways. Whether these effects are due to discomfort based on violation of norms concerning acceptable levels of visual attention, or to arousal of emotional states according to the feedback process postulated by Tomkins (1962) and Izard (1971), is moot. The point to be made is that such effects are possible. Given the large number of studies in which confederate gaze has been manipulated, it is surprising that this experience has not been hitherto reported.

The observation just discussed suggests that subjects' impressions of confederates who have been asked to gaze in unusual ways (see Exline, Fairweather, Hine, & Argyle, reported in Exline, 1972) could be affected as much by behaviors arising from the confederates' discomfort (or arousal) in being asked to gaze in unusual ways as by the manipulated gaze level alone. Rosenthal (1966) has shown that knowledge of hypotheses being tested can affect the behavior of an experimenter in unconscious but systematic ways. We suggest that knowledge that one is carrying out instructions to gaze at and away from others in non-normative fashion can similarly affect other aspects of confederates' behavior.

Several implications follow: (1) Confederates who are asked to manipulate their gaze should be trained until the experimenter is satisfied that they can produce the required gaze without affecting other aspects of their behavior. If they cannot, they should not be used. (2) Studies that provide no clear evidence that the confederates' concomitant behavior has been unaffected by gaze-level manipulations should probably be replicated with appropriate checks reported. (3) The observations in question suggest a line of research. What aspects, if any, of a confederate's behavior are concomitantly affected when the gaze manipulation is first attempted? Are certain kinds of confederates (e.g., men vs. women, those who are highly Machiavellian vs. those who are less so, culture group *A* vs. culture group *B*, etc.) more likely to be affected when carrying out the manipulation? In short, what appears to be a methodological issue may, in fact, lead to theoretical research.

3.4. One-way versus two-way interaction

The issue in this section is whether to record the gaze behavior of one, two, or more interactants (see also Scherer & Ekman, Section 1.3). Theoretically, this decision relates to the investigator's conceptualization of the unit of analysis. If the primary focus of the investigation is upon the responses or reactions of individuals to social stimuli emitted by one of the interactants, then, most likely, only the behavior of an identified subject will be measured. On the other hand, if a dyad, triad, or other group is considered to be the unit of analysis, the behavior of all participants will be noted.

From a methodological point of view, several issues must be considered. Investigators who control the gaze behavior of a confederate will record only the actions of the subject (e.g., Aiello, 1972; Exline et al., 1965). When the confederate is trained to gaze steadily at the subject, this procedure poses no serious problem (e.g., Exline et al., 1965), although it is always advisable to check the presentation of any independent or controlled variable. However, if the confederate's behavior is allowed to vary, failing to measure the visual behavior of the confederate puts one in the position of lacking accurate information regarding the presentation of the independent variable.

Furthermore, certain gaze variables that may be of interest to the experimenter cannot be obtained unless data from both participants are available. Mutual gaze, the extent to which the two participants simultaneously look into each other's eyes, would be an example of such a variable.

Measuring the gaze of both participants can create difficulties. It must be possible to position observers so that each can be in a direct line with the person to be coded. If the researcher wishes to measure mutual gaze, the recording equipment used to collect coded information from observers must be sophisticated enough to provide for the ready integration of information from both observers. If, for example, only stopwatches are available, it will be difficult if not impossible to determine simultaneous looking accurately, though recent work by Lazzerini, Stephenson, and Neave (1978) suggests that under some circumstances reasonable estimates of mutual gaze can be derived from accurate recordings of each participant separately.

3.5. Choice of behaviors measured

Investigators have focused upon two broad categories of behavior in measuring visual interaction. First, the perceptions and interpretations of gaze-related phenomena have been assessed through the use of questionnaires. Second, various gaze behaviors of subjects and confederates have been assessed by human observers. Whereas some studies are concerned with one or the other category, many incorporate both.

Perceptions of another's gaze

A number of aspects of perceptions of another's gaze have been investigated, for example, normative expectations, awareness of gaze level, impressions of the looker's strength or weakness, and so on, with the methods of assessment used being dependent upon the specific question asked.

The expected degree of comfort associated with receiving various amounts of gaze from hypothetical others was reported by Exline (1972). Subjects completed a questionnaire in which they reported how comfortable they would be when hypothetically, speaking to, listening to, or in mutual silence with others of their own and different age and sex who gazed at them 50% of the time, 100% of the time, or not at all. The greatest anticipated comfort was reported for a situation in which the respondent expected to be looked at about 50% of the time; the least, for that in which a woman anticipated receiving a 100% look in mutual silence from an older man.

Implicit in this approach is the assumption that persons are, at some level, aware of the gaze of those with whom they interact. This assumption has been tested by investigators who have asked naive subjects to estimate the amount of time they were looked at by an interaction partner. Results were mixed: Argyle and Williams (1969) concluded that subjects were relatively insensitive to the amount of gaze received from a confederate, whereas Ellsworth and Ross (1975) found subjects' estimates of a co-interactant's gaze to be ranked in direct concurrence with the gaze condition (high or low) in which they found themselves. The conflicting results suggest the existence of mediating variables that influence the perception of the salience of another's gaze, because in spite of the fact that their subjects were said to be relatively insensitive, Argyle and Williams (1969) did find positive correlations ranging from 0.49 to 0.65 between the subjects' feeling of being observed and their judgment of the amount of gaze received from a co-interactant. Perhaps the feeling of being looked at is related to a tendency to be self-aware. Given Duval and Wicklund's (1972) postulate of objective self-awareness (in which a person looks inward, self-examining), this would be an interesting line of research to pursue.

It would also be interesting to consider the extent to which people are aware of their *own* gaze level and its effect upon the behavior of others. Attribution research indicates that people are frequently not aware of their impact on others. An individual tends to attribute the cause of another's behavior to the other's personality, without considering the possible influence of his or her own behavior on the situation (Jones & Nisbett, 1971). The impact of interpersonal gaze, then, might sometimes occur independent of the looker's awareness.

Lastly, the meaning associated with various patterns of gaze has been assessed by requesting respondents to give, via questionnaires, their impressions of persons they view on videotape or film (Kleinke, Meeker, & La Fong, 1974), or of persons with whom they have actually interacted (Argyle et al., 1974). A variety of questionnaire types have been used – the semantic differential technique, Likert scales, Guttman scales, and so on. See Nunnally (1978) for a fuller description of appropriate scales. Two familiar dimensions run through this literature: those of evaluation and potency. Depending on the context of the interaction, giving visual attention to another can indicate a positive or negative evaluation of that other, or a dominant or deferent orientation toward him or her (Ellsworth & Carlsmith, 1968; Exline et al., 1975; Exline & Winters, 1965).

We have described but a few of the many ways in which the perception of another's gaze has been treated. Without attempting to be exhaustive, we have suggested other approaches that could be fruitfully pursued. In any event, we believe that investigators of gaze interaction would be wise to obtain, routinely, data concerning subjects' awareness of a co-interactant's gaze – particularly when gaze is experimentally manipulated.

Gaze variables

The study of visual behavior, as a socially significant variable, has primarily been concerned with an individual's tendency to look at (in the eyes, eye region, or face) or away from his or her co-conversant. These two mutually exclusive states may be represented, as in Figure 3.2, by the use of numerals 1 (look at) and 0 (look away).

The extent to which a person looks at and/or away from another person may be quantified by employing several different measures:

1. Frequency: the number of times a person looks at a conversational partner.
2. Total duration: the number of seconds during which the person looks at this partner.
3. Proportion of time (or percentage): the proportion of a specified interaction category, for example, the total period while looking, speaking, and so on, during which the person looks at his or her partner. This measure is especially appropriate when the duration of the interaction varies for different dyads.

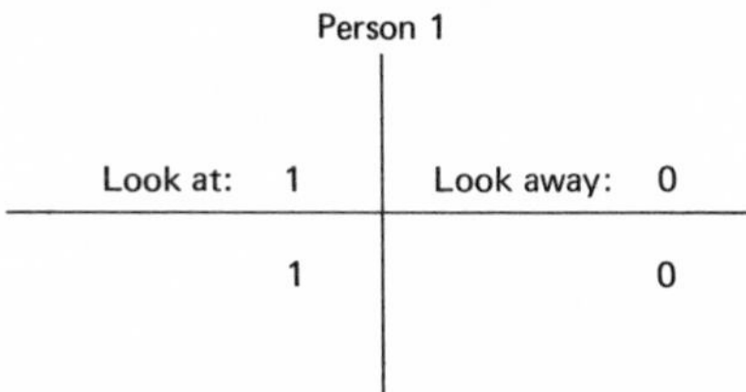

Figure 3.2. Representation of the gaze behavior of one individual (Person 1): looking at (1) and away from (0) an interaction partner.

4. Average duration: the mean or average duration of the individual glances at the partner. Although the mean is the measure of central tendency typically reported by gaze researchers, it is important to note that the frequency distribution of glances is *J*-shaped and would therefore be more appropriately described by the median.
5. Standard deviation of glances: the standard deviation associated with the average duration of glances that would provide information regarding the variability of glances.

The extent to which a person looks another in the face, regardless of what the other does, is referred to as *total gaze*. Thus we may speak of the frequency, duration, proportion, mean, and standard deviation of total gaze. Argyle and Ingham (1972), just to give one of many examples, measured the proportion and average duration of total gaze and found both to increase as the distance between interactants increased.

When the visual behavior of both members of a dyad is considered, the number of possibilities is expanded, as depicted in Figure 3.3. Each participant may look either at or away from his or her partner, so that four mutually exclusive categories are produced: mutual gaze at one's partner, one-way looking by either participant, and mutual looking away from one's partner. Again each of these variables may be recorded as frequency, duration, proportion, mean, and standard duration.

Mutual gaze, the time during which two interactants gaze into each others eyes (faces) simultaneously, has proved to be the most investigated of the gaze variables. In some instances this has been a necessary consequence of employing a continuously gazing confederate (e.g., Exline et al., 1965; Exline & Winters, 1965; Kleinke & Pohlen, 1971; Kleinke, Staneski, & Berger, 1975). Level of mutual gaze has been related to topic intimacy (Exline, Jones, & Maciorowski, 1977; Rohner & Aiello, 1975; Weiss & Keys, 1975) and to interpersonal distance (Argyle & Ingham, 1972; Goldberg, Kiesler, & Collins, 1969; Russo, 1975).

Several years ago, Strongman and Champness (1968) suggested that

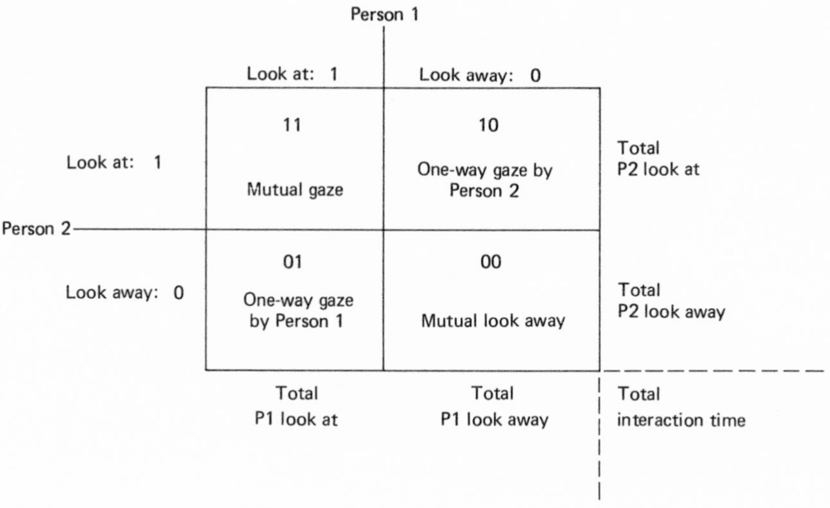

Figure 3.3. Representation of the gaze behavior of two individuals.

the incidence of mutual gaze might be fruitfully compared to a chance model:

> If chance robots are indulging in directed gaze, where looking toward is "on" and looking away is "off", the amount of mutual "on" which occurs can be calculated probabilistically. Thus, if total time is a, robot 1's "on" total during this time is (c1) and robots 2's is (c2), then the total time during which they are both "on", i.e., when by chance, they indulge in EC, is given by $(c_1 \times c_2) / a^2$.
>
> This can, of course, be compared with actual EC time. [P. 385]

This quoted formula was further refined by Argyle and Ingham (1972) to correct for differences in looking typically associated with periods when one is speaking to as opposed to listening to one's partner. Rutter, Stephenson, Lazzerini, Ayling, and White (1977) and Lazzerini et al. (1978) applied the Strongman and Champness formula to data from several of their own experiments. They considered the total gazes of two freely interacting conversants to be independent of each other and proceeded to multiply these two durations together to obtain an expected joint occurrence of mutual gaze (Rutter et al., 1977). They found the expected mutual gaze so computed to be virtually identical to the observed mutual gaze. Using the same logic but applying more sophisticated procedures, Lazzerini et al. (1978) obtained the same results. On the basis of these two investigations, the authors argue that because the gaze of the two participants in a dyad is independent, mutual gaze is the chance result of their co-occurrence and hence is not a particularly commanding variable. Clearly, this position is quite different from the conclusions of anecdotal and experimental reports.

One might question, however, the basic assumption on which their analysis is based. The observed duration of total gaze for each participant would not seem to be appropriate to the development of a chance model of gaze; the observed total gaze already is, we would argue, dependent upon the presence of the other person. First, consider that gaze is typically recorded as a dichotomous variable: gaze at the partner (1), gaze away from the partner (0). The expected chance occurrence of such a system would be 0.50; and the expected joint occurrence of two systems $0.50 \times 0.50 = 0.25$. One can carry the analysis further, however. Consider a person alone in a room who is able to look at anything desired. The probability of this person's gazing at any one point in the room can be computed. Now bring another person into the room. The eye–face region of this second person constitutes a small portion of the first person's visual field (provided interpersonal distance is maintained at a social level) and thus would be associated with an even smaller expected total gaze than 0.50, and consequently smaller mutual gaze than 0.25. But clearly, when two people converse, they spend much more than these expected minuscule proportions gazing at one another. Another human is a socially significant event that captures far more of our attention, and thus our visual focus, than a truly chance model would predict.

Research has demonstrated that there is important information to be gained by considering whether the gazer is speaking to or listening to his or her partner (Ellyson et al., 1979; Exline et al., 1975). The matrix of mutually exclusive categories integrating both speech and gaze for two participants is given in Figure 3.4. As in previous figures, the numeral 1 represents action, either looking or speaking, and 0 represents looking away from or listening to the conversational partner. (For completeness, it should again be pointed out that one may consider the frequency, duration, proportion, mean, and standard deviation of these variables.) Exline et al. (1975) found look–speak/look–listen patterns that differentiated occupants of high- and low-power positions in a problem-solving dyad. This pattern showed the mean difference between looking while listening and looking while speaking to be positive for occupants of

		Person 1: Look 0 Speak 0	Person 1: Look 0 Speak 1	Person 1: Look 1 Speak 0	Person 1: Look 1 Speak 1	
Person 2	Look 0 Speak 0	(1) 0000	(2) 0001	(3) 0010	(4) 0011	P2 totals
	Look 0 Speak 1	(5) 0100	(6) 0101	(7) 0110	(8) 0111	
	Look 1 Speak 0	(9) 1000	(10) 1001	(11) 1010	(12) 1011	
	Look 1 Speak 1	(13) 1100	(14) 1101	(15) 1110	(16) 1111	
		P1 totals				Total interaction time

Figure 3.4. Representation of categories of visual and speech behavior of two participants: looking at or speaking to the interaction partner (1) and not looking at or speaking to the partner (0).

low-power positions and negative for occupants of high-power positions. It is interesting to learn that the patterns were replicated when subjects were categorized by their personal orientations toward controlling others, rather than by the power inherent in the positions to which they were assigned. The pattern characteristic of the occupant of the high-power position was the same as that for the highly control-oriented person, whereas the low-power position pattern matched that of the person whose control orientation was low.

Although the matrix in Figure 3.4 represents all possible categories resulting from the intersection of the speech and gaze of two persons, the contents of the individual cells are not typically studied. The variables most often considered are constructed by collapsing across cells. For example, P1's percentage of look–listen, the proportion of P2's speaking time during which P1 is gazing at P2, is computed by summing the contents of cells 7, 8, 15, and 16 and then dividing by the sum of 5, 6, 7, 8, 13, 14, 15, and 16. Other variables of interest may be obtained in the same manner by summing.[4]

In addition to the duration measures of visual attention just mentioned (most of which treat the phenomena by considering behavior summed over time), the diagram in Figure 3.3, for example, encourages the analysis of visual behavior in terms of dyadic states. Given a predetermined time base, one can analyze dyadic interaction by means of transitions from state to state. By sampling the record every 0.5 second, for example, one can determine which of four dyadic states exists at that moment. By such means one can accumulate a transition matrix showing the probability of any dyadic state's maintaining itself or proceeding to any other dyadic state in the next 0.5 second.

If the initial state is one of mutual gaze (*P*1:1, *P*2:1), and this is followed 0.5 second later by another mutual gaze state, and 0.5 second later by a gaze aversion by *P*1 only, the record would read (*P*1:1, *P*2:1), (*P*1:1, *P*2:1), (*P*1:0, *P*2:1). The sequence shows two transitions: mutual gaze, followed by another mutual gaze, proceeding to a one-way gaze by *P*2. As Stern (1974) has shown, the transition matrix can be converted to a state-transition diagram permitting representation of the number and probability of transitions. Such a technique permits analyses of true dyadic gaze interaction, and can be used to study relationships that cannot be investigated when gaze is measured only by summed durations.

Stern (1974), for example, has used the transitional probability analyses of gaze recorded during mother–infant play to investigate such questions as: "Does maternal gaze alter the probability of the infant initiating a gaze at her, and does it alter the probability of his terminating a gaze at her?" (p. 203). His analysis indicates that a mother's gaze at her infant increases the probability of the infant's initiating a gaze at her, and also that all infants are less likely to avert the gaze if the mother is looking at them.

Such a technique can be generalized to the study of gaze patterns among adults. It could be used to determine, for example, if, and under what conditions, one member of a dyad is more likely to initiate and/or break a mutual dyadic gaze than is the other. Adding the variable speech–silence, as in Figure 3.4, increases the total possible number of states to be sampled to 16, and permits investigation of look–speak/look–listen relationships of various kinds of dyads in terms of transitional probabilities. Hedge, Everitt, and Frith (1978), for example, investigated the role of eye gaze in controlling the flow of verbal conversation by examining just such a 16 × 16 transitional probability matrix. Their results indicate that gaze plays a more important role in controlling the dialogue of friends than of strangers. Hedge et al. were also able to demonstrate that a first-order Markov chain model adequately described the gross temporal aspects of gaze and speech during the dyadic interactions they observed. In addition, the relationship between power and looking described by Exline et al. (1975) could be readily analyzed to determine whether the low-power or the high-power person is more likely to break an established mutual gaze when the low-power person, the high-power person, or no one speaks. Analyzing gaze data by means of computing and comparing transitional probabilities enables the investigator to carry out increasingly rich and fine-grained analyses of behaviors over the course of an interaction, analyses that the typically employed summary measures do not permit.

Few investigators have examined the interrelationships within the potentially large set of gaze variables. Kendon and Cook (1969) and Duncan and Fiske (1977) represent welcome exceptions. Kendon and Cook found percentage, mean, and frequency of total gaze, look–listen, look–speak, and mutual gaze to be significantly ($r = 0.27$) and sometimes substantially (e.g., $r = 0.70$ to 0.88) intercorrelated. In our own lab, we have also found this to be the case. Several hundred experiments in the last 20 years have demonstrated interpersonal gaze to be an important social event. It would seem important to examine closely the different gaze variables and their relationship to each other and to other variables, in order to determine if all are truly socially significant or if their statistical significance in some instances might not be due to the correlations between variables.

The behavior of persons in freely interacting dyads tends to be correlated with the behavior produced by their partners. In the context of the visual interaction literature, for example, Coutts and Schneider (1975) report the correlation for frequency and duration of glances between same-sex interaction partners to range from -0.31 (n.s.) to -0.66 ($p < 0.01$). In mixed-sex dyads the correlations were positive and of approximately the same magnitude. These correlations have implications for the analysis of data from the dyadic situations in which they occur. It would be inappropriate to enter scores from each dyad member into an analysis that requires statistically independent data points. If the focus of attention is mutual gaze, both parties contribute to the one shared score and the statistical problem of correlation does not exist (see, e.g., Hore, 1970; Rubin, 1970; Russo, 1975). The appropriate analysis of behaviors other than shared ones, however, requires consideration of the correlation. One suggestion would be to compute the mean score for dyad members and compute further analyses on these means rather than the original scores. One could also analyze the data from but one member of a dyad and discard those from the other. Both of these solutions sacrifice the efforts that went into the participation of *two* subjects. Coutts and Schneider (1975) offer a more economical solution. They treat "dyads" as a within-subject or correlated-means factor with two levels: person 1 and person 2. Dyad members are randomly assigned to either one of these positions. The suitability of each of these suggestions will depend upon the particular experimental context; however, some sort of adjustment for the correlation would seem to be essential for acceptable data analysis.

Gaze is clearly only part of one's total potentially communicative display behavior. The impact of the display on a receiver is likely to depend upon the interrelationships among the various components, including speech, posture, gestures, facial expressions, and so on. To date, only a few investigators (e.g., Duncan & Fiske, 1977) have studied relationships between gaze and variables other than speech; with the increasing availability of laboratory computers, however, gaze behavior in relation to other nonverbal behaviors is likely to be increasingly studied. For example, one might expect gaze and hand–arm gestures to covary – especially gestures associated with speech. Speech-related gestures would probably become meaningless arm waving if one's partner were not looking; and how do you discover a partner's gaze direction but by looking?

Thus far we have considered only the categories of looking at and looking away from the eyes or face of another person. These categories are by far the most often studied. Other aspects of visual behavior have been investigated, however.

A number of researchers have become interested in more refined analysis of the broad category of looking away. The direction of away gaze (conjugate lateral eye movement) has been studied in relation to cerebral hemisphere dominance (Libby, 1970). Gur (1975) reports that when a questioner sat behind the subject, right-handed persons glanced away to the left when solving spatial problems and glanced to the right when posed verbal problems. When faced by the questioner, however, the same subjects tended to look away in predominantly one direction, either left or right, regardless of the type of problem. The typical procedure in such research is to request the participant to gaze straight ahead, either at the eyes of the questioner or into space, when each question is asked. When subjects begin to speak, observers then record the direction of the initial gaze deviation.

Direction of gaze has also been studied during the silent expression of emotion. Exline et al. (1979) report that when recounting sad personal experiences, subjects spend more time gazing downward than directly at an interviewer, and reverse the pattern when recounting happy personal experiences. These differences in direction patterns, when taken in conjunction with facial displays (Ekman, 1972; Izard, 1971), may well constitute a package of appropriate concomitances that can aid decoders in correctly discriminating among the affects contained in the different personal experiences described by each stimulus person. Further research, of course, is required to establish if it is possible to determine the relative contributions to the accurate assessment of affect displays of gaze direction, facial expression, and – when nonverbal sound is added – paravocal information (Scherer, 1979; Chapter 4).

Clearly, there are many other qualities of visual behavior that would seem, intuitively, to provide information for a viewer. In addition to the direction and duration of fixations, one might consider the speed of movement between fixations. People tend to differ in their degree of eye movement. Some persons are relatively steady in their visual behavior, looking and looking away only after several seconds of fixation, whereas others may be described as flickering in their gaze pattern. Their eyes dart about, resting only briefly on any target. In addition to individual differences in gaze patterns, situational factors can also play a role. A listener who has grown bored might become unable to maintain a steady gaze at his partner and show such boredom by shifting focus from spot to spot. The researcher might also consider the facial surround of the eyes, the action of the muscles of the eye pocket (sleepy vs. wide awake), the position and movement of the brows, and the general expression of the face. The direction of gaze provides important information for a receiver about a person's focus of attention, be it on the receiver, on another, or on something else. Finally, the facial display accompanying the gaze is undoubtedly a major factor in the interpretation of the nature of the interest implied by the presence or absence of visual attention. Gaze researchers could build upon the extensive work of Ekman (1972), Ekman, Friesen, and Ellsworth (1972), and Izard (1971, 1977) concerning the measurement and meaning of facial expression, in order to investigate the relationships between gaze direction and facial displays. Is there, for example, a close coordination in time between the fixation of the gaze on the eye region or face of another and the activation of the muscle groups associated with joy? Is the deviation or direction of the deviation of the gaze coordinate with major changes in facial muscle activity? The methods of assessing facial expression described by Ekman (Chapter 2) should be very useful in studying relationships between gaze and facial expression.

The significance of any of the gaze-related variables mentioned here will depend upon the ability to detect their presence validly and reliably. These measurements are typically made by human observers, and it is to the observer's ability to make such judgments that we now turn.

3.6. Behavioral observation

The task of determining the direction, frequency, and duration of a person's gaze has proved problematic. Typically, a human observer is called upon to view an interaction, either live or recorded, and to indicate the extent of the visual behavior of the participants. It is important to consider the reliability and validity of such measures and the relative merits of observing live as compared to recorded action.

Reliability and validity of measures obtained from human observers

There is evidence to indicate that human observers, under optimal conditions, are quite reliable in determining various aspects of a person's visual behavior. For example, in a study directed at the question of reliability (Exline, 1972), 10 males and 10 females were interviewed for approximately 5 minutes each by a continuously gazing male interviewer. The incidence of the subjects' gaze at the interviewer was simultaneously recorded by the interviewer and by an observer positioned directly behind the interviewer on the other side of a one-way vision mirror. Discrepancies of 0.10 second or larger were considered errors. The average proportions of overlap for the two records were 0.905, 0.942, and 0.916 for the first 15 seconds, the middle 250 seconds, and the last 15 seconds, respectively.

Fehr (1981) obtained similar results with data coded from videotapes. Twenty-eight freely interacting female dyads were recorded while describing personal experiences to each other. The interactions varied from 5 to 20 minutes in duration. The tapes were viewed on two separate occasions by different observers. The correlations between coding sessions for the proportion of total gaze, look–speak, look–listen, one–way gaze, mutual gaze, and mutual no-look ranged from 0.88 to 0.99.

Other investigators have obtained similar reliabilities when training observers to code visual behavior for studies dealing with substantive issues. Respectable reliabilities have been obtained for the recording of total time (Fugita, 1974), frequency (Fugita, 1974), mutual gaze (Rubin, 1970), and away gazes on both a horizontal and a vertical plane (Exline et al., 1979; Gur, 1975; Libby, 1970). See Argyle and Cook (1976) for a summary of the reliability data. An interpretation of these reliabilities follows a discussion of the variables affecting the validity of gaze recording.

The fairly respectable reliabilities obtained for the observation of interpersonal gaze are meaningful only if it can be demonstrated that the measures are valid, that is, that the direction, frequency, and duration of gaze are actually correctly ascertained. It is this aspect of coding visual interaction that is the most problematic. The available evidence indicates that humans are not as accurate as desired in determining when others look them directly in the eye(s). (See Argyle & Cook, 1976; Exline & Fehr, 1978; and Harper, Wiens, & Matarazzo, 1978, for other reviews of the following material.)

Krüger and Hückstedt (1969) argued that if there exists a special phenomenon of "eye contact," subjects should be able to discriminate gazes into their eyes from gazes to other parts of their faces. However, only 35% of the judgments were correct at 80 cm, and only 10% at 200 cm. These results were replicated by Ellgring (1970).

Gibson and Pick (1963) investigated subjects' abilities to discriminate gazes at them (to the bridge of the nose) from gazes away from their faces. This study is usually cited by investigators as evidence for the validity of gaze measurement; however, von Cranach and Ellgring (1973) provide cogent criticisms of this favorable interpretation of Gibson and Pick's data. Von Cranach and Ellgring direct our attention to the large proportions of off-the-face gazes, 40% of the gazes to the left and 36% of the gazes to the right, which are judged as gazes at the face. Also, when the sender's head is turned 30° to the right or left, correct judgments drop off to 52% and 36%, respectively.

Other aspects of the observation situation have been investigated by von Cranach and his colleagues. Krüger and Hückstedt (1969) determined that errors in receivers' judgments increase as distance between sender and receiver increases, as gaze duration decreases, and as the sender's head deviates from a straight-on position. Head position plays an even greater role in reducing the accuracy of observers' judgments. Also, observer error increases with an increase in angular displacement away from the direct line of regard between the sender and receiver. Furthermore, von Cranach, Schmid, and Vogel (1969) found a considerable decrement in correct responses when gaze and head movements preceded the fixation to be judged.

The decrease in validity associated with an increase in sender–receiver distance has posed a particular problem for adequate testing of aspects of Argyle and Dean's (1965) Equilibrium Model of human interaction. It has been suggested that as interpersonal distance between dyad members increases, interpersonal gaze will increase. Stephenson and Rutter (1970) report that increased interpersonal distance produced increased errors of measurement: A larger number of non-face gazes were judged as face gazes. They suggest that the typically recorded increase in gaze with increased distance is due to measurement artifact. To investigate this question further, Stephenson, Rutter, and Dore (1973) videotaped participants interacting at different distances. Through the use of a zoom lens they were able to make the televised images identical despite the fact that interpersonal distance actually varied. Increased gaze was still observed for greater distances, and they concluded that their findings supported the equilibrium hypothesis. It is unclear, however, whether they have actually removed all sources of bias associated with distance. Although the televised image was the same size in the different conditions, the degree of eye movement necessary to shift focus from the eyes to other parts of the face, or to other points either on or off the body, would still be much smaller, and thus more difficult to discriminate, at greater distances.

Although such reports raise disquieting questions concerning almost 20 years of visual interaction research, several alternative explanations of the data are tenable. First, the circumstances under which the validity data have necessarily been collected tend to be relatively stilted when compared to free interaction. To obtain information about the validity of measurement, precise knowledge of the fixation point and duration of a looker's gaze must be obtained to serve as the criterion against which observer recordings are compared. This criterion has been obtained by using procedures that enable the experimenter to specify, at any given point, exactly where each gaze is focused, the length of its duration, and the angle from which it is sent. Stringent controls over a sender's visual behavior are required to ensure that such criteria are met. Senders and receivers typically use chin rests to ensure stable lines of regard. They wear head sets in order to receive directions about fixation points and the duration of the look. They do not converse with each other. Instrumentation developed to register the fixation points of the gaze automatically has, to date, proven to be equally restrictive and cumbersome, requiring chin rests to keep head and eyes in fixed positions, or obtrusive and bizarre-looking helmets with apparatus covering one eye (e.g., the Mackworth eye-marker camera). Validity data have thus been collected under extremely restrictive circumstances quite different from ordinary social interaction. The results of such studies may well be restricted to the relatively unusual and socially sterile settings that produce such data.

Vine (1971) has compared reliability of observations obtained in such restrictive settings with reliabilities obtained from observer recordings in more natural interaction. He filmed two interchanges, one highly controlled and one in which two individuals interacted freely. The inter- and intrarater reliabilities increased from 73.8% to 93.8% and from 76.4% to 96.2%, respectively, when the free rather than the controlled interaction was observed. Noting that there was nothing to suggest that the observers' ability to discriminate gaze direction improved between the two sessions, Vine argued that gaze in spontaneous interaction situations is easier to record because interactants look either at or well away from each other. This would imply that the discriminations that were difficult for receivers (observers) in the validity studies are not required in uncontrolled interactions. Although Vine's study is not, strictly speaking, a validity study (one cannot obtain true validity from measures of reliability alone), his results nevertheless suggest that in free social interaction the discriminations required of an observer may be more easily achieved.

It is also Argyle's (1970) contention that, in natural situations, people look either at or well away from interaction partners. We too have noticed this, especially when one partner is engaged in returning the glance of the other. However, when one member of a dyad looks away from his or her partner for a few seconds, the partner frequently uses this opportunity to attend closely to areas of the other's body that are considered socially inappropriate to be examining when receiving the other's visual attention. We speculate that decreases in the validity of measurement occur mainly in such low gaze situations.

Exline (1972) has argued that where the receiver thinks the sender looks is more important than where the sender does precisely focus. Thus gazes close to the eyes probably will be reacted to as if they were fixed precisely on the eye or eyes, and will be responded to as such. Because fairly high reliabilities have been obtained between the findings of receivers and observers of a sender's gaze (e.g., Exline, 1972), observers may be said to be making socially valid judgments. There are occasions, however, when it is important to know just where on a receiver's face the sender focuses. This is particularly true when the investigator is interested either in the sender's feelings of involvement with the other or in the overall level of dyadic involvement. Less involvement could result if true mutuality of gaze is absent because one or both senders closely scrutinize the other's nose or mouth.

At present the most convincing evidence that one can place faith in observer recordings of gaze stems from the experimental work of von Cranach and Ellgring (1973). Their work suggests that the validity of observer measurement improves after training sessions in which observers are provided feedback concerning the actual direction of a sender's gaze.

The ideal solution to the validity question discussed here would be to be able to measure gaze direction in a situation in which the sender's gaze did not need to be controlled. It would then be possible to design experiments to test our assumptions about the distribution of interpersonal gaze. Techniques for measuring eye fixations developed in the context of reading research may help us to meet this objective. Several of the oculometers currently available allow for moment-to-moment tracking of eye movement without obtrusive head gear or contact lenses. Although there are some restrictions in mobility, subjects may move their heads as much as 15 cm in any direction before tracking is lost.

Until further information is obtained regarding the validity of visual interaction measurement, we would like to offer the following suggestions, gleaned from the literature and our own work, for creating a recording situation maximally conducive to the collection of valid and reliable data:

1. Have dyad members face each other directly.
2. Place observers or TV cameras directly behind receivers.
3. Keep the sender–receiver distance as small as possible.
4. Test the visual acuity of observers.
5. Train observers with feedback trials.
6. Have some eye level lighting to reduce shadows in the eye pocket.
7. Obtain reliability estimates from all observers.
8. Schedule fatigue breaks into coding sessions. Observers may relieve the eye strain associated with long-term focusing on the eyes of a sender by moving their heads while keeping their eyes focused on the target. The head movement changes the muscles used for focusing.

Recorded versus live interactions

Two issues (at least) require consideration in the comparison of live and recorded interactions: (1) the ability to obtain reliable and valid measurements in each situation, and (2) the relative obtrusiveness of various observation techniques (see also Scherer & Ekman, Section 1.3).

As already described, Fehr (1981) obtained respectable reliabilities from videotape recordings. The validity problems encountered in live interactions would probably generalize to recorded interactions; so an investigator would be well advised to place cameras in the locations where observers would provide the most accurate data, that is, directly behind the person with whom the sender is interacting. Antis, Mayhew, and Morley (1969) recorded more errors of judgment with a televised than with a live image. They attributed the greater television error to the curvature of the screen. They recorded, however, a dummy head with movable eyes. The "gaze" of these eyes was controlled in the manner typical of the psychophysical validity studies. It is possible that placing observers directly in front of the screen and recording more natural interactions would reduce this effect. Prior to employing televised or film recordings, it would be advisable to compare gaze recordings made of the live interaction with those made of the recordings to ensure reliability.

With respect to the question of obtrusiveness, experience and data suggest that the method of observation may alter the visual behavior of interactants in ways not necessarily conducive to the primary focus of an investigation. Risser, Dovidio, and Faltot (1977) compared the gaze behavior of persons who were interviewed under five conditions that differed in the degree of obtrusiveness of visual observation and/or recording devices. Subjects in all conditions knew that they were to be audiotaped, and a microphone and speaker box were clearly visible. Visual observation was varied so that subjects were (1) not aware that they were observed, (2) aware of but unable to see recording equipment, (3) able to see a TV camera with a small lens, (4) able to see a TV camera with a large zoom lens, or (5) able to see a one-way vision mirror. Subjects who were aware of being recorded (conditions 2–5) demonstrated a significant preference for looking away from rather than toward the recording equipment (including the mirror). Subjects who were unaware of being observed and/or recorded (condition 1) showed no such gaze-direction preference. Other aspects of subjects' behavior, as well as their perceptions of the interviewer, were affected. Significantly more of those who were aware that their behavior was being recorded brought their hands to their faces than did those who were unaware of the recording. Also, participants who knew they were being observed described themselves as anxious and reported being more anxious about the equipment. This was particularly true when the recording device was the camera with large lens. Such data provide evidence in favor of using hidden and unannounced observation techniques to record visual interaction.

We recognize that we are raising an ethical question when we point up the methodological benefits to be derived from covert recording of behavior (see also Wallbott, Section A.7). Present regulations do permit such unobtrusive recording if potential benefits outweigh potential harm. In the present case, the benefits include a less reactive measure of visual interaction (as indicated by the work of Risser et al.), which could not be otherwise obtained. Very few subjects indicate concern about the recording when it is subsequently disclosed to them. The general nature of a project is explained to subjects prior to their participation. They are asked to sign a certificate of informed consent indicating that they are aware that they do not have to participate in the project; that, should they agree to begin, they may withdraw from participation at any time; and that they do not have to answer questions they do not wish to answer. Following such data collection, we explain our action and ask participants to sign a second consent form pertaining to the use of the data. If consent is not forthcoming, we immediately erase the tape and excuse the person from further participation in the study.

There are research questions, however, that require relatively obtrusive techniques. For example, when attempting to compare visual, vocal, and visual–vocal communication, the investigator must use equipment that permits control over the channels that carry information back and forth between the interactants. The interpersonal communications laboratory designed by Peter Bricker at Bell Laboratories (Bricker & Wish, 1978) provides for such comparisons. Participants may interact face-to-face or via a telecommunication system that allows for the control of both audio and video channels. In the latter case, subjects are seated in front of a screen on which they view the face and shoulders of the interaction partner. Significant from the perspective of visual interaction research is the fact that participants may look each other in the eye through this system by means of the use of a front-surface mirror and a beam splitter. Similar systems have also been assembled by Shea and Rosenfeld (1976) and by Wellens (1978). The eye engagement provided by this system would seem to permit participants greater involvement in an ongoing conversation while reducing somewhat the obtrusiveness of the intervening equipment. Future research employing such systems will provide information regarding the advantages and disadvantages of videophones, which currently do not provide for eye contact per se.

3.7. Data-recording equipment

There exist numerous methods of recording visual interaction data. The decision concerning which one to choose revolves around (1) expense,

(2) the gaze variables of interest, (3) the context of measurement, and (4) the investigator's sophistication with certain techniques.

The simplest and least expensive technique is to tally the frequency of occurrence of some aspect of gaze behavior. It would be possible to get a rough estimate of duration by checking the presence or absence of the category of interest at regular intervals.

Stopwatches, especially cumulative stopwatches, provide the possibility of obtaining duration information. Two watches are needed: One is used to time the total duration of the interaction; the other is started with the onset of a gaze and stopped at the offset. A cumulative stopwatch will sum these durations. The seconds of looking divided by the total time of the session results in the proportion of looking for one person. If the observer has a third arm, a coordinated foot, or a helper, he or she could also obtain information concerning the frequency of looking, which when divided into the duration of looking would result in the average duration of gazes.

Both of these procedures (check sheets and stopwatches) provide information concerning only the gaze of one person and one gaze variable category (total looking). Variables dependent upon the behavior of two interactants, such as mutual gaze or look–listen, and variables dependent upon making two measurements on the same person, such as look–speak, cannot be obtained readily by these methods.

There are several systems available that permit simultaneous recording and integration of several input channels. A system costing a few hundred dollars that enables one to obtain information about several people simultaneously is a pen record machine such as the Esterline-Angus event recorder. At least four input channels are desirable for gaze research because this number allows for the recording of speech and gaze for two persons. Four observers are required simultaneously, one for each channel. Each observer hand holds a two-state switch, which is depressed for the duration of action on the channel in question, speech or gaze. (Microswitches are recommended because they are lightweight and operate easily without fatiguing the hand – a problem when the cheaper spring-loaded switches are used.) A pen is connected to each switch. When the switch is closed, the pen deflects on the steadily rolling graph paper. The number of graph blocks encompassed by the deflection provides duration information. Frequency is indicated by the number of deflections. Variables dependent upon the state of other variables are determined by counting the blocks associated with joint deflections.

Tallying the frequencies and durations for several variables for several minutes for each dyad is very time-consuming, and the likelihood of computational error is great. Computer systems, if available, provide many advantages over pen record machines. The variables accessible are the same, but the ease and accuracy of access increase greatly. There are on the market numerous mini-computers (e.g., Digital Equipment Company's PDP 11/03) that allow for input channels identical to those of the pen record machines. A program must be written, one that scans the input channels and stores information concerning the duration of switch closures for each set of switch configurations. These raw data are then summarized to produce the gaze variables of interest.

With most computer systems, it is possible to purchase or construct peripheral devices that can record data for processing in the computer at a later time. For example, the microswitches may be connected to a cassette tape recorder that stores the data on tape. This procedure would allow a portable data-recording system, serviceable in the field or laboratory. For the construction and analysis of variables of interest the contents of the tape would be fed into the parent machine. This would appear to be the ideal choice of recording equipment: It allows for flexibility of recording location, several input channels, and machine computation of variables.

3.8. Conclusions

We have described how social psychologists and other investigators of human communication have conceptualized, measured, and recorded gaze behavior between and among human interactants. Early studies had suggested that the investigation of gaze behavior would be both promising and simple. It was judged to be an activity that was shared by, that linked together, and that could powerfully affect all sighted human beings. It was directly observable and discrete. The researcher did not have to infer its existence as a variable from interpretations of other activity, but could, investigators believed, clearly state when it began, how long it lasted, when it stopped, and how frequently it occurred. Moreover, by appropriately placing observers, investigators believed that they could reasonably approximate its target and, most important, measure it unobtrusively. Gaze, in short, impressed them as an important psychological variable that could be measured in a nonreactive fashion. Investigators positioned their observers behind one-way vision mirrors and went to work.

By now it should be apparent that the wise investigator will not innocently assume that to locate a room with one-way vision mirrors (or obtain cameras with powerful telephoto lenses) and hire a group of keen-eyed observers equipped with recording devices will assure reliable and accurate collection of the gaze behavior that will test his or her hypotheses.

In this chapter, we have attempted to show that the recording and assessment of gaze requires a number of critical and interlocking decisions that, beginning with the researcher's theoretical approach and the specific relationship of interest, will determine the nature of later decisions concerning site, use of confederates, equipment, and specific indexes of gaze. Certain decisions will bear on the question whether the measurement is or is not reactive (e.g., will observing through visible mirrors affect the nature of a subject's visual attention?), and others could create uncontrolled forces that may affect relationships of interest (the use, for example, of continuously looking confederates to simplify the measurement of mutual gaze may well affect the obtained level of such a phenomenon). Still other decisions, such as the distance at which to locate observers, will determine the appropriateness of the gaze measure used – whether it should be defined as a head orientation, a face look, an eye look, and so forth.

We hope that our discussion of these issues will be useful to future investigators as they conceptualize their problems and implement the designs they have constructed to collect the gaze data of interest to them. We still believe that human gaze behavior provides a promising and powerful means of gaining understanding of human interaction, impact, and communication. We sincerely hope that the issues we have raised will be seen as challenges to be overcome, rather than as barriers to discourage further research.

Notes

1. Later subdivided into *eye gaze* and *face gaze* by Harper, Wiens, and Matarazzo (1978).
2. See Section 3.5 on measures obtained from human observers.
3. LaFrance and Mayo (1976) were able to record only looking-while-listening behavior in their field study of conversations. Because the first study in their report apparently found an interesting relationship between look–listen and look–speak behavior in the laboratory, it would have been to their advantage to have been able to code both such patterns in the field.
4. It is important to note that computer programs written to cumulate instances of the 16 categories may not obtain the correct information regarding the average duration of states dependent on only two channels (e.g., look–speak), rather than four channels. It is necessary to cumulate data by one, two, and four channels to get the correct averages.

References

Aiello, J. R. A test of equilibrium theory: Visual interaction in relation to orientation distance and sex of interactants. *Psychonomic Science*, 1972, *26*(6), 335–336.

Antis, S. M., Mayhew, J. W., & Morley, T. The perception of where a face or television "portrait" is looking. *American Journal of Psychology*, 1969, *82*, 474–489.

Argyle, M. Eye-contact and distance: A reply to Stephenson and Rutter. *British Journal of Psychology*, 1970, *61*(3), 395–396.

Argyle, M. Nonverbal communication in human social interaction. In R. A. Hinde (Ed.), *Non-verbal communication*. Cambridge: Cambridge University Press, 1972.

Argyle, M., & Cook, M. *Gaze and mutual gaze*. Cambridge: Cambridge University Press, 1976.

Argyle, M., & Dean, J. Eye-contact, distance and affiliation. *Sociometry*, 1965, *28*, 289–304.

Argyle, M., & Ingham, R. Gaze, mutual gaze, and proximity. *Semiotica*, 1972, *6*(1), 32–49.

Argyle, M., Lefebvre, L., & Cook, M. The meaning of five patterns of gaze. *European Journal of Social Psychology*, 1974, *4*(2), 125–136.

Argyle, M., & Williams, M. Observer or observed?: A reversible perception in person perception. *Sociometry*, 1969, *32*, 396–412.

Birdwhistell, R. L. *Kinesics and context*. Philadelphia: University of Pennsylvania Press, 1970.

Blurton Jones, N. Characteristics of ethological studies of human behaviour. In N. Blurton Jones (Ed.), *Ethological studies of child behaviour*. Cambridge: Cambridge University Press, 1972.

Bricker, P. D., & Wish, M. A new program of research on interpersonal communication: Laboratory facility and some early results (Paper 34.3). *Conference Record, National Telecommunications Conference*, 1978, *3*, 1–5.

Cary, M. S. Does civil inattention exist in pedestrian passing? *Journal of Personality and Social Psychology*, 1978, *36*(11), 1185–1193.

Chance, M. R. A. Attention structure as the basis of primate rank order. *Man*, 1967, *2*, 503–518.

Cline, M. G. The perception of where a person is looking. *American Journal of Psychology*, 1967, *80*, 41–50.

Coutts, L. M. & Schneider, F. W. Visual behavior in an unfocused interaction as a function of sex and distance. *Journal of Experimental Social Psychology*, 1975, *11*, 64–77.

Duncan, S., Jr. Nonverbal communication. *Psychological Bulletin*, 1969, *72*, 118–137.

Duncan, S., Jr., & Fiske, D. W. *Face-to-face interaction*. Hillsdale, N.J.: Erlbaum, 1977.

Duval, S., & Wicklund, R. A. *A theory of objective self-awareness*. New York: Academic Press, 1972.

Eibl-Eibesfeldt, I. *Ethology: The biology of behavior*. New York: Holt, Rinehart & Winston, 1970.

Ekman, P. Universals and cultural differences in facial expression of emotion. In J. R. Cole (Ed.), *Nebraska Symposium on Motivation* (Vol. 19). Lincoln: University of Nebraska Press, 1972.

Ekman, P., Friesen, M. V., & Ellsworth, P. C. *Emotion in the human face: Guidelines for research and an integration of findings*. New York: Pergamon Press, 1972.

Ellgring, J. H. Die Beurteilung des Blickes auf Punkte innerhalb des Gesichtes. *Zeitschrift für Experimentelle und Angewandte Psychologie*, 1970, *17*, 600–607.

Ellgring, J. H., & von Cranach, M. Process of learning in the recognition of eye-signals. *European Journal of Social Psychology*, 1972, *2(1), 33–43.*

Ellsworth, P. C. Direct gaze as a social stimulus: The example of aggression. In P. Pliner, L. Krames, & T. Alloway (Eds.), *Nonverbal communication of aggression*. New York: Plenum, 1975.

Ellsworth, P. C., & Carlsmith, J. M. Effects of eye contact and verbal content on affective response to a dyadic interaction. *Journal of Personality and Social Psychology*, 1968, *100*, 15–20.

Ellsworth, P. C., Carlsmith, M., & Henson, A. The stare as a stimulus to flight in human subjects: A series of field experiments. *Journal of Personality and Social Psychology*, 1972, *19*, 302–311.

Ellsworth, P. C., & Langer, E. J. Staring and approach: An interpretation of the stare as a nonspecific activator. *Journal of Personality and Social Psychology*, 1976, *33*(1), 117–122.

Ellsworth, P. C., & Ludwig, L. Visual behavior in social interaction. *Journal of Communication*, 1972, *22*, 375–403.

Ellsworth, P., & Ross, L. Intimacy in response to direct gaze. *Journal of Experimental Social Psychology*, 1975, *11*, 592–613.

Ellyson, S. L., Dovidio, J. F., Corson, R. L., and Vinicur, D. L. Visual dominance behavior in female dyads: Situational and personality factors. *Social Psychology Quarterly*, 1980, *43*(3), 328–336.

Exline, R. V. Explorations in the process of person perception: Visual interaction in relation to competition, sex and need for affiliation. *Journal of Personality*, 1963, *31*(1), 1–20.

Exline, R. V. *The effect of a stare upon the line of movement of a pedestrian on a public walkway*. Unpublished manuscript, University of Delaware, 1971.

Exline, R. V. The glances of power and preference. In J. R. Cole (Ed), *Nebraska Symposium on Motivation* (Vol. 19). Lincoln: University of Nebraska Press, 1972.

Exline, R. V., Ellyson, S. L., & Long, B. Visual behavior as an aspect of power role relationships. In P. Pliner, L. Krames, & T. Alloway (Eds.), *Nonverbal communication of aggression*. New York: Plenum, 1975.

Exline, R. V., & Fehr, B. J. Applications of semiosis to the study of visual interaction. In A. W. Siegman & S. Feldstein (Eds.), *Nonverbal behavior and communication*. Hillsdale, N.J.: Erlbaum, 1978.

Exline, R. V., Gray, D., & Schuette, D. Visual behavior in a dyad as affected by interview content and sex of respondent. *Journal of Personality and Social Psychology*, 1965, *1*, 201–209.

Exline, R. V., Jones, P., & Maciorowski, K. *Race, affiliation-conflict theory and mutual visual attention during conversation*. Paper presented at the annual convention of the American Psychological Association, San Francisco, 1977.

Exline, R. V., Parades, A., Gottheil, E., & Winkelmayer, R. Gaze patterns of normals and schizophrenics retelling happy, sad, and angry experiences. In C. E. Izard (Ed.), *Emotions in personality and psychopathology*. New York: Plenum, 1979.

Exline, R. V., Thibaut, J., Hickey, C. B., & Gumpert, P. Visual interaction in relation to Machiavellianism and an unethical act. In R. Christie & F. Geis (Eds.), *Studies in Machiavellianism*. New York: Academic Press, 1970.

Exline, R. V., & Winters, L. C. Affective relations and mutual glances in dyads. In S. S. Tomkins & C. E. Izard (Eds.), *Affect, cognition and personality*. New York: Springer, 1965.

Exline, R. V., & Yellin, A. Eye contact as a sign between man and monkey. *Proceedings of the XIXth International Congress of Psychology*, 1971, p. 199. (Summary)

Fehr, B. J. *Visual interaction in the laboratory and in the field.* Unpublished manuscript, University of Delaware, 1968.

Fehr, B. J. *The communication of evaluation through the use of interpersonal gaze in same- and interracial female dyads*. Unpublished doctoral dissertation, University of Delaware, 1981.

Fugita, S. S. Effects of anxiety and approval on visual interaction. *Journal of Personality and Social Psychology*, 1974, *29*(4), 586–592.

Garfinkel, H. *Studies in ethnomethodology*. Englewood Cliffs, N.J.: Prentice-Hall, 1967.

Gibson, J. J., & Pick, R. B. Perception of another person's looking behavior. *American Journal of Psychology*, 1963, *76*, 386–394.

Goffman, E. *Asylums*. Garden City, N.Y.: Doubleday, 1961.

Goffman, E. *Behavior in public places*. New York: Free Press, 1963.

Goldberg, G. N., Kiesler, C. A., & Collins, B. E. Visual behavior and face-to-face distance during interaction. *Sociometry*, 1969, *32*, 43–53.

Gur, R. E. Conjugate lateral eye movement as an index of hemispheric activation. *Journal of Personality and Social Psychology*, 1975, *31*, 751–757.

Harper, R. G., Wiens, A. N., & Matarazzo, J. D. *Nonverbal communication: The state of the art*. New York: Wiley, 1978.

Hedge, B. J., Everitt, B. S., & Frith, C. B. The role of gaze in dialogue. *Acta Psychologia*, 1978, *42*, 453–475.

Hooff, J. A. R. A. M. van. Facial expressions in higher primates. *Symposia of the Zoological Society of London*, 1962, *8*, 97–125.

Hore, T. Social class differences in some aspects of the nonverbal communication between mother and preschool child. *Australian Journal of Psychology*, 1970, *22*(1), 21–27.

Hutt, J. J., & Hutt, C. (Eds.). *Behaviour studies in psychiatry*. Oxford: Pergamon Press, 1970.

Izard, C. E. *The face of emotion*. New York: Appleton-Century-Crofts, 1971.

Izard, C. E. *Human emotions*. New York: Plenum, 1977.

Jones, E. E., & Nisbett, R. E. *The actor and the observer: Divergent perceptions on the causes of behavior*. New York: General Learning Press, 1971.

Kendon, A. Some functions of gaze-direction in social interaction. *Acta Psychologica*, 1967, *26*, 22–63.

Kendon, A., & Cook, M. The consistency of gaze patterns in social interaction. *British Journal of Psychology*, 1969, *60*, 481–494.

Kendon, A., & Ferber, A. A description of some human greetings. In R. P. Michael and J. H. Croock (Eds.), *Comparative ecology and behaviour of primates*. New York: Academic Press, 1973.

Kirkland, J., & Lewis, C. Glance, look, gaze, and stare: A vocabulary for eye-fixation research. *Perceptual and Motor Skills*, 1976, *43*(3), 1278.

Kleck, R. E., & Nuessle, W. Congruence between indicative and communicative functions of eye contact in interpersonal relations. *British Journal of Social and Clinical Psychology*, 1968, *1*, 241–246.

Kleinke, C. L. Compliance to requests made by gazing and touching experimenter in field settings. *Journal of Experimental Social Psychology*, 1977, *13*, 218–223.

Kleinke, C. L., Meeker, F. B., & La Fong, C. Effects of gaze, touch, and use of name on evaluation of "engaged" couples. *Journal of Research in Personality*, 1974, *1*, 368–373.

Kleinke, C. L. & Pohlen, P. D. Affective and emotional responses as a function of other person's gaze and cooperativeness in a two-person game. *Journal of Personality and Social Psychology*, 1971, *17*, 308–313.

Kleinke, C. L., Staneski, R. A., & Berger, D. E. Evaluation of an interviewer as a function of interviewer gaze, reinforcement of subject gaze and interviewer attractiveness. *Journal of Personality and Social Psychology*, 1975, *31*, 115–122.

Krüger, K., & Hückstedt, B. Die Beurteilung von Blickrichtungen. *Zeitschrift für Experimentelle und Angewandte Psychologie*, 1969, *16*, 452–472.

LaFrance, M., & Mayo, C. Racial differences in gaze behavior during conversations: Two systematic observational studies. *Journal of Personality and Social Psychology*, 1976, *33*(5), 547–552.

Lambert, W. W., & Lambert, W. E. *Social psychology*. Englewood Cliffs, N.J.: Prentice-Hall, 1964.

Lazzerini, A. J., Stephenson, G. M., & Neave, H. Eye-contact in dyads: A test of the independence hypothesis. *British Journal of Social and Clinical Psychology*, 1978, *17*, 227–229.

LeCompte, W. F., & Rosenfeld, H. M. Effects of minimal eye contact in the instruction period on impressions of the experimenter. *Journal of Experimental Social Psychology*, 1971, *7*, 211–220.

Libby, W. L., Jr. Eye contact and direction of looking as stable individual difference. *Journal of Experimental Research in Personality*, 1970, *4*, 303–312.

Lorenz, K. Ueber die Bildung des Instinktbegriffes. *Naturwissenschaft*, 1937, *25*, 289–331.

Lorenz, K. The comparative method in studying innate behaviour patterns. *Symposium of the Society of Experimental Biology*, 1950, *4*, 221–268.

Marsh, K. H. *Visual behavior of a listener, involvement of a speaker, and impression formation in observers*. Unpublished master's thesis, University of Delaware, 1970.

Mead, G. H. *Mind, self and society*. Chicago. University of Chicago Press, 1934.

Nunnally, J. C. *Psychometric theory* (2nd ed.). New York: McGraw-Hill, 1978.

Risser, D. T., Dovidio, J. F., & Faltot, J. *The relative merits of five observational methodologies using cameras and one-way mirrors*. Paper presented at the annual convention of the Eastern Psychological Association, Boston, April 1977.

Rohner, S. J., & Aiello, J. R. *The effect of topic intimacy on interaction behaviors*. Paper presented at the meeting of the Eastern Psychological Association, New York, 1975.

Rosenthal, R. *Experimenter effects in behavioral research*. New York: Appleton-Century-Crofts, 1966.

Rubin, Z. Measurement of romantic love. *Journal of Personality and Social Psychology*, 1970, *16*, 265–273.

Russo, N. F. Eye contact, interpersonal distance, and the equilibrium theory. *Journal of Personality and Social Psychology*, 1975, *31*, 497–502.

Rutter, D. R., Stephenson, G. M., Lazzerini, A. J., Ayling, K., & White, P. A. Eye contact: A chance product of individual looking? *British Journal of Social and Clinical Psychology*, 1977, *16*, 191–192.

Scheflen, A. Natural history method in psychotherapy. In L. A. Gottschalk & A. H. Auerbach (Eds.), *Methods of research in psychotherapy*. New York: Appleton-Century-Crofts, 1966.

Scherer, K. R. Nonlinguistic vocal indicators of emotion and psychopathology. In C. E. Izard (Ed.), *Emotions in personality and psychopathology*. New York: Plenum, 1979.

Shea, M., & Rosenfeld, H. Functional employment of nonverbal social reinforcers in dyadic learning. *Journal of Personality and Social Psychology*, 1976, *34*(2), 228–239.

Simmel, G. Sociology of the senses: Visual interaction. In R. E. Park and E. W. Burgess (Eds.), *Introduction to the science of sociology*. Chicago: University of Chicago Press, 1921.

Snyder, M., Grether, J., & Keller, K. Staring and compliance: A field experiment on hitchhiking. *Journal of Applied Social Psychology*, 1974, *4*(2), 165–170.

Stephenson, G. M., & Rutter, D. R. Eye-contact, distance and affiliation: A reevaluation. *British Journal of Psychology*, 1970, *61*, 385–393.

Stephenson, G. M., Rutter, D. R., & Dore, S. R. Visual interaction and distance. *British Journal of Psychology*, 1973, *64*(2), 251–257.

Stern, D. Mother and infant at play. In M. Lewis and L. Rosenbaum (Eds.), *The effect of the infant on its caretaker*. New York: Wiley, 1974.

Strongman, K. T., & Champness, B. G. Dominance hierarchies and conflict in eye contact. *Acta Psychologica*, 1968, *28*, 376–86.

Tinbergen, E. A., & Tinbergen, N. *Advances in ethology*, 1972, *10*, 1–53.

Tinbergen, N. *The Study of instinct*. London: Oxford University Press, 1951.

Tinbergen, N. Ethology and stress diseases. *Science*, 1974, *185*, 20–27.

Tomkins, S. S. *Affect, imagery, consciousness*. Vol. 1: *The positive affects*. New York: Springer, 1962.

Vine, I. Judgment of direction of gaze: An interpretation of discrepant results. *British Journal of Social and Clinical Psychology*, 1971, *10*(4), 320–331.

von Cranach, M. The role of orienting behavior in human interaction. In A. H. Esser (Ed.), *Behavior and environment: The use of space by animals and man*. New York: Plenum, 1971.

von Cranach, M., & Ellgring, J. H. Problems in the recognition of gaze direction. In M. von Cranach & I. Vine (Eds.), *Social communications and movement*. New York: Academic Press, 1973.

von Cranach, M., Schmid, R., & Vogel, M. V. Ueber einige Bedingungen des Zusammenhanges von Lidschlag und Blickwendung. *Psychologische Forschung*, 1969, *33*, 68–78.

von Cranach, M., & Vine, I. Introduction. In M. von Cranach and I. Vine (Eds.), *Social communication and movement*. New York: Academic Press, 1973.

Weiss, M., & Keys, C. *The influence of proxemic variables on dyadic interaction between peers*. Paper presented at the annual convention of the American Psychological Association, Chicago, 1975.

Wellens, A. R. A device that provides eye-to-eye video perspective for interactive behavior. *Behavior Research Methods and Instrumentation*, 1978, *10*, 25–26.

4. Methods of research on vocal communication: paradigms and parameters

KLAUS R. SCHERER

The large majority of studies of nonverbal behavior are concerned with nonvocal phenomena such as gaze, facial expression, or body movement. The neglect of vocal phenomena such as pitch and voice quality may stem in part from the methodological difficulties connected with the storage and analysis of sound. Apart from these methodological deterrents, however, many researchers in nonverbal communication seem to regard most vocal activity as governed by the rules of the language code and thus not properly nonverbal behavior. This assumption is quite unjustified. Though it is true that speech is a vocal activity much of which is verbal, there are a large number of human vocalizations that are essentially nonlinguistic (such as involuntary affect vocalizations). Furthermore, not all aspects of speech are verbal or linguistic in nature. Any utterance humans produce is also characterized by a large number of nonlinguistic or nonverbal – at best "paralinguistic" – aspects, such as intonation, voice quality, rhythm, and pausing.[1] Such phenomena constitute an analog nonverbal signal system that intermeshes with and modulates the predominantly digital verbal or linguistic code.

This chapter is meant as an introductory overview of the methods available for study of vocal communication. It is intended primarily for researchers new to the area of vocal behavior research who require a short, readable survey of the relevant methodology. In attempting such a broad survey, it is impossible to avoid simplifying many complex issues and omitting a large number of important aspects of the topics covered. Anyone intending to engage in research on vocal behavior should consult the specialized references listed throughout the text, particularly if acoustic analyses are being planned.

4.1. The social functions of vocal behavior

Because speech is a comparatively recent addition to the human repertoire of communication systems, it is highly likely that our speechless forefathers had to make do for millennia with the same nonverbal signaling systems used by most subhuman species. We all know that humans still use nonverbal signals along with language, and there is a strong likelihood that many of these nonverbal signaling devices are essentially phylogenetically continuous (C. Darwin, 1872; Ekman, 1973; K. R. Scherer, 1979a, 1981a). Phylogenetic continuity of nonverbal signal systems would not be surprising, because both the social functions of these signals and the physiological mechanisms that produce them may be highly similar in man and animals. For example, any kind of social organization based on enduring relationships between individuals and structural properties of groups requires a set of "markers" for the biological and social identity of individuals, their transitory states (cognitive, affective, and intentional), and their relationships to other individuals (see K. R. Scherer, 1977c/1979; K. R. Scherer & Giles, 1979). The observer of such markers is thus able to place the sender in a social matrix formed by the sender's enduring biological and psychological characteristics as well as by the sender's membership in various social categories. The observer can also gauge the present state of his or her relationship to the sender and infer the latter's affect state and behavioral intentions. Without such information transfer, flexible behavioral responses and complex social interactions would not be possible (see Giles, Scherer, & Taylor, 1979, pp. 348–351).

Animal vocalizations serve many of these functions, for example, the marking of individual identity, age, sex, group membership, and status, as well as affect states and impending behavioral acts (see Marler & Hamilton, 1966; Sebeok, 1968, 1977; W. J. Smith, 1977). It can be shown that nonlinguistic vocalizations and nonverbal aspects of speech serve many of the same functions for humans. They mark individual identity (Giles et al., 1979; Tosi, 1979), age (Helfrich, 1979), sex (P. M. Smith, 1979), personality (K. R. Scherer, 1979b; Siegman, 1978), social class (Robinson, 1979), membership in ethnic and racial groups (Giles, 1979), and many other aspects of social-structural patterns and social situations in which individuals may find themselves (P. Brown & Fraser, 1979; P. Brown & Levinson, 1979). Furthermore, there can be little doubt that human vocal behavior communicates emotional states very effectively (K. R. Scherer, 1979a, 1981a), and although there is less research, it is most likely that interpersonal relationships such as liking or dominance–

submission are also well reflected in a number of vocal characteristics (Feldstein & Welkowitz, 1978; Harper, Wiens, & Matarazzo, 1978, pp. 20–67; K. R. Scherer, 1979c; Siegman, 1978, 1979). Thus, not only does one seem to be justified in assuming a large degree of phylogenetic continuity of vocal signal systems, they seem to play a major role in human social communication.

During evolution, language and speech were superimposed on a primitive, analog vocal signaling system. Because speech uses the same voice-production mechanism and many of the same acoustic features as the more primitive nonverbal system, we find an intriguing intermeshing of verbal and nonverbal aspects in human sound production (in addition to some pure remnants of the earlier nonverbal system, such as spontaneous affect vocalizations; see K. R. Scherer, 1977a, 1981a). The mixture of a digital, symbolic communicative code with very special design features (see Hockett, 1960) and a more primitive analog signaling system, both using vocalization as a vehicle for information transmission, has been baffling for both linguists and students of nonverbal communication. With few exceptions, linguists have tended to ban such analog characteristics of human speech from their domain of inquiry or, at most, have relegated paralinguistic phenomena to a marginal position in the canon of their science. Nonverbal communication researchers, on the other hand, have often regarded such paralinguistic phenomena as predominantly linguistic and verbal (particularly because the distinction between vocal and verbal does not seem to be generally made).

The relative neglect of nonverbal aspects of speech is all the more regrettable because the very mixture of digital and analog aspects of human vocalization renders this communication modality exceptionally powerful. Through speech, humans can at the same time communicate symbolic meaning via language, with all the advantages that the design features of language command, and reveal information about their biological and social identity, transitory states, and relationship to the listener via a nonverbal vocal signaling system. A particular advantage of the latter is that it is coded continuously (rather than discretely) and probabilistically (rather than invariantly; see Giles et al., 1979, pp. 360–375; K. R. Scherer, 1977b/1979, 1980); different shades or degrees of strength of an underlying state can be communicated through continuously changing or graded vocal signals, and probabilistic coding ensures a high degree of negotiability of the meaning conveyed. Giles et al. (1979) point out that

> in social interaction, there are norms governing the emission and elicitation of information on intimate issues. These might include

> how the other feels about you, his relationships with others you like, and his views on trade unions and socialism. Given that we do not interrogate people directly about their feelings on such issues and because they may be reluctant to self-disclose particularly threatening information, the monitoring of various speech markers is a singularly important means by which an individual can glean such information. Moreover, while individuals may wish to avoid verbalizing certain feelings and making specific information about themselves more public, there may be other issues (e.g. their achievements, kindnesses, power) which they would like to make more explicit but about which they feel restrained from communicating directly. Once again, the subtle use of speech markers indicative of these psychological states may be the mechanism whereby these emotionally charged ideas are brought inferentially to the attention of another more appropriately. [P. 345]

Although the amalgamation of digital linguistic and analog nonverbal meaning in human speech vocalization renders this communication mode exceptionally flexible and powerful, it also makes it exceptionally difficult to study scientifically. As already mentioned, one of the major problems is that many of the acoustic parameters that serve to communicate linguistic information may also have nonverbal marking functions. For example, the variation of fundamental frequency (F_0) of the voice (perceived as pitch; see Appendixes A and B) can serve both to communicate syntactic information, indicating, for example, whether an utterance is intended as a question or a statement, and to reveal information about the emotional state of the speaker. Thus in many cases the same parameters used to infer specific linguistic aspects of speech must be used to assess nonlinguistic aspects of meaning. One way to conceptualize this duality is to assume that many acoustic parameters of speech vocalization are constrained by linguistic rules in such a way that they can vary only within fairly narrow boundaries, but the variation of the parameter within these boundaries may be free to indicate social characteristics or transient states of the speaker. For example, the speaker must produce a vowel with formant frequencies in specific regions of the frequency spectrum in order to allow vowel recognition by the listener (see Appendix B on formants). However, formant frequencies may vary slightly within the acceptable frequency regions, thereby indicating information about the psychological state of the speaker (see Section 4.6). In the following sections of this chapter, those parameters of human vocalization most likely to carry information about social and biological identity, affect states and intentions, and relationships to others are discussed in detail.

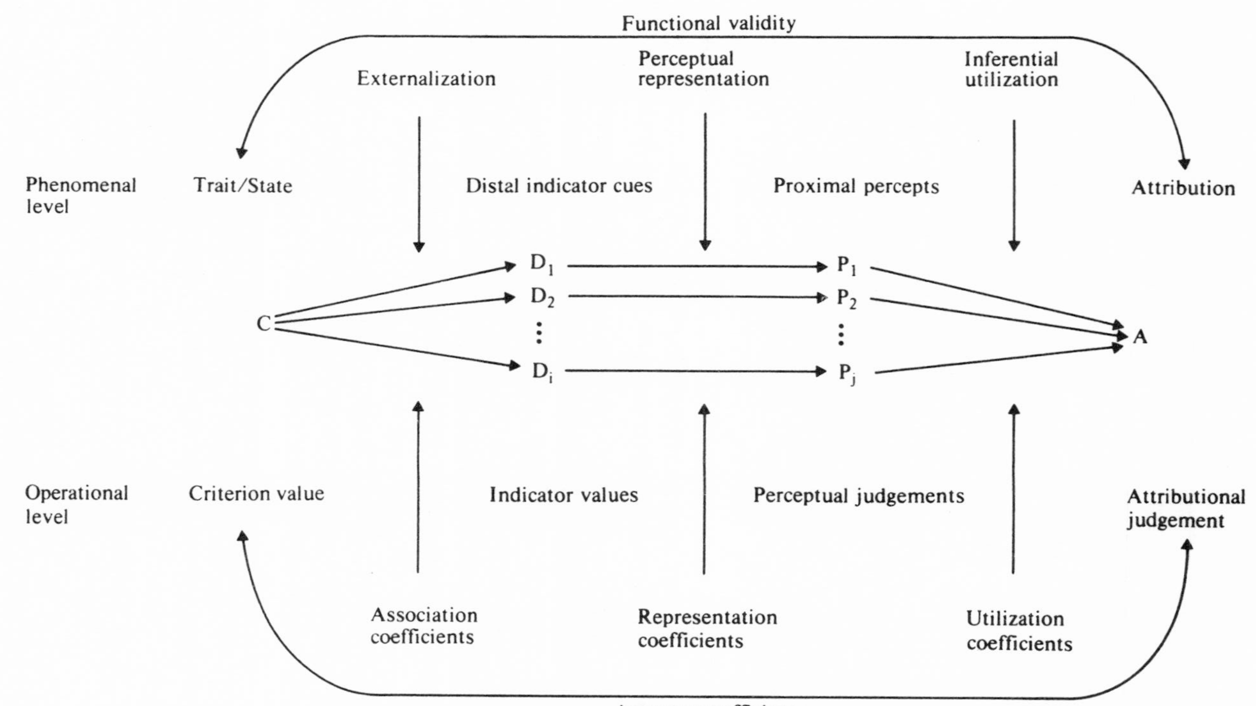

Figure 4.1. A modified version of the Brunswikian lens model. *Source:* K. R. Scherer and Giles, 1979

4.2. A paradigm for the study of nonverbal behavior

Before we turn to a detailed discussion of the parameters that describe human vocalization and of the procedures that can be used to assess them, let us consider a more general research paradigm that, in addition to suggesting a particular approach to research in this area, will help to structure the following review. K. R. Scherer (1974a, 1978) has proposed a modified version of the Brunswikian lens model (Brunswik, 1956) as an appropriate paradigm for research on nonverbal behavior, because it includes the expression, information transmission, and impression aspects of nonverbal communication and thus highlights the communicative nature of these processes. The model, reproduced in Figure 4.1, specifies that a particular trait or state of a sender is externalized or expressed in distal indicator cues, that is, characteristics of the sender's nonverbal behavior that can be objectively measured. These distal cues are perceived by an observer and represented as proximal percepts in his or her cognitive structures. On the basis of such proximal percepts, the observer arrives at an attribution about the sender's traits or states (which the observer assumes, are reflected by the distal indicator cues) on the basis of a set of inference rules. It can be shown that if the operationalized variables corresponding to these phenomena, that is, criterion values, indicator values, perceptual judgments, and attributional judgments, are measured independently, the adequacy of the model and the role of the particular cues studied can be assessed empirically using path analytic methods (K. R. Scherer, 1974a, 1978).

As an example, Figure 4.2 shows a lens model used in a study of extroversion inferences from vocal cues. A model of this sort allows us to determine the externalization or expression of a particular trait or state in a number of objectively measurable distal cues, the perception (or misperception) of these cues, the pattern of inference rules used to arrive at a particular attribution, and the accuracy of the judgment. Although, in this case, American judges do better than chance in inferring the extroversion of speakers on the basis of content-masked voice cues alone, similar models show why they are less accurate for other traits. Inaccuracy can result from a lack of externalization (i.e., the absence of distal cues for a particular trait or state), or from misperception of the distal cues, or from inference rules that do not adequately reflect the externalization patterns. Though the model is static in the sense that it does not, in its present form, contain feedback or interaction sequences, it represents important aspects of the communication processes underlying interactive behavior (see Scherer & Ekman, Sec-

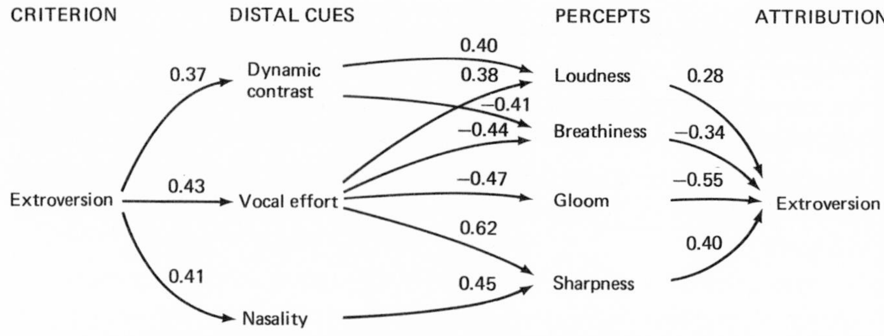

Figure 4.2. Example of a Brunswikian lens model approach for study of the accuracy of extroversion inference. Curvilinear arrows indicate hypothetically assumed causal relationships. Strengths of the relationships are indicated by Pearson *r*s (n = 24). Other intercorrelations among variables have been omitted to simplify the figure. *Source:* K. R. Scherer, 1978

tion 1.2, for a discussion of research priorities concerning the individual vs. the interaction as focus).

If one adopts the lens model paradigm to study the expression and impression aspects of nonverbal communication, it is necessary to obtain objective measures of traits or states of the sender and of the distal cues in the vocal or nonvocal behavior, as well as subjective measures of the proximal percepts and attributions of observers. This chapter is primarily concerned with the discussion of the methods available for measure of distal and proximal cues of human vocalization.

4.3. The segmentation of vocal behavior

The expression *flow of speech* nicely characterizes the continuity of spoken language, which, unlike written language, does not offer a ready-made hierarchy of units such as letters, words, sentences, paragraphs, and so on. In speech the only "natural" demarcations are often the beginnings and endings of utterances, which can be as short as a yes or no or as long as a sermon. Generally, the stream of speech has to be segmented for purposes of analysis, to allow the quantitative description of fairly homogeneous and thus comparable parts of an utterance (see also Rosenfeld, Section 5.5). Researchers can construct hierarchies of segments in which lower-level segments, such as words, constitute a higher-level segment, such as a sentence. The choice of segments and their demarcation depends both on the nature of the parameter to be assessed and on the specific research aims.

There are two major types of segmentation – physical and perceptual. For physical segmentation, boundaries are determined exclusively on the basis of physical criteria, that is, patterns of events or sound energy distribution; whereas perceptual segmentation requires that the human information-processing system demarcate segments on the basis of prior categorization.

Physical segmentation is often chosen if automatic processing of speech via electroacoustic equipment is desired. The simplest type of physical segmentation is cutting up the speech flow into fixed-length time slots, for example, consecutive 300-millisecond periods. Their length can be the result of many factors: limitation of the analysis equipment, theoretical considerations, or constraints of the analysis conditions (e.g., temporal resolution depending on sampling rate in digital analysis; see Bricker & Pruzansky, 1980).

One type of physical segmentation consists of the differentiation between sound periods and silent periods on the basis of presence or absence of sound energy (and often uses fixed-length time slots as lower-order segments). This approach is primarily used in interaction chronography, the automatic detection of sound–silence (or "on–off") patterns in dyadic conversation (Chapple, 1948; Feldstein & Welkowitz, 1978; Jaffe & Feldstein, 1970; Matarazzo, Wiens, & Saslow, 1965). Finally, physical segments can be defined (and automatically detected) by the periodic or nonperiodic portions of the speech wave form resulting in voiced and unvoiced segments (see Appendix B). For voiced segments, the individual cycles or periods of the wave are sometimes used as even more molecular segments.

For perceptual segmentation similar criteria can be employed. For example, rather than using a hardware energy detector, one can use a human listener to determine sound and silence portions within an utterance. The results of these two types of segmentation do not always match, because the human listener is affected by his or her expectations concerning the presence of short silent portions in articulated speech and may not detect or report these silences.

Most of the perceptual segments normally used to cut up speech are derived from phonology and linguistics. Obvious examples are phonemes (single speech sounds), morphemes (the minimal meaningful units of language), clauses (subdivisions of a sentence each containing a subject and a predicate), and sentences. Although the phonological and lexical units such as phonemes, syllables (combinations of phonemes), and morphemes are fairly easy to delimit and categorize, this classification is more difficult for the more molar units such as clauses and sentences, because one rarely finds "well-formed" sentences, in the classic linguistic sense, in spoken language. One possible way of avoiding this problem is to segment phonemic clauses (Boomer, 1978; Dittmann & Llewellyn, 1967; Trager & Smith, 1951/1957). These units are defined by prosodic features of speech, like the occurrence of a primary stress and a juncture pause in a portion of speech.

Other potential perceptual segments are defined by criteria involving speech content, such as the marking of speech acts (Gottschalk & Gleser, 1969; Morley & Stephenson, 1977; Wish, D'Andrade, & Goodnow, 1980). Some more formal molar perceptual segments are turns (periods of a conversation during which a speaker holds the floor) or conversations or monologues as a whole. Of course, many more types of perceptual segments involving categorizations by human listeners are possible. For example, a student of rhetoric may attempt to segment a monologue into different types of arguments. Sociolinguists try to distinguish segments of conversations determined by particular topics. Anthropologists may attempt to segment verbal interactions according to the type of functions fulfilled: greetings, leave-takings, and the like. These examples show that there is virtually no limit to the perceptual segments that can be differentiated in verbal utterances on the basis of structural or functional criteria.

One major problem that is often overlooked in naive approaches to segmentation is that the human observer is a fallible segmenter, and so the reliability of the segmentation procedure must be assured. This is particularly important in cases where content or functional criteria are used for the segmentation, rather than more formal criteria requiring less inference from the observer.

In the general case, segments consist of many *units of analysis*. Units of analysis are those portions of segments which form the basis for obtaining a value for some parameter; for example, pauses may be the units for the parameter *average length of silent pauses* per segment (e.g., an utterance); 20-millisecond stretches of speech arbitrarily demarcated in the voiced portions of the speech signal could be the units for *average fundamental frequency* (see Appendix B). One either computes means and variability measures for the values of the parameters assessed on the basis of these units or plots these values across the segment (e.g., an intonation contour as a plot of F_0 values across an utterance). For both of these types of measurement a reasonably large number of units per segment is needed in order to assure stability of average values or, in the case of sequential analysis, reliability of change patterns. The choice (and demarcation) of segments and units of analysis is often not only one of the most difficult methodological steps but also one of the decisive prerequisites for proper analysis conditions and adequate interpretation of acoustic analyses. Thus the issue of the appropriate units and segments of analysis should not be treated lightly. Often it is not just a technical issue of analysis conditions but is intricately connected with theoretical notions concerning the phenomenon to be analyzed and the type of question to be investigated. The optimal relationship between units and segments depends both on the level of description or the type of measurement and on the nature of the parameters being measured.

4.4. Levels of description of vocal behavior

Human vocalization is produced by the joint action of respiratory, phonatory, and articulatory processes (a short review of the voice-production process is given in Appendix A). Consequently, each vocalization can be characterized on a number of levels: (1) the physiological level, including description of nerve impulses, or muscle innervation patterns that form the basis for the action of the structures involved in the voice-production process; (2) the phonatory–articulatory level, including description of the position and/or movement of the major structures involved, such as the vocal folds or the tongue; and (3) the acoustic level, including description of characteristics of the speech wave form emanating from the mouth (see Appendix B).

Different objective methods are available for study of characteristics of vocal behavior on each of these levels, such as electromyography for the measurement of muscle innervation on the physiological level, high-speed or X-ray film for study of the movement of articulators and the phonation mechanism on the phonatory–articulatory level, and electro-acoustic analysis of wave forms on the acoustical level. However, given our knowledge about relationships between audible characteristics of sound waves and acoustic features, their phonatory–articulatory origin, and, to some extent, the physiological patterns involved, it is also possible to use auditory evaluation via expert coding or rating to characterize vocalization, albeit less accurately, on each of these levels (see Scherer & Ekman, Section 1.4). Often speech experts attempting such auditory evaluation will use some of the objective measurement instruments mentioned, such as sound spectrographs or other devices (see Appendix C), as auxiliary means.

Even though the various levels of description are obviously not independent of one another (for example, each articulatory setting of the vocal tract can, in principle, be reduced to the specific underlying physiological pattern of muscle innervation), it is important to keep these levels clearly differentiated. First, in many cases we do not yet know the relationship between one level of description and another (for example, the exact phonatory–articulatory setting responsible for the specific pattern of acoustic parameters); and second, in some cases, different processes on one level may lead to the same result on another level (for example, several different phonation patterns might lead to the same acoustic parameter in the spectrum).

Many of the category systems that have been proposed for paralinguistic phenomena (Crystal, 1969, 1975; Key, 1977, pp. 92–100; Laver & Hutcheson, 1972, pp. 11–14; Poyatos, 1976; Trager, 1958) do not differentiate among levels of description, a factor that makes it impossible to compare the various labels or categories – leaving aside the problems of reliable operationalization of the concepts. In many such systems, additional complications are created by the inclusion of linguistic criteria such as "juncture," sender intentions such as "manipulation attempts," listener interpretations such as "complaining voice," or cultural norms such as "overhigh pitch." Because of these shortcomings and because most of these systems have been relatively rarely used in empirical research, they will not be systematically surveyed, compared, or critically assessed in this chapter. The major concern is the description of parameters that can be objectively assessed for each level of description or that seem useful for subjective measures of proximal cues in the perception process.

4.5. The physiological and phonatory–articulatory levels

Most of the methods available for the description of speech (or vocalization generally) on the physiological level are very technical and require the researcher to have a high level of expertise. Among the methods adopted by physiologists are the assessment of breathing patterns with the help of a number of different devices (e.g., thermistors to measure temperature differences between inhaled and exhaled air or strain gauges to measure chest movement) or electromyographic measurement of muscle activity (using surface or needle electrodes). Though the use of such objective measurement devices is too costly and complicated, as well as too obtrusive, for most research on nonverbal behavior, there may be ways of assessing variables on the physiological level by somewhat simpler procedures. In those cases where physiological processes or correlates thereof are visible, observational methods or coding procedures can be used. For example, changes in some actions of the facial musculature, particularly around the mouth, may play an important role in assessing the effect of arousal on articulatory processes. It might be possible to score some of those muscle action changes using Ekman and Friesen's Facial Action Coding System (see Ekman, Chapter 2).

Unfortunately, most of the muscles that contribute to speech production are not readily visible and cannot be assessed in this way. This is the case, for example, with the musculature regulating phonation (intra- and extralaryngeal muscles). Breathing, on the other hand, might be amenable to observation; either its visible correlates (such as chest movement and mouth opening) or its auditory correlates (such as exhalation or inhalation noises) might be assessed. Unfortunately, the possibilities for such observation appear to be very limited, and the accuracy and validity of data obtained in such a way are very much open to investigation.

Precise measurement of vocalizations on the phonatory–articulatory level of description is also restricted to experts with access to sophisticated apparatus. For example, high-speed motion picture cameras in combination with laryngeal mirrors can be used to film the movement of the vocal folds, allowing exact determination of duration and shape of glottal openings. X-ray films of the movement of articulatory structures, displaying the speed of movement and the relationship of the major articulators to each other, can be produced. Moreover, electrodes can be placed on various surfaces within the vocal apparatus, such as the tongue and the hard palate, and computer-assessed plots of type and duration of contact among parts of the articulators can be obtained in this way (see Abbs & Watkin, 1976). But clearly, such methods are of little use for nonverbal behavior researchers desiring to obtain practicable measurements of vocalization for a fairly large number of speakers.

One possible approach to obtaining phonatory–articulatory variables is use of auditory assessment techniques in which experts attempt to infer the nature of the phonatory and articulatory processes that have produced a particular audible sound. Most speech scientists and phoneticians are able to infer many aspects of the nature of the production process on the basis of acoustic patterns, because during their training they will frequently have attempted to produce certain sound patterns, trying to control the phonation and articulation apparatus, and will have observed the resulting acoustic patterns in the process. Furthermore, they have access to the accumulated knowledge about the relationship between particular phonation and articulation processes and the resulting acoustic patterns of sound waves. Such auditory assessment procedures are often used to diagnose vocal pathology associated with unusual voice quality (Greene, 1964/1972; Perkins, 1971; Travis, 1971). For example, a *breathy* voice is due to incomplete closure of the vocal folds during phonation, which allows excess air to escape into the superior vocal tract. *Harsh* voice, on the other hand, is the description used for phonation characterized by hypertense musculature, which results in irregular periods of vocal fold opening. Similarly, as far as articulation processes are concerned, terms such as *slurred* or *clipped* refer to movements of the articulators that do not result in the ideal position for the production of certain sounds.

Auditory assessment of voice quality variables produced by phonatory or articulatory processes are very common in many coding schemes for paralinguistic phenomena (see Crystal, 1969, 1975; Key, 1977; Poyatos, 1976). As already mentioned, some researchers have used acoustic measurement techniques, such as sound spectrography, in addition to auditory evaluation, trying to base their inferences on evidence from acoustic–phonetic studies of the acoustic correlates of particular phonatory and articulatory processes. Unfortunately, the diverse use of the terms available for the description of phonation and articulation patterns has led to some confusion in the definition of particular concepts and the underlying processes. In most cases, experts using these concepts have developed somewhat idiosyncratic usage, and they have rarely bothered to obtain measures of reliability in applying their categories. Consequently, on the phonatory–articulatory level of description via auditory assessment, there has been some concern about the problem of assessing voice quality reliably.

Recently, Laver (1975, 1980) has proposed the first theoretically consistent and well-documented system of categories for the assessment of voice quality on the phonatory–articulatory level. The system is based on a phonetic model for the description of the long-term muscular adjustments, or settings, of the vocal apparatus in producing the normal voice. The major dimensions of the system are (1) the habitual settings of the supralaryngeal articulatory structures, such as velum, tongue, palate, lips, and so on, in determining the longitudinal and latitudinal axes of the vocal tract and the opening of the velum; (2) the phonation types produced by the laryngeal structures; and (3) the level of overall muscular tension. Table 4.1 contains a summary listing of the various categories for each of these dimensions. This system has been taught to

Table 4.1. *Summary listing of the categories proposed by Laver for the phonatory–articulatory description of voice quality*

Supralaryngeal settings		*Laryngeal settings*
Longitudinal axis settings:		*Simple phonation types:*
Labial	Labial protrusion	Modal voice
	Labiodentalization	Falsetto
Laryngeal	Raised larynx	Whisper
	Lowered larynx	Creak
Latitudinal axis settings:		*Compound phonation types:*
Labial	Close rounding	Whispery voice
	Open rounding	Whispery falsetto
	Lip-spreading	Creaky voice
Lingual		Creaky falsetto
Tip/blade	Tip articulation	Whispery creak
	Blade articulation	Whispery creaky voice
	Retroflex articulation	Whispery creaky falsetto
Tongue-body	Dentalized	Breathy voice
	Palato-alveolarized	Harsh voice
	Palatalized	Harsh falsetto
	Velarized	Harsh whispery voice
	Pharyngalized	Harsh whispery falsetto
	Laryngopharyngalized	Harsh creaky voice
Mandibular	Close jaw position	Harsh creaky falsetto
	Open jaw position	Harsh whispery creaky voice
	Protruded jaw position	
	Retracted jaw position	Harsh whispery creaky falsetto
Velopharyngeal settings:		
	Nasal	*Overall muscular tension settings:*
	Denasal	Tense voice
		Lax voice

Source: Laver and Hanson, 1981.

other researchers and is available as a potential research tool, although its reliability has not yet been reported.

4.6. The acoustic level of description

This is the most promising level of description for most of the research on nonverbal behavior, because acoustic parameters of speech can be obtained from tape recordings of utterances. Furthermore, parameters are well defined and can be extracted in a fairly straightforward manner, through the use of electroacoustic apparatus or digital computers. However, as we shall see, research using acoustic analysis is costly and time-consuming and requires some acoustic–phonetic expertise. This section reviews some of the parameters commonly extracted from speech that may be useful variables in nonverbal behavior research. (Appendix B provides a short summary of some of the basic concepts in acoustics for those readers unfamiliar with this area.)

Objective measurement of acoustic parameters

Human sounds are acoustically defined by parameters in the physical dimensions of time, frequency, and amplitude (see Appendix B). In this section parameters based on time (e.g., sound duration or pause length), on frequency (e.g., fundamental frequency of the voice), on amplitude (e.g., intensity of the voice), and on several of these dimensions (e.g., energy distribution in the frequency spectrum) (see also Shoup & Pfeifer, 1976; Wakita, 1976) will be reviewed. Vocal behaviors predominantly defined by verbal criteria, such as verbal productivity, fluency, speech disturbances, or speech style (see Mahl & Schulze, 1964; Sandall, 1977; K. R. Scherer, 1979b, pp. 160–176) will not be discussed.

Parameters based on time. Utterances generally consist of consecutive sound and silence segments. Electroacoustic equipment or digital analysis can be used to demarcate these segments and to measure their respective lengths in units of time. From this information a number of variables can be obtained. The basic measures are the total length of an utterance and the number and average duration of both sound and silence portions within it. Because the variables and assessment procedures in automated sound–silence analyses are extensively described elsewhere (Chapple, 1948; Feldstein & Welkowitz, 1978; Jaffe & Feldstein, 1970; Matarazzo & Wiens, 1972), the following discussion will be restricted to some of the problems likely to arise in using these methods.

In many cases, the number of sound or silence periods is divided by the length of an utterance or of the total speech output of a speaker in a specific situation (measured in time units or in number of linguistic units, such as syllables or words) in order to render these values comparable across speech samples of different lengths. Although total speech output is usually fairly easy to assess (at least within a recording session), *utterance* as an analysis segment is often difficult to define unequivocally in naturally occurring speech. Often, utterance as a standard of comparison for sound–silence measurement is defined as a speaker turn, that is, the time during which the speaker holds the floor (see West & Zimmermann, Chapter 9). Unfortunately, there is some disagreement about the exact definition of a turn. Depending on the concept of turn used, the definition may require that smooth turn-taking take place between two conversation partners and that they have a clear understanding of the rules involved. These requirements may not be met in the case of children or psychiatric patients, and they are frequently not met in heated discussions.

In cases like these, attempts to standardize measures of duration or occurrence of sound and silence portions require different units for standardization. One possibility is the use of fixed-length time slots, such as seconds or minutes. However, this procedure may be risky if vocalizations occur in bouts with long intermittent periods in which there is no vocal activity at all. In such cases the researcher will generally want to know the distribution of sound and silence within one of those bouts, rather than averaged over many fixed-length slots combining vocalization bouts and intermittent periods. In order to distinguish such bouts from intermittent periods, the investigator needs reliable criteria for the duration of silence required to determine that a vocalization bout has ended (see Fagen & Young, 1978; Stark, Rose, & McLagen, 1975).

Apart from the problems in defining appropriate segments for standardization and comparison, it is difficult to decide what units should be used to measure the length of these segments. As mentioned before, time units or formal linguistic units can be used. Because of possible differences in the tempo or rate of speech, the resulting ratios will differ widely, depending on which of these units is used. If the ratio is to be unaffected by rate of speech, it is advisable to use ratios based on syllables or other linguistic units for standardization. One time-based ratio that avoids some of these problems is the sound–silence ratio that measures total vocalization time (without silent periods) over the total duration of silent periods (Goldman-Eisler, 1968). However, this ratio, as well as most simple indexes of pause frequency, assume incorrectly that all silent periods can be treated in a functionally similar way. This assumption may frequently be unwarranted, because silent periods of different length may have widely varying functions (see Siegman, 1978, pp. 206–207). If this is the case, one is not justified in lumping all these silent periods together, because the resulting ratio is not very meaningful. For example, there are often silent periods in the acoustic speech wave form that are due to short delays in the readjustment of the articulatory setting between two phonemes, or to the syntactic structure of the sentence. To include such silent periods in a general sound–silence ratio may render this measure less meaningful and increase the general error variance. Therefore, silent portions below 200–300 milliseconds are often disregarded in counting silent periods or forming ratios. Unfortunately, the duration of such articulation- or syntax-based silent portions may vary, depending on the location in the utterance (Butcher, 1979), and may differ according to type of speech sample or speaker characteristics.

One possible way to avoid this problem is to tabulate a frequency distribution of classes of sound and silence periods of different lengths and prepare a histogram. If there are clear modes or peaks in the distribution, it may be possible to differentiate various types of silent periods (which may or may not have different functional implications).

The term *silent period* rather than *pause* has been used throughout this discussion. It is very important to maintain this distinction, because *pause* is not a true acoustic parameter. The notion of a pause seems to connote or imply that the speaker "intends" to continue to speak, and thus it requires an inference by the observer, whereas *silent period* refers just to absence of energy. Given sufficient empirical evidence, one might conclude that silent periods of a certain length can be regarded as pauses or even hesitation pauses. However, in the absence of such information, one has to reserve the term *pause* for perceptual assessment in which the listener not only uses the absence of energy as a criterion but also takes linguistic context and perceived speaker state into account.

If a conversation between two speakers is studied, a number of additional variables can be extracted from the pattern of sound and silence. Figure 4.3 shows the variables defined by Jaffe & Feldstein (1970) in "interaction chronography."[2] The assessment of the variables shown in Figure 4.3 is based on determining in regular intervals (usually 300 milliseconds) the presence or absence of energy in each of the two speakers' channels.

Feldstein and Welkowitz (1978) went to great pains to point out that they were not inferring the motivational state of the speaker – whether he or she *wanted* to interrupt, for example – from automatically assessed sound–silence patterns in conversations. Given that sound–silence sequences reveal little information about context or speaker intention, this is an important precaution in order to avoid treating as functionally equivalent events that may be rather different in their structure and function.

Although time-based parameters have been extensively used in nonverbal communication research, we are a long way from completely understanding their functions. Silent periods seem to be determined both by cognitive and affective (e.g., anxiety) states (Murray, 1971; Rochester, 1973; Siegman, 1978). There are relationships to personality

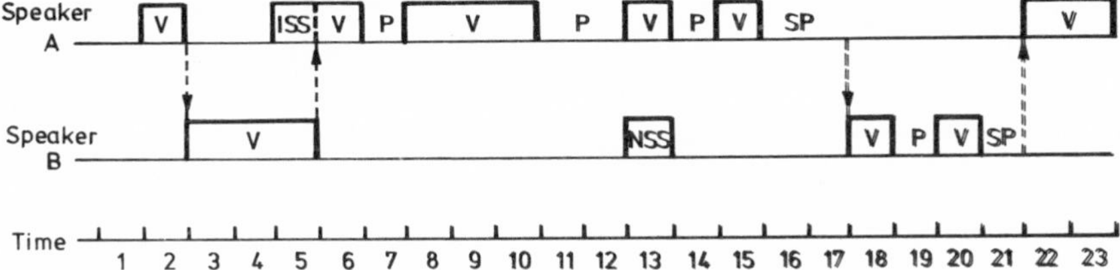

Figure 4.3. Temporal speech parameters in dyadic conversations: a diagrammatic representation of a conversational sequence. The numbered line at the bottom represents time in 300-millisecond units. *V* stands for vocalization, *P* for pause, and *SP* for switching pause (the silence that frequently occurs immediately prior to a change in the speaking turn). The arrows that point down denote the end of speaker *A*'s turns; the arrows that point up denote the end of speaker *B*'s turns. *ISS* and *NSS* stand for interruptive and noninterruptive simultaneous speech, respectively. *Source*: Feldstein & Welkowitz, 1978

traits, such as extroversion and trait anxiety, but these may differ depending on the length of the silent periods (Siegman, 1978, pp. 206–207) and on intercultural differences (K. R. Scherer, 1979b). Number and duration of sound–silence patterns in conversation also seem to play a major role in interaction regulation and the development of interpersonal relationships (Feldstein & Welkowitz, 1978; Matarazzo & Wiens, 1972; Siegman, 1979).

Parameters based on amplitude. The vertical excursions of the speech signal in the wave form shown in Figure 4.4 represent the sound pressure (transformed into voltage by the electrical response of a microphone). The amplitude of the wave form, the widest excursion from the baseline, reflects sound pressure, which is in turn related to the power or intensity of speech sounds, subjectively perceived as loudness.[3] Mean intensity of the signal can be obtained by computing the square of the pressure (voltage) value for specific time points of the signal and averaging these values. This mean can be expressed as a proportion of the intensity of a standard sound, and transformed into decibels (db). Although intensity is one of the easiest acoustical measures to obtain, it is also one of the most difficult to interpret. The intensity of the signal is dependent not only upon the vocal effort with which a vocalization is produced and the resulting pressure at the mouth of the speaker, but also on the direction in which the speaker faces in relation to the microphone and the distance to the microphone. The large number of extraneous factors affecting the intensity of recorded vocalization signals, including the difficulty of calibrating the amplification of the signal in sound recording, render a direct interpretation of intensity values virtually impossible.

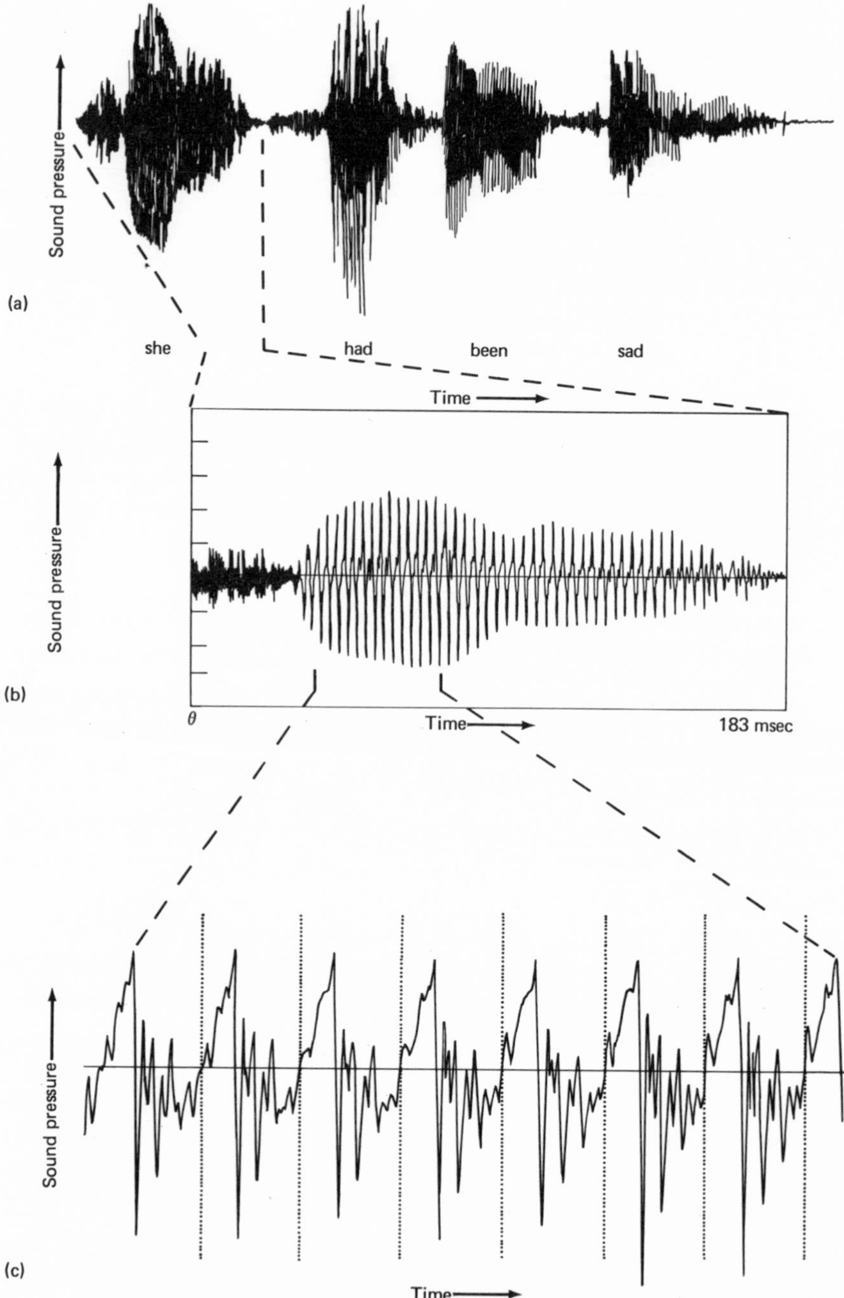

Figure 4.4. Illustration of a speech wave form with different degrees of temporal resolution. Time signal segments are given for (a) the utterance "She had been sad," (b) the word "she," and (c) a segment from the vowel [i:] showing demarcation of individual periods.

In order to compare the intensity of vocalizations of different speakers, the researcher must take great care to assure equality of the distance from each speaker to the microphone and control over the head direction of each speaker in relation to the microphone. In addition, a standard gain setting on the tape recorder has to be used. Even for consecutive measurements of the same speaker and the assessment of changes in vocalization intensity, similar precautions have to be taken. Unless the researcher is absolutely certain that these extraneous conditions are comparable for all speakers and recording sessions, intensity measures should be interpreted very cautiously.

If recording conditions have been controlled appropriately, the level and variation of intensity may be a potentially useful acoustic variable. There are some reports in the literature that intensity increases under stress (see K. R. Scherer, 1981b), but the evidence is still sparse. On the other hand, many studies of the vocal expression of emotion do show an increase in intensity of the voice for emotions characterized by excitement, such as anger and joy (K. R. Scherer, 1979a, p. 513). There is good evidence that extroverts speak with louder voices than introverts (K. R. Scherer, 1978, 1979b) and that confidence and persuasiveness may also be associated with higher intensity (K. R. Scherer, 1979c; K. R. Scherer, London, & Wolf, 1973), even though there seem to be major intercultural differences (see K. R. Scherer, 1979b). Intensity variations obviously play a major role in emphasis, as well as in turn-taking regulation (Duncan, 1972, 1973; Meltzer, Morris, & Hayes, 1971), and may indicate the nature of the relationship to an interaction partner (Natale, 1975). The potential importance of this parameter for nonverbal behavior research would seem to justify increased efforts to develop procedures for the objective measurement of intensity that avoid the many possible sources of artifact.

Parameters based on frequency. One of the most frequently used vocal parameters is the fundamental frequency (F_0) of the vocalization wave form. Figure 4.4c shows the time signal for the vowel [i:]; the individual periods of the wave form have been demarcated by vertical lines. Fundamental frequency (which is a major determinant of perceived pitch) is defined simply as the number of these periods per second (cycles per second = Hertz [Hz]; see Appendix B).

The fundamental frequency of a vocalization often changes rather rapidly. One can differentiate several types of variability: If even adjacent individual periods are somewhat different in length, so that an underlying irregularity in the vibration of the vocal folds is revealed, one talks of *jitter* or *perturbation*. Although the exact nature and the significance of jitter are still not very well known, it is assumed that there is a relationship to emotional arousal (Lieberman & Michaels, 1962; for a technical review of perturbation measures, see Davis, 1979).

Across longer segments fundamental frequency will vary rather extensively. Among the possible variability measures are F_0 range (F_0 maximum − F_0 minimum), F_0 variance or standard deviation, or interquartile distances of F_0, all for a chosen segment. One of the most important ways of looking at F_0 variability is a plot of consecutive F_0 values resulting in a curve or contour, as shown in Figure 4.5. F_0 curves, if determined for a linguistically meaningful segment, are referred to as *intonation contours*. These contours themselves are amenable to further feature extraction, such as the point of highest or lowest excursion, steepness of rise or fall, and a number of other characteristics, even though quantification or typological categorization of these parameters is still in the stage of development (M. V. Liberman, 1978; Stern & Wasserman, 1979; Takefuta, 1975).

F_0 is the vocal parameter that has yielded the most consistent evidence about externalization of speaker traits and states. Recent reviews of vocal correlates of stress, emotion, and psychopathology (K. R. Scherer, 1979a, 1981a, 1981b) show that an increase in arousal or excitation seems to be generally accompanied by F_0 increase. However, there are strong individual differences that may be due to response specificity or coping strategy. In a review of vocal correlates of personality, K. R. Scherer (1979b) concluded:

> Higher F_0 seems to be associated with a personality syndrome of competence and dominance in male American (and, to some extent, male German speakers) as well as with a syndrome of discipline/dependability in male German and female American speakers. An explanation in terms of habitually elevated level of arousal is suggested in both cases. [P. 157]

Furthermore, F_0 might be an interesting indicator of the role of arousal in interpersonal interaction: In a large-scale study of interactions between civil servants and clients, U. Scherer & K. R. Scherer (1980) found that civil servants judged as aggressive in dealing with particular types of clients showed elevated F_0 in talking to these clients.

Although the evidence for F_0 variability is somewhat less consistent, increased F_0 variability or range also seems to accompany heightened arousal (K. R. Scherer, 1979a; Williams & Stevens, 1981). F_0 variability is probably an important factor in expressiveness and may play a signifi-

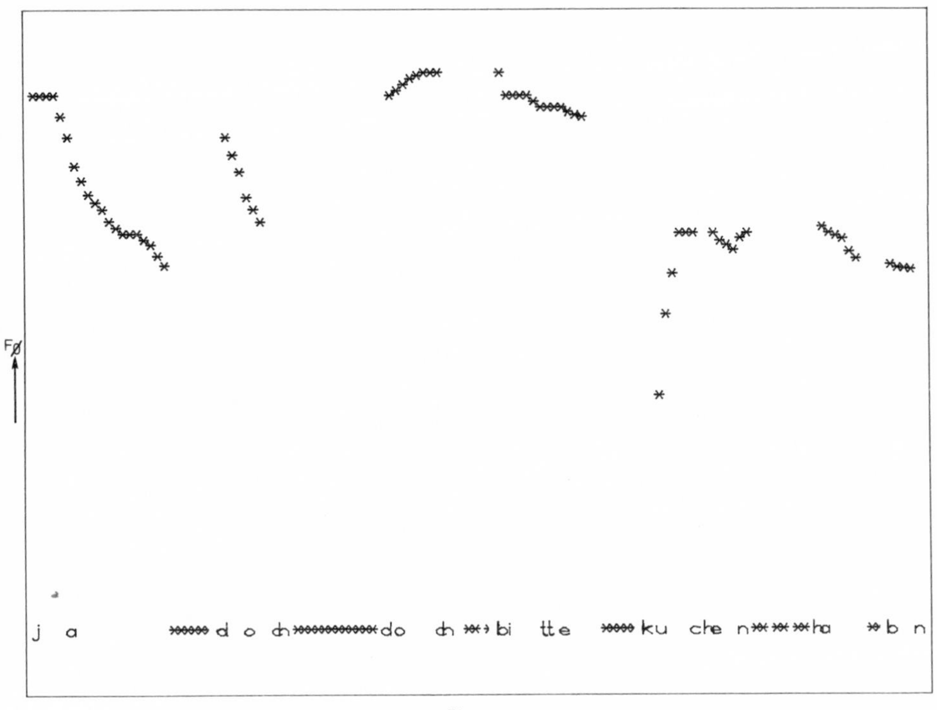

Figure 4.5. Intonation contour for a short utterance spoken by a 3-year-old German girl: "Ja . . . doch . . . doch bitte Kuchen haben" ("Yes . . . I do . . . I do want some cake please").

cant role in the communication of confidence and persuasiveness (K. R. Scherer, 1979c, pp. 104–105; K. R. Scherer et al., 1973).

The role of intonation contours in communicating emotion and attitudes has been shown early by Uldall (1960, 1964/1972). Unfortunately, there has been very little research in this area, although it seems to be common knowledge that slight variations in intonation contours convey subtle aspects of emotional and attitudinal meaning (M. V. Liberman, 1978).

Consequently, the study of mean F_0, F_0 range and variability, and F_0 contours promises to be one of the most fruitful and exciting approaches in vocal communication research. This is because of the strong effects of emotional arousal on the respiratory and phonatory mechanisms that produce F_0. Furthermore, the complex signal structure of F_0 changes

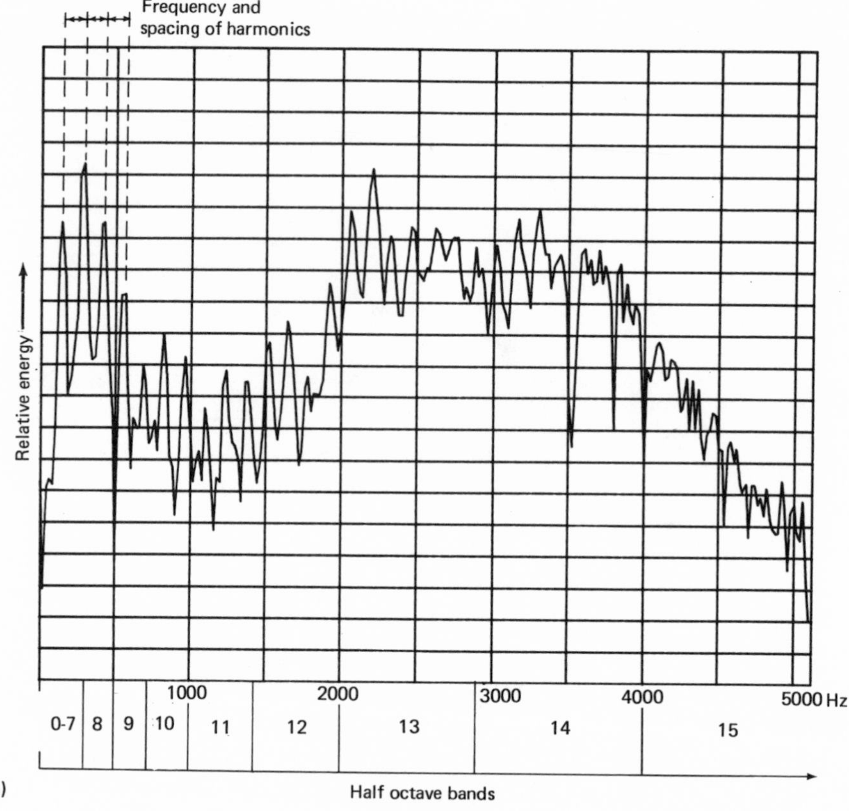

Figure 4.6. Spectra for the time signal segment from the vowel [i:] as shown in Figure 4.4c: (a) spectrum showing harmonics and vocal tract resonances; (b) smoothed spectrum (vocal tract filter function) showing the formants.

rapidly over time, allowing the encoding of highly differentiated messages.

Parameters based on frequency and amplitude. The spectrum, that is, the frequency-by-amplitude display of an acoustic wave form, yields measures of the harmonics and resonance characteristics or formants and various types of measures concerning the energy distribution in the frequency range (see Appendix B). Figure 4.6a shows the spectrum for a small portion of the signal displayed in Figure 4.4c. This spectrum contains both the harmonic structure of the voiced sound, that is, the multiples of the fundamental frequency (mostly determined by phonatory settings) and distinctive peaks, the formants that reflect the resonance characteristics of the vocal tract for the respective articulatory

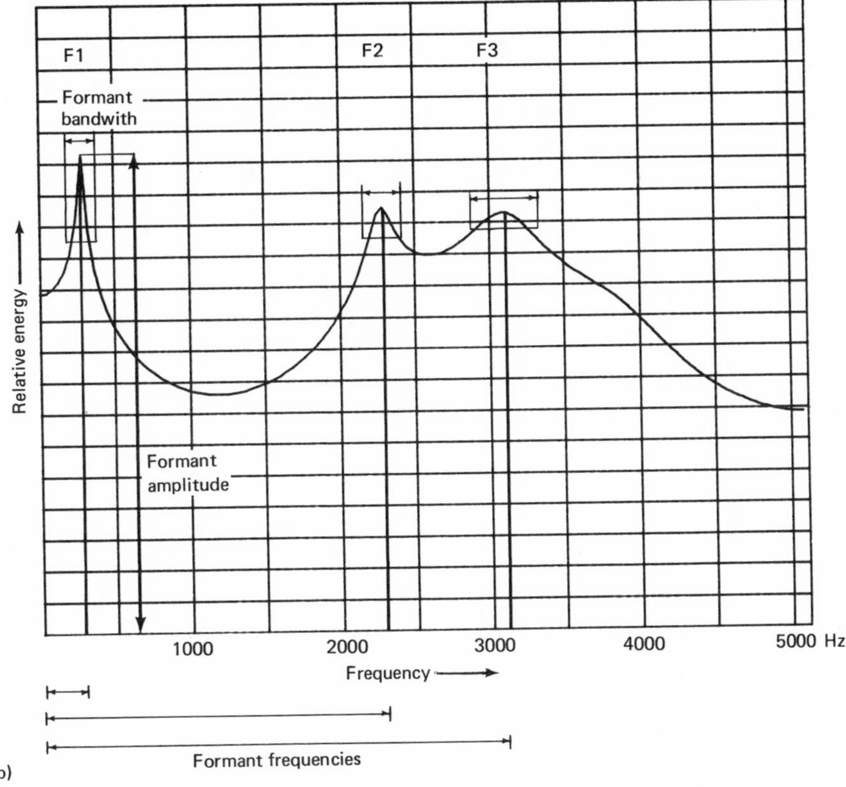

(b)

setting (shown in Figure 4.6b). Though the harmonics are rarely used for the extraction of acoustic parameters, the formants are among the most important spectral parameters. For each formant three types of variables can be computed, using appropriate analysis routines (see Appendix C): the frequency point at which the formant peak is located, the amplitude of this peak, and the bandwidth of the formant, represented by the transverse cut through the peak, as shown in Figure 4.6b. Whereas the spectrum in Figure 4.6b represents only one very small portion or *frame* of the original wave form in Figure 4.4c, Figures 4.7a and 4.7b show how formants can be displayed for several such frames in a row (see the ensuing discussion).

It will be noted from Figure 4.6 that formants, that is, the indicators of the resonance characteristics of the vocal tract for a particular articulato-

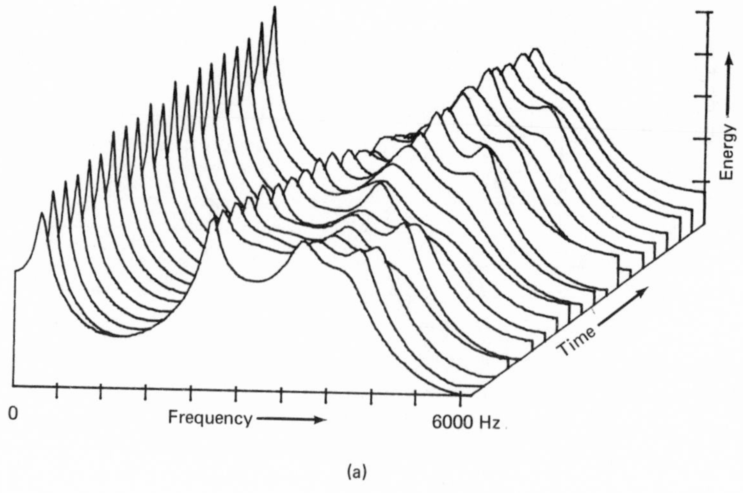

(a)

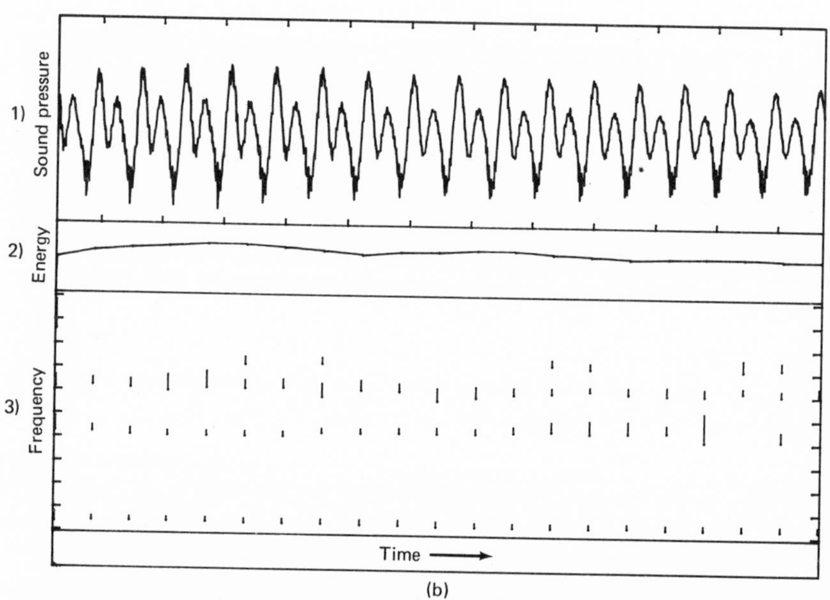

(b)

Figure 4.7. Changes of formant structure over time for the vowel [i:] as shown in Figure 4.4c: (a) three-dimensional plot; (b) plot of (1) time signal, (2) intensity, and (3) formant frequency and bandwidth.

ry setting, amplify particular harmonics of the fundamental frequency. Thus formants do not "create" energy; a formant peak in the spectrum can appear only if there is energy in the harmonics to support it. Because the harmonics as multiples of the fundamental frequency depend on the latter, formant frequency locations in the spectrum will differ somewhat from speaker to speaker and from utterance to utterance. Although listeners have no problems recognizing different vowels (see Lieberman, 1977, pp. 36–39), differential spacing of harmonics has important implications for the acoustic assessment of formant frequencies. It is much more difficult to obtain the appropriate acoustic parameters for voices with high F_0 (those of women and children) because their harmonics are spaced very widely, with the result that there are fewer harmonics within a particular frequency range.

Because of these difficulties, phonetic and electroacoustic speech analysis is often carried out with adult male voices exclusively. In addition, there is a high probability of artifacts in some of the analysis techniques if they are used for voices with very high F_0. Thus one has to be very careful in interpreting data obtained from an automatic acoustic analysis of such voices. In terms of formant frequencies, one safeguard is to compare the values obtained with published tables of formant values in particular languages (see Malecot, 1974; Minifie, 1973). Even though one cannot expect to find perfect correspondence between the values obtained in analysis and published values, there should be a fair degree of similarity, particularly in the relationships of the formants to each other (e.g., the distance between the first and second formant, etc.) and their general location.

It is the location of the formant frequencies and the relationships of the formants to each other that determine the perception of a certain vowel quality in speech recognition. Surprisingly, formant frequencies can vary rather widely for different speakers without apparent effect on the ability of listeners to decode the appropriate vowel quality accurately. The human ear and the speech-recognition apparatus seem to utilize some kind of normalization procedure whereby the general characteristics of the voice of the speaker, including fundamental frequency, are taken into account in the attempt to decode the type of vowel articulated by the speaker. In general, the locations of formants F1 to F3 are most important for vowel decoding and seem to be heavily determined by the particular articulatory setting for each vowel. Formants F4 to F6, on the other hand, vary less with different vowel qualities and seem to be more indicative of the general resonance of the particular speaker's vocal tract (see Fant, 1960; Minifie, 1973). It seems reasonable to assume that variations in the frequencies and relationships among these higher formants may be more useful for the detection of speaker-specific characteristics than the lower formants. However, as can be seen in Figure 4.7b, F5 and F6 or even higher formants are often difficult to determine.

Although the word *formant* is generally used in phonetics to describe the specific energy concentration characterizing particular vowels, it is possible to compute similar resonance peaks in the spectrum for nonlinguistic vocalizations, including infant vocalizations. In this case, however, it is not possible to check the results obtained against published values for particular vocal tract resonances, because such material is available for vowels and diphthongs only. Given the technical difficulties of analyzing voices with high fundamental frequency, frequencies often found for women and children, it becomes difficult to guard against possible artifacts.

Up to this point, the discussion has been restricted to the assessment of resonance characteristics for short fixed-length time slots or frames of 20–100 milliseconds. One can plot the formant values for several such frames, as shown in Figures 4.7a and 4.7b, to display the formant tracks or trajectories for a particular segment, often a vowel or word. Instead of plotting these trajectories, one can also compute average values for the formant frequencies, amplitudes, and bandwidths for such segments. Meaningful averaging of formant frequencies, however, can be made only for steady state vowels and vowellike phonations, because an average would become uninterpretable if it were based on the formants of two different vowels. On the basis of the formant frequencies for a segment such as that shown in Figure 4.7b, one can obtain a large number of different variables in addition to the averages. For example, one can determine both the lowest and the highest frequencies, the frequency at the midportion of a vowel (as well as bandwidth and amplitude for each of these cases), and a large number of derived conditional values and proportions, such as the frequency of formant F2 at the point where formant F1 has a maximum, the quotient between formant F1 and formant F2 (see the example in Figure 4.8), and so on. Goldstein (1976) has proposed several such measures in an attempt to use formant data for speaker-recognition purposes.

Whereas the averaging of formant values for segments longer than steady state portions of vowels is meaningless, the examination of formant trajectories beyond the boundary of the steady state portion of a vowel may yield important information about the nature of the transition from one vowel to the next or from vowel to consonant. These

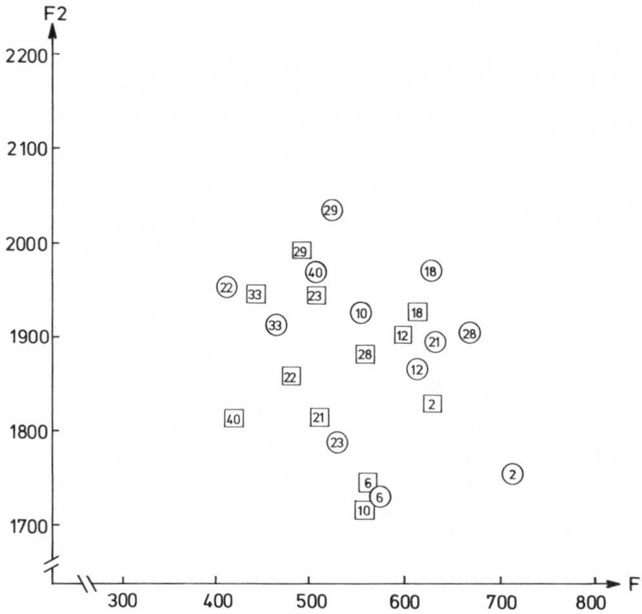

Figure 4.8. Plot of the frequencies of the first formant (F1) against the frequencies of the second formant (F2) for nine female schizophrenic patients before □ and after ○ therapy (vowel [eɪ] in *afraid*).

transitions are very important for speech recognition (C. J. Darwin, 1976; Fant, 1960; A. M. Liberman, Cooper, Shankweiler, & Studdert-Kennedy, 1967; Studdert-Kennedy, 1976), and they may provide important information about the manner of speaking – defining precise or slurred articulation, for example. At present, however, little is known about the exact nature of the variables that will have to be extracted from these transitions and their information value for nonlinguistic characteristics. It is to be expected that further research on transitions, analyzing their relevance for the diagnosis of speaker traits and states, may well prove worthwhile.

Formant data have as yet been used only rarely in vocal behavior research. However, theoretical considerations suggest that these parameters should be sensitive to articulation changes induced by emotional arousal (Hecker, Stevens, von Bismarck, & Williams, 1968; Williams & Stevens, 1972). Tolkmitt, Helfrich, Standke and Scherer (in press) studied changes in formant frequencies between an admission and a discharge interview for each of a group of psychiatric patients, finding changes that might reflect more precise articulation after therapy (see F1-by-F2 plot in Figure 4.8). In another study, formant frequencies for some vowels revealed significant interaction effects for the impact of task and emotional stressors on persons characterized by extreme repression or sensitization coping styles (K. R. Scherer & Tolkmitt, 1979). At this point, formant parameters and the changes they undergo as a function of nonlinguistic determinants are little understood. However, because it is unlikely that speakers actively attempt to manipulate their formant frequencies, as they may do for F_0, these parameters hold much promise for further research on vocal communication.

Averaging of spectral parameters is meaningful if it is performed across very lengthy segments of speech, for example, several sentences. In this case the context dependence of the spectral parameters owing to specific vowels and consonants is reduced because the specific characteristics of different sound segments will no longer predominate, and it may be possible to obtain a general, average picture of the energy distribution in the frequency spectrum of a specific voice in a particular speech situation. This is the assumption underlying the use of the long-term spectrum (LTS), which represents the average of individual spectra for fixed-length frames over a lengthy speech utterance. Figure 4.9 shows examples of two long-term spectra for a female subject describing (a) a stress film and (b) a film on pottery making.

Silent periods should be completely eliminated from the speech sample before the long-term spectra are computed. Otherwise, the spectra of the tape hiss or noise will distort the results. In addition to eliminating silent periods, it may be useful to compute separate long-term spectra for voiced and unvoiced portions of speech, given the different spectral characteristics of these two types of sound production.

Long-term average spectra indicate the characteristic distribution of energy over the frequency range in the voice of a speaker for a particular utterance. Such long-term average spectra have often been used in studies on automatic speaker recognition by computer, because they have been thought to represent the stable characteristics of a speaker's voice, independent of short-term variations caused by the nature of the linguistic segments. However, in most of these studies, speakers had to read lengthy passages of standard text in order to allow automatic speaker recognition with a modicum of success. As yet, there is little reliable information on the length of nonstandard natural speech utterances needed to obtain a stable long-term spectrum representative for a speaker's voice.

Although it is very easy to display long-term average spectra graphically, it is somewhat more difficult to interpret differences between speakers or speech situations meaningfully in these spectra (see Figure

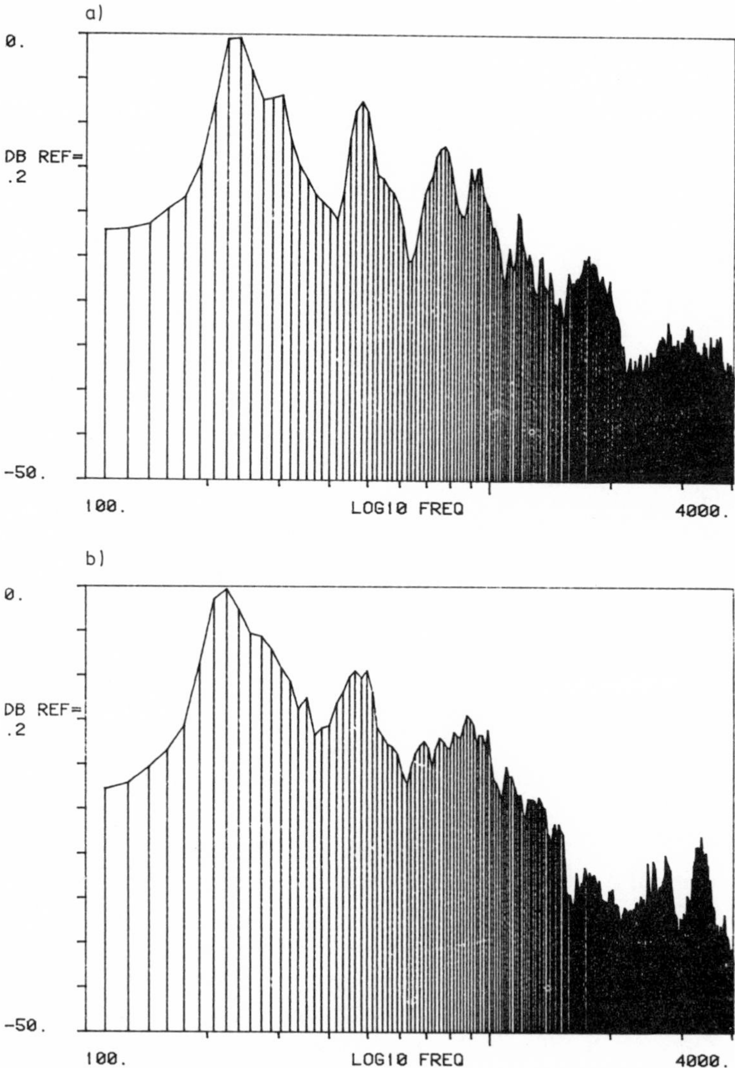

Figure 4.9. Long-term spectra (2 min of vocalization each) for a female speaker describing (a) a stress-inducing film on jaw surgery and (b) a film on pottery making.

4.9). Graphic displays of this sort may be useful for the development of hypotheses concerning relevant parameters, but the test of these hypotheses requires quantitative variables for statistical analysis. Depending on the type of acoustic analysis, the long-term average spectrum consists of several hundred discrete values. In order to reduce this mass of data one often averages values in specific frequency bands. For example, one could obtain energy averages for frequency bands with a width of 100 Hz: 0–100 Hz, 100–200 Hz, 200–300 Hz, and so on. Generally, however, logarithmic rather than linear scales are used in dividing the frequency spectrum into discrete bands, because this type of scaling seems to correspond better to the way in which our auditory apparatus processes spectral information (i.e., averaging over wider bands in the higher frequencies). The scales most often used are third-octave or half-octave bands (see Figure 4.6a). If a digital spectrum is obtained, the energy components within these bands are averaged arithmetically.

Long-term spectral analysis is frequently done with hardware filter banks that measure the average energy within these frequency bands (for further details see Appendix C). The use of such bands reduces the variables obtained from the long-term average spectrum to about 10 to 15, a number that can be reasonably handled in statistical analysis programs. However, owing to the scarcity of research in this area, little is known about the significance and diagnostic value of these bands. Some of the data reported in studies that have used filter bank spectra have to be interpreted with caution, because the effect of changes in fundamental frequency has not always been taken into account. Obviously, if fundamental frequency changes strongly, the proportion of energy within the bands in the region of the fundamental frequency can change dramatically, because F_0 usually carries most of the energy in the speech signal. Because this band-boundary-crossing phenomenon resulting from F_0 changes depends on whether the fundamental frequency range of a speaker falls within one of these bands or crosses boundaries, it may be very misleading to compare long-term average spectra for different speakers under different emotional conditions (see K. R. Scherer, 1979a, p. 506). One way to avoid such misinterpretation is to exclude from long-term spectra the frequency region below the upper range of fundamental frequency. If one wants to obtain data on spectral energy distribution changes that are completely independent of F_0 changes, one must also correct for changes in the location of the harmonics.

There is some indication in the literature that the ratio between the energy in the lower part of the frequency spectrum (using a cutoff point of 500 or 1,000 Hz) and the energy in the higher frequencies is an important parameter reflecting differences in phonation and the general tension of the vocal apparatus (Frøkjaer-Jensen & Prytz, 1976; Laver, 1975, 1980). Consequently, one can construct proportional indexes or low–high coefficients defined as proportion of energy below the cutoff point divided by proportion of energy above the cutoff point. At present, it is unclear which cutoff point, that is, 500 or 1,000 Hz, or some point in between, is optimal for this kind of quotient. It would be desirable to know more about the effect of particular phonatory adjustments and vocal tract characteristics on the long-term spectrum, in order to decide on the location of the cutoff point.

Even though energy distribution in long-term spectra was among the first acoustic parameters to be systematically studied (Friedhoff, Alpert, & Kurtzberg, 1964; Hargreaves & Starkweather, 1964; Ostwald, 1963, 1973), the evidence available is hardly conclusive. Some of the relevant studies of therapy effects in psychiatric patients or the effects of stress induction on normal subjects have shown evidence of spectral changes (Roessler & Lester, 1979; K. R. Scherer, 1979a; Simonov & Frolov, 1973; Tolkmitt et al., in press). However, neither the exact nature of the parameters to be used nor the magnitude of the effects is well established. Unlike F_0 or other clearly defined single parameters, the long-term spectrum does not provide a simple index of the energy distribution. Consequently, much further work is needed to construct valid parameters. The evidence available to date, as well as theoretical considerations, suggests that this might be very promising.

There has been little effort to extract additional information from the long-term spectrum. It is possible, however, that further variables could be obtained using these spectra. For example, the drop-off of energy with increasing frequency can be described by gradients of differential steepness for different speakers (see Davis, 1979). This drop-off might be indicative of differences in the harmonic structure of vowels or general characteristics of habitual vocal tract settings in articulation. Systematic research using regression line fitting through fairly linear parts of the long-term spectrum might yield some interesting variables in the form of regression coefficients. To date, there does not seem to have been any systematic research on the relationship of such variables to psychological traits or states of the speaker or to the nature of the interaction.

A summary of the major parameters in the acoustic analysis of speech that have been discussed within this section is provided in Table 4.2. This table also indicates the frequency of usage of the parameters and of

Table 4.2. *Major parameters in the acoustic analysis of speech*

Types of parameters (units in parentheses)	Distribution characteristics[a]			Time series	Proportions
	Mean	Variance	Range		
Time parameters (in seconds; basic unit: sound bursts)					
Occurrence and duration of sound bursts	C	R	R	R	C
Occurrence and duration of silence intervals	C	C	R	R	C
Frequency parameters (in Hz; basic unit: wave period or time slot)					
Fundamental frequency (F_0)	C	C	C	C	R
Formant frequency (F1 . . . F*n*)	C	R	C	C	C
Formant bandwidth (B1 . . . B*n*)	C	R	R	D	R
Intensity/energy parameters (in dB; basic unit: sound burst or time slot)					
Total energy of sound unit	C	C	C	C	C
Energy at F_0 and higher harmonics	P	P	P	R	P
Energy at formant frequencies	C	R	R	R	R
Average energy in frequency bands	C	R	R	D	R

Note: C = commonly used; R = rarely used; P = possible, but not yet established; D = dubious.

[a]Examples of parameter values within and across segments (e.g., vowels, words, sentences, utterances).

derived statistical measurements in the vocal communication literature. As pointed out before, however, frequency of use does not necessarily reflect a parameter's validity as an indicator of speaker traits and states, or its usefulness in studying nonverbal communication processes. The scarcity of research in this area is due more to lack of effort, probably because of the requirements for phonetic–acoustic expertise and expensive equipment, than to negative findings. However, the utility of a number of the parameters discussed can be determined only if further progress in acoustic–phonetic and socio-psychophonetic research is made. For example, the role of formant changes under stress cannot be properly evaluated unless the effect of physiological arousal on phonatory and articulatory structures and the effects of the latter on formant frequencies are better known. Similarly, formant differences between groups of speakers or speech situations need to be evaluated to determine whether listeners are able to perceive these differences and treat them as meaningful information. Thus a call for further research using acoustic parameters in vocal communication studies does not suffice. This research needs to be complemented by acoustic–phonetic, physiological, and socio-psychophonetic research that pays increased attention to the fact that the speaker is a social organism rather than a linguistic automaton.

Auditory assessment of acoustic parameters

Because the measurement of acoustic parameters is based on audible sound waves, it is possible to attempt auditory assessment of these parameters using human observers (see Scherer & Ekman, Section 1.4, for a discussion of various types of observers). Here a short overview of parameters or variables measured with the help of human observers, both expert and lay, will be provided.

Almost all of the objective parameters of an acoustic speech wave form that have already been discussed can be "heard" by judges and can consequently be assessed with the help of category systems and rating scales. However, owing to a number of factors, these auditorily assessed variables do not necessarily correlate very highly with objectively measured variables of the same acoustic parameters. Among these factors are the characteristics of the human hearing system (which does not function exactly like a filter bank analyzer or a digital computer); the fact that expectations and auditory habits, often based on certain aspects of a language and/or cultural norms, affect auditory impression; and the difficulty of translating an auditory impression into a quantitative judgment on a scale.

One of the most severe drawbacks of our auditory system as an acoustic measurement instrument is that it seems to be somewhat deficient in ability to isolate individual acoustic parameters (see Small, 1973b). For example, our judgment of the fundamental frequency of a voice, which is heard as pitch, is affected not only by F_0 itself but also by many other factors, including the energy distribution in the spectrum (Laver, 1975, p. 258; Small, 1973b, pp. 407–418). Similarly, the judgment of loudness of a voice is not a direct function of the amplitude or intensity of the speech wave but seems also to be affected by many variables, including spectral characteristics that may in part represent the vocal effort of the speaker (Lehiste, 1970, pp. 113–120; Small, 1973b, pp. 382–385). This integrative mode of functioning of the auditory system has its drawbacks for auditory acoustic analysis, but it is a major asset for speech recognition. As we have seen, listeners seem to be able to "normalize" various acoustic parameters, particularly formants, by relating them to specific characteristics of the speaker's voice.

Experts such as phonologists and phoneticians claim to be able to overcome these integrative perception tendencies of our hearing system. With some training they seem to achieve fairly satisfactory agreement among themselves on a number of acoustic parameters, such as pitch and loudness (see K. R. Scherer, 1974b). However, the correlations of such expert judgments with objective acoustic measurements are not at all well known, and although expert judges may agree among themselves, their ratings may not agree very well with objective analyses. This is a particular problem if not only the ranking of speakers but the assessment of some parametric value, such as fundamental frequency in Hertz or small differences between speech samples, is concerned (see Dittman & Wynne, 1961; Lieberman, 1965). Owing to these problems of differentiating and scaling parameters, most of the transcription systems or rating dimensions that have been proposed for assessment of paralinguistic variables have employed some kind of cultural norm or standard that is used as a baseline to which a particular speech pattern can be compared.

This is true, for example, for the paralinguistic transcription system proposed by Trager and Smith (1951/1957). This transcription system uses categories such as "overhigh" and "oversoft" to specify the characteristics of specific acoustic parameters. Even though there have been reports of satisfactory reliability, as well as validity, for this kind of transcription system (see Duncan, Rice, & Butler, 1968; Duncan & Rosenthal, 1968), there are a number of problems (see also Crystal & Quirk, 1964, pp. 21–23; Dittman & Wynne, 1961). For example, normative standards concerning the "correct" or "modal" level of loudness, pitch, and amplitude of voice may vary rather dramatically among different language communities, dialect groups, and even different social classes or subcultures within dialect groups. Furthermore, this system provides very few categories. These may not be sufficient to describe the range of observable voice changes or, in particular, to account for differences in emotional states. Finally, the system requires that the judges have a fair degree of linguistic expertise and prior training.

Attempts to develop rating systems based on the Trager–Smith approach that can be used by lay judges after some training with demonstration tapes (N. N. Markel, Meisels, & Houck, 1964) have not been very frequent, possibly because of the fundamental problem with the underlying assumptions concerning a modal or standard pattern of speech. Because these systems are heavily based on modal speech behavior, they would be very difficult to apply to an analysis of vocalizations in infants and children, where quite different standards apply. Even if one tried to use the speaker as his or her own baseline, that is, tried to assess deviation from normal speech patterns for this person, one would have severe problems with appropriate sampling procedures for obtaining a reasonable estimate of the person's modal speech patterns. Consequently, it may be advisable to use electroacoustic devices or digital processing rather than human judges, lay or expert, to measure distal cues in the form of purely acoustic parameters. There are as yet, however, no studies that systematically compare acoustic methods and judges for their ability to differentiate different traits or states of speakers on the basis of vocal cues.

4.7. Proximal cues of vocalization characteristics

In the preceding sections I have described parameters that serve to characterize vocalization by means of objective measurements, although some of them may be obtained via auditory expert judgment. The normal listener, however, is not an expert on voice and speech production and will probably perceive and evaluate the sounds that reach his or her ear in a different manner. The way in which objectively measurable distal cues of vocalization are perceptually represented as proximal cues is generally of little interest in studies focused on the investigation of the externalization aspect only. However, it does play an important role for studies focused on communication processes, specifically, for those dealing with the way in which perceivers utilize vocalization cues in person perception and attribution.

Unfortunately, the nature of the representation of proximal cues is not very well understood at present, and little research effort has been expended to date on this topic. For example, we do not know whether the categories that people use in processing the acoustic cues they hear are congruent with or comparable to the criteria that phoneticians and acousticians use. As already shown, human auditory perception does not simply register acoustic parameters. Furthermore, we may be unable to pick up fine differences of frequency, amplitude, or duration. Apart from these sensory restrictions, characteristics of the information processing, that is, the sorting into categories that are then used for further attribution, are virtually unknown.

As in many other areas where the way in which people use cues in information processing is studied, one approach to grasping the "folk categories" is to use the popularly available verbal labels that people use to refer to and converse about their proximal percepts. In this approach one operates under the assumption that people are likely to have invented verbal labels for categories which are important to them and about which they need to communicate. Unfortunately, there are a large number of open questions concerning the verbal codability of proximal percepts. For example, do the verbal labels that a language makes available for the description of voices and vocalizations determine the categories that the perceiver will eventually use in processing such stimuli? Or are those proximal percepts independent of linguistic labels and categories, so that they must be translated into linguistic terms if a need to communicate proximal percepts arises (as when researchers ask about them)?

One of the major problems in assessing proximal percepts of voice parameters via verbal labels is that many of the terms available, such as *strident*, *harsh*, and *shrill*, have very strong implied evaluative components. The implications are quite obvious for voice labels such as *gloomy*, *strong*, *nice*, or *clear*. It is interesting that many works of fiction use voice descriptions instead of personality or mood characterizations, presumably because the authors assume the existence of stereotypical inference links between particular types of voice descriptors and personality and mood categories. In general, research on voice and personality has shown that stereotypical inference rules linking particular vocal characteristics to personality traits are very strong (Kramer, 1963; K. R. Scherer, 1972).

In spite of many problems in attempts to assess proximal percepts of vocalization characteristics, it would seem necessary to make a concerted effort to study the nature of these percepts in order to understand the process of voice cue utilization (as specified in the Brunswikian lens model mentioned in Section 4.2). Obviously, one of the first steps is to attempt to develop rating scales that incorporate the verbal labels used in a particular culture to describe vocalization characteristics in folk

Table 4.3. *Scales for ratings of proximal vocal cues for voice quality and speech characteristics*

Voice quality	Speech characteristics
1. *Pleasantness* Clear Cultured Melodic Expressive Flexible Pleasant	1. *Precision* Fluent Distinct Poised Clear Articulated Precise Exact Controlled Meticulous
2. *Resonance* Masculine Strong Resonant Sonorous	2. *Rate* Fast Clipped Hasty Hurried
3. *Depth* Dark Deep	3. *Sloppiness* Fuzzy Monotonous Slurred Jerky Sloppy
4. *Breathiness* Breathy Broken Quavering	4. *Rhythm* Rhythmic Accentuated Cadenced Accented
5. *Warmth* Mellow Soothing Warm	5. *Affectation* Pathetic Mannered Crawling Affected
6. *Thinness* Effeminate Thin	6. *Regularity* Calm Regular Uniform
7. *High-pitch* High-pitched Light	
8. *Sharpness* Ringing Sharp	
9. *Loudness* Loud Penetrating	
10. *Harshness* Harsh Rough	
11. *Gloom* Gloomy Muffled	
12. *Hoarseness* Hoarse Throaty	
13. *Flatness* Flat	
14. *Nasality* Nasal	
15. *Dryness* Dry	

Note: Based on voice- and speech-attribute rating forms developed by K. R. Scherer (1970). The clusters proposed here result from preliminary factor analyses of American and German rater groups, including self-, peer, and stranger ratings.

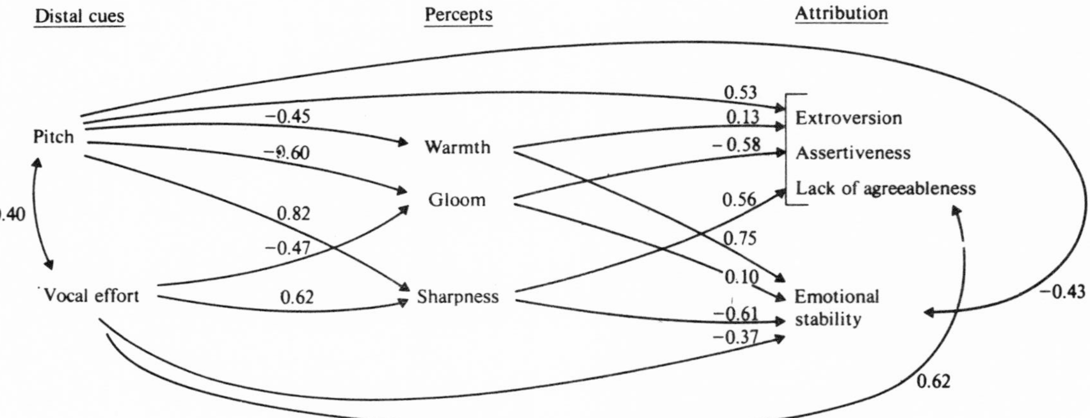

Figure 4.10. Partial lens model for personality inference from speech. Curvilinear arrows indicate hypothetically assumed causal relationships. Strengths of the relationships are indicated by Pearson *rs* ($n = 24$). Intercorrelations among variables for each type of measurement have been omitted to simplify the figure. *Source*: K. R. Scherer & Giles, 1979

terms. Table 4.3 shows two preliminary scales for ratings of proximal vocal cues, one for voice quality and one for speech attributes. These scales are based on a list of adjectives for the English language that was the result of a lengthy search of popular literature on voice quality and speech style (K. R. Scherer, 1970). Figure 4.10 shows an example of a partial Brunswikian lens model that illustrates the way in which proximal percepts described by such verbal labels are affected by objectively determined acoustic characteristics, on the one hand, and the way in which they are utilized in inferring personality, on the other hand. Such an analysis shows which cue configurations observers use to infer personality and affect characteristics from the voice.

The study of proximal percepts of voices and their utilization seems to be one of the most promising and untapped fields within vocal communication research. It would be conceivable, for example, to manipulate a variety of acoustic characteristics of standard utterances and observe the changes in verbal labels that are attached to these synthetic voices (and also to examine individual differences in the usage of these folk terms for voice quality and vocalization).

4.8. Inferences and attributions based on vocal behavior

In many studies of person perception and nonverbal communication it is of interest to investigate the inference processes and the resulting attributions on the bases of different types of voices and different aspects of vocal behavior. K. R. Scherer (1979c) has reviewed the techniques available for obtaining the stimulus material for such studies, including (1) encoding of specific sender states via role playing, (2) seminaturalistic studies of dyadic interaction or group processes, and (3) systematic manipulation of voice and speech cues. Each of these techniques has its particular advantages and disadvantages. Unfortunately, most studies in this area differ on many dimensions, including the type of stimulus material; it is therefore very hard to compare results.

It would be most useful to start with studies utilizing naturalistic or seminaturalistic vocalization material to investigate attribution, in order to obtain general notions concerning the importance of particular cues and the nature of the inference processes. This would also guarantee at least some degree of ecological representativeness. Given the natural restrictions on sampling of voices, states, and situations (see Scherer & Ekman, Section 1.3), it is advisable to follow up the results of such studies by using encoding or systematic manipulation techniques to explore the effects on attribution of different values of a specific

Table 4.4. *Emotional attributions significantly associated with acoustic parameters*

Acoustic parameters of tone sequences	Direction of effect	Emotion rating scales listed in decreasing order of associative strength
Amplitude variation	Small	Happiness, pleasantness, activity
	Large	Fear
Pitch variation	Small	Disgust, anger, fear, boredom
	Large	Happiness, pleasantness, activity, surprise
Pitch contour	Down	Boredom, pleasantness, sadness
	Up	Fear, surprise, anger, potency
Pitch level	Low	Boredom, pleasantness, sadness
	High	Surprise, potency, anger, fear, activity
Tempo	Slow	Sadness, boredom, disgust
	Fast	Activity, surprise, happiness, pleasantness, potency, fear, anger
Envelope	Round	Disgust, sadness, fear, boredom, potency
	Sharp	Pleasantness, happiness, surprise, activity
Filtration cutoff-level (number of harmonics)	Intermediate (few)	Pleasantness, boredom, happiness sadness
	High (many)	Potency, anger, disgust, fear, activity, surprise

Source: K. R. Scherer and Oshinsky, 1977.

parameter and of different combinations of parameters. In spite of many differences in methodology, studies on the attribution of personality from the voice (Apple, Streeter, & Krauss, 1979; B. L. Brown, Strong, & Rencher, 1975; K. R. Scherer, 1979b) indicate fairly strong inferential links between voice cues and personality inferences. For example, for male speakers a higher mean F_0 seems to be perceived as indicative of greater extroversion, assertiveness, confidence, and competence. Very high F_0, however, is interpreted in both males and females as effeminacy, immaturity, or emotional instability (see K. R. Scherer, 1979b, pp. 179–189). Similarly, there seem to be strong, culturally shared inference links between vocal cues and emotion attributions (Davitz, 1964; K. R. Scherer, 1974c, 1981a). Some representative results from a study by K. R. Scherer and Oshinsky (1977) are shown in Table 4.4.

Studies of the attribution from the voice of psychological traits and states (including attitudes and interpersonal relationships) may have many different purposes. One classic aim of person perception research has been the assessment of accuracy. As has been shown before, the use of a Brunswikian lens model types of research paradigm would seem to be a most promising approach to this problem.

Other kinds of research are geared toward assessing the nature of the cue utilization, rather than the accuracy per se. In such studies, it is most important to be able to specify which cues are used by the observer in inferring a particular trait or state and how the perceiver makes use of cue combinations. Scherer and his collaborators have proposed cue separation and recombination procedures to assess cue utilization in personality and emotion attribution from nonverbal behavior (K. R. Scherer, Scherer, Rosenthal, & Hall, 1977). Basically, such a procedure requires the analytic separation of particular cues, a procedure similar to multichannel experiments (Argyle, Alkema, & Gilmour, 1971; Bugental, Kaswan, & Love, 1970; Ekman, 1965; Ekman & Friesen, 1974; Mehrabian & Ferris, 1967; Rosenthal, 1966/1976) in which judges are presented with audio, video, or audiovisual records and attempts are made to assess the relative importance of auditory and visual cues (for a critique of some of these approaches see Ekman, Friesen, O'Sullivan & Scherer, 1980). In most cases, however, it is possible to break down the cues further, even within a channel of communication.

The isolation of particular characteristics of the vocal signal and the assessment of the information remaining and its utilization by listeners have a long history in the area of vocal behavior research. Soskin and Kauffmann (1961) and Starkweather (1956) were among the first to use content-filtered speech produced by low-pass filtering of the signal. In this procedure the speech signal is passed through a low-pass filter, which attenuates all the energy above a certain frequency, usually about 400 Hz (although this may differ for men and women), and passes the energy below that point. Additional distortion may be introduced to make it more difficult to understand whatever may be left of the content (Rogers, Scherer, & Rosenthal, 1971). Although this content-filtering technique is used in many studies only to eliminate the verbal aspect of speech content, it does of course also eliminate many voice quality cues, particularly those that are related to the energy distribution in the spectrum. The cues that are left after content filtering are mostly sequence cues, such as rhythm, pauses, and speed of speech, and some frequency cues, such as fundamental frequency.

K. R. Scherer (1971) has developed a masking technique that removes most of those sequence cues while leaving the frequency cues, which are relevant to voice quality, unchanged. This technique, called *randomized splicing*, consists of splicing of speech samples into small pieces of tape, randomly rearranging these pieces, and splicing them back together after having eliminated pauses. This technique removes most of the sequence cues in speech and retains the frequency cues (such as the spectral energy distribution). Although the result of this masking technique does not sound much like speech, it gives a very vivid and natural rendering of the voice quality of the speaker. Digital computers can be used to perform random splicing very quickly and effectively.

Random splicing and content filtering can be used singly and in combination to determine the role of sequence and frequency cues in trait and state attribution to a speaker (see K. R. Scherer, Koivumaki, & Rosenthal, 1972). Such masking techniques can be used in factorial designs, including cue isolation in other channels, as well (for example, comparison of static physiognomy in a photograph and dynamic expressive behavior shown in video clips [K. R. Scherer et al., 1977]). Studies of this sort allow us to determine not only the importance of specific cues in the attribution process and the strength of the inferential link between a cue and a particular attribute but also the effect of particular cue configurations.

Sophisticated electroacoustical equipment and digital computers can be used to separate and manipulate cues further and to produce a variety of cue combinations. For example, it is possible to isolate parameters such as fundamental frequency and amplitude of a particular speech sample and expose observers to just these (Lieberman & Michaels, 1962). One promising technique is the use of synthesis methods to produce many possible combinations of different parameter values for a number of cues. For example, K. R. Scherer (1974c; K. R. Scherer & Oshinsky, 1977) used a Moog synthesizer to vary different levels of seven acoustic cues systematically and studied the types of inferences observers drew from the stimuli resulting when these cues were combined in a factorial design. Judges strongly agreed in their inferences from particular combinations of cues (see Table 4.4 for an example of the results). B. L. Brown et al. (1975) and Apple et al. (1979) have used digital computers to resynthesize voices and change parameters such as fundamental frequency and speech tempo in order to study the personality traits judges attribute. This kind of methodological approach seems to be most promising for future research on inference processes from vocal cues.

4.9. Relationships between vocal and nonvocal nonverbal behaviors

The bulk of this chapter has been devoted to a discussion of various methods available for the study of vocal cues as communicated in the auditory channel. However, many researchers have pointed out that a strict separation of channels of communication and an exclusive study of any one of these is likely to miss the multichannel nature of human communication. Thus, after a period of research governed by single-channel approaches (owing in part to the many methodological difficulties, the complexity, and the expense of studying nonverbal cues), research is now turning toward multichannel approaches combining measures from different modalities of nonverbal behavior. (This issue is discussed in detail in Ekman & Scherer, Section 1.3.) In the present section some methodological possibilities for combining vocal measurements with other nonvocal variables will be described. Given that there are very few preliminary approaches to the multimodal study of nonverbal behavior, it is too early to attempt a systematic survey of potential methods and approaches. Therefore, the following examples, drawn largely from the work of our Giessen research group, are meant only to illustrate possibilities.

Moment-to-moment behavior plots

One approach to the study of the relationships between behaviors in different modalities or channels is a moment-to-moment or point-by-point plot of behavior sequences using some kind of graphic representation of behavioral elements. Condon and Ogston (1966) and Kendon (1970) have used this approach to study the synchrony between various nonverbal behaviors and vocal behaviors in highly molecular analyses of small segments of behavior. Generally, these investigators have used still-frame and slow-motion film analysis and observer coding to plot events in different channels within a common time base. Rosenfeld (1980; see also Section 5.5) has cogently criticized some of the methodology used and the results reported in these studies.

The Giessen research group has attempted to develop the technical facilities and the programs to prepare multimodality plots of nonverbal behavior, using acoustic analysis of speech by computer and observer or machine coding of gestural behavior as input. Figure 4.11 shows an example for such a plot, in which observer coding of gestures and head movement (based on an adaptation of the system proposed by Ekman & Friesen, 1972; see K. R. Scherer, Wallbott, & Scherer, 1979; Wallbott, Scherer, & Scherer, in preparation) was used. In this type of analysis the beginning and ending points of movement acts coded by observers are shown, with symbols indicating the type of movement coded. In the vocal channel, pauses, intensity, and fundamental frequency as determined by computer analysis of the corresponding speech sample are displayed for the same time base. Though the example given in Figure 4.11 shows a behavior score for just one actor, it is easy to plot a dyadic interaction by providing the same kind of display for both interactors with a common time base. Multimodality plots of this sort can be used for qualitative analyses, such as attempts to arrive at hypotheses about correspondences and sequences between vocal and nonvocal acts, or they can serve as the basis for more quantitative sequence analyses (see van Hooff, Chapter 7).

In addition to such plots, which combine observer-coded movement and computer-analyzed speech data, we have attempted to use movement tracking with digitalization devices (such as an ultrasonic pen or a pointer movable across the videoscreen, devices that allow us to store in a computer the coordinates of a particular point of the subject's body for each movement position; see also Rosenfeld, Section 5.5) in combination with speech measures on the same time base.

Behavior styles

Another approach is the combination of measurements from several behavior modalities aggregated over interactions or parts thereof. In a recent study of interactions between civil service officials and clients, my colleagues and I attempted to combine vocal and nonvocal nonverbal behaviors into indexes of *behavior styles* that might be characteristic of personality or attitudes toward interaction partners. This attempt was based on the assumption that different persons may use patterns of vocal and nonvocal nonverbal acts consistently and that observers see such combinations of acts as units of behavior style or appearance (see Scherer & Ekman, Section 1.1). On the basis of factor analyses of coded behavior data and computer-analyzed speech, as well as theoretical assumptions, we drew up the lists of behavior styles and the acts that constitute them that are given in Table 4.5. These behavior styles were then used as variables in statistical analyses, and interesting correlations both with personality and attitudes of the civil service officials and with attributions made by observers watching videotapes of the interactions were found (U. Scherer & Scherer, 1980).

INKREMENTIERUNGSWEITE 400

NAME DES KODIERERS K O D I E R E R A

%%%

ZEIT	RECHTE HAND	LINKE HAND	K O P F BEWEGUNG	K O P F ORIENTIERUNG	R U M P F ORIENTIERUNG	R U M P F POSITION	ZEIT	STILLE PAUSEN	STIMM LOS	F0 GRUNDFREQUENZ	LAUTSTAERKE	F0	TEXT
5:27:51	.	.	KI	<	1	.	5:27:51		@@				sich
5:27:55	.	.	KI	<	1	.	5:27:55					138.3	
5:27:59	.	.	KI	<	1	.	5:27:59					148.8	
5:27:63	.	.	KI	<	1	.	5:27:63					132.6	jetzt
5:27:67	.	.	KI	<	1	.	5:27:67					150.5	
5:27:71	.	.	KI	<	1	.	5:27:71		@@				
5:27:75	.	.	KI	<	1	.	5:27:75					163.	
5:27:79	----	.	KI	<	1	.	5:27:79					158.	
5:27:83	UI	.	KI	<	1	.	5:27:83					153.3	Sie
5:27:87	UI	.	KI	<	1	.	5:27:87		@@				
5:27:91	UI	.	KI	<	1	.	5:27:91					139.1	
5:27:95	UI	.	KI	<	1	.	5:27:95					144.6	
5:27:99	UI	.	KI	----	1	.	5:27:99					157.	
5:28: 3	UI	.	KI	!	1	.	5:28: 3					168.4	müssen
5:28: 7	UI	.	KI	!	1	.	5:28: 7					178.4	
5:28:11	UI	.	KI	!	1	.	5:28:11					184.1	
5:28:15	UI	.	KI	!	1	.	5:28:15					184.1	
5:28:19	UI	.	KI	!	1	.	5:28:19					201.5	
5:28:23	UI	.	KI	!	1	.	5:28:23					206.4	
5:28:27	UI	.	KI	!	1	.	5:28:27					208.1	jetzt
5:28:31	UI	.	KI	!	1	.	5:28:31					193.9	
5:28:35	UI	.	KI	!	1	.	5:28:35		@@				
5:28:39	UI	.	KI	!	1	.	5:28:39		@@				
5:28:43	UI	.	KI	!	1	.	5:28:43		@@				
5:28:47	UI	.	KI	!	1	.	5:28:47		@@				
5:28:51	UI	.	KI	!	1	.	5:28:51		@@				
5:28:55	UI	.	KI	!	1	.	5:28:55					181.5	
5:28:59	UI	.	KI	!	1	.	5:28:59					168.4	
5:28:63	UI	.	KI	!	1	.	5:28:63					154.2	
5:28:67	UI	.	KI	!	1	.	5:28:67		@@				umdenken
5:28:71	UI	.	KI	!	1	.	5:28:71		@@				
5:28:75	.	.	KI	!	1	.	5:28:75					110.8	
5:28:79	.	.	KI	!	1	.	5:28:79		@@				
5:28:83	.	.	KI	!	1	.	5:28:83		@@				
5:28:87	.	.	.	!	1	.	5:28:87					92.7	
5:28:91	.	.	.	!	1	.	5:28:91					105.3	
5:28:95	.	.	.	!	1	.	5:28:95		@@				
5:28:99	.	----	.	!	1	.	5:28:99						
5:29: 3	.	PV	.	!	1	.	5:29: 3						
5:29: 7	.	PV	.	!	1	.	5:29: 7						

Figure 4.11. Example of a multichannel computer plot for a public official's verbal utterance: "... sich jetzt ... sie müssen jetzt umdenken" ("You will have to reconsider now"). Explanatory notes by column numbers: (1) time base; (2) right hand (*Ul* = amplifying illustrator); (3) left hand (*PV* = position change; (4) head movement (*Kl* = head illustrator); (5) head orientation (< = head oriented toward partner, ! = head lowered); (6) body orientation (1 = lean forward); (7) body position; (8) time base; (9) silent pauses; (10) voiceless speech segments; (11) fundamental frequency (F_0, pitch); (12) loudness; (13) F_0 values. *Source*: K. R. Scherer, 1980

Table 4.5. *Verbal and nonverbal components of behavior styles of civil servants in interactions with clients*

Behavior style	Components (objectively measured)
Verbosity	Total verbal output in seconds
Domineering speech behavior	Many interruptions of the client Few interruptions by the client
Emotional manner of speaking	High F_0 variability Many head illustrators Many hand illustrators
Frequent listening responses	Many backchannel head nods Many vocal backchannel signals
Immediacy	Head often oriented toward the client Head rarely oriented toward the table Body rarely upright or leaning backward
Controlled expressive behavior	Many positions with hands touching each other Few repetitive adaptors Few pointing illustrators Relatively low F_0 with low F_0 variability
Preoccupation with records	Long silent periods Frequent handling of papers

The preceding examples are illustrative of the approaches that researchers in nonverbal communication might find useful in extending their work beyond the study of isolated modalities or channels. It should be noted, however, that such multimodality measurement approaches can succeed only to the degree that conceptually and methodologically sound measurements are available for each individual modality. Thus the step toward multimodal analysis of nonverbal behavior is of necessity the end result of careful methodological development in the assessment of vocal and nonvocal nonverbal behavior.

Appendix A. The Process of Voice Production

In order to facilitate understanding of the description of acoustic parameters given in this chapter, this appendix provides a short overview of the basic structures and processes involved in voice production (see Appendix B for

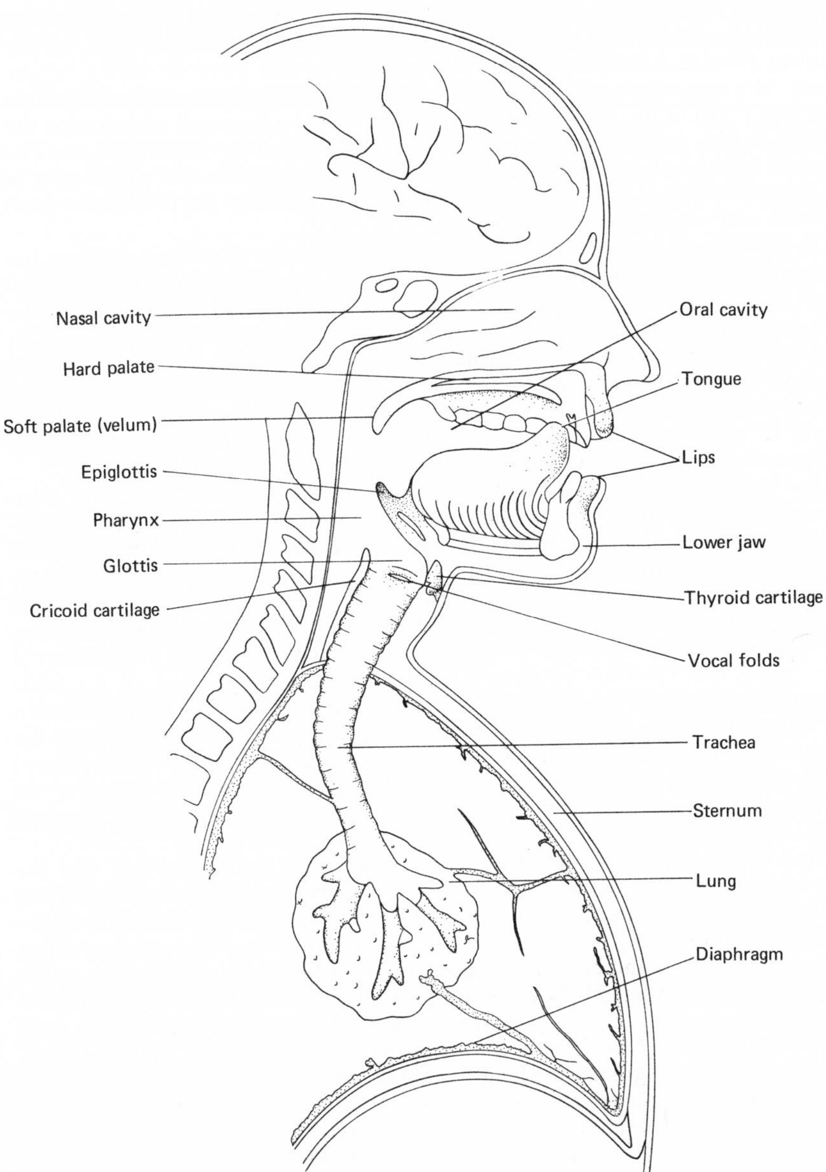

Figure 4.12. Schematic diagram of the human vocal mechanism.

explanation of some of the acoustic concepts used here). For more extensive discussions of this topic the reader is referred to Fant (1960), Flanagan (1965/1972), Lieberman (1977), Minifie, Hixon, and Williams (1973), and Zemlin (1968).

Figure 4.12 shows a schematic diagram of the human vocal tract and the structures involved in phonation and articulation. The basis of all sound making with the human vocal apparatus is air flow through the vocal tract, mostly during exhalation (although sound production is also possible during inhalation). The type of sound depends on whether the air flow passes freely through the lower part of the vocal tract, the opening between the vocal folds (called the *glottis*) in the larynx, or whether the vocal folds impede the flow of air. The former case results in *unvoiced* sound (which characterizes the production of many consonants), the latter case in *voiced* sound (used for the production of all vowels and some consonants).

In the case of unvoiced sounds, in which the air that is pressed up from the lungs passes the glottis freely, air turbulence occurs at the point of major vocal tract constriction (for example, the small mouth opening in the articulation of the consonant [s]). The turbulence constitutes a sound source, producing "noise" in the form of an aperiodic wave form. This sound source sets the air in the vocal tract in vibration, and owing to the specific resonances of the vocal tract for the particular articulatory setting, the flat spectrum of the noise will be filtered and parts of the frequency spectrum will be amplified or attenuated (see the subsequent discussion in this appendix, and also Appendix B).

For voiced sounds, the air pressed up from the lungs is prevented from passing through the glottis because the vocal folds are adducted. This impedance results in an increase in subglottal air pressure. If the subglottal pressure surpasses a certain level, the vocal folds are forced open and a puff of air is released into the supralaryngeal vocal tract, setting the air within it into vibration. The sudden decrease of pressure in the glottis after this release (along with other factors) allows the vocal folds to close again, starting a repetition of the cycle. The vibration produced by the opening and closing of the folds constitutes a periodic sound source with a quasi-triangular wave form, as shown in Figure 4.13. The peak of each triangular pulse represents the point of the greatest opening of the glottis, whereas the intervals between pulses represent periods when the glottis is closed. The periodicity of these glottal pulses, the rate of vibration of the vocal folds, represents the fundamental frequency of the voice (F_0).

This very simplified description may have given the impression that the opening and closing of the folds – and thereby the fundamental frequency of glottal pulses – is determined exclusively by the subglottal pressure. The subglottal pressure is only one factor, however. The human larynx is an exceedingly complex structure, and both the tension and the adduction and abduction of the vocal folds are regulated by a large number of extra- and intralaryngeal muscles, which act in combination to produce a laryngeal setting for voicing. The most important factors are the length, thickness, mass, and tension of the vocal folds. In other words, the greater the length and the tension, and the smaller the mass and thickness, of these ligaments, the faster they open and close and the higher the fundamental frequency will be. The details of the phonation processes (sound production by vocal fold action) and the role of the structures involved, particularly of the various muscles, are not yet completely known (see Broad, 1973; Flanagan, 1965/1972; Harris, 1974; Lieberman, 1974; MacNeilage & Ladefoged, 1976; Sawashima, 1974).

As shown elsewhere (K. R. Scherer, 1979a), the laryngeal setting in phonation is likely to be strongly affected by emotional arousal. The effects of psychological factors on the larynx are demonstrated by the rather frequent psychogenic voice pathologies involving phonation problems (see Greene, 1964/1972; Moses, 1954; Perkins, 1971). K. R. Scherer (1979a) has hypothesized that higher muscle

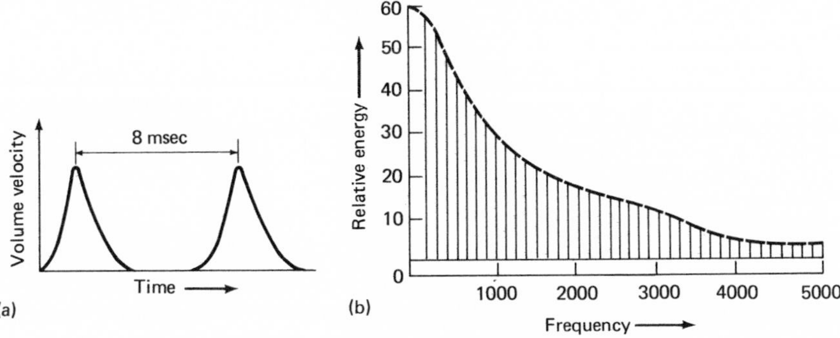

Figure 4.13. Wave form produced by the opening and closing of the vocal folds and the resulting spectrum: (a) time signal of wave form; (b) spectrum.

tension during psychological arousal could change the laryngeal setting so as to produce glottal pulses with higher fundamental frequency.

In addition, the shape of the triangular glottal wave form may be affected by these factors. Depending on the muscular forces that act on the vocal folds, the glottal pulse reflecting the nature of the opening and closing phases could differ quite strongly. For example, if the vocal folds are very tense and strongly compressed, the opening and closing phases might be more explosive, causing steeper onset and termination gradients in the triangular glottal pulse wave form.

The glottal pulses pass through the *acoustical filter* of the vocal tract. This process is shown in Figure 4.14, which illustrates the *source-filter theory* of speech production accepted by most speech scientists today. As a result of the glottal pulse's passage through the transfer function of the vocal tract, some of the harmonics in the spectrum of the pulse are amplified and others are attenuated. Both effects depend on the resonance characteristics of the specific articulatory setting in the vocal tract. Wave form 4.14c shows the result of this filtering process in the time domain, and wave form 4.14f its equivalent in the frequency domain. It is this type of wave form, radiating at the mouth of the speaker (and its spectrum), that serves as the basis for the objective measurement of acoustic criteria.

Thus a speech wave form (and its spectrum) combines two quite different independent sources of influence: the glottal wave or pulse (determined by the subglottal pressure and the laryngeal setting) and the vocal tract resonance characteristics (transfer or filter function, mainly determined by the supralaryngeal articulatory setting). Although it will be methodologically difficult, an attempt should be made to differentiate acoustic parameters according to the factor that primarily determines them, the glottal source or the vocal tract shape (see J. D. Markel & Gray, 1976), because it is possible that the laryngeal setting and the vocal tract shape are differentially affected by psychological factors.

It should be pointed out that the preceding discussion of the processes of voice production is rather simplified and that many factors have not even been mentioned. This is also true for the determinants of the acoustic speech wave form and its spectrum. For example, the effects of the impedance of the vocal

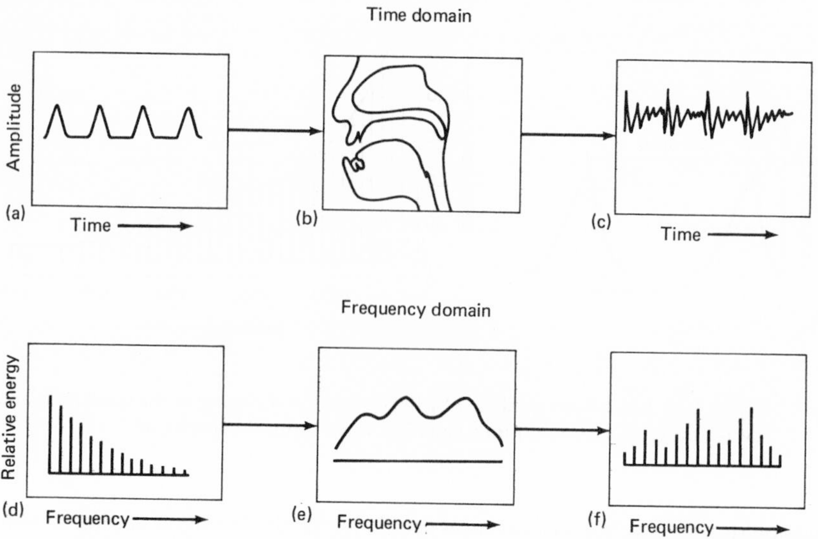

Figure 4.14. Source-filter model of speech production: (a) glottal wave; (b) vocal tract shape; (c) radiated sound wave; (d) glottal spectrum; (e) vocal tract transfer function; (f) acoustic spectrum at mouth opening. *Source:* Adapted from Fant, 1960

tract walls, of friction, and of radiation loss have not been discussed, nor have phase relationships between the components of the complex wave form (see Flanagan, 1965/1972; J. D. Markel & Gray, 1976). However, there seems to be consensus that the glottal excitation and the vocal tract resonance characteristics are by far the most important determinants of the acoustic characteristics of the speech wave form.

Appendix B. A short introduction to speech acoustics

Audible speech, like any other sound, consists of sound waves. In order to understand the rationale for the extraction of various acoustic parameters from these sound waves, one must have a basic understanding of some of the fundamental properties of wave forms. In this appendix some basic notions in acoustics are introduced. For a more detailed treatment of this material the reader is referred to Denes and Pinson (1963/1972), Fry (1979), Ladefoged (1962), or Small (1973a).

The simplest case of a sound wave form is the sinusoidal wave form shown in Figure 4.15a. As most readers will remember from their physics courses, this graph maps the periodic variation of air pressure over time that has been produced by a vibrating sound source, such as a tuning fork. Figure 4.15a displays the sound wave in the time and amplitude dimensions. (Because

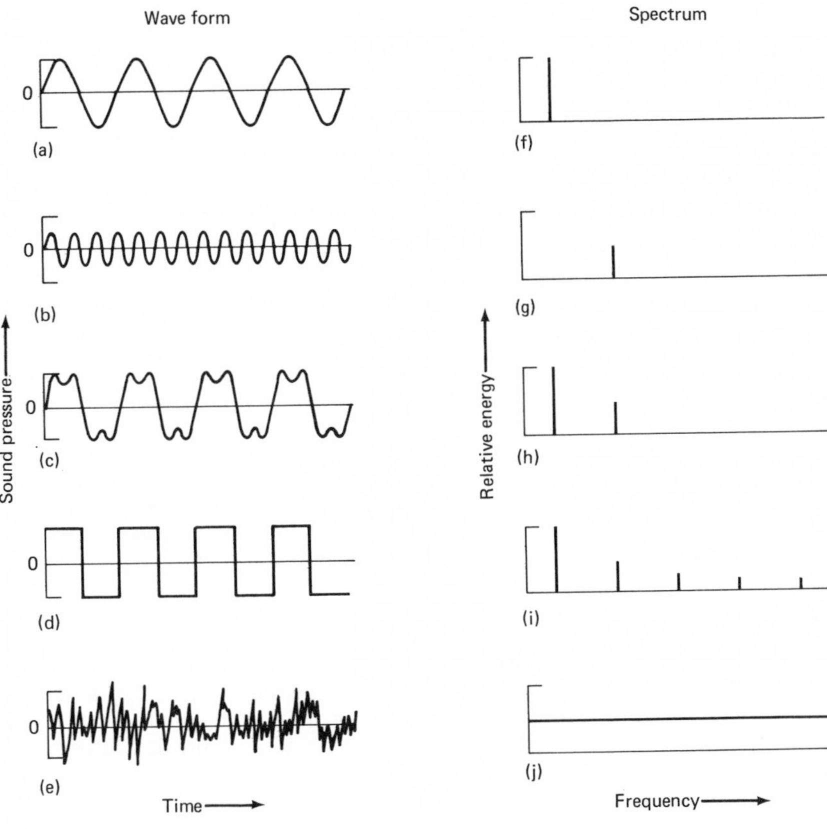

Figure 4.15. Wave forms and their spectra: (a, f) low-frequency sine wave; (b, g) high-frequency sine wave; (c, h) complex waveform, composite of (a, f) and (b, g); (d,i) square wave; (e, j) noise.

amplitude is always one of the terms used in displaying properties of wave forms, we will call this type of description *display in the time domain.*) Sinusoidal wave forms change in a regular, periodic fashion, going through complete cycles, as shown in Figure 4.15. The number of cycles per second indicates the periodicity or frequency of the wave measured in Hertz (Hz). The wave form can also be represented as a frequency, (displayed in an amplitude-by-frequency plot). This display, which is called the *spectrum* of the wave, shows the amplitude of the wave form at its frequency in the frequency range, as shown in Figure 4.15f.

Most sound waves are much more complex than the simple sinusoid in Figure 4.15, but as the French mathematician Fourier has shown, it is possible to decompose any complex wave to sinusoid components (via Fourier analysis). Every periodic complex wave consists of combinations of many simple sinusoid wave forms with different frequencies. In the example shown in Figure 4.15, the complex wave (c) consists of the sinusoidal components (a) and (b), which differ in periodicity or frequency. Consequently, the spectrum of the complex wave (c) shows the amplitude for the two sinusoidal components at their respective frequencies.

As shown in Figure 4.15, the periodicity of the complex wave is determined by the sinusoidal component with the lowest frequency. This component wave form determines how many cycles per second appear in the complex wave form. Therefore the frequency of the lowest sinusoidal component of a complex wave is called fundamental frequency, or F_0.

In Fourier analysis, complex waves are decomposed into constituent sinusoids with frequencies that are integral multiples of the fundamental frequency. For example, a complex wave with $F_0 = 100$ might be decomposed into constituent sinusoids with frequencies of 300, 500, 700, and so on. These frequencies, called *harmonics*, represent energy concentrations in the frequency domain, as shown in the spectrum of the complex wave form (see Figure 4.15h). Figure 4.15 presents three types of complex wave forms (Figure 4.15c, d, e) with the corresponding spectra showing the harmonic structure (Figure 4.15h, i, j). Whether harmonics are odd or even multiples or both depends on the type of complex wave form. Similarly, the decrease of the amplitude in the higher harmonics as one goes up in the frequency range depends on the nature of the complex wave form (or conversely, the complex wave form is determined by the frequency and amplitude of the higher harmonics).

We can now consider a typical speech wave form. Figure 4.4b showed the wave form (or"time signal") for the word *she*. Clearly, this wave form is not uniform throughout. The first part looks like wave form 4.15e; it is nonperiodic; whereas the second part of the wave form is periodic, as in Figure 4.15c. However, the wave form in Figure 4.4b is not quite comparable to those in Figure 4.15, because the Figure 4.4b wave is the result of acoustical filtering by the human vocal tract.

Acoustic tubes such as the vocal tract have the attribute of amplifying specific frequencies in the source spectrum (i.e., the spectrum of the wave form produced by the excitation source). Because the resonance characteristics of an acoustical tube determine which frequencies of the source spectrum are boosted and which are attenuated, and because the tube passes (and amplifies) some and retains (by attenuation) other frequencies, it is called an acoustical filter. These resonance characteristics of an acoustical filter are called *transfer function* (see Appendix A). Figure 4.16 shows the resonant frequencies of a uniform acoustic tube 17 cm in length and 4 cm in diameter. The resonance characteristics of this tube are described by those parts of the frequency range for which the spectral energy of the incoming wave form is amplified. These resonant frequencies, which show up as peaks in the spectrum of the filtered wave form, are called *formants* and numbered from lowest to highest (from 1 upward, often symbolized F1, F2, etc.). If wave form (a) in Figure 4.13 were to be filtered by the transfer function for this tube, the spectrum of the resulting wave form would look like the display in Figure 4.16b. This particular tube is an idealized model of the vocal tract of an adult male speaker that is useful for theoretical purposes. In reality, the vocal tract shape is much more complex, and – most importantly – it changes shape continuously in the process of articulation. Figure 4.16c shows the formant structure of wave form 4.13a as filtered by a real human vocal tract; in this case the vocal tract is shaped for the articulation of a wide-open vowel [æ], as in the word *had*.

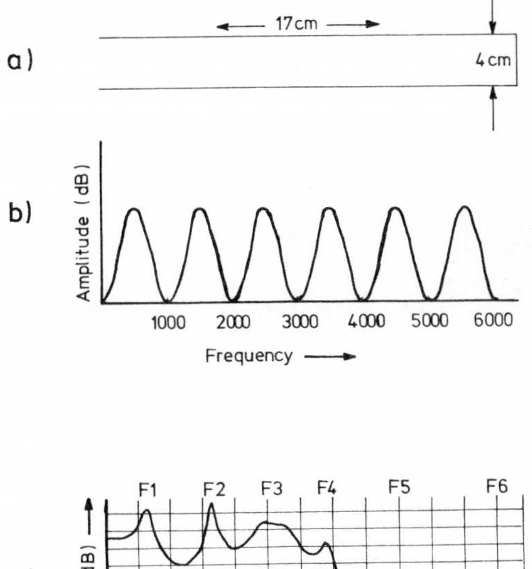

Figure 4.16. Comparison of resonance characteristics by location of formants (F1–F5): (a) uniform acoustical tube; (b) natural resonance characteristics of (a); (c) human vocal tract resonance characteristics.

Appendix C. Measurement Procedures and Equipment

The concepts and study methods needed for the analysis of sounds come from a number of disciplines, such as acoustics, mathematics, physiology, phonetics, and electrical engineering. In spite of advances in those disciplines in the first part of the century, it is the telephone that has had the biggest impact on the development of appropriate methods for the objective analysis of vocal sounds. In the interest of limiting precious channel capacity in telephone lines, electrical engineers have attempted to isolate those parts of the speech signal required for the intelligibility of speech. One of the essential advances in this effort has been the development of equipment to make speech visible, the sound spectrograph or sonagraph (see the discussion later in this appendix; see also Potter, Kopp, & Green, 1947), which has been frequently used in speech research. Many other methods are available today, however. In this section some of the options available for objective acoustic analysis will be reviewed briefly.

The most convenient procedure for acoustic analysis is the recording of some kind of vocalization sample onto magnetic tape and the application of acoustical analysis to the speech wave forms stored on the tape. However, fairly high recording quality is required for this analysis. Wallbott (Technical Appendix)

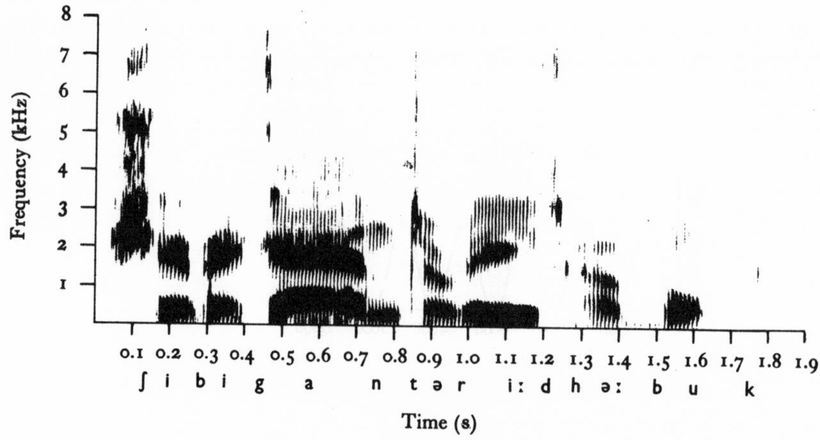

Figure 4.17. Spectrogram of "She began to read her book." *Source*: Fry, 1979

provides an overview of the prerequisites and procedures for high-quality audio recording.

For measurements in the time domain, that is, direct measurements on the time signal, it may be sufficient to display the speech wave form on a storage oscillograph (possibly taking a photograph of the display). Obviously, this is a very time-consuming procedure because only very short portions of the acoustic wave form can be examined at a time. It is much more convenient to use FM tape recorders, if they are available, or to play back speech samples at lower speed and to use a paper tape recorder to plot the speech wave form. Measurements of speech intensity are also fairly straightforward, because simple electroacoustic equipment can be used to measure changes in the power of the recorded signal. As with the speech wave form, it is convenient to plot the intensity continuously on graph paper to have a permanent record.

A large number of devices are available for obtaining the spectrum of a speech or vocalization wave form. Unfortunately, most of these are quite expensive and difficult to use without lengthy prior experience. The oldest and most established device is the sound spectrograph, which produces three-dimensional representations of speech spectra, with frequency plotted on the vertical axis and time on the horizontal axis, and amplitude represented by the degree to which the paper or a videoscreen is darkened (Agnello, 1975; Lieberman, 1977, pp. 46–67). Figure 4.17 shows a spectrogram of a short utterance.

Filter banks and real-time spectrum analyzers measure the energy of the signal in particular frequency bands, thus providing spectra of sounds in real time. Most modern spectrum analyzers offer the option of storing the spectral values on some kind of storage medium for further analysis. There are also some commercially available devices for F_0 extraction.

By far the most flexible and at the same time most expensive and demanding analysis is speech analysis via digital computer (see Wakita, 1976). Generally, small laboratory computers (such as the PDP 11) with analog-to-digital (A/D) and digital-to-analog (D/A) conversion periphery are used for such analyses. It is also possible to analyze digitized speech on large high-speed computers in university computing centers if the appropriate software is available. It is to be expected that such analyses will be greatly facilitated by technological advances in the years to come and by the increasing availability of appropriate software (see J. D. Markel & Gray, 1976; Digital Signal Processing Committee IEEE, 1979; for sample programs).

However, even if digital speech-analysis techniques become more readily available, researchers will still have to be very careful to select the proper analysis conditions and to detect artifacts, which can occur very easily. Consequently, researchers should be warned about using highly sophisticated techniques without satisfactory knowledge of the acoustics of speech and the specific bases of the analysis programs employed. In addition, the difficulties inherent in preparing speech samples in appropriate form for analysis and in the statistical treatment of the data obtained by digital analysis should not be underestimated.

Acknowledgments

Much of the work of the Giessen research group reported in this chapter has been done by Hede Helfrich, Ursula Scherer, Reiner Standke, Frank Tolkmitt, and Harald Wallbott. These people have also provided helpful comments and support for the preparation of the chapter. I gratefully acknowledge comments by Paul Ekman, Stanley Feldstein, Robert Rosenthal, and an anonymous reviewer, while assuming full responsibility for any shortcomings that remain despite the excellent advice.

Notes

1. In this chapter no attempt is made to define terms such as *paralinguistic, extralinguistic, nonlinguistic, nonverbal, paraverbal,* or *prosodic,* or to propose a solution to the inconsistent use of this terminology in the literature. For such attempts, the reader is referred to Crystal (1969), Key (1977), Laver & Hutcheson (1972), and Poyatos (1976). The term *vocal behavior* is used for phenomena produced by the vocal apparatus of a speaker and received by the auditory sense organs of a hearer. The term *vocalization* is used for such phenomena, whether voiced or unvoiced sounds are produced. The *linguisticity* or *verbality* of such phenomena, i.e., the degree to which they are seen as part of the language code, is difficult to determine as long as there is no consensus about the exact nature and the boundaries of this code, even within the field of linguistics.
2. Their *switching pause* is termed *latency* in interview studies, in which one speaker's utterances are always questions and the latency of the answer, i.e., the silent period from the end of the question until the onset of the answer, reflects a reaction time.
3. The relationships among amplitude, pressure, power, energy, and intensity, as well as loudness, are too complex to be discussed here. The reader is referred to Small (1973a, pp. 21–26, 1973b, pp. 381–385) for a detailed discussion. The terms are used somewhat loosely in this chapter to avoid cumbersome technical detail. Similarly, the relationship of sound pressure to electroacoustic measures cannot be treated in detail.

References

Abbs, J. H., & Watkin, K. L. Instrumentation for the study of speech physiology. In N. J. Lass (Ed.), *Contemporary issues in experimental phonetics*. New York: Academic Press, 1976.

Agnello, J. G. Measurements and analysis of visible speech. In S. Singh (Ed.), *Measurement procedures in speech, hearing, and language*. Baltimore: University Park Press, 1975.

Apple, W., Streeter, L. A., & Krauss, R. M. Effects of pitch and speech rate on personal attributions. *Journal of Personality and Social Psychology*, 1979, *37*(5), 715–727.

Argyle, M., Alkema, F., & Gilmour, R. The communication of friendly and hostile attitudes by verbal and non-verbal signals. *European Journal of Social Psychology*, 1971, *1*, 385–402.

Boomer, D. S. The phonemic clause: Speech unit in human communication. In A. W. Siegman & S. Feldstein (Eds.), *Nonverbal behavior and communication*. New York: Wiley, 1978.

Bricker, P. D., & Pruzansky, S. The validation of automatic methods for measuring conversational speech activity. *Behavior Research Methods and Instrumentation*, 1980, *12*, 499–508.

Broad, D. J. Phonation. In F. D. Minifie, T. J. Hixon, & F. Williams (Eds.), *Normal aspects of speech, hearing, and language*. Englewood Cliffs, N.J.: Prentice-Hall, 1973.

Brown, B. L., Strong, W. J., & Rencher, A. C. Acoustic determinants of perceptions of personality from speech. *International Journal of the Sociology of Language*, 1975, *6*, 11–32.

Brown, P., & Fraser, C. Speech as a marker of situation. In K. R. Scherer & H. Giles (Eds.), *Social markers in speech*. Cambridge: Cambridge University Press, 1979.

Brown, P., & Levinson, S. Social structure, groups and interaction. In K. R. Scherer & H. Giles (Eds.), *Social markers in speech*. Cambridge: Cambridge University Press, 1979.

Brunswik, E. *Perception and the representative design of psychological experiments*. Berkeley & Los Angeles: University of California Press, 1956.

Bugental, D., Kaswan, J., & Love, L. Perception of contradictory meanings conveyed by verbal and nonverbal channels. *Journal of Personality and Social Psychology*, 1970, *16*, 647–655.

Butcher, A. R. Pause and syntactic structure. *Arbeitsberichte des Instituts für Phonetik an der Universität Kiel*, 1979, *12*, 293–301.

Chapple, E. D. The interaction chronograph: Its evolution and present application. *Personnel*, 1948, *25*, 295–307.

Condon, W. S., & Ogston, W. D. Soundfilm analysis of normal and pathological behavior patterns. *Journal of Nervous and Mental Disease*, 1966, *143*, 338–347.

Crystal, D. *Prosodic systems and intonation in English*. Cambridge: Cambridge University Press, 1969.

Crystal, D. *The English tone of the voice*. London: Arnold, 1975.

Crystal, D., & Quirk, R. *Systems of prosodic and paralinguistic features in English*. The Hague: Mouton, 1964.

Darwin, C. *The expression of the emotions in man and animals*. London: John Murray, 1872.

Darwin, C. J. The perception of speech. In E. C. Carterette & M. P. Friedman (Eds.), *Handbook of perception*. Vol. 7: *Language and speech*. New York: Academic Press, 1976.

Davis, S. B. Acoustic characteristics of normal and pathological voices. In N. Lass (Ed.), *Speech and language: Advances in basic research and practice* (Vol. 1). New York: Academic Press, 1979.

Davitz, J. R. A review of research concerned with facial and vocal expressions of emotion. In J. R. Davitz (Ed.), *The communication of emotional meaning*. New York: McGraw-Hill, 1964.

Denes, P. B., & Pinson, E. N. *The speech chain: The physics and biology of spoken language*. Garden City, N.Y.: Doubleday, Anchor Press, 1972. (1st ed., 1963.)

Digital Signal Processing Committee IEEE (Ed.). *Programs for digital signal processing*. New York: IEEE Press, 1979.

Dittman, A. T., & Llewellyn, L. G. The phonemic clause as a unit of speech decoding. *Journal of Personality and Social Psychology*, 1967, *6*, 341–349.

Dittman, A. T. & Wynne, L. C. Linguistic techniques and the analysis of emotionality of interviews. *Journal of Abnormal and Social Psychology*, 1961, *63*, 201–204.

Duncan, S. D., Jr. Some signals and rules for taking speaking turns in conversations. *Journal of Personality and Social Psychology*, 1972, *23*, 283–292.

Duncan, S. D., Jr. Toward a grammar for dyadic conversations. *Semiotica*, 1973, *9*, 29–46.

Duncan, S. D., Jr., Rice, L. N., & Butler, J. M. Therapists' paralanguage in peak and poor psychotherapy hours. *Journal of Abnormal Psychology*, 1968, *73*, 566–570.

Duncan, S. D., Jr., & Rosenthal, R. Vocal emphasis in experimenters' instruction reading as unintended determinant of subjects' responses. *Language and Speech*, 1968, *11*, 20–26.

Ekman, P. Differential communication of affect by head and body cues. *Journal of Personality and Social Psychology*, 1965, *2*, 726–735.

Ekman, P. (Ed.). *Darwin and facial expression: A century of research in review*. New York: Academic Press, 1973.

Ekman, P., & Friesen, W. V. Hand movements. *Journal of Communication*, 1972, *22*, 353–374.

Ekman, P., & Friesen, W. V. Detecting deception from the body or face. *Journal of Personality and Social Psychology*, 1974, *29*, 288–298.

Ekman, P., Friesen, W. V., O'Sullivan, M., & Scherer, K. R. Relative importance of face, body and speech in judgments of personality and affect. *Journal of Personality and Social Psychology*, 1980, *38*, 270–277.

Fagen, R. M., & Young, D. Y. Temporal patterns of behavior: Durations, intervals, latencies, and sequences. In P. W. Colgan (Ed.), *Quantitative ethology*. New York: Wiley, 1978.

Fant, G. *Acoustic theory of speech production*. The Hague: Mouton, 1960.

Feldstein, S., & Welkowitz, J. A chronography of conversation: In defense of an objective approach. In A. W. Siegman & S. Feldstein (Eds.), *Nonverbal behavior and communication*. Hillsdale, N.J.: Erlbaum, 1978.

Flanagan, J. L. *Speech analysis, synthesis and perception* (2nd ed.). New York: Springer, 1972. (1st ed., 1965.)

Friedhoff, A. J., Alpert, M., & Kurtzberg, R. L. An electro-acoustic analysis of the effects of stress on voice. *Journal of Neuropsychiatry*, 1964, *5*, 266–272.

Frøkjaer-Jensen, B., & Prytz, S. Registration of voice quality. *Bruel and Kjaer Technical Review*, 1976, *3*, 3–17.

Fry, D. B. *The physics of speech*. Cambridge: Cambridge University Press, 1979.

Giles, H. Ethnicity markers in speech. In K. R. Scherer & H. Giles (Eds.), *Social markers in speech*. Cambridge: Cambridge University Press, 1979.

Giles, H., Scherer, K. R., & Taylor, D. M. Speech markers in social interaction. In K. R. Scherer & H. Giles (Eds.), *Social markers in speech*. Cambridge: Cambridge University Press, 1979.

Goldman-Eisler, F. *Psycholinguistics: experiments in spontaneous speech*. New York: Academic Press, 1968.

Goldstein, U. G. Speaker-identifying features based on formant tracks. *Journal of the Acoustical Society of America*, 1976, *59*, 176–182.

Gottschalk, L. A., & Gleser, G. C. *The measurement of psychological states through the content analysis of verbal behavior*. Berkeley & Los Angeles: University of California Press, 1969.

Greene, M. C. L. *The voice and its disorders*. New York: Pitman, 1972. (1st ed., 1964.)

Hargreaves, W. A., & Starkweather, J. A. Voice quality changes in depression. *Language and Speech*, 1964, *7*, 84–88.

Harper, R. G., Wiens, A. N., & Matarazzo, J. D. *Nonverbal communication: The state of the art*. New York: Wiley, 1978.

Harris, K. S. Physiological aspects of articulatory behavior. In T. A. Sebeok (Ed.), *Current trends in linguistics*. Vol. 12: *Linguistics and adjacent arts and sciences*. The Hague: Mouton, 1974.

Hecker, M. H. L., Stevens, K. N., von Bismarck, G., & Williams, C. E. Manifestations of task-induced stress in the acoustic speech signal. *Journal of the Acoustical Society of America*, 1968, *44*, 993–1001.

Helfrich, H. Age markers in speech. In K. R. Scherer & H. Giles (Eds.), *Social markers in speech*. Cambridge: Cambridge University Press, 1979.

Hockett, C. F. Logical considerations in the study of animal communication. In W. E. Lanyon & W. N. Tavolga (Eds.), *Animal sounds and communication*. Washington, D.C.: American Institute of Biological Sciences, 1960.

Jaffe, J., & Feldstein, S. Stochastic models of the time patterns of dialogue, *Rhythms of dialogue*. New York: Academic Press, 1970.

Kendon, A. Movement coordination in social interaction: Some examples described. *Acta Psychologica*, 1970, *32*, 100–125.

Key, M. R. *Nonverbal communication: A research guide and bibliography*. Metuchen, N.J.: Scarecrow Press, 1977.

Kramer, E. Judgment of personal characteristics and emotions from nonverbal properties. *Psychological Bulletin*, 1963, *60*, 408–420.

Ladefoged, P. *Elements of acoustic phonetics*. Chicago: University of Chicago Press, 1962.

Laver, J. *Individual features in voice quality*. Unpublished doctoral dissertation, University of Edinburgh, 1975.

Laver, J. *The phonetic description of voice quality*. Cambridge: Cambridge University Press, 1980.

Laver, J., & Hanson, R. Describing the normal voice. In J. Darby (Ed.), *Speech evaluation in psychiatry*. New York: Grune & Stratton, 1981.

Laver, J., & Hutcheson, S. (Eds.). *Communication in face to face interaction*. Harmondsworth: Penguin, 1972.

Lehiste, I. (Ed.). *Suprasegmentals*. Cambridge, Mass.: MIT Press, 1970.

Liberman, A. M., Cooper, F. S., Shankweiler, D. P., & Studdert-Kennedy, M. The perception of the speech code. *Psychological Review*, 1967, *74*, 431–461.

Liberman, M. V. *The intonational system of English*. Bloomington: Indiana University Linguistics Club, 1978.

Lieberman, P. On the acoustic basis of the perception of intonation by linguists. *Word*, 1965, *21*, 40–54.

Lieberman, P. A study of prosodic features. In T. A. Sebeok (Ed.), *Current trends in linguistics*. Vol. 12: *Linguistics and adjacent arts and sciences*. The Hague: Mouton, 1974.

Lieberman, P. *Speech physiology and acoustic phonetics: An introduction*. New York: Macmillan, 1977.

Lieberman, P., & Michaels, S. B. Some aspects of fundamental frequency and envelope amplitudes as related to the emotional content of speech. *Journal of the Acoustical Society of America*, 1962, *34*, 922–927.

MacNeilage, P., & Ladefoged, P. The production of speech and language. In E. C. Carterette & M. P. Friedman (Eds.), *Handbook of perception*. Vol. 7: *Language and speech*. New York: Academic Press, 1976.

Mahl, G. F., & Schulze, G. Psychological research in the extralinguistic area. In T. Sebeok, A. S. Hayes, & M. C. Bateson (Eds.), *Approaches to semiotics*. The Hague: Mouton, 1964.

Malecot, A. Cross-language phonetics. In T. A. Sebeok (Ed.), *Current trends in linguistics*. The Hague: Mouton, 1974.

Markel, J. D., & Gray, A. H. T. *Linear prediction of speech*. New York: Springer-Verlag, 1976.

Markel, N. N., Meisels, M., & Houck, J. E. Judging personality from voice quality. *Journal of Abnormal and Social Psychology*, 1964, *69*, 458–463.

Marler, P. R., & Hamilton, W. J. *Mechanisms of animal behaviour. New York: Wiley*, 1966.

Matarazzo, J. D., & Wiens, A. N. *The interview: Research on its anatomy and structure*. Chicago: Aldine-Atherton, 1972.

Matarazzo, J. D., Wiens, A. N., & Saslow, G. Studies in interview speech behavior. In L. Krasner & L. P. Ullmann (Eds.), *Research in behavior modification*. New York: Holt, Rinehart & Winston, 1965.

Mehrabian, A., & Ferris, S. R. Inference of attitudes from nonverbal communication in two channels. *Journal of Consulting Psychology*, 1967, *31*, 248–252.

Meltzer, L., Morris, W. N., & Hayes, D. P. Interruption outcomes and vocal amplitude: Explorations in social psychophysics. *Journal of Personality and Social Psychology*, 1971, *18*, 392–402.

Minifie, F. D. Speech acoustics. In F. D. Minifie, T. J. Hixon, & F. Williams (Eds.), *Normal aspects of speech, hearing, and language*. Englewood Cliffs, N.J.: Prentice-Hall, 1973.

Minifie, F. D., Hixon, T. J., & Williams, R. (Eds.). *Normal aspects of speech, hearing and language*. Englewood Cliffs, N.J.: Prentice Hall, 1973.

Morley, I., & Stephenson, G. *The social psychology of bargaining*. London: George Allen & Unwin, 1977.

Moses, P. *The voice of neurosis*. New York: Grune & Stratton, 1954.

Murray, D. C. Talk, silence, and anxiety. *Psychological Bulletin*, 1971, *75*, 244–260.

Natale, M. Convergence of mean vocal intensity in dyadic communication as a function of social desirability. *Journal of Personality and Social Psychology*, 1975, *32*, 790–804.

Ostwald, P. *Soundmaking: The acoustic communication of emotion*. Springfield, Ill.: Charles C. Thomas, 1963.

Ostwald, P. *The semiotics of human sound*. The Hague: Mouton, 1973.

Perkins, W. H. *Speech pathology*. St. Louis: C. V. Mosby, 1971.

Potter, R. K., Kopp, G. A., & Green, H. C. *Visible speech*. New York: Van Nostrand, 1947.

Poyatos, F. *Man beyond words: Theory and methodology of nonverbal communication*. New York: New York State English Council, 1976.

Robinson, W. P. Speech markers and social class. In K. R. Scherer & H. Giles (Eds.), *Social markers in speech*. Cambridge: Cambridge University Press, 1979.

Rochester, S. R. The significance of pauses in spontaneous speech. *Journal of Psycholinguistic Research*, 1973, *2*, 51–81.

Roessler, R., & Lester, J. W. Vocal patterns in anxiety. In W. E. Fann, A. D.

Pokorny, I. Koracau, & R. L. Williams (Eds.), *Phenomenology and treatment of anxiety*. New York: Spectrum, 1979.

Rogers, P. L., Scherer, K. R., & Rosenthal, R. Content-filtering human speech: A simple electronic system. *Behavioral Research Methods and Instrumentation*, 1971, *3*, 16–18.

Rosenfeld, H. M. Whither interactional synchrony? In K. Bloom (Ed.), *Prospective issues in infant research*. Hillsdale, N.J.: Erlbaum, 1980.

Rosenthal, R. *Experimenter effects in behavioral research* (enlarged ed.). New York: Irvington, 1976. (Originally published, New York: Appleton-Century-Crofts, 1966.)

Sandell, R. *Linguistic style and persuasion*. London: Academic Press, 1977.

Sawashima, M. Laryngeal research in experimental phonetics. In T. A. Sebeok (Ed.), *Current trends in linguistics*. Vol. 12: *Linguistics and adjacent arts and sciences*. The Hague: Mouton, 1974.

Scherer, K. R. *Attribution of personality from voice: A cross-cultural study on dynamics of interpersonal perception*. Unpublished doctoral dissertation, Harvard University, 1970.

Scherer, K. R. Randomized splicing: A note on a simple technique for masking speech content. *Journal of Experimental Research in Personality*, 1971, *5*, 155–159.

Scherer, K. R. Judging personality from voice: A cross-cultural approach to an old issue in interpersonal perception. *Journal of Personality*, 1972, *40*, 191–210.

Scherer, K. R. Persönlichkeit, Stimmqualität und Persönlichkeitsattribution: Pfadanalytische Untersuchungen zu nonverbalen Kommunikationsprozessen. In L. H. Eckensberger & U. S. Eckensberger (Eds.), *Bericht über den 28. Kongress der Deutschen Gesellschaft für Psychologie* (Vol. 3). Göttingen: Hogrefe, 1974. (a)

Scherer, K. R. Voice quality analysis of American and German speakers. *Journal of Psycholinguistic Research*, 1974, *3*, 281–290. (b)

Scherer, K. R. Acoustic concomitants of emotional dimensions: Judging affect from synthesized tone sequences. In S. Weitz (Ed.), *Nonverbal communication*. New York: Oxford University Press, 1974. (c)

Scherer, K. R. Affektlaute und vokale Embleme. In R. Posner & H. P. Reinecke (Eds.), *Zeichenprozesse – Semiotische Forschung in den Einzelwissenschaften*. Wiesbaden: Athenaion, 1977. (a)

Scherer, K. R. Die Funktionen des nonverbalen Verhaltens im Gespräch. In D. Wegner (Ed.), *Gesprächsanalyse*. Hamburg: Buske, 1977. (b) (Reprinted in K. R. Scherer & H. G. Wallbott (Eds.), *Nonverbale Kommunikation*. Weinheim & Basel: Beltz, 1979.)

Scherer, K. R. Kommunikation. In T. Herrmann, P. R. Hofstätter, H. P. Huber, & F. E. Weinert (Eds.), *Handbuch psychologischer Grundbegriffe*. München: Kösel, 1977. (c) (Reprinted in K. R. Scherer & H. G. Wallbott (Eds.), *Nonverbale Kommunikation*. Weinheim & Basel: Beltz, 1979.)

Scherer, K. R. Inference rules in personality attribution from voice quality: The loud voice of extraversion. *European Journal of Social Psychology*, 1978, *8*, 467–487.

Scherer, K. R. Nonlinguistic vocal indicators of emotion and psychopathology. In C. E. Izard (Ed.), *Emotions in personality and psychopathology*. New York: Plenum, 1979. (a)

Scherer, K. R. Personality markers in speech. In K. R. Scherer & H. Giles (Eds.), *Social markers in speech*. Cambridge: Cambridge University Press, 1979. (b)

Scherer, K. R. Voice and speech correlates of perceived social influence. In H. Giles & R. St. Clair (Eds.), *The social psychology of language*. London: Blackwell, 1979. (c)

Scherer, K. R. The functions of nonverbal signs in conversation. In R. St. Clair & H. Giles (Eds.), *The social and psychological contexts of language*. Hillsdale, N.J.: Erlbaum, 1980.

Scherer, K. R. Speech and emotional states. In J. Darby (Ed.), *The evaluation of speech in psychiatry*. New York: Grune & Stratton, 1981. (a)

Scherer, K. R. Vocal indicators of stress. In J. Darby (Ed.), *Speech evaluation in psychiatry*. New York: Grune & Stratton, 1981. (b)

Scherer, K. R. & Giles, H. (Eds.). *Social markers in speech*. Cambridge: Cambridge University Press, 1979.

Scherer, K. R., Koivumaki, J., & Rosenthal, R. Minimal cues in the vocal communication of affect: Judging emotions from content-masked speech. *Journal of Psycholinguistic Research*, 1972, *1*, 269–285.

Scherer, K. R., London, H., & Wolf, J. The voice of confidence: Paralinguistic cues and audience evaluation. *Journal of Research in Personality*, 1973, *7*, 31–44.

Scherer, K. R., & Oshinsky, J. S. Cue utilization in emotion attribution from auditory stimuli. *Motivation and Emotion*, 1977, *1*, 331–346.

Scherer, K. R., Scherer, U., Rosenthal, R., & Hall, J. A. Differential attribution of personality based on multichannel presentation of verbal and nonverbal cues. *Psychological Research*, 1977, *39*, 221–247.

Scherer, K. R., & Tolkmitt, F. The effect of stress and task variation on formant location. *Journal of the Acoustical Society of America* (Suppl. 1), 1979, *66*, 512. (Abstract)

Scherer, K. R., Wallbott, H. G., & Scherer, U. Methoden zur Klassifikation von Bewegungsverhalten: Ein funktionaler Ansatz. *Zeitschrift für Semiotik*, 1979, *1*, 187–202.

Scherer, U., & Scherer, K. R. Psychological factors in bureaucratic encounters: Determinants and effects of interactions between officials and clients. In W. T. Singleton, P. Spurgeon, & R. B. Stammers (Eds.), *The analysis of social skill*. New York: Plenum, 1980.

Sebeok, T. A. (Ed.). *Animal communication: Techniques of study and results of research*. Bloomington: Indiana University Press, 1968.

Sebeok. T. A. (Ed.). *How animals communicate*. Bloomington: Indiana University Press, 1977.

Shoup, J., & Pfeifer, L. L. Acoustic characteristics of speech sounds. In N. J. Lass (Ed.), *Contemporary issues in experimental phonetics*. New York: Academic Press, 1976.

Siegman, A. W. The telltale voice: Nonverbal messages of verbal communication. In A. W. Siegman & S. Feldstein (Eds.), *Nonverbal behavior and communication*. Hillsdale, N.J.: Erlbaum, 1978.

Siegman, A. W. The voice of attraction: Vocal correlates of interpersonal attraction in the interview. In A. W. Siegman & S. Feldstein (Eds.), *Of speech and time*. Hillsdale, N.J.: Erlbaum, 1979.

Simonov, P. V., & Frolov, M. V. Utilisation of human voice for estimation of man's emotional stress and state of mind. *Aerospace Medicine*, 1973, *44*, 256–258.

Small, A. M. Acoustics. In F. D. Minifie, T. J. Hixon, & F. Williams (Eds.), *Normal aspects of speech, hearing, and language*. Englewood Cliffs, N.J.: Prentice-Hall, 1973. (a)

Small, A. M. Psychoacoustics. In F. D. Minifie, T. J. Hixon, & F. Williams (Eds.),

Normal aspects of speech, hearing, and language. Englewood Cliffs, N.J.: Prentice-Hall, 1973. (b)

Smith, P. M. Sex markers in speech. In K. R. Scherer & H. Giles (Eds.), *Social markers in speech*. Cambridge: Cambridge University Press, 1979.

Smith, W. J. *The behaviour of communicating: The ethological approach*. Cambridge, Mass.: Harvard University Press, 1977.

Soskin, W. F., & Kauffman, P. E. Judgement of emotion in word-free voice samples. *Journal of Communication,* 1961, 11, 73–80.

Stark, R. E., Rose, S. N., & McLagen, M. Features of infant sounds: The first eight weeks of life. *Journal of Child Language*, 1975, *2*, 205–221.

Starkweather, J. A. The communication value of content-free speech. *American Journal of Psychology*, 1956, *69*, 121–123.

Stern, D. N., & Wasserman, G. A. *Intonation contours as units of information in maternal speech to pre-linguistic infants*. Paper presented at the meeting of the Society for Research on Child Development, San Francisco, 1979.

Studdert-Kennedy, M. Speech perception. In N. J. Lass (Ed.), *Contemporary issues in experimental phonetics*. New York: Academic Press, 1976.

Takefuta, Y. Analysis of intonation. In S. Singh (Ed.), *Measurement procedures in speech, hearing, and language*. Baltimore: University Park Press, 1975.

Tolkmitt, F., Helfrich, H., Standke, R., & Scherer, K. R. Vocal indicators of psychiatric treatment effects in depressives and schizophrenics. *Journal of Communication Disorders,* in press.

Tosi, O. *Voice identification: Theory and legal applications*. Baltimore: University Park Press, 1979.

Trager, G. L. Paralanguage: A first approximation. *Studies in Linguistics*, 1958, *13*, 1–12.

Trager, G. L. & Smith, H. L., Jr. *An outline of English structure*. Washington, D.C.: American Council of Learned Societies, 1957. (1st ed., 1951.)

Travis, L. E. (Ed.). *Handbook of speech pathology and audiology*. New York: Appleton-Century-Crofts, 1971.

Uldall, E. Attitudinal meanings conveyed by intonation contours. *Language and Speech*, 1960, *3*, 223–234.

Uldall, E. Dimensions of meaning in intonation. In D. Abercrombie et al. (Eds.), *In honour of Daniel Jones*. London: Longman, 1964. (Reprinted in D. Bolinger (Ed.), *Intonation: Selected readings*. Harmondsworth: Penguin, 1972.)

Wakita, H. Instrumentation for the study of speech acoustics. In N. J. Lass (Ed.), *Contemporary issues in experimental phonetics*. New York: Academic Press, 1976.

Wallbott, H. G., Scherer, K. R., & Scherer, U. *Analysemethoden nonverbalen Verhaltens*. Manuscript in preparation, University of Giessen.

Williams, C. E., & Stevens, K. N. Emotions and speech: Some acoustical correlates. *Journal of the Acoustical Society of America*, 1972, *52*, 1238–1250.

Williams, C. E., & Stevens, K. N. Vocal correlates of emotional states. In J. Darby (Ed.), *The evaluation of speech in psychiatry*. New York: Grune & Stratton, 1981.

Wish, M., D'Andrade, R. G., & Goodnow, J. E. Dimensions of interpersonal communication: Correspondence between structures for speech acts and bipolar scales. *Journal of Personality and Social Psychology*, 1980, *38*, 848–860.

Zemlin, W. R. *Speech and hearing science: Anatomy and physiology*. Englewood Cliffs, N.J.: Prentice-Hall, 1968.

5. Measurement of body motion and orientation

HOWARD M. ROSENFELD

5.1. Introduction

Body motion is selected as a separate area of study within the field of nonverbal communication for both structural and functional reasons. Structurally, the domain of body motion is based on spatiotemporal displacements of the skeletal system. The skeletal system, which consists of a complex and differentiated set of interrelated body parts, is capable of contributing to the accomplishment of a variety of tasks or functions.

Two major subclasses of the uses of the skeletal system may be referred to as its instrumental and its referential functions.[1] In its instrumental usage, skeletal action directly contributes to the performance of some task. Examples of commonplace instrumental functions of body motion are maintenance of an upright posture to counter the force of gravity, reorientation and relocation of the body or its parts so as to relate to objects in the external world, manipulations of external objects, and relief of physical discomforts by means of self-contact responses. In its instrumental usage the function of an act usually is readily apparent from its form. Measurement of instrumental functions of body motion is important to a variety of basic and applied sciences, such as physiology, biomechanics, sports kinesiology, and ergonomics or work adaptation.

To the student of nonverbal communication, the skeletal system is of importance primarily because of its involvement in referential communication. In the referential usage of the skeletal system, movements of the body serve as referents (signs, symbols, or indexes) of other characteristics of the actor, such as social status, personality, and state of mind. Often the form of the act is not directly related to its referent. In such cases the degree to which the act is attributed a particular communicative function depends upon shared experience by its perceivers.

In general, the parts of the skeletal system are differentially involved in instrumental and referential acts. In primates, the legs and trunk commonly are occupied in the persisting instrumental problem of countering the force of gravity and in a variety of activities that require spatial relocation. The hands are occasionally implicated in these two functions – providing leverage for raising the body from a sitting position, for example, or serving as a counterbalancing force in walking. But the hands are available to a much greater extent than the legs for object manipulation and referential communication. Furthermore, although the lower limbs are structurally more capable of performing feats of strength, the upper limbs are better adapted for the speed and versatility required of an efficient referential communicative system. In addition, though participants in social interaction are directing most of their visual attention to each other's faces, where the most important organs for vocal and emotional communication are located, their field of vision also permits simultaneous perception of actions of the head and often of the hands as well.

Clearly, there are exceptions to these generalizations. For example, dancers emphasize the lower body in their referential communication, and acrobats can locomote on their hands. But, in general, in the published literature on nonverbal communication, more attention has been paid to the activities of the hands, and secondarily the head, than to other components of the skeletal system.

In its referential usage, the skeletal system may act alone or in conjunction with speech or other bodily systems, such as gaze and facial expression, and in relationship to external objects. Sometimes a particular bodily act may serve both instrumental and referential functions. For example, the way a person walks may represent not only the instrumental act of relocation but also more general personality traits (Allport & Vernon, 1933/1967). A raised fist may be an initial phase of an aggressive action as well as a gesture of threat (McGrew, 1972). Certain arm and head movements associated with the beginning of conversational speech may be instrumental in the construction of utterances and may simultaneously indicate to the listener that the speaker does not wish to be interrupted (Dittmann, 1972b).

At the level of skeletal action, functional body motions often are extremely complex. They may involve a variety of body parts in a differentiated series of displacements over space and time. Although in the United States a conversational listener commonly conveys an affirmative reaction by a simple vertical nod of the head, the comparable message in Ceylon has been described as "curving the chin in a downward leftward arc . . . , often accompanied by an indescribably beautiful parakineme of back-of-right-hand cupped in upward-facing-palm of the left hand, plus-or-minus the additional kineme of a crossed-ankle curtsey" (LaBarre, 1964, p. 198). Precise measurement of such actions would appear to be a forbidding task. Yet most people most of the time are very proficient at using their bodies for social communication and also quite successful in interpreting the complex movements of other persons. Although they may not be able to articulate the physical bases of their actions and perceptions, they are able to apply a variety of ordinary language labels to complex bodily actions with considerable consensus.

Is it not possible, then, in conducting research on communication through body motion, to avoid the complexities of precise physical measurement and to rely upon consensual labeling by observers? For many research purposes, it is sufficient merely to note correctly that a particular type of functional act has occurred. In many circumstances observers can perform this task competently. But the observational capacities of the observer can become overburdened in many other circumstances, for example, when ordinary language terms are ambiguous, when the choice between alternative categories requires fine discriminations, when action is very complex and rapid, and when precise detail needs to be recorded. In such cases the observer may need to be aided, or even replaced, by special conceptual and physical tools.

Ordinary language is richly endowed with labels referring to functional acts for which neither a dictionary nor common experience is sufficient to assure reliable applications to observed behavior. For example, people disagree about whether an "aggressive" act must display evidence of forceful motion (versus, say, a mild squeeze on a trigger or a whispered insult), of intent to harm (versus accidental harm), and of anger (versus, say, the indifference of the hired hit man). It might be relatively easy to discriminate most aggressive acts from most "friendly" ones, but it would be more difficult to differentiate them from the "rough and tumble play" with which they have many components in common (McGrew, 1972).

One can reduce these problems by providing observers with more specific operational definitions of categories; for example, aggression may be defined as "hitting" (G. R. Patterson & Cobb, 1971). In such cases the observer is required to act less as an interpreter of behavior than as an instrument of measurement – a human ruler, timer, and calculator. But even the trained observer has a limited capacity to simulate the scope or accuracy of measuring devices and the memory and calculation capacity of computers.

Furthermore, there simply may be no consensually acceptable operational definition available for certain socially important functional concepts. In such cases it may be necessary first to establish critical conditions under which the behavior of interest is likely to occur, and comparison conditions under which it is not likely to occur. By comparing the details of behavior in the two conditions one may then objectively derive an operational definition of the concept, which in turn may be used in further research (Rosenfeld, 1972).

It is important to be able to specify – either in advance or as the result of research – attributes of functional movements that are "criterial" for identifying those movements and for discriminating them from other functional acts in one's definitional system. Criterial features may differ, depending upon level of analysis and instrument of measurement. For example, a handshake greeting can be described as a large set of temporally coordinated muscular contractions, or as a simpler set of spatiotemporal displacements of segments of a limb, or as a set of more molar components (grasp, squeeze, pump), or simply as a subjectively understood "handshake." The activities assessed at the different levels may or may not be highly correlated.

Considering that different researchers may identify the same category of action on the basis of different levels of analysis, or even different features at the same level, it is essential that a comprehensive approach to analysis be capable of comparing levels of measurement systematically. The system should be able to describe any body motions at a common basic level of measurement. It also should be capable of transforming its common denominators into higher levels of complexity or abstraction. Such a system then would be capable of interrelating measurements at all levels of analysis, from elementary behavioral components, through complex behavioral configurations, to observer-defined designations.

It should be emphasized that objective, reductive analysis is not being recommended here as the only legitimate method of measurement, nor is intersubjective consensus being ruled out as a useful research tool. The argument is rather that the capacity for objective elementary analysis is necessary for a science of bodily communication, although the desirability of its actual application will depend upon specific research purposes and available opportunities for data collection.

This chapter offers a general conceptual framework for the measurement of functional body motions and configurations, ranging from the molecular to the molar levels of analysis. A variety of physical and conceptual tools of measurement of bodily communication are discussed in terms of the framework. References to research involving measurement of body motion are selected primarily for their illustrative value. It is beyond the scope of the chapter to attempt to review systematically all existing studies in which measurement of body motion is included, or to give complete historical accounts of the development of common categories of measurement. Rather, the major goal is to provide a comprehensive framework that will be applicable to the analysis and evaluation of existing systems and to the construction of new methods of measuring body motion. A variety of existing measurement systems and their applications will be discussed following the presentation of the framework.

There appears to be an emerging consensus regarding the fundamental features that should be included in a generally applicable system for measuring body motion. There must be a basic taxonomy of movable parts of the body, including identification of those specific points on the parts which are most central for the description of movements. The critical body points need to be locatable within temporal and spatial dimensions of the environment. Furthermore, it is necessary to specify the elementary features of motion that result from the displacements of body parts in a spatiotemporal framework. Logical rules must be provided for transformation of elementary features of motion into more abstract features and more complex configurations. Another important task is the specification of the relationship between the physical properties of body motion and the perception and labeling of body motion by observers. Finally, tools for efficient and reliable measurement, as well as procedures for the validation of functional inferences, are needed for both observational and direct analysis.

5.2. Fundamental issues in measuring movement

Body part taxonomies

There is general agreement among both experts and laypersons on the identification of basic parts of the body that are sources of movement. Essentially, the movable skeletal system consists of a set of bony segments connected at joints. The trunk, which is bounded at the top by the neck and head and at the bottom by the hips, is the center of a symmetrical "tree structure" whose branches are the upper and lower appendages (arms and legs), which, in turn, branch out into the fingers and toes.

For efficient measurement of movements at a molecular behavioral level, it is necessary to know the capacity for movement of each segment and of various combinations of segments (see Laban, 1975). The ranges, speeds, and forces of movement of different body segments are constrained by the different kinds of joints, muscles, and locations of attachments of muscles to the segments, as well as by the bony structures of the segments themselves. Thus the serious researcher probably would benefit from consulting a standard textbook on the anatomic foundations of kinesiology (e.g., Logan & McKinney, 1977).

Although the body and its subparts consist of three-dimensional objects, it is not necessary to be attentive to every point on the surface of each moving part. Most researchers who use the body part taxonomy direct their attention to certain points that are considered critical for discrimination between movements (see Figure 5.1). The most commonly chosen points are the apexes of the angles formed at the joints between adjacent segments (for example, a point on a knuckle, wrist, elbow, and so on) and also the center of mass of a segment (for example, a point near the center of the forearm). These selected points and the lines through segments that connect them are salient objects of perception as well as efficient bases for direct measurement and analysis.

There is an additional way in which the body is involved in functional movements, one that requires a more elaborated taxonomy. This is as an *object* of orientation, contact, and manipulation. One very obvious, molar distinction between body parts considered as objects of action is the body of the actor (self-directed) versus the body of another person (socially directed).

A variety of researchers – for example, Greenbaum and Rosenfeld (1980 [see Table 5.7]), Jourard (1966), Krout (1935), and Mahl (1968) – also have assigned special importance to the specific parts of the body with which one makes contact. Relevant parts of the body as an object of action include the segments and joints of the skeletal system as well as other organs of the body, such as the surface of the cranium, eyes, ears, mouth, the areas covering the heart and stomach, and the organs of elimination and sex. Many common terms referring to body motion can be understood only by considering both sources and objects of motion, for example, a *slap, hug,* or *scratch.* Of course, a complete conception of objects of orientation would encompass all significant objects in the environment in addition to the bodies of persons. These would include objects associated with the body, such as clothing or cigarettes (Scheflen, 1964, 1965), and also less tangible objects of reference, such as speech (Ekman & Friesen, 1969b; Freedman & Hoffman, 1967; Rosenfeld, 1966b). At least half of the 29 gestures listed by McGrew (1972) require objects of orientation for their definition (see Table 5.6).

Figure 5.1. Locations of critical points and lines on the body for analysis of movement. *Source:* Hay, 1978, p. 137.

Spatial frames of reference

Motion of the body occurs in three-dimensional space. Thus it can be described accurately by locating the body parts along three orthogonal coordinates. The coordinates themselves, however, can be located simultaneously within several frames of reference. The two most basic types of reference systems are the anatomic (see Logan & McKinney, 1977) and the environmental (see Golani, 1976); each can be further subdivided into more specific frames of reference.

From an *anatomic* perspective, the location of a body part can be identified with respect to axes defined by other parts of the body. It is traditional in the field of anatomic kinesiology to identify three orthogonal planes that are defined relative to a baseline position of the body. In this standard position, referred to as the basic anatomic position, the body is considered to be erect with the arms at the sides and the palms

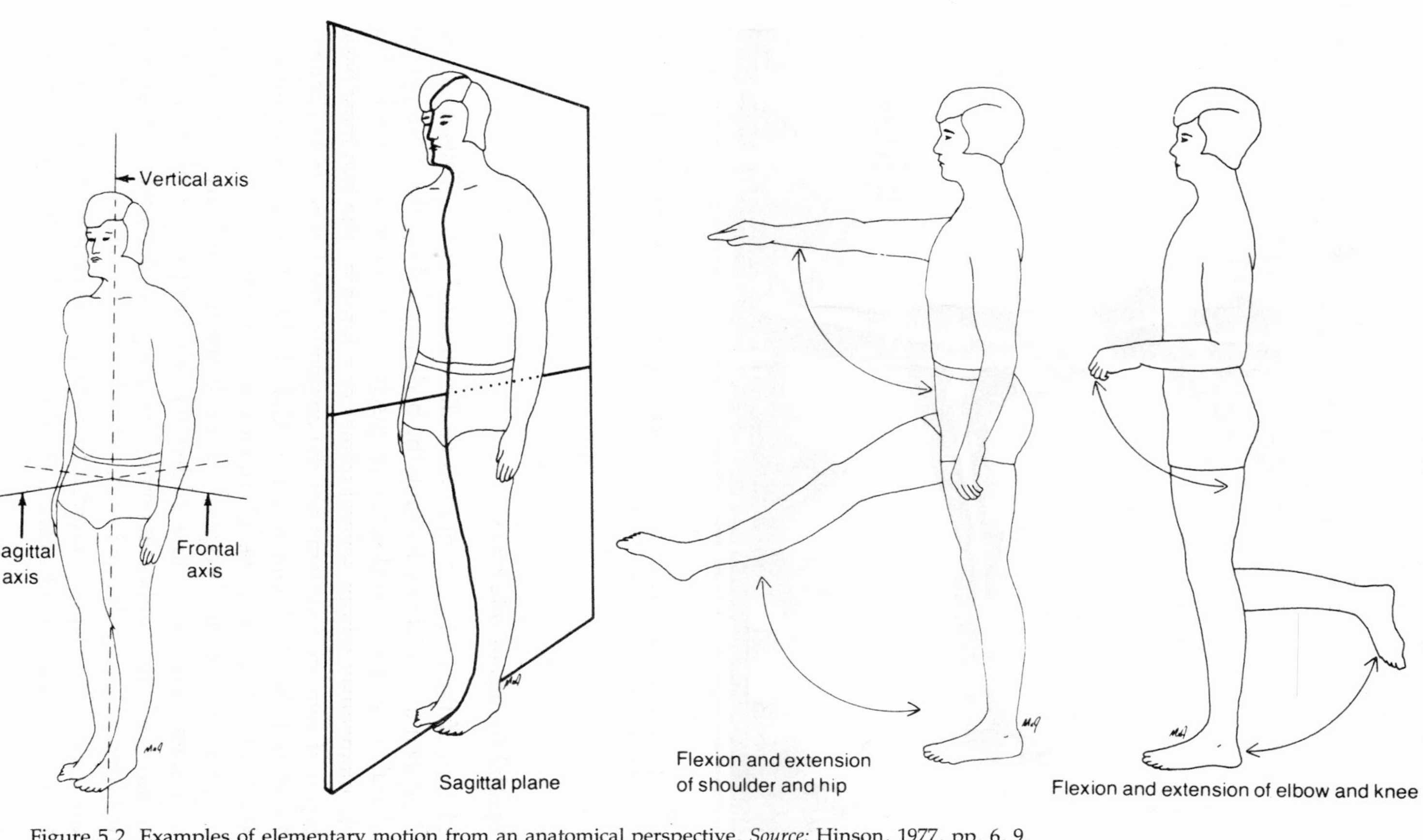

Figure 5.2. Examples of elementary motion from an anatomical perspective. *Source:* Hinson, 1977, pp. 6, 9.

of the hands facing forward. The sagittal or anteroposterior plane divides the long axis of the body into the right and left halves; the lateral or frontal plane divides the long axis into front and back halves; and the transverse or horizontal plane divides the body into upper and lower portions. Of course, actual movements may occur in multiple planes, including diagonal ones. But any point on the body at any moment can be located according to the intersection of three orthogonal spatial dimensions (see Figure 5.2).

A segment of the body may be viewed as a rigid line that can rotate about its associated joint. Thus any point of interest on the segment can be considered to be located on the periphery of a sphere whose radius is defined by the bone connecting the body point to the joint at the center of the sphere (see Figures 5.3 and 5.12). Furthermore, many of the segments of the body can be viewed as peripheral components of a connected tree structure of jointed segments located in a set of overlapping spheres. Consequently, the location of the joint at the center of a sphere of action may change owing to the relocation of another connected segment that is anatomically nearer to the center of the body. That is, the location of the sphere around any joint can itself move around in the environment during a movement that involves more than one segment in a tree structure. For example, in a pointing motion, the hand may rotate laterally at the wrist, but the wrist itself also may be displaced because of rotation of the forearm around the elbow joint. The pointing action also could be accompanied by rotation of the upper arm around the shoulder or of the trunk around the waist, or by the displacement of the entire body owing to action of the legs or feet, or by any combination of these movements. Methods for identifying and interrelating spatial relocations of body parts will be discussed in later sections on tools of measurement and quantitative analysis.

From an *environmental* perspective, a moving body part can be located along dimensions defined with respect to objects in the world external to the body. One general environmental framework is based upon the polar axis of our planet and the gravitational forces acting upon us. From this global perspective, movement can occur in relation to any point on the surface of the earth in north–south, east–west, and up–down axes. Often the investigator is interested in the location of body parts relative to a particular object in the environment. In such cases, the location of the object itself can serve as the origin of a three-dimensional space within which the body moves. The location of the moving body part can then be described according to its angle of

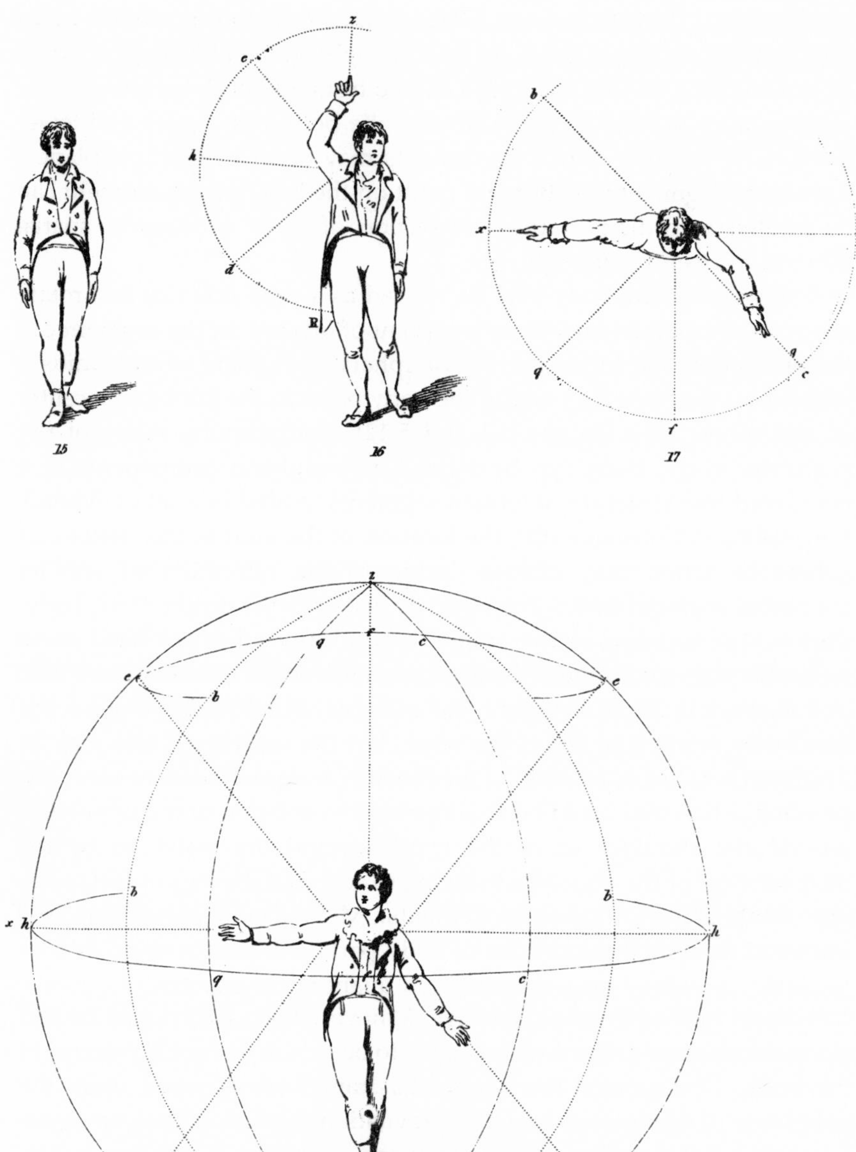

Figure 5.3. Planes and spheres of hand movement relative to the shoulder joint in oratorical delivery. *Source:* Austin, 1806/1966, plate 2.

approach or avoidance and its proximity to the object (see figures 5.5, 5.13, 5.17, and 5.18).

Temporal frames of reference

A complete framework for the characterization of movement requires the addition of a temporal dimension to the above-mentioned conceptions of physical components and spatial frames of reference. It is important to be aware that different treatments of time can affect the way in which a given bodily action is measured and interpreted. People usually think of the temporal dimension in terms of conventional units (seconds, minutes, etc.) of movement of clocks that are universally synchronized to regular external physical rhythms, such as the rotation of the earth and the oscillations of crystals. Subjective experiences of time (e.g., slow, fast) may deviate from the objective standards, however, causing problems of observational reliability. Also, other kinds of temporal distributions, such as biological and psychological rhythms, may be used in research. For example, one may be interested in the degree to which one person synchronizes his or her movements to rhythmic properties of another person's movements (Condon, 1979; Golani, 1976; Rosenfeld, 1981). In that case, the periodic properties of the latter person's movement, even if irregular, can serve as the objective "clock" according to which the first person's motions are assessed.

Certain research advantages can accrue from intentional manipulations of the temporal dimension in ways that are alien to everyday experience. Various recording techniques permit the artificial slowing or stopping of records of action, in order to obtain more detail than is available through real-time assessment. Conversely, the artificially speeding up of time can reveal structural features of action that are masked by the detail of real-time experience.

Sometimes the appropriate size of temporal or sequential unit will have been established in prior research. For example, inasmuch as most human reaction times to meaningful stimuli have been found to have a minimal latency of 0.1 second (Harter & White, 1968), studies of this aspect of movement should use minimal time units of less than 0.1 second. Studies of movements that apparently need little or no cognitive mediation may require even smaller minimal units; for example, the analysis of synchronization of body movement to phonetic changes in speech (Condon, 1979) apparently requires minimal units of 0.04 second or less (see Figure 5.20). In the study of movements that regulate speaker turns in conversations, Duncan (Duncan & Fiske, 1977) selected the syllable as his minimal sequential unit. His finding that the signals actually occurred in conjunction with larger phraselike units should aid other researchers who are interested in this topic in the selection of a more efficient unit. Duncan's finding also served to validate the work of earlier researchers who had selected the phraselike unit as their sequential level of analysis (e.g., Dittmann & Llewellyn, 1969).

Segmentation of movements

To discriminate between and to categorize specific body motions within a prolonged action sequence, it is necessary to be able to identify the boundaries of the separate motions. Specification of boundaries of discrete actions is particularly difficult when motion is very complex. For example, action persisting over an extended period of time may include many body parts, activated in different but overlapping time periods, with relatively fluid transitions between changes in direction, speed, and force. Criteria for discriminating boundaries vary widely, ranging from the relatively implicit and observer defined (e.g., Newtson, Engquist, & Bois, 1977) to the more explicit and statistically defined (e.g., Bobbitt, Gourevitch, Miller, & Jensen, 1969).

For those problems in which observation of movement is the tool of measurement, an important consideration is how the human observer perceptually segments movements in the temporal dimension (Johansson, 1973; Newtson et al., 1977). For example, when is a pause in a sequence of motions perceived to be part of a single unitary movement, and when is it considered to be a transitional period between a pair of unitary movements? In a three-cycle head nod, if there is a longer pause between the second and third cycles than between the first and second, how large must the difference be in order for the event to be scored as one long event rather than two shorter ones? The answer is important for understanding the social labeling of movement and its physical basis and also for obtaining interobserver reliability of measurement.

To identify socially meaningful pauses, it may be necessary to present motion pictures to informants at the real-time rate with which they are familiar. But to identify the physical structure of pauses that are perceived as intraunit versus interunit features, it may be necessary also to analyze the film in slow motion so that the relationship of timing to perception can be determined. In any case, the elementary unit of time selected should be small enough to permit assessment of all discriminable changes that are likely to be critical to the meaning of a pattern of movement.

If one seeks an empirical criterion for segmentation, then one can use statistical criteria for identifying discontinuities in interval lengths, such as log-survivor functions, and for identifying sequential dependencies between different categories of interval, such as Markov chains (see van Hooff, Chapter 7). Hayes, Meltzer, and Wolf (1970) exemplify three levels of empirically derived sequential units, using data from the domain of vocalization rates in conversation. They demonstrate the very important point that the conclusions one draws about the relationships among sequences of behavioral acts can vary depending upon the level of molarity one has chosen in the analysis of the acts.

One simple conceptual scheme for considering changes in patterns of movement is a two-dimensional matrix in which one dimension consists of elementary units of time and the other of designated movable parts of the body. The entry of each cell in this matrix is the spatial location of each body part in each time unit. Each discriminable type of entry for location of a body part or set of parts, or each sequence of identical entries, may be considered to constitute a different type of elementary *position,* and each discriminable change from one temporal unit to the adjacent subsequent temporal unit may be considered to constitute a different type of elementary *motion* (see Ekman & Friesen, 1967; Golani, 1976; see also Figure 5.13).

If a position or a type of transition is repeated across adjacent units, then the series of elementary events may be coded as a unit (e.g., standing or reaching). Thus a series of elementary units can be summarized as a smaller series of variable-length extended units (see Bobbitt et al., 1969; Hayes et al., 1970; Rosenfeld & Remmers, 1981). Of course, decisions can be made to subdivide extended units according to additional criteria, such as arbitrary divisions of length or intensity (e.g., standing for a short rather than a long time or gesturing calmly rather than intensely). Similarly, criteria can be specified by which a set of adjacent extended units can be combined into a more complex unit (e.g., clenching and then shaking a fist).

Features of movement

Fundamentally, all movement consists of the displacement of body parts in space and time. Displacements of body parts through space and time may be viewed as continuous functions. But sometimes it is useful to consider motion as if it consisted of a series of discrete locations of body parts in discrete time intervals. In fact, motion-picture and videotape records of body motion literally are composed of a series of discrete temporal images. The most elementary description of a movement – the common denominator that permits comparison of any movements – is the specification of the spatial location of each relevant body part over sequential units of time.

The complete spatiotemporal pattern of displacements of a complex set of body parts that are physiologically interrelated in various ways (e.g., by tree structure or by bilateral symmetry), or what Golani (1976) refers to as the "multidimensional concatenation" of movement, is in itself an unwieldy descriptive concept. Usually, the description of a smaller number of more molar or abstract features is sufficient to characterize the type of movement and to discriminate it from other types.

The field of anatomic kinesiology has established a relatively extensive vocabulary referring to directions of displacement (see Logan & McKinney, 1977). Its elementary concepts of movement incorporate the anatomical position as the frame of reference, as well as such additional anatomical considerations as rotation of segments at specific joints, structural differences between joints, and muscular forces that give rise to motion. Given the widespread usage of concepts of anatomic kinesiology in the assessment of communicative movements, several key terms will be noted here (see also Figure 5.2).

The terms for motion in the frontal plane include *abduction* and *adduction* (sideways limb movements respectively away from and toward the midline of the body, such as the lateral movements of the upper arm in the production of semaphore code), and *hyperadduction* (for example, the extreme lateral extension of the thumb in the American hitchhiking symbol, assuming the basic anatomic reference position in which the palm of the hand is facing forward). Other frontal motions are *ulnar* and *radial deviation*, referring to motion of the hand in the directions of the little finger and the thumb, respectively; an example would be the lateral movements of the hand at the wrist joint in waving goodbye. Another frontal motion is *elevation* of the shoulder girdle, as in a shrug.

In the sagittal plane, *flexion* and *extension* refer to decreases and increases in the angle of body segments at joints; *hyperextension* would include the backward rotation of the leg at the hip in preparation for a kick. Movement in the transverse plane includes *rotation* around a part's own central axis, as in the turning of a door knob. Rotational subcategories include the *pronation* of the wrist (its rotation around the radial-ulnar joint in the forearm to a position 180° from the anatomic position, which is as far as any single joint will permit) and its *supination* (rotation back to the anatomic position).

There also are terms for motion in multiple planes (spherical space), such as the cone-shaped *circumduction* of the arm in a windmill pitch of a softball. Logan and McKinney (1977) list a variety of kinesiologic terms that tend to be used interchangeably in practice. For example, *sideways tilting* of the spinal column is referred to sometimes as abduction and other times as lateral flexion, and the subsequent return of the spine to the anatomic position may be referred to as adduction or as *reduction*.

It should be emphasized that an advantage of this kinesiologic vernacular is the consistency of its implication of the anatomic frame of reference in the specification of direction of motion. The absence of such consistency in definitions of motion was humorously demonstrated in a cartoon in a book on Labanotation (Hutchinson, 1961, p. 196), in which supine customers in a barber shop responded differently to a gun wielder's demand, "Hands up!" One customer extended his arms behind his head and thus toward the wall, whereas the other reached his arms toward the ceiling.

In this context it should be noted that frames of reference other than the anatomical may be more appropriate for certain kinds of research. In studies of social relationships a subject's movements usually are most meaningfully described in comparison to the location of another person. In these cases it would be preferable to use terms such as *sociofugal* (Hall, 1963, 1974) to describe the direction of the action. The anatomical perspective, in contrast, usually is appropriate for the description of emotion, personality, sports, dance, and other events that tend to be substantially independent of social and environmental objects.

Once a basic category of body part displacement has been identified, the movement can be further specified by a variety of summary features. Some of these are objectively definable by mathematical formulae and can be directly transformed into their higher-order derivatives (see Grieve, Miller, Mitchelson, & Smith, 1975; Gustafsson & Lanshammar, 1977; Logan & McKinney, 1977). Perhaps the most fundamental features are simply duration and distance. A commonly employed set of higher-order derivatives, computed from difference equations and referring to the rate of temporal displacement, is velocity (distance/time) and acceleration (rate of change in velocity). Even higher-order derivatives are possible, for example, jerk or rate of change in acceleration, but these are rarely applied in research on bodily communication. Other basic dimensions of movement that require assessment of the mass of the body part and of objects of impact are momentum (mass × velocity) and force (mass × acceleration).

It should be noted that the application of any of these abstractions to an act within given temporal boundaries assumes that the movement is in a "steady state," that is, that the attribution holds throughout the entire time period. An acceptable substitute for a steady state assumption might be the averaging of a measure that varies with reasonable regularity during the period, for example, the average amplitude (vertical distance) of cycles of head nodding (Rosenfeld & McRoberts, 1979). Repetitions of event categories within a coherent behavior sequence can be described in conventional measures of frequency or rate (number of occurrences per time) and period (time intervals between peaks of occurrences). Also, to the degree that there are differences or irregularities in the distinguishable components of an extended action, it might be considered relevant to compute summary indexes of diversity (e.g., a ratio of types of different acts to total number of acts; see Frey and von Cranach, 1973).

Other summary properties of movements can be constructed from relationships of moving body parts to each other and to external objects that may or may not move. For example, in an unpublished manuscript, Frey and Pool (1976) offer an objective definition of hand "openness" that can be directly measured from pictures of action. Their measure of openness is a straightforward assessment of the average of the lateral distances of the hands from the trunk of the body over a series of time units.

Frey and Pool also claim to have combined elementary spatiotemporal properties to form such parameters of movement as expansion, illustration, taxis, reaching out, concordance of hand movements, concordance of positions, imitation of movement, and distance variation among interaction partners. In addition, they note that they have constructed objective indexes of many higher-order observational categories proposed by the ethologists Brannigan and Humphries (1972), such as nod, bob, shrug, crouch, swing, shuffle, threat, and akimbo. Of course, the degree to which such objective measures correspond to what ethologists or other researchers actually identify through observation of verbally defined categories can be determined only by the simultaneous application of observational and direct measurement methods to the same data, and the analysis of their degree of correspondence. Frey and Pool have not reported doing this.

Loci of measurement

Implicit in the foregoing discussion were the notions that communicative bodily acts can be assessed at several different locations in space and time and that methods of measurement tend to differ depending upon the location selected for assessment. The various loci at which a bodily act can be assessed might best be illustrated by reference to a model of message transmission that was developed by communication engineers (Shannon & Weaver, 1949). In this model an item of information travels from a source to a destination and undergoes various transformations in the process.

To adapt the model to our purposes we might view a bodily message (e.g., an emotion or an intention) as originating in the brain of the sender. The result is a particular pattern of activation of efferent neurons, which is transduced into a pattern of muscular contractions, which in turn is transformed into angular motions of the body segments at the joints, and which also is reflected in a pattern of movement of the surfaces of the body segments in space. Light reflected off the body parts, in turn, evokes a sequence of activities in an observer – sensation, perception and finally interpretation of this message.

It is theoretically possible to assess the message at any of the various locations just noted. However, as a practical matter, there can be substantial disparity between measures of the same act at the different loci, owing to noise associated both with the message and with the available methods of measurement. Table 5.1 lists some of the kinds of records of movement that can be obtained at different loci of measurement, along with corresponding recording devices. At this time one cannot assess the neural representation of most bodily messages at a useful level of precision. Muscular contractions can be assessed, but they are only weakly correlated with the measures of the movements of segments that follow them (Grieve et al., 1975). Assessment of actual movements of the skeletal system at the levels of joints and segments can be accomplished with great precision under certain circumstances. But thus far the most common locus of measurement has been at the level of the observer.

5.3. Observational measurement

Basic issues

The preference for human observers over other instruments of measurement in the study of communication by body motion is not difficult to understand. Human observers are ubiquitous, ready-made, sophisticated measuring instruments. Through both genetic endowment and everyday experience the normal person is capable of recognizing an

Table 5.1. *Relationships among locus of measurement, recording instruments, and recorded data*

Locus of measurement	Recording instruments	Recorded data
Direct measurement		
Neurons	Microelectrodes	Firing pattern
Muscles	Electromyograph	Contractions
Skeleton	Stabilimeter	Motion of body
	Accelerometer	Acceleration of segment
	Dynamometer	Force
	Hodometer	Locomotion coordinates
	Goniometer	Angular displacement
	Optoelectronic monitor	Motion coordinates of segments
Film or videotape	Camera	Picture
Observer-mediated measurement		
Observation of film or tape	Graphic input device	Spatial coordinates of segments
	Motion analyzer	Categorization and timing
	Event recorder	
Observation of behavior	Notation	Symbols
	Natural language recording	Informal description

extensive number of complex patterns of movement and applying a rich vocabulary in order to describe the perceived patterns.

Considering the capacity of the body to engage in complex configurations of relative motion of segments, and the additional fact that the bodies and eyes of observers of action commonly are simultaneously in motion, it is a remarkable feat for the observer accurately and consistently to identify coherent categories of displacement. Thus it is very important to understand the particular strengths and limitations of the human observer as an instrument of assessment of body motion. How much are the movement-recognition skills of observers based on a common genetic endowment? How much is their emergence dependent on maturational processes, on experience in object perception, and on development of movement-related vocabulary? What is the relationship between the actual physical features of moving stimuli and their perception? To what degree is movement perception based on gestalt properties, more specific structural properties, and elementary features? At what ages can the human being be recruited as an observer of particular forms of movement, at an acceptable level of reliability? More questions have been raised here than there is space or evidence to answer. However, several recent findings relevant to the perception of body motion, and its developmental antecedants, will be reviewed briefly.

Even young infants display many of the basic skills required for perception of movements. By the age of approximately 2 months, infants visually track moving stimuli (Nelson, 1971) and are sensitive to cues of relative motion of objects (Lasky & Gogel, 1978). If one accepts the assumption that increase in motor activity indicates preference for a visual stimulus, then the infant shows evidence of preference for moving stimuli of intermediate complexity (Haith, Kessen, & Collins, 1969). On the basis of variations in rate of habituation of response to visual stimulation, there is evidence that infants make a variety of subtle distinctions between features of moving stimuli (E. J. Gibson, Owsley, & Johnston, 1978). A basic feature that is assumed to underlie infant attention to particular forms of motion is violation of expectations about subsequent events in a coherent sequence (E. J. Gibson et al., 1978; Haith et al., 1969). Of course, with greater experience, the nature of events that constitute a violation is likely to change.

By 5 months infants show evidence of identifying the persistence of moving objects on the basis of common features and trajectory, and by 9 months they recognize object permanence (Moore, Borton, & Darby, 1978). The theory that infants are innately disposed to perceive causal relationships between temporally associated events (J. J. Gibson, 1966; Michotte, 1963), also has received empirical support (Borton, 1979). Another feature of motion to which infants are sensitive by at least 2 months of age is looming of objects toward them (Yonas & Peterson, 1979).

Around the end of the first year of life, infants also show rapid progress in the development of skill in the verbal representation of objects. Recent research in linguistic development indicates that the earliest forms of communicative speech involve a coordination of verbal referents to objects with nonverbal orientations toward both the objects and the human recipients of the messages (e.g., Sugarman, in press). Presumably, if one were to inspect the contents of the rapidly developing vocabulary of the child in the early years, one would also find a proliferation of terms referring to features and categories of body motion.

But there also are disadvantages in using the available perceptual and verbal skills of observers as a tool for the identification of body motion. In particular, the relationship between the movement patterns of actors and the perceptual labeling of the movements by observers is not always clear. Many of our common labels for patterns of movement lack explicit operational definitions (as in the case of *aggression,* discussed earlier). They are useful for purposes of identifying occurrences of body motion only to the degree that they are reliably usable, that is, consensually applicable across independent observations of the same class of movements.

Also, for some purposes, such as automated analysis of movement and training of skills in movement, the reliability of observation of even globally defined events may not be sufficient. In such cases it usually is necessary to define categories precisely in terms of common denominators such as elementary features and structures. Again, more evidence is needed not only of the physical acts that correlate with verbal identification of categories, but also of the general perceptual processes that are involved. Thus research on the psychophysics of motion perception is very important for the development of a systematic approach to the measurement and analysis of body motion.

Mature observers do show some limits in their ability to detect movements accurately. They tend not to perceive motion when objects are displaced at a rate of less than 5° of arc per second (Yarbos, 1967), and their tracking becomes more latent as object velocity increases, with losses in visual acuity apparent for objects moving more than about 60° per second (Reading, 1972).

Current theory and research on adult perception of patterns (Reed, 1978) indicates that it may be very difficult to identify the elementary physical properties underlying the perceptual identification and discrimination of many of the complex verbal categories referring to body motion that abound in the literature. To apply an objective system of physical measurement to such higher-order, observationally based constructs requires that valid definitions be available at a minimum of three levels of perceptual analysis – features, structures, and topological organizations. *Feature* theory assumes that observers take account of such elementary parameters as lines, and that they describe them in terms of such elementary attributes as length. *Structural* theory further assumes the operation of principles for identifying relationships between features (e.g., for deciding which lines in a configuration tend to

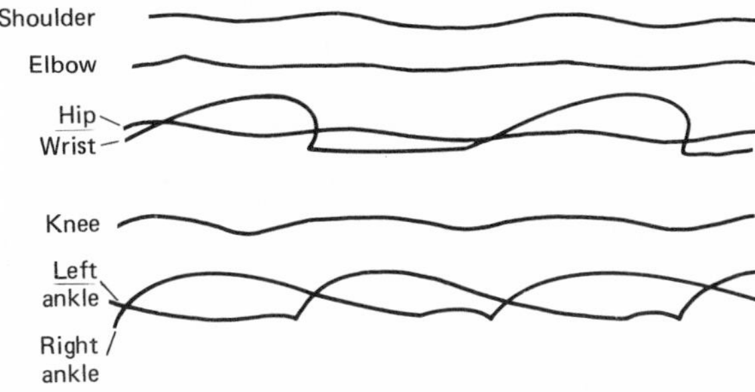

Figure 5.4. Filmed motion paths of six right-side joints and the left ankle of a walking person. *Source:* Johansson, 1973, p. 203.

be grouped together). Another tenable alternative is *topological* theory, which assumes that the observer identifies an overall organization without necessarily starting with a feature analysis.

Thus far, little is known about which models apply to the events referred to by many of the myriad body motion categories that are employed in everyday language, as well as in theory and research on nonverbal communication. Wallbott (1980) has made some preliminary efforts to classify categories from the literature on expressive hand movements along a multidimensional scale ranging from elementary features to gestalt categories. Substantial progress toward identifying perceptual processes underlying the identification of some categories of body motion has been made by Johansson (1973, 1978), who offers a vector-analytic model to account for his experimental evidence that the spontaneous labeling of a stimulus array as a person *walking* can be evoked by the simulated movement in two-dimensional space of as few as five points on the body (hip, knees, ankles; see Figure 5.4). In this model the attribution that a person is walking in a plane perpendicular to the observer is based upon common motion of the points. The perception of movement in a plane away from the observer is based upon common recession of the points on the perpendicular two-dimensional screen toward a theoretical point of convergence in space. Restle (1979) claims that Johansson's data can be incorporated into an even more general information-theoretical model of memory coding.

Admittedly, walking is by no means representative of the complexity of patterns of body motion that commonly are labeled by observers. But the successful experimental analysis of the relationship between elementary features of movement and the perception of walking may portend the development of similar objective analyses of other molar behavior patterns. Such research should be particularly useful for identifying specific aspects of disagreement between coders of the same events.

Other researchers have studied the relationship of characteristics of more complex and varied human activities to the observer's identification of boundaries between behavioral units. In a 1977 study, Newtson found that typically perceived breakpoints in the flow of behavioral episodes presented on videotapes commonly occur after changes in locations of four to six body parts (Newtson et al., 1977). In other studies, he has found that the level of molarity of perceptions of given behavioral episodes is influenced by minor disturbances (Newtson, 1973). For example, smaller-sized meaningful units are perceived after the introduction of a single unexpected activity in a prolonged behavioral episode, even though no changes have occurred in the subsequent events. Also, more molar units are likely to be perceived if the observer can see evidence of the periodic completion of a product during the performance of briefer repetitive activities, such as a nail's being driven in after several strokes of a hammer (Newtson, Rindner, Miller, & La Cross, 1978). Although a good theoretical explanation of these results has not yet been put to the test, Newtson prefers a cognitive model in which the observer actively compares preexisting conceptual patterns to the observed patterns of behavior. A major implication of Newtson's findings for present purposes is that the observer-generated labeling of complex episodes of body motion can vary with relatively small changes in observer perspective or in behavioral structure and context.

Thus it is important to specify the observational conditions under which reliable measurements can be obtained. Unfortunately, little systematic research has been done on the parameters that affect reliability of observation of body motion. In fact, many researchers do not assess or report reliability coefficients at all. Among those who do report reliability, the coefficients of agreement or correlation commonly are 0.90 or better on scales in which perfect agreement is 1.00. To some degree this high level must reflect the selective inclusion of observational procedures that meet conventional standards of reliability in the scientific community. It does not necessarily mean that all potentially meaningful categories of body motion are observable at a comparable level of agreement.

A great many variables are likely to affect reliability of observation in the domain of body motion. These include the complexity of the behaviors to be scored, their rates of occurrence, explicitness of definitions and of notational methods, training of observers, and such situational characteristics as lighting, distance of observer from subject, and angle of observation relative to the plane of motion. Many of these problems are shared with other domains of behavior, and therefore general principles of observation (e.g., Bickman, 1976) are likely to generalize substantially to the body motion domain.

Periodically, researchers do report evidence of variables that affect reliability of observation of body motion. For example, McDowall (1979) reported increasingly reliable observations of occurrence of elementary displacements of body segments, from a film of a group of conversants, as the size of the observational interval increased from one to six film frames (see Table 5.2). Similarly, Rosenfeld and McRoberts (1979) obtained increasingly reliable assessments of basic features of head nods from videotape records as the scoring interval increased from 0.1 second to 0.7 second (see Table 5.3). Such information is important for the study of certain problems; for example, Condon's (1979) work on synchrony of body motions with phonetic changes requires almost perfect reliability within filmed intervals as small as 0.033 second (see Rosenfeld, 1981).

Another example relates to the problem of how heavy an observational load can be placed on an observer before reliability breaks down. During the course of an automated study of rates of vocal participation of 18 pairs of conversants (Rosenfeld & Sullwold, 1969), I collected some heretofore unreported data on the effect of the observational load placed on a pair of experienced observers upon their reliability in scoring movements of several parts of the body of the designated subject. The five categories referred to relatively simple movement configurations of the sort that commonly are included in both conversational and ethological studies – social gaze, head nods, smiles, gesticulations (speech-related hand movements) and self-manipulations, as briefly defined by Rosenfeld (1966b). The independent observers scored each variable by pressing one of five piano-key switches throughout the occurrence of each category of movement that they perceived while watching the subject closely through a one-way window at a distance of about 2.4 m. The interobserver reliability scores consisted of the correlation across subjects between the number of 2-second intervals in an Esterline-Angus multichannel event recording in which the observers marked the occurrence of a particular category.

The observers simultaneously observed a designated subject for 2-minute periods under one of three sets of instructions – to observe only the three variables located in the head and face area (social gaze, head nods, and smiles), to observe only the two variables involving movement of the hands (gesticulations and self-manipulations), or to

Table 5.2. *Intraobserver reliabilities recorded for nine body parts at the one- to six-frame units of agreement*

Observer	Units of agreement	Body parts[a] 1	2	3	4	5	6	7	8	9
1	1	0.35[b]	0.27[b]	0.22	0.50[c]	0.71[c]	0.29[b]	0.36[b]	0.36[c]	0
	2	0.92[c]	0.56[c]	0.22	0.67[c]	0.67[c]	0.42	0.46	0.50[b]	0
	3	0.67	0.40	0.83[c]	0.67[b]	0.67[b]	0.55	0.70[b]	0.75[c]	0.33
	4	1.00[c]	0.56	0.57	0.75	1.00[c]	0.75[b]	0.50	0.75	1.00[c]
	5	1.00[b]	0.43	0.67	0.71	1.00[c]	0.75	0.67	1.00[c]	0.33
	6	1.00[b]	0.57	0.83	0.67	0.75	0.67	0.86	0.83	1.00[b]
2	1	0.14	0.09	0.27[b]	0.25	0.18	0.21	0.15	0.13	0
	2	0.33	0.33	0.40	0.67[c]	0.44[b]	0.70[c]	0.67[c]	0.29	0
	3	0.33	0.71[c]	0.40	0.88[c]	0.43	0.60	0.56	1.00[c]	0.50
	4	0.56	0.71[b]	0.40	0.75	0.67[b]	1.00[c]	0.75[b]	0.50	0.50
	5	0.63	0.83[b]	0.71	1.00[c]	0.83[b]	0.88	0.67	0.50	0.50
	6	0.57	1.00[b]	0.75	1.00[b]	0.75	1.00	0.75	0.60	0.50
3	1	0.31[b]	0.22	0.25	0.56[c]	0.06	0.13	0.15	0.07	0
	2	0.62[c]	0.37	0.43[b]	0.75[c]	0.23	0.29	0.44	0.25	0
	3	0.67	0.22	0.67[b]	0.75[c]	0.15	0.33	0.57	0.27	0.50
	4	0.80	0.37	0.67[b]	0.86[b]	0.30	0.60	0.82	0.50	0.50
	5	0.67	0.43	1.00[c]	0.71	0.33	0.63	0.70	0.71	0
	6	1.00	0.57	1.00[b]	0.67	0.57	0.57	1.00	0.57	0.50
4	1	0.36[b]	0.15	0.25	0.18	0.30	0.17	0.89[c]	0.29[b]	0
	2	0.58[c]	0.50[b]	0.25	0.44[b]	0.41	0.40	0.89[c]	0.50[b]	0
	3	0.46	0.56	0.63[b]	0.63[b]	0.67	0.33	0.88[c]	0.60[b]	0.33
	4	0.60	0.75	0.50	0.63	0.80	0.57	1.00[c]	0.60	0.33
	5	0.56	1.00[c]	0.57	0.83[b]	0.70	0.75	0.88	0.80[b]	0.33
	6	1.00	1.00[b]	0.83	0.80	0.88	0.50	1.00	1.00[b]	1.00[b]
5	1	0.46[c]	0.27[b]	0.08	0.33[b]	0.50[c]	0.08	0.33[b]	0.13	0
	2	0.58[c]	0.40	0.18	0.33	0.67[c]	0.08	0.85[c]	0.50[b]	0
	3	0.89[c]	0.44	0.50	0.33	0.83[c]	0.18	0.75	0.80[c]	0
	4	0.89[b]	0.50	0.22	0.40	0.80[b]	0.11	1.00[b]	0.50	0
	5	0.88	0.80[b]	0.67	0.63	0.67	0.25	0.80	0.80[b]	0
	6	1.00[b]	0.67	0.83	1.00[b]	1.00[b]	0.50	1.00	1.00[b]	0

[a]Body parts analyzed: (1) head; (2) upper right arm; (3) lower right arm; (4) right hand; (5) upper left arm; (6) lower left arm; (7) left hand; (8) right foot; (9) left foot.
[b]$p < 0.05$. [c]$p < 0.01$.
Source: McDowall, 1979, pp. 82–83.

observe all five variables simultaneously (see Table 5.4). Under the first two sets of instructions, reliability coefficients for the three body motion categories averaged 0.96 (range 0.92 – 0.99). Under the third set of instructions these reliabilities dropped to an average of 0.56 (range

Table 5.3. *Intercoder reliability coefficients for two features of head nods in videotaped behavior samples before and after intercoder review of discrepancies*

Head nod feature	Error permitted	Mean % agreement[a] Pre	Post
Number of changes in direction	None	50	58
	1 change	83	90
	2	93	97
	3	96	99
Duration (0.1-sec intervals)	0 sec	10	21
	0.1	32	49
	0.2	50	74
	0.3	58	85
	0.4	65	91
	0.5	72	94
	0.6	81	96
	0.7	81	98

[a]Mean percentage agreement based on four overlapping pairs of coders.
Source: Data from Rosenfeld and McRoberts, 1979.

Table 5.4. *Effect of amount of information to be coded on intercoder reliability correlations*

Movement category	Amount to code: Head or hands	Head and hands
Head nod	0.92	0.45
Gesticulation	0.98	0.79
Self-manipulation	0.99	0.44

Note: All categories in the table were coded as frequencies of separate occurrences.
Source: Direct observational data on 14 subjects from my own unpublished study.

0.44 – 0.79). The substantial drop in reliability probably was affected both by the increased range of the visual field required for the observation and by the increased requirements for key pressing.

In the study under discussion, a comparison was also made of the coding reliability for frequencies of discrete acts and total duration of acts in the three categories, when hands and head were observed on separate occasions. Although frequency and duration of head nods correlated 0.93, the interobserver correlation for frequency (0.92) was substantially higher than that for duration (0.65). Gesticulation frequency and duration also correlated 0.93, but they were equally reliable. Self-manipulation frequency and duration correlated only 0.29, and the duration measure was only slightly less reliable (0.92) than was that for frequency (0.99).

Friesen, Ekman, and Wallbott (1979) similarly reported that frequency and duration of illustrative hand movements correlated (rho) 0.98. The *emblematic* (the term is defined in the subsequent discussion of psychosocial models) category *shrug* had a frequency – duration correlation of 0.85. (In the Rosenfeld study just cited, the category of gesticulation included both illustrative and emblematic movement.) However, unlike Rosenfeld, Friesen et al. found a high correlation (0.88) between frequency and duration of manipulations. Similarly, Freedman, O'Hanlon, Oltman, and Witkin (1972) reported interobserver correlations for "body-focused" movement (similar to self-manipulations) of 0.99 for discrete occurrences and of 0.92 for continuous scores. In general, then, frequency and duration of movements during conversation tend to be quite highly correlated. As Friesen et al. point out, frequency is the preferable measure in the sense that it requires less work of the coder.

Sensitization and training of observers

One way to enhance the natural capacities of the observer as an instrument of body motion measurement is to provide special training. At least two philosophies have guided recommendations for such experiences. One of these emphasizes the value of the observer as a natural pattern recognizer. The corresponding special experiences given the observer are opportunities to become more familiar with the kinds of movements to be coded and thus more sensitized to their structural properties. In the ethological approach to the study of human behavior, which heavily emphasizes the domain of body motion, it has been reported that more experienced observers tend to be both more attentive to details of behavior and more likely to perceive complex patterns of action (Hutt & Hutt, 1974). However, the extent to which such changes also are influenced by theoretical predilections is not clear.

Condon (1979) recommended general sensitization opportunities with the data to be scored as a preliminary step before observers code the visual and verbal channels of motion-picture records for the locations of points of segmentation. Unfortunately, such sensitization experiences also run the risk of increasing the probability that perceived correspondences in the two distributions will be the result more of the reinforcement of perceptual biases in the observer than of the improved detection of organized behavior patterns in the subject (see Rosenfeld, 1981).

The other philosophy of training is that the observer can be improved as an objective measuring device, that is, as an accurate detector of explicitly definable characteristics of action. It is commonly reported in research publications that reliability is enhanced as researchers become more familiar with measuring instruments, as opportunities for application increase, and as feedback on performance is provided. Most coding schemes for body motion are based on verbal definitions. However, training with visual models (still or motion pictures of actual or simulated configurations) is likely to be particularly effective when researchers are observing complex behaviors that are commonly perceived at the gestalt level.

Billman and McDevitt (1980) reported average interrater reliabilities (percentage of agreement), on 18 ethological categories adapted from Blurton Jones (1972), over their final three training sessions. The respective percentages were 86, 95, and 92, indicating modest improvement. However, the training procedures were not specified.

Similarly, Rosenfeld and McRoberts (1979) computed intercoder reliabilities on the assessment of features of head nods before and after pairs of independent coders had an opportunity to discuss their bases of disagreements and to review them on videotape. Table 5.3 shows their changes in percentage of agreement for several features, with the agreements computed for varying degrees of temporal "error." Clearly the opportunities for discussion improved reliability. Without systematic control over the information exchanged between coders, however, it is not possible to improve the written coding definitions to benefit future coders. Of course, one could use the improved coding scores along with the videotaped examples as nonverbal models for future coders.

In a study of body motion during interaction between infants and their mothers (see Rosenfeld & Remmers, 1981), intercoder discrepancies were used as the basis for improving the coding system. An assistant and I developed an initial coding system and obtained initial reliability scores. A subsequent coder, using only the written definitions, obtained lower agreement with the first assistant's scores on several categories. This third coder scrutinized the videotapes for objective bases of disagreement and found several previously unspecified assumptions shared by the original coders. These were made explicit in a revision of the coding system. Table 5.5 shows the

Table 5.5. *Intercoder reliability (% agreement) on coding of movements of mothers with infants, as a function of coder collaboration and time interval*

Category	Occurrences[a]			Starts[a]		
	Coders 1, 2	Coders 2, 3 (pre)[b]	Coders 2, 3 (post)[b]	Coders 1, 2 (unit lag 0)	Coders 1, 2 (unit lag 1)	Coders 1, 2 (unit lag 2)
Orient head	89	97	—	47	84	84
Manipulate object	82	32	70	27	61	73
Contact infant	70	86	—	30	67	85
Relocate self	95	50	82	36	70	70

[a]Occurrence scores refer to presence of act during interval; start scores to initiation of act during interval (0.5 sec).
[b]Coder 3 relied on the written and verbal definitions of Coders 1 and 2 during the "pre" code and on revisions of the written code for the "post" code.
Source: Date from my own unpublished study.

reliabilities obtained for four movement categories of mothers. This table also shows, as did the studies by McDowall (1979) and Rosenfeld and McRoberts (1979), that reliability of coding the temporal location of the initiation of movements improves as the size of the temporal unit increases.

Sometimes reliability can be improved by combining subcategories into a larger superordinate category. For example, consider the coding of head orientation for the studies by Gunnell (1979) and Rosenfeld and Hancks (1980). The intercoder percentage of agreement for occurrence of head shifts toward a conversational partner within brief periods at the ends of utterances was 73. However, the reliabilities of subcategories were lower (e.g., 44 for head turn, 25 for head lower, 57 for head point). On the other hand, Friesen et al. (1979) obtained higher correlations between frequency and duration when manipulations of the subject's own body were subdivided into brief (rho = 0.84) and long (rho = 0.88) than when these categories were combined (rho = 0.68).

Finally, there are some indications that definitions requiring finer discriminations by observers are less reliably codable. Among the intimacy-related movements listed by Mehrabian (1972), the lowest reliabilities were for sideways lean (0.63), which was measured in degrees from the upright, and for hand relaxation (0.66), which required judgments of amount of tension. The highest reliabilities were for number of leg movements (0.97), and for distance (0.95), which required counting floor tiles.

5.4. Physical tools of measurement and analysis

In previous sections of this chapter I have mentioned the advantages of observers as instruments of measurement, particularly their existing skills in the recognition and verbal labeling of complex behavior patterns and their capacity to enhance these skills through training and practice. Observational measurement can be further improved through the employment of culturally developed artifacts that serve to extend the observer's perceptual, cognitive, and motor capacities. These nonhuman tools of measurement can improve the quantity, quality, and efficiency of observation. In some cases they can even serve as substitutes for observation.

Instrumentation can help overcome such limitations in observers as restricted field of vision (including inability to see objects behind themselves, behind subjects, or behind obstacles located between observer and subjects), inconsistency and inaccuracy in estimation of spatial and temporal parameters (especially when visual events are highly detailed and rapidly changing), limited memory capacity (especially for delayed coding), inability to identify the physical and psychological determinants of their perceptual differentiation and integration of components of movement (in case there are problems of reliability and validity), and limited computational abilities. Inasmuch as similar limitations affect observers in all domains of nonverbal communication, extensive discussion of general compensatory devices is not appropriate in this chapter (but see Bickman, 1976; Hutt & Hutt, 1974; Sackett, 1978).

Certain devices are particularly important in the measurement of body motion, however, owing to the complexity of action of which the skeletal system is capable, and particularly to the fact that its activities can include the entire span of the human body in three spatial dimensions, thereby taxing the natural observational apparatus of the observer. Among the tools to be discussed are those that facilitate the perceptual accuracy of live observations, the notational recording and reconstruction of perceived events, the recording of iconic representations of movements, the notational recording and reconstruction of iconic representations, the direct measurement of movement parameters, and the quantitative analysis of recorded parameters (see Table 5.1).

Often it is necessary to measure body motion in real time – for example, when immediate feedback must be given to subjects about their behavior or when it is not possible to obtain adequate photographic representations for later analysis. Real-time analysis of body motion can be enhanced by such conventional observational aids as telescopes and periscopes, rangefinders, and spatial landmarks, especially when observers are distant or hidden from subjects.

Most observational studies can benefit from event-recording devices, especially those that permit the observer to give persistent visual attention to the subject. The most versatile varieties currently available are small, lightweight, portable, and battery operated devices, with manual operation of a keyboard that permits alpha-numeric coding of any size category system, along with automatic synchronization to a real-time clock; these devices store the time-coded event sequences in a compact memory bank that can be directly interfaced into a digital computer.[2] Earlier varieties of event-recording devices stored events on separate channels of multitrack tape recorders or of multitrack strip-chart recorders (e.g., the popular Esterline-Angus 20-channel event recorder). Although all such methods preserve the temporal locations of events (e.g., the start and stop times), the strip-chart method has the drawback that the coded data must be transduced either by hand or by optical scanner before being entered into a computer.

Alternatively, the researcher who is operating on a low budget or wishes to be unencumbered by complex apparatus may get by simply with paper and pencil. For example, in one study of relatively uncomplicated categories of observed movement – head nods, speech-related gesticulations, and self-manipulations – the observers successfully marked letters corresponding to each category down a strip of adding-machine tape, without diverting visual attention from the subject (Rosenfeld, 1966b).

Other notational systems employ more iconic codes, that is, pictorial representations (see the illustrations in Key, 1977). Simple pictorial symbols representing body parts and orientations (e.g., Bakken, 1977; Birdwhistell, 1952, 1970 [see Figure 5.22]; Hall, 1963, 1974 [see Figures 5.17 and 5.18]) are useful for real-time descriptions of configurations of movement for which no conventional verbal labels have yet been coined. More elaborate iconic representations, ranging from realistic drawings (e.g., Austin, 1806/1966 [see Figure 5.3]; Efron, 1941/1972 [see Figure 5.21]; Mahl, 1968; Scheflen, 1965) to more abstract representations (e.g., Davis, 1979 [see Figures 5.15 and 5.16]; Golani, 1976 [see Figures 5.12 and 5.13]), may be too complex for use in real-time observation. But they are useful as off-line transformations of recorded data because of their efficiency for representation of critical configurations. Also technology is available for computer animation of movement.[3]

Perhaps it is stretching the concept of iconicity too far, but the taking of pictures of movements may be considered to be a very literal form of iconic representation. Direct motion pictures and open-shutter still pictures are two-dimensional representations in discrete time intervals that can preserve a tremendous amount of information about the spatiotemporal properties of real movements. A variety of special equipment for acquiring direct visual records of body motion, as well as advice about their usage, is available (see Gottschalk & Auerback, 1966; Grieve et al., 1975; Hutt & Hutt, 1974; Logan & McKinney, 1977; Wallbott, Technical Appendix).

Motion-picture film and, more recently, videotape have been the most popular recording materials. Devices for enhancing photographed movement include lenses varying in field of view and light sensitivity, film materials varying in light sensitivity and resolution, variable-speed recording by cameras and tape recorders, special lighting techniques to enhance detail, multiple angled mirrors or multiple synchronized cameras for three-dimensional recording of movement, and a host of rules of operation regarding such matters as camera placement, camera movement, and the identification of critical reference points or dimensions. Examples of conventional wisdom particularly applicable to the study of body motion are that high-velocity body movements are likely to blur on film frames when the camera speed is less than 32 frames per second, and thus that observer agreement on elementary changes in movement may require a "window" of several such frames (e.g., McDowall, 1979), and that lenses located farther away from the subject produce less spatial distortion owing to parallax error.

In addition to cost, a further disadvantage of filming rather than direct coding is that the filmed data remain to be coded. The coding of filmed representations of body motion can, of course, be accomplished by means of most of the observational methods that are applicable to the observation of behavior in real time. Real-time playback of motion pictures may be preferred if the purpose of the playback is to estimate how the actual observer or participant would have perceived the behavior. It also may be sufficiently reliable and valid for particular research goals.

An advantage of filmed recording is the opportunity to review the same record for purposes of identifying more information, and at a higher level of reliability, than can be processed at real time. The viewing and reviewing process can include variations in the rate of playback – fast motion to detect patterns that may be obscured by the detail of normal speed and slow motion to enhance the accurate detection of more molecular activities (see Figure 5.20). Special motion-analysis equipment can be used to optimize variable-speed analysis (see Kendon, Chapter 8; Wallbott, Technical Appendix).

To the degree that movement is viewed as a discrete time sequence, it also is possible to code single pictures or still frames from motion pictures for their configurations and spatial coordinates. Some researchers go through the intermediate step of tracing selected parts from projected films for this purpose (see Hutt & Hutt, 1974). To code a sequence of iconic images at the most elementary level – in terms of the spatial coordinates of the body points of interest – it is necessary to be able to identify the coordinate dimensions. Early efforts relied upon such techniques as independently identifying the distance between reference points in the environment and estimating their corresponding transformations on film (e.g., Efron, 1941/1972) and the addition of background grids visible in the film (see Hutt & Hutt, 1974; Logan & McKinney, 1977).

Another method for recording distances and angles is the superimposition of grids over images to be coded. In one simple predecessor of this technique, used for the assessment of interpersonal orientation and distance in two-person interactions, a protractor was placed over the spot on the floor of the environment where one person was located, and a tape measure at the pivot of the protractor was extended to the location of the other person, to provide measures of interpersonal distance and angle of orientation (Rosenfeld, 1965). In subsequent versions, temporary concentric circles and radii emanating at regular angles were taped to the floor where a reference person would be located, then recorded on slides (Breck & Rosenfeld, 1977 [see Figure 5.5]) or videotapes (Sussman & Rosenfeld, in press), and then removed from the floor. Then the subjects were filmed or videotaped by the same cameras, and the two images (dimensions and subjects) were subsequently superimposed on projection screens or video monitors. Intercoder agreement on intersubject chair placement distances to the nearest inch was better than 99%.

A wide variety of sophisticated, semiautomated methods for identifying spatial coordinates from pictures is now available. Figure 5.6 shows a Vanguard Film Analyzer for the observer-mediated identification of two-dimensional coordinates from moving-picture film. Various periph-

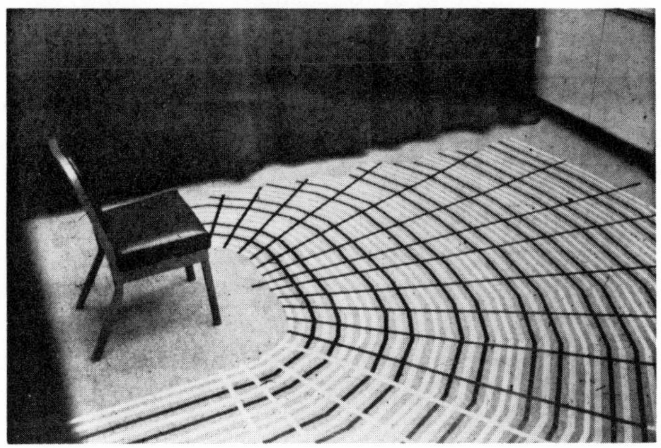

Figure 5.5. Removable-tape protractor for assessment of interpersonal distance and angle of orientation. *Source:* Breck and Rosenfeld, 1977.

Figure 5.6. Vanguard Film Analyzer for observer-mediated coding of two-dimensional coordinates of behavior. *Source:* Miller and Nelson, 1973, p. 142.

eral devices can be added, in order to facilitate entry of the coordinates into a computer (see Miller & Nelson, 1973). Another alternative is the graphic table, such as the Graf Pen device in which a film image is projected onto a graphic tablet. In the past, these graphic input devices were used more in cartography than in nonverbal communication studies. A typical form uses a mechanical or optical cursor that can be moved about above the surface to be coded (see Carau, 1979). The movable cursor is related by mechanical or electrical connections to the two-dimensional spatial coordinates of the surface, so that its location by the observer above any point on the screen permits an automatic readout of the coordinates of the intersecting lines. (Note, however, that devices using two-dimensional microphone pickups from a stylus may be susceptible to sound interference from other sources.)

Particularly useful for the study of body motion is the application of graphic input devices to television monitors (see Figure 5.7). In addition to providing the coordinates defining the length and width of the surface, this method can also be used to superimpose arbitrarily placeable coordinates on the screen. Actions can thus be described with reference to other movable body parts or to movable objects, as well as to the fixed environment (Frey & Pool, 1976; also see Futrelle, 1973).

If the motion of a subject is at right angles to the camera, and thus also to the observer of the film, it usually is not difficult to identify the two-dimensional coordinates of movement. If only a two-dimensional picture is available, it might be possible to estimate motion in the third dimension on the basis of such cues as the relative size of the object on the screen, or the amount of light the object reflects from a fixed light source in the environment. Efron (1941/1972) describes some clever techniques for estimating motion in the third dimension from two-dimensional film, using photographed simulations from models of moving body parts and trigonometric calculations. But there is a more accurate way of identifying coordinates of movement in two- or three-dimensional space.

For some purposes research on body motion requires extremely precise measurement of displacement – for example, in the study of sports kinesiology and rehabilitative medicine. The ideal measuring technique in such circumstances is the completely automated optoelectronic measuring device. A currently workable example is the SELLSPOT system.[4] In this technique, critical body points of the subject are designated, and tiny light-emitting diodes are placed upon each point. Thin wires connect the lights to a portable battery, which distributes momentary power to them in extremely rapid sequences. Multiple

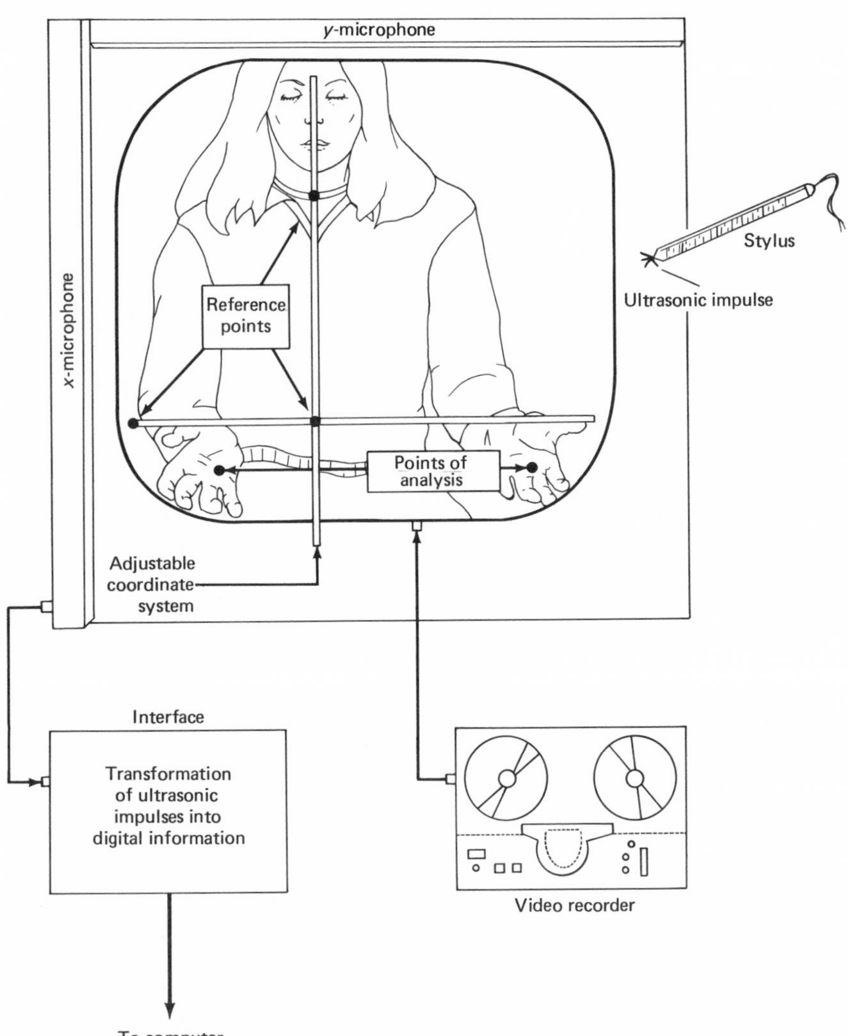

Figure 5.7. An adaptation of a graphic computer input device for coding two-dimensional coordinates from videotape. The microphones pick up the ultrasonic impulse released by the stylus when pressed down at any point on the video screen. The respective *xy* coordinates as given by the microphone response are digitally entered into a computer. *Source:* Adapted from Wallbott, 1980.

optoelectronic monitors, which are temporally synchronized to the pulsing cycle of the lights, record the spatial location of each light in three dimensions, and transmit the spatial coordinates of each lighted point to a computer. Gustafsson and Lanshammar (1977) provided an automatic analysis of gait using the SELLSPOT system. In addition, they

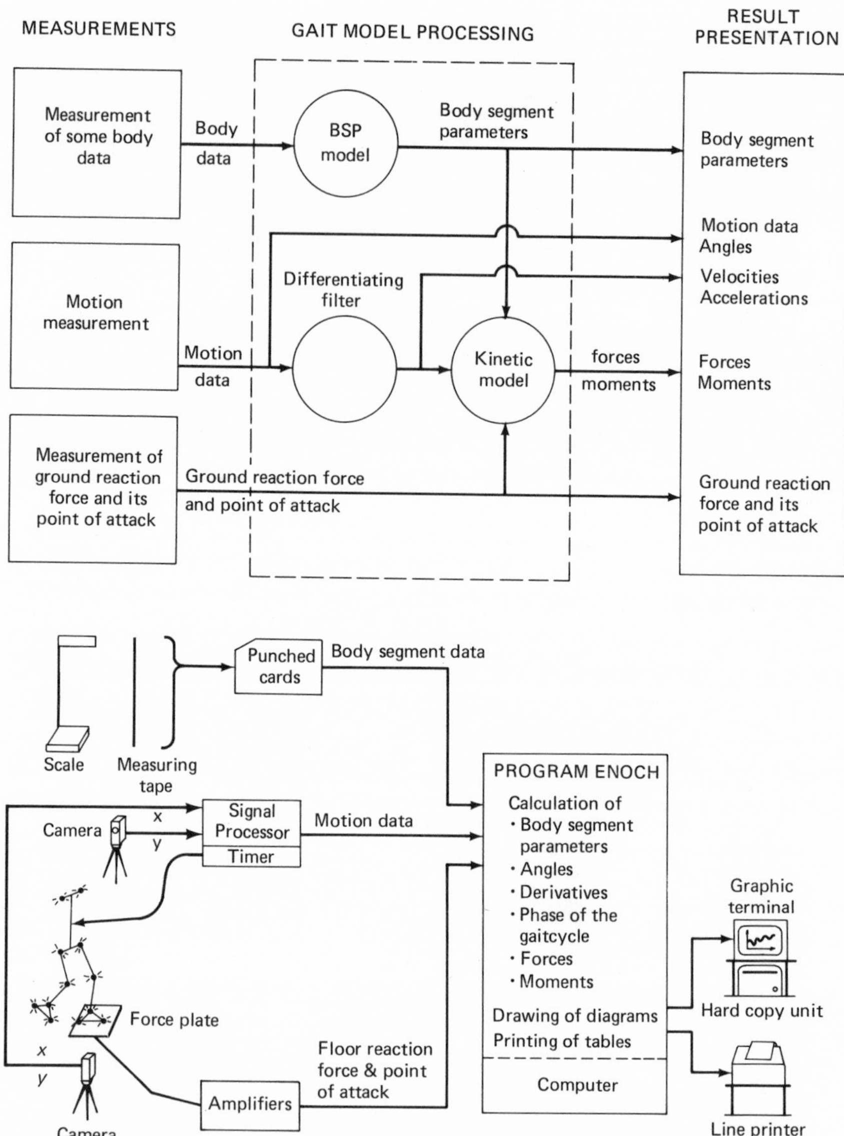

Figure 5.8. The ENOCH system for gait analysis: *top,* functional view; *bottom,* technical realization. *Source:* Gustafsson and Lanshammar, 1977, pp. 22, 24.

made direct assessments of the force of gait with dynametric devices (force plates; cf. Grieve et al., 1975), which were integrated with the body motion data by means of an automated system labeled ENOCH (see Figures 5.8 and 5.9).

Whereas the optoelectronic method requires maintenance of direct

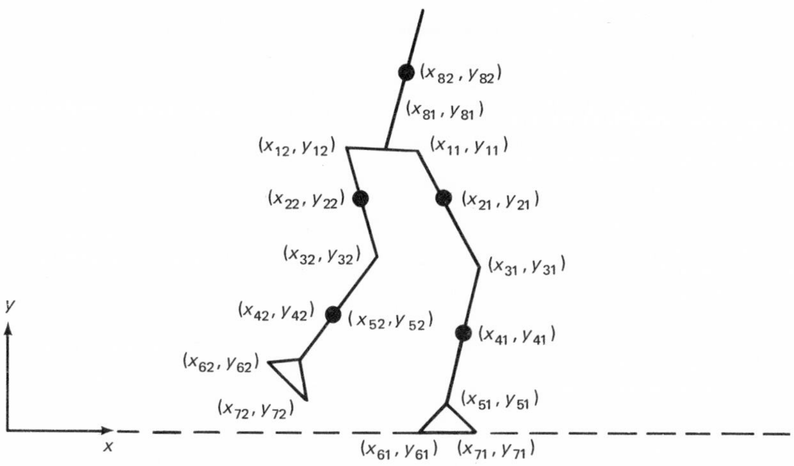

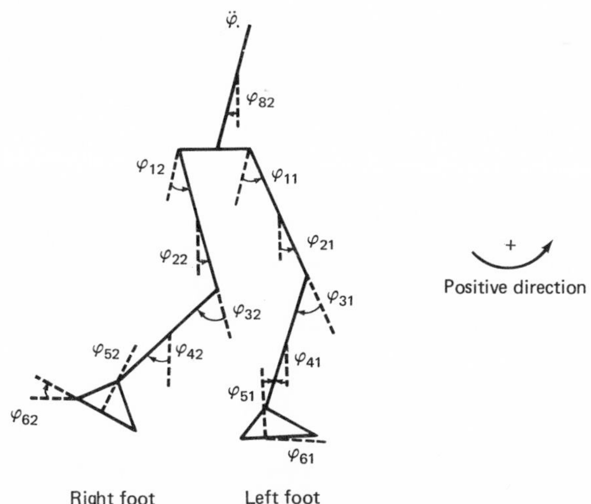

Figure 5.9. Cartesian coordinates *(top)* and angular displacements *(bottom)* in gait analysis. *Source:* Gustafsson and Lanshammar, 1977, p. 131.

light contact between the moving subject and a recording device in a fixed location of the environment, other direct measurement instruments are attached to the body. One standard tool is the electrogoniometer, placed at the joints of connected segments, which automatically assesses the angle of displacement of a motion by means of potentiometers (Gollnick & Karpovitch, 1964 [see Figure 5.10]; Grieve et al., 1975).

Another set of devices simply assesses amount of motion of the body.

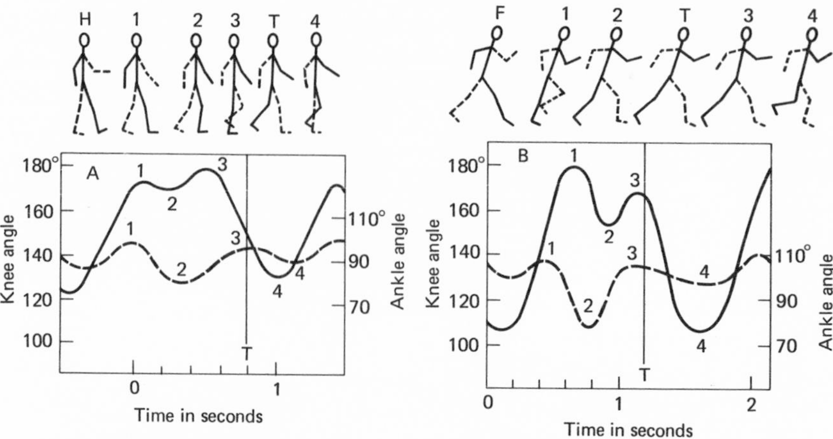

Figure 5.10. Direct goniographic recording of the right knee and right ankle in walking and running: Solid line = knee; broken line = ankle; *A* = walking on horizontal at 2.5 mph with 120 steps per min; *B* = running on horizontal at 5.0 mph with natural cadence; *H* = heel contact in walking; *F* = foot contact (in running); *T* = toe lift; knee (1) = first extension, (2) = shock absorption; (3) = second extension, (4) = greatest flexion; ankle (1) = first extension, (2) = flexion during support phase, (3) = second extension, (4) = flexion during swing phase. *Source:* Gollnick and Karpovitch, 1964, p. 360.

Gross motor activity of animals in cages, infants in cribs, and children in chairs has commonly been measured by stabilimeters consisting of transducers sensitive to movement of environmental objects or enclosures (e.g., Lewis & Wilson, 1970). Movements of several different body segments can be simultaneously assessed by the use of accelerometers consisting of motion-sensitive transducers attached to each part (Dittmann & Llewellyn, 1969).

Most of these direct measurement techniques have the potential disadvantage of producing reactive effects in subjects, owing to their awareness of being assessed, as well as possible physical constraints on action. A more subtle device is the hodometer for assessing paths of locomotion of subjects, in which a grid of pneumatically operated switches in pillows beneath a carpet unobtrusively records the locations of footfalls (Bechtel, 1970).

5.5. Quantitative analysis

Assuming that the elementary features of body motion can be described quantitatively, the problem of summarizing the data so that they can be characterized in an efficient and meaningful way remains. Mathematical formulas and corresponding computer programs for reduction of quantitative data are indispensable tools for a scientific system of analyzing communicative body movements and configurations. Reference has been made to two such methods – the fully automated ENOCH system for the direct remote analysis of locomotion (Gustafsson & Lanshammar, 1977) and a semiautomated system for analyzing videotapes of movement (Frey & Pool, 1976). In both cases, the elementary quantitative data to be analyzed consist of the spatial coordinates of particular body parts over temporal units.

The classic notational systems for representing the locations of events in space can be found in standard geometry books (e.g., Olmsted, 1947). They are the Cartesian or, alternatively, the polar coordinates of the events. Cartesian coordinates are sets of two or three numbers referring to the location of a point at the intersection of orthogonal dimensions describing two- or three-dimensional space.

To describe a movement of a body part, it is necessary to assess coordinates for at least two temporal units (e.g., start and stop positions). If the event to be described is a static position, its location can be compared to the location of a prior position or a standard baseline position. Examples of referent positions are the standard anatomical position described earlier or some conventional configuration of the body, such as the position it assumes when sitting upright in a chair. The two-dimensional polar coordinates of a position are the radius (the segment, e.g., forearm) connecting the moving point of interest (e.g., wrist) to its origin (e.g., elbow joint), and its angle of displacement from a reference dimension (e.g., horizontal axis). The Cartesian and polar descriptions of a displacement are functionally equivalent mathematical representations, as will be shown in a subsequent example.

If the investigator is interested in orientation toward an environmental or social object, then a standard external referent will be appropriate. For example, in one study of the use of chair placement as a means of ingratiation by subjects, the standard orientation was defined as a line from the center of the subject's chair to the center of the object person's chair. This was compared to the line from the center of the subject's chair through the center of the front of the subject's chair. It was hypothesized that the size of the angle formed by the two lines indicated the degree to which the subject communicated an interest in a close relationship by means of chair placement. Comparison to subjects in a noningratiating control condition failed to validate the hypothesis, although a second hypothesis that shorter distance between chairs reflects ingratiation was verified (Rosenfeld, 1965). In a similar vein, subsequent studies have studied direction of lean and amount of postural asymmetry as indicators of social attitude (Mehrabian, 1972).

To illustrate the application of spatial notation, consider that one's data consist of a videotape of a handshake greeting, recorded with the camera perpendicular to the line of action. Suppose that the current object of interest is the movement of the hand in the two-dimensional plane of the video monitor on which the videotape is played back. Further assume that the hand movement is considered to result from rotation of the forearm, pivoting at the elbow (the wrist is assumed to be rigid). Suppose that we project a pair of orthogonal spatial dimensions through the elbow point – a vertical line or y axis for displacement in the up–down direction and a horizontal line or x axis representing the forward–backward direction.

The Cartesian coordinates of the center of the hand at any moment (film frame) during the handshake are simply the pair of numerical values representing its projection onto the x and y axes. The polar coordinates of the same location are the length of the line (radius) connecting the elbow to the hand and the angle (theta) formed by the segment and a referential axis (say, the x axis).

Further assume that a line is added connecting the hand to the x axis, so that a right triangle is formed joining the hand, the elbow, and the point connecting the hand to the x axis. The Cartesian and polar descriptions would be interchangeable because, by the Pythagorean theorem, the radius equals the square root of the sum of the squared sides of a right triangle; and theta is the angle whose tangent is the y side divided by the x side. The actual displacement of the hand in space during a time interval, owing to rotation at the elbow, is describable as the arc of the circle formed at the outer point of the radius. (By coincidence, one of the two long bones of the forearm happens to be called the radius.)

To complicate the matter slightly, consider that the motion of the forearm occurred in a plane other than that of the filmed image, for example, obliquely away from the camera. Suppose that by using the estimating techniques discussed earlier, or by adding a second camera at right angles to the first, we were able to assess the three-dimensional Cartesian coordinates of the location of the hand. The polar (or, in this case, spherical) equivalents of the Cartesian coordinates of the sphere of action would require assessment of the length of the radius, as before, and of two orthogonal angles to characterize the location of the hand within its conical field of action. The actual displacement of the hand from one moment to another would now be described as an arc on the surface of a sphere, rather than as an arc of a circle.

Figure 5.11. Rotation and translation of body parts during movement. Here the cyclist translates his upper body along a horizontal path by means of rotation of his legs. *Source:* Hay, 1978, p. 13.

Let us complicate the example further. Very likely the displacement of the hand in space in a handshaking episode is attributable not only to motion of the forearm, but to the extension of the upper arm as well. To have a more complete record of the motion, it is necessary to relocate the orthogonal spatial dimensions through the shoulder joint and to determine the coordinates of the upper arm, just as was done for the lower arm. But given the tree structure of the limbs, it is obvious that the two sets of coordinates are not independent. The position of the hand can be defined by its location relative to the shoulder as well as to the elbow. It is not difficult to imagine variations on this theme in which a larger number of body segments are interrelated; for example, the handshake may be accompanied by a bow, which will involve rotation of the trunk in the displacement of the hand.

Fortunately, there are quantitative procedures that permit interrelation of a series of connected segments so that they can be described in relation to each other (e.g., the location of the hand can be described relative to the shoulder or to the other hand; see also Figure 5.11). These procedures transform the set of coordinates describing each point into *homogeneous coordinates*. This transformation can be accomplished by *rotation* of the axes of the displaced point to match those of the reference point and *translation* of the location of the displaced point to the values of the reference sphere. The matrices within which the coordinates of displacement of each connected body part are defined can be multiplied to derive the relative displacements of more remotely connected parts. The reader is referred to Newman and Sproull (1979) for more detail.

What difference does it make which of all these alternatives one selects in describing motion? For one thing, certain kinds of instruments require certain notations; for example, the direct measurement of movements by goniometers attached to joints requires angle of displacement as the elementary measure. A more important consideration is related to the perception of motion. As noted earlier, it is not always clear what physical cues an observer uses in assigning observed behavior to a particular verbal category of action. Take the case of rating the friendliness of a handshake greeting. Is the critical characteristic the movement of the hand in the frontal plane? If so, does the observer attend only to the motion of the hand, or perhaps also to the angle at the elbow? Would different ratings result from differential attention to the two areas? Might the observer also be attentive to the degree to which the subject extends the hand forward (owing to upper arm rotation at the shoulder), and might the observer perhaps give extra weight to the inclusion of a bow of the trunk? Without the capacity for relating perceptual categories to common denominators of physical action, and to their mathematical derivatives, it is unlikely that the study of body motion can progress far as a scientific endeavor.

5.6. Research applications

For the researcher who is seeking the "right" method for measuring body motion, the extreme diversity of existing measurement systems may appear confusing and frustrating. But methods should be viewed as tools for answering substantive and theoretical questions. Many of the existing methods differ in their appropriateness for answering different questions; and a wide variety of theoretical and substantive questions concerning body motion have been posed in the literature. On the other hand, when different researchers use different methods to answer very similar questions, it is legitimate to ask which alternative is preferable. The answer must depend ultimately upon comparison of the information gained to the human and material costs of the different methods. Thus far, there have been few systematic studies of the relative effectiveness and efficiency of different measurement systems for the study of different problems of nonverbal communication through body motion.

Inasmuch as existing systems for measuring body motion have been devised for a variety of substantive purposes and derived from a variety of theoretical perspectives, they tend to vary along multiple dimensions. It is beyond the scope of this chapter to attempt to catalogue the extensive empirical literature on body motion to achieve a comprehensive factorial structure of methodology. It is hoped, however, that the conceptual structure presented here will aid the reader who is interested in making such comparisons. In the present section, relationships between broad categories of problems and of methods are discussed, along with some examples from the research literature.

Although the classification of substantive problems and of methods into discrete categories is necessarily somewhat arbitrary, several distinctions are useful for analytic purposes. A basic difference between substantive areas corresponds to the distinction made early in this chapter between instrumental and referential functions. The instrumental category is concerned with movements involved in a variety of skills, whereas the referential category is concerned with movements and positions that serve as indicators of other characteristics of actors.

Within the instrumental and referential realms, a further distinction can be made between personal and social aspects. The personal category of skills includes such acts as normal locomotion (Gustafsson & Lanshammar, 1977), athletic activities (Grieve et al., 1975; Logan & McKinney, 1977), and drawing (Connolly & Elliott, 1972). At the social level of skills are such subcategories as signaling deference and avoiding social conflicts (Greenbaum & Rosenfeld, 1978; McGrew, 1972), establishing social relationships (Greenbaum & Rosenfeld, 1980), and performing various tasks involved in carrying out face-to-face conversations (Goffman, 1963; Kendon, 1973, 1977). Some skills are more difficult to label as personal or social, for example, sign language (Stokoe, 1972), dancing (Laban, 1975), and job performance (Lamb & Turner, 1969).

In the referential category are movements and configurations associated with individual and group differences. At the individual level a basic substantive distinction can be made between indicators of general arousal (Freedman & Hoffman, 1967), and more specific states of mind, such as emotions (Ekman & Friesen, 1969b), motives (Rosenfeld, 1966a, 1966b), attitudes (Mehrabian, 1972), and memories (Mahl, 1968). At the group level, referential characteristics serve to discriminate memberships in different social categories (Birdwhistell, 1970; Efron 1941/1972; Hewes, 1955).

These categories are not mutually exclusive. Persons in a given behavior setting may exhibit configurations of body motion from any, several, or all of the areas; and they may do so simultaneously or sequentially. For example, individual and group differences in referential communication style can affect the abilities of mixed combinations of interactants to regulate their social relationships skillfully (Giles & Powesland, 1975).

Regarding the classification of methodology, a basic distinction can be made between elementary systems of measurement and higher-order systems. Elementary systems emphasize minimal components of movement, whereas higher-order systems emphasize complex functional configurations as their basic units. The higher-order systems may or may not use more elementary features to define their categories.

In general, different elementary systems tend to have similar categories of measurement, owing to their common grounding in the fundamentals of anatomy and kinesiology (see Birdwhistell, 1952; Eshkol, 1973; Laban, 1975). In contrast, higher-order systems tend to differ from each other because each provides complex measures that pertain to particular theoretical and substantive problems (see Ekman & Friesen, 1969b; McGrew, 1972).

In principle, elementary systems should be more generally applicable across problem areas than are higher-order systems. In fact, however, most elementary systems have had relatively limited application. One likely reason is that they have tended to be more costly and difficult to apply. This problem should be reduced as technological innovations become more available.

There tends to be a rough association between level of methodological analysis and type of substantive problem. In general, elementary levels of analysis have been applied to the study of personal skills, whereas higher-order systems have been applied to studies of referential communication. A likely reason is that skills often require formal training, which in turn requires specific information about the performance of elementary components of action. In contrast, many complex referential acts are more likely to be learned unintentionally through modeling processes, rather than by training in components. Correspondingly, investigators more often are interested in identifying the occurrence of referential acts than in modifying their performance. Thus the common experience of observers, perhaps aided by simple verbal definitions and visual models, may prove adequate for measurement of many referential categories, such as emblems (Ekman & Friesen, 1969b), at a gestalt level.

5.7. Models and systems of measurement

Although every empirical study of body motion is based upon methods of measurement, not all such studies are methodologically systematic. A systematic approach to measurement consists of logically coherent and efficient concepts and procedures selected for their applicability to a domain of substantive interests. In this section some major systems will be briefly identified on the basis of the explicit or implicit theoretical models underlying their construction. It should be realized, however, that this effort to categorize researchers is bound to contain some "error of measurement," owing to the complexity of many of the measurement schemes being considered, as well as to biases in the person who does the categorizing.

Biomechanical models

The most elementary systems of analysis are modeled upon well-established principles of physical science. In particular, they draw upon the laws of mechanics as applied to anatomical constructions. They also commonly use the notational and computational principles of solid geometry.

Users of biomechanical models are particularly likely to rely upon technical apparatus for the direct measurement of behavior. Because such methods are relatively free of human error, reliability of measurement seldom is assessed. However, there is still a risk of accumulation of small errors when a variety of elementary measurements is assessed, transformed, and integrated (Grieve et al., 1975).

Several prominent systems for the measurement of body motion are based upon the elementary segmental structure of the skeletal system. The well-established field of anatomic kinesiology, with its terminology for description of elementary movements (Logan & McKinney, 1977), most commonly has been used in research on instrumental uses of the body. Grieve et al. (1975) describe a diverse array of tools for the objective, elementary measurement of motion and for computation of some higher-order derivatives. They also provide sophisticated discussions of approprate occasions for the usage of the methods, although they do not deal with the special problems of application of these methods to the analysis of complex referential communicative processes. Some initial efforts toward extending the applicability of the principles of anatomic kinesiology to referential communicative acts have been made by Higgins (1977) and Wallbott (1980).

One of the most generally applicable systems of measurement was developed in Israel by Eshkol and Wachmann (see Eshkol, 1973). Golani (1976) has offered an excellent, comprehensive discussion of the system, including its theoretical assumptions, its past and potential applications to substantive questions, and the location of source materials.[5] The system allows full description of any action in terms of the angles of all limb displacements within overlapping spheres of action (see Figure

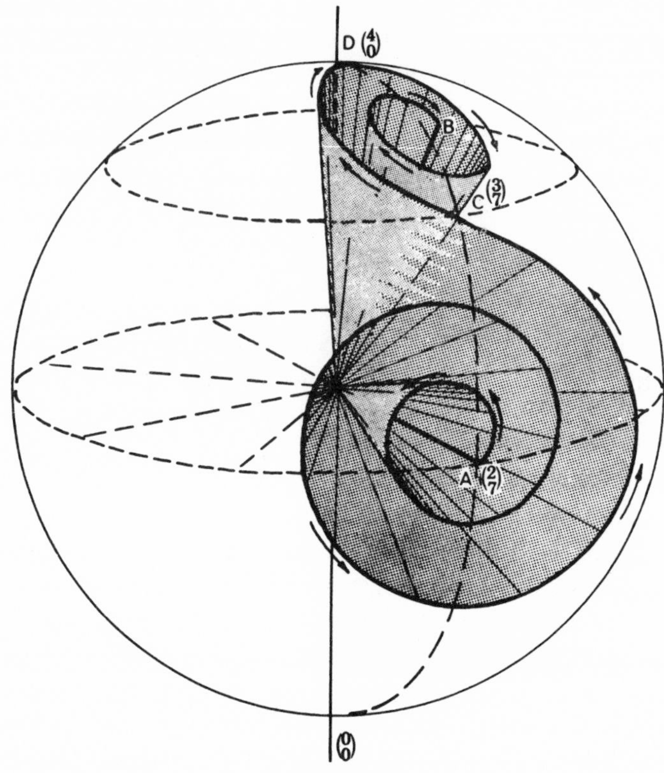

Figure 5.12. Eshkol and Wachmann analysis: The extremity of a limb segment moves on the surface of an imaginary sphere. *Source:* Golani, 1976, p. 74

5.12). Thus a movement can be reconstructed in the absence of prior structural or functional definitions. The spheres of action themselves can be located within any frame or frames of reference, such as the standard anatomical position, other baseline body positions, or environmental and social objects. This choice is left to the researcher. The size of the sectors in a sphere of rotation is selected according to the needs for precision in spatial discrimination of the particular investigation. For example, instead of plotting the location of a body part at a particular moment according to its location on 360° scales of longitude or latitude, the investigator may decide that only eight sectors, each covering 45°, should provide sufficient resolution.

The notation system conveys both discrete and continuous properties of movement. As described by Golani (1976), in any selected coordinate system

> *an actual elementary movement is defined as a movement performed by a limb segment, and is specified by four variables: the initial position; the angle between the moving limb and the axis of movement; the sense of the movement (clockwise or anticlockwise); and the speed of the movement.* A constant rate of change in the first of the last of the above variables still defines one elementary movement. A discrete change in any of these variables terminates one movement and starts another. [P. 76, original emphasis]

Golani noted that the Eshkol–Wachmann system has been applied, not only to his own analyses of courtship patterns and sexual relationships among golden jackals (see Figure 5.13) and among Tasmanian devils, but also to body motion in physical education, physiotherapy, dance, sign language, and graphic art. Newtson et al. (1977) used the system to explore the relationship between instrumental categories of actors' behavior and the ways such behavior was segmented by observers.

The act of walking has been particularly well analyzed at the elementary level. The sophisticated elementary analyses and simulations of walking conducted by Johansson (1973) provide evidence about some of the basic psychophysical processes involved in the perception of body motion. The analysis of motion perception is extremely important for relating the observational and direct measurement levels of analysis. It is to be hoped that Johansson's approach will be applied productively to complex referential communicative acts, so that the efficient methods of elementary analysis used by Gustafsson and Lanshammar (1977) and those proposed by Frey and Pool (1976) can be more extensively used.

Inasmuch as infancy is a period in which motor behavior develops from relatively diffuse to more coordinated states, it is not surprising that anatomic notation and elementary movement analysis are also commonly employed on research on infants. Hutt and Hutt (1974) review and evaluate the methods used in several studies of infant development. Examples are the early studies by Gesell (1935; Gesell & Halverson, 1942), which included the use of slow-motion analysis of films, spatial grids, matrices for the coding of acts by body part and time units, and the coding of still positions and movements at both molecular and molar levels. Among the findings was the identification of the development of increasingly complex, symmetrical arm extensions. These are likely to be precursors to the development of instrumental skills such as object manipulation, and to referential acts such as deictic or pointing gestures (see Jancovic, Devoe, & Wiener, 1975). Another example is the research of Kessen and his colleagues (Kessen, Hendry, & Leutzendorff, 1961; Kessen, Leutzendorff, & Stoutsenberger, 1967),

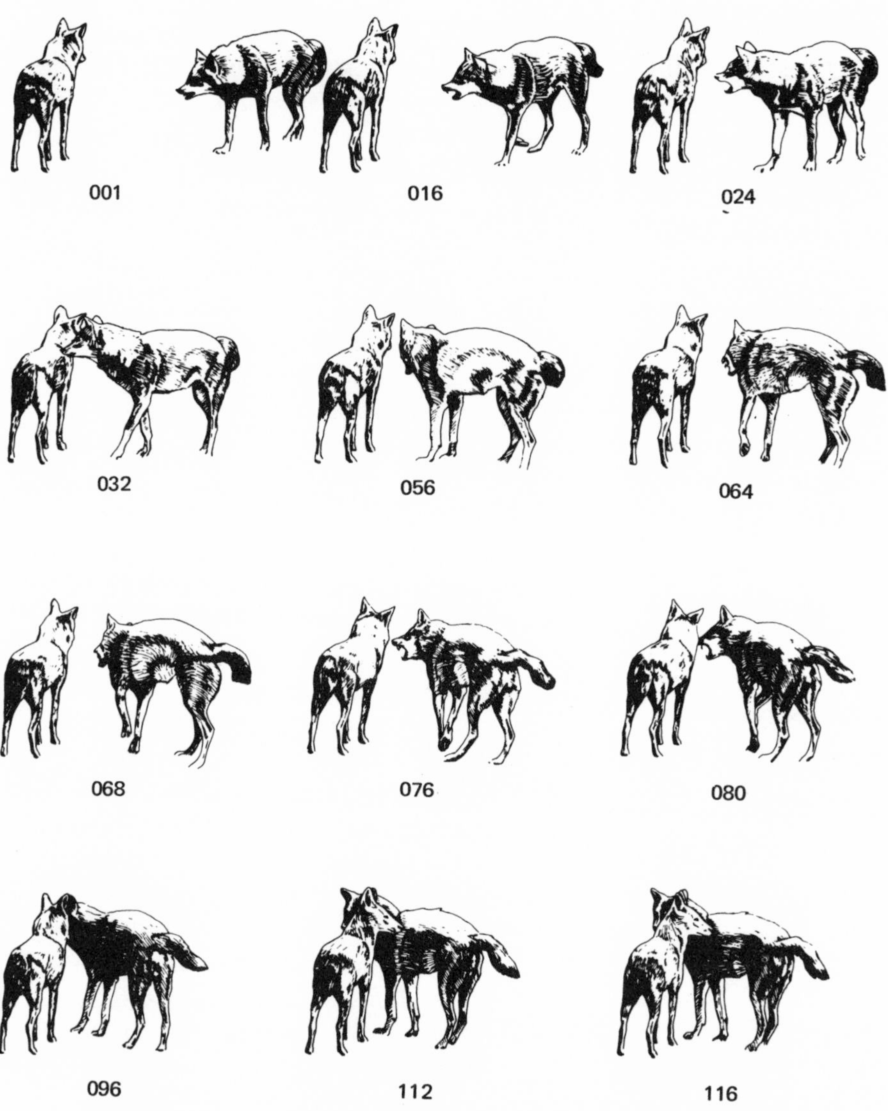

Figure 5.13. Application of the Eshkol and Wachmann system to the analysis of 5 sec of precopulatory motor interaction of golden jackals. The same 24-frames-per-second 16-mm film was used for both drawings and notation, with numerals indicating frame numbers. Drawings were made of beginning or end of actual

who noted that the measurement of body point displacements from sampled frames of motion pictures provides more replicable, as well as more detailed, data about infant movement than had been available from earlier research using stabilimeters.

Although the concepts of anatomic kinesiology have been applied

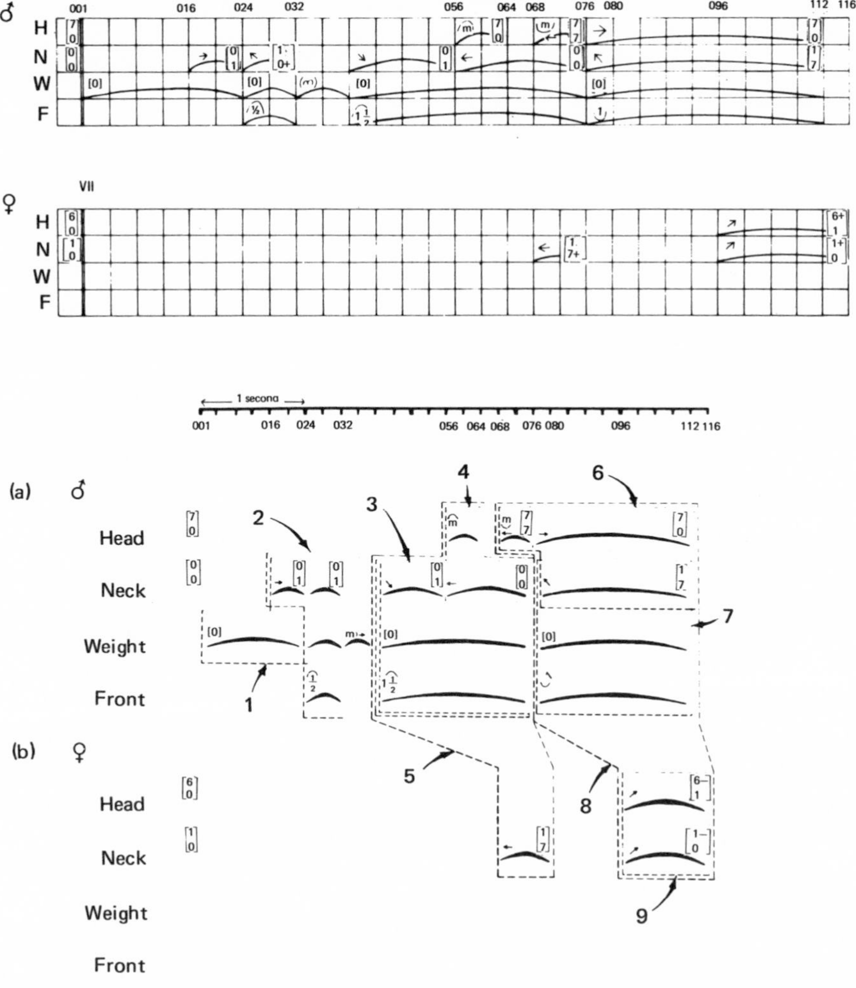

movements; the male is on the right. Section (a) provides notation of the concatenate. Section (b) adds superimposition of routes of convergence. *Source:* Golani, 1976, pp. 102, 103.

primarily to the analysis of physical skills, they also have been used for the identification of basic structural properties of face-to-face interaction, at both the personal and social levels (Condon, 1979; Kendon, 1972). However, these will be discussed elsewhere, within the context of the theoretical model to which each is most closely related.

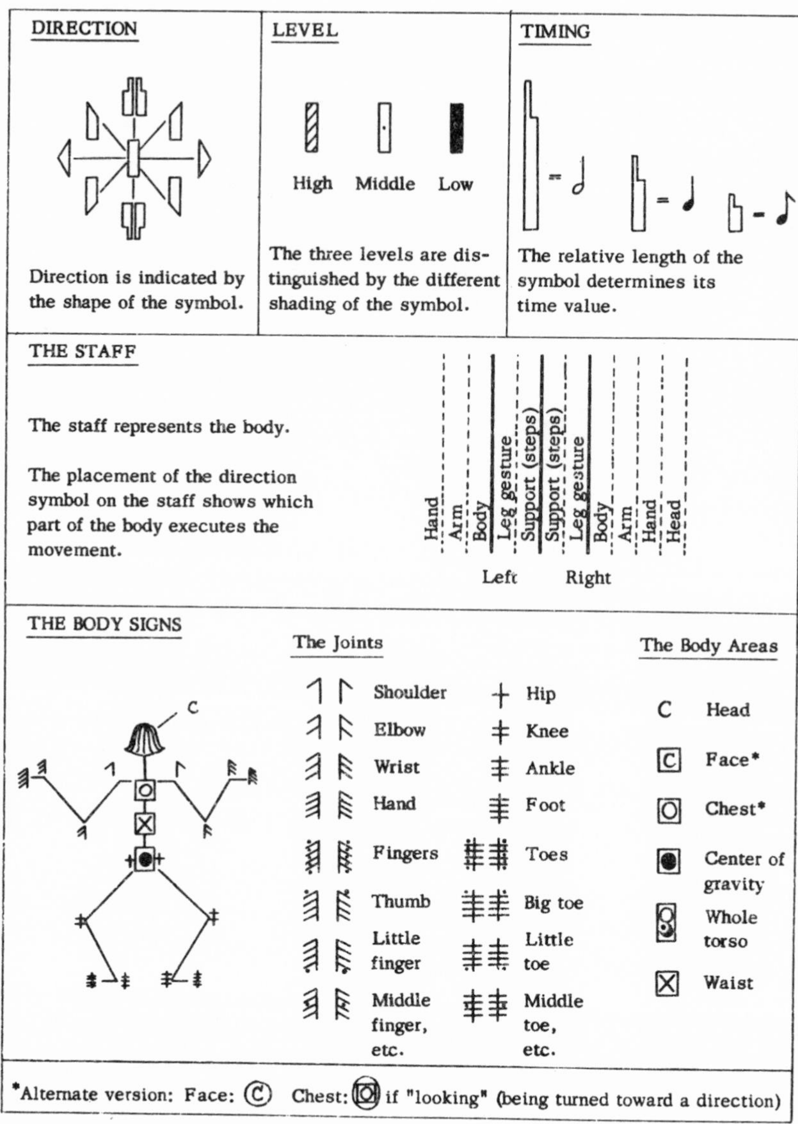

Figure 5.14. Some symbols used in Labanotation. *Source:* Hutchinson, 1961, p. 263.

The musical analogy

According to Laban (1975), the development of his well-known notational system was motivated by the model of musical notation systems. Laban sought a similar degree of precision, efficiency, generality of application, and qualitative elegance. The Laban system, like the Eshkol–Wachmann system, was strongly influenced by an interest in dance and also claims broad applicability to other areas of interest.

However, Laban puts more emphasis on qualitative and subjective features of movement than does Eshkol.

The system includes a basic segmentation of the skeletal system (see Figure 5.14), although with more differentiation of the feet than is characteristic of most other systems (e.g., sole, top, instep, heel). It also includes some basic kinesiological terms (e.g., rotations, measured in eights of a circle), spatial terms (e.g., straight and circular paths, small versus large range of space utilized), and terms for object relationships (e.g., touch, carry). The length of the symbol is varied to show duration of action. Of particular significance in Labanotation is the use of symbols to reflect qualitative aspects of body motion, referred to under the general categories *effort* and *shape*. For example, movements are described according to their fluency, strength, weakness, relaxation, and resistance.

In addition to its application to dance and to dance therapy, Labanotation has been applied to the analysis of athletics, industrial performance (Lamb & Turner, 1969), and motor discharge in infant development (Kestenberg, 1965). A general discussion of the potential of the Laban system for the analysis of nonverbal communication and detailed illustrations of its application to the description of some human greetings are provided by Davis (1979 [see Figures 5.15 and 5.16]). Although there is no doubt that the qualitative terms in the notational system reflect many subjective conceptions of motion that are prominent in everyday language, it remains to be determined how reliably such features can be observed.

Biosocial models

The ethological approach to the analysis of body motion is based upon both a theoretical model and a distinctive method (Blurton Jones, 1972; McGrew, 1972). Biological evolutionary theory underlies the ethologist's search for adaptive patterns of behavior among members of a species observed in their natural environment. Thus its concepts emphasize such general functions as the management of conflict through *agonistic* behavior and the promotion of productive social relationships through *bonding* behaviors. It is not surprising that many of the categories in the recently emerging field of *human* ethology are similar to categories previously developed for analysis of other species.

The most active application of ethological concepts to human behavior appears in analyses of children's peer interactions in schools and playgrounds. Extensive lists of such ethologically relevant behaviors are available in the writings of Blurton Jones (1972), McGrew (1972 [see

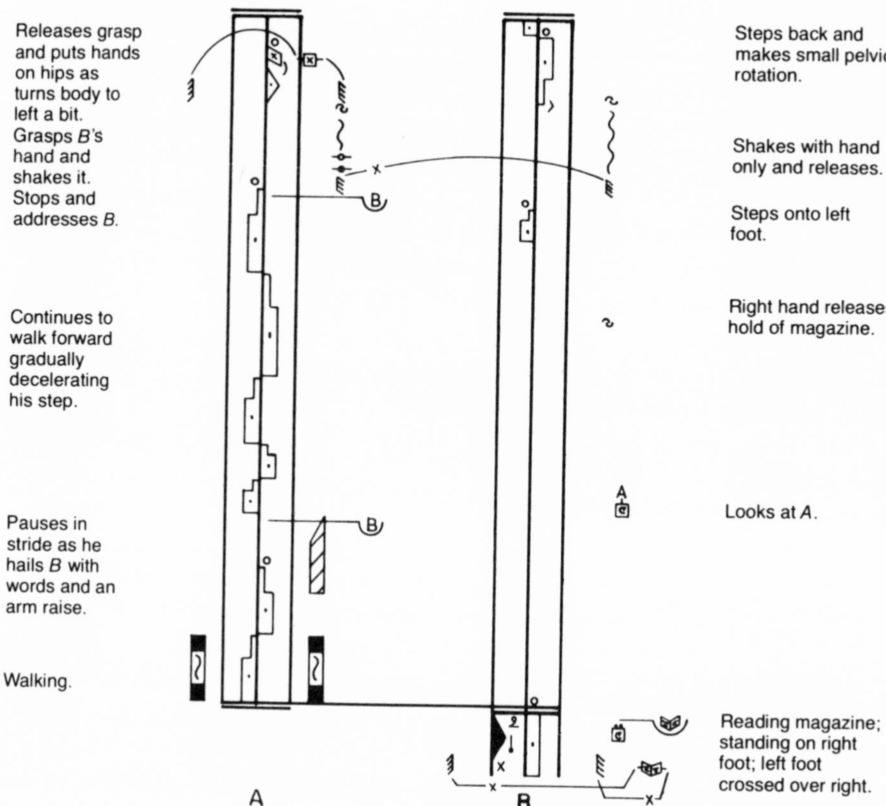

Releases grasp and puts hands on hips as turns body to left a bit.
Grasps B's hand and shakes it.
Stops and addresses B.
Continues to walk forward gradually decelerating his step.
Pauses in stride as he hails B with words and an arm raise.
Walking.
Steps back and makes small pelvic rotation.
Shakes with hand only and releases.
Steps onto left foot.
Right hand releases hold of magazine.
Looks at A.
Reading magazine; standing on right foot; left foot crossed over right.
A
B

This is a record of a greeting sequence in which *A* hails, approaches, and initiates handshaking with a rather reticent *B*. The movement of each person is shown on individual staffs: *A* and *B*. These are connected by means of the horizontal line at the bottom, indicating that the sequences are done simultaneously. The notation is read from the bottom up. Symbols below the first connecting line show *B*'s position. Placement of symbols in columns, as well as individual body part symbols, represent the body part which is used. The vertical center line divides the body right and left. The length of the symbols shows length of time of the movement. Locomotion is shown in the center columns (= forward steps for *A*). Arm and other body gestures are placed in the outer columns (for example, *A* hails *B* with arm right forward diagonal high:). Relationships are shown through the use of various types of bows, for example, *B* holding magazine with hands:

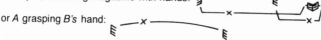

or *A* grasping *B's* hand:

Figure 5.15. Application of Labanotation to a greeting sequence. *Source:* Davis, 1979, p. 185, notation by James Pforsich.

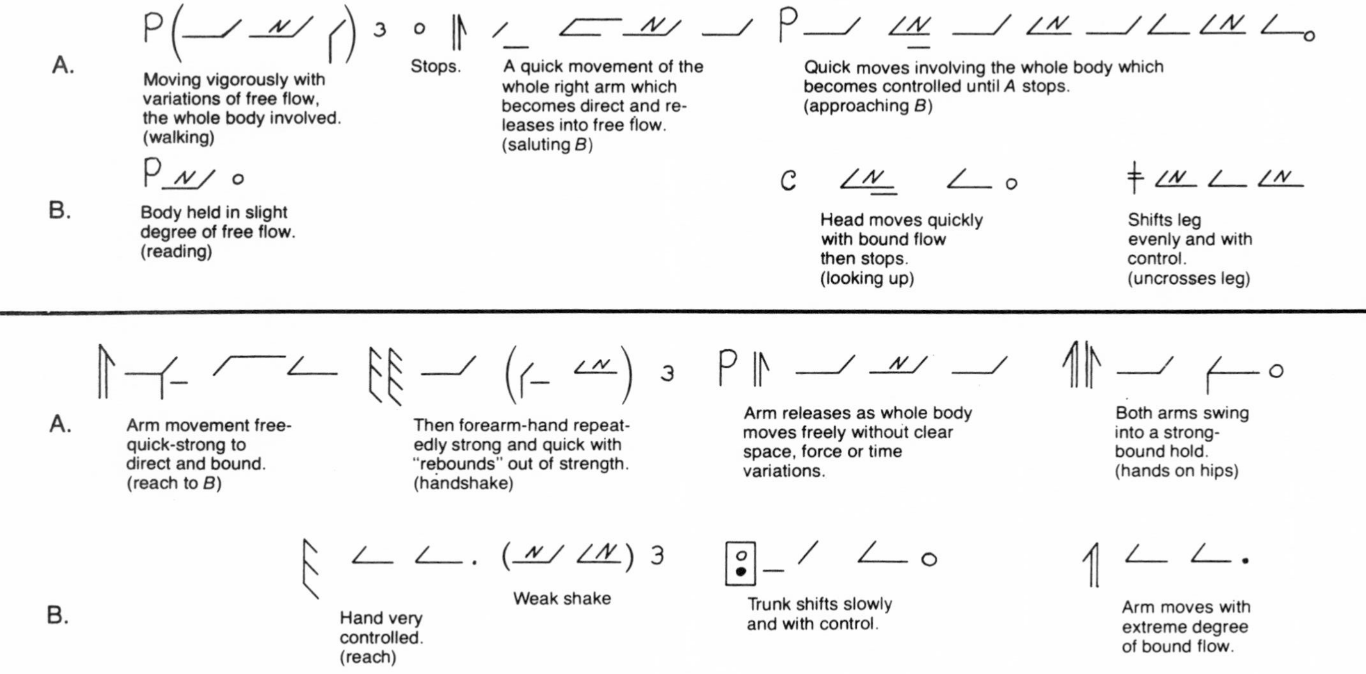
A.
Moving vigorously with variations of free flow, the whole body involved. (walking)
3
Stops.
A quick movement of the whole right arm which becomes direct and re-leases into free flow. (saluting B)
Quick moves involving the whole body which becomes controlled until A stops. (approaching B)
B.
Body held in slight degree of free flow. (reading)
Head moves quickly with bound flow then stops. (looking up)
Shifts leg evenly and with control. (uncrosses leg)
A.
Arm movement free-quick-strong to direct and bound. (reach to B)
Then forearm-hand repeat-edly strong and quick with "rebounds" out of strength. (handshake)
3
Arm releases as whole body moves freely without clear space, force or time variations.
Both arms swing into a strong-bound hold. (hands on hips)
B.
Hand very controlled. (reach)
Weak shake
3
Trunk shifts slowly and with control.
Arm moves with extreme degree of bound flow.

This recording of the same handshake greeting shows two very different movement patterns. *A* is vigorous, free-swinging, and postural. *B* maintains a bland, controlled, and restricted manner. The basic effort symbols have a diagonal stroke in common (for example ⌈ = strong, ∠ = bound, ⌐ = direct, —´ = slow). The body part symbols are abstracted from a stick figure (for example ‖ = whole arm, ⋶ = forearm-hand, ⁞ = whole trunk) except for P which indicates a "postural" movement (one which involves the whole body). Effort flow in notation form is often denoted in terms of degree (.—/ = very free, —/ = free, N/ = neutral or somewhat free, ∠N = neutral or slightly bound, ∠ = bound, ∠. = very bound).

Figure 5.16. Effort notation of a handshake greeting. *Source:* Davis, 1979, p. 189.

Table 5.6]), and Hutt and Hutt (1974). For more than 100 motor activities of children, McGrew provides extensive operational definitions at the level of elementary movement, along with reliability coefficients and summaries of validating evidence. Hutt and Hutt (1974) add data on frequency of occurrence and duration, along with briefer definitions of McGrew's categories. The categories typically are grouped topographically, according to the major body part involved (e.g., head, upper limb), as well as functionally, according to relationships to social and nonsocial objects. Examples of the categories are head nod, hit, scratch, reach, crouch, and march. The verbal definitions of the categories include elementary features of anatomic kinesiology. For example, in the head nod, "the head is moved forward and backward on the condyles resting on the atlas vertebra, resulting in the face moving down and up" (McGrew, 1972, p. 57). McGrew differentiated aggression and rough-and-tumble play in children on the basis of overlapping structures of a large number of simpler classes of behavior.

A substantial number of McGrew's categories are listed in Table 5.6. Among the categories for which he provided reliability coefficients in his 1972 book, I counted at least 46 that involved body motion. The coefficients of agreement between McGrew and another observer on the coding of body motion categories from videotapes of children's behavior averaged about 85%, with a range of 60–100%. My inspection of the most reliable and least reliable categories did not indicate any particular bases to account for the differences.

Fagen and Goldman (1977) offered statistical criteria for estimating when one has reached the point of diminishing returns in looking for new entries for an ethogram. As the reader may also recall, Frey and Pool (1976) claimed to have constructed precise definitions of many of the ethological concepts of Brannigan and Humphries at a sufficiently elementary level to permit their semiautomated measurement from videotape records.

Some ethologists have claimed to have identified movements that are characteristic of virtually all humans (e.g., Eibl-Eibesfeldt, 1972). At the level of body motion the purported universals include social "attachment" responses of infants to caregivers (Bowlby, 1969) and head-tilting "appeasement" responses in children (H. F. Montagner, personal communication, Sept. 7, 1979). But to the degree that human behavior is culturally acquired (Birdwhistell, 1970; LaBarre, 1964) and cognitively controlled, one would expect human movements to show considerably more variability than those of other species. For example, it has been observed that female pedestrians differ from male pedestrians in their

Table 5.6. *Ethogram of preschool children's behavior patterns, arranged by body parts involved*

I. Facial
1. Bared teeth
2. Blink
3. Eyebrow flash
4. Eyes closed
5. Grin face
6. Low frown
7. Mouth open
8. Narrow eyes
9. Normal face
10. Nose wrinkle
11. Play face
12. Pout
13. Pucker face
14. Red face
15. Smile
16. Wide eyes

II. Head
1. Bite
2. Blow
3. Chew lips
4. Chin in
5. Face thrust
6. Gaze fixate
7. Glance
8. Grind teeth
9. Head nod
10. Head shake
11. Head tilt
12. Kiss
13. Laugh
14. Lick
15. Look
16. Mouth
17. Spit
18. Swallow
19. Tongue out
20. Verbalize
21. Vocalize
22. Weep
23. Yawn

III. Gestures
1. Automanipulate
    - Finger
    - Fumble
2. Beat
    - Incomplete
    - Object
    - Open
    - Up
3. Beckon
4. Clap hands
5. Digit suck
6. Drop
7. Fist
8. Forearm raise
9. Forearm sweep
10. Hand cover
11. Hand on back
12. Hold hands
13. Hold out
14. Knock
15. Pat
16. Pinch
17. Point
18. Pull
19. Punch
    - Incomplete
    - Object
    - Open
    - Side
20. Push
21. Reach
22. Repel
23. Scratch
24. Shake
25. Snatch
26. Throw
27. Tickle
28. Underarm throw
29. Wave

IV. Leg
1. Kick
    - Incomplete
    - Up
2. Shuffle
3. Stamp

V. Gross
1. Arms akimbo
2. Body oppose
3. Fall
4. Flinch
5. Hug
6. Jump
7. Lean back
8. Lean forward
9. Physical contact
10. Quick hop
11. Rock
12. Shoulder hug
13. Shrug
14. Stretch
15. Turn
16. Wrestle

VI. Posture
1. Climb
2. Crouch
3. Immobile
4. Kneel
5. Lie
6. Play crouch
7. Sit
8. Slope
9. Stand

VII. Locomotion
1. Back
2. Back step
3. Chase
4. Crawl
5. Flee
6. Gallop
7. March
8. Miscellaneous Locomotion
9. Run
10. Sidle
11. Sidle step
12. Skip
13. Step
14. Walk

Source: McGrew, 1972.

speed of departure from a staring stranger (Ellsworth, Carlsmith, & Henson, 1972; Konečni, Libuser, Morton, & Ebbesen, 1975); yet no sex differences were found in similar circumstances when the subjects who were stared at were drivers of cars (Greenbaum & Rosenfeld, 1978). One possible reason for the difference, suggested by the latter authors, was that the sexually dimorphic characteristics relevant to speed of walking, such as length of legs and body weight, were irrelevant for the pedal-depressing response required for acceleration of a car.

Thus the use of any category of human behavior as an *index* of a particular psychological state is questionable on the grounds that virtually all behavior is susceptible to social influence processes. This point is emphasized by social learning theorists and perhaps overemphasized by cultural relativists, both of which groups will be considered in the context of other models. But to give a concrete example, interpersonal proximity often is used as an index of intimacy, whereas it is only one of a variety of alternatives that can serve the same function: for example, orientation of head or trunk or legs, or body lean, or touch (Argyle & Dean, 1965; Mehrabian, 1972; M. L. Patterson, 1973). Similarly, the use of clinging may or may not be reinforced as an attachment response (Gewirtz, 1969). Thus the attribution of particular functions to many naturally occurring forms of movement may require either substantial contextual qualification (e.g., cultural or situational) or probabilistic inference.

It is possible to use the ethological method without necessarily accepting the evolutionary theory. This was done in a recent study by Greenbaum and Rosenfeld (1980) of the closest phase of greetings in an airport setting. The authors initially identified components of physical greeting on the basis of intuitive discriminations of body parts involved and configuration of movement. After interobserver reliability coefficients on the features were inspected, they used the processes of *splitting* (subdividing) and *lumping* (combining) until seven reliably observable categories of body contact were ultimately obtained. The categories and their coefficients of agreement are shown in Table 5.7.

Several of the categories were found to be differentially associated with order of occurrence in the greeting process, and others were associated with sex differences. Both order and sex were used as criterion variables for interpreting the functions of categories in the setting. Among the findings were that kissing typically occurred early and hand-to-upper-body later in the sequences, and that male-to-male greetings were characterized by handshakes, whereas female and cross-sex dyads commonly engaged in mutual embraces.

In another study of greetings (Kendon & Ferber, 1973), when the

Table 5.7. *Interobserver reliability coefficients for seven commonly observed categories of body contact during greetings at an airport*

Category	% agreement
Mutual lip kiss	75
Face kiss	75
Mutual face contact	80
Handshake	100
Handhold	67
Hand to upper body	82
Embrace	96

Source: Data from Greenbaum and Rosenfeld, 1980.

process was initiated between subjects at a far distance, the most typical body motion was the head toss. The authors sensibly interpreted this head toss as an initial acknowledgement of the participants' interest in each other, and its occurrence appeared to increase the probability that the subjects would follow up with more intimate response forms. It is interesting to compare this interpretation with the finding of Morris, Collett, Marsh, and O'Shaughnessy (1979), whose research will be described in more detail later, that the head toss more typically was interpreted as a symbol of hostility (see Figure 5.19). One possible explanation of the difference is context; Kendon's subjects were American and Morris's were European, and Morris et al. presented the head toss to subjects out of any social setting context. But Morris claimed that among his own subjects the difference between the two kinds of interpretation was attributable to topography; that is, those who attributed the greeting function to the head toss had mistaken it for the very similar head "jerk." This, therefore, is another example of the need for caution in asserting the necessary and sufficient conditions for a particular movement to have a particular referential function.

A biosocial model with a much stronger cultural emphasis than is characteristic among ethologists is the "proxemics" system of Hall (1963, 1974). Hall emphasizes the use of the body to regulate the degree to which individuals expose their sensory receptors to one another. He postulates that eight dimensions of behavior are relevant to the regulation of interpersonal exposure and provides simple coding rules and notations for discrete locations on each dimension (see Figures 5.17 and 5.18). At the level of body motion, as presently defined, his dimensions include postural identifiers (prone, standing, sitting, or squatting),

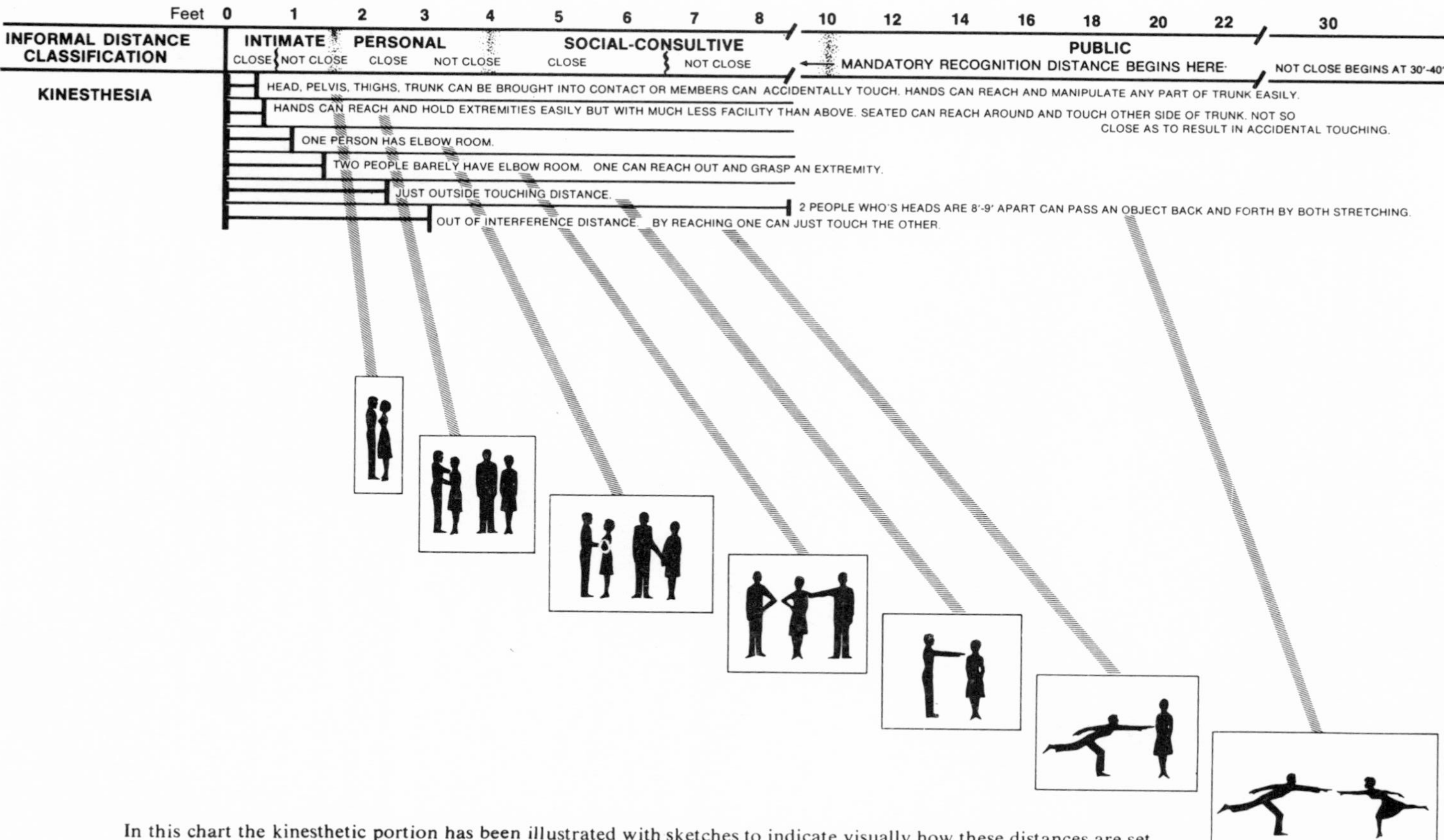

In this chart the kinesthetic portion has been illustrated with sketches to indicate visually how these distances are set.

Figure 5.17. Functional implications of proxemic zones. *Source:* Hall, 1979, p. 307.

This scale measures the distance between the subjects, employing the body's own measuring rods; that is, the distances are based on what people can do with their arms, legs, and bodies, and are formulated according to four basic potential touching distances:

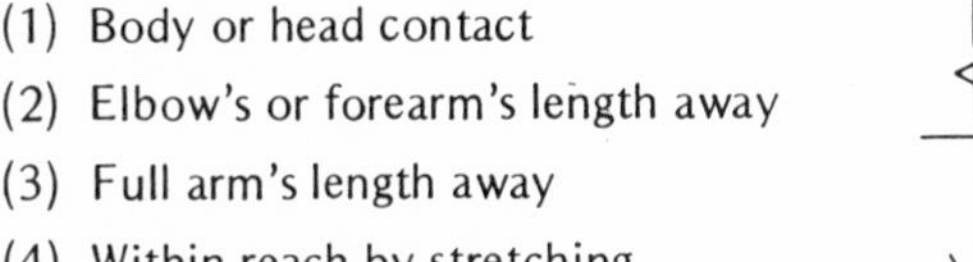

(1) Body or head contact

(2) Elbow's or forearm's length away

(3) Full arm's length away

(4) Within reach by stretching (body leaning, arm and leg extended)

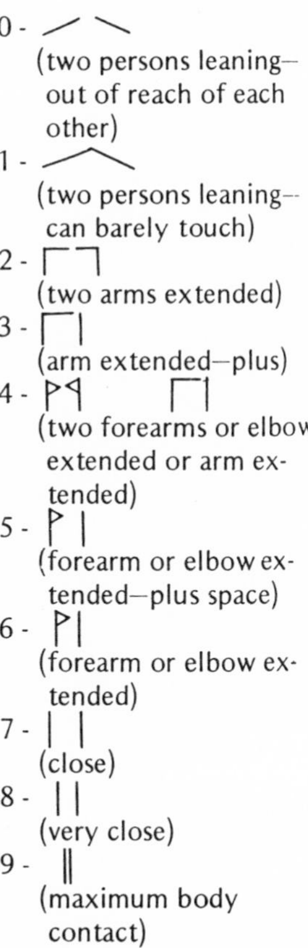

Figure 5.18. Proxemic notation for body distance between persons. *Source:* Hall, 1974, p. 58.

sociofugal–sociopetal orientation (measured by direction and angle), kinesthetic factors (capacity for touching), and forms of touching.

A major focus of Hall's research has been the identification of cultures that differ in contact norms and the study of the interpersonal problems that result from intercultural encounters between members of the respective groups. Research on the relationship of culture to proxemics generally has suffered either from absence of statistical significance tests or from confounding of culture with such intimacy-associated variables as topic and language. These variables were controlled in a recent study by Sussman and Rosenfeld (in press), in which proximity was shown to be independently affected by culture, sex, and language. Through the superimposition of grid lines on projected pictures of subjects, the authors were also able to obtain virtually perfect intercoder reliability on distance and angle of orientation of chair placement. A similar measurement procedure, used by Breck and Rosenfeld (1977), is shown in Figure 5.5.

A biosocial model also is implicit in Morris et al.'s (1979) study of cultural similarities and differences in the use of gesture. According to the preface of their book, "Each of these actions has a particular history – sometimes personal, sometimes cultural, and sometimes more deeply biological" (pp. xi–xii). They studied the distribution of 20 hand and head gestures (see Figure 5.19) over 40 locations, mostly in Europe. They illustrated each gesture by a drawing and described it in ordinary language terms referring to body parts that serve as sources and objects of action, their structural configurations, and the quantitative and qualitative features of their movements. For example, the first-listed gesture, the "fingertips kiss," was described as follows:

> The tips of the fingers and thumb of the right hand are presented together and pointed towards the gesturer's own lips. At the same time the hand is raised towards the lips and the fingertips are lightly kissed. As soon as the kissing movement of the mouth has been made, the hand is tossed lightly forward into the air, the fingers opening out away from one another as this second movement is executed. [P. 2]

Variations in the form of each gesture were also described. For example,

> The true fingertips kiss is usually a rather gentle performance, the movement having little vigour, but when it is imitated by foreigners who do not normally employ it, it is nearly always heavily over-emphasized. When used frequently, it often lacks the actual hand-to-lips contact, the fingertips stopping just short of the mouth. [P. 2]

Visual presentation of this gesture was meaningful to about half of the informants in the study, primarily to those in continental Europe where its dominant interpretation was "praise." In Italy it more often communicated "salutation."

The basis for selecting the 20 items was not fully specified. However, the method of identifying their meanings was to present drawings of each gesture to 30 adult male informants selected at random in public places and to ask them if the gesture was used locally, and if so what it meant. If the informants were unsure about the drawings, the researchers enacted the gesture for them. The results showed the number of informants in each location who provided each of several varieties of meaning.

Although Morris et al. noted that what they referred to as gestures were equivalent to what other researchers have called *emblems* (cf. Efron,

Figure 5.19. Twenty gestures studied cross-nationally. *Source:* Morris, Collett, Marsh, and O'Shaughnessy, 1979, p. XXVI

1941/1972), the methodological criteria employed in studies of emblems by Ekman (1975) were much stricter. One important implication of the difference in operational definition is that different researchers who seek to identify cultural "emblems" or "gestures," as subjectively understood, are likely to obtain different results because of methodological differences.

Morris et al. did note one common basis for disagreement among informants. This was *gesture blurring,* in which an informant unfamiliar with a gesture would attribute to it the meaning of the gesture that was most similar to it in his own culture. The back-translation method used in Ekman's (1975) study of emblems tends to prevent this problem from confounding the results; the method will be discussed in a later section on psychosocial models.

Another monumental study of cultural differences was conducted by Hewes in 1955. Hewes's focus was on static postural positions (e.g., standing, squatting, sitting) that were interpretable largely on the basis of different requisites for instrumental activity in different societies. Working from photographs, Hewes provided an extensive set of drawings revealing both gross and subtle variations.

Among the most clearly biological perspectives on movements involved in social interaction is the theory of *interactional synchrony* proposed by Condon (1979). Although his interests were more theoretical than methodological, Condon's methods remain noteworthy because they are very controversial (see Rosenfeld, 1981). Condon selected the fundamental units and movements used by anatomic kinesiologists for the purpose of demonstrating precise interpersonal synchronization of nonverbal behavior at the elementary level among conversational participants, including newborn infants, children, and adults. Inasmuch as he anticipated that the points of synchronization would correspond to phoneme changes in speech, it was necessary to assess elementary movements across time frames smaller than the duration of phonemes (see Figure 5.20). This task required special photographic equipment such as high-speed cameras and single-frame projectors. Condon's entries in his two-dimensional coding matrix of body part by film frame included kinesiological terms such as *flexion, rotation, extension, adduction,* and *pronation,* along with terms for direction and speed. He thereby implicitly allowed for evidence of the selective synchronization of different body parts and different forms of displacement, viewed from the basic anatomic perspective. However, no differential synchronization by body part or movement was reported.

Condon reported very high interobserver reliability in the coding of

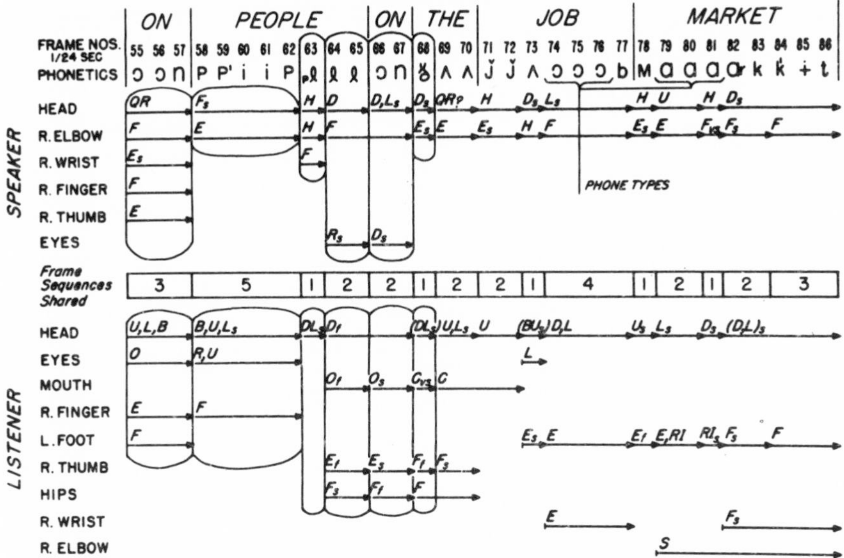

Figure 5.20. An example of synchrony of body movements: self- and interactional synchrony with "process units" circled (24-frames-per-second film). QR = incline right; *F* = forward or flex (depending on body part); *H* = hold (not moving); *D* = down; *L* = left; *E* = extend; *P* = pronate; *C* = close; *RI* = rotate inward; *RO* = rotate outward; *AD* = adduct; *U* = up; *S* = supinate; *B* = back. The subscripts refer to speed: *s* = slight; *f* = fast; *vs* = very slight. *Source:* Condon and Sander, 1974, p. 458.

the movements across single frames at 0.033-second intervals, with coefficients of agreement averaging in the mid-90s. Rosenfeld (1981) estimated that to obtain this level of reliability, coders of the films would need to have virtually complete implicit agreement on the definition of just-noticeable displacements and on that of boundary points between several subjectively defined ranges in velocity per displacement (e.g., fast, slight, very slight). In an attempt to achieve independent replication of Condon's evidence of nonverbal synchrony among conversing adults, McDowall (1979) obtained intercoder reliability coefficients averaging only around 20% at the single-frame level. McDowall's reliability approached Condon's level only when the coding unit was increased in size up to six frames (see Table 5.2). Additional methodological problems related to the assessment of interactional synchrony are discussed in Rosenfeld (1981).

A landmark study that provided an extremely potent negative reply to Nazi therories about the biological basis of gestures associated with ethnic groups was performed by Efron (1941/1972). This study also is noteworthy for its many methodological innovations. Efron developed,

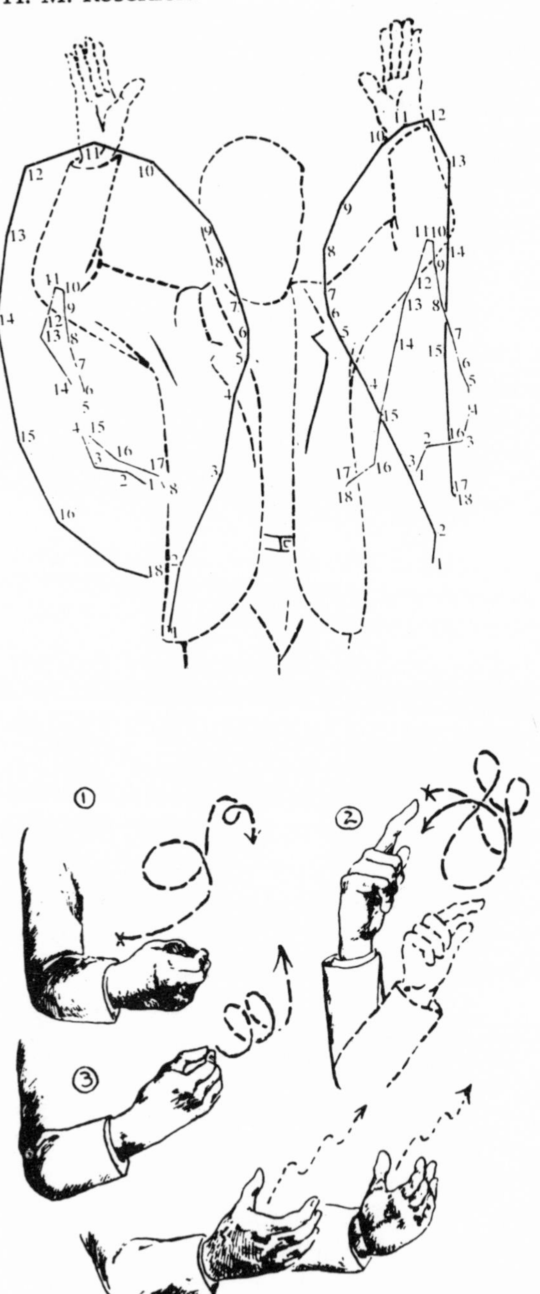

Figure 5.21. Examples of cultural differences in gestures: *top*, wide radius of movement from the shoulder of a traditional Italian; *bottom*, sinuous gesture of a ghetto Jew. *Source:* Efron, 1941/1972, pp. 166, 177.

and applied to an extensive number of subjects, an impressive array of tools for the observation, recording, notation, simulation, and interpretation of configurations of movement, particularly movement involving the hands. He was able to document effectively the differences between the relatively fluid speech-related hand movements of southern Italian immigrants to the United States and the relatively discontinuous movements of northern European Jewish immigrants (see Figure 5.21). He also demonstrated the disappearance of these differences with acculturation experiences in the United States. Efron's carefully developed categories and definitions of emblematic and illustrative movements were a major influence on the systematic conceptualization developed by Ekman and Friesen (1969b).

Social structural models

The *kinesics* notational system of Birdwhistell (1952, 1970) probably is among the best-known methods in the field of nonverbal communication. It is based upon the viewpoint that human communication is an integrated multichannel process, shaped primarily by cultural experiences. Birdwhistell objected to the isolation of nonverbal communication from its larger communicative context. He further assumed that communicative nonverbal behavior is organized according to structural linguistic principles. Thus he proposed a hierarchy of units of nonverbal behavior, ranging from the elementary *kineme* (cf. phoneme) to the more molar and meaningful *kinemorph,* which in turn can be located within larger kinemorphic constructions. He also proposed that nonverbal behavior can function to mark points of stress and segmentation of speech, in ways analogous to vocal prosodic characteristics.

Thus far, publication of Birdwhistell's system has been restricted to a loose collection of essays based upon diverse observations of American subjects, and relatively extensive lists of proposed units with simple notational recording symbols (see Figure 5.22). In the notational system, the body is divided into major regions and subregions corresponding to the anatomy of the skeletal system. Many of the proposed units refer to static configurations, akin to "shape" concepts of Labanotation, for example, slumped spine, drooped shoulders, and curled fingers. A smaller number reflect "effort"-like conceptions, for example, tense hands and stiff fingers.

The substantially incomplete status of the kinesics system, compared to other basic systems of measurement, can be partly attributed to the

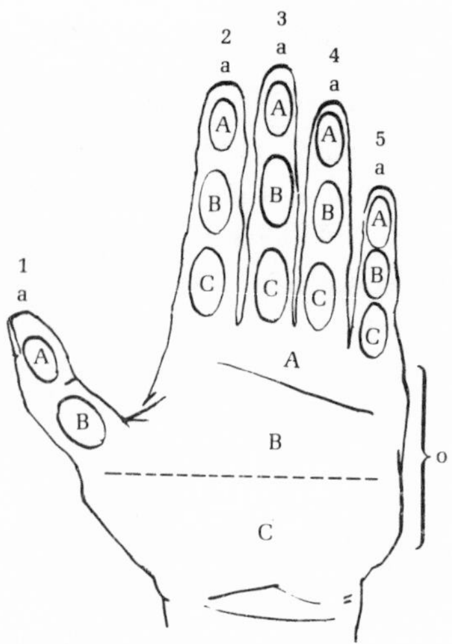

TOTAL HAND

(L) 11111 — Hand extended (lax). No finger touching another.

(L) $\underline{11111}$ — Hand extended (tense). No fingers touching.

(L) 5 — Hand extended, lax or tense (tension indicated by —). Fingers each touching neighboring finger.

(L) 131 — First finger not touching second; second, third, and fourth touching along length; fifth finger not touching others.

(L) ⌉$\underline{1}_{\supset}$ $3_{\cup}$ — All crooking notation follows logic shown above for single fingers. Figure shown illustrates "Thumb (1) crooked posteriorly and not touching other fingers; fingers 3, 4, and 5 touching along length and with a curl; finger two (2) not touching with a tense hook.

(L) 1 $\overset{\text{C-BC}}{2}$ $3_{\cup}$ — Notation for joint touching is placed over the numerical finger-indicating figure. Figure shown illustrates: 1 extended (lax); 2 C touching 3 at joints B and C, with 2 extended (lax); 3, 4, 5 touching along length and in curl.

(L) +4 — Fist (lax), thumb outside over fingers 2, 3. (In this case conventionality eliminates necessity for 1's contact points on posterior portions of 2 and 3.) Tense indicated by —.

(L) $\overset{\frown}{14}$ — Capped fist, thumb continuing radial line and touching 1A to 2BC.

Figure 5.22. Examples of kinesic categories of hand configuration. *Source:* Birdwhistell, 1970, pp. 268, 270

inherent difficulty of collecting validating evidence. The attribution of communicative significance to any configuration of body motion, from Birdwhistell's perspective, depends upon evidence of consistency of occurrence within contextual surroundings. It is difficult to assert when sufficient evidence of that sort has been collected. But until the contextual consistencies have been demonstrated, any unit studied in the system remains a hypothesis. Birdwhistell's system has been criticized in particular for its linguistic analogy, on the grounds that much communicative nonverbal behavior lacks the discrete quality of linguistic units (Dittmann, 1971, 1978).

It also should be noted that Birdwhistell's domain of kinesics is not synonymous with the domain of body motion as defined in this chapter. Kinesics applies to all discriminable movements of the organs of the body, including such nonskeletal actions as the eye and lip muscular movements involved in facial expression, which are treated as separate domains in the present volume. Also, the kinesics system excludes, or at least minimizes, touch.

A somewhat less controversial analogy between the structure of body motion and of speech has been made in the analysis of sign language (see Dittmann, 1978), which may be considered a formal system of referential movements as well as a social skill. With regard to American Sign Language, Stokoe (1972) suggested that the signs are constructions of basic elements that are functionally comparable to the spoken phoneme. Each sign is describable as a unique combination of three classes of *cheremes:* the *tabula,* which describes the locations on the body at which the signing takes place (e.g., face, trunk); the *designator,* or configuration of the hand (e.g., flat, curved, contracted); and the *signation,* or movement (e.g., upward, away from signer, circular). A notational system for describing the cheremes of American Sign Language is provided by Stokoe, Casterline and Croneberg (1976).

Social-structural models based more on a broad interpersonal systems perspective than on a linguistic analogy have had a strong following among students of communication in the United States. Particularly influential were the members of the "Palo Alto" group (e.g., Watzlawick, Beavin, & Jackson, 1967). A related interdisciplinary group of well-known social scientists was not able to achieve the integrated theory it sought. The latter group's long-expected interdisciplinary book, to be entitled *The Natural History of an Interview* (McQuown, 1971), finally came to rest in draft form in the microfilm archives of the University of Chicago. The manuscript documents the wide array of difficulties that probably must be faced in any major endeavor to integrate multiple perspectives.

The social-structural perspective of Goffman (e.g., 1963) has had a continuing major influence on researchers in all areas of communicative study. Goffman, who initially developed a dramaturgical model of interpersonal relationships, has offered many insights into the role of body motion in the maintenance of social order. Kendon (1972, 1973, 1977; see also Chapter 8), in particular, has applied microanalytic methods in the study of the major varieties of interpersonal relationship emphasized by Goffman. These include such events as greetings, the initiation of focused conversation, and the packaging of information within the conversational process – topics of interest to many disciplines.[6] Kendon's work heavily emphasizes the frame-by-frame analysis of motion pictures of elementary movements and also his own ability to detect structural organization within behavioral complexities. Although he usually does not apply formal statistical analysis in his intensive studies, his detailed observations have influenced others to follow up with more confirmatory forms of research (e.g., Greenbaum & Rosenfeld, 1980).

Psychosocial models

Many of the measures of body motion that appear in the literature on nonverbal communication developed out of interests in the analysis of personality characteristics, particularly as they are related to mental health. Most treatments of mental disorders have emphasized psychotherapeutic processes based upon face-to-face interaction. Thus it is not surprising that many investigators use a mixture of nonverbal categories or dimensions referring to emotional states and also to the process of verbal communication. In general, biosocial models are associated with eclectic, multilevel measurements.

Psychologists long have been fascinated by the idea that the most private feelings and thoughts of an individual may be unintentionally revealed through nonverbal behavior. Inasmuch as the face is actively recognized and attended to as the major organ for expressing different emotional states, it has been proposed that movements of the lower body are particularly likely to be an unmonitored and uninhibited, if meager, source of emotional information (Ekman & Friesen, 1969b).

There is an extensive literature describing the kinds of body motion that purportedly reflect private and often repressed emotional states and associated cognitions (see literature reviewed by Kestenberg, 1965; Mahl, 1968; Mehrabian, 1972). Much of the earlier literature stemmed from a combination of psychoanalytic theory and associated clinical observations, in which verbal correlates of body motion served as a major validating criterion, whereas more recent studies have emphasized experimental criteria.

Body movement has been implicated in the expression of emotion in a variety of ways. Many investigators, particularly those with a psychoanalytic orientation, have reported that rate of motor activity reflects general level of emotional arousal (e.g., Kestenberg, 1965). Researchers have shown that an increase in rate of limb activity in conversational situations can result from a variety of arousing events, often with a positive affective component. Persistently higher rates of certain speech-associated limb movements may result from a general improvement in state of mental health (Ekman & Friesen, 1972); situational increases in arm gesticulations may result from arousal of affiliative motivation (Rosenfeld, 1966b); and momentary hand activation at the initiation of speech may result from cognitive tasks such as the need to construct a complex conversational utterance (Dittmann, 1972b). Note, however, that movements of the upper limbs and head that accompany speech also can function to facilitate exchange or regulation of verbal information. The latter functional usage will be discussed in a subsequent section on social relationships.

Negative emotional states are likely to be reflected in self-contact behaviors, as well as object-contact responses. The self-contact actions have been referred to by many labels, including *synkinetic* movements (Allport & Vernon, 1933/1967), *autistic* movements (Krout, 1935), *self-manipulations* (Rosenfeld, 1966b), *body-focused* movements (Freedman & Hoffman, 1967), *self-adaptors* (Ekman & Friesen, 1969b), and *body manipulators* (Ekman, 1977). The functional implication of discomfort in some of these concepts has been validated in a variety of ways. The movements have been found to increase in response to experimentally induced withdrawal of socially supportive nonverbal behavior (Rosenfeld, 1967); and their rate of occurrence has been found to be correlated with ratings of anxiety, guilt, and deceptiveness (Ekman & Friesen, 1972), as well as disapproval (Rosenfeld, 1966a). Several of these researchers, among others, have hypothesized and occasionally verified that the nature of the body parts involved (e.g., hand to head), as well as the nature of the act (e.g., rub versus scratch), may be associated symbolically with particular states of emotion. However, there is a widespread tendency, particularly in the popular literature, to interpret functions on the gratuitous basis of face validity.

Emotional information also has been attributed to more complex configurations and movements. Specific emotional states have been attributed by observers to stick figures of different postural configurations (Rosenberg & Langer, 1965), although such configurations have not been commonly employed in the observation of naturally occurring behavior. Ekman and Friesen (1967) presented evidence that movements of the body are more likely to reflect particular emotions than are static positions. Other complex configurations related to the expression of interpersonal emotional and attitudinal states will be discussed in the context of social relationships.

From the various studies of self-contact behavior reviewed here, it is obvious that there is an excessive proliferation of ordinary language terms, all referring to a relatively coherent class of self-contact behaviors as defined at the elementary level. Some researchers have attempted to simplify the diversity of concepts in this and other areas of nonverbal communication by proposing the application of simpler factorial structures from other domains of behavior, such as small-group research (Kogan, Wimberger, & Bobbitt, 1969) and semantic analysis (Mehrabian, 1972). Thus far no such factorial structure has gained wide acceptance in the area of referential communication through body motion. The lack of clear or consensual definitions of functional concepts referring to state of mind is a major obstacle to the functional cataloguing of body motion. As one progresses from restricted conceptions of emotion (e.g., Ekman & Friesen, 1969) to more elaborate conceptions of personality that include motives (e.g., Rosenfeld, 1966a, 1966b), attitudes (e.g., Mehrabian, 1972), and cognitions (e.g., Mahl, 1968, 1977), a much broader range of movements is likely to be included.

Nevertheless, it should be of at least heuristic value to inspect the concepts and methods of some of the pioneering efforts to study the role of body motion in the expression of personality, broadly conceived. For example, Allport & Vernon (1933/1967) initiated a noteworthy early effort to bring the emerging tools of scientific psychology to bear upon the comprehensive analysis of the expression of persisting personality characteristics. The numerous categories of movement that they included covered the entire range of levels of measurement, from simple displacements of specific body parts to vague qualitative terms from ordinary language usage. They paid particular attention to style of walking as a personality trait, including such measures as length of stride, elasticity, and mincing quality. Around the same time, Krout (e.g., 1935) also conducted a wide range of innovative scientific investigations into the personal functions of body movement.

A substantial amount of research has been conducted on the uses of body motion and orientation during the process of face-to-face conversation. Ekman and Friesen (1969b) suggested a set of five functional categories for the analysis of conversational interaction. The categories were labeled according to their functions, although the authors also specified behavioral features characteristic of each category. Body motion is strongly involved in four of their five categories, the exception being emotional expression through facial configurations. One of the remaining four categories – body manipulators – was discussed in the earlier section on personal characteristics. Whereas affect displays and body manipulations are conceptually, and often empirically, independent of the exchange of verbal information in conversations, the remaining three categories – emblems, illustrators, and regulators – are intimately connected to verbal communication. Each category can be further divided into a variety of subclasses. Scoring procedures and information on reliability and validity of emblems and illustrators (and adaptors) are described in recent publications (Friesen et al., 1979; also see Scherer, Wallbott, & Scherer, 1979).

Following Efron (1941/1972), the category of *emblems* is defined as body motions or configurations that are used by a culture to refer to simple messages that are consensually translatable into a word or simple phrase (e.g., a shrug). In their cross-cultural studies of emblems, Ekman and his colleagues (Ekman, 1975; Johnson, Ekman, & Friesen, 1975) used a back-translation method in which some participants demonstrated how particular verbal concepts are nonverbally expressed (the encoding method) and other participants responded to visual presentations of the acts with verbal labels (the decoding method). Thus far Ekman and his co-workers have found that most cultures have a repertoire of a couple of hundred emblems, some shared with other cultures and some unique. As noted earlier, although emblems are similar in form to the movements that Morris et al. (1979) referred to as gestures, Ekman's criteria for two-way translation, as well as for a high level of consensus, are likely to result in the selection of different contents in the category. Emblems also are similar in form to the symbolic movements studied by Mahl (1968, 1977), except that the latter were identified on the basis of their significance to the individual patient and not to the culture as a whole.

Illustrators refer to motions, primarily of the hands, that follow speech rhythm and that function to mark certain structural properties of the speech content, such as terms to be given special emphasis and boundaries of particular ideational units. Ekman and Friesen (1972) define eight subclasses of illustrators on the basis of both form of motion and its relationship to verbal material.

Other researchers have studied movements equivalent to illustrators in detailed analyses of small segments of motion-picture film or videotape. On the basis of his observations of therapist–client interactions in psychiatric settings, Scheflen (1964, 1965) suggested that many bodily movements are hierarchically organized, corresponding to different levels of molarity of verbal production. He distinguished three levels: *points*, which commonly are marked by brief head movements; *positions*, often marked by postural shifts; and *presentations*, marked by relocation of the body.

Kendon (1977) followed up these ideas in intensive microanalyses of several segments of filmed conversations, and offered illustrative evidence of a five-level system of movements, corresponding roughly to linguistic units of phrase, sentence, paragraph, and combinations thereof. He, too, observed that larger speech units were accompanied by larger motions, which generally consisted of more expansive ranges of movements and the inclusion of body parts of grosser size and lower probability of movement. For example, changes in smaller verbal units are likely to be marked by brief movements of the fingers, changes in larger units by sweeps of the arm, and changes in still larger units by shifts in posture. In addition, Kendon noted that peaks in intensity of movement tend to occur at high-information locations during speech – in pauses during which utterances presumably are constructed, and at the least predictable words in phrases. The studies by Scheflen and Kendon also indicate that although individuals differ in their characteristic forms of movement per level, each person still differentiates among levels. A variety of illustrative motions is also described by Birdwhistell (1970).

An earlier section reviewed research showing that rate of illustrative movements during speech tends to indicate level of arousal and enthusiasm, and that stylistic differences in illustrative movements tend to discriminate certain cultures from others. A less well researched area is the effectiveness of illustrators in promoting verbal information exchange (cf. Cohen, 1977). In this capacity the function of illustrators is similar to that of the final category, regulators.

Regulators, which are movements that guide the participation of members of conversations, have not been studied as thoroughly as the other categories; a general review of the research is provided by Rosenfeld (1978). Most attention has been paid to the regulation of speaking turns. Duncan and Fiske (1977) performed intensive microanalyses of several conversations to determine what kinds of nonlinguistic cues are predictive of such turn properties as smooth speaker switching and states of simultaneous talk. Their study was valuable in demonstrating that, to identify the significant signals, conversations need not be segmented into units smaller than the phonemic clause, a prosodic unit roughly corresponding to a phrase. Of particular interest was their finding that a held gesticulation – a hand or arm movement that is not returned to resting position – is a particularly potent signal for retaining or taking over the speaking turn. This is a good example of the interface between illustration and regulation.

The regulator concept also pertains to more specific interactive processes within speaking turns. Of particular interest is the phenomenon of the *back channel* (Yngve, 1970) or *listener response* (Dittmann, 1972b), in which a person in the listener role gives a brief verbal reaction such as "mhm," or a nonverbal equivalent, which is not considered sufficient to constitute a change in speaker role. Statistical analysis of the role of body motion in speaker switching and in listener responding was presented in two recent studies of 20 independent conversational dyads (Gunnell, 1979; Rosenfeld & Hancks, 1980). Whereas previous researchers used either contextual behavioral variables or experimental manipulations as criteria for interpreting regulatory functions of nonverbal behavior, Gunnell used both criteria simultaneously. By differentially motivating subjects to be cooperative rather than competitive in the apportionment of the speaking turn, she was able to differentiate between rule-enforcing and rule-breaking activities at critical junctures (contexts) in speech. A major finding was that a speaker's head pointing toward the listener functioned to elicit a listener response rather than a shift in turns; competitive subjects, however, tended to take advantage of their brief dominance during the listener response by immediately grabbing the floor.

Rosenfeld and Hancks (1980) focused upon variations in the nonverbal structure of listener responses and the degree to which their differences were predictable from the nonverbal structure of the preceding speaker response. Factor analyses of the nonverbal behaviors revealed seven varieties of listener responses and four varieties of speaker antecedents. The most potent speaker configuration of nonverbal behaviors, labeled *active ending,* was composed of a multiplicity of movements, including subsets of postural shift toward the listener, head movements toward the listener, brief head nods, and incomplete gesticulations. Active ending was a significant predictor of such listener movements as brief head nodding and leaning forward prior to the speaker's completion of utterance, but not of normal-sized postutterance head nods.

The body movement most strongly implicated in research on regulators is the head nod. Most researchers have treated the head nod as a single binary event, scoring it as either occurring or not occurring (e.g., McGrew, 1972; Rosenfeld, 1966a, 1966b, 1967). It has been hypothesized, however, that the function of the head nod may differ depending upon variations in its features and in its timing (Birdwhistell, 1970; Dittmann & Llewellyn, 1968; Rosenfeld, 1972). Some confirmatory evidence was provided in the aforementioned study by Rosenfeld and Hancks (1980).

A detailed statistical analysis of the effects of features of the topography of head nods upon their interpretation was conducted by Rosenfeld and McRoberts (1979). They studied such features as number of cycles, excursiveness, total movement, total time, and rate of movement. Using videotapes, with opportunities for repeated viewing, they were able to score the location of features within a 0.2-second period (see Table 5.3).

Body motion also is central in another category of behavior that is considered to be indicative of positive mental health and interpersonal relationships. This is *congruence*, or *synchrony*, which refers to the degree to which different channels or modalities of nonverbal communication communicate compatible information (Ruesch, 1955; Scheflen, 1964, 1965). Gross synchrony between the limb configurations of interacting persons is widely accepted as a general index of interpersonal rapport (see Trout & Rosenfeld, 1980); and both intrapersonal and interpersonal synchrony at an elementary level have been implicated as an index of mental health (Condon, 1979).

In pioneering, nonstatistical studies of therapist–client interactions in psychotherapeutic settings, Scheflen (1964, 1965) observed that, during periods of verbalized and experienced rapport, the participants tended to match each other's configurations of posture and limbs. The congruence could be a direct match or a mirror image. It typically took the form of copying of the other person's limb configurations for a period of time; common forms are folding of arms and crossing of legs.

Trout and Rosenfeld (1980) systematically manipulated the occurrence of interpersonal congruence of limbs in videotapes of simulated psychotherapy sessions. They also cross-classified the congruence variable with three degrees of postural lean (forward, upright, and backward), which also has been considered to be an indicator of interpersonal attitude (Mehrabian, 1972). In the Trout and Rosenfeld study, observers of the videotapes attributed significantly greater rapport to the congruent-limb episodes than to the noncongruent ones. The effect of forward lean was substantially greater than that of congruence; however, in contrast to Mehrabian's findings, upright and backward lean were undifferentiated.

Many of the categories of body motion discussed in this section on social behavior appear in a variety of empirical studies of conversation undertaken from other theoretical perspectives. For example, in a series of efforts to derive and validate a nonverbal index of motivation for approval, Rosenfeld (1966a, 1966b) found repeated evidence of the functional significance of gesticulations (Ekman & Friesen's illustrators) and head nods (primarily regulators). Under increased motivation to win approval, women were particularly prone to increase gesticulations, and men to increase head nods. Actual approval received, however, was strongly related only to the head nods, regardless of sex of actor. The discrepancy between the relation of the nonverbal categories to criteria of intention and the relation of these categories to criteria of reception (of approval) attests to the importance of considering both of these criteria in the analysis of communicative function, a point also emphasized by Ekman and Friesen (1969b) and by Wiener, Devoe, Rubinow, and Geller (1972).

Social learning models

Many researchers have attempted to discover where particular communicative body motions come from. Examples given in this chapter have included variations in body motion as a function of age and of culture. Although acquisition of forms of movement clearly is associated with differences between age and culture, these variables do not identify the psychological processes that are involved. They are particularly inadequate for the purpose of accounting for individual differences within age and culture groups and for the promotion of learning of more effective forms of action.

Social learning theory (Bandura, 1977; Gewirtz, 1969) offers a basic set of principles to account for both the acquisition and the performance of any form of behavior. Like the ethological model and the social-structural models, it focuses upon the immediate context of behavior for its major explanatory criteria. But in addition, the social learning model emphasizes the implications of repetitive patterns of contextual relationships for the modification of response forms. Major contextual variables are social reinforcers – those that follow particular responses with sufficient reliability to result in the increased probability of performing the response in the future – and models – observed behaviors that increase the probability that an observer will match them.

Although no systematic attempt has been made to apply a social learning approach to nonverbal behavior, body motion has been studied for its modeling and reinforcing functions as well as for its responsiveness to social learning processes. A few examples from my own research follow here.

Working from the accumulation of evidence that conversants tend to reciprocate smiles and head nods (Rosenfeld, 1966b), I demonstrated that performance of these response classes could be extinguished if a conversational partner systematically withheld reciprocation (Rosenfeld, 1967). Also, in a recent study of nonverbal reinforcement of learning, my colleague and I found that the performance of students was affected by the contingent presentation of such emblems as head nods and head shakes (Shea & Rosenfeld, 1976). But the most interesting results of the latter study were obtained as a result of experimental manipulations that evoked variations in subtlety of teacher nonverbal behavior. It was found that forms of teacher body movement differed substantially, depending upon whether the teachers were motivated to be overtly clear or very subtle (Shea & Rosenfeld, 1976; Rosenfeld, Shea, & Greenbaum, 1979). In the overt condition, teachers mostly used highly excursive head nods and head shakes to indicate positive and negative reactions to student performance. But in the subtle condition, where nonverbal behavior was implicitly prohibited but necessary for effective teaching, the teachers exhibited an entirely different kind of nonverbal response to poor performance. This was termed the *fallen face,* consisting of a slackening of the lower jaw along with a general loss of muscular tonus in the face. Technically, the jaw is a joint, and thus the fallen face belongs in the study of body motion, although it also happens to be one component of the facial emotion of surprise (Ekman, Chapter 2).

Thus far, little is known about the course of development of the nonverbal activities that typically accompany conversations (see Rosenfeld, 1980; Schaffer, 1977). In general, it has been found that children increasingly approximate adult forms (De Long, 1974; Jancovic et al., 1975) and perceptions (Rosenfeld, Shea, & Greenbaum, 1975, 1979) of functional movements and that their responses at critical junctures are less probable and more latent than are those of adults (Dittmann, 1972a).

Finally, it should be noted that there has been a recent increase in interest in the general issue of training "social skills," among both social psychologists (e.g., Trower, Bryant, & Argyle, 1978) and applied behavior analysts. Consequently, there is likely to be greater application of elementary notation and of social learning models to the study of referential social communication through body motion.

5.8. Conclusions

Systems of measurement are valuable only as tools for enhancing understanding of functional questions. In the complex field of nonverbal communication it is convenient to organize methods of measurement according to limited subsystems of behavior, even though many functional acts involve the interaction of multiple behavioral subsystems. Most of the behavioral subsystems attended to in the study of nonverbal communication emphasize highly specialized organs in localized areas of the body and particularly the region of the head – the visual system, the vocal and auditory systems, and the facial musculature system.

Most of the remainder of the body has also been attributed major importance in nonverbal communication, but there has been little consensus about how to organize discussion of it. This is easily demonstrated by a comparison of contemporary textbooks: Mehrabian (1972) provides a single chapter on "posture and position"; Knapp (1978) offers separate chapters on "physical behavior" and "touching behavior"; Harper, Wiens, and Matarazzo (1976) have separate chapters on "kinesics" (emphasizing both Ekman and Birdwhistell) and "proxemics" (including touch); Argyle (1975) has separate chapters on "gestures and bodily movements," "posture," "bodily contact," and "spatial behavior." In addition, major categoric systems for measuring nonverbal communication, such as those of Birdwhistell, Ekman, and McGrew, differ in their inclusion of the various behavior subsystems.

In the present chapter, I decided to focus upon the skeletal system in the analysis of body motion and orientation. The skeletal system underlies most, although not all, of the behaviors attended to by the authors just named. In particular, it can be dealt with as a *coherent physical system*. Its actions can be analyzed in terms of the well-understood laws of biomechanics and their particular expression in anatomic kinesiology, and efficiently notated and quantitatively analyzed in terms of solid geometry.

The major problem faced in the analysis of communication through body motion is how to deal with the tremendous complexity of biomechanical actions involved in most meaningful forms of movement. It is impractical to assess the minute details of spatiotemporal displacement and their organization for every event of interest. Fortunately, it often also is unnecessary to do so, because most people are capable of automatically abstracting and integrating much detail in their perception of functional acts, and also because great detail and precision are not necessary for many research purposes.

In selecting methods of measuring body motion, the rule of parsimony should be followed. One should do no more work than is necessary to answer functional questions, but no less, either. It is wasteful to assess movement at a microanalytic level, only to analyze it for gross rates of occurrence of reliably perceivable configurations. It is equally foolish to collect data at a more molar level than is required for answering questions regarding precise temporal location.

The most essential requisite for deciding upon levels and units of measurement is the specification of *criterial* features of the functional categories in one's system of nonverbal behavior. Criterial features should be specified at the highest level of abstraction or organization that is consistent with the clear identification of one's concepts and their discrimination from each other. The highest degree of organization is the gestalt or topological level, in which the pattern of motion is understood as a whole. Typically it is best expressed to an observer by a pictorial model and by well-understood normal language terms, such as *shrug*. Otherwise it may be necessary to specify measures at the level of more elementary structural properties of behavior, as in McGrew's system for ethological analysis and Ekman's system for conversational analysis. If these prove insufficient, it may be necessary to go to an even more elementary feature analysis, as in the systems of Birdwhistell, Laban, and Eshkol.

A comprehensive approach to the measurement of functional body acts must have the capacity to work at all of these levels, and to interrelate the various levels. In this chapter I have suggested basic requisites for comprehensive measurement, starting at the most elementary levels and working up to the more complex ones. I paid particular attention to the problem of how actual physical movement is related to the perception of that movement, an issue that is critical for the development of automated measurement systems intended to simulate observational processes.

I have reviewed a wide range of examples of empirical research employing systems and measures of body motion, selecting studies that were useful for illustrating particular issues regarding measurement. Even this limited sample of the literature has revealed a great diversity of measures, particularly at the more complex levels of analysis. Part of this diversity is attributable to the highly differentiated usage of communicative movements by people and to the fact that they live in various societies, each of which has developed its own conventions regarding nonverbal expression.

Much of the diversity in measures also is attributable to the relatively early stage of development of the field of nonverbal communication. Communicative movements are of interest to researchers in a wide variety of social and behavioral sciences. Thus far, a variety of conceptual models has been borrowed, including mechanics, evolutionary biology, music, dance, and linguistics. Until there is consensus on substantive issues and theoretical models, there is unlikely to be consensus on measures.

I have noted certain correspondences between substantive interests and level of measurement. In general, instrumental acts of body motion, particularly what might be called physical skills, tend to be studied at the more elementary behavioral levels that are useful for training purposes. In contrast, referential (indexical and symbolic) acts tend to be analyzed at a more holistic perceptual level, which is adequate for the typical purpose of identifying their occurrence. A current trend toward the promotion of social skills and communicative competence, however, may require increasing use of elementary levels in the analysis of referential acts. Fortunately, the technology, both hardware and software, for conducting efficient analyses at the elementary level is developing rapidly.

Particularly problematic is the desire of many investigators to provide measures that can serve as reliable indexes of particular functional acts. Often very similar movements are involved in different functions all of which are of interest to the investigator, as in aggression versus playful fighting among children. Also, similar acts may have opposite functions in different cultures, as in the expression of affirmation and negation through head movement. Thus it is important to identify the limiting forms and contexts for any indexical inference. The more clearly such constraints are specified, the more certain, or less probabilistic, will be the functional usage.

The specification of indexical measures ultimately is a matter of validation. Current methods of validation range from soft criteria to hard criteria. In the popularized literature, and among many professionals as well, there is a tendency to interpret measures on the basis of face validity or naive theory. Many researchers depend upon their experience in scientific training, theoretical study, and extensive observation as their basis for interpreting body motion. Others depend upon contextual criteria, which are subject to being confounded with other possible explanatory variables, or upon experimental criteria, which may not generalize to natural situations. Both sorts of criteria offer unique contributions to validation, and they can be combined effectively in the same studies.

Overall, the future of measurement of body motion for the study of nonverbal communication looks very bright. A large number of investigators are working on the problem, a substantial data base is being accumulated, and research is becoming increasingly sophisticated at both the conceptual and the technological level.

Acknowledgments

I wish to express my appreciation to Bruce Duncan, Chuck Nelson, and Harald Wallbott for their help in providing reference materials, and my gratitude to Bill Remmers for his generous and useful technical consultations. Preparation of this chapter was supported in part by National Institute for Child Health and Human Development Grants HD-002528, administered through the Kansas Center for Research in Mental Retardation and Human Development, and by grants from the Biomedical Sciences Support Fund (No. 4673-5706) and the General Research Fund (No. 3909-038) at the University of Kansas.

Notes

1. Mahl (1968) similarly discriminated between *instrumental* and *symbolic* functions. The term *referential* was selected in this chapter because it carries less implication of intent than does *symbolic*. The present use of *referential* should not be confused with uses of that term to apply to a particular experimental task (e.g., Glucksberg, Krauss, & Higgins, 1975), although the usages are compatible. Also, *referential* should be discriminated from *inferential* functions, which pertain to interpretation of behavior by observers, regardless of its function for the performer.
2. Two examples are the DATAMYTE (Electro-General Corporation, 14960 Industrial Road, Minnetonka, Minn. 55343) and the MORE Field Recorder (Observational Systems, 1103 Grand Avenue, Seattle, Wash. 98122)
3. Among active workers in branches of computer graphics relevant to the study of body motion are Lance Williams and Ephraim Cohen at the New York Institute for Technology, Norman Badler at the University of Pennsylvania, and Ed Catmull at Lucasfilm, Ltd. in San Anselmo, CA. Computer simulation of sports movements is being developed by Gideon Ariel at Coto Research in Trabuco Canyon, CA , and Peter Cavenaugh at Pennsylvania State University. For general reference materials see the journal *Computer Graphics* and also the publications of SIGGRAPH (graphics subgroup of the Association for Computing Machinery).
4. The SELLSPOT system is provided by Selcom, Box 4032, S-433 04, Partille, Sweden.
5. According to Golani (1976), publications on the Eshkol and Wachmann notation system can be obtained in the United States from Dr. Anneliz

Hoymans, Department of Physical Education, University of I
Champaign, Urbana, Ill. 61801, and in Israel from the Move
Society, 75 Arlozorov Street, Holon, Israel 58327.

6. Other researchers have performed exploratory investigations o
of body motion in the leave-taking process (Bakken, 1977;
Friedrich, & Shulman, 1973).

References

Allport, G. W., & Vernon, P. E. *Studies in expressive movement*. New York: Hafner, 1967. (Originally published, New York: Macmillan, 1933.)

Argyle, M. *Bodily communication*. London: Methuen, 1975.

Argyle, M., & Dean, J. Eye-contact, distance and affiliation. *Sociometry*, 1965, *28*, 289–304.

Austin, G. *Chironomia; or, a treatise on rhetorical delivery: Comprehending many precepts, both ancient and modern, for the proper regulation of the voice, the countenance, and gesture: Together with an investigation of the elements of gesture, and a new method for the notation thereof: Illustrated by many figures*. Carbondale: Southern Illinois University Press, 1966. (Originally published, London, 1806.)

Bakken, D. Saying goodbye: An observational study of parting rituals. *Man–Environment Systems*, 1977, *7*, 95–105.

Bandura, A. *Social learning theory*. Englewood Cliffs, N.J.: Prentice-Hall, 1977.

Bechtel, R. B. Human movement and architecture. In H. M. Proshansky, W. H. Ittelson, & L. G. Rivlin (Eds.), *Environmental psychology: Man and his physical setting*. New York: Holt, Rinehart & Winston, 1970.

Bickman, L. Observational methods. In C. Selltiz, L. S. Wrightsman, & S. W. Cook [Eds.], *Research methods in social relations* (3rd ed.). New York: Holt, Rinehart & Winston, 1976.

Billman, J., & McDevitt, S. C. Convergence of parent and observer ratings of temperament with observations of peer interaction in nursery school. *Child Development*, 1980, *51*, 395–400.

Birdwhistell, R. L. *Introduction to kinesics*. Louisville: University of Louisville, 1952.

Birdwhistell, R. L. *Kinesics and context: Essays on body motion communication*. Philadelphia: University of Pennsylvania Press, 1970.

Blurton Jones, N. (Ed.). *Ethological studies of child behaviour*. Cambridge: Cambridge University Press, 1972.

Bobbitt, R.A., Gourevitch, V. P., Miller, L. E., & Jensen, G. D. The dynamics of social interactive behavior: A computerized procedure for analyzing trends, patterns, and sequences. *Psychological Bulletin*, 1969, *71*, 110–121.

Borton, R. W. *The perception of causality in infants*. Paper presented at the meeting of the Society for Research in Child Development, San Francisco, 1979.

Bowlby, J. *Attachment and loss: I. Attachment*. London: Hogarth Press, 1969.

Brannigan, C., & Humphries, D. Human non-verbal behaviour: A means of communication. In N. G. Blurton Jones (Ed.), *Ethological studies of child behaviour*. Cambridge: Cambridge University Press, 1972.

Breck, B. E., & Rosenfeld, H. M. *Effects of topical discomfort and participant gender on conversational distance*. Paper presented at the meeting of the American Psychological Association, San Francisco, 1977.

Carau, F. Which graphic input for computers? *Electronic Engineering Times*, November 5, 1979, pp. 49–52.

Cohen, A. A. The communicative functions of hand illustrators. *Journal of Communication*, 1977, *27*, 54–63.

Condon, W. S. An analysis of behavioral organization. In S. Weitz (Ed.), *Nonverbal communication: Readings with commentary* (2nd ed.) New York: Oxford University Press, 1979.

Condon, W. S., & Sander, L. W. Synchrony demonstrated between movements of the neonate and adult speech. *Child Development*, 1974, *45*, 456–462.

Connolly, K., & Elliott, J. The evolution and ontogeny of hand function. In N. Blurton Jones (Ed.), *Ethological studies of child behaviour*. Cambridge: Cambridge University Press, 1972.

Davis, M. Laban analysis of nonverbal communication. In S. Weitz (Ed.), *Nonverbal communication: Readings with commentary (2nd ed.), New York: Oxford University Press, 1979.*

De Long, A. J. Kinesic signals at utterance boundaries in preschool children. *Semiotica*, 1974, *11*, 43–73.

Dittmann, A. T. Review of *Kinesics and context* by R. L. Birdwhistell. *Psychiatry*, 1971, *34*, 334–342.

Dittmann, A. T. Developmental factors in conversational behavior. *Journal of Communication*, 1972, *22*, 404–423. (a)

Dittmann, A. T. The body movement–speech rhythm relationship as a cue to speech encoding. In A. W. Siegman & B. Pope (Eds.), *Studies in dyadic communication*. New York: Pergamon Press, 1972. (b)

Dittmann, A. T. The role of body motion in communication. In A. W. Siegman & S. Feldstein (Eds.), *Nonverbal behavior and communication*. Hillsdale, N.J.: Erlbaum, 1978.

Dittmann, A. T., & Llewellyn, L. G. Relationship between vocalizations and head nods as listener responses. *Journal of Personality and Social Psychology*, 1968, *9*, 79–84.

Dittmann, A. T., & Llewellyn, L. G. Body movement and speech rhythm in social conversation. *Journal of Personality and Social Psychology*, *1969*, *11*, 98–106.

Duncan, S., Jr., & Fiske, D. W. *Face-to-face interaction: Research, methods, and theory*. New York: Wiley, 1977.

Efron, D. *Gesture and environment: A tentative study of some spatio-temporal and "linguistic" aspects of the gestural behavior of Eastern Jews and Southern Italians in New York City, living under similar as well as different environmental conditions.* New York: King's Crown Press, 1941. (Reprinted as *Gesture, Race and Culture*. The Hague: Mouton, 1972.)

Eibl-Eibesfeldt, I. Similarities and differences between cultures in expressive movements. In R. A. Hinde (Ed.), *Nonverbal communication*. Cambridge: Cambridge University Press, 1972.

Ekman, P. Movements with precise meaning. *Journal of Communication*, 1975, *26*, 14–26.

Ekman, P. Biological and cultural contributions to body and facial movement. In J. Blacking (Ed.), *The anthropology of the body* (A.A.A. Monograph 15). London: Academic Press, 1977.

Ekman, P., & Friesen, W. V. Head and body cues in the judgment of emotion: A reformulation. *Perceptual and Motor Skills*, 1967, *24*, 711–724.

Ekman, P., & Friesen, W. V. Nonverbal leakage and clues to deception. *Psychiatry*, 1969, *32*, 88–105. (a)

Ekman, P., & Friesen, W. V. The repertoire of nonverbal behavior: Categories, origins, usage, and coding. *Semiotica*, 1969, *1*, 49–98. (b)

Ekman, P., & Friesen, W. V. Hand movements. *Journal of Communication*, 1972, *22*, 353–374.

Ellsworth, P. C., Carlsmith, J. M., & Henson, A. The stare as a stimulus to flight in human subjects. *Journal of Personality and Social Psychology*, 1972, *21*, 302–311.

Eshkol, N. *Moving, writing, reading*. Tel Aviv: Movement Notation Society, 1973.

Fagen, R. M., & Goldman, R. N. Behavioral catalog analysis methods. *Animal Behavior*, 1977, *25*, 261–274.

Freedman, N., & Hoffman, S. P. Kinetic behavior in altered clinical states: Approach to objective interviews. *Perceptual and Motor Skills*, 1967, *24*, 527–539.

Freedman, N., O'Hanlon, J., Oltman, P., & Witkin, H. A. The imprint of psychological differentiation on kinetic behavior in varying communicative contexts. *Journal of Abnormal Psychology*, 1972, *79*, 239–258.

Frey, S., & Pool, J. *A new approach to the analysis of visible behavior*. Unpublished manuscript, Forschungsberichte aus dem Psychologischen Institut, Universität Bern, 1976.

Frey, S., & von Cranach, M. A method for the assessment of body movement variability. In M. von Cranach & I. Vine (Eds.), *Social communication and movement*. London: Academic Press, 1973.

Friesen, W. V., Ekman, P., & Wallbott, H. Measuring hand movements. *Journal of Nonverbal Behavior*, 1979, *4*, 22–29.

Futrelle, R. P. GALATEA: A proposed system for computer-aided analysis of movie films and videotape. *University of Chicago Institute for Computer Research Quarterly Report*, 1973, No. 37.

Gesell, A. Cinemanalysis: A method of behavior study. *Journal of Genetic Psychology*, 1935, *47*, 3–16.

Gesell, A., & Halverson, H. M. The daily maturation of infant behavior: A cinema study of postures, movements, and laterality. *Journal of Genetic Psychology*, 1942, *61*, 3–32.

Gewirtz, J. L. Mechanisms of social learning: Some roles of stimulation and behavior in early human development. In D. A. Goslin (Ed.), *Handbook of socialization theory and research*. Chicago: Rand-McNally, 1969.

Gibson, E. J., Owsley, C. J., & Johnston, J. Perception of invariants by five-month-old infants: Differentiation of two types of motion. *Developmental Psychology*, 1978, *14*, 407–415.

Gibson, J. J. *The senses considered as perceptual systems*. Boston: Houghton Mifflin, 1966.

Giles, H., & Powesland, P. F. *Speech style and social evaluation*. London: Academic Press, 1975.

Glucksberg, S., Krauss, R., & Higgins, E. T. The development of referential communication skills. In F. D. Horowitz, M. E. Hetherington, S. Scarr-Salapatek, & G. M. Siegel (Eds.), *Review of child development research* (Vol. 4). Chicago: University of Chicago Press, 1975.

Goffman, E. *Behavior in public places: Notes on the social organization of gatherings*. New York: Free Press, 1963.

Golani, I. Homeostatic motor processes in mammalian interactions: A choreography of display. In P. P. G. Bateson & P. H. Klopfer (Eds.), *Perspectives in ethology* (Vol. 2). New York: Plenum, 1976.

Gollnick, P. D., & Karpovitch, P. V. Electrogoniometric study of locomotion and of some athletic movements. *Research Quarterly*, 1964, *35*, 357–369.

Gottschalk, L. A., & Auerback, A. H. (Eds.). *Methods of research in psychotherapy*. New York: Appleton-Century-Crofts, 1966.

Greenbaum, P., & Rosenfeld, H. M. Patterns of avoidance in response to interpersonal staring and proximity: Effects of bystanders on drivers at a traffic intersection. *Journal of Personality and Social Psychology*, 1978, *36*, 575–587.

Greenbaum, P. E., & Rosenfeld, H. M. Varieties of touching in greetings: Sequential structure and sex-related differences. *Journal of Nonverbal Behavior*, 1980, *5*, 13–25.

Grieve, D. W., Miller, D. I., Mitchelson, J. P., & Smith, A. J. *Techniques for the analysis of human movement*. London: Lepus Books, 1975.

Gunnell, P. K. *Conversational role regulation for dyads in cooperative and competitive floor-apportionment conditions*. Unpublished doctoral dissertation, University of Kansas, 1979.

Gustafsson, L., & Lanshammar, H. *ENOCH: An integrated system for measurement and analysis of human gait*. Uppsala, Sweden: Institute of Technology, 1977.

Haith, M. M., Kessen, W., & Collins, D. Response of the human infant to level of complexity of intermittent visual movement. *Journal of Experimental Child Psychology*, 1969, *7*, 52–69.

Hall, E. T. A system for the notation of proxemic behavior. *American Anthropologist*, 1963, *65*, 1003–1026.

Hall, E. T. *Handbook for proxemic research*. Washington, D.C.: Society for the Anthropology of Visual Communication, 1974.

Hall, E. T. Proxemics. In S. Weitz (Ed.), *Nonverbal communication: Readings with commentary* (2nd ed.). New York: Oxford University Press, 1979.

Harper, R. G., Wiens, A. N., & Matarazzo, J. D. *Nonverbal communication: The state of the art*. New York: Wiley, 1976.

Harter, M. R., & White, C. T. Periodicity within reaction time distributions and electromyograms. *Quarterly Journal of Experimental Psychology*, 1968, *20*, 157–166.

Hay, J. G. *The biomechanics of sports techniques*. Englewood Cliffs, N.J.: Prentice-Hall, 1978.

Hayes, D. P., Meltzer, L., & Wolf, G. Substantive conclusions are dependent upon techniques of measurement. *Behavioral Science*, 1970, *15*, 265–268.

Hewes, G. W. World distribution of certain postural habits. *American Anthropologist*, 1955, *57*, 231–244.

Higgins, J. R. *Human movement: An integrated approach*. St. Louis: C. V. Mosby, 1977.

Hinson, M. M. *Kinesiology*. Dubuque, Iowa: W. C. Brown, 1977.

Hutchinson, A. *Labanotation*. New York: New Directions, 1961.

Hutt, S. J., & Hutt, C. *Direct observation and measurement of behavior*. Springfield, Ill.: Charles C. Thomas, 1974.

Jancovic, M. A., Devoe, S., & Wiener, M. Age-related changes in hand and arm movements as nonverbal communication: Some conceptualizations and an empirical exploration. *Child Development*, 1975, *46*, 922–928.

Johansson, G. Visual perception of biological motion and a model for its analysis. *Perception and Psychophysics*, 1973, *14*, 201–211.

Johansson, G. Visual event perception. In R. Held, H. W. Leibowitz, & H. L. Teuber (Eds.) *Handbook of sensory physiology*. Vol. 8: *Perception*. Berlin: Springer-Verlag, 1978.

Johnson, H. G., Ekman, P., & Friesen, W. V. Communicative body movements: American emblems. *Semiotica*, 1975, *15*, 335–353.

Jourard, S. An exploratory study of body accessibility. *British Journal of Social and Clinical Psychology*, 1966, *5*, 221–231.

Kendon, A. Some relationships between body motion and speech: An analysis of an example. In A. W. Siegman & B. Pope (Eds.) *Studies in dyadic communication.* New York: Pergamon Press, 1972.

Kendon, A. The role of visible behaviour in the organization of social interaction. In M. von Cranach & I. Vine (Eds.), *Social communication and movement.* London: Academic Press, 1973.

Kendon, A. *Studies in the behavior of social interaction.* Bloomington: Indiana University, 1977.

Kendon, A., & Ferber, A. A description of some human greetings. In R. P. Michael & J. H. Crook (Eds.), *Comparative ecology and behavior of primates.* New York: Academic Press, 1973.

Kessen, W., Hendry, L. S., & Leutzendorff, A. Measurement of movement in the human newborn: A new technique. *Child Development,* 1961, *32,* 95–105.

Kessen, W., Leutzendorff, A. M., & Stoutsenberger, K. Age, food deprivation, nonnutritive sucking, and movement in the human newborn. *Journal of Comparative and Physiological Psychology,* 1967, *63,* 82–86.

Kestenberg, J. S. The role of movement patterns in development: I. Rhythms of movement. *Psychoanalytic Quarterly,* 1965, *34,* 1–36.

Key, M. R. *Nonverbal communication: A research guide and bibliography.* Metuchen, N.J.: Scarecrow Press, 1977.

Knapp, M. L. *Nonverbal communication in human interaction* (2nd ed.). New York: Holt, Rinehart & Winston, 1978.

Knapp, M. L., Hart, R. P., Friedrich, G. W., & Shulman, G. M. The rhetoric of goodbye: Verbal and nonverbal correlates of leave-taking. *Speech Monographs,* 1973, *40,* 182–198.

Kogan, K. L., Wimberger, H. C., & Bobbitt, R. A. Analysis of mother–child interaction in young mental retardates. *Child Development,* 1969, *40,* 799–812.

Konečni, V. J., Libuser, L., Morton, H., & Ebbesen, E. Effects of a violation of personal space on escape and helping responses. *Journal of Experimental Social Psychology,* 1975, *11,* 288–299.

Krout, M. H. Autistic gestures: An experimental study in symbolic movement. *Psychological Monographs,* 1935, *46,* 119–120.

Laban, R. *Principles of dance and movement notation* (2nd ed.). London: MacDonald & Evans, 1975.

LaBarre, W. Paralinguistics, kinesics, and cultural anthropology. In T. A. Sebeok, A. S. Hayes, & M. C. Bateson (Eds.), *Approaches to semiotics.* The Hague: Mouton, 1964.

Lamb, W., & Turner, D. *Management behaviour.* New York: International Universities Press, 1969.

Lasky, R. E., & Gogel, W. C. The perception of relative motion by young infants. *Perception,* 1978, *7,* 617–623.

Lewis, M., & Wilson, L. Infant stabilimeter. *Journal of Experimental Child Psychology,* 1970, *10,* 52–56.

Logan, G. A., & McKinney, W. C. *Anatomic kinesiology* (2nd ed.). Dubuque, Iowa: W. C. Brown, 1977.

Mahl, G. F. Gestures and body movements. *Research in Psychotherapy,* 1968, *3,* 295–346.

Mahl, G. F. Body movement, ideation, and verbalization during psychoanalysis. In N. Freedman & S. Grand (Eds.), *Communicative structure and psychic structure.* New York: Plenum, 1977.

McDowall, J. J. Microanalysis of filmed movement: The reliability of boundary detection by observers. *Environmental Psychology and Nonverbal Behaviour,* 1979, *3,* 77–88.

McGrew, W. C. *An ethological study of children's behavior*. New York: Academic Press, 1972.

McQuown, N. A. (Ed.). *The natural history of an interview*. Microfilm Collection of Manuscripts on Cultural Anthropology, 15th Series, University of Chicago, Joseph Regenstein Library, Department of Photoduplication, 1971.

Mehrabian, A. *Nonverbal Communication*. Chicago: Aldine–Atherton, 1972.

Michotte, A. *The perception of causality*. London: Methuen, 1963.

Miller. D. I., & Nelson, R. C. *The biomechanics of sport: A research approach*. Philadelphia: Lea & Febiger, 1973.

Moore, M. K., Borton, R. W., & Darby, B. L. Visual tracking in young infants: Evidence for object identity or object permanence? *Journal of Experimental Child Psychology*, 1978, *25*, 183–197.

Morris, D., Collett, P., Marsh, P., & O'Shaughnessy, M. *Gestures: Their origins and distribution*. New York: Stein & Day, 1979.

Nelson, K. E. Accommodation of visual tracking patterns in human infants to object movement patterns. *Journal of Experimental Child Psychology*, 1971, *12*, 182–196.

Newman, W. M., & Sproull, R. F. *Principles of interactive graphics*. New York: McGraw-Hill, 1979.

Newtson, D. Attribution and the unit of perception of ongoing behavior. *Journal of Personality and Social Psychology*, 1973, *28*, 28–38.

Newtson, D., Engquist, G., & Bois, J. The objective basis of behavior units. *Journal of Personality and Social Psychology*, 1977, *35*, 847–862.

Newtson, D., Rindner, R., Miller, R., & La Cross, K. Effects of availability of feature changes in behavior segmentation. *Journal of Experimental Social Psychology*, 1978, *14*, 379–388.

Olmsted, J. M. H. *Solid analytic geometry*. New York: Appleton–Century Crofts, 1947.

Patterson, G. R., & Cobb, J. A. A dyadic analysis of "aggressive" behaviors. In J. P. Hill (Ed.), *Minnesota Symposia on Child Psychology* (Vol. 5). Minneapolis: University of Minnesota Press, 1971.

Patterson, M. L. Compensation in nonverbal immediacy behaviors: A review. *Sociometry*, 1973, *36*, 237–252.

Reading, V. M. Visual resolution as measured by dynamic and static tests. *Pflugers Archiv*, 1972, *333*, 17–26.

Reed, S. K. Schemes and theories of pattern recognition. In E. C. Catterette & M. P. Friedman (Eds.), *Handbook of perception* (Vol. 9). New York: Academic Press, 1978.

Restle, F. Coding theory of the perception of motion configurations. *Psychological Review*, 1979, *66*, 1–24.

Rosenberg, B. G., & Langer, J. A study of postural–gestural communication. *Journal of Personality and Social Psychology*, 1965, 2, 593–597.

Rosenfeld, H. M. Effect of an approval-seeking induction on interpersonal proximity. *Psychological Reports*, 1965, *17*, 120–122.

Rosenfeld, H. M. Approval-seeking and approval-inducing functions of verbal and nonverbal responses in the dyad. *Journal of Personality and Social Psychology*, 1966, *4*, 597–605. (a)

Rosenfeld, H. M. Instrumental affiliative functions of facial and gestural expressions. *Journal of Personality and Social Psychology*, 1966, *4*, 65–72. (b)

Rosenfeld, H. M. Nonverbal reciprocation of approval: An experimental analysis. *Journal of Experimental Social Psychology*, 1967, *3*, 102–111.

Rosenfeld, H. M. The experimental analysis of interpersonal influence processes. *Journal of Communication*, 1972, *22*, 424–442.

Rosenfeld, H. M. Conversational control functions of nonverbal behavior. In A. W. Siegman & S. Feldstein (Eds.), *Nonverbal behavior and communication.* Hillsdale, N.J.: Erlbaum, 1978.

Rosenfeld, H. M. Whither interactional synchrony? In K. Bloom (Ed.), *Prospective issues in infancy research.* Hillsdale, N.J.: Erlbaum, 1981.

Rosenfeld, H. M., & Hancks, M. The nonverbal context of verbal listener responses. In M. R. Key (Ed.), *The relationship of verbal and nonverbal communication.* The Hague: Mouton, 1980.

Rosenfeld, H. M., & McRoberts, R. *Relationship of topographical features, verbal and nonverbal context, and ratings of head nods.* Unpublished manuscript, University of Kansas, 1979.

Rosenfeld, H. M., & Remmers, W. Searching for temporal relationships. In B. Hoffer & R. St. Clair (Eds.), *Developmental kinesics: the emerging paradigm.* Baltimore: University Park Press, 1981.

Rosenfeld, H. M., Shea, M., & Greenbaum, P. *Developmental trends in the recognition of normative facial emblems of "right" and "wrong" by normal children from grades 1 to 5.* Paper presented at the meeting of the Society for Research in Child Development, Denver, 1975.

Rosenfeld, H. M., Shea, M., & Greenbaum, P. Facial emblems of "right" and "wrong": Topographical analysis and derivation of a recognition test. *Semiotica,* 1979, *26,* 15–34.

Rosenfeld, H. M., & Sullwold, V. Optimal informational discrepancies for persistent communication. *Behavioral Science,* 1969, *14,* 303–315.

Ruesch, J. Nonverbal language and therapy. *Psychiatry,* 1955, *18,* 323–330.

Sackett, G. P. (Ed.). *Observing behavior.* Baltimore: University Park Press, 1978.

Schaffer, H. R. (Ed.). *Studies in mother–infant interaction.* London: Academic Press, 1977.

Scheflen, A. E. The significance of posture in communication systems. *Psychiatry,* 1964, *27,* 316–331.

Scheflen, A. E. *Stream and structure of communicational behavior: Context analysis of a psychotherapy session* (Behavioral Studies Monograph No. 1). Philadelphia: Western Pennsylvania Psychiatric Institute, 1965.

Scherer, K. R., Wallbott, H. G., & Scherer, U. Methoden zur Klassifikation von Bewegungsverhalten: Ein funktionaler Ansatz. *Semiotik,* 1979, *1,* 177–192.

Shannon, C. E., & Weaver, W. *The mathematical theory of communication.* Urbana: University of Illinois Press, 1949.

Shea, M., & Rosenfeld, H. M. Functional employment of nonverbal social reinforcers in dyadic learning. *Journal of Personality and Social Psychology,* 1976, *34,* 228–239.

Stokoe, W. C. *Semiotics and human sign languages.* The Hague: Mouton, 1972.

Stokoe, W. C., Casterline, D. C., & Croneberg, C. G. *A dictionary of American sign language on linguistic principles.* Silver Spring, Md.: Linstok Press, 1976.

Sugarman, S. The development of preverbal communication: Its contribution and limits in promoting the development of language. In R. L. Schiefelbusch & J. Pickar (Eds.), *Communicative competence: Acquisition and intervention.* Baltimore: University Park Press, in press.

Sussman, N. M., & Rosenfeld, H. M. *Influence of culture, language and sex: Influences on interpersonal distancing. Journal of Personality and Social Psychology,* in press.

Trout, D. L., & Rosenfeld, H. M. The effect of postural lean and body congruence on the judgment of psychotherapeutic rapport. *Journal of Nonverbal Behavior,* 1980, *4,* 176–190.

Trower, P., Bryant, B., & Argyle, M. *Social skills and mental health.* London: Methuen, 1978.

Wallbott, H. G. The measurement of human expression. In W. von Raffler-Engel (Ed.), *Aspects of nonverbal communication.* Lisse: Swets & Zeitlinger, 1980.

Watzlawick, P., Beavin, J., & Jackson, D. *The pragmatics of human communication.* New York: Norton, 1967.

Wiener, M., Devoe, S., Rubinow, S., & Geller, J. Nonverbal behavior and nonverbal communication. *Psychological Review,* 1972, *79,* 185–214.

Yarbos, A. L. *Eye movements and vision.* New York: Plenum, 1967.

Yngve, V. H. On getting a word in edgewise. In M. A. Campbell (Ed.), *Papers from the sixth regional meeting, Chicago Linguistic Society.* Chicago: University of Chicago Department of Linguistics, 1970.

Yonas, A., & Peterson, L. *Responsiveness in newborns to optical information for collision.* Paper presented at the meeting of the Society for Research in Child Development, San Francisco, 1979.

6. Conducting judgment studies

ROBERT ROSENTHAL

6.1. The nature of judgment studies

Some dimensions of judgment studies

Research in nonverbal communication very often requires the use of observers, coders, raters, decoders, or judges. Although distinctions among these classes of human (or at least animate) responders are possible, I shall not distinguish among them here but rather shall use these terms more or less interchangeably.

Judgment studies may focus on nonverbal behaviors considered as independent variables; for instance, when the corners of the mouth rise, do judges rate subjects as being happier? Judgment studies may also focus on nonverbal behaviors considered as dependent variables; for instance, when subjects are made happier, are the corners of the subjects' mouths judged as having risen more?

Judgment studies may employ a variety of metrics, from physical units of measurement to psychological units of measurement. For example, the movement of the corner of the mouth can be given in millimeters, whereas judges' ratings of happiness may be given on a continuum ranging from *not at all happy* to *very happy*, perhaps on a scale of 7 points.

The judgments employed in a judgment study may vary dramatically in their reliability. Thus judgments based on physical units of measurement are often more reliable than are judgments based on psychological units of measurement, although, for some purposes, the latter may be higher in validity despite their being lower in reliability (Rosenthal, 1966). This may be because a lower degree of social meaning is inherent in the more molecular physical units of measurement than in the more molar psychological units of measurement. Table 6.1 shows some of the dimensions upon which it is possible to classify various judgment studies.

Table 6.1. *Dimensions tending to distinguish various types of judgment studies*

Dimension	Examples		
Type of variable	Dependent	vs.	independent variables
Measurement units	Physical	vs.	psychological units
Reliability	Lower	vs.	higher levels
Social meaning	Lower	vs.	higher levels

The judgment study model

The underlying model of a basic judgment study is shown in Figure 6.1. One or more encoders characterized by one or more attributes (e.g., traits, states, etc.) (*A*) are observed by one or more decoders who make one or more judgments (C) about the encoders on the basis of selectively presented nonverbal behavior (*B*). The *AB* arrow refers to the relationship between the encoder's actual attribute (e.g., state) and the encoder's nonverbal behavior. The *AB* arrow reflects the primary interest of the investigator who wishes to employ the nonverbal behavior as the dependent variable. The *BC* arrow reflects the primary interest of the investigator who wishes to employ the nonverbal behavior as the independent variable. The *AC* arrow reflects the primary interest of the investigator interested in the relationship between the encoder's attribute and the decoders' judgment, i.e., the decoders' accuracy.

The nonverbal behavior (*B*) presented to the decoders tends to be highly selected as part of the research design. Investigators interested in facial expressions might present still photographs of the face (e.g., Ekman, 1973), whereas investigators interested in tone of voice might present speech that is content standard (Davitz, 1964), randomized spliced (Scherer, 1971), or content filtered (Rogers, Scherer, & Rosenthal, 1971). Investigators interested in comparing the relative efficiency of cues carried in various channels of nonverbal communication might provide access to different channels of nonverbal cues (e.g., face, body, tone of voice [Rosenthal, Hall, DiMatteo, Rogers, & Archer, 1979; Scherer, Scherer, Hall, & Rosenthal, 1977]).

To summarize the simple judgment model, then, we have encoder attributes, say, states (*A*), manifested behaviorally (*B*) and decoded by judges (C). The states then generate both the nonverbal behaviors and the decoders' judgments.

A more complex judgment study model based on Brunswik's (1956) lens model has been described by Scherer (1978).

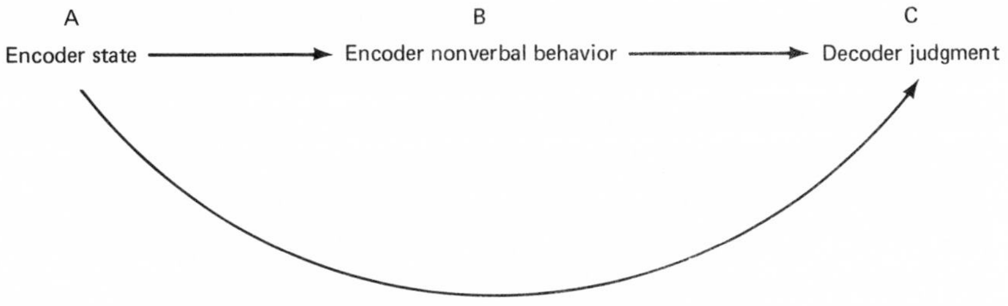

Figure 6.1. A simple Model of judgment studies.

The purposes of judgment studies

Judgment studies serve many purposes. In terms of our simple model of judgment studies (Figure 6.1), the focus of a judgment study may be on the encoder state or other attribute (*A*); the encoder's nonverbal behavior (*B*); the decoder's judgment itself (*C*); the *AB*, *AC*, and *BC* arrows; or the *ABC* chain.

Encoder state. Suppose we wanted to develop a system for the diagnosis of anxiety in college students from various nonverbal cues. Suppose further that we had available film clips of 30 students being interviewed. Before we could correlate various nonverbal behaviors with the degree of anxiety of the students we would have to ascertain their actual anxiety level. One way of defining the students' actual level of anxiety might be to show the 30 film clips to a sample of experienced clinical psychologists or other experts on anxiety and obtain ratings of the degree of anxiety shown by each college student. The mean rating of anxiety of each stimulus person (encoder) becomes the operational definition of the true state of the encoder. Note that our emphasis here was on defining the encoder state, *not* on specifying the cues that might have led the expert judges to decide what ratings they would give. In addition, note that this particular judgment study, done for the purpose of estimating parameters (mean anxiety), rather than establishing relationships, was a kind of preliminary study to be followed up by a study linking the state of anxiety to the nonverbal concomitants (an *AB* arrow) (Rosenthal & Rosnow, 1975a).

Encoder nonverbal behavior. Suppose we wanted to study the mediation of teacher expectancy effects (Rosenthal, 1966, 1969, 1974, 1976; Rosenthal & Jacobson, 1968; Rosenthal & Rubin, 1978). One of our hypotheses might be that teachers who expect more from their students treat them more warmly. Furthermore, we may believe that this warmth will be expressed in part through tone of voice. Before we can examine the relationship between teachers' expectations and teachers' warmth in tone of voice, however, we must be able to define tonal warmth. One way of defining warmth would be to ask judges to make ratings of the degree of warmth shown in the content-filtered voices of teachers talking to their students. The mean rating of warmth obtained for each stimulus teacher's content-filtered voice becomes the definition of the warmth of the nonverbal behavior. The purpose of this particular judgment study, like that of the one just described, would be to estimate parameters (mean warmth), rather than establish relationships. As such it might serve as a kind of preliminary study that would be followed up by a study relating the nonverbal behavior to a teacher state or some other type of variable. Such studies have been conducted with the focus on the tone of voice shown by, for example, physicians and mothers (Milmoe, Novey, Kagan, & Rosenthal, 1968; Milmoe, Rosenthal, Blane, Chafetz, & Wolf, 1967).

Decoder judgment. In the case of the two purposes of judgment studies described so far, judges' ratings were employed to provide definitions of encoder states and encoder nonverbal behavior, usually in the context of a preliminary study, or a simple descriptive study (e.g., what proportion of experimenters smile at their research subjects? [Rosenthal, 1967]). Sometimes, however, it is the judgments themselves that we want to study. The interpretation of nonverbal cues may depend heavily on personal characteristics of the judges. Thus we might not be surprised to find that aggressive, delinquent boys will tend to interpret nonverbal cues as more aggressive than would less aggressive boys (Nasby, DePaulo & Hayden, 1979). Or we might be interested to learn that blind children may be more sensitive to tone-of-voice cues (content filtered and randomized spliced) than are sighted children (Rosenthal et al., 1979).

AB arrows. If we record therapists' expectations for their patients and observe their nonverbal behaviors as they interact with their patients, we have the ingredients of an *AB* arrow study. Therapists' nonverbal behaviors could be defined by measurements of muscle movements in millimeters or voice changes in hertz or by judgments of warmth, pride, esteem, and expectation, as rated on 9-point scales. In either case, we regard the nonverbal behaviors as the dependent variable, and the therapists' expectations as the independent variable.

BC arrows. A common type of *BC* arrow judgment study might experimentally manipulate various encoder nonverbal cues and observe the effects on decoders' ratings of various encoder characteristics (e.g., H. S. Friedman, 1976, 1978, 1979a). Questions addressed might include: Are smiling faces rated as more friendly? Are voices with greater pitch range judged more pleasant? Are louder voices judged more extroverted? (Scherer, 1970, 1978, 1979a, 1979b; Scherer, Koivumaki, & Rosenthal, 1972; Scherer & Oshinsky, 1977; Scherer, Rosenthal & Koivumaki, 1972).

AC arrows. *AC* arrow judgment studies are common in the general research domains of clinical diagnosis and person perception. The general paradigm is to ask decoders to assess the encoders' true attributes (e.g., diagnosis, anxiety level, adjustment level) and to correlate decoders' judgments with independently determined definitions of encoders' true traits or states. Thus, for example, clinicians' ratings of adjustment and anxiety might be correlated with encoders' scores on various subscales of such tests as the Minnesota Multiphasic Personality Inventory, or scores based on the Rorscharch, Thematic Apperception Test, or life history data.

When *AC* arrow judgment studies are employed in research on nonverbal communication it is often in the context of "accuracy" studies. Encoders may, for example, show a variety of posed or spontaneous affects, and judgments of these affects made by decoders are then evaluated for accuracy. Sometimes these accuracy studies are conducted to learn the degree to which judges show better than chance accuracy (Allport, 1924; Ekman, 1965a, 1973). At other times they are conducted to establish individual differences among the judges in degree of accuracy shown. These individual differences in decoding accuracy may then be correlated with a variety of personal attributes of the judges (e.g., gender, age, ethnicity, psychopathology, cognitive attributes, personality attributes, etc. [Rosenthal et al., 1979]). It should be noted that such individual difference studies can be meaningfully conducted even when the mean level of accuracy shown by the entire sample of judges does not exceed the chance expectation level, as in comparisons of people scoring above chance with those scoring below chance.

ABC chains. Sometimes we are simultaneously interested in the *AB* arrow and the *BC* arrow; such studies can be viewed as studies of the *ABC* chain. Suppose we want to study the mediation of teacher expectancy effects. We begin with a sample of teachers known to vary in their expectations for their pupils' intellectual performance, that is, known to vary in encoder states (*A*). These teachers are observed interacting with pupils for whom they hold high and low expectations, and a sample of judges rates the teachers' behavior on degree of smiling, forward lean, and eye contact, that is, encoder nonverbal behaviors (*B*). Finally, a sample of judges rates the nonverbal behavior of the teachers for degree of overall warmth and favorableness of expectancy; that is, this sample makes decoder judgments (*C*) of a fairly molar type. We are now in a position to examine the effects of teacher expectation on teacher nonverbal behavior and the social impact of these effects on nonverbal behavior, all in the same study.

Designing judgment studies

The particular purpose of any judgment study should determine the particular procedures of that study. Given the diversity of purposes of judgment studies already discussed, it is not possible to prescribe the detailed procedures that should be employed for any particular study. However, because judgment studies do have certain communalities, it is possible to discuss issues likely to be confronted in many of them. In the following sections I address some of these issues.

6.2. Sampling judges

How many judges shall we employ in a judgment study in which our primary interest is in the encoders rather than the judges, and who should they be? The major factors determining the answers to these questions are (1) the average reliability coefficient (*r*) between pairs of judges chosen at random from a prescribed population and (2) the nature of the population of judges to which we want to generalize our results.

Effective reliability

Suppose our goal is to establish the definition of the encoder's state (*A*) or of some encoder nonverbal behavior (*B*). We might decide to employ judges' ratings for our definition. As we shall see shortly, if the reliability coefficient (any product moment correlation such as *r*, point biserial *r*, or phi) is very low we will require more judges than if the reliability coefficient is very high. Just how many judges to employ is a question for which some useful guidelines can be presented (Rosenthal, 1973; Uno, Koivumaki, & Rosenthal, 1972).

If we had a sample of teachers whose nonverbal warmth we wanted to establish, we might begin by having two judges rate each teacher's warmth on the basis of the videotaped behavior of each teacher. The correlation coefficient reflecting the reliability of the two judges' ratings would be computed to give us our best (and only) estimate of the correlation likely to be obtained between any two judges drawn from the same population of judges. This correlation coefficient, then, is clearly useful; but it is not a very good estimate of the reliability of our variable, which is not the rating of warmth made by a single judge but rather the mean of two judges' ratings. Suppose, for example, that the correlation between our two judges' ratings of warmth were 0.50; the reliability of the mean of the two judges' ratings, the "effective" reliability, would then be 0.67, not 0.50. Intuition suggests that we should gain in reliability in adding the ratings of a second judge because the second judges' random errors should tend to cancel those of the first judge. Intuition suggests further that adding more judges, all of whom agree with one another to about the same degree, defined by a mean interjudge correlation coefficient of 0.50 for this example, should further increase our effective reliability. Our intuition would be supported by an old and well-known result reported independently by Charles Spearman and William Brown in 1910 (Walker & Lev, 1953). With notation altered to suit our current purpose, the well-known Spearman–Brown result is

$$R = \frac{nr}{1 + (n - 1)r} \tag{1}$$

where R = "effective" reliability, n = number of judges, r = mean reliability among all n judges (i.e., mean of $[n\,(n - 1)\,/\,2]$ correlations).

Use of this formula depends on the assumption that a comparable group of judges would show comparable mean reliability among themselves and with the actual group of judges available to us. This assumption is virtually the same as the assumption that all pairs of judges show essentially the same degree of reliability.

As an aid to investigators employing these and related methods, Table 6.2, employing the Spearman–Brown formula, has been prepared. This table gives the effective reliability, R, for each of several values of n, the number of judges making the observations, and r, the mean reliability among the judges; it is intended to facilitate the rapid obtaining of approximate answers to each of the following questions:

Table 6.2. *Effective reliability of the mean of judges' ratings*

Number of judges	Mean reliability (r)																		
(n)	05	10	15	20	25	30	35	40	45	50	55	60	65	70	75	80	85	90	95
1	05	10	15	20	25	30	35	40	45	50	55	60	65	70	75	80	85	90	95
2	10	18	26	33	40	46	52	57	62	67	71	75	79	82	86	89	92	95	97
3	14	25	35	43	50	56	62	67	71	75	79	82	85	88	90	92	94	96	98
4	17	31	41	50	57	63	68	73	77	80	83	86	88	90	92	94	96	97	*a*
5	21	36	47	56	62	68	73	77	80	83	86	88	90	92	94	95	97	98	*a*
6	24	40	51	60	67	72	76	80	83	86	88	90	92	93	95	96	97	98	*a*
7	27	44	55	64	70	75	79	82	85	88	90	91	93	94	95	97	98	98	*a*
8	30	47	59	67	73	77	81	84	87	89	91	92	94	95	96	97	98	*a*	*a*
9	32	50	61	69	75	79	83	86	88	90	92	93	94	95	96	97	98	*a*	*a*
10	34	53	64	71	77	81	84	87	89	91	92	94	95	96	97	98	98	*a*	*a*
12	39	57	68	75	80	84	87	89	91	92	94	95	96	97	97	98	*a*	*a*	*b*
14	42	61	71	78	82	86	88	90	92	93	94	95	96	97	98	98	*a*	*a*	*b*
16	46	64	74	80	84	87	90	91	93	94	95	96	97	97	98	98	*a*	*a*	*b*
18	49	67	76	82	86	89	91	92	94	95	96	96	97	98	98	*a*	*a*	*a*	*b*
20	51	69	78	83	87	90	92	93	94	95	96	97	97	98	98	*a*	*a*	*a*	*b*
24	56	73	81	86	89	91	93	94	95	96	97	97	98	98	*a*	*a*	*a*	*b*	*b*
28	60	76	83	88	90	92	94	95	96	97	97	98	98	98	*a*	*a*	*a*	*b*	*b*
32	63	78	85	89	91	93	95	96	96	97	98	98	98	*a*	*a*	*a*	*a*	*b*	*b*
36	65	80	86	90	92	94	95	96	97	97	98	98	*a*	*a*	*a*	*a*	*b*	*b*	*b*
40	68	82	88	91	93	94	96	96	97	98	98	98	*a*	*a*	*a*	*a*	*b*	*b*	*b*
50	72	85	90	93	94	96	96	97	98	98	98	*a*	*a*	*a*	*a*	*b*	*b*	*b*	*b*
60	76	87	91	94	95	96	97	98	98	98	*a*	*a*	*a*	*a*	*a*	*b*	*b*	*b*	*b*
80	81	90	93	95	96	97	98	98	98	*a*	*a*	*a*	*a*	*a*	*b*	*b*	*b*	*b*	*b*
100	84	92	95	96	97	98	98	*a*	*a*	*a*	*a*	*a*	*a*	*b*	*b*	*b*	*b*	*b*	*b*

Note: Decimal points omitted. [a]Approximately 0.99. [b]Approximately 1.00.

1. Given an obtained or estimated mean reliability, r, and a sample of n judges, what is the approximate effective reliability, R, of the mean of the judges' ratings? The value of R is read from the table at the intersection of the appropriate row (n) and column (r).
2. Given the value of the obtained or desired effective reliability, R, and the number, n, of judges available, what will be the approximate value of the required mean reliability, r? For the answer, we read across the row corresponding to the n of judges available until we reach the value of R closest to the one desired; the value of r is then read as the corresponding column heading.
3. Given an obtained or estimated mean reliability, r, and the obtained or desired effective reliability, R, what is the approximate number (n) of judges required? For this answer we read down the column corresponding to the mean reliability, r until we reach the value of R closest to the one desired; the value of n is then read as the corresponding row title.

Product moment correlations. It should be noted that the mean reliability (r) of Table 6.2 is to be a product moment correlation coefficient such as

Pearson's *r*, the point biserial *r*, or the phi coefficient. It is not appropriate to employ such indexes of "reliability" as percentage agreement – number of agreements (*A*) divided by the sum of agreements (*A*) and disagreements (*D*), $A/(A + D)$ – or net agreements – $A - D)/(A + D)$. These indexes not only should be avoided in any use of Table 6.2 but should be avoided in general because of the greatly misleading results that they can yield. For example, suppose two judges were to evaluate 100 film clips for the presence or absence of frowning behavior. If both the judges saw frowns in 98 of the film clips and disagreed only twice they would show 98% agreement; yet the χ^2 testing the significance of the product moment correlation phi would be essentially zero! Thus two judges who shared the same perceptual bias (e.g., almost all behavior is a frown) could consistently earn nearly perfect agreement scores while their actual correlation would be essentially zero with one another (phi = 0.01).

Reliability and analysis of variance

When there are only two judges whose reliability is to be evaluated it is hard to beat the convenience of a product moment correlation coefficient for an appropriate index of reliability. As the number of judges grows larger, however, working with correlation coefficients can become inconvenient. For example, suppose we employed 40 judges and wanted to compute both their mean reliability ($\bar{r}$) and their effective reliability (*R*). Table 6.2 could get us *R* from knowing $\bar{r}$, but to get $\bar{r}$ we would have to compute $(40 \times 39)/2 = 780$ correlation coefficients. That is not hard work for computers, but averaging the 780 coefficients to get $\bar{r}$ is very hard work for investigators or their programmers. There is an easier way, and it involves the analysis of variance.

Table 6.3 shows a simple example of three judges rating the nonverbal behavior of five encoders on a scale of 1 to 7, and Table 6.4 shows the analysis of variance of these data. Our computations require only the use of the last column in Table 6.4, the column of mean squares (Guilford, 1954). Examination of computational formulas (2) and (3) shows that they tell us how well the judges can discriminate among the sampling units (e.g., people). In these formulas judges' disagreements are subtracted (e.g., *MS* encoders − *MS* residuals) divided by a standardizing quantity, and judges' rating biases or main effects are controlled for.

Table 6.3. *Judges' ratings of nonverbal behavior*

	Judges			
Encoders	*A*	*B*	*C*	Σ
1	5	6	7	18
2	3	6	4	13
3	3	4	6	13
4	2	2	3	7
5	1	4	4	9
Σ	14	22	24	60

Table 6.4. *Analysis of variance of judges' ratings*

Source	*SS*	*df*	*MS*
Encoders	24.0	4	6.00
Judges	11.2	2	5.60
Residual	6.8	8	0.85

Our estimate of *R*, the effective reliability of the ratings of *all* the judges, is given by

$$R \text{ (est.)} = \frac{MS \text{ encoders} - MS \text{ residual}}{MS \text{ encoders}} \tag{2}$$

Our estimate of *r*, the mean reliability or the reliability of a *single* average judge, is given by

$$r \text{ (est.)} = \frac{MS \text{ encoders} - MS \text{ residual}}{MS \text{ encoders} + (n - 1)\, MS \text{ residual}} \tag{3}$$

where n is the number of judges as before (formula [3] is known as the intraclass correlation.) For our example of Tables 6.3 and 6.4 we have

$$R \text{ (est.)} = \frac{6.00 - 0.85}{6.00} = 0.858$$

and

$$r \text{ (est.)} = \frac{6.00 - 0.85}{6.00 + (3 - 1)\, 0.85} = 0.669$$

In the present example it will be easy to compare the results of the analysis of variance approach with the more cumbersome correlational approach. Thus the correlations (r) between pairs of judges (r_{AB}, r_{BC}, and r_{AC}) are 0.645, 0.582, and 0.800, respectively, and the mean intercorrelation is 0.676, which differs by only 0.007 from the estimate (0.669) obtained by means of the analysis of variance approach.

If we were employing only the correlational approach we would apply the Spearman–Brown formula (1) to our mean reliability of 0.676 to find R, the effective reliability. That result is

$$R = \frac{(3)(0.676)}{1 + (3 - 1)(0.676)} = 0.862$$

which differs by only 0.004 from the estimate (0.858) obtained by means of the analysis of variance approach. In general, the differences obtained between the correlational approach and the analysis of variance approach are quite small (Guilford, 1954).

It should be noted that in our present simple example the correlational approach was not an onerous one to employ, with only three correlations to compute. As the number of judges increased, however, we would find ourselves more and more grateful for the analysis of variance approach.

Reliability and principal components

In situations were the ratings made by all judges have been intercorrelated, and a principal-components analysis is readily available, another very efficient alternative for estimating the reliability of the total set of judges is available. Armor (1974) has developed an index, *theta*, that is based on the unrotated first principal component (where a principal component is a factor extracted from a correlation matrix employing unity [1.00] in the diagonal of the correlation matrix). The formula for *theta* is

$$\theta = \frac{n}{n - 1}\left(\frac{L - 1}{L}\right) \tag{4}$$

where n is the number of judges and L is the latent root or eigenvalue of the first unrotated principal component. The latent root is the sum of the squared factor loadings for any given factor and can be thought of as the amount of variance in the judges' ratings accounted for by that factor.

Factor analytic computer programs generally give latent roots or eigenvalues for each factor extracted, so θ is very easy to obtain in practice.

Reporting reliabilities

Assuming that we have done our reliability analyses well, how shall we report our results? Ideally, reports of reliability analyses should include both the mean reliability (the reliability of a single judge) and the effective reliability (reliability of the total set of judges or of the mean judgments). The reader needs to know the latter reliability (R) because that is, in fact, the reliability of the variable employed in most cases. However, if this reliability is reported without explanation, the reader may not be aware that the reliability of any one judge's ratings is likely to be lower, often substantially so. A reader may note a reported reliability of 0.80 based on 12 judges' ratings and decide that the variable is sufficiently reliable for his or her purposes. This reader may then employ a single judge, only to find later that this single judge was operating at a reliability of 0.25, not 0.80. Reporting both reliabilities avoids such misunderstandings.

Split-sample reliabilities. A related source of misunderstanding is the reporting of correlations between a mean judge of one type and a mean judge of another type. For example, suppose we had 10 male and 10 female judges, or 10 black and 10 white judges. One sometimes sees in the literature the reliability of the mean male and mean female judge, or that of the mean black and mean white judge. Such correlations of the mean ratings made by all judges of one type with the mean ratings made by judges of another type can be very useful, but they should not be reported as reliabilities without the explanation that these correlations might be substantially higher than the average correlation between any one male and any one female judge, or between any one black and any one white judge. The reasons for this are those discussed in the earlier section on effective reliability.

Trimming judges. It sometimes happens that when we examine the intercorrelations among our judges we find one that is very much out of line with all the others. Perhaps this judge tends to obtain negative correlations with other judges, or at least to show clearly lower reliabilities with other judges than is typical for the correlation matrix. If this "unreliable" judge were dropped from the data the resulting estimates of reliability would be biased, that is, made to appear too reliable. If a judge must be dropped, the resulting bias can be reduced by equitable trimming. Thus, if the lowest-agreeing judge is dropped, the highest-agreeing judge is also dropped; if the two lowest-agreeing judges are dropped, the two highest-agreeing judges are also dropped; and so on. Experience suggests that, when large samples of judges are employed, the effects of trimming judges are small, as is the need for trimming. When the sample of judges is small, we may feel a stronger need to drop a judge, but doing so is more likely to leave a residual biased estimate of reliability. A safe procedure is to do all analyses with and without the trimming of judges and to report the differences in results from data with and without the trimming. Although the method of trimming judges seems not yet to have been systematically applied, the theoretical foundations for it can be seen in the work of Mosteller and Rourke (1973) and Tukey (1977).

Judge characteristics

So far in this discussion of the sampling of judges we have not considered systematic differences among our judges. Typically, there is no special interest in individual differences among judges when we consider issues of reliability. We simply decide on the type of judges we want, for instance, college students, clinical psychologists, linguists, dance therapists, mothers, and so on, and then regard each judge within that sample as to some degree equivalent to or interchangeable with any other judge within that sample.

Sometimes, however, our interest focuses directly on individual differences among judges – for example, when we want to know about the relationships of these individual differences to accuracy (or systematic inaccuracy) of encoding and decoding nonverbal behavior. Interest in such relationships has been increasing (Buck, 1979; DePaulo & Rosenthal, 1979a; DiMatteo, 1979; H. S. Friedman, 1979b; Hall, 1979; Nasby, DePaulo, & Hayden, 1979; Rosenthal, 1979d; Rosenthal & DePaulo, 1979; Rosenthal et al., 1979; Uno et al. 1972; Weitz, 1979; Zuckerman & Larrance, 1979).

The types of variables that have been studied for their degree of relationship to skill in decoding nonverbal cues include judges' age, sex, cultural background, cognitive attributes, psychosocial attributes, special skills and impairments, training, and experience (e.g., Rosenthal et al., 1979).

If we are planning a judgment study and want simply a prototypic sample of judges, we may be content to select a sample of college or high school students. If our aim is simply to define the encoder's state or the encoder's nonverbal behavior by means of the judges' ratings, we need not even be overly concerned about the common problem of volunteer bias (Rosenthal & Rosnow, 1975b). If our interest, however, is to estimate the average degree of accuracy for the population selected (e.g., students), we should be aware of the potentially large effects of volunteer bias.

Recent research with high school students has suggested that the correlation between volunteering for behavioral research and accuracy of decoding nonverbal cues may be on the order of 0.40 (Rosenthal et al., 1979). Such a correlation reflects the situation obtained when 70% of the volunteers and only 30% of the nonvolunteers achieve the median level of accuracy, with about half the judges being volunteers and half nonvolunteers (Rosenthal & Rubin, in press).

Sometimes our intent in a judgment study is not to find prototypic judges but the "best" judges for our purpose. Thus, if we wanted judgments of nonverbal cues to psychoses, we might want clinical psychologists or psychiatrists for our judges. If we wanted judgments of nonverbal cues to discomfort in infants, we might want pediatricians, developmental psychologists, or mothers. If we wanted judgments of nonverbal cues of persuasiveness, we might want trial lawyers, fundamentalist clergymen, or salespersons.

Maximizing judge accuracy. If there is no very specialized type of judgment we are after, but we would like to obtain the highest level of accuracy possible in a general way, we might want to select our judges on the basis of prior research suggesting characteristics of those more sensitive to nonverbal cues. A recent review of research suggests that to optimize overall sensitivity we might select judges who are female, of college age, cognitively complex, and psychiatrically unimpaired (Rosenthal et al., 1979). Actors, students of nonverbal communication, and students of visual arts tend to perform better than do members of other occupational groups; and among teachers and clinicians, the more effective teachers and clinicians are likely to be the better decoders of nonverbal cues (Rosenthal et al., 1979). Finally, if we were to base our selection of more accurate judges of nonverbal behavior on psychosocial variables, we might want to consider results of the type shown in Table 6.5, based on research reported elsewhere in detail (Rosenthal et al., 1979). Users of Table 6.5 should note that the correlations given are medians of varying

Table 6.5. *Psychosocial variables likely to be useful in selecting judges of greater than average sensitivity to nonverbal cues* ($r \geq 0.20$)

Variables	Number of studies	Median *r*	Equivalent to increasing success rate[a] From	To
Volunteering for research	2	0.40	0.30	0.70
Achievement potential	5	0.31	0.34	0.66
Social–religious values	1	0.28	0.36	0.64
Interpersonal adequacy	5	0.25	0.38	0.62
Democratic orientation	2	0.24	0.38	0.62
Intellectual and interest modes	5	0.23	0.38	0.62
Maturity	5	0.22	0.39	0.61
Interpersonal sensitivity	22	0.22	0.39	0.61
Task orientation	1	0.21	0.40	0.60
Nondogmatism	2	0.20	0.40	0.60
Spouse's report of nonverbal sensitivity	2	0.20	0.40	0.60

Note: For this table, sensitivity to nonverbal cues was defined by performance on the Profile of Nonverbal Sensitivity (PONS) test (Rosenthal, Hall, DiMatteo, Rogers, & Archer, 1979).
[a]Based on the Binomial Effect Size Display (Rosenthal & Rubin, in press).

numbers of studies conducted; greater confidence may be placed in those relationships based on a larger number of studies. Even in those cases, however, it is possible for any *one* study to show a much higher or a much lower correlation than the median.

6.3. Sampling encoders

The basic issues that must be faced in a sampling of encoders are very similar to the issues that must be faced in a sampling of judges. One decision that must be made is how many encoders to employ. Should the researcher's finite resources be allocated to increasing the number of encoders (with a concomitant decrease in the number of scenes encoded by each sender) or to increasing the number of scenes encoded by each sender (with a concomitant decrease in the number of encoders)? The purpose of a recent study was to address this question in a preliminary manner by comparing the internal consistency of tests using many encoders, each sending the same scene, with the internal consistency of a standardized test using a single encoder who sends many different scenes (Rosenthal, Hall, & Zuckerman, 1978).

When this question is rephrased as a substantive rather than methodological one, it may become more generally interesting: Am I, as a judge of other people's nonverbal communication, more consistent in the accuracy of my repeated judgments of a single other person than I am in the accuracy of my single judgments of a host of different people? To put this still another way, could the accuracy of my future judgments of the single person be predicted better than could the accuracy of my future judgments of new people?

Tests employing many encoders

My co-workers and I made two tests using many encoders. The procedural details are given elsewhere (Zuckerman, Hall, DeFrank, & Rosenthal, 1976). Here it is enough to say that two groups of encoders ($n = 30, 29$) were videotaped while they reacted spontaneously to four different videotaped scenarios (pleasant adult–child interaction, comedy scene, murder scene, and auto accident). Encoders were also videotaped while talking about the four scenarios and while *trying* to communicate via facial expression the nature of the stimuli they had been exposed to. Thus each encoder sent 12 scenes: four scenarios in each of three modes (spontaneous, talking, and posed). For each group of encoders, a group of 30 judges decoded the encoders' scenes by viewing those scenes on a videotape and making multiple-choice judgments about which one of the four scenarios was being expressed in each. These judgments were then scored for accuracy.

For each of our two samples of encoders (and separately for each of the 12 encodings), we were able to intercorrelate the accuracy scores earned by the encoders. In psychometric terms, encoders were analogous to test items and judges were analogous to test-taking subjects. The average of the intercorrelations among single test items, or among senders in this case, when corrected for the number of test items (or encoders) by the Spearman–Brown procedure described earlier, becomes an index of internal consistency known as *K-R* 20, coefficient alpha, or effective reliability (*R*) (Guilford, 1954; Rosenthal, 1973).

Test employing one encoder

Our goal was to compare the length-corrected internal consistency coefficients based on intercorrelations among encoders encoding the

Table 6.6. *Length-corrected internal consistency coefficients for two many-encoder tests*

	Pleasant scene		Unpleasant scene		
Mode	Child	Comedy	Murder	Accident	Mean
Test A					
Spontaneous	0.96	0.91	0.94	0.98	0.95
Talking	0.67	0.82	0.85	0.94	0.82
Posed	0.86	0.77	0.92	0.96	0.88
Mean	0.83	0.83	0.90	0.96	0.88
Test B					
Spontaneous	0.92	0.89	0.93	0.93	0.92
Talking	0.71	0.31	0.89	0.52	0.61
Posed	0.67	0.91	0.81	0.90	0.82
Mean	0.77	0.70	0.88	0.78	0.78
Grand mean	0.80	0.77	0.89	0.87	0.83

same scene in the same mode (the many-encoder tests just described) with the intercorrelations among many different scenes sent by the same encoder. The latter intercorrelations were already available from psychometric research conducted with the Profile of Nonverbal Sensitivity (PONS) test (Rosenthal et al., 1979). In that test 20 different scenes are encoded by a single sender in 11 different channels of nonverbal communication (e.g., face, body, content-filtered speech, random-spliced speech, and various combinations of these), yielding 220 different items. In the study reported in Rosenthal et al. (1979), the internal consistency coefficient for the 220-item PONS test was 0.86 for the norm group of nearly 500 high school students. When the analogous internal consistency coefficient was computed for the 20 scenes showing only the face (i.e., the modality employed in the many-sender tests), the reliability was nearly identical (0.88) after correcting for the difference in length (from 20 to 220 items) by the Spearman–Brown procedure described earlier (Guilford, 1954; Rosenthal, 1973).

Internal consistency data

Table 6.6 shows the internal consistency coefficients for our many-encoder tests: two samples of encoders in three modes of sending each of the four scenes. All coefficients of internal consistency are corrected using the Spearman–Brown formula to the same number of items as the PONS (220). This is done merely to make results of one kind of test comparable to the results of the other; because coefficients of internal consistency go up as the number of test items goes up, it is essential to control for that fact when comparing two such coefficients. (It would have been equally informative, though somewhat unusual in practice, to apply the Spearman–Brown formula downward from the 220-item length to the 30-item length for the single-encoder test.) The grand mean of all 24 alphas of Table 6.6 was 0.83, and the grand median was 0.90. Because all of the items of the PONS test were posed, it was of specific interest also to note that the mean and median internal consistencies of Table 6.6 for just the posed scenes were 0.85 and 0.88, respectively. The latter value was identical to the internal consistency coefficient for the face items of the PONS corrected for length. In short, the reliability of the ability to decode different encoders sending the same scenes was, on the average, the same as the reliability of the ability to decode different scenes sent by the same encoder.

Table 6.7 shows the analysis of variance of the data of Table 6.6. The three factors were (1) test (two groups of encoders), (2) mode (spontaneous, talking, or posed), and (3) scene (child, comedy, murder, and accident). The last factor was decomposed into a contrast for pleasant versus unpleasant scenes, with the two pleasant and the two unpleasant scenes nested within those categories. The purpose of this analysis was not to test for significance in particular but to examine the relative magnitude of effects. Results showed that encoder equivalence (internal consistency) was greatest for spontaneous encoding, lowest for talking about a stimulus, and intermediate for posed encoding. Although the magnitude of the effect was smaller, there was also a tendency for greater sender equivalence with unpleasant scenes (0.88) than for pleasant ones (0.78). In the PONS test internal consistency was similarly greater for unpleasant than pleasant scenes (0.87 versus 0.81).

Implications

We found that the consistency of the ability to decode different encoders sending the same scenes was essentially identical to the consistency of the ability to decode one encoder sending different scenes. This in no way means, however, that being able to decode one encoder assures being able to decode a different encoder. Indeed, applying the Spearman–Brown formula in the downward direction from our standard length of 220 items shows that the average correlation between ability to

Table 6.7. *Analysis of variance of length-corrected internal consistency coefficients for two many-encoder tests*

Source	*SS*	*df*	*MS*	*F*	*p*	eta
Test	0.0590	1	0.0590	[a]		
Mode	0.1953	2	0.0976	6.92[b]	0.006	0.65
(Scene	0.0608	3	0.0202)			
Pleasantness	0.0570	1	0.0570	4.04[c]	0.06	0.42
Residual	0.0038	2	0.0019	[d]		
Test × mode	0.0391	2	0.0196	[d]		
(Test × scene	0.0202	3	0.0067)			
Test × pleasantness	0.0001	1	0.0001	[d]		
Test × residual	0.0201	2	0.0101	[d]		
(Mode × scene	0.0650	6	0.0108)			
Mode × pleasantness	0.0218	2	0.0109	[d]		
Mode × residual	0.0432	4	0.0108	[d]		
(Test × mode × scene	0.1396	6	0.0233)			
Test × mode × pleasantness	0.0028	2	0.0014	[d]		
Test × mode × residual	0.1368	4	0.0342	[d]		
Pooled residual	0.2677	19	0.0141			

[a]Untestable.
[b]Mean alphas for spontaneous, talking, and posed modes were 0.93, 0.71, and 0.85, respectively.
[c]Mean alphas for pleasant and unpleasant scenes were 0.78 and 0.88, respectively.
[d]Pooled.

decode any two encoders encoding only a *single item* is very low ($r = 0.03$), but *just* as high as the correlation between ability to decode any two scenes encoded by a single encoder ($r = 0.03$).

What our results do indicate is that no greater gain in generality results from adding encoders sending the same scene than from adding different scenes encoded by the same sender. Our results provide no basis for deciding whether a decoding task should employ more encoders (and fewer scenes) or more scenes (and fewer encoders). Only further empirical research with new stimulus materials can inform us whether there are circumstances under which any particular combination of j senders and k scenes (where $j \times k = n$ stimuli) would be optimal (e.g., in the sense of maximizing validity coefficients) for any specific research purpose. Thus there is no sense in which our results should be interpreted as an argument for employing either only a single sender or only a single scene.

Further research might show that internal consistency would go up for judgments of a more homogeneous group of many encoders (e.g., all of one sex) or for judgments of a more homogeneous group of scenes or affects sent by a single sender. For the researcher, however, increases in validity owing to increased internal consistency of this sort might be offset for some purposes by a loss of generality in the stimulus materials. In short, we may have to pay for increases in internal consistency with a decrease in external validity.

Encoder sampling and decoder validity. The foregoing discussion assumes that we do indeed want to generalize to encoders and to the variety of scenes or affects encoded by them. The stimulus sampling required to permit such generalization is often highly desirable and probably is practiced too rarely (Brunswik, 1956; Clark, 1973; Ekman, Friesen, & Ellsworth, 1972; Hammond, 1954; Rosenthal, 1966). Before we leave this discussion, however, it should be pointed out that there are times when our goals are more modest and when there is no intrinsic interest in generalizing to encoders. Such would be the case when our intent is only to differentiate among decoders.

Suppose, for example, that we want to develop a test that would differentiate psychotherapists of greater and lesser sensitivity to the nonverbal cues of their patients. The validity of our test might be assessed by the correlation between test scores and ratings of the therapists made by their supervisors, their peers, and their patients. Suppose further that we select one male and one female encoder to portray 50 scenes or affects, the nonverbal aspects of which are to be decoded by our psychotherapist decoders. Our test might turn out to have fairly substantial validity coefficients (e.g., 0.30 [Cohen, 1977; Rosenthal & Rubin, in press]), even though one male and one female encoder will not normally permit secure generalization to the parent populations of male and female encoders. In short, it is not necessary to be able to generalize to a population of *encoders* when our goal is only to generalize to a population of *decoders*. Sometimes we want to be able to generalize to both the population of decoders and the population of encoders, and that situation raises interesting questions of data analysis that will be discussed shortly.

Encoder characteristics

So far in this discussion of the sampling of encoders we have not considered systematic individual differences (e.g., traits, states) among our encoders. Typically, there is no special interest in individual differences among encoders when we consider issues of generalizability over encoders. We simply decide on the type of encoders we want –

college students, actors, children, or some other category – and then regard each encoder within that sample as to some degree equivalent to or interchangeable with any other encoder within that sample. Indeed, much of the pioneering work on nonverbal aspects of emotion expression has been within the biological framework that emphasizes the basic similarities of the encoding of emotions even cross-culturally (Darwin, 1872/1965; Ekman, 1973; Izard, 1971).

There are times, however, when our interest does focus directly on individual differences among encoders for example, when we want to know about the relationships of these individual differences to accuracy of encoding nonverbal behavior (Rosenthal, 1979d). Compared to the wealth of studies examining the personal correlates of nonverbal decoding ability, there are relatively few studies examining the personal correlates of nonverbal encoding ability (Knapp, 1978). Among the better-established findings are those suggesting that females are better encoders than males (Hall, 1979) and that better encoders are less responsive electrodermally than are poorer encoders (for an overview of this literature see Buck, 1979).

6.4. Simultaneous sampling

We have seen that there is a growing tradition of research on individual differences among judges in the ability to decode nonverbal cues and a more recent tradition of research on individual differences among encoders in the ability to encode nonverbal cues. Still more recent is the investigation of individual differences in skill at nonverbal decoding and encoding in the same study (e.g., DePaulo & Rosenthal, 1979d; Zuckerman et al., 1976; Zuckerman, Lipets, Koivumaki, & Rosenthal, 1975). This is a very desirable development, one permitting the examination of personal correlates of both encoding and decoding skills, as well as the examination of the relationship between the skills of decoding and encoding nonverbal cues.

The purpose of the present section is to call attention to, and to suggest solutions for, a special problem created when both decoders and encoders are included in the same analysis. This problem is also found in other studies of person perception and, more broadly, in any study in which groups of judges make observations of groups of stimulus persons. Briefly, the problem is that regarding encoders as a between-subjects factor and decoders as a within-encoders (i.e., repeated measures) factor can yield tests of significance that are markedly different from those based on an equally defensible analysis regarding decoders as a between-subjects factor and encoders as a within-decoders (i.e., repeated measures) factor. In a recent study (Rosenthal & DePaulo, 1980), we found that when decoders were regarded as a between-subjects factor, sex of decoder made no significant difference, $F(1, 34) = 1.77$, but when decoders were regarded as a within-encoders factor, the *same data* showed an enormous effect of decoder gender, with $F(1, 34) = 35.60$! In what follows this problem is explained in some detail and solutions are suggested (Rosenthal & DePaulo, 1980). To anticipate the discussion somewhat, the problem and its solutions are associated with the greater precision of repeated measures (within sampling units) than of ordinary between-sampling-units analyses because of the correlation with each other of the levels of a repeated measures factor (Winer, 1971).

The encoder–decoder data matrix

In a hypothetical example, four encoders, two males and two females, have each encoded one positive affect and one negative affect. Four decoders, two males and two females, have rated each of the two encodings of each of the four encoders. For each pair of encodings by a single encoder, the decoder's rating of the negative affect (on a scale of positiveness) is subtracted from the decoder's rating of the positive affect. These difference scores are shown in Table 6.8. A large difference score means both that a given decoder has done a good job of decoding that encoder's affects and that the encoder has done a good job of encoding the two affects. The row (or decoder) means define the individual differences among decoders, whereas the column (or encoder) means define the individual differences among the encoders.

The key source of the problem is that the standard analysis of these data is a two-way analysis of variance with either encoders or decoders as the between-subjects factor and the other as the within-subjects factor. Depending on one's purpose, one is equally justified in calling the encoders or the decoders the between factor. If encoders are regarded as the between factor because we wish to generalize to encoders, each decoder's score is a repeated measurement of the encoder's skill. If decoders are regarded as the between factor because we wish to generalize to decoders, each encoder's score is a repeated measurement of the decoder's skill.

A standard analysis of variance of the data of Table 6.8 is shown in Table 6.9. For the sake of this example, the encoder factor was arbitrarily chosen as the between factor, and the decoder factor was the within factor. The data of Table 6.8 were chosen so that the results of the

Table 6.8. *Illustration of the results of a study of encoding and decoding skill: hypothetical data*

	Male encoders		Female encoders		
Decoders	1	2	3	4	Mean
Male					
1	1	0	3	2	1.5
2	0	−1	2	1	0.5
Female					
3	3	2	3	2	2.5
4	2	1	2	1	1.5
Mean	1.5	0.5	2.5	1.5	1.5

Note: Subtable of means

	Encoders		
Decoders	Male	Female	Mean
Male	0.0	2.0	1.0
Female	2.0	2.0	2.0
Mean	1.0	2.0	1.5

Table 6.9. *Standard analysis of the results of a study of encoding and decoding skill*

Source	*df*	*MS*	*F*	eta
Between encoders				
Encoder gender (*E*)	1	2.00	2.00	0.71
Encoders within gender (*R*)[a]	2	1.00	—	
Within encoders				
Decoder gender (*D*)	1	2.00	∞	1.00
DE	1	2.00	∞	1.00
DR[a]	2	0.00	—	

Note: This table is based on eight observations obtained from four encoders each observed twice; once for the average female decoder and once for the average male decoder.

[a]Error terms for the just preceding sources.

analysis would be identical if the labels *encoders* and *decoders* were interchanged. The encoder gender effect, a between-subject effect of Table 6.9. was not significant, with an *F* of only 2.00. However, the decoder gender effect, a within-subjects effect, was very significant, with $F = \infty$. This great difference in the value of F was obtained despite the fact that the sex-of-encoder and sex-of-decoder effects were of identical size, as defined by the column and row means of Table 6.8. The data of Table 6.8 could also have been analyzed by regarding decoders as the between-subjects factor and encoders as the within-subjects factor. That analysis would have yielded results showing a nonsignificant effect of decoder gender ($F = 2.00$) but a very significant effect of encoder gender ($F = \infty$). These analyses suggest that when encoder or decoder effects are viewed as within-subjects effects they may be more significant statistically than when they are viewed as between-subjects effects, even if they are of exactly the same size.

Actual analyses of encoder–decoder data

To document that the results of the preceding illustration are reasonably realistic, I offer here the results of a series of analyses of real data investigating sex differences in skill at encoding and decoding nonverbal cues.

The details of the research are given elsewhere (DePaulo & Rosenthal, 1979b). Here it is sufficient to note that 38 encoders, 20 males and 18 females, were videotaped while describing (1) a person they liked (*like*), (2) one they disliked (*dislike*), (3) one they both liked and disliked (*ambivalent*), (4) the person they really liked as though they disliked that person (*like as though dislike*), and (5) the person they really disliked as though they liked that person (*dislike as though like*). The first two descriptions, then, were of pure affects, the third description was of mixed affect, and the last two descriptions were of deceptive affects.

The same 38 persons serving as encoders also served as decoders. Half the male and half the female encoders served as the decoders for the remaining half; Encoders 1–19 were decoded by encoders 20–38, and encoders 20–38 were decoded by encoders 1–19. For each of the five encodings made by encoders an accuracy-of-encoding score was computed for each decoder. For example, accuracy of encoding (or decoding) *like* might be defined by the ratings of liking given to the *like* encoding minus the ratings of liking given to the *dislike* encoding.

Table 6.10 shows the F ratios obtained when the independent variables of encoder gender and decoder gender were studied by means of both a between-subjects analysis and a within-subjects analysis for the five different dependent variables, the accuracy scores. For both encoder

Table 6.10. F *tests obtained in actual studies of nonverbal communication skill as a function of type of analysis*

Dependent variable	Independent variable			
	Encoder gender: between analysis	Encoder gender: within analysis	Decoder gender: between analysis	Decoder gender: within analysis
Like	8.30[a]	19.60[b]	1.77	35.60[b]
Dislike	4.53[c]	10.81[a]	0.78	13.29[b]
Ambivalent	1.43	9.38[a]	1.66	8.16[a]
Like as though dislike	0.17	0.71	1.24	1.55
Dislike as though like	3.62	7.13[a]	0.00	0.10
Median	3.62	9.38[a]	1.24	8.16[a]

Note: Dfs for all *Fs* = 1, 34.
[a] $p < 0.01$, etas range from 0.42 to 0.49. [b] $p < 0.001$, etas range from 0.53 to 0.72. [c] $p < 0.05$, eta = 0.34.

and decoder gender the within-subjects analysis led to larger *F* ratios than did the between-subjects analysis. For the 10 *F* ratios obtained when the independent variable was a between-subjects factor, the median *F* was 1.54 ($p = 0.222$); for the 10 *F* ratios obtained when the same independent variable was a within-subjects factor, the median *F* was 8.77 ($p = 0.006$).

The *F* ratios of Table 6.10 were transformed to normalized ranks (Walker & Lev, 1953), and a 2 × 2 × 5 analysis of variance – type of analysis (between/within) × type of independent variable (encoder) gender/decoder gender) × type of dependent variable (*like* accuracy/ *dislike* accuracy . . . *dislike as though like* accuracy) – was computed, not primarily for purposes of significance testing but for examination of relative magnitudes of effects. Table 6.11 shows the results of this analysis. Type of analysis made a very big difference, but neither the type of independent variable (encoder vs. decoder gender) nor the interaction of the independent variable with the type of analysis showed a detectable effect. The mean square for the dependent variable (regarded as a random effect), though not testable (unless the pooled error is viewed conservatively as an estimate of σ_e^2), was very substantial, with an eta of 0.792 (F [4, 12]) = 5.04, $p = 0.013$, but this is a very conservative estimate). This simply means that some types of nonverbal encoding and decoding skills show larger effects of encoder and decoder gender

Table 6.11. *Analysis of variance of results of studies of nonverbal communication skill obtained as function of type of analysis*

	Basic analysis				Pooled error	
Source	*df*	*MS*	*F* (1, 4)	*p*	*F* (1, 12)	*p*
Dependent variable (*R*)	4	223.88	[a]		[a]	
Type of analysis (*A*)	1	405.00	14.40[b]	0.019	9.12[c,d]	0.011
AR	4	28.12	[a]		[a]	
Independent variable (*B*)	1	57.80	<1	—	1.30	0.276
BR	4	87.92	[a]		[a]	
BA	1	28.80	1.68	0.265	<1	—
BAR	4	17.18	[a]		[a]	
Pooled error (*AR, BR, BAR*)	12	44.41				

Note: This analysis was based on normalized ranks of original *F* ratios. The analysis based on the untransformed date yielded essentially the same results.
[a]Not testable. [b]Effect-size eta = 0.88.
[c]Effect-size eta = 0.66; *df* (1,12) based on original untransformed data = 8.68, $p = 0.012$.

than do other such skills. In the present studies the "pure" affects (liking and disliking) showed greater sex differences in nonverbal skill than did the deceptive affects, $r = 0.777$ (F [1, 12] = 18.29, $p = 0.001$).

The analyses presented show clearly that the choice of analysis (between vs. within subjects) can make a substantial difference in the inferences we draw via standard analyses from our studies about both encoder and decoder effects, because of the greater power of within-subject effects. There is less of an analytic problem, however, when we consider the interaction of encoder and decoder effects. That is because, no matter which factor, encoder or decoder, is considered a between and which is considered a within factor, the interaction of these two is always a within factor. For the five dependent variables of our study we computed the interaction of encoder and decoder gender, once for encoder as the between factor and once for decoder as the between factor. None of the 10*F*s was significant. The five *F*s obtained when encoder was the between factor ranged from 0.00 to 2.06, with a median of 0.10, whereas the five *F*s obtained when decoder was the between factor ranged from 0.01 to 3.55, with a median of 0.08. For the five dependent variables, the correlation (r) between the F for interaction obtained when encoder was the between factor and the F obtained when decoder was the between factor was 0.998, $df = 3$, $p < 0.0001$. For the purpose of testing the interaction of encoder and decoder effects, therefore, it appears to make rather little difference whether we consider the encoders or the decoders as the between factor.

A solution through expanded analysis

We have seen, both for our hypothetical example and for our real data, that the statistical significance of studies of individual differences in nonverbal communication may depend heavily on whether the encoder or the decoder factor is regarded as the between-subjects factor, rather than the within-subjects factor, because of the greater power of repeated measures factors. Although the implications for analysis and statistical inference have apparently not been noted previously, it seems that investigators have generally made their decisions about analysis on the basis of the relative sizes of samples of encoders and decoders (and Hall, 1980, has shown that investigators employing larger samples of encoders tend to employ smaller samples of decoders, $r = -0.47$). Thus, if 50 subjects are to decode the nonverbal cues of 1 male and 1 female encoder, it is the decoders that will be regarded as the between-subjects factor, and the 2 encoders will be regarded as the two levels of the within-decoders factor. Or, if 2 judges, 1 black and 1 white, are to decode the behavior of 30 classroom teachers, it is the encoder factor that will be regarded as the between-subjects factor, and the 2 decoders will be regarded as two levels of the within-encoder factor.

Such usage is not unequivocally wrong. It does appear, however, that the implications of the practice should be clear. Whatever the basis of the decision, the between-factor type of analysis permits generalization of results to the population of which the encoders or decoders may be viewed as a random sample. However, because between-subjects error terms are typically larger than within-subject error terms, these analyses will lead to smaller *F*s. The within-factor type of analysis does not permit generalization of the results, that is, estimates of effects, to the population of which the encoders or decoders may be viewed as a random sample. That is, the within factor is typically analyzed as a fixed effect, whereas the between factor is typically analyzed as a random effect. The loss in generality that occurs for the within-subject analysis is accompanied, however, by relatively larger *F*s, because within-subject (repeated measures) error terms are typically smaller than between-subject error terms – sometimes *much* smaller because of the correlated nature of repeated measures.

If we want to be able to generalize to populations of both encoders and decoders, we must expand the typical model of the analysis of

Table 6.12. *Expanded model analysis of results of a study of encoding and decoding skill*

Source	*df*	*MS*	*F*	eta
Between encoders				
Encoder gender (*E*)	1	4.00	2.00	0.71
Encoders with gender (*R*)[a]	2	2.00[b]		
Within encoders				
Decoder gender (*D*)	1	4.00	∞[c]	1.00
DE	1	4.00	∞[d]	1.00
DR[a]	2	0.00		
Decoders within gender (*S*)	2	2.00[b]	∞	
SE	2	0.00		
SR	4	0.00		

[a]Standard error terms for the just preceding sources.
[b]Can be tested against *SR* if desired.
[c]Decoders viewed as fixed effects. If decoders are viewed as random effects, *D* is tested against *S*, decoders within gender, and $F = 2.00$.
[d]Decoders viewed as fixed effects. If decoders are viewed as random effects, *DE* is tested against *SE* and *F* remains unchanged in this example.

encoder–decoder data matrices. This expansion does not require any new statistical principles, only the application of generally known ideas to this particular problem (Snedecor & Cochran, 1967; Winer, 1971). Table 6.12 shows an example of the expanded analysis required, in which the encoder factor has been arbitrarily regarded as the between-subjects factor. The data analyzed are those of Table 6.8. The first five sources of variance of Table 6.12 are the same as those shown in the standard analysis of Table 6.9. The last three sources of variance of Table 6.12 are new; they represent: (1) decoders nested within each decoder gender (*S*), (2) the interaction of these nested decoders with the gender of the encoder (*SE*), and (3) the interaction of decoders nested within each decoder gender with encoders nested within each encoder gender (*SR*).

The first of these new terms (*S*) provides the error term against which we test the effect of decoder gender (*D*) if we want to be able to generalize to decoders other than those who happen to be in our study. This term (*S*) is analogous to the error term (*R*), or encoders nested within encoder gender, which is the error term used to test the effect of encoder gender (*E*).

The second new term (*SE*) provides the error term against which we test the effect of the interaction of encoder gender and decoder gender (*DE*) if we want to be able to generalize that interaction to decoders other than those who happen to be in our study.

The third new term (*SR*) provides the error term against which we could test the effect of encoders nested within encoder gender (*R*) as well as the effect of decoders nested within decoder gender (*S*), although in practice there may be little reason to want such tests. Of some theoretical interest, however, may be the comparison of the components of variance associated with individual differences among encoders and decoders. These can be computed from the relations among the mean squares for *R*, *S*, and *SR*.

For the data of Table 6.8 the expanded analysis of Table 6.12 yields the same results as does the standard analysis of Table 6.9 when decoders are regarded as fixed, with *F*s for encoder gender, decoder gender, and their interaction of 2.00, ∞, and ∞, respectively. However, if decoders are viewed as a random factor, these *F*s become 2.00, 2.00, and ∞ (see footnotes of Table 6.12). In this example only the *F* for decoder gender was affected by our use of the enlarged model for analysis. In other examples the *F* for interaction might also be affected by our use of the enlarged model. However, the effect of encoder gender is always unaffected by our use of the expanded model. It should also be emphasized that in the expanded model either the encoder or the decoder effect can serve as the between-subjects factor.

Computation of the enlarged model analysis is straightforward and leads to a far richer yield of information than does the standard model analysis (i.e., eight vs. five sources of variance). However, if only the main effects of encoder and decoder attributes (e.g., gender) were of interest, the appropriate tests for both encoder and decoder effects could be made by performing the standard analysis of Table 6.9 twice, once with encoders as the between-subjects effect and once with decoders as the between-subjects effect. Inferences made about the two between effects would then permit generalization to other encoders and decoders, whereas inferences about the two within effects and the interactions could not be generalized to other encoders or decoders.

In summary, then, whenever encoders and decoders are included in the same analysis, special attention must be paid to whether each of these factors is to be regarded as a between- or within-subject factor and whether each is to be regarded as a fixed or a random effect (Snedecor & Cochran, 1967; Winer, 1971).

6.5. Stimulus selection

Once the encoders have been selected for a judgment study, further selection must be made of the precise aspects of the encoders' nonverbal behavior that will serve as the stimulus materials for the judges. Suppose, for example, that we have selected as our encoders a group of classroom teachers who have been videotaped for 30 minutes on each of three different occasions. Suppose further that we have calculated that 6 minutes of videotape per teacher is all we will have time to show to our judges, given the total number of teachers in our sample. How shall we select the 6 minutes from the 90 minutes?

Behavior sampling

We might decide that we should have a sample of teacher behavior from each of the three videotape recording occasions. Perhaps we will decide to choose the first 40 seconds, the last 40 seconds, and the midmost 40 seconds of the behavior we are studying from each of the three occasions. In this sampling procedure, we will be sure to examine at least some of the behavior of the early, middle, and late periods of each of the occasions of observation. Although the particular selection of segments to be judged must depend on the particular purpose, it seems to be wise to sample systematically the various occasions of observation, the phases of each occasion of observation, and the types of specific behavior we want to present to our judges for evaluation. It should be noted, however, that one price we pay for this systematic, objective sampling procedure is the possibility that particular behavior sequences will be interrupted by the beginning or end of the time sample. This problems tends to diminish as the length of each time sample is increased.

To illustrate sampling the types of specific behavior of interest we consider further our example of videotaped teachers. Our theory of teaching might hold that to understand teaching behavior we must know how teachers interact with (1) the class as a group and (2) individual students. We might decide, therefore, that half our stimuli will be selected from teacher interactions with the class as a whole, and the remaining half of our stimuli will be selected from teacher interactions with individual students. Table 6.13 illustrates a sampling plan that "stratifies" or "blocks" on three different variables: (1) type of classroom behavior, (2) phase of each teaching occasion, and (3) occasion of teaching. Judges' ratings are thus available for each combination of

Table 6.13. *Illustrative plan for sampling nonverbal behavior*

	Class-directed classroom behavior			Individual-directed classroom behavior		
Occasion	Beginning	Middle	End	Beginning	Middle	End
First						
Second						
Third						

Note: Each element of this sampling plan consists of a 20-second stimulus presentation.

levels of the three independent variables of Table 6.13, and analyses of judges' ratings will tell us whether teacher nonverbal behavior differs detectably as a function of type of classroom interaction (directed to the class or directed to the individual), phase of interaction (beginning, middle, end), or occasion (first, second, third), or as a function of interactions among these three variables.

Modality sampling

Suppose we have decided on a sampling plan for our judgment study, perhaps one like that shown in Table 6.13. What shall be the specific stimuli presented to our judges? Depending on how we have videotaped the interactions, we could present any subset of the following aspects of behavior, and the listing is only a sampling:

I. Video only; no audio
   A. Face only
      1. All of face
      2. Part of face
   B. Body only
      1. All of body
      2. Part of body
   C. Face plus body
      1. All of face plus body
      2. Parts of face plus body (e.g., upper half of face blacked out)
   D. Interpersonal distance cues

II. Audio only; no video
   A. Full sound track
      1. Natural speech
      2. Standard content
      3. Foreign language

B. Content removed
1. Content filtered
2. Randomized spliced
3. Speech played backwards

III. Verbal only (transcript)

IV. Combinations of above

The specific nature of our research question must determine the type of nonverbal cues we will present to our judges. However, it can be seen from this nonexhaustive listing that the same basic material can serve many times over as stimulus materials in different "channels" of nonverbal communication. The resources of real life ordinarily will not permit our employing the many forms of stimulus material that might be interesting and important.

Clip length. How we decide the question of the specific type of nonverbal stimuli to employ also has implications for the length of each stimulus clip. Although it has been established that considerable nonverbal information can be communicated in just 2 seconds in both the video and audio channels (Rosenthal et al., 1979), there may be interactions of channel and length of exposure such that changes in length of exposure will affect the information value of different channels in different ways. For example, we know that considerable nonverbal information can be extracted from face or body cues exposed for only 1 or 3 twenty-fourths of a second, but it seems unlikely that as much nonverbal information could be extracted from tone-of-voice cues exposed for such short periods.

Stimulus sampling. Once again, depending on our purpose, we may want to ensure an adequate representation of the various attributes that have been identified reliably in the various modalities. Thus, for example, a number of affects have been reliably differentiated in facial expressions (Ekman, 1973; Ekman et al., 1972; Izard, 1971, 1977), and we may want to assess individual differences in judges' ability to decode these various affects. Further, various workers have found a number of dimensions onto which it seems possible to map the various affects (for reviews of this work see, e.g., Ekman et al., 1972; Rosenthal et al., 1979), and we may want to assess individual differences in judges' ability to decode behavior varying along one or more of these dimensions. Examples of the affects that have been reliably described are happiness, disgust, surprise, sadness, anger, and fear; examples of the dimensions that have been described are positive–negative, dominant–submissive, and intense–controlled.

Posed versus spontaneous encoding

An important decision to be made in the process of selecting stimuli is whether to employ posed or spontaneous encoding. On a priori grounds, but not on empirical grounds, we might prefer spontaneous over posed stimuli because it is ultimately the encoding and decoding of everyday nonverbal cues about which we want to make inferences. It would be an error of logic, however, though a common one, to assume that because our ultimate interest is in spontaneous nonverbal cues, a better index of accuracy could be constructed from the use of such stimuli. Surface similarities between models and things modeled are no guarantee of predictive utility, (e.g., it would be unwise to assume that the experimental stresses imposed on a perfect 15-cm model of a giant commercial airliner would provide sufficient information about the airliner's real-life resistance to stress). A model's utility lies in our knowing the relationship between the properties of the model and the thing modeled (Kaplan, 1964). At the present time we do not know whether real-life stimuli would be better or worse than or not different from posed stimuli in permitting us to predict accuracy in decoding of everyday nonverbal cues. What is known, however, that is useful to our understanding of any measure of nonverbal accuracy, is that those people who are good at decoding posed stimuli are also good at decoding spontaneous stimuli ($r = 0.58$, $p < 0.001$ [Zuckerman et al., 1976]; and $r = 0.32$, $p < 0.02$ [Zuckerman, Larrance, Hall, DeFrank, and Rosenthal, 1979]; in addition, people, who "send" more accurately in the posed mode are also better at sending in the spontaneous mode (in four studies $r = 0.35$ [Buck, 1975]; $r = 0.75$ [Cunningham, 1977]; $r = 0.46$ [Zuckerman et al., 1976]; $r = 0.40$ [Zuckerman et al., 1979]).

Size of sample of stimuli

Once we have decided whether to employ posed or spontaneous encoding, who our encoders shall be, how we shall sample their behavior, and what modality of stimuli will be employed (e.g., video or audio), we must still decide how many stimuli to employ altogether. That question is one of the most difficult to answer, because it depends to a great extent on the total number of encoders. Earlier, evidence was presented to show that there might be an even trade-off between the number of encoders encoding a given affect and the number of affects or scenarios encoded by each encoder. Only further research can tell us for what purpose we should employ what balance of j encoders each encoding k scenes.

6.6. Stimulus presentation

Medium of presentation

In addition to making decisions about stimulus sampling, the investigator must select a medium of presentation for the stimuli. For example, the selected behavior could be recorded on film or videotape, on a still photograph, in an artist's representational or stylized drawing, on audiotape, or on a combination of such media. Because real-life behavior flows in time, film and videotape, each accompanied by sound, are the potentially most informative media for total cues available. However, if the focus were on facial expressions or on tone of voice, still photos or audiotape alone might be quite sufficient to the purpose at hand. As we might expect, the amount of nonverbal information in still photographs appears to be greater than that found in drawings, and the amount of nonverbal information in film or videotape appears to be greater than that found in still photographs (Ekman et al., 1972; see also the earlier discussion of modality sampling).

All of these media of presentation have in common that the stimulus materials are preserved more or less permanently so that they can be analyzed and reanalyzed. There are times, however, when the stimulus presentation is in a live mode, either because live interaction is what we want to study or because we cannot obtain a more permanent record of the interaction. For example, if we were interested in a teacher's nonverbal behavior, but were unable to make a permanent record via film or videotape, we might employ classroom observers to record various aspects of teachers' nonverbal behaviors. Because we cannot replay live behavior to conduct a reliability analysis, it is especially important that we employ enough observers for each nonverbal variable being judged to get our effective reliability (R) to an acceptable level.

Maximizing efficiency of design

In recent years, investigators of nonverbal communication processes have become increasingly interested in the simultaneous investigation of two or more channels of nonverbal communication (DePaulo, Rosenthal, Eisenstat, Rogers, & Finkelstein, 1978; Ekman, 1965b; Ekman & Friesen, 1969, 1974; Ekman, Friesen, & Scherer, 1976; Littlepage & Pineault, 1978; Maier & Thurber, 1968; Rosenthal, 1964, 1966; Rosenthal, Fode, Friedman, & Vikan, 1960; Rosenthal et al., 1979; Scherer et al., 1977; Zuckerman, DeFrank, Hall, Larrance, & Rosenthal, 1979; Zuckerman et al., 1976).

Table 6.14. *Illustrative experimental design*

	Length of exposure (in msec)[a]			
Channel	50	150	450	1,350
Face				
Body				

[a]The four exposure lengths were selected to be linear in their logs.

In these multichannel studies, judges are required to rate behaviors in two or more channels of nonverbal communication. In addition to channel differences, other variables such as length of exposure of the stimulus material may be of interest. As we have more questions to ask of differences among stimulus modalities, media, length, and so on, we can achieve greater and greater statistical power (and thereby help to keep down the increased cost of collecting more information) by designing our stimulus material array so as to form a fully crossed factorial analysis of variance with judges as the sampling units and the factors of the experimental design as largely, but not exclusively, within-subjects factors.

An illustrative design. Let us say that we wanted to compare the information conveyed in facial expressions and in body movements as these occurred in various everyday life situations. Suppose, in addition, that we wanted to evaluate the relative amounts of nonverbal information conveyed in exposure lengths of 50, 150, 450, and 1,350 msec. The experimental design is shown in Table 6.14. If we had n judges available to participate in our research we could assign one-eighth of them to each of our eight experimental conditions and analyze the experiment as a 2×4 factorial analysis of variance with both factors as between-subjects factors. In most cases, however, we could have a far more powerful design if we had each of our n judges make ratings in all eight of the experimental conditions. Our analysis would still be a 2×4 analysis of variance, but now both factors would be within-subjects factors. Depending on the degree of correlation of ratings made under the eight different conditions, we might be able to conduct our within-subjects analysis with far fewer judges than would be required for the between-subjects analysis. Table 6.15 shows the analyses of variance (without planned contrasts). To keep the total number of df equal, the within-

Table 6.15. *Analysis of variance: between- versus within-subjects models*

Between model		Within model	
Source	*df*	Source	*df*
Channel	1	Channel	1
Exposure length	3	Channel × subjects[a]	9
Chan. × expos. length	3	Exposure length	3
Subjects in conditions[a]	72	Expos. length × subjects[a]	27
		Chan. × expos. length	3
		Chan. × expos. length × subj.[a]	27
		Subjects	9
Total	79	Total	79

[a]Error terms for the just preceding sources.

subjects model was assigned only 10 judges, each operating in all eight conditions; the between-subjects model was assigned 80 judges, 10 of whom operated in each of the eight conditions. In many situations, the within-subjects model will serve us more efficiently (i.e., with greater statistical power) than the between-subjects model, because the error terms will tend to be smaller. Within-subjects analyses are often characterized by a risk of such time-related effects as fatigue and carry-over effects. Procedures for dealing with these problems will be taken up in the section on counterbalancing and blocking.

A more complex design. More complex designs than that shown in Table 6.14 have also been usefully employed. Earlier, in the section on sampling encoders, I described the PONS test designed to measure sensitivity to nonverbal cues found in 11 different channels – face, body, face + body, randomized spliced (RS), content filtered (CF), face + RS, Face + CF, body + RS, body + CF, face + body + RS, face + body + CF. Within each of these 11 channels, half the items were positive in affect and half were negative in affect. Within the positive and negative items found in each of the 11 channels, half were dominant in interpersonal orientation and half were submissive.

Table 6.16 shows the experimental design. There are four levels of video information (no cues, body cues, face cues, face + body cues), three levels of audio information (no cues, RS cues, CF cues), two levels of affect (positive, negative), and two levels of interpersonal orientation (dominant, submissive). Accordingly, decoding accuracy scores for any person or group taking the PONS test can be analyzed as a 4 × 3 × 2 × 2

Table 6.16. *A more complex experimental design*

	Video							
Audio	No cues neg.	No cues pos.	Body cues neg.	Body cues pos.	Face cues neg.	Face cues pos.	Body + face cues neg.	Body + face cues pos.
No cues								
Dominant	[a]	[a]						
Submissive	[a]	[a]						
RS cues								
Dominant								
Submissive								
CF cues								
Dominant								
Submissive								

Note: Five stimulus items occur in each cell of the 2 × 2 × 3 × 2 × 2 design.
[a]Empty cells in design; in statistical analysis these cells are given chance accuracy level scores (Rosenthal, Hall, DiMatteo, Rogers, & Archer, 1979).

repeated measures analysis of variance. However, the four levels of the video factor can be more efficiently rewritten as a 2 × 2 design (face present/face absent × body present/body absent), so that our four-factor design becomes a five-factor (2 × 2 × 3 × 2 × 2) design. For some purposes, a sixth factor of order of presentation, or learning, is added. Thus, within each combination of channel and type of scene, there are five items that can be arranged for analysis into the order in which they are shown in the PONS test. This order or learning factor, with its five levels, is fully crossed with the five factors just listed. The 1-degree-of-freedom (*df*) contrast for linear trend is an overall index of improvement over time in PONS performance. Individuals and groups can, therefore, be compared for their degrees of learning as well as their levels of performance. In addition, the interaction of the 1-*df* learning contrast with other 1-*df* contrasts provides interesting information on such questions as which channels show greater learning and which content quadrants show greater learning, and various combinations of these questions.

It should be noted that our data-analytic model does not make frequent use of all 11 channels or of all combinations of channels and affect quadrants. Though the model employs all this information, it employs it in a more efficient and reliable manner by subdividing parts of the 11-channel profile into larger subsections than channels based only upon 20 scenes each. Thus all scenes employing the face can be compared to all scenes not employing the face, all scenes employing the body can be compared to all scenes not employing the body, all scenes employing audio information can be compared to all scenes not employing audio information, and so on. This series of comparisons, or contrasts, is appreciably more reliable and powerful than the simultaneous examination of all 11 channels. This improvement in reliability and power will be discussed in more detail in the section on focused *F* tests.

Counterbalancing and blocking

Suppose we decide to conduct the experiment of Table 6.14 as a within-subjects design with 8 stimuli to be presented in each of the 8 experimental conditions. How shall we decide the sequence of presentation of the 64 stimuli that are to be presented to our judges? Our first thought might be to arrange the 64 stimuli randomly; however, experience and reflection suggest that this procedure leaves too much to chance. Bad luck in the selection of the random sequence can leave us with a serious problem of confounding. (This problem of confounding is likely to be serious only when we select a small number of random sequences. With a large number of random sequences there is much less chance of a serious problem of confounding.)

In our example, a certain channel (face or body) or exposure length (50, 150, 450, 1,350 msec) may wind up heavily overrepresented in certain regions of the random sequence, so that apparent effects of channel or exposure length are really effects of serial position of stimulus presentation. If the random sequencing of stimuli has put substantially more than half the body channel items into the last half of the test, and if scores (e.g., ratings, accuracy, etc.) for the body channel are found to be lower than those for the face channel, we cannot tell whether body channel scores are really lower or whether there was only a boredom or fatigue effect that lowered performance on all stimuli presented late (an effect that just happened to apply to body items more than to face items because of our particular randomization sequence).

Blocking plans. The problem of confounding can be avoided to a great extent by the procedure of blocking on serial position. Alternative blocking plans for our present example include:

1. Let the first 32 items of the 64 include 4 stimuli from each of the 8 experimental conditions (2 channels × 4 exposure lengths). The 4 stimuli from each condition to be presented in the first 32 items are selected at

Table 6.17. *Latin square for presentation of 64 stimuli*

Block	Order of presentation within blocks							
	1	2	3	4	5	6	7	8
First	*A*	*B*	*C*	*D*	*E*	*F*	*G*	*H*
Second	*B*	*C*	*D*	*E*	*F*	*G*	*H*	*A*
Third	*C*	*D*	*E*	*F*	*G*	*H*	*A*	*B*
Fourth	*D*	*E*	*F*	*G*	*H*	*A*	*B*	*C*
Fifth	*E*	*F*	*G*	*H*	*A*	*B*	*C*	*D*
Sixth	*F*	*G*	*H*	*A*	*B*	*C*	*D*	*E*
Seventh	*G*	*H*	*A*	*B*	*C*	*D*	*E*	*F*
Eighth	*H*	*A*	*B*	*C*	*D*	*E*	*F*	*G*

random, and the sequence of presentation of the first 32 items is also decided randomly. The sequence of the last 32 items may be decided randomly, or the sequence of the first 32 items can be run in reverse so as to equalize the average serial position of each of the 8 experimental conditions.

2. Let the first 16 items of the 64 include 2 stimuli from each of the 8 experimental conditions. The 2 stimuli per condition are assigned at random to each of the 4 blocks of 16 items each. The presentation sequence for the 4 blocks of stimuli may be random, or 2 may be random while the remaining two are simple reversals of the 2 random sequences.
3. Let the first 8 items of the 64 include 1 stimulus from each of the 8 experimental conditions. The particular stimulus per condition is assigned at random to each of the 8 blocks of 8 items each. The presentation sequence for the 8 blocks of stimuli: (*a*) may be random for all 8; (*b*) may be random for 4 with the remainder as simple reversals of these 4; (*c*) may be fully counterbalanced in a Latin square.

The advantage of the Latin square is that each of the 8 experimental conditions will occur once and only once in each of the 8 blocks of stimuli and once and only once in each order of presentation within blocks, so that the mean serial position of each of the 8 conditions will be identical. Table 6.17 illustrates a Latin square we could employ for the study under discussion.

Carry-over effects. Whenever we employ the powerful within-subjects designs, we must consider whether there will be any reasonable risk of carry-over effects. That is, will the performance on the second item be affected by the *particular* item that preceded it, or, more generally, will the performance on the *k*th item be affected by the particular sequence of $(k - 1)$ items preceding the *k*th item?

When each subject is measured repeatedly on items representing the experimental conditions, and when counterbalancing and blocking have

Table 6.18. *Design and analysis of an experiment testing for carry-over effects*

A. Design

Group		Order 1	Order 2	Order 3
I	10 Judges	*A*	*B*	*C*
II	10 Judges	*B*	*C*	*A*
III	10 Judges	*C*	*A*	*B*

B. Analysis (prior to contrasts)

Source	*df*
Between judges	29
Sequence	2
Judges within sequences	27
Within judges	60
Order	2
Channel (order × sequence)	2
Residual	56

been properly employed, carry-over effects are not likely to invalidate the inferences we would like to draw. However, if we want to be *certain* of eliminating the risk of carryover effects, we can design our studies to employ both a within- and a between-subjects design so that we can (1) have the unaffected results of the between-subjects design if there *are* carry-over effects and (2) have the more precise, powerful results of the within-subjects design as well, if there are *no* carry-over effects. Table 6.18 presents the design and analysis of an experiment to test for the major substantive hypothesis as well as the hypothesis of carry-over effects.

Suppose we have 30 judges who are to make ratings of stimuli derived from three channels: face (*A*), body (*B*), and tone of voice (*C*). Assume the common situation wherein it is difficult to obtain judges in the first place, but once they have been obtained, it costs little more to have them make a few more ratings. Thus it would be very efficient to have each judge rate all three channels. To avoid confounding we counterbalance as shown in Table 6.18. Our judges are randomly assigned to our three sequences of presentation of stimuli (*ABC, BCA, CAB*). However, we are concerned about possible carry-over effects. The analysis of the data shown in Table 6.18 yields a test that tells whether sequence of presentation (e.g., ABC) of stimuli makes a difference and whether the order of presentation (e.g., presented first) makes a difference. If they do not make a difference (say a small and nonsignificant *F*), we feel comforted and can employ the full 90 observations provided by our 30 judges. If they *do* make a difference and we want an estimate of channel differences unaffected by carry-over effects, we analyze only the data obtained from the stimuli we presented to the judges *first*; that is, the face stimuli as rated by group I, the body stimuli as rated by group II, and the tone-of-voice stimuli as rated by group III. It should be noted, however, that this act of purification is not without its cost: We lose 60 observations in the process!

Judging sessions

So far in this discussion of stimulus presentation I have not dealt explicitly with the issue of the total length of time required to judge all of the encoder behavior we want to have evaluated. The more items of behavior we want to have judged, the longer the exposure time of each item, and the longer the period of time required for judges to make their ratings, the longer will be the total length of service required of each judge.

If the duration of a session required to make all ratings is too long, we may invite our judges back for future sessions to finish their rating task. Inviting our judges back for a second session runs the risk of introducing an effect of judging session owing to judge fatigue, boredom, or practice, or owing to such extraneous factors as changes in the environmental situation from one judging session to the next. This procedure also runs the risk that some judges will not return and their data will then be lost. If we employed six judges in the first session and only four appear for the second session, we will have lost one-third of our data. An alternative to having judges come back for subsequent sessions is to employ more judges, each judging fewer encoder behaviors; thus k times as many judges each judge only $1/k$ times as many items.

Suppose we decide to divide the total stimulus material we want to have rated into two halves ($k = 2$), each to be rated by a different group of judges. Our procedures for conducting such a study should minimize the danger of confounding characteristics of the particular items presented in each half with the differences in rating behavior between the two groups of judges. Simple random assignment of items to halves could result in serious confounding problems, and we should employ the principles of counterbalancing and blocking described earlier to minimize these problems. Each half of the stimuli set should be as nearly

Table 6.19. *Equivalent halves of stimuli presented in two judging sessions*

	Judging session	
	First	Second
Judge group I	Half *A*	Half *B*
Judge group II	Half *B*	Half *A*

equal to the other in type of item and number of items per type as possible.

Even if we could be sure that all of the judges employed in one session would be available for a second rating session, it could be very helpful to create two equivalent halves of our stimulus materials. In that way we could avoid confounding the particular half of the items (*A* or *B*) with the judging session (1 or 2). Table 6.19 presents the appropriate design; half the judges are randomly assigned to the sequence *AB* and half are randomly assigned to the sequence *BA*.

Independence of judges. It is customary when presenting encoder behaviors to judges to employ judges in groups. This is an efficient procedure, in that we can collect a great deal of data in just a single session. It would be very costly indeed if we had to present all our encoder behaviors to judges working just one at a time. There is, however, a frequently unrecognized and potentially serious risk in this custom of having judges work in groups. That risk is the loss of independence of their ratings. Judges working in the same session may make ratings that are correlated with those of other judges for many different reasons: Judges glance at one another's ratings; and judges are similarly affected by the mood and manner of the experimenter and of other judges in that judging session, the examinations that may be coming the next day, the fact that they are missing their favorite television show, the rainstorm outside, the evening news, and so on. (It should be noted that the issue here is not the effect on the mean ratings made by any group of judges but the effect on the degree of similarity of the judges' ratings within a given group.)

If it is an explicit goal of the research to generalize to judges, the statistical tests of significance of the phenomena in which we are interested (e.g., differences between channels) require that judges' ratings be completely independent. If judges' ratings are not independent, the *df* for the denominators of our *F* tests are a function no longer of the number of judges but rather of the number of *groups* of judges. Thus, if there is only a single group of judges, *no tests of significance are possible*. An alternative to the inefficient procedure of having all judging sessions take place with only a single judge (to avoid losing judges' independence) is available, and it requires employing several groups of judges.

Testing for independence. The basic strategy is to permit us to test for judge independence and to base our decision regarding tests of significance on the information provided by the experiment. Suppose we want to compare ratings made on the basis of encoder behavior presented in three channels: face, body, and tone of voice. We have 40 judges available, 20 females and 20 males. If we present the stimuli to all 40 judges at a single session we will not be able to assess the independence of the judges and hence may have no defensible significance test available. If we present the stimuli to one judge at a time it will require 40 rating sessions, an inefficiency we may not be able to afford. We can afford, let's say, to have judges make their ratings in one of four sessions. Table 6.20 presents the design and analysis of our illustrative experiment.

Of the 40 judges, 5 female and 5 male judges are assigned at random to each of our four judging sessions, and each judge rates behavior in all three channels of face, body, and tone. Suppose our first question is whether the average ratings made by male and female judges are significantly different in the population from which our judges have been sampled. Our temptation is to test the sex-of-judges effect against the judges-within-conditions effect, so that our error term will have 32 *df*. Unfortunately, we may not be justified in making this test. The appropriate test of our hypothesis is to test the sex effect against the sex × groups interaction, the latter error term having only 3 *df*! However, if the sex × groups interaction is neither significant nor large (say, less than 2.0 [Green & Tukey, 1960]) when tested against the judges-within-conditions effect, these two terms may be pooled, and the new term will then serve as the error term for the sex-of-judge effect. Optionally, the groups effect may also be pooled into this new error term. Poolability, as defined by a sufficiently small *F*, is an alternative way of stating that judges' ratings made within conditions are essentially independent.

Our primary interest in the present study is in the within-judge effects of channel and channel × sex. Our temptation is to test both effects against the channel × judges interaction with 64 *df*. Again, we may not

Table 6.20. *Design and analysis of an experiment testing for judge independence*

A. Design

	Female judges			Male judges		
Channel:	Face	Body	Tone	Face	Body	Tone
Judge group I						
Judge group II						
Judge group III						
Judge group IV						

B. Analysis (prior to contrasts)

Source	*df*
Between judges	39
Sex of judges	1
Groups	3
Sex × groups	3
Judges within conditions	32
Within judges	80
Channels	2
Channels × sex	2
Channels × groups	6
Channels × sex × groups	6
Channels × judges	64

be justified in doing so. The proper error term for the channels effect is the channels × groups interaction, and the proper error term for the channels × sex interaction is the channels × sex × groups interaction. Each of the latter two error terms has only 6 *df*, rather than the 64 *df* we would no doubt prefer. However, if the channels × groups interaction is poolable with the channels × judges interaction, we may use this new pooled error term to test for the channels effect; and if the channels × sex × groups interaction is poolable with the channels × judges interaction, we may use this new pooled error term to test for the channels × sex interaction. Testing for poolability is very much like testing for independence of judges within sessions; when $F = 1.00$, the correlation among judges (the intraclass correlation) is 0. (We should note that this low intraclass correlation does not mean low interjudge reliability. That reliability depends on the *difference* between the channels effect and its error term, and on the *difference* between the channels × sex effect and *its* error term.)

When we achieve poolability in this design we not only gain the power to which we are entitled, we have also set our minds at rest that our observations have been independent. But suppose our tests for poolability suggest that pooling is not warranted (e.g., F is significant and/or greater than 2.00)? That leaves us in the difficult situation of having to use as error terms the effects of groups of judges or the interactions of groups of judges with other variables (e.g., sex, channels, etc). These error terms ordinarily have few *df*, and we must be satisfied with the lower power that usually is a consequence of fewer *df* in the error term. Nevertheless, it is better to have an accurate test of significance with *known* low power than an inaccurate test with *apparent* great power. If we have developed the very desirable habit of always reporting an effect-size estimate along with our tests of significance, the "penalty" we pay for proper inference will be very much minimized. More will be said on effect-size estimation and reporting in a subsequent section.

6.7. Judges' responses

I have talked often of judges' ratings, evaluations, observations, and judgments, but I have not yet been very explicit about the precise nature of the dependent variable, the judge's response. What shall be the format in which the judges make their responses?

There are two great traditions of response format in the area of nonverbal communication, the *categorical* and the *dimensional*, and each has been used in a wide variety of research studies (e.g., Argyle, 1975; Buck, 1979; DePaulo & Rosenthal, 1979a, 1979b; Ekman, 1973; Ekman et al., 1972; Izard, 1971, 1977; Mehrabian, 1970; Rosenthal, 1966, 1979d; Scherer, 1979a, 1979b; Zuckerman et al., 1979; Zuckerman et al., 1976). The categorical response format presents the judge with two or more response alternatives of which one (usually) is selected. The dimensional response format presents the judge with some form of more or less continuous rating scale (e.g., 1–5, 1–7, or 1–9) on which one numerical value is to be circled, crossed out, or otherwise selected.

There is no evidence to suggest that either of these response formats is uniformly superior, but each seems especially well suited to certain research questions and orientations. For example, if one holds a theory that there are *m* basic emotions, it is reasonable to employ a categorical response format including some or all of these *m* basic emotions (Ekman, 1973; Izard, 1971). If one holds a view that nonverbal cues can be mapped into a semantic space of three dimensions, it is reasonable to employ a dimensional response format tapping the three dimensions of semantic space (Osgood, 1966). In this section I shall consider some of the issues arising in the use of various formats of judges' responses.

Categorical formats

Suppose we wanted to assess judges' accuracy at decoding the affects in 60 content-filtered speech samples. The samples were chosen to represent six emotions studied by Ekman (1973): anger, disgust, fear, happiness, sadness, and surprise. Of the 60 items, 10 were intended to represent each of the six affects. One response format might simply list all six emotions and ask the judges to circle the one that was most like the affect represented in the sample of content-filtered speech. Judges' total accuracy score would simply be the number of affects out of 60 that were correctly chosen. In this example, the frequency of correct alternatives was properly balanced so that all six emotions occurred equally often (10 times). The advantage of this balancing is that a judge who is biased to see all affects as anger will still only score at the chance level of 10 out of 60. If the frequency of correct response alternatives had not been balanced, those judges biased to rate all affects in a certain way would earn accuracy scores too high. (A little further on, I shall discuss the effects of guessing in more detail.)

Making use of more of the data. For some research purposes, in studies of nonverbal accuracy, the total accuracy score may be all the data we want from each judge. However, much more often than we realize at present, it may be advisable for us to look more closely at our data, not only for purposes of testing specific hypotheses, but also to see what the data might have to teach us in a spirit of exploratory data analysis (Tukey, 1977).

For example, in addition to the total accuracy score, we can construct six separate accuracy scores, one for each of the emotions. Doing so generates a profile of accuracy scores, and judges or groups of judges can be compared on their profiles as well as on their total scores. Comparing judges on their profiles means comparing them on each of the elements (affects, in this case) taken one at a time, several at a time, or all at once. When we compare profiles we can proceed in several ways. One way is to think of our six-score profile as a single point located in a six-dimensional space so that we can compute distances (similarities) among points or judges. Another way is to correlate the six scores of each judge with the six scores of other judges. Similarity in this case is given not by distance but by similarity in the shape of the profile

Table 6.21. *Full data matrix for one judge, employing a categorical response format*

	Correct category						
Chosen category	Anger	Disgust	Fear	Happiness	Sadness	Surprise	Σ
Anger	8[a]	4	3	1	2	2	20
Disgust	1	4[a]	2	1	3	1	12
Fear	1	1	3[a]	2	1	2	10
Happiness	0	0	0	3[a]	0	1	4
Sadness	0	1	2	1	4[a]	2	10
Surprise	0	0	0	2	0	2[a]	4
Σ	10	10	10	10	10	10	60

[a]Items scored as accurate; total accuracy = 24.

as summarized by a product–moment correlation of some kind (e.g., Pearson's or Spearman's).

Rich as the yield in accuracy scores may be from the simple illustrative study under discussion, considerably more can be learned by a still closer look at the judges' responses, one that permits analysis of judges' errors as well as accuracies (Tomkins & McCarter, 1964; see also my discussion later in this chapter of the two-step model of response quantification). Table 6.21 shows an illustrative full data matrix that summarizes all 60 of the judge's responses. For each of the correct categories of emotion, given in the columns, we can see the distribution of responses according to the category chosen by the judge, given in the rows. This illustrative judge correctly identified 8 of the 10 anger stimuli but missed 2; one was mistakenly called disgust, and the other was mistakenly called fear.

The column totals of the full data matrix are fixed by the design of the study. In this case, each column totals 10 because we were careful to balance our set of stimuli for the frequency with which each emotion was the correct alternative. The row totals define the judge's bias. Fully unbiased judges, regardless of their total level of accuracy, would show no real differences among their row totals. The illustrative judge of Table 6.21 did show a significant bias, $\chi^2(5) = 17.6$, $p = 0.0035$, that was characterized by choosing the category anger too often and the categories happiness and surprise not often enough.

The bias of seeing too much of one category (e.g., anger) tends to inflate accuracy for the biased category. Thus, if there were perfect bias for one category (e.g., anger), all categories chosen would be *that* category and all items for which that category (i.e., anger) was the correct answer would be scored correct. Accordingly, there tends to be a positive correlation between bias toward a category and accuracy in that category. For the data of Table 6.21 the correlation between bias (the column on the far right) and accuracy (the entry of each column with the superscript *a*) is 0.93, $p = 0.007$. Because the accuracy score is one component of the row total, or bias, we naturally expect a positive correlation between accuracy and bias. It often happens, however, that even when the row total is corrected for accuracy by subtracting the accurately categorized items from the row total, the correlation between accuracy and bias remains. For the data of Table 6.21, for example, the row totals of 20, 12, 10, 4, 10, 4 become 12, 8, 7, 1, 6, 2 when corrected by the accuracy scores of 8, 4, 3, 3, 4, 2, that is, when this last set is subtracted from the first. Still, the correlation between these accuracy scores and the accuracy-corrected bias scores remains substantial: $r(4) = 0.85$, $p = 0.033$. We could also compute our test for bias on the accuracy-corrected row totals, if we should want an estimate of bias that omitted items categorized accurately. In this example, the test for bias remains significant when we employ the accuracy-corrected row totals, $\chi^2(5) = 13.67$, $p = 0.018$.

Further insight into the patterning of responses made in a full data matrix of the type shown in Table 6.21 can often be obtained by examining the differences between each cell entry and the value expected for that cell entry given its row and column total (row total × column total ÷ grand total). These differences, or residuals, highlight the frequencies that are much too large or much too small and are, therefore, in need of close examination. An additional procedure for gaining such insight is a procedure called *standardizing the margins* developed by Mosteller (1968) and described in a more elementary context by Rosenthal & Rosnow (1975a). The procedure shows what the cell entries are like after the row totals have been made equal to each other and the column totals have all been made equal to each other.

Number of categories. In the illustration we have been discussing, it was reasonable to employ a categorical format of six alternatives. Often the design of the research requires only two or three response alternatives; and when the needs of the research speak clearly on the number of alternatives or categories to employ, we should listen. Frequently, however, there is no clear theoretical reason to prefer any particular number of categories; and that was the situation in our development of the PONS test (Rosenthal et al., 1979). That test presents judges with 220 items of nonverbal behavior and asks them to select one of just two alternatives as the correct response. From a theoretical point of view, there was no reason to employ only two alternatives. We might just as well have used three, four, or even five. Indeed, everything else being equal, tests tend to be more reliable when the number of alternatives is increased (Nunnally, 1978, pp. 652–653).

Our choice of only two alternatives or categories was based more on intuition than on strong evidence. We felt that with a test so long (220 items meant 45 minutes administration time with two response alternatives), adding even a third alternative might prove to make the task too onerous and perhaps too time-consuming as well. There is a very real logistic advantage in having tests or judging tasks kept under 50 or 45 minutes: They can be more easily administered to intact classes of secondary school and college students.

In a test or judging task, if more categories can be employed without sacrificing other desirable features of the task, there is a practical benefit to be had. It becomes easier to assess the probability that a *particular* judge has shown accuracy greater than chance. Normally, when samples of judges are employed, this is not a great advantage, because the number of judges gives us the power to establish that judges, in the aggregate, can do better than chance in decoding nonverbal cues. In clinical contexts, however, or in selection contexts, where we are very much interested in evaluating the performance of a single patient or applicant, a larger number of alternatives per item is very useful, especially when we must keep the total number of items administered fairly low.

Table 6.22 shows the number of items required to show a single judge to be significantly accurate for each of several numbers of response alternatives. If our criterion of real accuracy were accuracy at a one-tailed p of 0.005, we would require 9 items having only 2 response categories, but only 3 items having 6 response categories. Thus, if we wanted to evaluate nonverbal accuracy in each of 11 channels, as in the PONS test, we would require 99 items with only 2 alternatives, but only 33 items with 6 alternatives. Table 6.22 is useful not only for research applications in which only a single judge has been employed but also in clinical applications where we may wish to establish the accuracy of individual clinicians.

Effects of guessing. The second column of Table 6.22 shows the probability of obtaining a correct response by random selection of a response

Table 6.22. *Minimum number of items required to establish an individual judge's accuracy at various levels of significance*

		Significance levels (one-tailed)				
Number of alternatives	Chance level	0.10	0.05	0.01	0.005	0.001
2	0.50	4	5	7	9	10
3	0.33	3	3	5	5	7
4	0.25	2	3	4	4	5
5	0.20	2	2	3	4	5
6	0.17	2	2	3	3	4
7	0.14	2	2	3	3	4
8	0.12	2	2	3	3	4
9	0.11	2	2	3	3	4
10	0.10	1	2	2	3	3
11	0.09	1	2	2	3	3
12	0.08	1	2	2	3	3

alternative (guessing) as a function of the number of response categories or alternatives. With only 2 categories we have a probability of 0.50 of guessing the correct category; with 10 categories we have a probability of only 0.10. Therefore, if we had a test of 100 items, we would regard a score of 50 correct quite differently if the number of alternatives (A) were 2 or 10. If A were 2, the performance would be no better than chance; if A were 10, the performance would be very substantially better than chance: $\chi^2(1) = 178$, $Z > 13$, p close to 0. Our evaluation of the effects of guessing on the level of a judge's accuracy, then, depends heavily on the number of response alternatives.

Under many conditions, we may not be concerned with estimation of a judge's actual level of accuracy. In a great deal of research on individual differences, for example, we may be concerned only with judges' relative position on a distribution of accuracy scores. In such cases the number of response categories per item need not concern us. At other times, however, we do want some estimate of how well a judge or group of judges has done, taking into account the effect of successful guessing as a function of the number of response alternatives. The standard estimate is given by Nunnally (1978). The number of items that are correct after adjustment for guessing (R adjusted) is a function of the number of items that are correct, or right (R); the number of items that are incorrect, or wrong (W); and the number of categories of response for each item (A). The adjusted number correct is given by

$$R \text{ adjusted} = R - \frac{W}{A - 1}$$

Thus, if we answer 50 of 100 items correctly, we will earn an adjusted score of 0 if there are only 2 alternatives per item, because we did not do any better than randomly choosing (guessing). However, had there been 10 alternatives, our adjusted score would have been 44.4. Table 6.23 gives the adjusted accuracy scores for a 100-item test for varying numbers of response alternatives. The first column gives the number of correctly answered items (R) in steps of 5. The second column gives the number of incorrectly answered items (W), which is simply $100 - R$ for this table. In each column of the body of the table, a perfectly chance level of performance is given by an adjusted accuracy score of 0. Because Table 6.23 employs steps of 5 in the number of items correct, a nearly exact score of 0 is not found in each column; however, interpolation can be used to find the level of approximate 0 or any other value located between adjacent entries. A more precise location for 0 values of adjusted accuracy scores for Table 6.23 is given by

$$R = \frac{100}{A}$$

or, more generally, by

$$R = \frac{K}{A}$$

where K is the total number of items, or $R + W$.

The relationship by which the total number of items (K) is the sum of the right (R) and wrong (W) answers holds only if we score as wrong any items that are omitted. However, scoring omitted items as 0 gives them too little credit in computing R. It seems preferable to credit omitted items with the score that would be obtained by purely random guessing, i.e., the reciprocal of the number of alternatives ($1/A$). Thus, if there are two categories of response, we credit omitted items with 0.5 points; if there are three response alternatives, we credit omitted items with 0.33 points; and so on (Nunnally, 1978, p. 650; Rosenthal et al., 1979). Because judges often know more than they think they do, and because factors other than actual skill at nonverbal decoding affect the frequency of omitted items, it seems best to do all one can to avoid omitted items. Judges can usually be successfully urged to leave no blanks. If blanks *are* left and we do not credit them with $1/A$ points, we run the risk of having people who don't like to guess scoring significantly *below* chance.

Table 6.23. *Estimated accuracy adjusted for guessing (100-item test)*

		Number of alternatives								
Number right	Number wrong	2	3	4	5	6	7	8	9	10
100	0	100	100	100	100	100	100	100	100	100
95	5	90	92.5	93.3	93.8	94	94.2	94.3	94.4	94.4
90	10	80	85.0	86.7	87.5	88	88.3	88.6	88.8	88.9
85	15	70	77.5	80.0	81.2	82	82.5	82.9	83.1	83.3
80	20	60	70.0	73.3	75.0	76	76.7	77.1	77.5	77.8
75	25	50	62.5	66.7	68.8	70	70.8	71.4	71.9	72.2
70	30	40	55.0	60.0	62.5	64	65.0	65.7	66.2	66.7
65	35	30	47.5	53.3	56.2	58	59.2	60.0	60.6	61.1
60	40	20	40.0	46.7	50.0	52	53.3	54.3	55.0	55.6
55	45	10	32.5	40.0	43.8	46	47.5	48.6	49.4	50.0
50	50	0	25.0	33.3	37.5	40	41.7	42.9	43.8	44.4
45	55	−10	17.5	26.7	31.2	34	35.8	37.1	38.1	38.9
40	60	−20	10.0	20.0	25.0	28	30.0	31.4	32.5	33.3
35	65	−30	2.5	13.3	18.8	22	24.2	25.7	26.9	27.8
30	70	−40	−5.0	6.7	12.5	16	18.3	20.0	21.2	22.2
25	75	−50	−12.5	0.0	6.2	10	12.5	14.3	15.6	16.7
20	80	−60	−20.0	−6.7	0.0	4	6.7	8.6	10.0	11.1
15	85	−70	−27.5	−13.3	−6.2	−2	0.8	2.9	4.4	5.6
10	90	−80	−35.0	−20.0	−12.5	−8	−5.0	−2.9	−1.2	0.0
5	95	−90	−42.5	−26.7	−18.8	−14	−10.8	−8.6	−6.9	−5.6
0	100	−100	−50.0	−33.3	−25.0	−20	−16.7	−14.3	−12.5	−11.1

Level of accuracy. So far I have talked only of the effect on item difficulty, or lack of "guessability," of an extrinsic factor of format: the number of response alternatives. There are also intrinsic factors contributing to item difficulty, for example, length of stimulus exposure time, quality of stimulus materials, and the like. From the point of view of developing psychometrically sound stimulus materials or tests, what should be the level of difficulty of the items? If there were two response alternatives, an average accuracy rate of 50% would clearly be undesirable, because that would suggest that judges were unable to decode the nonverbal materials at a rate better than chance. Similarly, if there were two response alternatives, an average accuracy rate of 100% would be undesirable, because no individual differences in accuracy could be assessed, and because we would have no idea of how much more difficult the task might have been made without the average accuracy level dropping noticeably.

There is no uniformly correct answer to the question of a desirable level of average accuracy for stimulus materials of varying numbers of response categories. As a very rough rule of thumb, however, we might expect reasonably good performance (e.g., discrimination power) from items with accuracy adjusted for guessing (*R* adjusted) of approximately 0.7. Table 6.23 can be employed to obtain the raw score accuracies (*R*) equivalent to the adjusted accuracies for each column (number of categories). For most practical application, the raw score accuracies (*R*) equivalent to the adjusted accuracy of 0.7 will range between 0.7 and 0.85, the latter value for the situation of only two response alternatives, the former value for the situation of a larger number of response alternatives (Guilford, 1954, p. 391; Nunnally, 1978, p. 273).

The two-step model of response quantification. Suppose we ask our judges to select one of six emotions as the correct one. We must first quantify the response in some way before our computer, animate or inanimate, can take the next step. Quantification in this case is very conveniently carried out by *dichotomous coding,* that is, assigning the value 1 to the chosen category and the value 0 to *all* the categories that were not chosen. If the response alternatives were (*A*) anger, (*B*) disgust, (*C*) fear, (*D*) happiness, (*E*) sadness, (*F*) surprise, and we selected *C*, fear, we would record the score of 1 for *C*, fear, and the score of 0 for alternatives *A*, *B*, *D*, *E*, and *F*. It should be noted that what we have quantified is the judge's response, not whether the response is correct or incorrect. After we have quantified the judge's response, we will ordinarily want to score that response as accurate or inaccurate. In the simplest case, where one of the response alternatives has been defined by the investigators as the correct one, an item is counted correct if the judge has assigned the value 1 to the alternative defined as the correct one. (It should be noted that for the example under discussion there is a strong empirical basis for scoring certain errors as more serious than others [Ekman et al., 1972; Izard, 1971; Tomkins & McCarter, 1964]. On these grounds, Ekman [personal communication, 1979] has long suggested that we should take account of the evidence on difficulty level, or likelihood of confusion of affects, in our scoring of accuracy.)

The procedure advocated here is thus a two-step procedure:

1. Recording the response quantitatively (assigning 1 or 0 to each response alternative)
2. Scoring the response as accurate – that is, 1 – if the response alternative scored 1 was the one designated as correct by the investigators, and as inaccurate – that is, 0 – if the response alternative scored 1 was not the one designated as correct by the investigators.

Why do we need step (1)? Why don't we simply score each item as correct or incorrect in the first place, that is, score the item 1 if the judge's selection was the correct one and 0 if the judge's selection was the incorrect one? Sometimes, for some purposes, that is indeed a reasonable procedure, but there are two basic reasons for the two-step procedure. The first is that computers, the inanimate kind, generally require the two-step procedure. In the first step we tell the computer what the judge's response was; in the second, the computer tells us whether it was correct or incorrect, depending on what we have told the computer to say. The second reason is that if we skip the first step we have thrown away a great deal of information for that item, if the item is answered incorrectly (see Table 6.21): For any item of A alternatives, there are $A-1$ incorrect alternatives, and if a judge misses an item we cannot identify the wrong alternative that attracted his or her vote. A full data matrix of the type shown in Table 6.21 is possible only if we use the two-step procedure. If we skip step (1), the rich yield of Table 6.21 is reduced in the best case to only the table's diagonal values, and in the worst case to only the total number of correct responses. We may feel sure at the time of the research that we are not interested in judges' biases or sources of confusion, and we may decide, therefore, to skip step (1) of our two-step procedure. Experience suggests, however, that we often do discover a need to look at these variables at some future time. It is therefore more efficient to design the quantification procedure with that possibility in mind.

Finally, there are situations in which the focus of research is entirely on step (1) – there is no step (2). That, for example, is the case for research on characteristic or "average" nonverbal demeanor (DePaulo & Rosenthal, 1979a, 1979b, in press). Personal correlates of these characteristic nonverbal demeanors are being investigated. More generally, of course, it is the case that *all* research in which judges' responses provide the definition of encoder state is research involving only step (1), whether judges are asked to employ categorical formats or other formats to be discussed later in this section.

Multiple response quantification. So far in the discussion I have assumed that in research on nonverbal decoding accuracy, only one of the categories offered as an alternative is the correct one. We need not restrict ourselves to that situation, however. Suppose, for example, that we wanted to replicate research suggesting that female superiority at decoding nonverbal cues was greater for more negative affects (Hall, 1979; Rosenthal et al., 1979). If we were employing the six response alternatives we have been discussing, we might decide that four of them comprised clearly negative affects (anger, disgust, fear, sadness), whereas the remaining two (happiness, surprise) did not. We might decide to form two categories of response: the four negative categories and the two nonnegative categories. For our first step, then, we would score as 1 *all* of the negative affects if any one of them was chosen and we would score as 0 *both* of the nonnegative affects if either one of them was chosen. For our second step, we would score the item as correct if the new larger category (negative, nonnegative) that was selected by the judge was the correct new category.

The example that we have chosen to examine here is made more complex by having the probability of a correct guess vary with the new category of the correct alternative. Thus, when the correct answer is a negative affect, the probability of guessing it correctly is 0.67; when the correct answer is a nonnegative affect, the probability of guessing it correctly is only 0.33. A judge whose response bias was to see all affects as negative would earn a score of 67% correct if our test represented the basic six emotions equally often. A judge whose response bias was to see all affects as nonnegative would earn a score of only 33% correct in the same case. If we wanted to make our test equally fair to persons of both types of bias, we would simply ensure that the total number of times negative and nonnegative alternatives were the correct answer had been made equal.

Category ranking. I began this discussion of response quantification by describing the simple case of coding one response alternative as 1 and all others as 0. I then discussed the somewhat more complex case of coding each of several response alternatives as 1 and the remaining response alternatives as 0. More complex forms of response quantification are also available. For example, judges may be asked to rank all of the response categories from most to least appropriate as a label for the nonverbal behavior serving as the stimulus item. This is a potentially more precise and discriminating procedure, usable whenever the investigators are able to rank the response alternatives from "most correct answer" to "least correct answer." (This *criterion ranking* is not always easy to achieve, but it does not differ in principle from the selection of just one correct answer in the more traditional procedures; see e.g., Ekman et al., 1972; Rosenthal et al., 1979.) Table 6.24 shows some hypothetical results for this ranking procedure. The first column lists the six response categories for a single item, and the second lists the ranking that has been defined as correct by the investigators. Four judges (*A, B, C, D*) have responded to this item by ranking the categories from most to least correct.

Two of the judges (*A* and *B*) would have been scored as correct if the item had been scored dichotomously, because they ranked as most correct (rank of 1) the same item the investigators defined as most correct. Two of the judges (*C* and *D*) would have been scored as incorrect if the item had been scored dichotomously, because they did not rank as the most correct the item that the investigators defined as most correct.

The third from the last row of Table 6.24 gives the correlation between the ranks assigned by the judge in that column and the ranks assigned by the investigators. The two judges who were correct when this item was scored dichotomously differed substantially from each other in their degree of correlation with the criterion ranking; one judge agreed perfectly (rho = +1.00), the other actually showed a slightly negative correlation (rho = −0.14) with the criterion ranking.

The two judges who were both incorrect when this item was scored dichotomously differed even more from each other. One of these judges disagreed perfectly with the criterion ranking (rho = −1.00), whereas the other agreed very strongly (rho = 0.94). It is especially noteworthy that one of the judges who was incorrect by the dichotomous scoring criterion (judge *C*) was very much more accurate by the more sensitive category-ranking criterion than one of the judges who was correct by the dichotomous scoring criterion (judge *B*).

One of the advantages of this procedure of category ranking is that we can employ fewer items per judge to establish that judges are more accurate than random guessers. For example, for a given item listing six response categories, a correct choice defined dichotomously has a probability of 0.17 of occurring by chance (random guessing). However, a perfectly accurate ranking performance has a probability of only 0.0014. If very small errors are made, as for judge *C*, the probability is only 0.01, and even if *none* of the ranks agree with the criterion ranks but

Table 6.24. *Illustrative results of four rankings of six response categories for one item*

Response categories	Criterion ranking	Judges' rankings with "correct response"		Judges' rankings with "incorrect response"	
		A	*B*	*C*	*D*
Happiness	1	1	1	2	6
Surprise	2	2	6	1	5
Anger	3	3	5	3	4
Fear	4	4	4	4	3
Disgust	5	5	3	5	2
Sadness	6	6	2	6	1
Rank correlation with criterion ranking		1.00	−0.14	0.94	−1.00
Dichotomous scoring		1	1	0	0
Sum of squared differences in ranks (ΣD^2)		0	40	2	70

are never off by more than one, the probability is still only 0.03, enough to establish statistically significant accuracy of nonverbal decoding with only a single item.

When the method of category ranking is employed, the correlation coefficient obtained for each item will be the more precise and efficient the greater is the number of response alternatives. Thus, if there are only two response alternatives, ranking them tells us no more than does selecting just one of them; the probability of getting it right by dichotomous scoring or of getting it perfectly right by ranking is still only 0.5. Even with as few as three response alternatives, however, the method of category ranking adds precision, and for only four response alternatives, a perfect ranking is significantly superior to random guessing, at $p = 0.04$, whereas a correct response by dichotomous scoring could occur by guessing with a probability of 0.25.

If we decide to employ category ranking, we could compute for each judge the mean (or median) correlation between his or her ranking of the categories and the criterion ranking of each of the items. This average correlation would be that judge's overall accuracy score. The formula for the correlation (rho) reflecting accuracy for each item is

$$\text{rho} = 1 - \left(\frac{6}{A^3 - A}\right) \Sigma D^2$$

where A is the number of categories or response alternatives and D is the difference between a judge's assigned rank and the criterion rank. Each of these Ds is squared, and these squared Ds are added to get ΣD^2. For many practical purposes, it turns out that we do not need to compute rho at all. For any data-analytic purpose other than estimating rho itself, we can do just as well using ΣD^2 instead of rho, because these quantities are perfectly correlated within a given study employing the same number of response alternatives (A) throughout.

Suppose we were comparing the nonverbal sensitivity of three groups of judges. We could work with the quantity ΣD^2 for each item, compute a mean ΣD^2 for each judge and for each group, and compute our test statistic (e.g., F) on these ΣD^2s. We could even report ΣD^2s as the means of our three groups and stop there, because the metric ΣD^2 has meaning in and of itself when the number of alternatives is constant. If, however, we wanted to compute the mean rho for accuracy for each of our three groups, we could do so simply by employing our mean ΣD^2s in the formula for rho just given. We can use Table 6.24 as an illustration. If we wanted the mean accuracy score of all four judges we could add the ΣD^2s given in the bottom row, take the mean (which equals 28), and substitute it into the formula for rho. Or we could simply average the four rhos of Table 6.24 and get precisely the same answer: Mean rho = 0.24, or rho of mean $\Sigma D^2 = 0.24$.

Dimensional formats

The dimensional response format usually presents judges with some form of more or less continuous rating scale. For example, judges may be asked to rate the degree of hostility in the tone of voice of a physician talking about alcoholic patients (e.g., Milmoe et al., 1967). Judges may be given anywhere between 2 and 20 or more scale points to choose from to indicate the level of hostility they perceive in the doctor's tone of voice.

Relating the formats. There is an interesting relationship between the dimensional and categorical response formats that is not generally recognized. A categorical response format with A alternatives to choose from is analogous to a set of A rating scales each offering only two scale points. Thus the categorical response format offering the alternatives

A. Angry_________
B. Happy_________
C. Sad _________

with the instruction to select one or more is analogous to the dimensional response format

A. Angry 0________1

B. Happy 0________1

C. Sad 0________1

with the instruction to rate the nonverbal behavior on each of the three rating scales offered. The end points (0 and 1) of the rating scale might be labeled *absent* = *0*, *present* = *1*; *low* = *0*, *high* = *1*; *does not apply* = *0*, *does apply* = *1*, or something similar. However we may choose to label the end points, both the categorical and the dimensional response formats will give us one of two possible scores for each category or each dimension, where 0 for the dimensional is the same as unselected for the categorical, and where 1 for the dimensional is the same as selected for the categorical.

Scale points and labels. The advantage of the dimensional response format begins to appear as the number of scale points increases. The greatest benefits to reliability accrue as we go from 2 to 7 scale points, but it may still be beneficial to reliability to employ up to 11 scale points (Nunnally, 1978). Indeed, there are some circumstances in which as many as 20 scale points will prove useful (Guilford, 1954; Rosenthal, 1966, 1976). From a very practical point of view, there are some advantages to employing 9 or 10 scale points – enough to reap most of the benefits of added reliability but not too many for keeping each judge's response at a single digit, which can effect some economies of data processing (the two choices would be 1–9 and 0–9, the former if a neutral midpoint is desired, the latter if not).

There is no clear agreement on the optimal number of labels to employ for our judges' rating scales. As a minimum, of course, we want to label the end points of our scale (e.g., *warm–not warm, warm–cold, not cold–cold*). Some additional benefits may accrue if we label some or all of the intermediate scale points. A useful practical solution is to label all the scale points when there are few of them (say 5 or less) and label only the areas of the rating scale when there are many. For example, in a 9- or 10-point rating scale of warmth, we might label the end points *not at all warm* and *very warm*, and distribute the 3 interior labels – *somewhat warm, moderately warm* and *quite warm* – so that the 5 labels will be approximately equidistant. This would be an example of a unipolar scale, one that runs from the absence of a characteristic to a great deal of the characteristic. An example of a bipolar scale, one that runs from a great amount of one characteristic to a great amount of its opposite, might be a 9- or 10-point scale of warmth labeled as *very cold* and *very warm* at the end points, with *somewhat cold, neither cold nor warm,* and *somewhat warm,* as the interior labels to be spaced along the rating scale. (Some special problems of bipolar scales will be discussed shortly.)

It is easier to find nonredundant labels for bipolar scales, and some researchers might want to employ more than 5 labels for the *cold–warm* scale we have been considering. An example of the use of 9 labels might be *very cold, quite cold, moderately cold, somewhat cold, neither cold nor warm, somewhat warm, moderately warm, quite warm, very warm.* Experience suggests that judges used to making ratings (e.g., college students, college graduates, most high school students) can do about as well with just a few labels on a rating scale as with many such labels. Different judges will tend to use different sections of the rating scales more frequently, but these biases do *not* affect the judges' reliability.

When designing rating scales for judgment studies, it is less confusing to judges and data processors always to place higher numbers on the right, because most judges and data processors will have learned in elementary school that numbers increase to the right. In addition, given the choice of placing the "good end" – for example, *warm, friendly, empathic* – on the left or on the right, experience suggests it is wiser to place it on the right. Although there *may* be a tendency for the grand mean ratings to increase somewhat thereby, it is likely that on the average, errors of judging, of coding, and of interpretation will be reduced by this practice (Guilford, 1954, p. 268). Numbers on our rating scales should of course be placed equidistantly apart, and the physical format of the sheet of rating scales should be designed to make it unlikely that scales could be overlooked.

The two-step model. A major advantage of the dimensional response format over the categorical response format is that, for any given dimension, we have relatively much greater precision of judgment than we do for any one of the categories of the categorical response format, assuming that we employ at least 3 scale points. Another advantage is that our judges' ratings in the dimensional format come "ready to use." That is, step (1) of the two-step model of response quantification described earlier is very easily accomplished: The rating *is* step (1). Often step (1) is all we need – when we are employing judges to define the encoder's true state, for example. However, if we want to assess the judge's accuracy, step (2) is required, and step (2) may be more complicated for the dimensional than for the categorical format.

In the case of the categorical format, step (2) required only that we compare the judge's response to the criterion. If the judge's response agreed with the criterion (e.g., both listed happy as 1 and all other responses as 0), it was defined as correct. In the case of the dimensional format, however, there is no direct way to decide whether the judge's response agrees with the criterion. For example, suppose we have members of a group of encoders describe in an honest way someone they like and someone they dislike, and describe in a dishonest way someone they really like, pretending to dislike the person, and someone they really dislike, pretending to like the person. We then ask the judges to rate these four encodings of each of the encoders on a 9-point scale of deceptiveness (DePaulo & Rosenthal, 1979a, 1979b, in press). How shall we score judges' accuracy in decoding the encoders' deception?

Suppose we simply averaged the ratings of deceptiveness given to the dishonest encodings. Could we say that judges who rated dishonest encodings as more deceptive than did other judges were more accurate than the other judges? There are two reasons why we might not want to do that. First, we might feel that not all the dishonest encodings were maximally dishonest, and so we might not want to define as most accurate those judges who labeled all dishonest encodings as maximally dishonest. Second, there might be some judges who rated *all* behavior as deceptive whether the encodings were deceptive or not.

Comparison ratings. Rather than average the ratings of deceptiveness given to dishonest encodings, we would do better to introduce a comparison rating against which to evaluate judges' ratings of the deceptiveness of the dishonest encodings. In the present example, we might compute the average rating of deceptiveness made when the encoder was instructed to be honest and subtract that average rating from the average rating of deceptiveness made when the encoder was instructed to be dishonest. The greater this difference score, the greater the extent to which that judge was able to differentiate between the encoders' honest and dishonest states. Thus a judge who saw deception everywhere and assigned a rating of 9 to all encodings would earn a difference score or accuracy score of 0. If we had not subtracted this judge's ratings of deceptiveness on the comparison stimuli, we would have scored this judge as maximally accurate instead of as completely inaccurate.

The general principle for forming accuracy scores of this type is to subtract the average rating on dimension x of stimuli that should show little x from the average rating on dimension x of stimuli that should show much x. The major advantages of this type of accuracy score are that it (1) adjusts for a judge's response bias and (2) permits finer gradations of accuracy than the all-or-none levels of accuracy ordinarily employed with categorical response formats. This type of accuracy score does require, however, that each judge make at least two ratings for each accuracy score required. The judge's accuracy for that pair of ratings is defined by the difference between the rating that should be higher if the judge is accurate and the rating that should be lower.

Bipolar versus unipolar scales. The difference between bipolar and unipolar scales was briefly noted earlier in this section. Bipolar scales run from a great amount of a characteristic to a great amount of its opposite (e.g., *warm–cold*), whereas unipolar scales run from a great amount of a characteristic to the absence of that characteristic (e.g., *warm–not warm; cold–not cold*).

For many practical purposes it seems not to matter much whether we employ bipolar or unipolar scales; the correlation between judges' ratings of warmth on a scale of *warm–cold* and a scale of *warm–not warm* is likely to be quite substantial, perhaps as high as the retest reliability of either rating. Experience also suggests however, that the expected negative correlation between ratings of *warm–not warm* and *cold–not cold* is not necessarily as high as we might expect. This potentially low correlation between unipolar rating scales that appear to be opposites has been superbly documented in recent work on masculinity–femininity (e.g., Bem, 1974; Spence and Helmreich, 1978).

This research has shown that the correlation between the unipolar scales of masculine and feminine is sufficiently poor that it is possible to identify about as many people who score high on both or low on both, as people who are high on one and low on the other.

More specific to research in nonverbal communication, DePaulo and Rosenthal (1979a, 1979b, in press) have employed scales of liking and disliking as unipolar scales. Despite substantial negative correlations between ratings on these unipolar scales, we have found it possible to identify encodings in which a person being described is both liked and disliked considerably. We employ this as an operational definition of an ambivalent interpersonal affect. We have also found it possible to identify encodings in which a person being described is neither liked nor disliked. We employ this as an operational definition of an indifferent interpersonal affect.

The lesson to us of these recent developments has been that it may be worth employing more unipolar scales (e.g., like *and* dislike scales rather than one like–dislike scale) in hopes of turning up other surprises.

Categories as dimensions. We can combine the characteristics of dimensional formats with those of categorical formats. Suppose, for example,

Table 6.25. *Illustrative profile of ratings of six categories of emotion*

Categories of emotion	Not at all 1	Somewhat 2	3	Moderately 4	5	6	Quite 7	8	Very 9
Angry	1	(2)	3	4	5	6	7	8	9
Disgusted	1	2	3	4	5	(6)	7	8	9
Fearful	1	2	3	4	5	6	7	(8)	9
Happy	(1)	2	3	4	5	6	7	8	9
Sad	1	2	3	4	(5)	6	7	8	9
Surprised	1	2	3	4	5	6	(7)	8	9

that we wanted to evaluate encoders' nonverbal behavior for the presence of six emotions or affects studied by Ekman (1973). We could ask judges to rate the degree of presence of each of these emotions on a 9-point scale. Table 6.25 shows an illustrative profile of the rated presence of the six emotions listed in the first column.

Employing categories as dimension (i.e., rating categories) is similar in spirit to the method of category ranking described earlier. However, there are several advantages to the former. First, in the method of category ranking, the number of categories to be ranked defines the number of scale points to be employed. In the method of category rating, we are free to decide the number of scale points and how they are to be labeled. Second, in category ranking, the distance between any two adjacent ranks is forced to be the same, but in category rating, the rated difference between adjacent ranks can more accurately reflect the judge's assessment of the difference. Table 6.25 illustrates this. If we had employed category ranking, the distance between *happy* and *sad* (two units) would be treated as equivalent to the distance between *fearful* and *disgusted* (two units). However, the judge's actual rating of these emotions showed the distance between *happy* and *sad* to be much greater (four units) than the distance between *fearful* and *disgusted* (two units).

A third advantage of the method of rating categories over the method of ranking categories, applicable to studies evaluating judges' accuracy, is that it gives greater statistical power to reject the hypothesis that the judge is performing in a purely random (i.e., nonaccurate) manner. This gain in statistical power is not dramatic, but it is most noticeable when the number of alternatives is small. Thus, where there are only three or four categories, it is not possible to reject the null hypothesis of no accuracy at $p = 0.01$ by the method of category ranking, even when rankings are in perfect agreement with the criterion rankings; however, even when there are only three or four categories, it is possible to reject the null hypothesis of no accuracy at $p = 0.01$ by the method of category rating.

Table 6.26 shows the degree of correlation required for both methods to demonstrate significant levels of accuracy. For any number of alternatives (A), it requires a lower correlation to reject the null hypothesis of no accuracy when category rating is employed than when category ranking is employed. As the number of alternatives grows larger, however, the advantage of category rating becomes smaller. But by far the most dramatic information of Table 6.26 is the listing of the probabilities of accurate guessing for various numbers of alternatives when the selection of only a single category is employed. Even with 12 alternatives, it is not possible to reject the null hypothesis of no accuracy by the category selection method. Thus, although category rating may be more powerful than category ranking, both are *very* dramatically superior to simple category selection.

It is not only for purposes of testing accuracy for statistical significance that both category ranking and category rating are superior to category selection. The former two methods both provide greater potential than the latter for scoring partial credit in cases of partial accuracy and for analyzing the nature of the errors made, in order to investigate both the source of errors for judges in general and individual differences among judges in factors associated with their mistakes in judgment.

The matter of partial credit may be especially important when we are working with a fairly homogeneous group of judges and/or are asking each one to judge very few items. In the limiting case of a single item per judge, we might be unable to distinguish between two judges both of whom "missed" the item as defined by category selection, but one of whom was very accurate ($r = 0.94$) while the other very inaccurate ($r = -1.00$) in the sense of agreement with the profile of criterion ratings (see Table 6.24).

The methods of category ranking and category rating thus permit the correlation, for each item, of each judge's ranking or rating with (1) the criterion ranking or rating, or (2) the grand mean rating by all judges. In addition, however, these methods also permit, for each item, the correlation with one another of the ratings of individual judges. Investigators interested in individual differences in judges' ratings would be able

Table 6.26. *Degree of agreement between judges' responses and the criterion required for establishing significant accuracy for a single item*

Number of alternatives (A)	Category selection: p of accurate guess	Category ranking[a]		Category rating[b]	
		0.05	0.01	0.05	0.01
3	0.33	—	—	0.99	1.00
4	0.25	1.00	—	0.90	0.98
5	0.20	0.90	1.00	0.80	0.93
6	0.17	0.83	0.94	0.73	0.88
7	0.14	0.71	0.89	0.67	0.83
8	0.12	0.64	0.83	0.62	0.79
9	0.11	0.60	0.78	0.58	0.75
10	0.10	0.56	0.75	0.55	0.72
11	0.09	0.53	0.73	0.52	0.68
12	0.08	0.51	0.71	0.50	0.66

[a]From Siegel, 1956. [b]From Walker and Lev, 1953.

to group, cluster, or factor judges into judge types, whose personal characteristics could then be investigated.

Open-ended formats

Teachers' folklore has it that good objective test items (e.g., multiple-choice items) are difficult to construct but easy to score, whereas good subjective (essay) test items are relatively easy to construct but difficult to score. Open-ended response formats are like essay examinations. Judges may be asked simply to report, in their own words, the type of affect they have just seen or heard, the type of person who would behave in such a way, the type of situation in which one might find such behavior and so on.

Judges' responses to an open-ended format are likely to yield a quite diverse set of reactions that would be very useful for generating research (or clinical) hypotheses, but that usually require considerable effort to quantify, if they are to be employed for hypothesis testing.

Diversity. In the categorical and dimensional formats, the investigator decides which categories or dimensions are required by, or at least useful to, the purposes of the research. In the open-ended, or free-response, formats, it is the judges who decide which categories or dimensions are to be employed. To some degree, the nature of the stimulus materials determines the categories or dimensions that are likely to be employed. To some degree, too, however, the individual characteristics of the judges determine the categories or dimensions that will be employed. Some judges, for example, are likely to employ some category or dimension of power much more often than others, whereas other judges are likely to employ some category or dimension of affection much more often. Depending on the stimulus characteristics, there will be varying degrees of diversity among judges in their evaluations of encoders' nonverbal behavior.

The value to the investigator of introducing greater diversity into judges' response formats is that judges may see or hear things that the investigator neither planned to look or listen for nor was able to see or hear when assessing the stimulus materials. Thus open-ended response formats are especially valuable in *pilot work* designed to generate the categories and/or dimensions to be employed in the more formal research to follow.

In addition to their use in pilot studies, open-ended formats can be employed as a *parallel enrichment procedure.* In this usage, a sample of judges is employed, some of whom are to make categorical and/or dimensional responses, and some of whom are to make open-ended responses. The quantitative data produced by the former subset of judges are then augmented by the more lively, realistic-sounding descriptions of the latter subset of judges. Hypothesis testing is based on the quantitative data, whereas hypothesis generating (and perhaps the feeling of "understanding") is based on the qualitative data produced by the judges employing open-ended formats. This very promising procedure, because it requires more judges, does of course increase research costs to some degree.

Quantification. Just about any kind of judge's response can be quantified, but usually the quantification of open-ended responses costs more, in time, effort, and often, money, than does the quantification of categorical or dimensional responses. The two most common approaches are (1) the *content-analytic* approach and (2) the *higher-order judges' approach.*

The content-analytic approach may employ either predetermined or inductively derived content categories, and each judge's open-ended response is coded as falling into one or more of a set of exhaustive content categories. (Content categories can be made exhaustive by the addition of the category *other.*) Each item of encoder nonverbal behavior is then scored as 1 or 0 for each of the content categories that have been generated either a priori or on the basis of the categories found in the set of open-ended responses. In short, the content-analytic approach is quantified just like the categorical response format's step (1). The practical differences are that the content-analytic procedure (1) usually yields a much larger number of categories than does the categorical procedure, and (2) provides no guarantee that categories of interest to the investigator will even be considered by judges.

The higher-order judge's approach employs an additional sample of judges who judge the open-ended responses on a series of dimensions (or categories) that have been selected by the investigator. The higher-order judge might be asked, for example, to rate an open-ended response on a 9-point scale reflecting to what degree the responder felt that the encoder's behavior was warm.

Although both practical experience and psychometric considerations have a great deal to offer us in deciding what type of response format we might want to employ to achieve any particular type of goal, we could benefit greatly from research designed specifically to test the relative merits of the various response formats, their variant forms, and the various combinations in which they might be employed.

Accuracy, error, and response bias

Much of the research on nonverbal communication has shown an interest in judges' accuracy. In my discussion of categorical and dimensional response format, I described methods for quantifying the accuracy of judges' responses, including methods designed to minimize the effects of various forms of response bias, or at least to permit us to estimate the type and degree of such biases. Much more could be said of the problem of quantifying accuracy in nonverbal communication. An excellent introduction to some of the technical issues, general to various fields of interpersonal judgment, has been provided by Cline (1964), and the response bias built into some types of answer formats has been discussed by Rosenthal et al. (1979, pp. 35–37, 116–117).

The problem of the quantification of accuracy seems somewhat less central to the open-ended format, if only because that format is not used so frequently in the assessment of judges' accuracy. In principle, of course, it could be.

In general, response biases can be viewed in three ways: (1) as a source of artifact impairing our effective quantification of accuracy scores, (2) as a source of information about interesting individual differences among judges, and (3) as a source of information about the workings in general of the senses and the mind of "the" human observer, or of subtypes of the human observer. An interesting recent example of viewing response biases in all three ways is given by Nasby et al. (1979).

6.8. The analysis of individual and sets of judgment studies

The analysis of the results of judgment studies, like the analysis of any other type of study, is closely linked to the design of those studies. In this discussion of judgment studies there has been a great deal said about their design. This is not the place to be detailed in the discussion of their analysis, but a few special issues must be considered.

Focused *F* tests

Much of the business of research in nonverbal communication is carried out by means of analyses of variance, ordinarily culminating in one or more *F* tests that are reported as "the results" of the research. "The results" of course, are the entire table of means, the table of variance, and much more. Here we focus only on the *F* tests themselves and how we can make them work harder for us. The rule of thumb is easy: Never (*almost* never) employ an *F* test in an analysis of variance, analysis of covariance, or multivariate analysis of variance that is unfocused, that is, that has more than a single *df* in the numerator of the *F* test. In most cases, unfocused *F*s address questions in which we are not really interested – questions of the form, Are there likely to be some differences of some kinds among some of the groups in our study? That is the kind of question we ask when we examine the decoding ability of judges at five age levels and report the *F* for age levels with 4 *df* in the numerator. Such unfocused *F* tests are very likely to lead to the conclusion that there are no real differences when it is quite likely that there actually are.

Contrasts. What is the alternative to the unfocused *F*? The focused *F* is an *F* of 1 *df* in the numerator. Some *F*s come that way – for example, any two groups – and the rest can be made to speak to us in focused fashion via a contrast (Rosenthal, 1979a; Snedecor & Cochran, 1967). In the example of comparing five age groups for nonverbal decoding ability, we might compute two contrasts: one for linear trend, and one for quadratic trend. The contrast for linear trend would tell us (with the possibility of an *F* 4 times as large as for the unfocused *F* test) whether decoding gets better or worse as people get older, a question of almost certain interest to the investigator. The quadratic trend contrast would tell us whether the older and younger groups tend to be more like each other than either is like the medium age groups. Not only do contrasts provide clearer answers to clearer questions, their consistent use often leads to improved experimental designs.

Variable reduction. What are we to do if we have a large number of dependent variables? Shouldn't we do some analyses that test "everything all at once," the various "multivariate" procedures? The principle of focused testing still applies, but we have the complication in some of the multivariate procedures that we cannot readily interpret just what the significant effect is. A practical and reasonable general procedure is to begin by reducing the total number of dependent variables to a smaller number by some procedure like cluster analysis, principal components, or factor analysis, and then treating the new "super variables" separately. Experience suggests that for most workaday purposes, refinements like weighting by factor loadings are not very robust. It seems preferable to employ unit weighting, that is, averaging the normalized variables that are to contribute to the super variable (see Dawes, 1979, for procedures very similar in spirit). The great advantage of variable reduction is that our new super variables are almost always behaviorally meaningful, and the tests of significance and effect-size estimations based on them are usually immediately interpretable.

Effect-size estimates

Every time an investigator reports an effect's level of significance, there is an associated magnitude of effect or effect size. This effect size should be reported routinely to give the reader a feeling for the size of the phenomenon under discussion. With small sample sizes, nonsignificant results can be quite large in terms of effect sizes, and with very large sample sizes, results that are just barely significant can be quite small in terms of effect size.

An excellent and detailed discussion of effect-size estimators is given by Cohen (1977), and I will note only two of them here; both have been widely used and are widely useful (H. Friedman, 1968; Rosenthal, 1979b, 1979c; Rosenthal & Rosnow, 1975b; Rosenthal & Rubin, 1978, 1979, in press). The first of these effect-size estimators is simply r, the Pearson product moment correlation. It can be estimated readily from an F test by the equation

$$r = \left(\frac{F}{F + df\ \text{error}} \right)^{1/2}$$

when df for the numerator of F is 1. It is to be hoped that that will almost always be the case. If df for the numerator of F is 2 or greater the equation becomes

$$\text{eta} = \left(\frac{(df\ \text{numerator})\ (F)}{(df\ \text{numerator})\ (F) + df\ \text{error}} \right)^{1/2}$$

where eta is the general index of correlation (i.e., not necessarily linear).

The second effect-size estimator (d), is defined by Cohen (1977) as the difference between the two group means divided by the standard deviation common to the two groups. The quantity

$$d = \frac{M_1 - M_2}{\sigma}$$

can usually be estimated from F with 1 df in the numerator by

$$d = \frac{2\sqrt{F}}{\sqrt{df_{\text{error}}}}$$

Finally we should note that d and r are related by

$$d = \frac{2r}{\sqrt{1 - r^2}} \quad \text{and} \quad r = \frac{d}{\sqrt{d^2 + 4}}$$

Summarizing research domains

Even after a well-done analysis of a judgment study, we are not quite finished. We will want to put our results into the context of other studies of that type. Our results may or may not agree with the results of these other studies that have been done. There is a growing literature suggesting how we may summarize the results of an entire series of studies with respect to effect-size estimation (Glass, 1976; Hall, 1979; Rosenthal & Rubin, 1978, 1979, 1981; Smith & Glass, 1977) and significance testing (Rosenthal, 1978; 1979b, 1979c); and some of this work has been brought together to facilitate its general use (Rosenthal, 1980).

The general principles are simple. For any area of research, we average the effect size for all the studies done, but with blocking on subtypes of study. We can then average the effect sizes, noting whether they vary greatly from block to block. The significance testing for a series of studies can be done in many ways. The easiest and most versatile is probably the method of adding Zs (Rosenthal, 1978).

For each of the studies we wish to summarize, we compute as accurate a p value as we can, always using a one-tail p. Each p is then transformed into its standard normal deviate equivalent (Z) by using standard tables. These Z values are always signed + if in the predicted direction, one-tail, and − if in the unpredicted direction, one-tail. The new Z associated with the p of the combined set of results is simply given by

$$Z = \frac{\Sigma Z}{\sqrt{n}}$$

That is, we add the signed Zs and divide that sum by the square root of the number of studies we are combining.

The systematic, quantitative assessment of the area of research in which we are interested has many benefits. It gives us a very strong basis for deciding about the null hypothesis if that is our interest; when done well, it gives us our best estimates of the importance of the effect, (e.g., Smith & Glass, 1977); it gives us indications of factors affecting the magnitude of the effect; it suggests where the research with the highest payoff might be; and finally, it reminds us that though our study is the most important judging study of all, it is likely, in the long run, to be one of a set of results, all of which, together, make the field move forward.

Acknowledgments

Preparation of this chapter was supported by the National Science Foundation and greatly influenced and improved by what I learned over the years from Bella M. DePaulo, Judith A. Hall, Donald B. Rubin, and Miron Zuckerman. Earlier drafts were read and improved by Rita Coleman, Bella DePaulo, Paul Ekman, Judy Hall, Klaus Scherer, and Miron Zuckerman.

References

Allport, F. H. *Social psychology*. Boston: Houghton Mifflin, 1924.

Argyle, M. *Bodily communication*. New York: International Universities Press, 1975.

Armor, D. J. Theta reliability and factor scaling. In H. L. Costner (Ed.) *Sociological methodology, 1973–1974*. San Francisco: Jossey-Bass, 1974.

Bem, S. L. The measurement of psychological androgyny. *Journal of Consulting and Clinical Psychology*, 1974, *42*, 155–162.

Brunswik, E. *Perception and the representative design of psychological experiments*. Berkeley & Los Angeles: University of California Press, 1956.

Buck, R. Nonverbal communication of affect in children. *Journal of Personality and Social Psychology*, 1975, *31*, 644–653.

Buck, R. Individual differences in nonverbal sending accuracy and electrodermal responding: The externalizing-internalizing dimension. In R. Rosenthal (Ed.), *Skill in nonverbal communication: Individual differences*. Cambridge, Mass.: Oelgeschlager, Gunn, & Hain, 1979.

Clark, H. H. The language-as-fixed-effect fallacy: A critique of language statistics in psychological research. *Journal of Verbal Learning and Verbal Behavior*, 1973, *12*, 335–359.

Cline, V. B. Interpersonal perception. In B.A. Maher (Ed.), *Progress in experimental personality research* (Vol. 1). New York: Academic Press, 1964.

Cohen, J. *Statistical power analysis for the behavioral sciences* (Rev. ed.). New York: Academic Press, 1977.

Cunningham, M. R. Personality and the structure of the nonverbal communication of emotion. *Journal of Personality*, 1977, *45*, 564–584.

Darwin, C. *The expression of the emotions in man and animals.* Chicago; University of Chicago Press, 1965. (Originally published, 1872.)

Davitz, J. R. *The communication of emotional meaning.* New York: McGraw-Hill, 1964.

Dawes, R. M. The robust beauty of improper linear models in decision making. *American Psychologist*, 1979, *34*, 571–582.

DePaulo, B. M., & Rosenthal, R. Ambivalence, discrepancy, and deception in nonverbal communication. In R. Rosenthal (Ed.), *Skill in nonverbal communication: Individual differences.* Cambridge, Mass.: Oelgeschlager, Gunn & Hain, 1979. (a)

DePaulo, B. M., & Rosenthal, R. Telling lies. *Journal of Personality and Social Psychology*, 1979, *37*, 1713–1722. (b)

DePaulo, B. M., & Rosenthal, R. Measuring the development of nonverbal sensivitity. In C. E. Izard (Ed.), *Measurement of emotions in infants and children.* New York: Cambridge University Press, in press.

DePaulo, B. M., Rosenthal, R., Eisenstat, R. A., Rogers, P. L., & Finkelstein, S. Decoding discrepant nonverbal cues. *Journal of Personality and Social Psychology*, 1978, *36*, 313–323.

DiMatteo, M. R. Nonverbal skill and the physician–patient relationship. In R. Rosenthal (Ed.). *Skill in nonverbal communication: Individual differences.* Cambridge, Mass.: Oelgeschlager, Gunn & Hain, 1979.

Ekman, P. Communication through nonverbal behavior: A source of information about an interpersonal relationship. In S. S. Tomkins and C. Izard (Eds.), *Affect, cognition and personality.* New York: Springer, 1965. (a).

Ekman, P. Differential communication of affect by head and body cues. *Journal of Personality and Social Psychology*, 1965, *2*, 725–735. (b)

Ekman, P. Cross-cultural studies of facial expression. In P. Ekman (Ed.), *Darwin and facial expression: A century of research in review.* New York: Academic Press, 1973.

Ekman, P., & Friesen, W. V. Nonverbal leakage and clues to deception. *Psychiatry*, 1969, *32*, 88–106.

Ekman, P. & Friesen, W. V. Detecting deception from the body or face. *Journal of Personality and Social Psychology*, 1974, *29*, 288–298.

Ekman, P., Friesen, W. V., & Ellsworth, P. *Emotion in the human face: Guidelines for research and an integration of findings.* New York: Pergamon Press, 1972.

Ekman, P., Friesen, W. V., & Scherer, K. R. Body movement and voice pitch in deceptive interaction. *Semiotica*, 1976, *16* (1), 23–27.

Friedman, H. Magnitude of experimental effect and a table for its rapid estimation. *Psychological Bulletin*, 1968, *70*, 245–251.

Friedman, H. S. *About face: The role of facial expressions of emotion in the verbal communication of meaning.* Unpublished doctoral dissertation, Harvard University, 1976.

Friedman, H. S. The relative strength of verbal versus nonverbal cues. *Personality and Social Psychology Bulletin*, 1978, *4*, 147–150.

Friedman, H. S. The interactive effects of facial expressions of emotion and verbal messages on perceptions of affective meaning. *Journal of Experimental Social Psychology*, 1979, *15*, 453–469. (a)

Friedman, H. S. The concept of skill in nonverbal communication: Implications for understanding social interaction. In R. Rosenthal, (Ed.), *Skill in nonverbal communication: Individual differences.* Cambridge, Mass.: Oelgeschlager, Gunn & Hain, 1979. (b)

Glass, G. V. *Primary, secondary, and meta-analysis of research.* Paper presented at the meeting of the American Educational Research Association, San Francisco, April 1976.

Green, B. F., & Tukey, J. W. Complex analyses of variance: General problems. *Psychometrika*, 1960, *25*, 127–152.
Guilford, J. P. *Psychometric methods* (2nd ed.). New York: McGraw-Hill, 1954.
Hall, J. A. Gender, gender-roles, and nonverbal communication skills. In R. Rosenthal (Ed.), *Skill in nonverbal communication: Individual differences*. Cambridge, Mass.: Oelgeschlager, Gunn & Hain, 1979.
Hall, J. A. Gender differences in nonverbal communication skill. In R. Rosenthal (Ed.), *New directions for methodology of vocal and behavioral science: Quantitative assessment of research domains*. San Francisco: Jossey-Bass, 1980, No. 5.
Hammond, K. R. Representative vs. systematic design in clinical psychology. *Psychological Bulletin*, 1954, *51*, 150–159.
Izard, C. E. *The face of emotion*. New York: Appleton-Century-Crofts, 1971.
Izard, C. E. *Human emotions*. New York: Plenum, 1977.
Kaplan, A. *The conduct of inquiry*. San Francisco: Chandler, 1964.
Knapp, M. L. *Nonverbal communication in human interaction* (2nd ed.). New York: Holt, Rinehart & Winston, 1978.
Littlepage, G., & Pineault, T. Verbal, facial, and paralinguistic cues to the detection of truth and lying. *Personality and Social Psychology Bulletin*, 1978, *4*, 461–464.
Maier, N. R. F., & Thurber, J. A. Accuracy of judgments of deception when an interview is watched, heard, and read. *Personnel Psychology*, 1968, *21*, 23–30.
Mehrabian, A. A semantic space for nonverbal behavior. *Journal of Consulting and Clinical Psychology*, 1970, *35*, 248–257.
Milmoe, S., Novey, M. S., Kagan, J., & Rosenthal, R. The mother's voice: Postdictor of aspects of her baby's behavior. *Proceedings of the 76th Annual Convention of the American Psychological Association*, 1968, pp. 463–464.
Milmoe, S., Rosenthal, R., Blane, H. T., Chafetz, M. E., & Wolf, I. The doctor's voice: Postdictor of successful referral of alcoholic patients. *Journal of Abnormal Psychology*, 1967, *72*, 78–84.
Mosteller, F. Association and estimation in contingency tables. *Journal of the American Statistical Association*, 1968, *63*, 1–28.
Mosteller, F., & Rourke, R. E. K. *Sturdy statistics*. Reading, Mass.: Addision-Wesley, 1973.
Nasby, W., DePaulo, B. M., & Hayden, B. *An attributional bias among aggressive boys to interpret unambiguous social stimuli as displays of hostility*. Unpublished manuscript, Harvard University, 1979.
Nunnally, J. C. *Psychometric theory* (2nd ed.). New York: McGraw-Hill, 1978.
Osgood, C. E. Dimensionality of the semantic space for communication via facial expressions. *Scandinavian Journal of Psychology*, 1966, *7*, 1–30.
Rogers, P. L., Scherer, K. R., & Rosenthal, R. Content-filtering human speech: A simple electronic system. *Behavior Research Methods and Instrumentation*, 1971, *3*, 16–18.
Rosenthal, R. The effect of the experimenter on the results of psychological research. In B. A. Maher (Ed.), *Progress in experimental personality research* (Vol. 1). New York: Academic Press, 1964.
Rosenthal, R. *Experimenter effects in behavioral research*. New York: Appleton-Century-Crofts, 1966.
Rosenthal, R. Covert communication in the psychological experiment. *Psychological Bulletin*, 1967, *67*, 356–367.
Rosenthal, R. Interpersonal expectations: Effects of the experimenter's hypothesis. In R. Rosenthal and R. L. Rosnow (Eds.), *Artifact in behavioral research*. New York: Academic Press, 1969.
Rosenthal, R. Estimating effective reliabilities in studies that employ judges' ratings. *Journal of Clinical Psychology*, 1973, *29*, 342–345.

Rosenthal, R. *On the social psychology of the self-fulfilling prophecy: Further evidence for Pygmalion effects and their mediating mechanisms* (Module 53). New York: MSS Modular Publications, 1974.

Rosenthal, R. *Experimenter effects in behavioral research* (Rev. ed.). New York, Irvington, 1976.

Rosenthal, R. Combining results of independent studies. *Psychological Bulletin*, 1978, *85*, 185–193.

Rosenthal, R. *Contrasts in behavioral research*. Unpublished manuscript, Harvard University, 1979. (a)

Rosenthal, R. The "file drawer problem" and tolerance for null results. *Psychological Bulletin*, 1979, *86*, 638–641. (b)

Rosenthal, R. Replications and their relative utilities. *Replications in Social Psychology*, 1979, *1*, 15–23. (c)

Rosenthal, R. (Ed.). *New directions for methodology of social and behavioral science: Quantitative assessment of research domains*. San Francisco: Jossey-Bass, 1980, No. 5.

Rosenthal, R., & DePaulo, B. M. Sex differences in accommodation in nonverbal communication. In R. Rosenthal (Ed.), *Skill in nonverbal communication: Individual differences*. Cambridge, Mass.: Oelgeschlager, Gunn & Hain, 1979.

Rosenthal, R. & DePaulo, B. M. Encoders vs decoders as units of analysis in research in nonverbal communication. *Journal of Nonverbal Behavior*, 1980, *5*, 92–103.

Rosenthal, R., Fode, K. L., Friedman, C. J., & Vikan, L. L. Subjects' perception of their experimenter under conditions of experimenter bias. *Perceptual and Motor Skills*, 1960, *11*, 325–331.

Rosenthal, R., Hall, J. A., DiMatteo, M. R., Rogers, P. L., & Archer, D. *Sensitivity to nonverbal communication: The PONS test*. Baltimore: Johns Hopkins University Press, 1979.

Rosenthal, R., Hall, J. A., & Zuckerman, M. The relative equivalence of senders in studies of nonverbal encoding and decoding. *Environmental Psychology and Nonverbal Behavior*, 1978, *2*, 161–166.

Rosenthal, R., & Jacobson, L. *Pygmalion in the classroom*. New York: Holt, Rinehart & Winston, 1968.

Rosenthal, R., & Rosnow, R. L. *Primer of methods for the behavioral sciences*. New York, Wiley, 1975. (a)

Rosenthal, R., & Rosnow, R. L. *The volunteer subject*. New York: Wiley-Interscience, 1975. (b)

Rosenthal, R., & Rubin, D. B. Interpersonal expectancy effects: The first 345 studies. *Behavioral and Brain Sciences*, 1978, *3*, 377–415.

Rosenthal, R., & Rubin, D. B. Comparing significance levels of independent studies. *Psychological Bulletin*, 1979, *86*, 1165–1168.

Rosenthal, R., & Rubin, D. B. A simple, general purpose display of magnitude of experimental effect. *Journal of Educational Psychology*, in press.

Scherer. K. R. *Non-verbale Kommunikation*. Hamburg: Helmut Buske Verlag, 1970.

Scherer, K. R. Randomized-splicing: A note on a simple technique for masking speech content. *Journal of Experimental Research in Personality*, 1971, *5*, 155–159.

Scherer, K. R. Personality inference from voice quality: The loud voice of extroversion. *European Journal of Social Psychology*, 1978, *8*, 467–487.

Scherer, K. R. Acoustic concomitants of emotional dimensions: Judging affect from synthesized tone sequences. In S. Weitz (Ed.), *Nonverbal communication: Readings with commentary* (2nd ed.). New York: Oxford University Press, 1979. (a)

Scherer, K. R. Voice and speech correlates of perceived social influence in simulated juries. In H. Giles & R. St. Clair (Eds.). *Language and social psychology*. Oxford: Basil Blackwell, 1979. (b)

Scherer, K. R., Koivumaki, J., & Rosenthal, R. Minimal cues in the vocal communication of affect: Judging emotions from content-masked speech. *Journal of Psycholinguistic Research*, 1972, *1*, 269–285.

Scherer, K. R., & Oshinsky, J. S. Cue utilization in emotion attribution from auditory stimuli. *Motivation and Emotion*, 1977, *1*, 331–346.

Scherer, K. R., Rosenthal, R., & Koivumaki, J. Mediating interpersonal expectancies via vocal cues: Differential speech intensity as a means of social influence. *European Journal of Social Psychology*, 1972, *2*, 163–175.

Scherer, K. R., Scherer, U., Hall, J. A., & Rosenthal, R. Differential attribution of personality based on multi-channel presentation of verbal and nonverbal cues. *Psychological Research*, 1977, *39*, 221–247.

Siegel, S. *Nonparametric statistics for the behavioral sciences*. New York: McGraw-Hill, 1956.

Smith, M. L., & Glass, G. V. Meta-analysis of psychotherapy outcome studies. *American Psychologist*, 1977, *32*, 752–760.

Snedecor, G. W., & Cochran, W. G. *Statistical methods* (6th ed.). Ames: Iowa State University Press, 1967.

Spence, J. T., & Helmreich, R. *Masculinity and femininity: Their psychological dimensions, correlates, and antecedents*. Austin: University of Texas Press, 1978.

Tomkins, S. S., & McCarter, R. What and where are the primary affects? Some evidence for a theory. *Perceptual and Motor Skills*, 1964, *18*, 119–158.

Tukey, J. W. *Exploratory data analysis*. Reading, Mass.: Addison-Wesley, 1977.

Uno, Y., Koivumaki, J. H., & Rosenthal, R. Unintended experimenter behavior as evaluated by Japanese and American observers. *Journal of Social Psychology*, 1972, *88*, 91–106.

Walker, H. M., & Lev, J. *Statistical inference*. New York: Henry Holt, 1953.

Weitz, S. Commentary. In R. Rosenthal (Ed.), *Skill in nonverbal communication: Individual differences*. Cambridge, Mass.: Oelgeschlager, Gunn & Hain, 1979.

Winer, B. J. *Statistical principles in experimental design* (2nd. ed.). New York: McGraw-Hill, 1971.

Zuckerman, M., DeFrank, R. S., Hall, J.A., Larrance, D. T., & Rosenthal, R. Facial and vocal cues of deception and honesty. *Journal of Experimental Social Psychology*, 1979, *15*, 378–396.

Zuckerman, M., Hall, J.A., DeFrank, R. S., & Rosenthal, R. Encoding and decoding of spontaneous and posed facial expressions. *Journal of Personality and Social Psychology*, 1976, *34*, 966–977.

Zuckerman, M., & Larrance, D. T. Individual differences in perceived encoding and decoding abilities. In R. Rosenthal (Ed.), *Skill in nonverbal communication: Individual differences*. Cambridge, Mass.: Oelgeschlager, Gunn & Hain, 1979.

Zuckerman, M., Larrance, D. T., Hall, J. A., DeFrank, R. S. & Rosenthal, R. Posed and spontaneous communication of emotion via facial and vocal cues. *Journal of Personality*, 1979, *47*, 712–733.

Zuckerman, M., Lipets, M. S., Koivumaki, J. H., & Rosenthal, R. Encoding and decoding nonverbal cues of emotion. *Journal of Personality and Social Psychology*, 1975, *32*, 1068–1076.

7. Categories and sequences of behavior: methods of description and analysis

J. A. R. A. M. VAN HOOFF

7.1. Introduction

Several times, in other chapters of this book, we have been reminded that behavior is structured and organized. Such statements sound almost like a tautology: Is not the active maintenance of an improbable structure the most characteristic aspect of all manifestations of life? Behavior is no exception. But because behavior is a process, rather than a material structure, its organization is an aspect of its transient nature. This organization is manifested in the patterning of movements and postures in space and in time.

Scientific endeavor seeks to describe this complex spatial and temporal structure objectively, to relate it to possible causes and effects, and, in so doing, to explain it in terms of its underlying principles, namely, the principles that organize and regulate the behavioral process. In order to achieve this aim we need to discover adequate quantitative methods. Various approaches have indeed been developed in recent years. In view of the complexity of the subject of investigation, however, it is not astonishing that some of the methods of analysis are not simple, and that many of the treatises on these methods do not make easy reading for the average student of behavior.

This difficulty has influenced the way in which I have chosen to treat the subject of the present chapter. A number of articles and books published in recent years give extensive, detailed surveys of the different methods and contain full references to the relevant literature (e.g., Cairns, 1977; Chatfield & Lemon, 1970; Colgan, 1978; Gottman, 1979; Gottman & Bakeman, 1979; Hazlett, 1977; Hinde & Stevenson, 1969; Hutt & Hutt, 1970; Kratochwill, 1978; Lamb, Suomi, & Stephenson, 1978; McFarland, 1974; Metz, 1974; Morgan, Simpson, Hanby, & Hall-Craggs, 1976; Sackett, 1977, 1978; Slater, 1973).

Another exhaustive review, therefore, hardly seemed warranted.

However, there is a need for an introductory survey of present methods, dealing with fundamental aspects. In this chapter an eclectic approach to the literature has been adopted, and simple illustrative numerical or graphical examples have been used instead of more concise mathematical notations. The focus of much of the work on the analysis of behavioral organization has been animal behavior; this is reflected in the examples selected here.

7.2. Behavior and behavioral interaction: a string of events in time

Behavior has been likened to a melody of movements and postures, adaptively composed to fulfill various requirements. The adequacy of these patterns is ultimately tested in their relative contribution to the propagation of an organism's genes. In many cases what promotes gene propagation promotes the survival of the organism (the notable exceptions being altruistic behaviors).

On closer examination the melody appears to consist of recurring themes and subthemes. These are made up of relatively invariant elementary patterns, which our Gestalt perception often recognizes easily, particularly in the behavior of our own species. Instances of such elementary patterns or acts are smiling, handshaking, shrugging, and so on. In other species we may recognize, for instance, zigzag dance, neighing, prancing, and the like. The ways in which we define these patterns objectively and precisely have not yet been worked out to everyone's satisfaction (see Rosenfeld, Section 5.5). I shall return to this matter in Section 7.3.

In this chapter the emphasis will be on the fact that these elementary patterns of movement and posture, which I shall call the *acts*, form a continuous string in time (an individual, whether animal or man, never does nothing). Again, our prescientific capacity to recognize patterns often tells us that these are not random strings. They are organized and therefore predictable. Our success as social beings in fact depends on our acuity in predicting and thus anticipating the behavior of our fellow creatures – a capacity that we share with practically all other animal forms. Scientific inquiry seeks to make the rules obtaining in these processes explicit and to explain them in terms of general underlying principles. This is an exercise consisting of two interacting approaches.

The first approach to understanding the organization or structure of behavior is to describe the patterns of the chains and detect laws of association. Although such descriptive analysis is of course guided by a priori concepts, on the whole one can do such analysis without paying attention to the specific factors that cause the associations and the consecutive steps in the behavioral chain. Descriptive knowledge automatically leads to the second approach and, indeed, directs it. This approach has to do with the "working" of behavior, in that it seeks to reveal the principles underlying the interaction of factors inside and outside the organism, and the programming structures in the organism. This chapter will focus on the descriptive analytical tools currently available.

The study of the organization of behavior can move in two directions. The first direction is guided by questions concerned with the sequential dependencies in the behavioral stream. Given a certain act, there are quite specific probabilities that consecutive acts will occur, and it is the nature and degree of these dependencies that one would like to reveal. This approach involves analyzing the behavioral flow (see Section 7.4) and can lead to the use of specific models for describing this flow. An obvious example is treatment of the behavioral flow as if it were a Markov chain[1] and application of information-theoretical approaches (see Section 7.6). The constraints in the behavioral flow have appeared to be more complex than can be accounted for by a Markov chain model, however. To accommodate these complexities, so-called grammatical models have been applied (see Section 7.8). The Markov model disregards the possible influence on the interdependencies of behavioral events of time factors such as the durations of events and the intervals between them. Various methods dealing with these aspects are discussed in Section 7.7.

Those who concentrate on the analysis of the interdependencies in the behavioral stream may treat this stream in one of two ways. They may restrict themselves to examining sequences within a particular individual. This choice does not necessarily indicate that they underestimate the influence of external factors, the most important of which may be the contiguous stream of behavior of fellow members of the species. For the time being they simply do not take into account these social influences and many other potential influences. Other people are particularly fascinated by social influences on behavior, as typified by communication, and seek to reveal the nature and extent of these influences (see also Scherer & Ekman, Section 1.1). To this end they take into account the behavioral streams of two interacting individuals by considering the acts of the two as elements of one string. Various ways in which this can be done will be treated at some length in this chapter.

The second direction taken in the study of behavioral organization is influenced by the notion that behavior can be regarded as a system of many different routines. Each routine consists of a set of acts, coordinated as instruments for the performance of a certain function. The adequacy of the performance of such a function is determined by whether or not it yields adaptive effects. This question is ultimately subject to the "judgment" of natural selection; and so, therefore, is the programming, that is, the causal mechanism that evokes specific acts at certain points in the routine. It is helpful if one thinks of the organization of the behavioral system as being hierarchical, as suggested by Tinbergen (1951) and Kortlandt (1955), and stressed more recently by Dawkins (1976). The essential implication of regarding behavior as a hierarchical set of functions is as follows: If circumstances call for the performance of a certain function, the presence or absence of specific aspects of these circumstances may determine which specific adjustments or subroutines will occur, and in the case of a multilevel hierarchy even more specific subroutines may be called for. More concretely: If I set out to make an omelet, I have to perform a number of acts, such as getting the eggs from the refrigerator and lighting the oven (unless it is lit already); in order to light the oven I may have to embark on the subroutine of finding matches in the drawer; if none are to be found there, I may have to go out to buy some, and therefore may have to fetch the bicycle, perhaps blow up the tires, and so on (see also Bindra, 1976, for a discussion of the articulation of planned action).

We end up with a model in which acts tend to occur in hierarchically nested series of specific clusters and subclusters. As these clusters will involve a number of behavioral elements occurring in close contingency over a certain period of time, a suitable way of revealing these behavioral clusters or categories, starting from behavior protocols, will be to analyze the temporal contingencies of behavior elements. If we succeed in recognizing such clusters, we can arrive at a more economical description of the ongoing behavior, namely, one using molar functional units instead of the molecular behavioral elements or acts. Use of such global units makes it feasible to record complex behavioral processes, such as polyadic social interactions (e.g., de Waal, 1978).

7.3. How to delimit behavior events and sample them

Behavior presents itself as a sequence of postures and movements. These are in fact patterns of effector states, which follow each other in time. The problem is whether we can objectively define the basic elements that constitute the stream. Can we delimit certain types of events or acts?

Among the behavioral sciences the discipline of ethology has always been most concerned with the description of natural behavior as the basis for further investigations into the causal and functional organization of behavior. The problems involved in such descriptions are well known. Nevertheless, ethological research does not seem to have been greatly hindered by these problems. Usually the ethography has been presented in a matter-of-fact style and the investigator has relied implicitly on his Gestalt-perceptive ability to form the right categories (Lorenz, 1967).

The less discrete the motor patterns are and the more variation they show, the greater the need for formal criteria to delimit them. This is especially true in the case of the expressive behavior of certain higher animals (see, e.g., Marler, 1959, 1965) and notably of our own species. Particularly in areas of behavior such as facial and vocal nonverbal expression, discreteness of patterns is the exception rather than the rule. Different structures, such as the elements of the face, can move partly or wholly independently; simultaneous combination of such behavioral components can result in a considerable number of patterns. The problems associated with the delimitation of expressive behavior have been treated at length in other chapters of this book (see Ekman, Chapter 2; Rosenfeld, Chapter 5).

One of the proposed methods for obtaining an objective classification is to represent every component as a vector in multidimensional space. The behavior pattern at any given time then is a multidimensional vector state, and the behavior is the succession of such vector states in time. Multidimensional-analysis methods, such as multidimensional scaling and cluster analysis (see Section 7.5) make it possible to discover certain modal clusters, that is, combinations that occur comparatively frequently. This method has been worked out by, for instance, Golani (1973, 1976) and Davies (1978).

In principle the modal combinations could be treated as the acts constituting the behavioral repertoire, and thus these separate consecutive acts could be regarded as being mutually exclusive events. Such a description may be necessary, because some of the analytical tools that I am going to discuss (e.g., Markovian and information-statistical methods: see Section 7.6) demand that events in a sequence be discrete and mutually exclusive. In practice, this is not always feasible. Bakeman (1978) shows the difficulty by pointing to descriptions of social interactions by Gottman. These descriptions emphasize the composite nature of such interactions and show that many aspects of behavior occur in parallel. Although the tools should of course be adapted to the problem, and not vice versa, one may be forced to make slight concessions in the ethography; for instance, one might treat simultaneously occurring patterns as if they were exclusive and followed each other mutually. The possible consequences of resulting artificialities should be borne in mind, however.

An important aspect in which units of behavior may differ is in their duration. Some units, such as a bark signaling alarm, have a duration of the same order of magnitude as the time-resolution scale that will be used for most purposes. One could call such a unit a *point event*. The incidence of point events is measured by frequency counts.

Other units, such as sleeping or grooming (e.g., in the case of a monkey), can last for various lengths of time. In the case of grooming, one might question whether it is an appropriate natural unit, because it can be split up into a number of molecular components, such as the hand and finger movements of the searching pattern (note that the term *searching pattern* expresses the fact that the elementary movements are coordinated in a rather stereotyped way that we recognize as a functional subroutine), the movements involved in swallowing the particles found, and so on. If the unit is split up it is reduced to its components, each of which can be treated as a point event. Again, the question whether such an approach is appropriate will depend on the scope of the analysis. If, however, it seems more sensible to treat the whole grooming pattern as a natural unit, then this unit will be a *lasting event*, and it may then be desirable to take its real-time duration into account as an additional variable.

The way in which the behavior is sampled depends on the recording possibilities available and should be guided by the kind of analysis that is wanted. J. Altmann (1974) has discussed the methods available at length; a summary can be found in Slater (1978). It may be sufficient, therefore, if I simply present a figure adapted from Slater, which illustrates that the type of sampling method is not without its consequences (Figure 7.1). The methods illustrated are *event-based* (time enters only in the form of discrete units, such as fixed sampling intervals). Some other kinds of sampling methods make use of real-time measurements (durations, intervals); recording these is much more complicated.

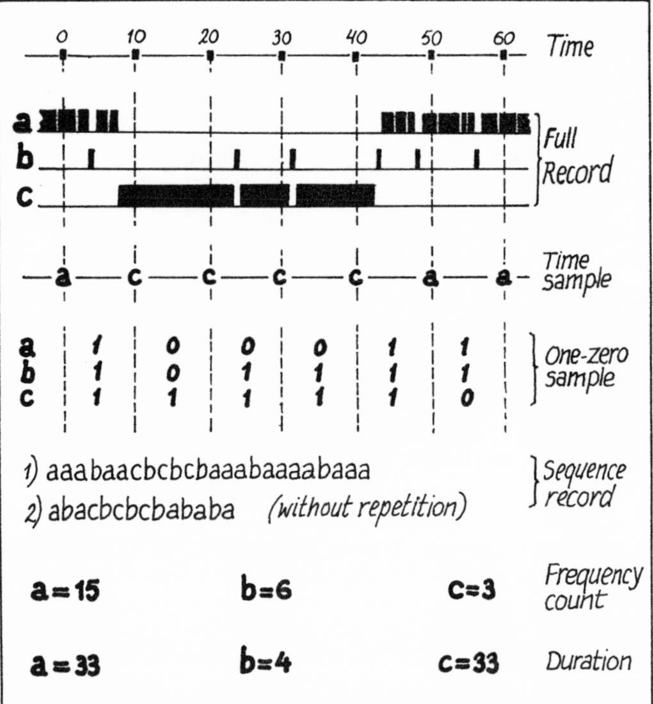

Figure 7.1. A few well-known methods of behavior sampling are applied to an imaginary behavior record to demonstrate the remarkable differences in the data structure obtain. *Source:* Adapted from Slater, 1978.

7.4. Sequential analysis: transition frequencies and behavior path diagrams

Patterns of transition frequencies

One of the classic and best-known schemes of behavioral process is that given by Tinbergen (1951) for the courtship behavior of the three-spined stickleback (Figure 7.2). It is in fact an interaction scheme. If every stickleback courtship sequence ran exactly like this, that is, if a given behavior element were *always* followed by another particular one, the process would be a deterministic sequence. Examples of such sequences are hard to find in animal behavior, particularly at a molar level, and this is certainly not one. In this case the *typical* sequence was inferred from numerous observations of actual sequences, many of which differed

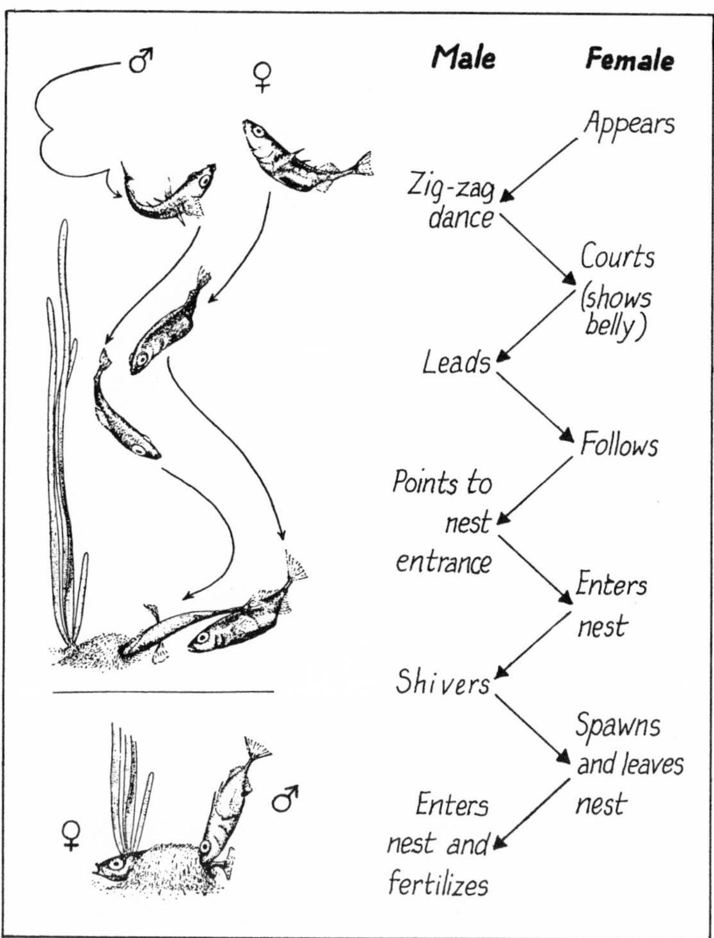

Figure 7.2. The classic example of a diagram of a typical interaction sequence is the one by Tinbergen (1951), showing the behaviors of a male three-spined stickleback in a reproductive mood and of a "ripe" female visiting his nesting territory.

because elements were omitted or repeated or the order was reversed. In other words, the behavioral contingencies turn out to be of a stochastic nature.

The empirical basis of a sequential analysis is a behavior protocol of many actual sequences. The transitions between elements can be scored in a transition frequency matrix; the row entries are, for instance, the preceding acts, and the column entries the succeeding acts (Figure 7.3). If the number of acts is not too large, one can begin to obtain some insight into the sequential organization from a pathway diagram.

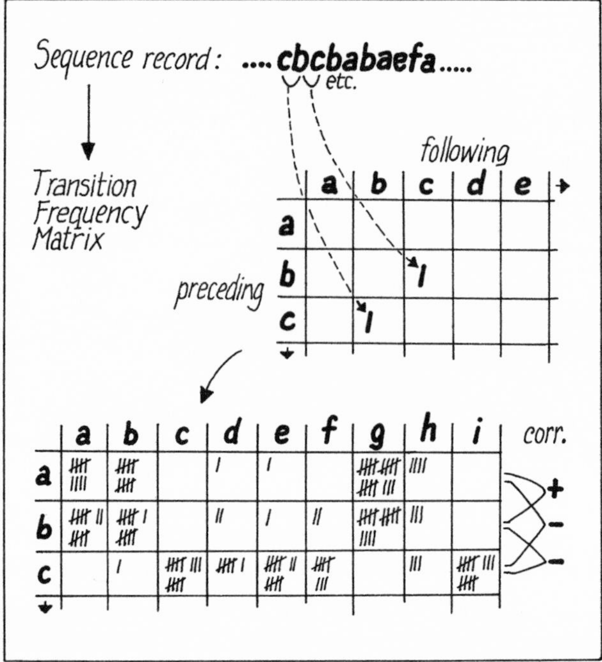

Figure 7.3. Schematic representation of the procedure of constructing a transition frequency matrix.

Sustare (1978), who has made a systematic survey of the ways in which aspects of the structure of behavior (and also social relations) can be presented visibly in the form of a diagram, calls such path diagrams kinematic graphs and gives several examples of their use in ethology. One possibility is an *auto-action path,* for the sequence of behavior elements in one animal. Such we have in the case of the distribution of transitions in the male ten-spined stickleback, as measured by Morris (1958) and portrayed in Figure 7.4. We can also have an *interaction path* for the sequence of alternating behavior elements of two interacting individuals. An instance is the palm diagram shown in Figure 7.2. In this case we have an "idealized" or typical path, arrived at by reducing the path diagram to the modal transition per behavior element. Another well-known example of such an auto-action path is the one given by Baerends, Brouwer, and Waterbolk (1955) for the courting behavior of the male guppy (Figure 7.5).

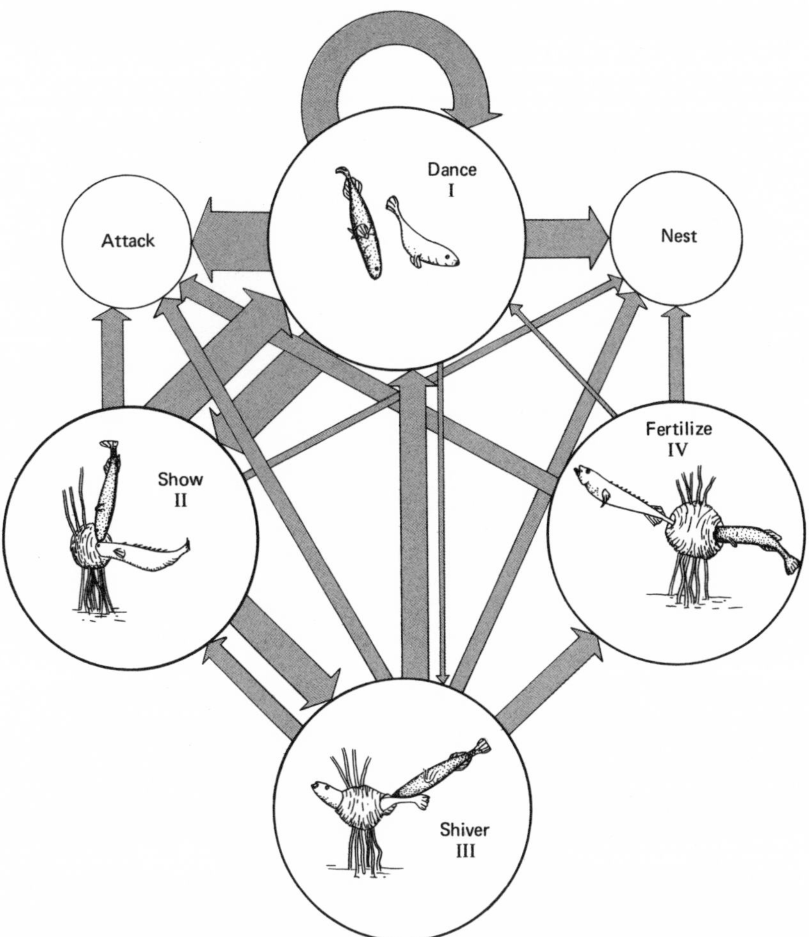

Figure 7.4. A kinematic graph of the sequence of activities shown by a male ten-spined stickleback in a reproductive mood (as shown by his black color) toward a female entering his territory. The width of an arrow represents the number of times a transition between two acts has been observed. *Source:* Marler and Hamilton, 1966, p. 191, based on data from Morris, 1958.

Comparison of the actual transitions with the random transition pattern

The representation rendered by the methods just noted is illuminating as long as the frequencies of the acts are not too different. Otherwise, these methods do not allow us to assess the relative importance of the transitions precisely. If the acts occur with differing frequencies (as is

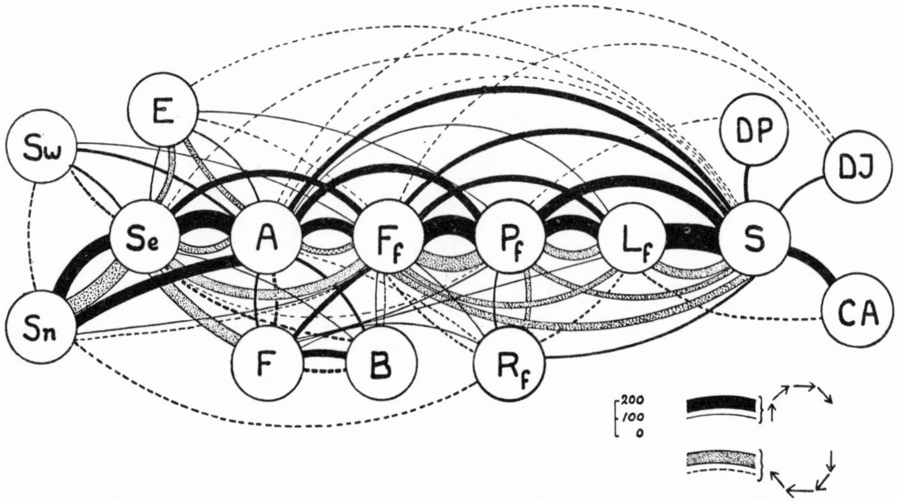

Figure 7.5. A kinematic graph of the courting behaviour of the male guppy. Black bands and continuous lines indicate transitions from the left to the right; hatched bands and dotted lines show transitions from the right to the left. The thickness of the bands indicates the frequency of the transitions. *Source:* Baerends, Brouwer, and Waterbolk, 1955, p. 262.

generally the case), then we may expect, on the basis of random combination, that there will be many transitions between frequently occurring elements and few between rarely occurring elements.

The way to overcome this problem is to compare the distribution of obtained transition frequencies with the distribution expected when the total frequencies of occurrence of the behavior elements are given. As a rule, the expected transition between two behavior elements is equal to the product of the respective row and column total in the transition matrix, divided by the sum total of transitions between all elements. In conventional notation:

$$e_{ij} = (o_{i*} \times o_{*j})/o_{**}$$

Once the values that can be expected on the basis of a random assocation of variables are known, it is of interest to investigate the extent to which the pattern found deviates from the pattern expected. Quantitative procedures that may be used have recently been reviewed at length in Colgan (1978), particularly in the contributions by Fagen and Young and by Colgan and Smith. A transition matrix differs from a contingency table *sensu stricto*, in that a behavior element enters it twice, first as the succeeding unit in a combination and next as the preceding unit in a new combination. Yet, for practical purposes, it can be treated as a contingency table and can be subjected to statistical procedures such as χ^2 (Bartlett, 1951, cited in Slater, 1973). Methods for analyzing such tables have recently been presented in a concise and very comprehensible manner by Everitt (1977).

A first general test will certainly show that there is strong dependence, that is, that the actual behavior is, on the average, strongly influenced by the behavior immediately preceding it, because the transition matrix as a whole differs significantly from a random pattern.

We can obtain more detailed information about the structure of the behavior if we can identify the transition categories that explain this dependence, in other words, if we can establish whether the dependence is restricted to certain parts or to particular cells of the transition matrix. Various methods have been suggested for extracting this kind of information from matrices, some of which are discussed briefly by Everitt (1977). A very suitable method is the analysis of residuals, as suggested by Haberman (1973). We can express both the degree to which and the direction in which an observed transition frequency (o) deviates from that expected (e) by the following quotient:

$$q_{ij} = (o_{ij} - e_{ij})/\sqrt{e_{ij}}$$

The quotient is called the *standardized residual*, and an estimate of its variance is given by

$$v_{ij} = (1 - o_{i*}/o_{**})(1 - 0_{*j}/o_{**})$$

For each cell in the matrix we can now compute a so-called *adjusted residual:*

$$d_{ij} = q_{ij}/\sqrt{v_{ij}}$$

This is a normal deviate, and the significance of the dependence as expressed in q can be found in the tables of the normal distribution. A positive, statistically significant value for q indicates that an act facilitates or drives the other act concerned; a negative value indicates that the act inhibits the other act.

The inspection of first-order residuals

The results of the analysis just described can be summarized in a kinematic representation. The example given in Figure 7.6 illustrates the suggestive nature of such kinematographs. First of all, it shows that the behavior elements arrange themselves in groups or clusters the elements of which have more transition connections with each other than with "outsiders." On the basis of some functionally unambiguous elements, such groups can be recognized as functional systems in the sense discussed previously. One of the clearest groupings in this case is the one in the lower left corner, which has been identified as the system of social play behavior.

Secondly, the representation shows that some clusters have more unidirectional behavior flow than others. Thus in the play system all transition connections are bidirectional (in other words, that particular section of the transition matrix is very symmetrical), and most of the elements are interconnected. The simplest explanation for this is that the elements can follow each other in almost any order. In other sectors of the graph we find indications that sequences have a stronger unidirectional structure. This finding is supported by evidence that certain behavior elements tend to figure more often at the beginning of sequences of social behavior elements, whereas others occur more frequently at the end. Some elements are like spiders in a web, at the hub of many outgoing arrows, situated between clusters that otherwise have few connections. An example of such an element is *smooth approach.* Being a "beginner" of strings of social behavior elements, this element obviously is an instrumental act in different functional systems. In this respect its position differs clearly from that of displays such as *grunt bark* or *shrill bark,* which, therefore, are likely to carry much more specific meanings.

This type of analysis and its kinematographic representation have their limitations as tools for obtaining information about the structure of the behavior. One limitation is that, although the graph suggests the existence of certain sequential patterns, these cannot show up clearly in this kind of representation, because it is based solely on the estimated probability of the transition of a behavior element to its immediate successor. One cannot deduce from such an analysis whether the probability of this transition is also dependent on what has taken place before. S. B. Altmann (1965), however, has shown that if higher-order conditional probabilities are investigated, more stereotyped sequences may be revealed. Such matters are being tackled by more sophisticated

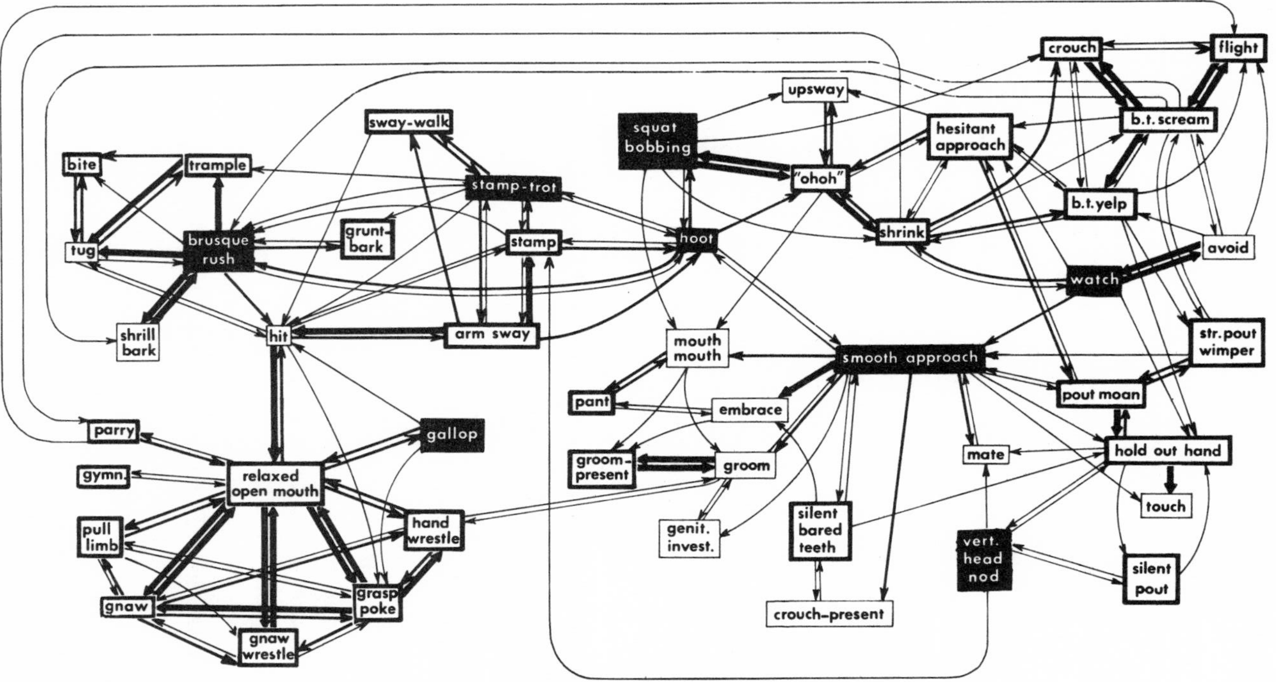

Figure 7.6. Kinematic graph of the principal within-animal transition during chimpanzee social interaction. Thick arrows correspond to a standardized residual $(q) > 15$, medium arrows to $q > 10$, and thin arrows to $q > 5$. Elements that tend to occur at the beginning of sequences of social interaction are set in a black frame; finishers are in a frame with a thin border; and elements that are not significantly more often beginners than finishers (and vice versa) are in a frame with a thick black border. *Source:* van Hooff, 1971, 1973.

methods, to which I shall return. Thus the behavior is being approached as if it were a Markov process. In order to characterize the degree of information transmitted in social communication systems, information-theoretical methods have been applied. Because the real world has appeared to be more complex than can be accounted for with the Markovian models underlying these methods, people dissatisfied with such models have gone on looking for methods that will provide a better representation of the aspects that interest them. This search has stimulated the development and application of, for instance, grammar models and semi-Markov models, described later.

Sample size and small expected frequencies. Some consideration should be given to sample size and small expected frequencies. Let us take sample size first. Fagen and Young (1978) report on recent simulation studies in which Fagen determined the minimum sample size required for assessing the significance of single cells in a matrix and for applying the information-theoretical approach, to be discussed shortly. If the number of behavior elements (the repertoire size) is R, then a sample of 10 R^2 behavioral acts would certainly be sufficient, 5 R^2 would be a borderline case, and 2 R^2 would definitely be unsuitable.

Everybody is familiar with the condition that the χ^2 statistic should not be applied if the expected values are too small. Generally a minimum value of 5 is recommended. A number of authors have investigated the validity of this condition (see Everitt, 1977, for a short summary and references) and have found that the rule is extremely conservative. Minimum values of even 0.5 appear to be generally acceptable, especially in the case of larger tables.

Note, too, that the nature of these statistics implies that a greater number of significant transitions will be found as the sample size increases, and that with smaller sample sizes, significant transitions in which a rare element is involved will have a comparatively greater chance of going unnoticed. Fagen and Young (1978) therefore emphasize that this method does not completely specify the true transition structure of the behavior, although it does indicate the predominant dependencies.

Treatment of the diagonal cells of the transition matrix. The computation just presented does not distinguish between the cells on the descending diagonal of the matrix and the other cells. The values in the diagonal cells (o_{ij} *for* $i = j$) refer to transitions of a behavior element from itself to itself, that is, repetitions of the same act.

In chimpanzee social behavior a gesture like *hold out hand* rarely lasts more than a few seconds, but it may be repeated after a short interval in the course of the same interaction. It can therefore be considered as a point event, and it would not be illogical to indicate in scoring that the element was preceded and succeeded by itself. By contrast, elements like *relaxed open mouth* or *play face* may last for some time and accompany a sequence of other elements, such as *gnaw-wrestling, hitting, gnawing, grasping, poking,* and so on. The problem of scoring transitions in simultaneous events can be partially avoided if one defines the behavioral elements in such a way that each combination of *relaxed open mouth,* say, with a different act is regarded as a separate, distinct element. This approach leads to a considerable increase in the number of behavioral variables, a problem that has been treated before. If, however, *relaxed open mouth* is considered as a separate unit, then whenever an accompanying element changes into another accompanying element, a transition can be considered to occur not only between the respective accompanying elements, but also between the *relaxed open mouth* and the succeeding accompanying element.

When van Hooff (1971) adopted this procedure he was confronted with the problem of whether at such a juncture in the behavioral stream *relaxed open mouth* should also be considered to pass into itself once. When he scored these auto-transitions, most of the diagonal transition frequencies turned out to be extremely high. Because of the arbitrariness involved and because it is wise to keep separate the issue of temporal contingencies of different acts and the issue of the durations and repetitiveness of acts, van Hooff decided to neglect the observed values of the diagonal entries altogether and to treat these as zero entries. The problem of the diagonal values has been treated in detail by Slater in his 1973 review of sequential analysis. Numerical examples presented in that review show that a high diagonal value enhances the expected values in the off-diagonal cells of the corresponding row and column; this increase is compensated by a decrease in the expected values in the other off-diagonal cells. Needless to say, this result can have a pronounced effect on which transitions are judged to be significant. The effect will be less marked the greater the dimension of the matrix. Slater found that for most of the transition matrices published in the literature, the act definitions were such that the descending diagonal cells did in fact reach high values.

Therefore, the values on the descending diagonal should preferably remain zero. But in order for them to do so, the computation of expected values should be modified: (1) The expected value in the descending diagonal cells should also be set to zero, and (2) the expected value that would have been obtained for a diagonal cell by the conventional computation should be distributed proportionally over the off-diagonal cells of the row and column concerned; this distribution ensures that the sum and column totals once more add up to their correct observed values. This is a complex computation that can be performed properly only by means of an iterative procedure; such a procedure has been presented by Goodman (1968). Lemon and Chatfield (1971) derived a computationally simpler solution for the estimation of e_{ij}:

$$e_{ij} = o_{i*} \times o_{*j}/(o_{**} - o_{j*})$$

This is the product of the relevant row and column totals, divided by the difference of the sum total and the row total of the same rank as the respective column. This solution, however, does not quite fulfill the above-mentioned condition (2). It yields expected values that differ increasingly from those obtained by means of the iterative method as the difference between the column and row totals increases.

Slater (1973) found that many researchers who had set their diagonal entries to zero did not apply these corrections. Such corrections matter if the matrices are small. When the dimension of the matrix increases, the corrections become less important, and in the case of the 53 × 53 matrix used by van Hooff (1971, 1973), the influence of the correction appeared to be negligible. However, because the correction is computationally simple, its use is always advisable. It should also be applied when, because of physical impossibility or for reasons of definition, one behavior simply cannot follow another. Slater and Ollason (1972), in a study of the temporal organization of the behavior of zebra finches kept in solitude, used behavioral units such as *feeding, drinking,* and *locomotion.* Because the feeding and drinking bowls were at different spots, *locomotion,* at least, had to occur between *feeding* and *drinking,* and their transition was a logical zero. The treatment of logical zeros has been considered extensively in Bishop, Fienberg, and Holland (1975, chap. 5).

Slater and Ollason's example offers a simple illustration of the influence the definition and selection of behavior units can have on the model that one obtains. If one were interested in revealing the extent to which eating and drinking, compared with other behavior patterns, are temporally contingent, one could, for instance, have circumvented the problem by selecting more molar inclusive behavior units, such as *go and feed* and *go and drink.*

7.5. Categories of behavior

In the instances just discussed, the emphasis was on the analysis of the sequential dependencies in the stream of behavior. As I have mentioned already, it is possible to regard behavior as a hierarchical system of functions.

Each of these functional subsystems mobilizes certain behavior elements, organizing them in adaptive patterns on the basis of internal programming rules that do not operate blindly but take account of the information fed into or fed back from the external situation. The concepts *behavior element* and *behavior system* as used in ethology (see Baerends, 1976) roughly correspond to the concepts *acts* and *actions* as used in psychology (e.g., Bindra, 1976).

In the lower animals, many acts or behavior elements are clearly connected with certain actions or functional systems; so they can even be used as unambiguous parameters for the activation of such systems. In the stickleback, for instance, the functional connection of such elementary patterns as *gluing, digging,* or *zigzag dance* is unambiguous. In higher animals, particularly in man, such exclusive connections of a particular motor pattern (act) with a specific function are less prevalent. And such connections as do exist tend to get lost if a molecular description of the behavior is used. This applies particularly to elementary acts that are used in some technical context; one and the same act may be incorporated in diverse actions or functional routines. Thus the elementary pattern *grasping* as such has a purely restricted immediate functional implication; knowledge about the functional role of the pattern is obtained if more is known about the way in which it is integrated with other elementary patterns and about contextual aspects of the behavioral syndrome. More direct connections are probably found in the case of those acts whose primary role is in direct social interaction and emotional expression. The functional associations evoked by terms such as, for instance, *smiling* or *shaking a fist* are illustrative.

In the kinematograph given for the social behavior elements of the chimpanzee (Figure 7.6), certain groupings that might represent functional systems can be seen. However, it should be realized that the picture is based on the most significant transitions, which constitute only 6% of the total number (2,756) of possible combinations in the relevant matrix of transition frequencies. So rather limited use is made of the available information. Besides, the transitions that occur significantly *less* often than expected by chance are not represented at all. Finally, the present simple two-dimensional representation fails to accommodate all the relations properly; obviously, if we are to depict this system of temporal proximities in a system of spatial proximities, we shall need more dimensions.

Multivariate analysis of temporal relationships

Two actions often used in the same functional context may show up in the temporal contingencies of the behavior in two fundamentally different ways: First, one may follow the other rather consistently, with a higher frequency than expected; we shall refer to this as the aspect of *association*. Secondly, they may be alternative choices for the execution of certain functions; they may occupy a similar position in the organization of behavior (the aspect of *embeddedness*). For instance, filling a cup from the tap and scooping up water with the hands from a stream may both occur as a preliminary to drinking. Specific differing aspects in the context determine which of two subroutines the individual selects, but the fact that they occur at all is a result of causal factors common to both subroutines; these are concerned with the fact that the water balance of the organism deviates from the norm, and regulation processes to adjust this imbalance are activated. This means that these acts will rarely, if ever, follow each other. So the transition frequency of one of these acts into the other will be much lower than is expected on the basis of random combination. However, each will be *embedded* between other elementary patterns in a similar way, so that the *pattern* of their transitions to other elements will be correlated (see Baerends, 1976: Dawkins, 1976; Dawkins & Dawkins, 1976).

For this reason, in a classical study of the reproductive behavior of a freshwater fish, the bitterling, Wiepkema (1961) computed the correlations between the patterns of transition frequencies of each pair of social behavior elements shown during the reproductive period. In fact, he did not use the absolute transition frequencies, but used instead the index *o/e*, that is, the quotient of the observed transition frequency *(o)* and that frequency expected *(e)* on the basis of chance. His reasoning was that the different behavior elements did not appear to occur with the same frequency. Therefore, even random combination would have yielded high transition frequencies between frequently occurring elements, and low transition frequencies between rarely occurring elements. In order to avoid such a source of covariance, he used the quotient *o*/e.

Principal-component analysis of profiles of temporal contingency. Wiepkema (1961) expected that the different behavior elements would represent a limited number of functional systems. Previous ethological investigations carried out on a number of species led him to expect at least two major systems in the reproductive behavior in the territorial species he investigated, one representing a sexual and the other an aggressive attitude. Such systems or sets would be revealed by the fact that its member elements distinguish themselves from the other acts by their high mutual correlations; that is, they share an appreciable amount of common variance.

Principal-component analysis is a very suitable means for discovering dimensions of common variance in a set of mutual correlations. The method accounts for the intercorrelations of the variables in terms of a more restricted number of independent common factors that refer to underlying hypothetical sources of influence. It is a kind of factor analysis, but this differs from factor analysis in the strict sense in that it does not imply any a priori assumptions concerning the covariance structure, particularly concerning the existence of error variance.

Factor analysis is fairly widely known now, and there are a large number of fundamental and introductory textbooks to which the reader is referred for particulars (e.g., Comrey, 1973; Harman, 1967; Harris, 1975; Kim, 1975; Maxwell, 1977; Rummel, 1970; Ueberla, 1971).

From this material, Wiepkema extracted three principal components (see Figure 7.7), which explained the major part of the variance (namely, 90%). The degree to which the different acts were correlated with these components, in other words, the extent to which they were influenced by these common sources of variations, was found to be in substantial agreement with information obtained via other methods.

The method first used in this way by Wiepkema has since been applied by several other workers, not all of whom achieved equally satisfactory results. Thus, Burton (1970) and Balthazart (1972) studied combat behavior of male cichlid fishes of the genus *Tilapia* in order to establish whether factor analysis would explain the behavior elements shown during combat sequences as the expression of two major tendencies, namely, the tendencies to attack and to flee. The structure revealed was judged to be insufficiently in agreement with the a priori hypotheses for this species, which was already comparatively well known ethologically. Although the appearance of a clear attack component and flight component was in accordance with expectations, there was a substantial third component that could not be interpreted. Balthazart reported that the distributions of the transitions in his matrices were extremely skewed and that there were many zero cells. This indicates that the studied behavior had a rather strict sequential organization,

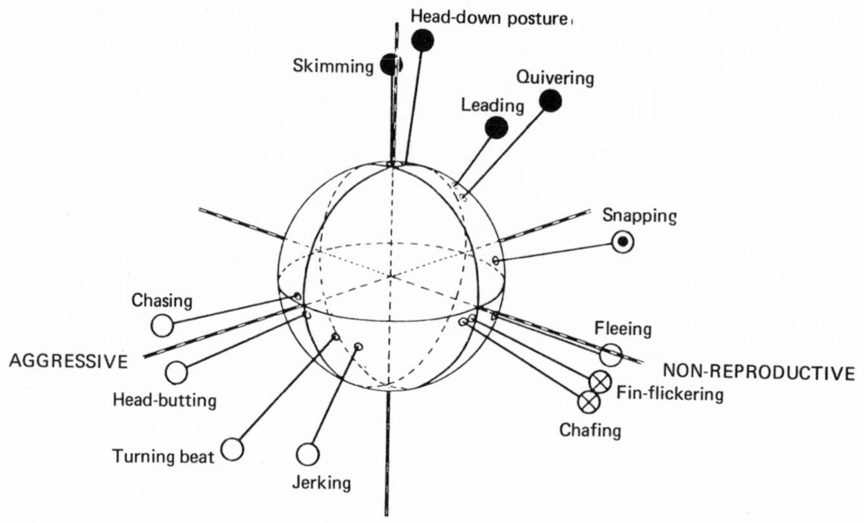

Figure 7.7. The results of a principal-component analysis of the transition patterns of the acts shown by a male bitterling in the reproductive situation. The acts have been arranged as vectors in space in such a manner that the cosine of the angle between any two of them is equal to the correlation of their transition patterns. Therefore, uncorrelated acts are at right angles, negatively correlated acts point into opposite directions, and positively correlated acts point in the same direction. To accommodate n acts in this way, n dimensions would be needed. However, if a number of acts are highly correlated, they will form a narrow vector bundle in this space. The analysis searches for those dimensions in the space in which the densest bundles lie, and it reduces the space to these main dimensions, projecting all vectors in these dimensions. The length of vector in the model indicates how large its projection is in the reduced space, that is, how well it can be explained in the resulting dimension components. *Source:* Adapted from Wiepkema, 1961.

which would be revealed better by studying the aspect of association than by considering that of embeddedness. From the author's comments it would seem that he did not quite distinguish these two aspects of organization and expected to reveal the association aspects by using a method directed at embeddedness. In 1973, Balthazart reported on a continuation study in which he had made use of the other measures of temporal contingency, namely, the frequency and duration of the behavior elements in arbitrarily chosen units of time (see Figure 7.8). He computed the correlation between the frequencies of two behavior elements over these units of time. This method is in fact a hybrid;

BEHAVIOR RECORD

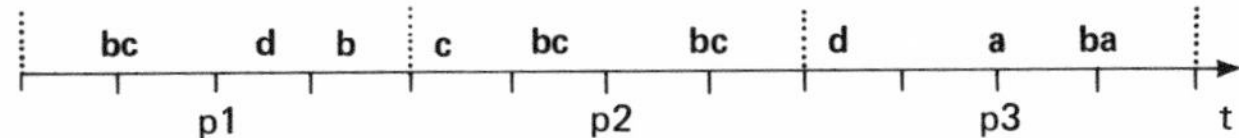

1. TRANSITION FREQUENCIES (A) and NEIGHBORSHIP FREQUENCIES (B); the latter is a symmetrical version of A. See also Figure 3.

(A)

	a	b	c	d
a	/	I		
b	I	/	IIII	
c		II	/	II
d	I	I		/

Corr.

(B)

	a	b	c	d
a	/	2		1
b	2	/	6	1
c		6	/	
d	1	1		/

Corr.

2. FREQUENCIES PER PERIOD. The record is divided into "periods" or "time bins" (p1, p2, p3 . . . pn): Frequencies (or durations) of acts per time bin are scored in a matrix.

	p1	p2	p3	-----	pn
a	0	0	2		...
b	2	2	1		...
c	1	3	0		...
d	1	0	1		...

Corr.

3. COMBINATION FREQUENCIES. For each combination of acts that occurs k times (k ⩾ 1) within a time bin, one score (A) or k scores (B) are entered in the combination matrix.

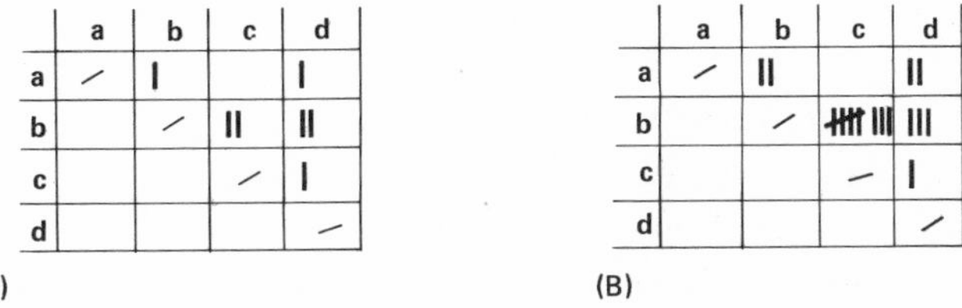

(A)

	a	b	c	d
a	/	I		I
b		/	II	II
c			/	I
d				/

(B)

	a	b	c	d
a	/	II		II
b		/	~~IIII~~ III	III
c			/	I
d				/

Figure 7.8. Schematic representation of several ways to measure the relationships of behavior elements on the basis of temporal contingency.

association and embeddedness cannot be distinguished by it, because association now is also reflected in the similarity of the transition profiles. Not only did Balthazart's correlation coefficients reach much higher values than with his previous method, but the principal-component analysis subsequently produced a more distinct picture, which was in much better agreement with the a priori hypothesis.

These studies go to show that the nature of the correlations subjected to the analysis are of great importance. Not only should the correlation be meaningful, but the data matrix should be suited to the computation of correlations.

An interesting aspect of the topic of frequency analysis as used by Balthazart is the choice of the length of the sample unit of time (the time bin): This has consequences for both method (2) and method (3) in Figure 7.8. There is no a priori criterion for this choice. The only thing certain is that with shorter periods one comes closer to 1–0 sampling (there is less and less chance that more than one behavior element occurs in the time bin). With long time bins the number of bins entering into the correlation computation gets smaller, but the number of behavior elements occurring in each bin increases. Correlations with the largest absolute values can be expected if the length of the time bin is on the order of the average length of time during which a behavior system is activated. If much longer time bins are chosen, the correlations are smoothed away. A further complicating factor is that the average length of time during which activation occurs may be different for different behavior systems. A solution to this problem is to do the same analysis several times with different time-bin lengths and to choose the solution with the most differentiated profile. Balthazart (1973) did precisely this. He even went one step further in that he chose a variable time-bin length, that is, the length of what he a priori considered to be a combat. After due compensations for the artifact of boosted correlations because of the differences in bin length (all elements have a chance to occur more frequently in longer bins), he found that this choice offered the most differentiated and meaningful solution.

A recommendation to treat correlations of frequencies in arbitrarily chosen periods with caution comes from the work of Delius (1969). He computed inter-act correlations for different period lengths and published a matrix of these correlations in which they were presented as a function of the period length. A remarkable result is that the correlations of two acts do not always vary monotonously with period length! This may reveal a nonstationarity that can, however, lead to investigations yielding a fuller insight into the relations between acts (see Section 7.7).

If one uses a matrix of transition frequency data as a starting point, two possibilities offer themselves. One can correlate two behavior elements either with the pattern of elements that follow each of them or with the pattern of preceding elements. The more the respective behavior elements tend to occur in sequences with a clear unidirectional structure, the more different the picture yielded by the two methods. This difference is difficult to interpret, however (Slater, 1973). For the investigation of the sequential aspects, other methods are more appropriate (see Sections 7.6 and 7.7), and it is better not to confuse the issue of directionality with that of behavior systems or categories.

In his investigation of the systems of social behavior in the chimpanzee, van Hooff (1970, 1973) therefore used neighborship frequencies (Figure 7.8, method [1*B*]). This method differed from the method just described in another respect as well. Instead of expressing the discrepancy between the observed and expected values by their quotient o/e, as the above-mentioned authors did, he used the standardized residual, $(o - e)/\sqrt{e}$; thus he hoped to boost the influence of the significant discrepancies and to reduce the influence of random or error variations.

This procedure had the intended effect. Application of the standardized residual yielded much better replicability, as was shown empirically when the total set of observations was split into three parts and the same analysis was applied to each part, once with the o/e quotient and once with the standardized residual (van Hooff, 1970).

It is important to realize that the outcome of component analysis is to a large extent determined by the selection of the sample over which the variables are measured. In the contingency matrix discussed here (Figure 7.8, method [1*B*]) every pair of behavior elements is compared for embeddedness (i.e., for the similarity of their profiles of contingencies). This similarity is expressed in a correlation coefficient. If two elements, say d and e, are being compared, the height of their correlation coefficient may depend heavily on the presence of certain other elements, say k and n, with which the neighborship scores of d and e are extremely high or low, so that these neighbors k and n contribute more than others to the total covariance of the two elements d and e. If the definition of the behavior is such that k and n are present in the repertoire list, this will promote the chance that common aspects of d and e will reveal themselves in a common component that explains a sufficient fraction of the total variance to merit the consideration of that component.

The influence on the outcome of the selection of variables may be demonstrated in another way, too. The choice of behavioral elements, though far from arbitrary, can vary, for instance, according to whether one operates as a "splitter" or a "lumper." One may have a priori reasons for lumping variables that a posteriori would indeed have proved to be highly correlated. By lumping them one reduces a particular contribution of common variance; consequently, one reduces the chance that this contribution will express itself as a principal component and raises the chance that other segments of covariance will reveal themselves as significant components.

In his analysis of chimpanzee social behavior, van Hooff (1971, 1973) turned these vicissitudes to advantage. In a first analysis of 53 behavior elements, five components were found on which at least a few behavior elements had their highest loading (in fact, all except one element had their highest loading on one of these five components). Next, the analysis was repeated with a new neighborship frequency matrix in which the behavior elements of *one* system were maintained, but those of the other four systems were conflated into four "category variables." Thus a further differentiation of each main system in the form of subsystems could show up. The results have been summarized in Figure 7.9.

Whereas the affinitive and the aggressive system did indeed differentiate further, the play system hardly did. In other words, the latter main system reflected a more homogeneous structure than the others. The picture is quite compatible with a priori expectations about the hierarchical structure of the behavior; there were no reasons to expect different kinds of play, but it could reasonably be assumed that there are different types of socially positive behavior.

Principal-component analysis of the distribution of acts over individuals. In the cases already described, behavior variables were compared for their patterns of transition frequencies or similar measures. For the purpose of that comparison, the data for a large number of individuals considered to represent a general "species" structure were pooled.

The individuals, however, are sources of variation themselves. Hitherto, the classic issue in factor analysis has been the relation between characteristics. This relation is determined by the similarity in the variation of the characteristics over individuals. The purpose of this kind of factor analysis is to find out the extent to which these characteristics have common sources of variance (this is generally known as the R-type analysis).

In the study of the structure of behavior, R-type analysis has a

Figure 7.9. The hierarchical organizational structure of 51 social behavior elements of the chimpanzee. This model of systems and subsystems is based on a number of component analyses of neighborship patterns, the results of which have been presented in tables 1–6 in van Hooff (1971, 1973). Compare Figure 7.6.

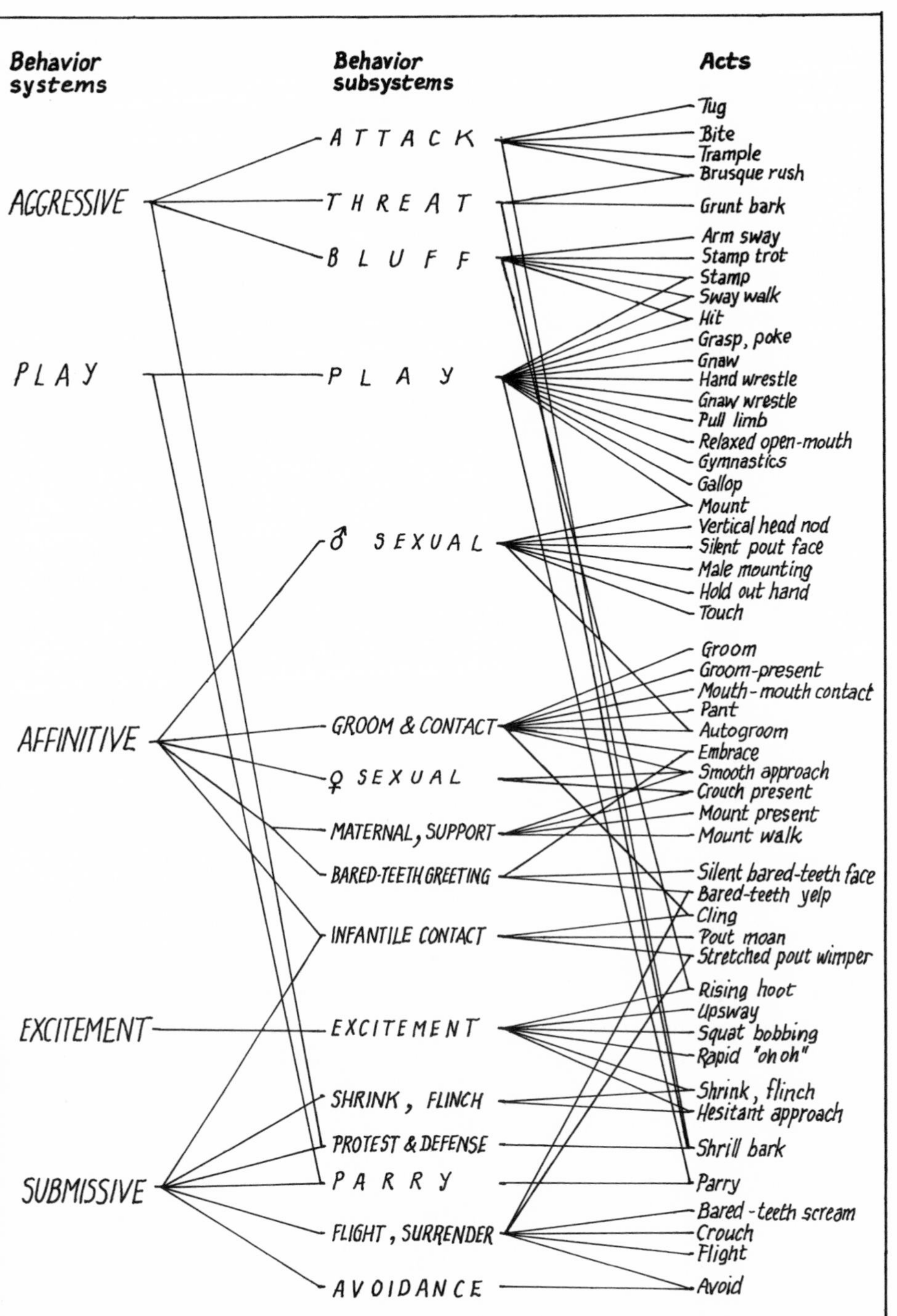

Behavior systems
Behavior subsystems
Acts
AGGRESSIVE
PLAY
AFFINITIVE
EXCITEMENT
SUBMISSIVE
ATTACK
THREAT
BLUFF
PLAY
♂ SEXUAL
GROOM & CONTACT
♀ SEXUAL
MATERNAL, SUPPORT
BARED-TEETH GREETING
INFANTILE CONTACT
EXCITEMENT
SHRINK, FLINCH
PROTEST & DEFENSE
PARRY
FLIGHT, SURRENDER
AVOIDANCE
Tug
Bite
Trample
Brusque rush
Grunt bark
Arm sway
Stamp trot
Stamp
Sway walk
Hit
Grasp, poke
Gnaw
Hand wrestle
Gnaw wrestle
Pull limb
Relaxed open-mouth
Gymnastics
Gallop
Mount
Vertical head nod
Silent pout face
Male mounting
Hold out hand
Touch
Groom
Groom-present
Mouth-mouth contact
Pant
Autogroom
Embrace
Smooth approach
Crouch present
Mount present
Mount walk
Silent bared-teeth face
Bared-teeth yelp
Cling
Pout moan
Stretched pout wimper
Rising hoot
Upsway
Squat bobbing
Rapid "oh oh"
Shrink, flinch
Hesitant approach
Shrill bark
Parry
Bared-teeth scream
Crouch
Flight
Avoid

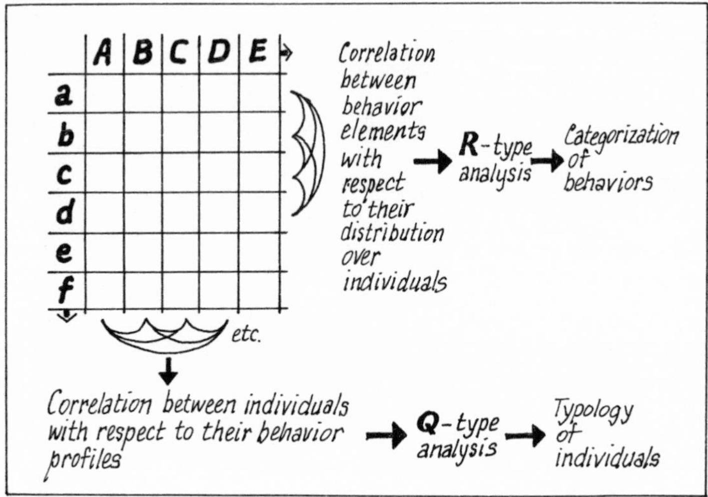

Figure 7.10 *Q*-type and *R*-type analyses.

meaningful application. Individuals occupy different positions in the social organization, positions reflected in their different choices of behavioral routines or systems. An individual in a "strong" position will need to pacify aggressive opponents comparatively rarely. Again, then, one may expect that behavior elements mobilized by the same (sub)system will covary in their distribution over individuals (see Figure 7.10) and, indeed, also over dyads of interacting individuals in the group (individual *A* may use a particular system in his interaction with, say, *C* and *D*, rather than with *E* and *F*).

An instance of such R-type analysis is found in the study by Aspey and Blankenship (1977) relating to categories of agonistic behavior of a wolf spider species. These authors correlated the score profiles of 20 behavior elements shown during male – male conflicts over 40 individuals and revealed four dimensions of variation, that is, four categories of agonistic behaviors. Analogous examples are a study by Frey and Pimentel (1978) on the fighting behavior of an anabantid fish species, and one by Noë, de Waal, and van Hooff (in press) on dominance interactions of chimpanzees. Being convinced that dominance is far from a unitary phenomenon, the latter authors performed a multidimensional analysis of the distribution – in a community of 19 grown-up chimpanzees – of 11 behavior variables and 2 measures of precedence, all of which would a priori be quite acceptable as dominance parameters. They did indeed reveal three types of dominance: "agonistic dominance," "bluff dominance," and "competitive dominance."

The score item used here is the interesting point. Dominance is an aspect of social relations! It was not the frequency with which individuals perform certain behaviors that proved to be of interest,[2] but the dyadic combinations of individuals in which these behaviors were seen; a *relational index* was chosen, therefore. Theoretically, every animal can perform and direct a particular behavior element toward each of the other 18 individuals, and it can receive that particular behavior from each of these individuals. If one animal gives to another individual more than he receives from that individual, that is, if the dyad is asymmetrical, one individual can be said to be dominant (or subordinate).

An individual can subsequently be characterized by a score consisting of the number of animals over which it is dominant minus the number to which it is subordinate; this difference is then divided by the total number of relationships (Figure 7.11). The score profiles of all the dominance parameters can at this point be compared and their correlations subjected to principal-component analysis. In choosing the appropriate measures one obviously has to be guided by the questions and their theoretical background, and this choice determines the relevance of the analysis as a whole.

For the sake of completeness, mention should be made of the reverse type of analysis, namely, Q-type analysis. Here *individuals* are compared and classified on the basis of their performance, or reception of behaviors (or other behavioral measures or characteristics). Such analysis may be applied in connection with the study of social structure (see, e.g., Fedigan, 1976).

Possibilities and limitations in the application of component analysis. The distributions of the measures used in studies such as those mentioned here are usually not normal. And the scale of measurement can often be regarded as no more than ordinal. Therefore, in most cases, rank correlations have been computed. Because the model of factor analysis supposes that the relations between the variables are expressed in the form of normal product moment correlations based on interval scales, formal objections can be made to this procedure. Thus a variable that is a linear combination of two others will be, for instance, equally correlated with each of them, provided that the variances of the two other variables are equal. This, however, will no longer be the case after these variables are transformed into ranks, as anybody can verify with a simple numerical example. Ranking procedures have nevertheless been used on the pragmatic assumption that in many cases they yield the best estimate of the structure of relations (see Ueberla, 1971). The procedure

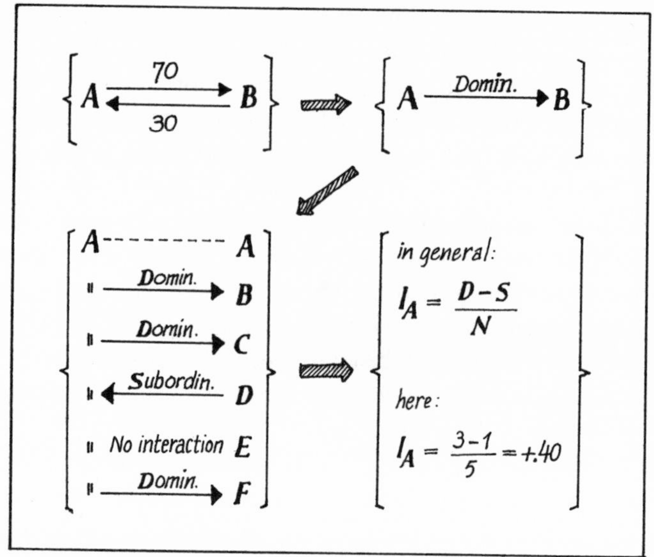

Figure 7.11. Derivation of a dominance parameter based on the number of relationships in which a given subject is dominant and the number in which it is subordinate.

finds empirical justification in Balthazart's (1972) comparison of different correlation methods.

This chapter is not the place to go into technical aspects of such methods as principal-component and factor analysis. For these the reader is referred to the literature mentioned earlier. Here I shall restrict myself to a few remarks concerning the reliability of the method.

If we had a matrix the scores of which had been generated at random, the correlation coefficients between the variables would have an average value of zero. Their average deviation from zero would tend to be greater the smaller the number of scores over which the correlation had been computed. Hence it is advisable to compute the correlations over many scores; a common recommendation is to have many more scores than there are variables. This precaution is certainly needed if, as is the case in normal practice, each cell entry in the matrix refers to one measurement of a characteristic in one individual. The chance that appreciable correlation coefficients merely reflect random covariation is very small if the entries refer to frequencies, the distribution of which has been found, by other methods, such as the computation of residuals, to deviate strongly from random (see Section 7.4). But even so, it is advisable to investigate whether the correlation matrix deviates sufficiently from random to justify component analysis (or other multidimensional analysis methods, for that matter). For this purpose a few tests have been proposed (they have been discussed by Dziuban and Shirkey, 1974).

A critical inspection of the correlation matrix is needed, because factor or component analysis performed even on randomly generated data will always yield a structure with a restricted number of main dimensions. In a critical article, Armstrong and Soelberg (1968) argue that it may well be possible to attach a more or less plausible explanation to such a random solution, and they show this in an empirical fashion with a fake experiment. Reviewing the psychological literature, they found that most authors who had applied these methods of analysis had not explicitly realized that their results might be randomly generated artifacts.

The trouble is that problems about how to establish the significance of such solutions have not yet been solved to everybody's satisfaction. There are empirically validated criteria concerning the number of factors or components that may be extracted: there are also tests based on more objective mathematical criteria (for detailed recommendations, see, for instance, Cattell, 1966; Ueberla, 1971). The most important criterion for judging a solution is whether it is meaningful and consistent.

Armstrong and Soelberg (1968) translate this reasoning into the following three types of operational advice. On the basis of *a priori hypotheses* (theoretical models, previous findings, or educated hunches), the researcher should specify beforehand the number of main dimensions, the variables loading together on them, and so on. Consistency could be investigated by *splitting the sample* into random subsamples and comparing the solutions, for instance, by correlating the factor loadings. Modern fast computers also enable researchers to run *Monte Carlo simulations* on samples of random data; this is a possibility particularly when samples are too small to be split. The simulated data should be comparable to the empirical data in sample size, distribution properties, and the like. Researchers can subsequently investigate whether actual results yield fewer components explaining a larger proportion of the variance and whether the loadings have greater absolute values.

Multidimensional scaling and cluster analysis. Factor and component analysis are sophisticated techniques. However, they are computationally complex. They are based on rather strict assumptions – for example, that there are in fact linear relations between the variates – even though they have by now appeared to be very robust in regard to departures from these assumptions. For these and other reasons, alternative methods of multivariate analysis, such as cluster analysis and multidimensional scaling, are enjoying popularity.

The object of multidimensional scaling is to represent the pattern of similarities and dissimilarities of a number of variables in the form of a geometrical representation. The greater the similarity between two variables, the closer they are placed in the spatial arrangement. There are metric methods where the distance parameter is related to the similarity parameter, and there are nonmetric methods where the similarity index is assigned ordinal value only. Application of these methods in the field of behavior research has been limited so far, and their selective advantages over other methods have still to be shown, a particular disadvantage being that the various methods that have been proposed involve elaborate computations. An advantage over methods such as factor and component analysis is that, whereas the latter methods are restricted to the use of correlation measures (in principle to Pearson's), multidimensional scaling allows various measures of similarity, association, or closeness (or the reverse – namely, dissimilarity or distance measures). For a discussion of such measures the reader is referred to Sneath and Sokal (1963) and Everitt (1974). There are a number of algorithms available for multidimensional scaling; the reader is referred to Spence (1978) for further details and references.

At first sight the multitude of methods of cluster analyses is rather bewildering. A very accessible treatment has recently been given by Everitt (1974). See also Cormack (1971), Everitt (1977), and DeGhett (1978), who also give detailed computational instructions. A very simple and easily readable introduction for ethologists is Morgan et al. (1976).

As the name implies, cluster analysis is concerned with discovering groups in sets of individuals, objects, or properties on the basis of some measure of similarity between them. Like multidimensional scaling, cluster analysis allows various measures of similarity, and not just correlation coefficients.

Most well known are the agglomerative techniques that result in a hierarchical structure of connectedness that can be represented by a "tree" or dendogram (see Figure 7.12). The ends of the branches represent the empirical elements. The points at which the branches connect indicate the level of connectedness of the respective elements and/or clusters.

In Figure 7.13 the procedure followed in two of the most popular methods is illustrated. Both methods begin by connecting in a first cluster those two elements that have a similarity index higher than the index of each with the other elements of the set. The level of connected-

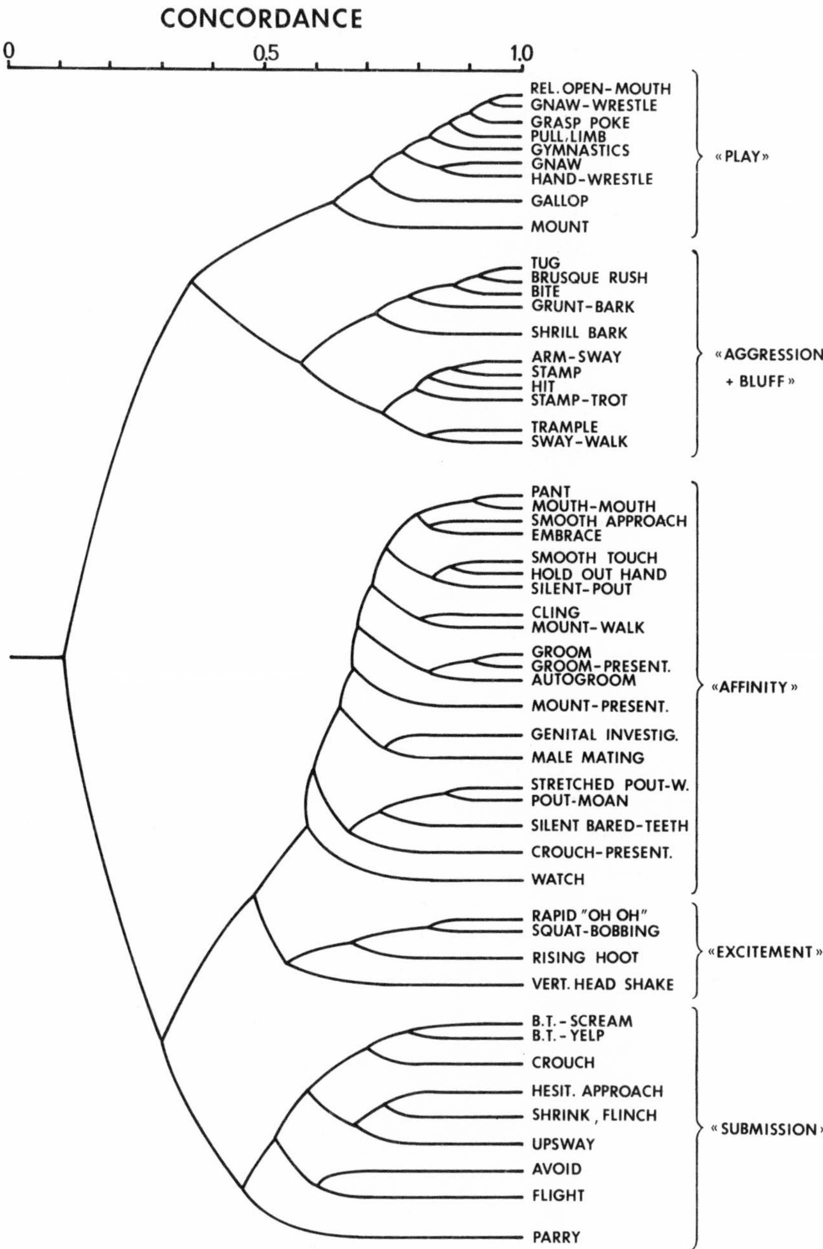

Figure 7.12. Results of a cluster analysis of the neighborship patterns of the social behavior elements of the chimpanzee. Compare with Figures 7.6 and 7.9. *Source:* van Hooff, 1971, 1973.

ness can be represented by the index of similarity or some ordinal derivative. The first cluster will be of (B) and (C) at Level 11. In the first method, called the *single linkage, nearest neighbor,* or *minimum distance* method, the similarity of the newly formed cluster to each of the remaining elements is set at a value equal to the highest value of similarity between each of its two composing elements and the respective remaining elements. Thus, the similarity of (BC) to (A) should be set at 10 (the choice being between (A) (B) = 10 and (A) (C) = 2). In the second method, the *complete linkage, farthest neighbor,* or *maximum distance* method, the new index is set at the lowest level of both possibilities. Therefore, (BC)(A) should be set at 2. In the matrix, thus reduced, the whole procedure is repeated until all the clusters have been incorporated into one cluster. The single linkage method leads to an assembly of clusters that have been formed on the weakest possible basis. The complete linkage method, on the other hand, yields clusters formed on the strongest possible basis. The results need not be the same. In the example of Figure 7.13, I have chosen a similarity matrix that highlights the differences between the methods: Whereas the conservative complete linkage method tends to generate distinct clusters, the single linkage method has a tendency, instead, to add elements to existing clusters and thus to form long "chains." This feature has been regarded as a disadvantage.

Both methods make rather limited use of the information available, in that the resulting cluster structure depends on only a limited number of the similarity indexes in the matrix. The larger the matrix, the larger the proportion of the similarity indexes that plays no role in the process. To overcome this problem, various alternative methods have been proposed, some rather complex; in these the levels of connectedness and/or the similarities of resulting clusters to the remaining elements are determined by some kind of averaging procedure; methods have been developed that use both weighted and unweighted averages.

The relative merits of component and cluster analysis

The merits of the different methods of cluster analysis are still the subject of discussion; there are various objections (*e.g.*, arbitrary choices, mathematical problems) to particularly the more complex agglomerative methods. In the light of these objections the single linkage method seems to find favor. The fact that the latter method leads to the notorious chaining, however, is one of the reasons why a number of pragmatists prefer the other methods (for a detailed review see Everitt,

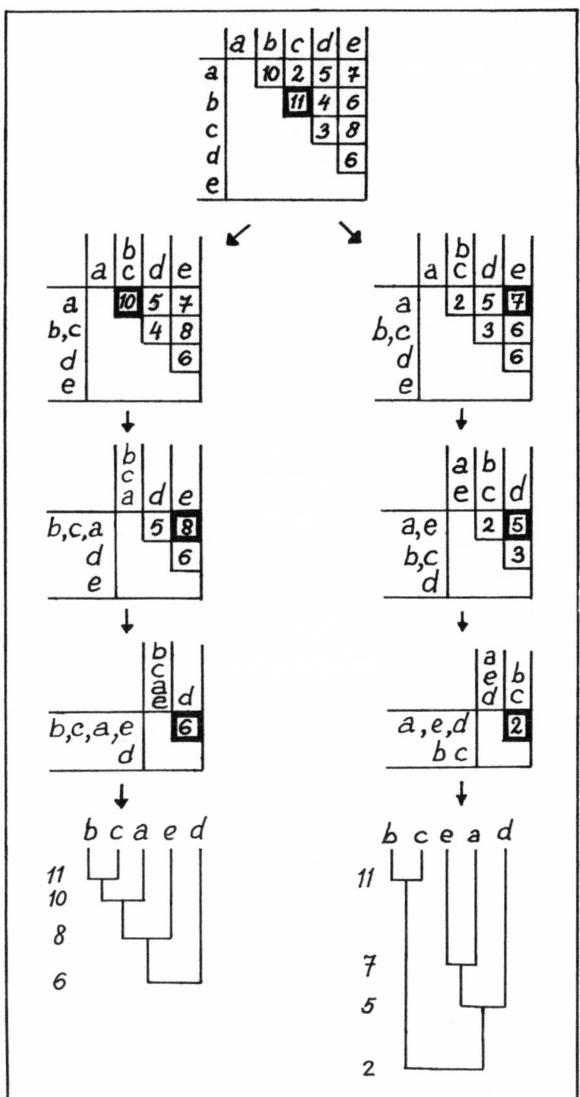

Figure 7.13. Examples of cluster analysis. The five variables whose similarity indexes are presented in the upper matrix are clustered according to the *single linkage, nearest neighbor,* or *minimum distance* method on the left, and on the right, according to the *complete linkage, farthest neighbor,* or *maximum distance* method.

1974). The methods mentioned are particularly well suited for revealing a hierarchical organization; in fact, it is inherent in the methods that they will show up a hierarchical organization even if it is not in the material. It is advisable, therefore, to use more than one multivariate method, to use procedures involving split halves, and, most important, to make a priori hypotheses explicit. Finally, Monte Carlo simulations might be used for comparison.

The biggest advantage of the multivariate methods is their data-reduction capability; they can generate molar units or indexes for the study of more complex phenomena (*e.g.*, the more parsimonious and therefore practical description of polyadic social interactions; see de Waal, 1978). These methods can be used as descriptive and exploratory devices and can help in the generation of new hypotheses. By uncovering more homogeneous subgroups in a hetereogeneous sample, even without reference to a preexisting classification scheme, they can provide insight into the underlying dimensions and suggest sources of variation (Aspey & Blankenship, 1977; Frey & Pimentel, 1978). So far, however, the testing capabilities of these methods remain limited. When forced to choose a method, one is attracted by the greater transparency of cluster methods, their less restrictive assumptions, and the fact that they make it possible to use a variety of similarity measures. The advantage of component and factor analytic methods is that the entire structure of similarities is taken into account, and consequently, such methods are less likely to be influenced by sampling fluctuations (Morf, Miller, & Syrotuik, 1976). Besides, these methods allow for the realistic possibility that a variable can be associated with more than one category. Thus the "genital presenting" shown by many primate species can be used both in the functional context of sexual invitation and in the context of appeasement achieved by remotivation of the partner. Particularly if the assumptions are met, the method of component analysis gives every indication of being very robust (Frey & Pimentel, 1978).

In all cases, however, the relevance of the results depends on the theoretical relevance of the measurement scores and the definition of similarities and differences used. As Aspey and Blankenship (1977) point out, though, these relevances are not always clear from the outset, and the methods may therefore also be used to explore the relevance of variables.

7.6. Sequential analyses: advanced event-based approaches

The dimensional and categorization approaches, treated in an earlier section, are not suitable for giving us insight into the sequential dynamics of the behavior processes. For that, I continue the theme treated in Section 7.4. There I reported on methods for establishing whether the pattern of observed dyadic combinations of preceding and succeeding behavior elements deviates from the pattern expected on the basis of random combination, given the different frequencies with which each of the elements occurs.

Markov chains

If there is a significant deviation from the pattern, that is, if preceding and succeeding events are not independent, we might consider the sequence to be a Markov chain. This is defined as a series of events in which the probability that a single event will occur depends on the event that immediately precedes it, but not on earlier events. This is the simplest form of dependency and is called a first-order Markov chain. It would seem counter-intuitive if, in behavior, acts earlier than the one immediately preceding a certain act had had no influence on this act. This intuition can be confirmed only by an empirical rejection of the first-order Markov model. This rejection can take the form of the procedure described in Section 7.4, by means of which the first-order dependency was established and the so-called zeroth-order Markov model – that is, one with no dependency – was rejected. In the next step one can check whether each *dyad*, given the different frequencies of dyadic combinations, follows the various acts that immediately precede it with proportionally equal frequencies. If this is the case, one can accept the first-order Markov model. If certain triadic combinations occur significantly more frequently or less frequently than expected, that is, if there are higher-order directive or inhibitive effects, one has to reject the first-order Markov model. Subsequently one can consider whether a second-order Markov model is acceptable or whether third-order or even higher-order dependencies must be assumed.

Such an approach is theoretically feasible and has even been applied in S. A. Altmann's (1965) classic study. Altmann could show that in interactive sequences of rhesus monkeys, higher-order dependencies (up to the fifth order) do exist. However, the number of possible combinations rises exponentially with increasing length of the sequence considered. With the sample sizes that are practically possible, the expected and observed frequencies of all these combinations will be so low as to make statistical inferences impossible (see Chatfield & Lemon, 1970, for a more formal treatment).

Lag sequential analysis

A question that intrigues the investigator of behavioral organization concerns the existence of possible important sequential patterns, recurrent themes in the melody of behavioral movement, so to speak. Most analyses have been restricted, in fact, to the dependencies between adjacent events, which cannot reveal such sequential themes. If a kinematic graph, such as the one presented in Figure 7.6, shows a preferential path of the form *ABC*, this does not necessarily imply that the actual sequences run in this way. One would like to know not only that there is a greater than average chance for *B* to follow *A* and for *C* to follow *B*, but also that *C* occurs more frequently than expected as the second event after *A*, that is, at lag 2.

Useful alternatives to higher-order Markovian analyses, which can reveal such sequential patterns, have been developed recently. Sackett (1974) introduced a method called "lag sequential analysis," which has been elaborated by Bakeman and Dabbs (1976). Similar methods have been described by Dawkins and Dawkins (1976) – the so-called curves of predictability – and by Douglas and Tweed (1979) – the so-called pre –post state histograms.

These methods allow one to discover dependencies not only between adjacent events, but also between events separated from each other by a given number of intercalated events. The principle of this lag sequential analysis is quite simple. For all occurrences of a given behavioral event *X*, one counts the number of times another event *Y* occurs at the successive *event slots* following (or preceding) act *X*. Douglas and Tweed, for instance, proceed to construct a histogram of these frequencies (Figure 7.14). In other words, if act *Y* occurs at event slots 3 and 7 following *X*, then the histogram counters for lag +3 and +7 will be incremented by the value 1. The result is a direct visual representation of the relationship between the respective acts. On the basis of the null hypothesis that *Y* occurs randomly at each event slot, the expected mean frequency can be computed. This and the 99% or 95% confidence bounds for each event slot can simply be plotted in the figure.

As we have seen earlier, it is recommended that the recording be such that an act cannot immediately follow itself. If it does not follow itself directly, the expected mean and the confidence bounds will oscillate at the early event slots neighboring act *X*. This oscillation will be damped as one gets farther away. This is easy to understand. Suppose we have three equiprobable events *A*, *B*, and *C*. Let *A* be our criterion event *X*.

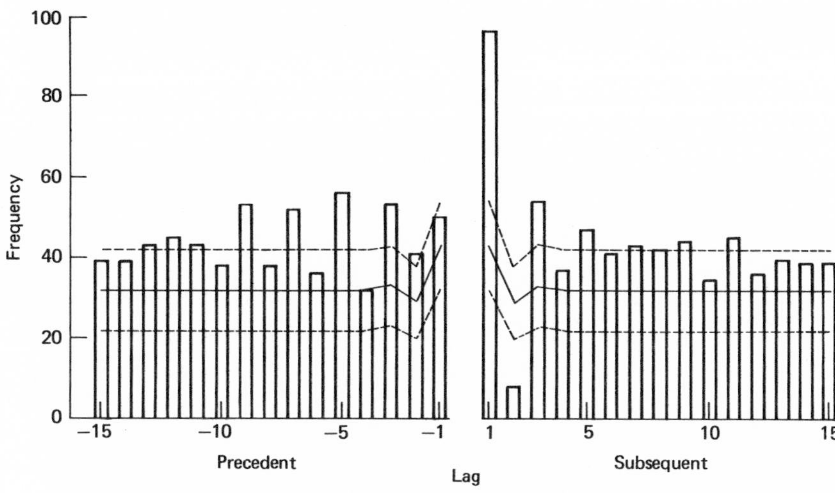

Figure 7.14. An example of lag sequential analysis, namely, a pre–post state histogram of two behaviors X and Y of the fly. The X behavior is represented at the lag 0, and the histogram shows the summed actual frequencies of the occurrence of the Y behavior at the successive event lags prior to or subsequent to every X. The solid line denotes the expected mean frequency of Y and the dashed lines the 95% confidence bounds. *Source:* Douglas and Tweed, 1979, p. 175.

Then the chance that B will occur at lag 1 is 50%. These 50% B acts will be followed solely by A and C. The 50% C acts, however, will be followed by A (25%) and B (25%). At the next slot, again, only one in two A and C acts (together 75%) will be followed by B (i.e., 37.5%). The successive probabilities of B are, therefore, 0.50, 0.25, 0.375, and the oscillation of p_B will damp out eventually at 33.3%.

Figure 7.15 gives the results of a lag sequential analysis presented by Gottman and Notarius (1978) and based upon the work of Sackett (1974). It concerns the interaction of rhesus monkey mothers and infants. In this case the ordinate represents the conditional probability of the Y act concerned. The X act is *gross activity* by the infant. Excessive peaks in the conditional probability profile, respectively at lag 1 for *pat–stroke–jiggle,* at lag 2 for *nurse,* and at lag 3 for *groom,* suggest that the mother reacts to gross activity of her infant with a rather typical sequential pattern. This finding can be examined further by using other behaviors in the sequence as the criterion act, for instance, by checking whether, in the mother's sequence, *pat–stroke–jiggle* is indeed followed with a predictable excessive probability by *nurse.* The method has also found application in a comparative study concerning marital interaction in nondis-

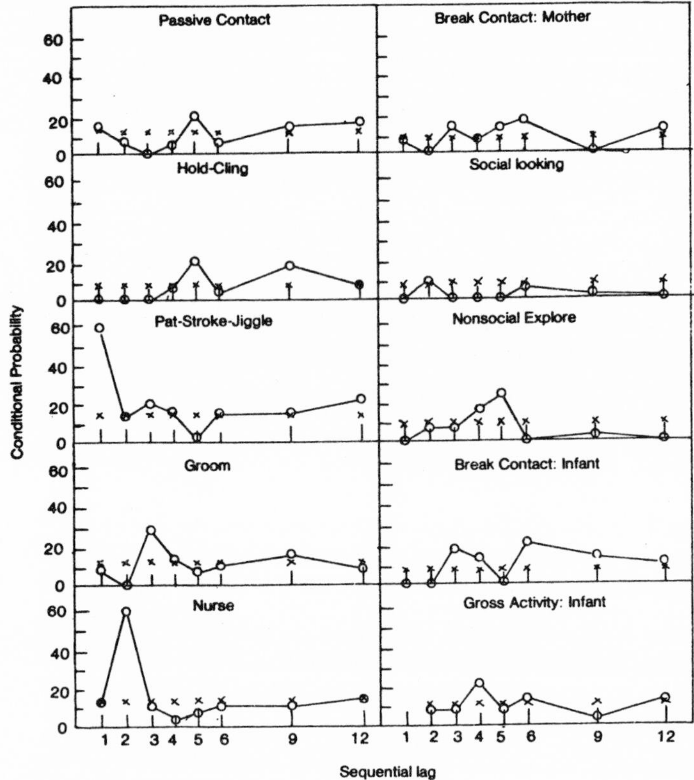

Figure 7.15. Lag sequential analysis of behaviors shown in the interaction between rhesus monkey mothers and infants. The X behavior is *gross activity* by the infant. *Source:* Gottman and Notarius, 1978, p. 272.

tressed and distressed couples by Gottman, Markman, and Notarius (1977). The proponents of this method emphasize its relative simplicity and its effectiveness.

Information-theoretical approaches

An alternative approach to the sequential dependencies in behavioral streams is provided by information theory. The novice will find a readable introduction in the essays of Attneave (1959) and Garner (1962). During the last 15 years or so there have been a number of applications of information theory in an ethological context. Reviews and references can be found in Raush (1972), Steinberg (1977), Losey

(1978), Gottman and Notarius (1978), and van den Bercken and Cools (1980a).

The basic concept in information theory is uncertainty, namely, the degree of uncertainty one has in predicting a certain event or in selecting a certain item in a given distribution of alternatives, or – conversely – the amount of information needed to remove this uncertainty).[3] This amount of information is expressed by the number of yes – no choices needed (bits). The basic reasoning, which leads to the well-known Shannon and Weaver (1949) formula for the average amount of information, is rendered schematically in Figure 7.16. For easier computation the following formula is often used, in which p_i has been replaced by its estimator n_i/N:

$$\hat{H} = \frac{1}{N}(N \log_2 N - \sum_{i=1}^{n} n_i \log n_i)$$

where n_i is the number of events of type i and N is the total number of all events.

Maximum uncertainty will exist when each of the alternative event types is equally probable, that is, when the distribution is completely random. For instance, in the case of eight alternatives, H_{max} will be 3. When the alternatives are not equiprobable, the uncertainty will be less ($<H_{max}$); in the extreme case where one alternative occurs always ($p = 1$) and the others never ($p = 0$), the uncertainty is smallest, namely 0; there is absolute certainty. The basic calculations in information theory are rather easy. If the data arrays are not too big, these calculations can be done fairly quickly even with a pocket calculator (to calculate base-two logarithms one must know that $\log_2 x = 3.3219 \log_{10} x = 1.4427 \log_e x$ and that log 0 should be assigned the value 0).

The application of the measure of information to the structure of behavior and to communication can be illustrated by the simple numerical examples of contingency matrices in Figure 7.17. Matrices A and B have the same marginal totals; therefore, the degree of uncertainty about the occurrence of an event of the X array $H(X)$ or the Y array $H(Y)$ is the same for A *and* B. The cell entries for the occurrence of XY combinations do differ, however. In the case of A, these are equal to what one would expect on the basis of random combination. In the case of B, they show a deviation from this pattern, which means that there is a dependency between X and Y. In other words, one is more likely to predict Y if one knows X, and conversely. Our numerical example shows that in the case of A, $H(XY)$ is the exact sum of $H(X)$ and $H(Y)$,

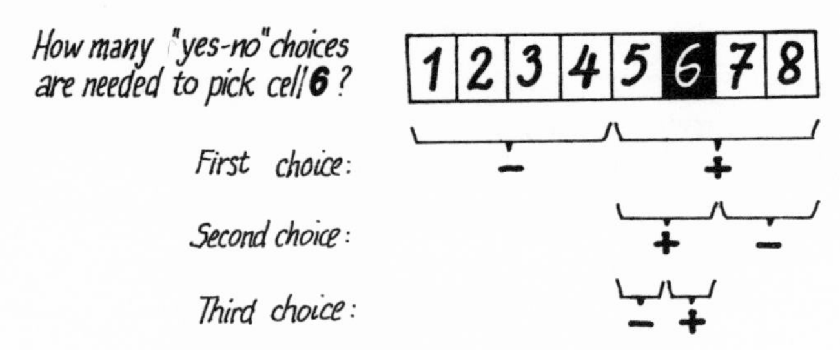

So with **8** items (**N=8**) **3** binary choices (**b=3**) are needed = **3 bits** of **information**

Here $2^3 = 8$	In general $2^b = N$	or $b = \log_2 N$
Here $p = 1/8$	In general $p = 1/N$	or $b = \log_2 1/p$

Convention: Amount of **Uncertainty** $H = \log_2 1/p$

In this case $p_1 = p_2 = p_3 = \ldots = p_8$. If however p's are not equal then: AVERAGE AMOUNT OF UNCERTAINTY is:

$$\hat{H} = \sum_{i=1}^{N} p_i \cdot \log_2 1/p_i$$

or

$$\hat{H} = -\Sigma p_i \cdot \log_2 p_i$$

$\hat{H}$ is maximal (uncertainty is greatest, or amount of information needed is greatest) when all possibilities (event types) are equiprobable [see **A**], and minimal when only ONE of the possible event types always occurs [see **C**]

A]	$p.\log_2 p$	B]	$p.\log_2 p$	C]	$p.\log_2 p$
$p_1 = .25$	$-.50$	$p_1 = .80$	$-.26$	$p_1 = 1.00$	0
$p_2 = .25$	$-.50$	$p_2 = .13$	$-.38$	$p_2 = 0$	0
$p_3 = .25$	$-.50$	$p_3 = .06$	$-.24$	$p_3 = 0$	0
$p_4 = .25$	$-.50$	$p_4 = .01$	$-.07$	$p_4 = 0$	0
	$\Sigma = -2.00$		$\Sigma = -0.95$		$\Sigma = 0$

Figure 7.16. Schematic derivation of the formula for the average amount of information.

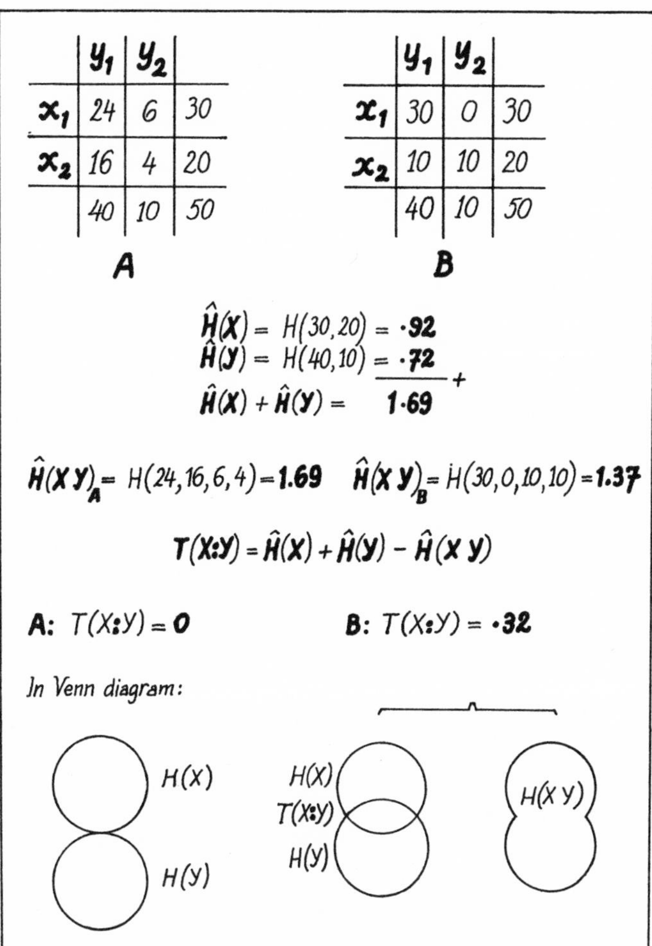

Figure 7.17. Example of the computational procedure for measuring the amount of information transmission between two processes (e.g., organisms) X and Y with the event types x_1 and x_2, and y_1 and y_2, respectively. Two data arrays have been given. In **A** the cell entries of the xy combinations are those that can be expected on the base of random combination; so there is no transmission of information. In **B**, on the other hand, there is such a transmission.

whereas in the case of B it is less. The difference $[H(X) + H(Y) - H(XY)]$ indicates the amount of information that is transmitted between X and Y (or that X and Y have in common). This is called the transmission $T(X{:}Y)$, or the covariability.

If the contingency diagram represents a matrix of transition frequencies, X being the behavior of I at a previous moment in time (I_{t-1}) and Y

being the present behavior of *I* (I_t), then $T(I_{t-1}:I_t)$ expresses the degree to which an animal's previous behavior determines its present behavior (i.e., its *auto-covariability*). If *X* represents the preceding behavior of a social companion *J*, (J_{t-1}), then $T(J_{t-1}:I_t)$ expresses the degree to which that companion's behavior has a determining influence (i.e., the *cross-covariability*).

These information-theoretical measures have been applied by a number of authors in their studies of aspects of communication in various species of animals. An early example is a study by Dingle (1969) on the interactions of Mantis shrimps. These animals inhabit rock cavities, which they defend fiercely, and they possess some conspicuous gestures that might have communicatory significance. The acts of two animals, experimentally brought into a situation of interaction for 60 minutes, were recorded alternately, so that an act of one animal was followed by an act of the other. The dyads of succession were entered in a transition matrix. However, the 60-minute period of confrontation was divided into 4 episodes, namely, 0–10 min, 10–20 min, 20–40 min, and 40–60 min. A transition matrix was made for each episode, and both the auto-individual and the cross-individual transmissions were computed. These transmissions appeared to be about equal. Part of the data is given in Figure 7.18. An interesting result is that both the information needed to predict the behavior of the individuals and the information transmitted between individuals reached a peak during the second 10-min episode. In other words, at that point the animals are most uncertain and take most account of the partner's behavior. This finding is in agreement with an impression gained in other ways, namely, that during this second episode the dominance relationships tend to be established.

Analyses along the same lines have been made by Hazlett and Bossert (1965) and Conant and Steinberg (1973). An interesting variant is the method used by Steinberg and Conant (1974), Hazlett and Estabrook (1974a, 1974b), and Rubenstein and Hazlett (1974) in that they also investigated the variation in the amount of information transmission. To this end they entered all the *first* behavior elements of a particular sequence on the *X* dimension of a transition matrix and all *second* acts on the *Y* dimension, and determined the amount of information transmitted. In this manner they gradually worked through the sequences by treating second and third elements in a similar manner and computing their transmission, and so on.

As we have seen, the two measures, auto-covariability and cross-covariability, enable us to compare the degree to which the antecedent

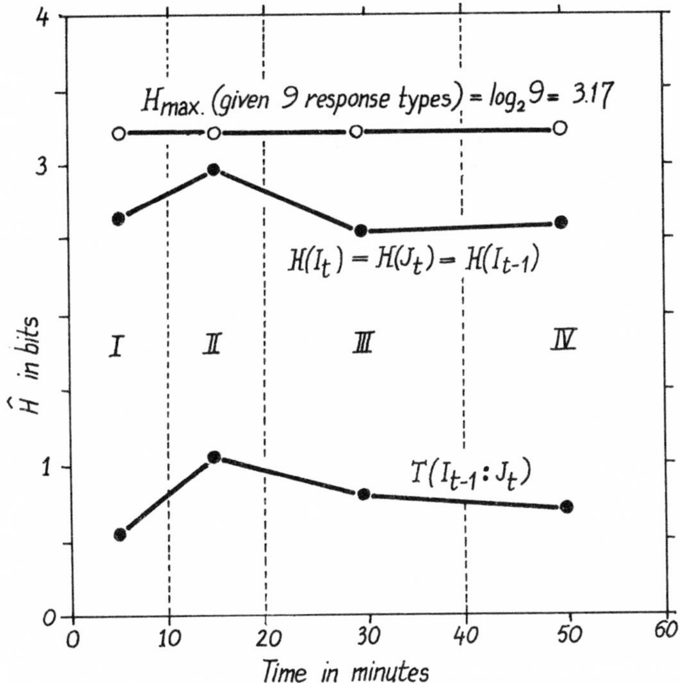

Figure 7.18. The average amount of uncertainty, $H(I_t) = H(J_t) = H(I_{t-1}) = H(J_{t-1})$, in the behavior of individuals and the amount of information transmitted between individuals, $T(I_{t-1}:J_t)$, during four successive phases of territorial conflict of pairs of Mantis shrimps. *Source:* Adapted from Dingle, 1969.

behavior of an individual and of the individual's partner constrain the individual's present behavior. At first one is inclined to consider the second type of constraint to be social communication, as indeed most authors have explicitly or implicitly done. In a recent series of articles, van den Bercken (1979) and van den Bercken and Cools (1980a, 1980b) have elaborated the information-statistical interaction model and have shown that different effects become confused if one assumes that interindividual transmission of information is identical to communication. The nature of this confusion becomes obvious if one realizes that the uncertainty measure (or variability measure) H is in fact a variance-like statistic, and that by analogy with variance statistics it is possible to decompose the variability of a sample variable I into independent components. This point is illustrated by the Venn diagram of Figure 7.19. The diagram shows that only segment c should be regarded as the communicative contribution that individual J makes to the reduction of the uncertainty in the behavior of I; segment b is an interaction

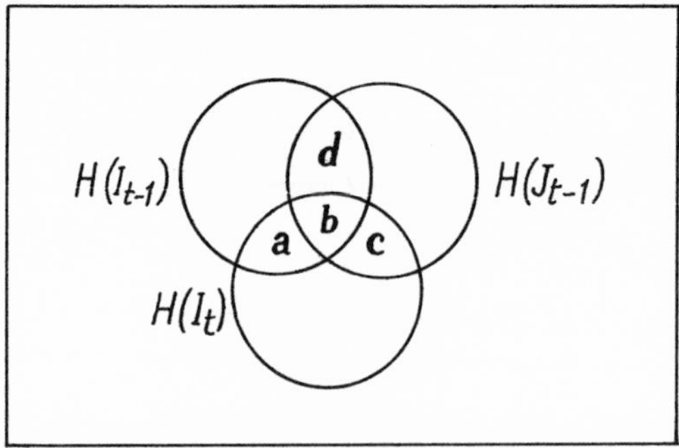

Figure 7.19. Venn diagram showing the different components of the covariability of the behavior of an individual I at time t with I's own previous behavior at time $t-1$ and that of I's partner J at time $t-1$.

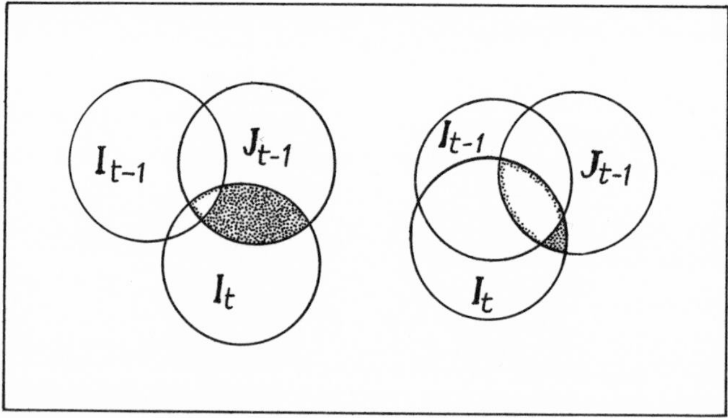

Figure 7.20. Venn diagram showing that the communication component of the transmission of information between two individuals J and I may vary partly independently of that transmission.

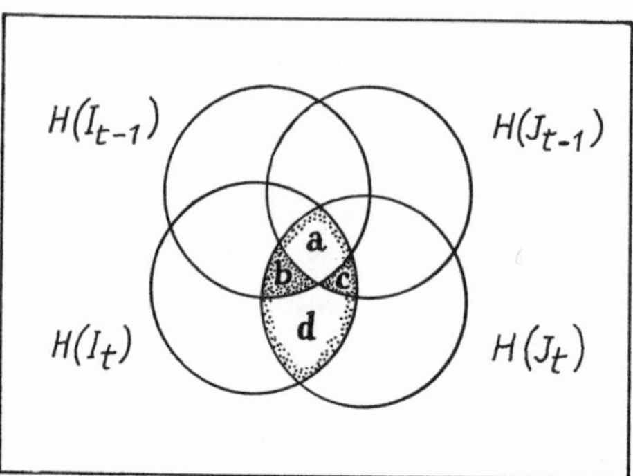

Figure 7.21. Venn diagram illustrating the relevant covariability components in the communication model of Marko (1966) and Hauske and Neuburger (1968).

component, because it also forms part of the covariability between I_{t-1} and J_{t-1}. This is no trivial consideration, as can be deduced from Figure 7.20, where the relative magnitudes of the components have been chosen differently. In both cases the transmission from J_{t-1} to I_t is about equal, but the communication component certainly is not. In a more implicit manner the same point has been made by Oden (1977) in an article about the partitioning of dependences. The different components can be computed quite simply from the formulae in Figure 7.22.

Van den Bercken (1979) applied the partial covariability measures in a neuroethological study concerning the function of the caudate nucleus; his hypothesis was that this brain structure is involved in the programming of ongoing behavior, in that it regulates the relationship between internal control (the execution of internal programs) and external control (the adjustment to influences from outside). He observed the free social interactions of triads of crab-eating macaques, one of which was chemically tele-stimulated in the caudate nucleus by drugs that either stimulated or inhibited the relevant neurotransmitter system. He did indeed find shifts in the relative amount of auto- and cross-covariability as compared to controls. The shifts were in opposite directions, the stimulator drug enhancing the intraindividual constraints (the macaque's "single-mindedness," so to speak), and the inhibitor both enhancing the interindividual constraints and simultaneously decreasing the intraindividual constraints. Van den Bercken could show that this was the case irrespective of the categories of behavior shown by the animals, that is, irrespective of their motivational state.

A slightly different line of thought concerning what can be understood as communication has been followed by Marko (1966) and by Hauske and Neuburger (1968), and has found application in the study of Mayer (1971). They have focused on the covariability between the present behavior of an animal I and that of its partner J, namely, $T(I_t{:}J_t)$; this is the oval consisting of the segments $a + b + c + d$ in Figure 7.21. They argue that this covariability between the simultaneous behavior states of two individuals must be due to causal influences that have preceded the present states – among others, the previous states of both I and J. Marko, therefore, divides $T(I_t{:}J_t)$ into the four components indicated. Of these, a is an aspect of the previous covariability, and only b and c, the partial cross-covariabilities $P(I_{t-1}{:}J_t)$ and $P(J_{t-1}{:}I_t)$, can be regarded as the communication components; d cannot be explained in terms of the previous behavior of I and J, but can be ascribed to external factors common to both individuals. Note that in this model the auto-covariability aspect has not been distinguished.

I shall not go further into the comparison of different methods. For

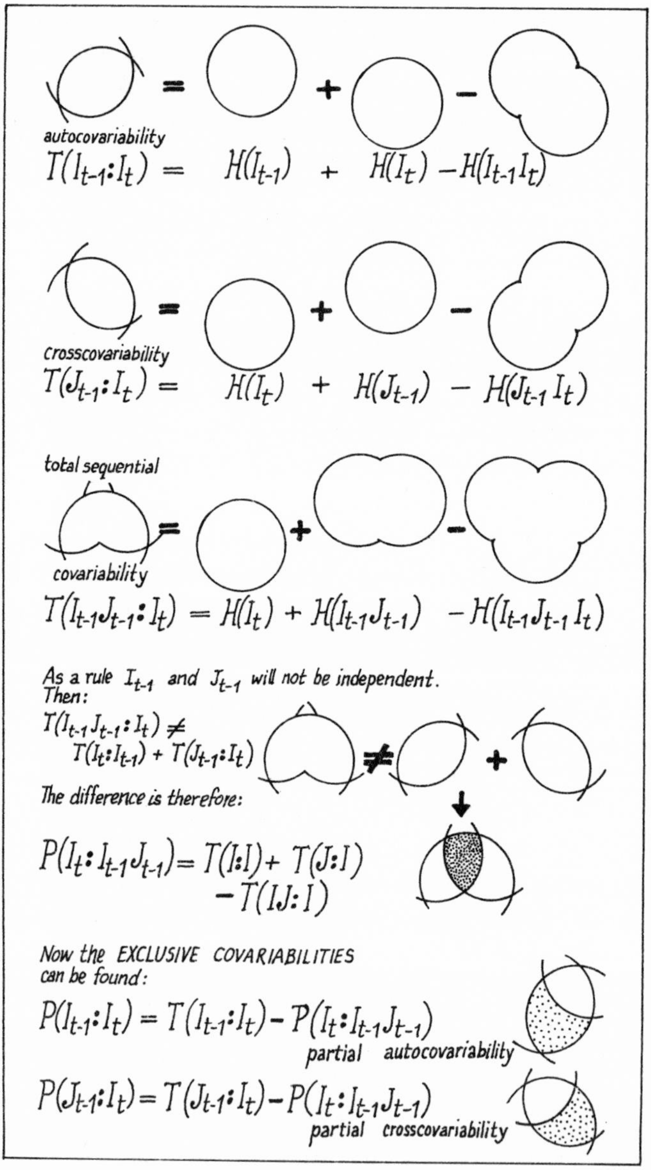

autocovariability

$$T(I_{t-1}:I_t) = H(I_{t-1}) + H(I_t) - H(I_{t-1}I_t)$$

crosscovariability

$$T(J_{t-1}:I_t) = H(I_t) + H(J_{t-1}) - H(J_{t-1}I_t)$$

total sequential covariability

$$T(I_{t-1}J_{t-1}:I_t) = H(I_t) + H(I_{t-1}J_{t-1}) - H(I_{t-1}J_{t-1}I_t)$$

As a rule I_{t-1} and J_{t-1} will not be independent. Then:

$$T(I_{t-1}J_{t-1}:I_t) \neq T(I_t:I_{t-1}) + T(J_{t-1}:I_t)$$

The difference is therefore:

$$P(I_t:I_{t-1}J_{t-1}) = T(I:I) + T(J:I) - T(IJ:I)$$

Now the EXCLUSIVE COVARIABILITIES can be found:

$$P(I_{t-1}:I_t) = T(I_{t-1}:I_t) - P(I_t:I_{t-1}J_{t-1})$$

partial autocovariability

$$P(J_{t-1}:I_t) = T(J_{t-1}:I_t) - P(I_t:I_{t-1}J_{t-1})$$

partial crosscovariability

Figure 7.22. Illustration of the computation of the possible interaction components between the behavior of an individual I at times $t-1$ and t and that of an individual J at time $t-1$ (see Figure 7.16). The computations are analogous to the one presented in Figure 7.17.

more detail, the reader is referred to the extensive review given by van den Bercken and Cools (1980a). These authors also go into matters concerning the computation of information-statistical measures. As a rule, the values of T and H are estimated from samples of behavior.

Generally, H is underestimated and T overestimated, because rare events may not be sampled. The correction of this bias has been discussed by Steinberg (1977) and Losey (1978). The latter author also reviews critically various methods that have been proposed for calculating the statistical confidence limits for information measures.

Restricted applicability of Markov and information-statistical approaches

Markov models and related information-theory models are based on the assumption that the systems investigated are stationary. There are two obvious sources of nonstationarity. Firstly, the behavior samples may differ in their statistical properties because they stem from different individuals who because of differences in aspects such as sex, age, social position, and the like, represent different systems. Secondly, in a given individual the probabilities of the occurrence of acts and their transition probabilities may change with time (*e.g.*, Lemon & Chatfield, 1971; Slater, 1973). Obviously, organisms are dynamic systems. Even if one takes pains to keep the external conditions as constant as possible, organisms will undergo motivational shifts, which will affect at least the zeroth-order probabilities. Such changes can be expected especially in the case of social interactions. As Slater (1973) points out, the two most likely reasons why two behaviors may be more closely associated in time than expected are that they share causal factors and therefore tend to occur in the same situations, or that one act stimulates the other in a particular way. Only the second type of contingency may be suitable for a rigorous Markov chain analysis. Because in most behavioral sequences both these aspects will be represented, Slater recommends that first-order sequence analysis (to reveal associations that might result from sequence effects) be combined with correlative techniques (suitable for revealing the "looser" associations that may result from common causal factors). A more critical attitude is adopted by Bekoff (1977), who in fact rejects Markovian analyses, unless stationarity is shown to exist.

However, one can also take the nonstationarity into account and use the information-statistical measures in a meaningful manner to demonstrate shifts in sequential dependencies, as in the instances already cited, that is, the studies of Dingle (1969) and Hazlett and Estabrook (1974a, 1974b). This was also done in a study by Mishler and Waxler (1975), concerning the sequential patterning of verbal interactions in human families. These authors computed the transmission measures for the dependency of behavior of family members on the previous behavior of their partners. However, in order to detect possible fluctuations in this covariability, they made use of a "moving window technique." The sequence record consisted of many short units. The "window," an episode of 50 such units, was moved over the record in steps of 1 unit, and for each window position the transmission measure was computed. These T measures were then plotted as a function of time. The resulting T curve shows peaks and valleys, indicating periods of strong and weak dependency, that is, periods in which a partner takes the other's behavior into account to greater and lesser degrees. Not only can such results lead to global discrimination (in the present study one could discriminate between families with normal and with schizophrenic children), they can also point to phases in the interaction that have particular significance because of their nature and circumstances.

Although information theory may be a general tool with wide applicability, it is in essence a global method, which measures average constraints of the interaction system under consideration but does not provide specific information about the meaning of individual elements (van den Bercken, 1979; Losey, 1978). For such specific questions one may use methods that involve more direct matrix inspection (e.g., the analysis of residuals or lag sequential analysis; see Section 7.4) or time series analysis (see Section 7.7).

A serious difficulty in Markovian and information-statistical approaches is that the way in which we define the behavioral events, establish the size of the repertoire, and determine the degree to which we split up the behavioral stream has far-reaching consequences for the magnitude of the information-statistical measures. In view of this, one should be very skeptical about any attempts to compare absolute measures, for instance, across species. The values can be compared only if the relevant criteria are identical.

Wilson (1975) has pointed out that there are important aspects of communication that cannot easily be revealed by the methods discussed here. These methods presuppose that behavior can be segmented in discrete events. How, then, are graded signals to be treated? The methods are based on patterns of contingency, which are rather closely and certainly homogeneously distributed in time. How is one to interpret signals that have a so-called primer or cumulative tonic effect, rather than a releaser effect, in other words, signals that act as motivational factors by slowly and gradually altering a receiver's readiness to respond in a particular manner (Schleidt, 1973). Both primer and releaser effects could also be related to the length of time the signal has acted on the receiver. Finally, some signals may cause highly significant responses to be released with a considerably latency.

	1.	2.	3.	4.	5.	6.	7.
1. Body shake	− (solid), + (open)						
2. Scratch			+	+			
3. Preen		+	+ (open)	−			
4. Stretch both wings	+	−		−	+	−	−
5. Wing & leg stretch				+			
6. Other groom						+ (open)	
7. Other behavior				+			

Figure 7.23. Matrix of the significant within-animal transitions in the plumage-maintenance behavior of the skylark. Two classes of transitions have been distinguished: those with intervals shorter than 1 minute (solid symbols on the left in each cell) and those with intervals longer than 1 minute (open symbols on the right). *Source:* Data from Delius, 1969.

7.7. Time as a factor in the interdependence of behavioral events

Figure 7.23 is particularly apt for showing the influence of time on the interdependence of behavioral events. The figure, taken from a study by Delius (1969) on the body- and plumage-care behavior of skylarks, is derived from a transition frequency matrix; in this matrix are recorded those transition doublets that deviate significantly from expectation either positively (+) or negatively (−). Because there was rather great variation in the intervals between the behavior elements, the procedure was carried out twice, first for those transitions with interevent intervals shorter than 1 minute and next for those with intervals longer than 1 minute. This matrix shows that the number of significant transitions decreases with larger intervals; so there is a diminution of the constraints owing to time. This is not contrary to our intuition. After 1 minute, however, new constraints show up, and so the organization structure changes with time. This is clearest in the case of the repetition of *body shake,* the performance of which introduces a refractory period, followed by a period of facilitation.

Clearly, what is needed are methods that can give more precise insight and detailed information about the relation between the (possible changes in) behavior probabilities and time. There are a number of methods that provide insight into the temporal distribution function of series of events. The general mathematical and statistical aspects of these methods, some of which are commonplace in the physical sciences, have been expounded in Cox and Lewis (1966). Because these approaches have been introduced in ethology by authors such as Hauske (1967), Delius (1969), and van der Kloot and Morse (1975), they are gradually finding wider application. For a review see Fagen and Young (1978). A thorough mathematical treatment of the different types of time-based probability distributions is to be found in Metz (1974).

Survivor curves of interact intervals and act durations

The simplest hypothesis is that different behavior acts occur independently; that is, the probabilities of their occurrence are not influenced by past history. For each given act this probability is constant through time (a Poisson process). As Figure 7.24 illustrates, this implies that the intervals between two given acts, as well as between repetitions of the same act, have an exponential distribution (Cox & Lewis, 1966). The most vivid way to represent such stochastic data is by a log-survivor or *ln*-survivor curve. If the data indeed represent a Poisson process, the log- or *ln*-survivor curve is a straight line, the slope of which indicates the termination rate of intervals between the respective events. Various types of distribution that deviate from the Poisson model can be visually recognized quite easily, because they deviate from a straight line.

Figure 7.25 gives the most typical examples of such types of distribution. Note that the *intervals* need not refer only to the time that passes before an act is succeeded by a particular other act, but may refer also to the time between the onset and the termination of a behavior: its *durations*. Finally, they may refer to time elapsed since a stimulus was applied and a response was scored; then they refer to *latencies*. The curve in Figure 7.25a shows an abundance of short intervals; that is, the intervals have an initial high likelihood of being ended. But as the interval survives for a longer time, its chance of being broken off is diminished. This can be interpreted in two ways: Either the factors that terminate the event decrease gradually after each initiating event, or the survivor curve is the combination of two or more straight lines; that is, it reflects at least two different termination processes. If the data refer to intervals between acts of the same type, these acts can be said to have a tendency to occur in bouts.

The convex curve of Figure 7.25b shows an increasing termination rate or *hazard* (cf. the intervals between birth and death). Obviously the factors causing the event that ends the interval are weak after the initiating event but gain in strength gradually (or perhaps even progres-

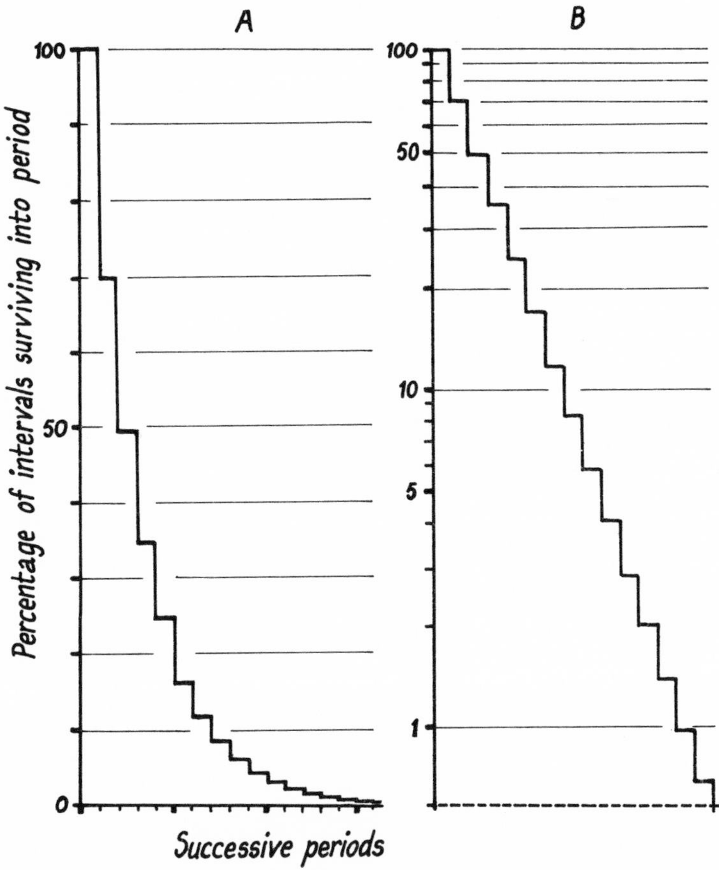

Figure 7.24. Survivor curve *(A)* and log-survivor curve *(B)* of interevent intervals. The abscissa represents the time, divided into periods of arbitrary length *t*. The ordinate represents the percentage of the intervals that survive through a given period. If the probability that a given event occurs to terminate the interval is constant through time, a constant fraction of the intervals surviving in the successive periods will be terminated. If the probability that the terminating event occurs in a period *t* is 0.3, then 30% of the intervals will be ended in period 1 and 70% will survive till period 2. Again, 70% of these (that is, 49% of the original population) will survive till period 3, and so on. The distribution of surviving intervals is exponential. As the example shows, the curve for the log-survivor distribution will be a straight line.

sively). If a survivor curve refers to durations of a behavior, a convex curve can be said to characterize a behavior of the "finisher" type (Fagen & Young, 1978), the completion of the behavior being dependent, for instance, on the building up of some result to a certain norm or limiting capacity, or on the depletion of some source of a given dimension. A straight curve – that is, one in which the ending occurs at random – can be said to characterize an interrupter type process, in which the

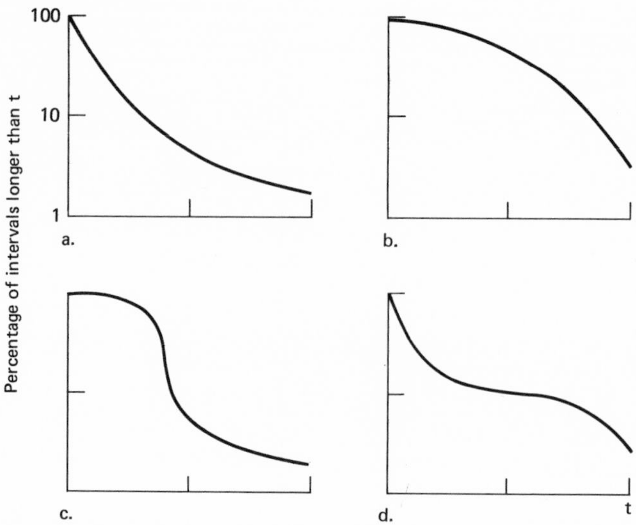

Figure 7.25. Various log survivors indicative of nonexponential interval distributions.

behavior is stopped by some unpredictable factor. If the respective causal factors for two (or more) behaviors tend to be present more or less simultaneously, the way in which the behaviors share the time is revealed by the distribution of the durations of these behaviors. If behavior *A* is of the "finisher" type, whereas the behavior *B* with which it alternates breaks at random, *A* can be said to be *controlling* *B* or to be *dominant* over *B* (McFarland, 1974). Which one is dominant, *A* or *B*, may depend on the relative strength of the respective causal factors; if they vary, switches in dominance between behaviors occur (for a detailed elaboration of the theoretical aspects of time sharing and the methodological aspects of its study, see Cohen & McFarland, 1979; McFarland & Lloyd, 1973; Silby & McCleery, 1976). The analogy with time sharing and turn taking in social interaction (for example, verbal intercourse) is obvious.

More complex log-survivor curves may be found. The example in Figure 7.25c indicates the existence of a rhythmic pattern, if it concerns intervals between acts of the same type. The example of Figure 7.25d could apply to life durations in a population with heavy infant mortality. A similar curve, presented by Fagen and Young (1978) for the inter-respiration interval lengths of a blue whale, suggests the existence of two distinct types of respiration and associated dive behavior.

If a log-survivor curve reveals nonstationarity, in that a probability of a transition in behavior changes in time, one may try to discover the sources of nonstationarity by investigating separately the interval distri-

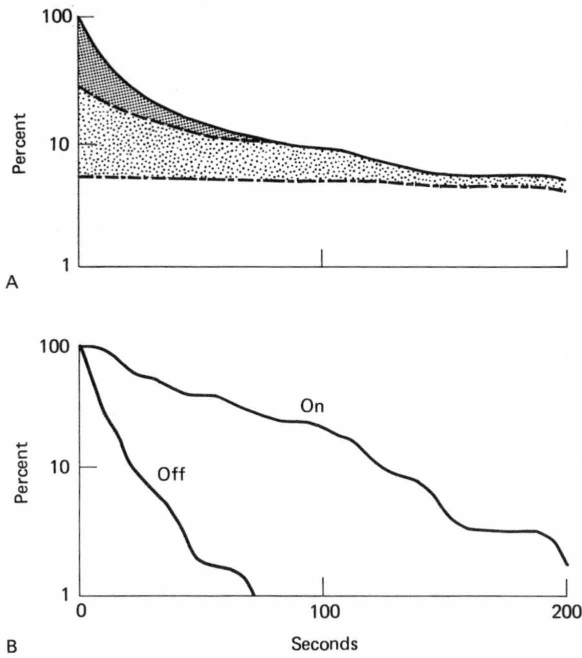

Figure 7.26. (A) Log-survivor curve of the durations of "on-mother" periods (*i.e.*, the infant is, at least partly, supported by the body of the mother) in a mother–infant pair of rhesus monkeys. The contributions of three different types of *on-mother* periods, namely, *off-nipple* (heavily speckled), *on-nipple* (lightly speckled), and *nursing* (unspeckled) have been indicated. (B) Log survivors of those on-mother periods that are terminated by the mother. Two types have been distinguished; in the one the infant is *on* and in the other *off* the nipple. This difference in condition is of great influence on the mother's behavior, as is evident from the different termination rates. These are both constant, as the log survivors do not differ significantly from a straight line. *Source:* Adapted from Dienske and Metz, 1977.

butions of certain subclasses of the process. This method was used in a study by Dienske and Metz (1977) on the regulation of contacts in mother – infant pairs of rhesus monkeys. This study makes extensive use of log-survivor methods. One aspect concerns *on-mother* contacts (the infant is sitting on the mother). Such contact episodes can be broken either by the child or by the mother. The log-survivor curve for the latter case is given in Figure 7.26 and is concave. If we separate the episodes that are ended by the mother into two types, those during which the child keeps a nipple in its mouth and those without a nipple in the mouth, then a straight log-survivor curve appears for each type of episode. In each situation then the mother's tendency to end the contact remains constant over time; in one situation ("nipple in mouth") it is lower than in the other, however. Thus the influence of various factors

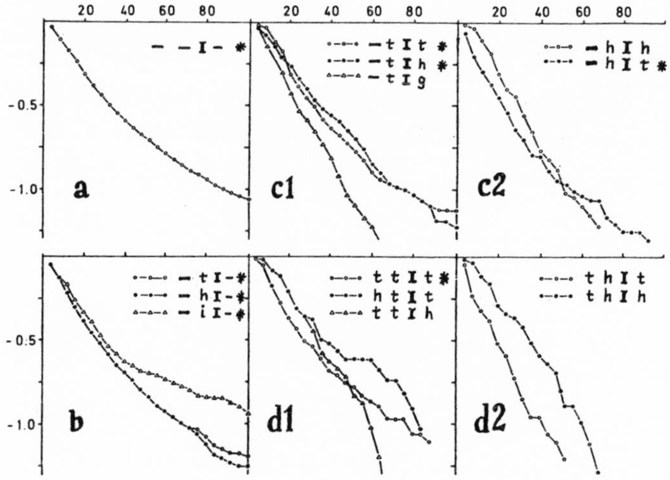

Figure 7.27. Log-survivor curves of various interevent intervals in the social-contact behavior of squirrel monkeys. The behavior units involved are: touching partner's head *(h)*, touching partner's trunk *(t)*, inspection of genitals *(i)*, and grasping partner's hips with both hands *(g)*. The curve of *a* is based on *all* interevent intervals *I*, irrespective of the nature of the bordering events (– – *I* –). The curve deviates significantly from a straight line, as is indicated by the asterisk. The fact that the curve is convex may imply that the sample of intervals consists of two or more samples from exponential distributions, each with a different termination rate. By specifying successively more bordering events of the intervals one may isolate different survivor functions indicating an influence of the specified event. If the resulting log survivors are still convex, specification of further events is indicated, until the resulting log survivors no longer differ from a straight line and the corresponding interval samples may be regarded as homogeneous. In *b* the preceding event is specified (– *m I* –). The log survivor for intervals initiated with *inspection of partner's genitals* clearly differs from those for intervals initiated by *touching partner's head* and *touching partner's trunk*. Each of the curves is still convex, suggesting that further differentiation is possible. In *c1* and *c2* the behavior that closes the interval is specified (– *m I n*). Again a few convex curves remain. In *d1* and *d2* a further preceding element is specified *(l m I n)*. One class of sample, namely, *t t I t*, still has a convex log survivor, indicating that even earlier events may make a difference. *Source:* Adapted from Pruscha and Maurus, 1979.

(circumstances, nature of the interactors, etc.) on a sequential process can be investigated. Another recent investigation along these lines has been done by Pruscha and Maurus (1979). They investigated certain interaction types in squirrel monkeys and differentiated these on the basis of log-survivor characteristics in more homogeneous subtypes (Figure 7.27). To establish whether an interval distribution is indeed a homogeneous Poisson distribution, van der Kloot and Morse (1975) recommend two tests.

It is interesting to compare the results of the classic transition frequency analysis as portrayed in Figure 7.23 with the results of an

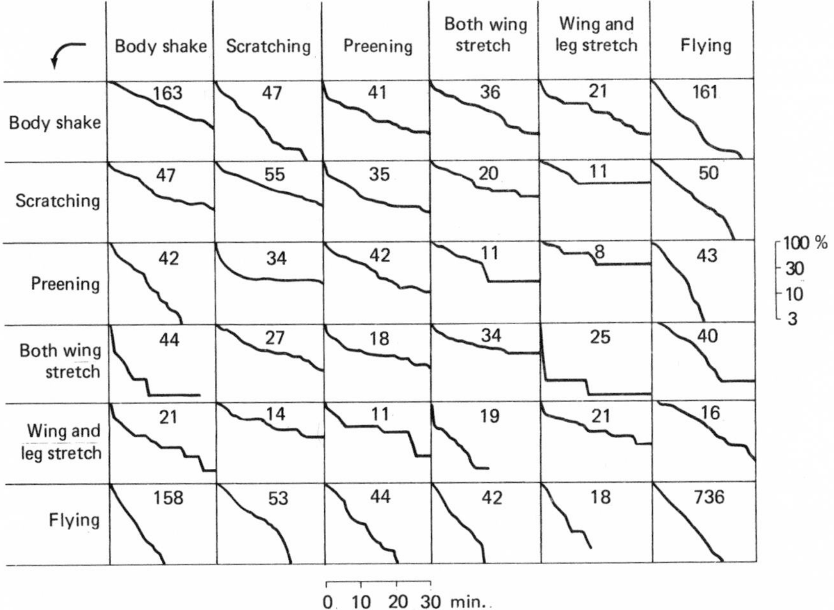

Figure 7.28. Log-survivor curves of the intervals between maintenance acts of skylarks. Top-row acts precede left-column ones. The ordinate gives, logarithmically, the percentage of interact intervals lasting longer than the time indicated on the abscissa. Small figures give the total number of the different interact intervals. *Source:* Delius, 1969, p. 159.

interval analysis in log-survivor form carried out on the same material, represented in Figure 7.28. Figure 7.23 revealed that the probability of the *body shake – body shake* transition changes considerably in time (by this method only those changes in transition probabilities which take place around the arbitrary demarcation point of 1 minute will be revealed). This altered probability is also reflected in the log-survivor curve. The curves clearly provide a more differentiated picture.

Time-lag correlation methods

There are alternative methods of investigating whether events in a time series are related to one another; in these, some correlation measure concerning their occurrence over a range of time lags is computed.

Figure 7.29 illustrates the principle of one such method, namely, a *coincidence count method* as applied by Heiligenberg (1973). The time scale of the behavior record is divided into a number of equally long sampling intervals or time bins. The length of the time bin chosen in this case is such that the different point events in the record fall into separate bins

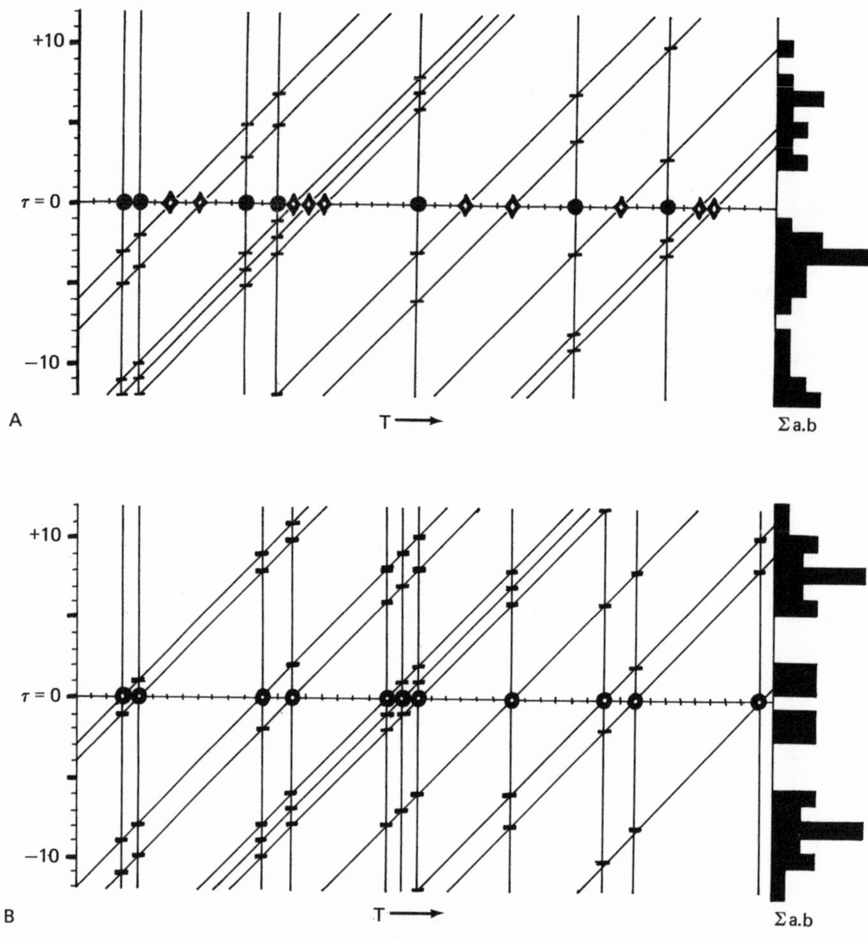

Figure 7.29. (A) Diagram of the method of cross-correlation with coincidence-frequency counts over a series of time lags τ: ● = behavior *a;* ◆ = behavior *b;* ✱ = coincidence. The behavior record over time *(T)* is given at τ = 0. The record of *b* is shifted with respect to the record of *a* with steps τ· For each respective time lag the number of coincidences (*ab* = 1) is summed in the histogram at the right. The histogram suggests that *b* tends to follow *a* with a modal delay of τ = 3 and that *a* tends not to be followed by *b* within 2τ units. (B) An auto-correlation can be made in an analogous manner. The histogram suggests that the event may occur in short bouts within 3τ units. These bouts tend to be repeated after about 8τ units.

(the presence in the record of acts with a noteworthy duration makes things more complicated, but I shall not go into this problem here). The presence of an act in a time bin is recorded with a score of 1, whereas its absence yields a score of 0. If we now shift the record of the one act along the record to the other act, increasing the time lag successively with one bin length, the product term of coinciding bins will be 1, provided that the two acts whose relation is to be investigated coincide. The sum of these products can be calculated for each time lag. Inspection of the profile of these product sums over the time lags can show peaks and valleys indicative of certain temporal dependencies.

Heiligenberg used the sum of the product terms to construct a product moment coefficient of correlation for each time lag. Note that this is a rather unconventional application. If one wants to obtain a good temporal resolution and therefore chooses comparatively short time bins, the acts will tend to occur in a minority of the time bins, and consequently, the coefficients will remain very low.

We can distinguish two main types of time-lag correlation methods. In the first type one relates the occurrence of identical acts as performed by only one individual in order to reveal patterns of repetition. This is called *serial correlation* or *auto-correlation.* In this case the correlation at time lag 0 will be 1, and the distribution of coefficients will be symmetrical around time lag 0. In the case of a fully random process, one would expect a level distribution. In the second type one relates the occurrence of two *different* acts; this is the so-called *cross-correlation.* Then, as a rule, the correlation at time lag 0 will be 0, and the distribution of the coefficients on either side of time lag 0 need *not* be symmetrical. One can use cross-correlations in three ways: first, to relate different acts in one and the same individual (*intraindividual cross-correlations*); secondly, to relate identical acts in different individuals; and thirdly, to relate different acts in different individuals (the latter two applications one could call *interindividual cross-correlations*).

Heiligenberg (1973) applied this method in a study of the intraindividual dependencies between social acts in the behavior of territorial males of the zebra fish (a cichlid species). In order to reveal the internal structuring of the behavior, he randomized as many external influences as possible, specifically, those coming from the social companions. He placed a number of juvenile conspecifics in each male's tank as stimulus objects and behavior targets. Juveniles are not yet able to give a structured answer to the agonistic and courtship activities of the territory owner; and in order to randomize the juveniles' responses even further, they were all blinded. The coincidence correlations between the acts of a male are shown in Figure 7.30. Heiligenberg went on to compare the empirically found correlation functions with theoretically calculated correlation functions on the assumption that the behavior is generated according to a renewal-process model. For the details of this sophisticated approach, the reader is referred to the original publication.

In Heiligenberg's study nearly all correlation functions leveled off

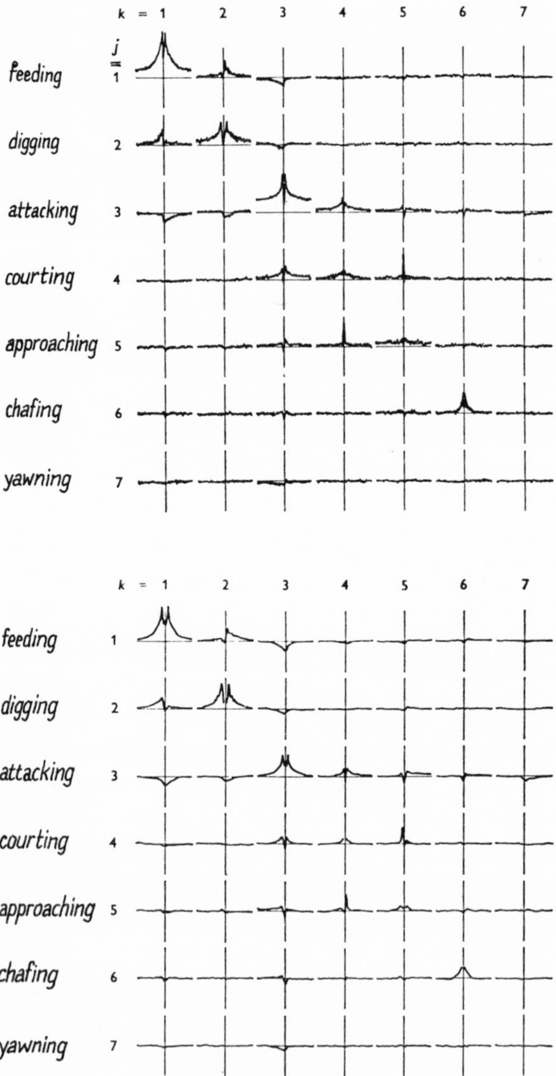

Figure 7.30. Time-lag coincidence correlations between 7 different behaviors of a cichlid fish species. Each of the 49 correlation functions is plotted in a graph, the abscissa of which ranges from -60 *(left)* to +60 *(right)* seconds with respect to the occurrence of the behavior in the row *(j)*. The ordinate represents the correlation coefficient and ranges from -0.05 to +0.05. The top matrix gives the empirical coincidence correlations, the bottom matrix gives the theoretical correlations under the assumption that the behavior is generated according to a *renewal-process* model. According to this model the probability that a certain event will occur depends only on the previous event and the time since that event. As soon as the event occurs, the probability is *reset* at the initial value and the process is renewed. To use an analogy: If you replace an old lamp bulb by a new one, the chance that it will wear

within 1 minute. Heiligenberg, however, suspected the existence of long-term fluctuations. He investigated these by means of an analogous method, the *frequency count method*. In this case one uses much longer time bins, and the frequency counts of an act per time bin are correlated.

The different methods of time-lag correlations were applied by van der Kloot and Morse (1975). In this study they investigated the dependencies of two courtship acts of red-breasted merganser ducks; to reveal the communication structure they determined auto- and cross-correlations within individuals and cross-correlations across individuals, of different as well as the same acts.

If periodicities are expected in a behavior, van der Kloot and Morse recommend yet another method of auto-correlation, which is well suited to revealing such periodicities, namely, *interval correlation*. Suppose the acts *a* are separated by intervals of different length, then the auto-correlation (or auto-covariances) can be calculated between two series of that same record of interval durations, shifted with respect to each other over a certain range of lags.

It is not difficult to imagine how an extension of the record with a periodic thickening and thinning of the occurrences of *a* would yield a string of correlation coefficients (or covariance measures) with repeated significant values. In practice the problem may be that the correlation-lag function may not always be unambiguous, and it may be difficult to determine whether a pattern represents chance variations from a nonperiodic process. The difficulty here is that the coefficients for different lags are not independent of each other. A Fourier analysis using the auto-covariances as coefficients is a well-known means of uncovering a periodicity. The variance is transformed from a time scale

Caption to Figure 7.30 (*cont.*)
out (and you will have to replace it once more) depends on the type of lamp bulb installed and on the time gone by since the replacement (the chance of wearing out will increase with time). The chance is *not* dependent, however, on the type of bulb installed the previous time and the length of time the previous bulb stayed intact. In other words, the intervals between successive replacements are independent. In connection with behavior, a renewal-process model implies that each behavioral event initiates a new state in which a certain probability function concerning the occurrence of subsequent behavior starts while the aftereffects of previous performances are being erased. Whether a renewal-process model is adequate can be investigated as follows: If subsequent intervals are indeed independent, execution of the same correlation procedure will yield the same correlation functions if the empirically found intervals are shuffled. In this case the correlation functions theoretically calculated on the basis of this assumption of independence did indeed yield a result that was judged insufficiently different from the empirical results to justify the acceptance of dependencies more complex than those of a renewal-process model.

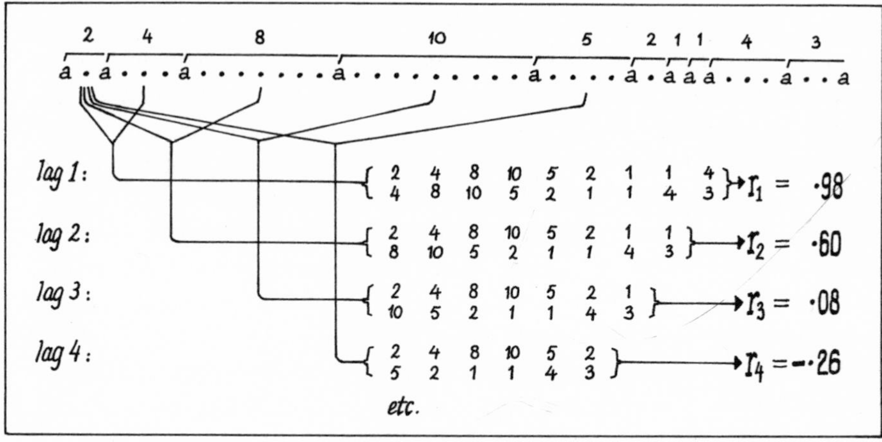

Figure 7.31. Schematic representation of the procedure of time-lag interval correlation.

to a frequency scale, a procedure that yields a so-called periodogram, the significance of which can be tested. For a detailed treatment of these methods and several alternatives, see van der Kloot and Morse (1975) and Fagen and Young (1978).

7.8. The phrase structure grammar model

In the preceding paragraphs we have seen that there are several possible ways of detecting orderliness in the serial process that we call behavior. Each of these ways highlights particular aspects of the organization. Thus categorization methods lead to a classification scheme in the form of a multilevel hierarchy. Sequential analyses culminate in Markovian or – if time is considered as a relevant aspect – in semi-Markovian concepts. S. A. Altmann (1965) was one of the early researchers who empirically investigated the possibility of behavior being a higher-order Markov process. He doubted whether such a model, although quite illuminative on aspects of the behavioral organization, would permit a comprehensive description of the behavior. The Markov model implies that an act depends to a certain extent on the last or antecedent event, to a lesser extent on the last but one event, and so on, in a monotonically decreasing function of the number of steps. Altmann pointed out, however, that "nested constraints" might exist, at least in human behavior. But even in the behavior of much more primitive animals, constraints exist that are at variance with a Markov model.

As early as 1941, Baerends had provided clear evidence for non-

Markovian constraints in connection with the "brood care" of an animal as simple as the digger wasp. The insect simultaneously takes care of several larvae, each of which has been deposited in a different burrow. The care for each larva is a rather fixed routine that, after the initial stage, operates almost independently of external feedback. The animal attends to its different young in turn. Returning to a particular young after an interval in which she has cared for the others but also has performed other behaviors, she picks up the routine at the point where she left off the last time. So she keeps a record and follows a time schedule, while functioning according to an action plan. Such a process, with dependencies of steps remote in time and interruptions by other behavior, defies explanation by a conventional Markov model. It is conceivable that there are, not only in human behavior (Miller, Galanter, & Pribram, 1960), but also in animal behavior, hierarchies of functions; thus, Kortlandt (1955) developed the idea of a hierarchical nesting of "appetites" on the basis of his studies of nest building behavior in cormorants. As Dawkins (1976) put it recently in a reappraisal of the concept of the hierarchical organization of behavior, often subsidiary goals are set up in the service of more global ones; thus decisions about possible actions in the distant future may be taken before decisions that concern the near future. The analogy with routines and subroutines imbedded therein, as found in programming instruction, is obvious.

Many years ago the structural analogy of nonverbal behavior and language was considered (S. A. Altmann, 1965), and in 1965 Marshall investigated the possibility of adapting the descriptive methods developed in psycholinguistics. He wrote a generative grammar for the reproductive behavior of the male pigeon. This unpublished work was discussed by Hutt and Hutt (1970) and Vowles (1970). Bodnár and van Baren-Kets (1974) applied the phrase structure grammar model to a category of human behavior. Before considering their study, let us have a quick look at the principles of this approach. More extensive expositions can be found in Hutt and Hutt (1970), Dawkins (1976), and Westman (1977).

Just like language, behavior consists of a finite number of elements, juxtaposed in strings according to a plan (the "rules"). This plan is supposed to constitute a hierarchical process in the organism, one that controls the order in which the operations are performed. One can distinguish groups of elements (words or, in our case, acts) that bear close statistical relationships to each other, closer than to members of other groups. These groups may be hierarchically nested in other groups. A linguistic example from Miller (1962), also used by Hutt and Hutt (1970), serves as a good illustration.

In the sentence *Bill hit the ball, the ball* is a more natural unit than *hit the;* we could replace *the ball* by *it*. Similarly, *hit the ball* is a more natural unit than *Bill hit the* and could be replaced by *acted.* Such units can be indicated by theoretical constructs such as *noun, verb, noun phrase, verb phrase,* and so on. These appear in certain orders, irrespective of their semantic meaning. A generative grammar is a theoretical system constructed to generate the sentences of the natural language by applying so-called production rules that make use of constructs such as those mentioned.

The complete utterance is referred to as the *sentence* **S** (in our case, sequence). It consists of an array of *terminal elements* (**a, b, c**) constituting the *terminal vocabulary* ($\mathbf{V_T}$); these are the words, and their behavioral "analoga" would be the acts. In addition, we need a *vocabulary of accessory elements,* $\mathbf{V_A}$ = [**A, B, C**]. These are hypothetical constructs. Note that **S** is also an element of $\mathbf{V_A}$. Finally there is a collection of *production rules* **P** of the form $\alpha \rightarrow \beta$; α and β can be elements of $\mathbf{V_T}$ and $\mathbf{V_A}$. A special class of grammars are the *probabilistic grammars* in which a certain probablity value is specified for the production of β from α: $\alpha \xrightarrow{P_{ij}} \beta$. A behavioral grammar will almost necessarily be a probabilistic grammar.

The following is a simple grammar:

$$\mathbf{V_T} = \{\mathbf{a, b}\}; \quad \mathbf{V_N} = \{\mathbf{S, A}\}$$

$$\mathbf{P} = \{\mathbf{S} \rightarrow \mathbf{aAa}, \quad \mathbf{A} \rightarrow \mathbf{a}, \quad \mathbf{A} \rightarrow \mathbf{bAb}\}$$

This grammar can generate sentences such as the following:

$$\mathbf{S} \rightarrow \mathbf{aAa} \rightarrow \mathbf{aaa}$$

$$\mathbf{S} \rightarrow \mathbf{aAa} \rightarrow \mathbf{abAba} \rightarrow \mathbf{ababa}$$

$$\mathbf{S} \rightarrow \mathbf{aAa} \rightarrow \mathbf{abAba} \rightarrow \mathbf{abbAbba} \rightarrow \mathbf{abbabba}$$

The sentence *Bill hit the ball* could be generated by the following grammar:

$\mathbf{V_T}$ = {Bill, John, Mary . . . , boy, girl, ball . . . , the, a . . . , hit, has . . .}

$\mathbf{V_A}$ = {**S,** noun phrase **NP**, verb phrase **VP**, article **A,** noun **N**, verb **V**}

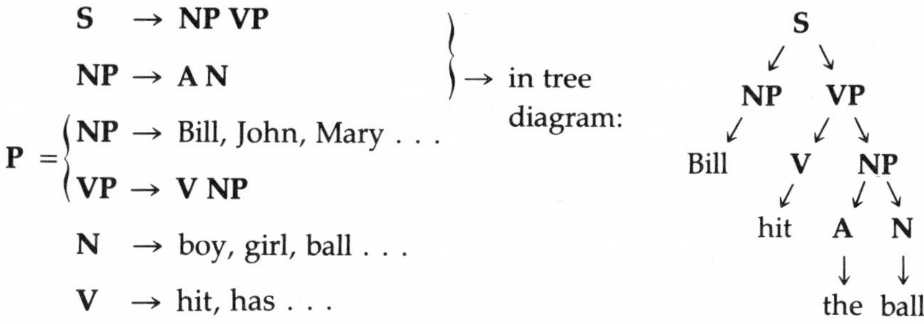

By further extension with recursive rules, a grammar can be composed that generates sentences such as *The boy, who has the ball, hit the girl.* This is an example of a non-Markovian chain with nested constraints.

Bodnár (1973, 1976) compared the behavior shown in a situation of free group social interaction by three categories of children: normal preschool children (2–4 years old), children with speech and hearing disorders (4–6 years), and mentally retarded children (mental age 2–4 years, physical age 8–15, IQ < 50). The behavior was compared in several respects. Although there were conspicuous differences in the level of activities and the relative frequencies of acts, he felt that more essential differences might be found in the organization of the behavior.

Using data-reduction techniques (e.g., principal-component and cluster analyses), he found several categories of behavior. One of these, present in each of the groups, could be termed *introvert* behavior. This behavior was considered suitable for a grammatical approach, one reason being that it is monologue.

The construction of the grammar for the normal children has been described by Bodnár and van Baren-Kets (1974). The principles outlined by Suppes (1970) were followed, and the terminal elements (the acts) were given. In this case they were

$$\mathbf{V_T} = \{\mathbf{a}, \mathbf{d}, \mathbf{r}, \mathbf{k}, \mathbf{o}, \mathbf{b}\}$$

a = auto-manipulation
d = thumb in mouth
r = rocking
k = looking around
o = observing
b = chin on breast

In this form of grammar construction, the sequences (uninterrupted strings of one or more of these acts) and their frequencies are empirically known (see Table 7.1). However, the selection of the accessory elements and the construction of production rules is an iterative process of the imagination that should be guided by parsimony and intuition. Finally, the probabilities of the production rules can be estimated from the table of sequence frequencies (Table 7.1). The grammar thus obtained can generate sequences, and the relative frequencies of the generated sequences to be expected in this way can be compared with those actually found. This comparison may lead to alterations in the grammar. The process is stopped as soon as no further improvements can be obtained in a parsimonious manner.

For the normal children three grammars were constructed. The accessory elements for grammar I and II were as follows:

$V_A = \{S, V, A, P, E, K, O, D, M\}$

V = visual attention
A = autistic behavior
P = passive visual behavior
E = external visual behavior
K = looking around > 5 seconds
O = observing > 5 seconds
D = thumb-sucking pattern
M = auto-manipulation pattern

The production rules for grammar I are given in Table 7.2; Figure 7.32 presents the tree diagram for grammar I. Comparison of the frequencies of the sequences expected on the basis of the grammar with the frequencies actually found (see Table 7.3) led to modifications, which resulted in grammar II. The tree diagram for grammar II is given in Figure 7.32b. One of the modifications was the introduction of a new terminal element, namely **l**, which was *looking for longer than 25 seconds*. Grammar II had a much better fit than I, according to the χ^2 criterion. Grammar III, which was an alternative design, had a much worse fit.

In 1976, Bodnár reported some preliminary results on the comparison of the behavior of the three categories of children. It was of interest to see whether the grammar developed for normal children would fit the data obtained for the other categories. Of course, the probabilities of the production rules had to be adjusted. If there was a good fit after this adjustment, it would be possible to conclude that the principles of organization were fundamentally similar. The expectation was that the fit with the data from the mentally retarded children would be bad, and this indeed was the case. Differences concerned perseverance effects and the positions of *rocking* and *auto-manipulation*. The fit to the data

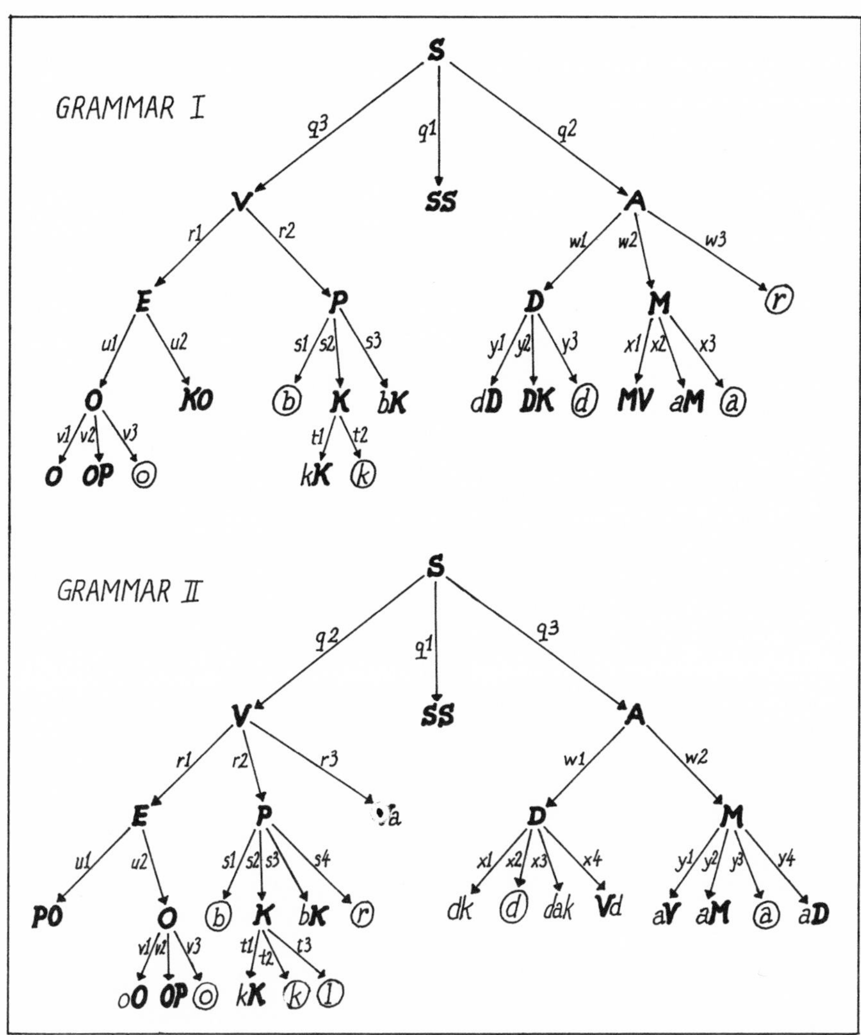

Figure 7.32. Tree diagrams of grammars I and II for the introvert behavior of preschool children. *Source:* Bodnár and van Baren-Kets, 1974, pp. 48, 54.

from the children with speech and hearing disorders was much better, as was expected (Bodnár, personal communication, 1979).

The example suggests that the grammatical methods may be useful for investigating hypotheses about behavioral organization. The methods have their limitations, though. With a greater number of variables, the number of production rules may increase so much as to render the method unpractical. There seems to be no way of knowing whether one has an optimal solution. Suboptimality becomes apparent only when a

Table 7.1. *Observed frequencies of sequences of introvert behavior in groups of normal preschool children*

k	493	kkoa	1	adkb	1	bkaak	1	dbk	2	obka	4
ko	46	kkobk	1	add	2	bkaa	1	dbkaa	1	obkaa	1
kok	2	kkooo	1	adbkk	1	bkaak	1	dboo	1	obod	1
koko	3	kka	4	ab	6	bkr	1	da	6	obob	3
kokok	2	kkakk	2	abk	3	bkddd	3	dak	26	oboo	1
kokk	1	kkakb	1	abka	1	bkbkb	1	dr	4	od	8
kokkk	3	kkad	2	abor	1	bko	12	drk	1	odo	1
koa	2	kkbkk	6	ar	2	bkokk	1	dro	1	oda	1
kobk	1	kkdkk	1	aa	23	bkobk	1	drda	1	odod	2
koo	9	kkrk	1	aak	2	bkoo	1	ddadk	1	odd	1
kook	1	kkrkk	1	aakak	1	bkooo	2	ddd	1	oddo	1
kookk	1	kkk	18	aakk	1	bkk	10	dddk	1	oddkk	1
kooda	1	kkko	2	aakd	1	bkko	2	dddd	4	odddk	1
kooo	1	kkkoa	1	aao	2	bkkbk	1	ddddd	3	or	1
ka	29	kkka	3	aaoo	1	bkkkk	1	o	631	ora	1
kak	4	kkkad	1	aad	1	bo	3	ok	40	oo	105
kakk	2	kkbk	1	aadk	1	bob	1	oko	5	ook	8
kaka	2	kkkk	9	aadkd	1	bobo	1	okok	1	ooko	1
kao	1	kkkka	1	aadkk	1	boo	2	okoo	3	ookk	1
kaoa	1	kkkkd	1	aab	1	booo	2	okook	1	ookoa	1
kaoo	1	kkkkk	19	aaa	5	bd	1	okooa	1	ood	1
kad	1	a	276	aaak	2	bdk	1	okooo	2	oodk	1
kaa	1	ak	21	aaakk	2	ba	1	oka	1	oob	2
kaak	1	ako	3	aaao	1	br	1	okako	1	oobk	7
kaakk	1	akooo	3	aaaa	3	bbka	1	okb	2	oobka	1
kaaa	2	aka	1	aaaak	1	d	48	okbk	4	oobko	1
kd	5	akak	1	aaaaa	3	dk	29	okr	1	ooa	9
kdk	3	akbk	1	r	25	dko	1	okk	2	ooak	1
kdko	1	akk	6	rk	5	dkok	1	okkok	1	ooaoo	1
kdkdk	1	akko	1	rkad	1	dkd	1	okkk	1	oodo	1

kdkdd	1	akka	1	rkk	1	dkdk	1	okkka	2	ooo	20
kdkkk	1	ao	30	ro	2	dkddk	1	okkkk	1	oook	2
kda	1	aokaa	1	rob	1	dka	2	oa	23	oooa	4
kdr	1	aoa	3	ror	1	dkadk	1	oao	4	oooao	1
kdda	1	aoao	3	roo	1	dkra	1	oaoa	1	ooobk	3
kb	3	aoaoo	1	ra	4	dkkk	1	oakbk	1	ooor	4
kbk	1	oad	1	rb	3	do	10	oabo	1	oooo	6
kbkaa	1	aobk	1	rbk	1	dok	1	oabk	2	ooook	1
kbkk	5	aoo	7	rd	1	doa	1	oabkk	1	ooooa	2
kbkkk	1	aook	1	rr	1	doaa	1	oaa	4	oooor	2
kboka	1	aooa	2	b	55	dod	1	oaabk	1	ooooo	3
kboo	1	ad	7	bk	144	doda	1	ob	5		
kk	31	adoo	1	bka	12	dobk	1	obk	25		
kko	1	ada	2	bkak	2	db	1	obko	5	Total:	2654

Source: Bodnár and van Baren-Kets, 1974, p. 65.

Table 7.2. *Production rules and associated probabilities of grammar I*

$S \xrightarrow{q_1} SS$	$P \xrightarrow{s_3} bK$	$O \xrightarrow{v_3} o$
$S \xrightarrow{q_2} V$	$K \xrightarrow{t_1} kK$	$A \xrightarrow{w_1} D$
$S \xrightarrow{q_3} A$	$K \xrightarrow{t_2} k$	$A \xrightarrow{w_2} M$
$V \xrightarrow{r_1} E$	$E \xrightarrow{u_1} O$	$A \xrightarrow{w_3} r$
$V \xrightarrow{r_2} P$	$E \xrightarrow{u_2} KO$	$M \xrightarrow{x_1} MV$
$P \xrightarrow{s_1} b$	$O \xrightarrow{v_1} oO$	$M \xrightarrow{x_2} aM$
$P \xrightarrow{s_2} K$	$O \xrightarrow{v_2} OP$	$M \xrightarrow{x_3} a$
$D \xrightarrow{y_1} dD$	$D \xrightarrow{y_2} DK$	$D \xrightarrow{y_3} d$

Source: Bodnár and van Baren-Kets, 1974, p. 46.

person with a brighter idea comes along. Finally, there is still some uncertainty about the best way of establishing goodness of fit (e.g., Hass & Wepman, 1972).

7.9. Conclusion

This review has been method oriented and not problem oriented. However it is intended to help the student of nonverbal communication to find the right tools for dealing with his or her problems.

The review shows that there is a great diversity of methods available to help us in detecting order and structure in sequences of elements of action and interaction. Gottman and Bakeman (1979) remind us that, even taken all together, these are no panacea. Certainly there is none that can be considered a single best and sovereign approach to all the problems of behavioral structure. This structure clearly cannot be commanded and all its aspects detected from one particular vantage point. Each of the methods has its particular sensitivities and limitations; it affords a specific survey of the matter. This urges us to be conscious about the nature of our questions in selecting a method and not to restrict ourselves too much in our choices.

Some of the methods that have been introduced during the last 15 years or so are rather complex and sophisticated. Even more important, they have become readily available in software libraries. The generally

Table 7.3. *Sequences of introvert behavior in groups of normal preschool children with observed frequencies ≥ 4*

S	Observed frequencies	Expected frequencies: Grammar I	Grammar II	Grammar III
k	493	411.3	424.6	346.6
ko	46	42.3	33.8	49.5
koo	9	7.6	5.8	2.8
ka	29	7.7	29.7	34.5
kak	4	0.4	0.2	1.0
kbkk	5	0.6	0.4	0.3
kd	5	3.2	10.9	12.5
kk	31	78.1	60.3	49.5
kka	4	1.5	4.2	0.8
kkbkk	6	0.1	0.1	0.3
kkk	18	14.8	8.6	4.5
kkkk	9	2.8	1.2	0.4
kkkkk	19	0.5	6.5	0.9
o	631	528.6	581.5	716.6
ok	40	25.3	41.1	59.4
oko	5	1.1	0.8	2.3
okbk	4	0.2	0.2	0.4
oa	23	10.0	40.7	41.4
oao	4	0.6	0.4	2.9
oaa	4	1.0	5.9	0.8
ob	5	5.1	8.3	6.6
obk	25	11.8	12.3	17.5
obko	5	0.4	0.2	0.7
obka	4	0.2	0.1	0.3
od	8	4.2	6.4	15.0
oo	105	95.2	99.4	32.9
ook	8	6.4	7.1	2.7
ooa	9	1.8	7.0	11.2
oobk	7	2.1	1.2	4.7
ooo	20	17.1	17.0	1.5
oooa	4	0.3	1.2	0.1
ooor	4	0.1	2.6	0.1
oooo	6	3.1	2.9	0.1
a	276	333.2	252.2	241.4
ak	21	16.6	16.9	34.5
akk	6	3.2	2.4	4.5
ao	30	21.4	23.1	41.4
aoo	7	3.8	4.0	1.9
ab	6	1.1	3.4	0.6
ad	7	2.6	6.3	1.3
aa	23	33.3	36.6	26.6
aaa	5	3.3	5.3	2.9
b	55	58.9	85.4	38.5
bk	144	137.1	127.3	102.1

Table 7.3 *(cont.)*

S	Observed frequencies	Expected frequencies: Grammar I	Grammar II	Grammar III
bko	12	4.1	10.1	14.6
bka	12	2.6	8.9	1.6
bkk	10	26.1	18.1	14.6
d	48	139.1	110.3	87.3
dk	29	2.3	46.7	12.5
do	10	4.2	1.0	12.5
da	6	2.6	0.9	1.3
dak	26	0.1	31.5	0.2
dr	4	0.4	0.1	0.1
dddd	4	0.4	0.0	0.2
r	25	55.2	38.1	26.7
rk	5	0.6	0.5	3.8
ra	4	1.0	0.3	0.4
Total	2,374	2,138.7	2,286.3	2,100.7
Rest	280	515.3	367.7	553.3
Degrees of freedom:		17	19	14
χ^2		314.7	189.4	362.9

Source: Bodnár and van Baren-Kets, 1974, p. 51.

laudable trend to apply quantitative methods stimulates the use of such sophisticated techniques; there is a risk, however, that these techniques may be chosen because of their availability, rather than because of their suitability for solving the scientific problems at hand. Recently, Bekoff (1977) emphasized that the methods should be adopted to the object of research and not vice versa. This author also stressed, as others had done before him, that the elegance of some of the methods should not tempt us to overlook the limitations imposed by the underlying assumptions. Especially in the case of Markov and information-statistical analyses, it is questionable whether the underlying assumptions are fulfilled. In some studies, such as those of van den Bercken and Cools (1980a, 1980b) the assumptions were obviously not fulfilled. In these studies information-theoretical measures were used in connection with the behavior of monkeys freely interacting in a group. Moreover, the results for a number of individuals were pooled. The assumption was, however, that possible fluctuations resulted in nonsystematic variation or increased noise and would not affect the conclusions drawn from the experiments. The question of the extent to which deviations from the assumptions can be regarded as "slight" will certainly continue to differentiate methodological purists and pragmatists. However, the burden of proof falls upon the latter.

The development of advanced mathematical methods enables investigators to master complex phenomena and to develop more "holistic" models. These methods, accordingly, may help us to acquire hitherto unattainable knowledge. Nevertheless, parsimony in the selection of the descriptive and analytical tools is still advisable (Fagen and Young, 1978). If a simple tool is adequate for the job, it should be given preference, if only because its use may make matters more understandable and communicable.

Notes

1. In its simplest form a Markov chain exists when in a sequence of different types of discrete, exclusive events, the probability that a certain event will occur at a given moment depends on the identity of the previous event in the chain, but not on earlier events; in other words, the past is considered to be represented in the antecedent event. In a Markov model the probability of occurrence of a given event is considered to be independent of the length of time elapsed since the previous event. If such a dependence does exist, however, the process can be described by using a so-called semi-Markov model (see Section 7.7).
2. The most dominant member of a group can show the behaviors indicating his status to all its fellow group members, but he need not do so frequently if his status is acknowledged. A low-ranking individual can display dominance indicators only to a few lower-ranking group members, but may do so very frequently to a particular individual.
3. The term *information* is often used in a confusing manner, namely, as an equivalent of *uncertainty*, whereas it is a complementary concept. For example, the common statement that a highly organized structure contains little information should be read to mean that there is little uncertainty left about its structure and that little information is needed to take away that uncertainty and to characterize that structure fully.

References

Altmann, J. Observational study of behaviour: Sampling Methods. *Behaviour*, 1974, *49*, 227–267.

Altmann, S. A. Sociobiology of rhesus monkeys: II. Stochastics of social communication. *Journal of Theoretical Biology*, *1965*, *8*, 490–522.

Armstrong, J. S., & Soelberg, P. On the interpretation of factor analysis. *Psychological Bulletin*, 1968, *70*, 361–364.

Aspey, W. P., & Blankenship, J.E. Spiders and snails and statistical tales: Application of multivariate analyses to diverse ethological data. In B. A. Hazlett (Ed.), *Quantitative methods in the study of animal behavior*. New York: Academic Press, 1977.

Attneave, F. *Applications of information theory to psychology*. New York: Holt, Rinehart & Winston, 1959.

Baerends, G. P. Fortpflanzungsverhalten und Orientierung der Grafwespe *Ammophila campestris* Jur. *Tijdschrift voor Entomologie*, 1941, *84*, 68–275.

Baerends, G. P. The functional organization of behaviour. *Animal Behavior*, 1976, *24*, 726–738.

Baerends, G. P., Brouwer, R., & Waterbolk, H. Tj. Ethological studies on *Lebistes reticulatus* (Peters). *Behaviour*, 1955, *8*, 248–334.

Bakeman, R. Untangling streams of behavior: Sequential analysis of observation data. In G. P. Sackett (Ed.), *Observing behavior* (Vol. 2). Baltimore: University Park Press, 1978.

Bakeman, R., & Dabbs, I. M. Social interaction observed: Some approaches to the analysis of behavior streams. *Personality and Social Psychology Bulletin*, 1976, *3*, 335–345.

Balthazart, J. Valideté de l'application de l'analyse factorielle à l'étude causale d'une séquence comportmentale avec un essai d'analyse du comportement agonistique chez *Tilapia macrochir* (Boulenger, 1912). *Annales de la Société Royale Zoologique de Belgique*, 1972, *102*, 3–34.

Balthazart, J. Analyse factorielle du comportement agonistique chez *Tilapia macrochir* (Boulenger, 1912). *Behaviour*, 1973, *46*, 37–72.

Bartlett, M. S. A further note on tests of significance in factor analysis. *British Journal of Statistical Psychology*, 1951, *4*, 1–2.

Bekoff, M. Quantitative studies of three areas of classical ethology: Social dominance, behavioral taxonomy and behavioral variability. In B. A. Hazlett (Ed.), *Quantitative methods in the study of animal behavior*. New York: Academic Press, 1977.

Bercken, J. van den. *Information-statistical analysis of social interaction in Java-monkeys applied in the neuro-ethology of the* nucleus caudatus. Unpublished doctoral dissertation, University of Nijmegen, 1979.

Bercken, J. H. L. van den, & Cools, A. R. Information-statistical analysis of social interaction and communication: An analysis-of-variance approach. *Animal Behavior*, 1980, *28*, 172–188.(a)

Bercken, J. H. L. van den, & Cools, A. R. Information-statistical analysis of factors determining ongoing behaviour and social interaction in Java monkeys *(Macaca fascicularis)*. *Animal Behavior*, 1980, *28*, 189–200.(b)

Bindra, D. *A theory of intelligent behavior*. New York: Wiley, 1976.

Bishop, Y. M. M., Fienberg, S. E., & Holland, P. W. *Discrete multivariate analysis*. Cambridge, Mass.: MIT Press, 1975.

Bodnár, F. A. De sociale gedragsstructuur van een groep zwakzinnige kinderen. *ZWO-jaarboek 1973*, pp. 165–170.

Bodnár, F. A. Humaan-ethologische verkenningen naar het gedrag van groepen kinderen. In J. de Wit, H. Bolle, & J. van Heel (Eds.), *Psychologen over het kind* (Vol. 4). Groningen: Tjeenk-Willink, 1976.

Bodnár, F. A., & Baren-Kets, E. J. van. Sequentiële analyse van gedragsobservaties bij jonge kinderen. *Nederlands Tijdschrift voor Psychologie*, 1974, *29*, 27–66.

Burton, J. Etude critique de l'analyse factorielle de la rivalité territoriale chez *Tilapia mossambica* Peters (Poisson cichlide). *Annales de la Société Royale Zoologique de Belgique*, 1970, *100*, 5–47.

Cairns, R. B. *The analysis of social interactions: Methods, issues and illustrations*. Hillsdale, N.J.: Erlbaum, 1979.

Cattell, R. B. *Handbook of multivariate experimental psychology*. (Chicago: Rand McNally, 1966.

Chatfield, C., & Lemon, R. E. Analysing sequences of behavioural events. *Journal of Theoretical Biology*, 1970, *29*, 427–445.

Cohen, S., & McFarland, D. Time-sharing as a mechanism for the control of behaviour sequences during courtship of the three-spined stickleback *(Gasterosteus aculeatus)*. *Animal Behavior*, 1979, *27*, 270–283.

Colgan, P. W. (Ed.). *Quantitative ethology*. New York: Wiley, 1978.
Colgan, P. W., and Smith, J. T. Multidimensional contingency table analysis. In P. W. Colgan (Ed.), *Quantitative ethology*. New York: Wiley, 1978.
Comrey, A. D. *A first course in factor analysis*. New York: Academic Press, 1973.
Conant, R. C., & Steinberg, J. B. Information exchanged in grasshopper interactions. *Information and Control*, 1973, *23*, 221–233.
Cormack, R. H. A review of classification. *Journal of the Royal Statistical Society*, 1971, *A134*, 321–367.
Cox, D. R., & Lewis, P. A. W. *The statistical analysis of series of events*. London: Methuen, 1966.
Davies, W. G. Cluster analysis applied to the classification of postures in the chilean flamingo *(Phoenicopterus chilensis)*. *Animal Behavior*, 1978, *26*, 381–388.
Dawkins, R. Hierarchical organisation: A candidate principle for ethology. In P. P. G. Bateson & R. A. Hinde (Eds.), *Growing points in ethology*. Cambridge: Cambridge University Press, 1976.
Dawkins, R., & Dawkins, M. Hierarchical organization and postural facilitation: Rules for grooming in flies. *Animal Behavior*, 1976, *24*, 739–755.
DeGhett, V. H. Hierarchical cluster analysis. In P. W. Colgan (Ed.), *Quantitative ethology*. New York: Wiley, 1978.
Delius, J. D. A stochastic analysis of the maintenance behaviour of skylarks. *Behaviour*, 1969, *33*, 137–178.
Dienske, H., & Metz, H. A. J. Mother – infant body contact in macaques: A time interval analysis. *Biology of Behavior*, 1977, *2*, 3–37.
Dingle, H. A statistical and information analysis of aggressive communication in the mantis shrimp *Gonadactylus bredini* Manning. *Primate Behaviour*, 1969, *17*, 561–575.
Douglas, J. M., & Tweed, R. L. Analysing the patterning of a sequence of discrete behavioural events. *Animal Behavior*, 1979, *27*, 1236–1252.
Dziuban, C. D., & Shirkey, E. C. When is a correlation matrix appropriate for factor analysis? *Psychological Bulletin*, 1974, *81*, 358–361.
Everitt, B. S. *Cluster analysis*. London: Heinemann, 1974.
Everitt, B. S. Cluster analysis and miscellaneous techniques. In A. E. Maxwell (Ed.), *Multivariate analysis in behavioural research*. London: Chapman & Hall, 1977.
Fagen, R. M., & Young, D. Y. Temporal patterns of behavior: Durations, intervals, latencies, and sequences. In P. W. Colgan (Ed.), *Quantitative ethology*. New York: Wiley, 1978.
Fedigan, L. M. A study of roles in Arishiyama West troop of Japanese monkeys *(Macaca fuscata)*. *Contributions to Primatology*, 1976, *9*, 1–95.
Frey, D. F., & Pimentel, R. A. Principal component analysis and factor analysis. In P. W. Colgan (Ed.), *Quantitative ethology*. New York: Wiley, 1978.
Garner, W. R. *Uncertainty and structure as psychological concepts*. New York: Wiley, 1962.
Golani, I. Non-metric analysis of behavioral interaction sequences in captive jackals *(Canis aureus* L.). *Behaviour*, 1973, *64*, 89–112.
Golani, I. Homeostatic motor processes in mammalian interactions: A choreography of display. In P. P. G. Bateson & P. H. Klopfer (Eds), *Perspectives in ethology* (Vol. 2). New York: Plenum, 1976.
Goodman, L. A. The analysis of cross-classified data: Independence, quasi-independence and interactions in contingency tables with or without missing entries. *Journal of the American Statistical Association*, 1968, *63*, 1091–1131.

Gottman, J. M. Detecting cyclicity in social interaction. *Psychological Bulletin, 1979, 86*, 338–348.

Gottman, J. M., & Bakeman, R. The sequential analysis of observational data. In M. E. Lamb, S. J. Suomi, & G. K. Stephenson (Eds.), *Social interaction analysis*. Madison: University of Wisconsin Press, 1979.

Gottman, J. M., Markman, H., & Notarius, C. The topography of marital conflict: A sequential analysis of verbal and non-verbal behavior. *Journal of Marriage and the Family*, 1977, *39*, 461–477.

Gottman, J. M., & Notarius, C. Sequential analysis of observational data using Markov chains. In T. R. Kratochwill (Ed.), *Single subject research: Strategies for evaluating change*. New York: Academic Press, 1978.

Haberman, S. J. The analysis of residuals in cross-classified tables. *Biometrics*, 1973, *29*, 205–220.

Harman, H. *Modern factor analysis*. Chicago: University of Chicago Press, 1967.

Harris, R. *A primer of multivariate analysis*. New York: Academic Press, 1975.

Hass, W. A., & Wepman, J. M. Information theory measures of grammatical goodness of fit. *Journal of Psycholinguistic Research*, 1972, *1*, 175–181.

Hauske, G. Stochastische und rhythmische Eigenschaften spontan auftretender Verhaltensweisen von Fischen. *Kybernetik*, 1967, *4*, 26–36.

Hauske, G., & Neuburger, E. Gerichtete Informationsgrössen zur Analyse gekoppelter Verhaltensweisen. *Kybernetik*, 1968, *4*, 171–181.

Hazlett, B. A. *Quantitative methods in the study of animal behavior*. New York: Academic Press, 1977.

Hazlett, B. A., & Bossert, W. H. A statistical analysis of the aggressive communication systems of some hermit crabs. *Animal Behavior*, 1965, *12*, 255–377.

Hazlett, B. A., & Estabrook, G. F. Examination of agonistic behavior by character analysis: I. The spider crab *Microphrys bicornutus*. *Behaviour*, 1974, *48*, 131–144. (a)

Hazlett, B. A., & Estabrook, G. F. Examination of agonistic behavior by character analysis: II. Hermit crabs. *Behaviour*, 1974, *49*, 88–110. (b)

Heiligenberg, W. Random processes describing the occurrence of behavioral patterns in a cichlid fish. *Animal Behavior*, 1973, *21*, 169–182.

Hinde, R. A., & Stevenson, J. G. Sequences of behaviour. *Advances in the Study of Behavior*, 1969, *2*, 267–296.

Hooff, J. A. R. A. M. van. A component analysis of the structure of the social behaviour of a semi-captive chimpanzee group. *Experientia*, 1970, *26*, 549–550.

Hooff, J. A. R. A. M. van. *Aspects of the social behaviour and communication in human and higher non-human primates*. Unpublished doctoral disseration, University of Utrecht, 1971.

Hooff, J. A. R. A. M. van. A structural analysis of the social behaviour of a semi-captive group of chimpanzees. In M. von Cranach & I. Vine (Eds.), *Expressive movement and non-verbal communication*. London: Academic Press, 1973.

Hutt, S. J., & Hutt, C. *Direct observation and measurement of behaviour*. Springfield, Ill.: Charles C. Thomas, 1970.

Kim, J. Factor analysis. In N. Nie et al. (Eds.), *Statistical package for the social sciences*. New York: McGraw Hill, 1975.

Kloot, W. van der, & Morse, M. J. A stochastic analysis of the display behaviour of the red-breasted merganser *(Mergus serrator)*. *Behaviour*, 1975, *54*, 181–216.

Kortlandt, A. Aspects and prospects of the concept of instinct (vicissitudes of the hierarchy theory). *Archives Néerlandaises Zoologie*, 1955, *11*, 155–284.

Kratochwill, T. R. *Single subject research: Strategies for evaluating change*. New York: Academic Press, 1978.

Lamb, M. E., Suomi, S. J., & Stephenson, G. R. *Social interaction analysis: Methodological issues*. Madison: University of Wisconsin Press, 1978,

Lemon, R. E., & Chatfield, C. Organization of song in cardinals. *Animal Behavior*, 1971, *19*, 1–17.

Lorenz, K. Gestaltwahrnehmung als Quelle wissenschaftlicher Erkenntniss. In Lorenz, *Ueber tierisches und menschliches Verhalten* (Vol. 2). Munich: Piper, 1967.

Losey, G. S. Information theory and communication. In P. W. Colgan (Ed.), *Quantitative ethology*. New York: Wiley, 1978.

Marko, H. Die Theorie der bidirektionalen Kommunikation und ihre Anwendung auf die Nachrichtenübermittlung zwischen Menschen (subjektive Information). *Kybernetik*, 1966, *3*, 128–136.

Marler, P. Developments in the study of animal communication. In P. R. Bell (Ed.), *Darwin's biological work*. Cambridge: Cambridge University Press, 1959.

Marler, P. Communication in monkeys and apes. In I. deVore (Ed.), *Primate behavior: Field studies of monkeys and apes*. New York: Holt, Rinehart & Winston, 1965.

Marler, P., & Hamilton, W. J. *Mechanisms of animal behavior*. New York: Wiley, 1966.

Marshall, J. C. *The syntax of reproductive behaviour in the male pigeon*. Unpublished research report, Medical Research Council, Psycholinguistics Unit, Oxford, 1965.

Maxwell, A. E. *Multivariate analysis in behavioural research*. London: Chapman & Hall; New York: Wiley, 1977.

Mayer, W. Gruppenverhalten von Totenkopfaffen unter besonderer Berücksichtigung der Kommunikationstheorie. *Kybernetik*, 1971, *8*, 59–68.

McFarland, D. J. Time-sharing as a behavioural phenomenon. In *Advances in the study of behaviour* (Vol. 5). London, New York: Academic Press, 1974.

McFarland, D. J., & Lloyd, I. Time-shared feeding and drinking. *Quarterly Journal of Experimental Psychology*, 1973, *25*, 48–61.

Metz, H. Stochastic models for the temporal fine structure of behaviour sequences. In D. McFarland (Ed.), *Motivational control systems analysis*. London: Academic Press, 1974.

Miller, G. A. Some psychological studies of grammar. *American Psychology*, 1962, *17*, 748–762.

Miller, G. A., Galanter, E., & Pribram, K. H. *Plans and the structure of behaviour*. New York: Holt, Rinehart & Winston, 1960.

Mishler, E. G., & Waxler, N. E. The sequential patterning of interaction in normal and schizophrenic families. *Family Process*, 1975, *14*, 17–50.

Morf, M. E., Miller, C. M., & Syrotuik, J. M. A comparison of cluster analysis and Q-factor analysis. *Journal of Clinical Psychology*, 1976, *32*, 59–64.

Morgan, B. J. T., Simpson, M. J. A., Hanby, J. P., & Hall-Craggs, J. H. Visualizing interaction and sequential data in animal behaviour: Theory and application of cluster-analysis methods. *Behaviour*, 1976, *56*, 1–43.

Morris, D. The behaviour of the ten-spined stickleback *(Pygostius pungitius* L.). *Behaviour Supplement*, 1958, *6*, 1–154.

Noë, R., Waal, F. B. M. de, & Hooff, J. A. R. A. M. van. Types of dominance in a chimpanzee colony. *Folia Primatologica*, in press.

Oden, N. Partitioning dependence in non-stationary behavioral sequences. In B. A. Hazlett (Ed.), *Quantitative methods in the study of animal behavior*. New York: Academic Press, 1977.

Pruscha, H., & Maurus, M. Analysis of the temporal structure of primate communication. *Behaviour*, 1979, *69*, 118–134.

Rausch, H. L. Process and change: A Markov model for interaction. *Family Process*, 1972, *11*, 275–298.

Rubenstein, D. I., & Hazlett, B. A. Examination of the agonistic behaviour of the crayfish *Oronectes virilis* by character analysis. *Behaviour*, 1974, *50*, 193–216.

Rummel, R. J. *Applied factor analysis*. Evanston: Northwestern University Press, 1970.

Sackett, G. P. *A nonparametric lag sequential analysis for studying dependency among responses in behaviour observation scoring systems*. Paper presented at the annual meeting of the Western Psychological Association, San Francisco, 1974.

Sackett, G. P. (Ed.). *Observing behavior* (Vol. 1). Baltimore: University Park Press, 1977.

Sackett, G. P. (Ed.). *Observing behavior* (Vol. 2). Baltimore: University Park Press, 1978.

Schleidt, W. Tonic communication: Continual effects of discrete signs in animal communication systems. *Journal of Theoretical Biology*, 1973, *42*, 359–386.

Shannon, C. E., & Weaver, W. *The mathematical theory of communication*. Urbana: University of Illinois Press, 1949.

Silby, R. M., & McCleery, R. H. The dominance boundary method of determining motivation state. *Animal behavior*, 1976, *24*, 108–125.

Slater, P. J. B. Describing sequences of behaviour. In P. P. G. Bateson & P. H. Klopfer (Eds), *Perspectives in ethology*. New York: Plenum, 1973.

Slater, P. J. B. Data collection. In P. W. Colgan (Ed.), *Quantitative ethology*. New York: Wiley, 1978.

Slater, P. J. B., & Ollason, J. C. The temporal pattern of behaviour in isolated male zebra finches: Transition analysis. *Behaviour*, 1972, *42*, 248–269.

Sneath, P. H. A., & Sokal, R. R. *Principles of numerical taxonomy*. London: Freeman, 1963.

Spence, I. Multidimensional scaling. In P. W. Colgan (Ed.), *Quantitative ethology*. New York: Wiley, 1978.

Steinberg, J. B. Information theory as an ethological tool. In B. A. Hazlett (Ed.), *Quantitative methods in the study of animal behavior*. New York: Academic Press, 1977.

Steinberg, J. B., & Conant, J. R. An informational analysis of the inter-male behaviour of the grasshopper *Chortophaga viridifasciata*. *Animal Behavior*, 1974, *22*, 617–627.

Suppes, P. Probabilistic grammars for natural languages. *Synthese*, 1970, *22*, 95–116.

Sustare, D. Systems diagrams. In P. W. Colgan (Ed.), *Quantitative ethology*. New York: Wiley, 1978.

Tembrock, G. Strukturmasse in der Analyse sequentieller Verhaltensereignisse. *Zoologische Jahrbuecher (Physiologie)*, 1978, *82*, 538–564.

Tinbergen, N. *The study of instinct*. Oxford: Oxford University Press, Clarendon Press, 1951.

Ueberla, K. *Faktorenanalyse: Eine systematische Einführung für Psychologen, Mediziner, Wirtschafts- und Sozialwissenschaftler*. Berlin: Springer, 1971.

Vowles, D. M. Neuroethology, evolution and grammar. In L. R. Aronson, E. Tobach, D. S. Lehrmann, & J. S. Rosenblatt (Eds.), *Development and evolution of behavior*. San Francisco: Freeman, 1970.

Waal, F. B. M. de. Exploitative and familiarity-dependent support strategies in a colony of semi-free living chimpanzees. *Behaviour*, 1978, *66*, 268–312.

Westman, R. S. Environmental languages and the functional bases of behavior.

In B. A. Hazlett (Ed.), *Quantitative methods in the study of animal behavior*. New York: Academic Press, 1977.

Wiepkema, P. R. An ethological analysis of the reproductive behaviour of the bitterling (*Rhodeus amarus* Bloch). *Archives Néerlandaises Zoologie*, 1961, *14*, 103–199.

Wilson, E. O. *Sociobiology: The New Synthesis*. Cambridge, Mass.: Harvard University Press, Belknap Press, 1975.

8. The organization of behavior in face-to-face interaction: observations on the development of a methodology

ADAM KENDON

In this chapter I shall discuss an approach to the study of face-to-face interaction in which the aim is to analyze what Erving Goffman (1967) has called the "ultimate behavioral materials" that people feed into social situations – the glances, postures, utterances, gestures, and positionings – and to discuss how these materials are organized and how they function in the creation of interactional events. In this approach it is supposed that occasions of interaction of any sort require for their accomplishment that the individuals who carry them off show certain patterns of behavioral organization. It is the aim of the work here to be discussed to describe what these patterns are.

The approach I am here concerned with has been termed by some a *structural* approach to the understanding of interaction (Duncan, 1969; Duncan & Fiske, 1977; see also Scherer & Ekman, Section 1.2). It represents a synthesis of several different lines of thought, including aspects of pragmatic social philosophy, interpersonal psychiatry, information theory and cybernetics, structural linguistics, and ethology. In what follows I shall sketch in some of the history of this synthesis, in particular seeking to show how the theoretical outlook that emerged as a result implies certain assumptions about the interaction process, which, in turn, give rise to a particular style of investigation. I shall then seek to illustrate an application of this investigatory style.

In view of the fact that the structural approach to interaction here being considered does not yet have a fully formalized methodology, it seems more appropriate to illustrate it by means of a case study of a specific investigation than to give an abstract review of techniques and methods as if these were well established. Accordingly, I shall review Kendon and Ferber's (1973) study of the structure of greeting encounters, giving an account of the alternative methodologies that were considered and trying to show how a particular view of behavioral organization and a particular approach to its analysis emerged as a result of the analysis that was undertaken. I shall endeavor to be particularly attentive to the way in which theoretical presuppositions predisposed us to particular kinds of practical actions as this investigation was begun.

8.1. The structural approach to analysis of face-to-face interaction

We may begin with a general characterization of the approach that will be discussed in this chapter. What are the kinds of questions this approach asks of interaction? What are the main assumptions upon which it proceeds?

Consider two people engaged in a handshake. We may ask, What actions must each perform in order for a handshake to be accomplished, and how must these actions be interrelated? Several things will be obvious at once. For one thing, the two individuals will have to be close enough to one another for them to be able to contact each other's hands, palm to palm, and they will have to be oriented to one another appropriately. This means that each will have to cooperate with the other as each moves in space in relation to the other. Each must recognize the other's movements and orientations in space as approaches preparatory for a handshake, and furthermore, each must be able to recognize that the other recognizes these movements for what they are. For what happens here is that the two individuals somehow come to share a common goal, that of getting into the proper position for a handshake.

We may ask, then, how is this common goal established? By what means do the two individuals come to establish that they share this common goal? We may note, further, that for the handshake to be accomplished, each must recognize the action of the other in extending his hand forward for what it is. Each must recognize this as an element in the interactional event *handshake,* and each must, furthermore, understand the position that such an element has in the overall sequence. It is easy to think of ways in which either participant could get his part of the handshake sequence wrong. He could extend his hand toward the other only after the other had ceased to extend his; he could come and stand side by side with the other, instead of facing him, and extend his hand laterally, away from the other person; he could hold his hand out with all fingers extended but spread, or with only the index finger extended, or with only the little finger extended. However, as a rule, people do not do these things. People do handshakes almost without thinking, and yet, in order to do them, they must enter into quite a complicated and delicate behavioral coordination: Each must behave in careful relationship to how the other behaves; each must employ particular bodily postures, head orientations, gaze directions, verbal utterances, voice modulations, and forelimb and head gestures, which are drawn in a way that each understands from a repertoire of such actions; and each must be seen by the other to be doing all these things in accordance with a plan of action of which each has knowledge.

It will be seen from this, perhaps, that it is possible to consider the behavior of handshakers, or indeed of people engaged in any sort of interaction, from a viewpoint that asks, not what the behavior can tell us about the individuals involved, but what can it tell us about what is required to accomplish the interaction. This is a communicational approach, for one is asking here what functions the various aspects of behavior and their deployment have for establishing, maintaining, and terminating the pattern of relationship between the actions of the participants in the interaction. In this approach we are looking for an understanding of what the interactive or communicative significance of action is, as it occurs within the interactional event being considered.

This approach has four leading assumptions.[1] First is the supposition that when people interact they come to participate in a system of behavioral relations that can be abstracted and considered as an object of study in its own right. This means that the focus of interest is on patterns of behavior and how they are interrelated in interaction, rather than on patterns of behavior as properties of individuals or classes of individuals.

Second, it is assumed that participants relate to one another through many different aspects of their behavior. Indeed, it is recognized that any aspect of behavior, and any form of action, even silence and immobility, can contribute to the interactional process.[2] Accordingly, in analyzing the processes of communication in interaction, we have to be prepared for the possibility that anything that is going on may be playing a part.

Third, it is supposed that the interactive functioning of any item of behavior in interaction depends upon its context of occurrence. Thus to focus only on smiles or only on gazes of a certain direction or only on particular hand movements or only on particular kinds of utterances, without seeing how these items are placed within the system of behavior as a whole, is not regarded as productive. Particular directions of gaze, let us say the act of looking at another person, acquire significance in the interaction only in virtue of the way they are patterned into relationships with other directions of gaze, with other actions of the face, head orientations, postural shifts, concurrent utterances. It is assumed, thus, that actions occur only in patterned relationships, and that an understanding of their communicational significance will be gained only through an account of such patterned relationships.[3]

The fourth assumption is that the units into which the behavior of the participants in interaction is organized, at any level of organization, have a characteristic or customary structure. That is to say, behavior is not constructed out of units or phrases whose pattern or form is completely different from any that have ever occurred before. As Scheflen (1973) has pointed out, the very occurrence of systemic patterned behavioral relations between people – the very phenomenon of interaction, that is – depends upon the ability of people to organize their behavior into patterns that have a predictable structure and organization. To accomplish a handshake, the two handshakers must be able to recognize what each is going to do, each step of the way; otherwise, neither would be able to coordinate his or her behavior with that of the other. But to recognize what the other is doing is possible only if the behavior of the other is familiar and the principles by which it is organized are commonly understood. It is one of the principal aims of the structural approach here being discussed to give an account of these typical or familiar patterns of behavior.

It will be seen that in this approach the concern is with what behavioral equipment people have available to them and how this equipment is deployed as they create occasions of interaction. It differs, for example, from a *psychological* approach, because it is not interested in explaining the behavior of individuals and it does not explore the ways in which specific aspects of behavior may be indexical of an individual's motivational or affective state (see also Ekman & Scherer, Section 1.2).

8.2. Sources of influence: a historical sketch

Throughout this chapter, I shall be concerned with the way in which the practical actions that one takes in analyzing behavior in interaction are predicated upon prior theoretical interpretations. One way to bring this out is to explore the evolution of a methodology. Accordingly, a brief sketch will be offered in which the specific influence of the several contributing lines of thought will be traced. I wish to suggest how the main assumptions of the approach to interaction we are here concerned with have arisen, and how they have led to certain assumptions about the communicational process that, in turn, imply a particular style of investigation.

It should be stressed that the sketch that follows is highly selective, for my intention here is to trace out only one line in the evolution of interaction studies. Many important contributions are left aside because, although they are essential for any general history of the development of interaction studies, they have played only an indirect role in the development of the structural approach.

The notion of *interaction* is a central one in much of social science. The term has been used to refer to a wide range of phenomena, and it has been defined in many different ways. Attempts to undertake explicit analyses of it began to appear in the 1930s (e.g., Chapple, 1939, 1940), and numerous schemes were devised for observing the acts of people in small groups (Heyns & Lippitt, 1954). In much of this work the focus of interest was upon various aspects of "group process," most notably the question how groups came to take decisions and how social structures in groups came to be established. It was supposed that this could be illuminated by means of a detailed study of how individual group members acted. The very large literature based on this general approach is exemplified in Hare, Borgatta, and Bales (1955) and surveyed in Hare (1962). It is notable, however, that in all of this work it is not so much the actual *behavior* of the interacting participants that is studied as the results of such behavior. Furthermore, in all of this work, what might be called the "machinery" of interaction is taken for granted. For example, an observer making observations of interaction, using any one of the very many different categorization schemes that have been devised (e.g., Bales, 1950), must be assumed to be able to recognize which participant is the speaker, to whom his or her speech is being addressed, who is and who is not a member of the group being observed, and the like. This observer is assumed, that is, to have a thorough understanding of the procedures or practices of interaction. It was never supposed that such procedures or practices could ever be an issue in themselves (see Kendon, 1975a). As Goffman (1971) has observed, interaction has rarely been treated as a subject matter in its own right. "Interaction practices," Goffman remarks, "have been used to illuminate other things, but themselves are treated as though they did not need to be defined or were not worth defining" (p. ix). The approach to interaction with which we are concerned in this chapter is one that does regard the practices of interaction as problematic. The historical sketch offered here deals with only those influences that appear to have contributed to the emergence of this kind of question.

Social behaviorism and interpersonal psychiatry

We may begin by going back to the first decade and a half of this century and note the emergence in sociology and social psychology of a concern with what, even then, was being referred to as *social interaction*. Georg Simmel had, as early as 1908, in his major work *Soziologie*, urged that the study of social interaction was *the* subject matter of sociology. As he put it elsewhere: "Society is merely the name for a number of individuals connected by interaction" (Simmel, 1950, p. 10). He went on, "If society is conceived as interaction among individuals, the description of the forms of this interaction is the science of society in its strictest and most essential sense" (1950, pp. 21–22). In consequence of this view, he gave early recognition to the importance of studying the actual behavioral forms of people in interaction, and in several different places in his work he discussed in some detail such forms as sociable conversation, coquetry, and, in a well-known passage from his *Soziologie* (excerpted by Park and Burgess in their early and influential reader *Introduction to the Science of Sociology* [Park & Burgess, 1921]), the "sociology of the senses," including such topics as the interactional significance of mutual eye-to-eye gaze.

Simmel's influence has been considerable; but of more direct importance to our immediate theme, it would appear, is the work of George Herbert Mead, who argued that the psychological properties of an individual, the individual's "mind" and "sense of self," are the emergent products of the process of interaction. Mead, much influenced as he was by Dewey and the philosophical outlook of pragmatism,[4] saw the meanings of such acts as gestures as lying in the responses made to them. A gesture is not to be understood in the first place as an expression; rather, it gains its significance from the way it is treated by a recipient. Meaning is thus born in the social process. "In the very beginning," Mead (1934) wrote, "the other person's gesture means what you are going to do about it" (p. 49). "Gesture," he said, "is the symbol of the result of the given social act of one organism insofar as it is responded to by another organism . . . as indicating that result" (p. 77).

Thus, in Mead's view, people can come to an understanding of their own actions and, ultimately, of themselves only through their perceptions of the way others behave toward them. Obviously, this is a reciprocal process. Mead supposed that people gradually come to internalize a conception of themselves that has its origin entirely in how they are treated by others. For what we consider ourselves to be, then, we are indebted to how others behave toward us. For Mead, as he himself puts it, "selves must be accounted for in terms of the social process, and in terms of communication" (1934, p. 49). Social relationships, accordingly, are not the consequences of previously developed selves' communicating; they are the emergent products of the process of interaction.

Mead's thinking has been very influential, but we may note here that one of its consequences has been to draw attention to the importance of studying the interpersonal process – and doing so directly – rather than studying the actions of people in isolation from one another. This interest in the interpersonal process was taken up by certain psychiatrists. Of particular interest to us is the work of Harry Stack Sullivan (1962, n.d.). Sullivan had taken up the study of schizophrenia, and he became convinced that it was to be understood as the consequence of interpersonal processes, rather than as an organically based cognitive or affective disorder of the individual (Sullivan, 1962). In his later work, Sullivan became much influenced by the work of Mead and others of the pragmatic school of social philosophy (Perry, 1964). He came to define psychiatry as "the study of interpersonal relations, emphasis being placed on the interaction of participants in a social situation, rather than being centered exclusively on the supposedly private economy of either one of those participants" (Sullivan, 1954, p. ix).

This way of thinking about psychological disturbance directed psychiatrists to the *interactive* process. Interest became focused upon the patient – therapist relationship; and the therapist, rather than being merely the mirror for the patient, one who reflected back the patient's own unconscious processes, or merely a tool for dissecting the patient's psyche, came to be understood as an essential component of a dyadic system. In consequence, some psychiatrists began to undertake a detailed analysis of the interactive process.[5]

It is not accidental, then, that the first attempts at a really detailed analysis of the interactive process were made in studies of psychiatric interviews, and that much of the pioneering work in the structural approach to the study of interaction has been done in this context.[6] In the first place, it was the interactionally oriented psychiatrists, such as Sullivan, who daily encountered interaction processes as something to contend with and think about. As they did so, there emerged considerable sensitivity to the full range of things that can happen in such interviews. An interpersonal psychiatrist, to be fully effective, would have to be fully aware of all the minutiae of actions – both those of the psychiatrist and those of the patient – and of how they are intertwined.

Thus the attempt of the structural approach to characterize how all of the aspects of behavior present in a social interaction contribute to that interaction, and thereby the attempt to grasp the communication process in all its complexity, can be seen as arising naturally from the kind of concern with the interactive process that a Sullivanian psychiatrist would have.

Information theory and cybernetics

Because of Mead's argument that the psychological properties of individuals are the emergent consequence of the interactive process, then, and because of his location of the emergence of language and symbolic meaning in that process, and also because of the developments in psychiatry for which Sullivan was so largely responsible, great interest came to be expressed in the details of the interpersonal process. Under the influence of concepts being developed in information theory and cybernetics, the process came to be formulated as one of communication. This formulation, owing in an important degree to Gregory Bateson (Ruesch & Bateson, 1951), had what appear to have been very significant consequences for the *kinds of questions* that came to be asked about interaction, *the kinds of phenomena* that came to be looked at, and the *strategy of investigation.*

The development in information theory under discussion here is the development of a way of measuring the amount of information that may be transmitted through a channel (e.g., Shannon & Weaver, 1949; Cherry, 1957). Shannon (among others) proposed making such measurements by determining the predictability of the signals that are being transmitted. Information, according to this theory, is conceived of as a measure of the relationship between a given signal and the possible number of different signals that could have been sent. Thus it will be very much easier to predict which state a signaling device will be in at any given time if it can be in only 1 of 2 states than if it can be in, say, 1 of 10 different states. The easier it is to predict the state of the device, the less information a given signal, upon receipt, is said to convey. Information, then, is measured as the reciprocal of predictability or redundancy.

For our present purposes, the point to bear in mind is that this treatment of information is a treatment of a property of signaling systems that is entirely general: It can be applied to *any signaling system whatever.* Any instance where you have something that has a repertoire of different states, if you have a receiver trying to predict what state it might be in, it could theoretically be analyzed in this way. This concept became important in the study of human interaction because it led to the idea that *all* detectable aspects of behavior can be approached through information theory. That is to say, any aspect of behavior that can be received by another can be regarded as potentially informative in this sense. Thus all aspects of behavior come to be of interest from an interactional or communicational viewpoint. Attention comes to be directed, in consequence, not just to deliberate speech and gesture, but also to posture and positioning, to seemingly unintentional actions, or to actions whose primary function would appear to have no relevance for communication. Such aspects of behavior had already, of course, begun to come under scrutiny for what they might reveal about unconscious motivations, owing to influences stemming from psychoanalysis.[7] However, the application of an information-theory orientation to human behavior in interaction led to a perspective that encouraged investigators to see that all aspects of behavior could be considered as "signal" and thus could participate in the interaction system that was the object of analysis (see Note 2 at the end of this chapter).

The actual application of the mathematical formulae derived by Shannon to measure rate of information transmission, channel capacity, signal-to-noise ratio and its relationship to redundancy, and so on has played a somewhat minor role in investigations of human communication, as it turns out. This, as McKay (1972), for example, has pointed out, is because it is so very difficult to know just how to make the appropriate measurements in actual cases. But the way of thinking that allowed theorists to conceive of an entirely general property of anything that could function informatively was very important in leading to the idea that all aspects of behavior in a situation of copresence could participate in the communication process. This, as we have seen, was one of the founding assumptions of the structural approach with which we are here concerned.

While information theory was being developed, and in close association with it, there were important developments in the mathematical analysis of self-regulating systems – or *cybernetics*, as it has come to be termed. This work, christened and largely pioneered by Norbert Wiener (1948), developed initially out of a need to find a way to design an antiaircraft gun that could automatically track its moving target. Here what was needed was, first, a way of continually informing the mechanism that controlled the gun's aim how much the aim varied from the desired direction, and then a way of adding to the aiming mechanism a means whereby the aim could be corrected in the light of this information about discrepancy. Thus, with a desired relationship to the target specified, a way of measuring the difference between the gun's actual direction and its desired direction had to be devised; then it was necessary to develop a way of transmitting this measurement of difference back to the controlling mechanism; and finally the system had to be so arranged that the greater the discrepancy, the more the controlling mechanism would act to reduce that discrepancy. The essential element here is that the action of the controlling mechanism was directed by information about the consequences of its own actions. This information was *fed back* to the controlling mechanism – and this is, of course, the central notion in what was then the new and, it should be stressed, entirely *general*, understanding of self-regulatory devices.

Now, as Wiener and others were quick to point out, this analysis made it possible to understand in a new way such self-regulating entities as organisms (Rosenblueth, Wiener, & Bigelow, 1943). They could be understood as negative feedback devices or cybernetic systems. To the extent that interpersonal events had become the object of attention – as they had, given the developments in social philosophy and psychiatry just discussed – it became apparent that these also could be thought about in cybernetic terms. Once again, as in the case of information theory, the ideas of cybernetics were developed at such a level of generality that it came to be seen as possible to apply them far beyond the context of their original development. With the general notions of information, information control, and feedback, or regulation in relation to a preset target value – with these general ideas at hand, it became possible to envision their application to a wide range of phenomena, and a new way of thinking became available.[8]

Before these ideas became current, interaction was often formulated as a stimulus response sequence in which *A*'s action serves as a stimulus to *B*, whose response in turn serves as a stimulus for *A*. Thus interaction sequences were likely to be thought of as linear chains of action.[9] It is possible that some kinds of interaction are best formulated in these terms. What I want to suggest here, however, is that if this is the prevailing model of the process, it encourages certain kinds of studies, in contrast to those that are encouraged if one adheres to a cybernetic model of the interaction process. As a consequence of the adoption of an information-theoretic and cybernetic formulation of the interaction process, new kinds of investigation came to be undertaken.

The linear chain model, first of all, directs one to analyze any instance of interaction as if it were an alternating sequence of discrete actions. It suggests that interaction is a discontinuous process, unidirectional, where each succeeding step in the sequence is considered to be only the consequence of the immediately preceding step.

In the second place, thinking of interaction as a linear, unidirectional chain encourages one to analyze it at a single level or organization only. The idea that there might be a number of different interactive chains going forward at the same time in an interactional event would be difficult to conceive of in this framework, because a unidirectional model causes one to think of individuals as separately acting on each other and separately responding. As a rule, one tends to think of individuals as doing only one thing at a time. Therefore, on this view of interaction, the focus tends to be on only one level of action at a time.

Third, the linear chain model tends to encourage interest only in the *novel outcomes* of any encounter. If one thinks in terms of a linear chain of cause and effect one is tempted to think about what happens in the end. Thus interest tends to be focused upon what happens as a result of an interaction. The fact that interactants have to take actions to maintain features of a social situation that do not change during its course tends to be overlooked.

On the other hand, once the actions of an individual in interaction are thought of as signals transmitting information to the other participant, rather than as stimuli causing responses, and once such actions are thought of, not as being produced as direct responses to the actions of the other, but as being carried out in consequence of the individual's own aims and plans (though nevertheless under some degree of guidance from information provided by the other's behavior), a new range of questions becomes available for investigation.

First, one comes to see that the actions of *P* and *Q* are not produced as a sequential chain, with each action appearing strictly as a consequence of the other's previous action. Rather, one sees that each participant is pursuing a line of action, but that each must adjust the actions that he or she takes in doing so in the light of information the other's actions provide. Just as the driver of a car, in seeking to keep the car on the road and to direct it toward a certain destination, must yet modify his or her actions in the light of information coming in about where the car is on the road, and what landmarks and signposts are being passed, so a participant in interaction must take into account how the other is acting in relation to his or her own actions. In interaction this is, of course, a reciprocal process. Thus one comes to see each participant as being under the continuous guidance of the other. In consequence, one's investigatory interest shifts to include a study of what *P* and *Q* are both doing at the same time: One becomes prepared to look, for example, at what *Q* is doing while *P* is speaking, at what *P* is doing while *Q* is listening, and the like. *Thus one comes to look at the nature of the behavioral relationship between P and Q as an ongoing phenomenon,* rather than first looking at what *P* does and then looking at what *Q* does.

Second, one comes to see that occasions of interaction may be organized at more than one level at once. If one thinks of interaction as a sequential organization of stimulus and response, one has to segment the behavior of the interactants into discrete pieces that will be regarded as responses. One then looks at each in succession, each being regarded as the consequence of the preceding. One is likely to look on a single level only, because one is trying to understand how the responses are chained together in sequence. On the other hand, if one views participants in interaction as self-regulatory beings whose actions are the resultant of plans executed under guidance from the feedback each provides the other, one is much more likely to entertain the notion of multiple simultaneous levels of organization in what is going on. This is because intentions, and the actions that execute them, have a hierarchical organization; thus, the information feedback guiding them must be matched in a hierarchical fashion (see Welford, 1958; Powers, 1974).

In analyzing a conversation between *P* and *Q*, for instance, one will recognize not only that each of *P*'s utterances is formulated under the guidance of moment-to-moment feedback from *Q* (e.g., whether *Q* is looking or nodding his head), but that the succession of *P*'s utterances may be linked into a higher order unit of, for example, a "persuasive sequence," and that whether, and the extent to which, *P* can carry this through will depend upon signals *Q* is giving him that refer, not so much to the action he is currently taking in respect to a specific current utterance of *P*, but to the more general level action of "patient listening," or whatever it may be. Further, *P* must be sensitive to aspects of *Q*'s behavior that let him know whether *Q* is maintaining an orientation and position indicative of his being willing to remain in conversation at all, and so on.

Third, as will perhaps be obvious from what has been said so far, adopting a cybernetic approach to interaction encourages one to attend not only to outcomes, or not mainly to outcomes; it also directs attention most particularly to the *ongoing process* of interaction. For not only is one concerned to see what happens in the end, one is also concerned to see how the actions of the participants come to be formulated and modified in relation to the informational feedback each provides the other, as the interaction is proceeding.

Fourth and finally, one's attention is also likely to be directed toward the *constant* aspects of an interaction. Because of the notion of dynamic equilibrium or homeostasis – to which cybernetics gave a precise and general formulation – it is recognized that, in such a self-regulatory system as an organism, its seemingly constant state is maintained in the face of continuous fluctuations in the environment. The same thing can be seen to be true of the conversation: It also takes place in a fluctuating environment with which both participants must continually deal. Furthermore, each must constantly monitor the other and adjust the longer-term aspects of his or her behavior – such as posture, bodily orientation, and positions – accordingly, in order to maintain the constant spatial and orientational relationship that must be sustained for a conversation. Accordingly, those aspects of the interactive process that have to do with maintaining the stability of the occasion become as important a subject for investigation as do those aspects that show change, development, and novelty.

Structural linguistics

The influence of ideas from information theory and cybernetics, then, was to direct attention to a new range of questions in studies of interaction. It led to an interest in process, rather than outcome, to an interest in how interactants behaved simultaneously and thereby mutually regulated one another's ongoing behavior; it led to an interest in the constant features of the interactive situation as well as an interest in change; it also led to an explicit recognition of the possible signal value of any aspect of behavior in the situation. That is, it led to a broadening of view about what behavior could be significant in interaction.

Now, for an item of behavior to have signal value, it must be understood to be part of a repertoire of alternative behaviors. To analyze behavior communicationally requires that we understand behavioral items as if they are part of a code. At the time when the implications of information theory and cybernetics were becoming clear, such an analysis was already available for language. The methods for deriving a description of a language code from acts of speech, extended to the analysis of body motion and other aspects of behavior, provided a way of thinking about such behavior that was compatible with a communication-theory orientation. This extension of linguistic method to behavior other than speech came about as a natural consequence of the development of linguistics as a method for the analysis of speakers, rather than of texts, and it has had an important influence on the structural approach we are here considering.

Linguistics in the United States, as it evolved under the influence first of Boas (1911), and then of Sapir (1921, 1949) and Bloomfield (1933), developed in close relationship with anthropology and was preoccupied with the task of producing systematic descriptions of American Indian languages, languages that had never been written down and whose structure was unknown. This meant that one of the first problems to be faced was that of finding out which sounds made by speakers of these languages were significant for what they were saying, and which were not. Because the languages were quite unknown, the researcher had no way of knowing what to exclude, and for this reason it was felt necessary to start by making complete transcriptions of all the vocal sounds of the informant. A great amount of effort, accordingly, was expended on the development of methods of notating speech sounds of all kinds. Once complete transcriptions were in hand, the investigator could begin to sort out the sounds that had been recorded into groups and to see whether they were functional linguistically or not. From this procedure developed the well-known techniques of contrastive analysis by which units in the language are established as different from one another if they are found to make a difference for the speakers of the language. The minimal pair technique was developed for establishing the repertoire of phonemes in a language and subsequently expanded to encompass the analysis of patterns of phonemes into minimal groupings or morphemes, which were regarded as serving as the building blocks of sentences.[10]

What was achieved was a methodology for establishing the functionally significant elements of a language by the analysis of the way in which living users of the language themselves perceived these elements. It was, thus, a methodology for working out the system of a language from the point of view of the speakers themselves. Also significant, it was a method that dealt directly with the analysis of *speech behavior*. In this it contrasted very markedly with the way linguistics had been developed hitherto, especially in Europe, where most work was done on written texts and where the problem of dealing with a speaker and deciding which aspects of his or her behavior were significant for the language was not the issue.

This approach to linguistics, with its emphasis on field work and its attendant problems of dealing with speech behavior, led naturally to an appreciation of the way in which speech as a social activity is embodied within a complex configuration of action, many aspects of which were seen to be significant for communication. Many of the pioneers of American linguistics – for example, Sapir and, most notably, Kenneth Pike – were very aware of this, and they suggested that the methods of analysis developed for abstracting the language code employed in speech could also be employed for the abstraction of code systems in other aspects of behavior. Sapir alluded to this possibility in several places in his writings. Pike (1967) explicitly developed the idea, to the point of suggesting that the structure of language, as he conceived of it, could provide a model for the structure of all human behavior.

Pike's attempts to extend the methodology of linguistic description to other kinds of social behavior were first published in preliminary form in 1954 (now available as Pike, 1967). At about the same time, Trager published his "first approximation" to the linguistic analysis of what he termed *paralanguage* (Trager, 1958); Birdwhistell began his efforts to apply the methodology of descriptive linguistics to body motion (Birdwhistell, 1952); and Hall, in collaboration with Trager, developed his attempts to analyze in this way interpersonal spacing and the social use of time (Hall, 1959, 1963, 1964, 1966, 1968, n.d.).[11]

The extension of the methods of descriptive linguistics to these other aspects of behavior had several consequences. The insistence in descriptive linguistics that one should attend, in the first instance, to as much of the speech behavior as possible, because one did not know at the outset what might be significant, led to the idea that, in the context of studies of interaction from a structural point of view, as much as possible of the observable behavior should be taken into account. This meant, of course, that emphasis was placed upon describing what one could observe, and efforts were also directed toward the development of transcription systems (although it is notable how little real progress was made in this respect).[12]

Additionally, as has already been indicated, the effort to extend the methods of descriptive linguistics to behavior other than speech meant that the researcher was assuming that it would be possible to abstract a system of elements whose organization could be studied in its own right. It was even supposed by some that investigators could find parallels in the organization of these systems of elements that would prove directly comparable to those proposed for language.

Ray L. Birdwhistell and the concept of kinesics

The most well known exponent of the extension of linguistic methods to behavior other than speech is perhaps Ray L. Birdwhistell, who coined the term *kinesics*, suggesting thereby that a study of the communicational functioning of body motion could be developed in a way that could parallel linguistics. Other writers, emphasizing other aspects of behavior, which they see as amenable to investigation according to a similar point of view, have proposed *proxemics*, for the study of spacing (Hall, 1963), and *tacesics*, for the study of touch (Kauffman, 1969).[13]

Birdwhistell's central idea is that bodily motion is patterned and that this patterning is to be understood in terms of an analysis into a repertoire of recurrent elements that occur in configurations constructed according to shared rules comparable in status to the rules of morphology and syntax in spoken language. Birdwhistell suggested that body motion could be analyzed into a repertoire of elements that were to be defined by informants, much as the repertoire of sound elements in a language is defined through work with informants. That is to say, the elements of body motion that are significant in a communication system, Birdwhistell argued, are those that are treated as significant by the users of the communication system themselves. Such significant elements were to be called *kinemes,* just as the significant elements in a spoken language are called phonemes.

An example may best illustrate the central notions of Birdwhistell's approach. In the face we may recognize several areas of articulation: the eyebrows, the lips, and so on. These areas can engage in many different actions, but from the point of view of understanding how elements of action in the face function communicatively, we must see that it is only those differences in articulation which make a difference to the communication process that are important, and it is in terms of these differences that the elementary components of the kinesic system are to be defined. Consider the eyebrows. They are capable of a number of different actions. They can be raised, they can have their inner corners drawn upwards, they can be lowered, and they can engage in certain combinations of these actions. We can undertake measurements of the muscular actions producing these different brow positions, and we may find that for each one of these actions the intensity or completeness of its accomplishment can vary continuously.[14] Whether the brows are raised or not makes a difference to the appearance of the face. A face with raised brows sends a different message from a face with brows in an unraised position. The question is, however, how much raising of the brows there has to be for it to make a difference to a perceiver of the face. Birdwhistell suggested that by examining how users of eyebrows themselves perceived these differences in communicational context, we could establish the repertoire of contrasting brow positions for a given community of brow users. Birdwhistell suggested that, by working with informants, we should be able to establish for each area of the body the repertoire of body positions and movements that would be perceived by members of the same communication community as significantly contrastive. We could, that is, establish the repertoire of kinemes for such a community.

Kinemes do not occur in isolation, of course, any more than phonemes do. They occur in patterns or combinations. Such combinations Birdwhistell termed *kinemorphs* (on an analogy with the linguistic term *morpheme*). And kinemorphs, of course, are themselves organized into more complex configurations termed *kinemorphic constructions.*

A long-distance greeting display, for example, can be seen as a combination of a particular bodily stance and a particular arm action and hand position. The entire combination would be regarded as a kinemorphic construction. The organizations found in the forelimb, the face and head, and the stance might be regarded as kinemorphs, and the components out of which those configurations are constructed might be identified as kinemes. Thus, in a long-distance greeting display, we often find the combination *head tilted back, eyebrows raised, mouth open, upper lip retracted to expose teeth* (see Eibl-Eibesfeldt, 1972; Kendon & Ferber, 1973). If, as we are supposing here, these elements have been established as kinemes, in the long distance greeting they have been combined in a characteristic way to form a head–face combination of a certain sort. And this combination or kinemorph is found in conjunction with other kinemorphs in a kinemorphic construction – in this case a person waving in greeting.

Birdwhistell, it will be seen, was proposing to employ for the analysis of body motion both the procedures of inquiry and the theoretical model that had been developed for language by such workers as Bloomfield (1933), Harris (1951), and, especially, Trager and Smith (1951) – to whom Birdwhistell acknowledges a particular debt.

Birdwhistell has published little about kinesics that would be regarded as more than programmatic, and it is only very recently that anyone has begun to take his suggestions sufficiently seriously to see if his model can apply, even to a limited range of body motion phenomena. Despite this, however, Birdwhistell has been very influential. His work has been highly effective in focusing attention upon the fact that people, in their body movements, do make use of repertoires of movement patterns that are shared culturally and cannot be accounted for by considering their significance for expression alone. Birdwhistell freed the study of body motion from a purely psychological approach. He showed, through his proposal for a kinesics, that it is equally important and possible to examine this behavior as if it is structured by those who use it into a code analogous to language.

The role of cinematography

Detailed studies of behavior structure, whether done in the context of social interaction or not, could not be undertaken without the availability of a recording technique that makes it possible to reinspect the behavior itself. Thus we could not have witnessed the emergence of the kinds of structural analysis of behavior in interaction that we are here concerned with if a recording technology such as cinematography had not developed. It is interesting to note that a most important impetus to the technical developments required for cinematography to become possible was provided by scientists and others who were interested in the analysis of the structure of movement. Eadweard Muybridge and Jules Marey were among those who laid the foundations of the technology required for taking photographs in rapid succession, an essential component of cinematography, and they were induced to undertake this study because of their interest in the analysis of movement. Though this original work dealt with animal motions, once cinematography was fully developed, it was almost immediately put to use in the recording and analysis of human behavior. Thus in 1895 the French anatomist Regnault began, at first with Marey's collaboration, a series of films that were intended for a comparative study of human movement patterns, such as walking, squatting, and tree climbing. A. C. Haddon, who mounted a major expedition from Cambridge University to the Torres Straits islands in 1898, made use of cinematography to record the behavior of the peoples he studied. Baldwin Spencer in 1901 began extensive filming of Australian aborigines for the purposes of making behavioral records.[15]

Subsequently, of course, cinematography has been extensively used by psychologists and others for the study of behavior (Michaelis, 1955). However, as I have argued elsewhere (Kendon, 1979a), the employment of this technology for the study of behavior in interaction did not begin until a conceptualization of the interaction process implying the use of cinematography as an investigative strategy had been developed. Once interaction was seen as a continuous process that could involve any aspect of behavior and that operated at multiple levels of organization simultaneously, the employment of audiovisual recording of interaction to provide specimens for analysis became appropriate. In spite of the fact that cinematography and sound recording had been available since the beginning of this century and were employed for the study of behavior from an early date, they were not used in the analysis of interaction until just 20 years ago, when this new conceptualization of the interaction process was first developed.

Today, with the ready availability of video recording and lightweight cinematographic equipment (see Wallbott, Technical Appendix) the use of behavior specimens in the study of interaction is increasingly widespread. The most recent area of expansion of this work has been the study of infant–mother interaction. It is striking that the conceptualizations of the interactive process being developed by workers in this area are very close to that developed in the approach we are here considering.[16]

The Natural History of an Interview: the collaboration at Palo Alto

The five influences or developments described so far all came together in 1956 at the Institute for Advanced Study at Palo Alto. In that year two psychiatrists who were deeply influenced by the interpersonal orientation that I have traced to Sullivan and Mead collaborated with two structural linguists and two anthropologists in an attempt to examine a single interactional event recorded on film, taking into account every possible aspect of the behavior of the participants. As far as I know, this was the first attempt to undertake such a structural analysis of behavior in interaction. The psychiatrists were Henry Brosin and Frieda Fromm-Reichman; the linguistic anthropologists were Norman McQuown and Charles Hockett; and the two anthropologists were Gregory Bateson and Ray Birdwhistell. Birdwhistell joined the collaboration because he was already known for his efforts to develop a linguisticlike analysis of body motion. Bateson, it is to be noted, is a particularly significant figure in this collaboration. He had, in 1938, in his work in Bali with Margaret Mead, pioneered the use of film and photography in the analysis of social behavior in natural settings. *Balinese Character* (Bateson & Mead, 1942), the publication that resulted from that collaboration, remains unmatched to this day; it can still be held up as a model for the comprehensive analysis of social behavior using the direct analysis of behavior specimens as its central technique.[17] But Bateson, as I have already noted, had also pioneered in the application of ideas from information theory to the analysis of interaction. Some of the key features of the new orientation to the study of interaction that I have mentioned probably owe more to Bateson than to anyone else. He had already published, in collaboration with Jurgen Ruesch (another important figure in these developments),[18] a book entitled *Communication: The Social Matrix of Psychiatry* (Ruesch & Bateson, 1951). The ideas expressed in that book were the direct outcome of Bateson's participation in the cybernetics conferences organized by the Josiah Macy, Jr., Foundation: At these conferences he met Norbert Wiener, whose work very much influenced him (Heims, 1977).

No publication emerged from the 1956 collaboration at Palo Alto, and those involved went their separate ways.[19] Birdwhistell joined Scheflen in Philadelphia, however, and the one consequence was Scheflen's highly important attempts to deal with the structure of complete interactional events: his analyses of psychotherapy sessions (Scheflen, 1963, 1964, 1966, 1973). Scheflen has also published several theoretical papers, including detailed expositions of the method of analysis that had originated in the 1956 Stanford collaboration. This method he has termed *context analysis*. Expositions of it may be found in Scheflen (1966, 1973), and commentaries have been provided by Bär (1974), McDermott and Wertz (1976), and Kendon (1979a).

A. E. Scheflen and context analysis

The central feature of context analysis, the feature from which the method gets its name, is the idea that patterns of behavior are described according to the contexts in which they occur. *Context*, for Scheflen, refers to whatever configuration of events or circumstances includes the unit being analyzed. He maintains that the significance of a unit of behavior cannot be stated except in terms of the contexts of occurrence of that unit. Context is, of course, a relative concept. In developing a context analysis of an interactional event the aim is to show how behavioral elements are patterned into larger configurations, and how these larger configurations are themselves patterned into configurations that include them, and so on up a hierarchy of levels of organization until one has reached the entire transaction. The transaction itself can, of course, also be considered as a unit, and a search can then be made for the contexts in which it occurs. Thus a unit of behavior considered by itself cannot be judged to have any significance, at least not from the point of view of its interactional function. Merely to count the frequency of smiles, say, or head nods or pipe lightings, within the course of a psychotherapy interview might be useful if we had some reason to believe that these behavioral items were correlates of some organismic state, but such counts would be of no use whatsoever if we were seeking to understand the functions these behavioral items might have in the transaction in question. For this purpose it is necessary to note carefully the configuration of behaviors within which such actions occur, and then to note the configurations within which such containing configurations are themselves contained. The outcome of a context analysis is an account of the structure of the interactional event in question in terms of the units out of which it is structured and the patterning that governs the development of those units.

Scheflen expounds the procedure of context analysis in five steps. The first of these is to gather an audiovisual record of the event one wishes to examine. Because the eventual goal in a context analysis is a complete account of the structure of the event in question, it is essential to have such a record (see "Ray L. Birdwhistell and the concept of kinesics," earlier in this section). The second step, according to Scheflen, is to make a comprehensive transcription of all the "behavioral events" that one can find in the specimen. In practice this means transcribing speech and all other behaviors onto a chart, so that the investigator can visually inspect the sequencing of the behavioral events. The third step is the analysis of the record into recurrent patterns or structural units. The fourth step involves a careful comparison of contexts to establish how recurrent patterns of action identified at a lower level of organization affect the nature of those contexts. In this analysis the investigator is seeking to find instances where the absence of an expected element can be observed, so that the consequences of such absence for the patterning of other behavior can be identified. From this the researcher can infer its communicative function within the context in question.

These first four steps all refer to processes of analysis that are done with a specimen of a single transaction, such as a psychotherapy session. Scheflen's fifth step, as he outlines it, refers to an expanding program of study in which the goal is to establish the contexts of occurrences for a transaction of the type that is being analyzed. In the case of a psychotherapy transaction, for instance, to continue the context analysis is to explore how that transaction, considered as a whole, occurs. Included here would be studies of the ecological conditions of the transaction, the persisting and preexisting social relationships between the participants, their individual characteristics, and the cultural and subcultural traditions of which they are a part. Scheflen's fifth step, which is really not a step of the same sort as the first four, but a whole program of investigation, goes well beyond our present scope of concern and will not be considered further here.

It should be stressed that the four-step sequence Scheflen proposes for this procedure is presented in this way for expository convenience only. As McQuown (1971a) has pointed out, and as Scheflen himself has acknowledged, the accomplishment of each step is to a large extent dependent upon the accomplishment of each of the others. For example, Scheflen suggests that the transcription of the behavioral events from the specimen precedes the delineation of recurrent units. Yet, as I shall explain again later, it is impossible to make any sort of a transcription without having some conception of the units into which the flow of behavior is to be divided. Thus, to the extent that a transcription is dependent upon a prior conception of units of organization, and to the extent that the making of the transcription is a step toward the further formulation of such units, the processes are interdependent and there is, in fact, a *cyclical* relationship between them.

This point becomes clear when we consider Scheflen's suggested solution to the problem of making the transcription comprehensive. It will be recalled that a central rule of the structural approach is that one cannot presuppose which aspects of behavior in an interaction are relevant for the communication process. Just as in the analysis of the structure of an unknown language one must begin by trying not to exclude any of the sounds that one's informant may make and must therefore produce a comprehensive transcription, so here, when considering the deployment of behavior in interaction, one must be prepared at the outset to take everything into consideration. As Scheflen (1966) has put it: "We do not decide beforehand what is trivial, what is redundant, or what alters the system. This is a *result* of the research" (p. 270). The requirement that the transcription be comprehensive seems to be an impossible one to meet, however. How could one ever transcribe "everything"? Scheflen's suggested solution is to point out that we do not have to do it all at once. He points out that behavior in interaction "is organized into standard structural units many of which are known through other research, recognizable at a glance and recordable with a stroke" (Scheflen 1966). Scheflen makes an analogy with the problem of trying to describe a baseball game:

> If you do not know the structural units of the game you will have to record thousands and thousands of fragments . . . For example, player number one opens his mouth, scratches arm, lifts bat, looks at player number seven, and so on. But if you do know the units and the system of notation you can codify the game on a single sheet.

In the case of the baseball game, of course, a good deal of the work we must do for common interactional occasions has been done for us, for a baseball game is already structured by a set of explicit rules. Interactional events, however, though their structural elements are not already written up – indeed, it is the very task of context analysis to establish these elements – are nevertheless *partly* understood by anyone who participates in them. That is, of course, any one of us. In beginning our transcription, thus, we should take full advantage of this partial understanding and begin by transcribing the units we *do* recognize. As we proceed, comparing our initial chart with the specimen, the transcription comes to be progressively refined and the organization of the whole event is gradually formulated.

It has to be admitted that this procedure has not been made fully explicit. As Scheflen has formulated it, many questions are left unanswered, and it probably would not be possible for a novice investigator to use Scheflen's exposition as a rule book for doing a context analysis. Much is left to the analyst's intuitive grasp of the behavior being examined and his or her ability to perceive the configurational structure of behavior. As I shall argue later, the mapping of the interactional event that appears, in Scheflen's formulation, to be put a step toward the goal of a context analysis actually seems to constitute the embodiment of the discoveries that it leads to.

Scheflen (1966) lays out, with the example of a therapist lighting a cigarette, a detailed illustration of the procedures to be followed in identifying a *structural unit* – a component part of the event one is trying to understand. One begins, according to him, by recognizing the event in the manner just described, recognizing it at a particular level of organization. In watching a greeting sequence, for instance, you may see something that you might label a *wave*. In watching a therapy session you see something you call *lighting a cigarette*.

In order to see whether this thing that you have recognized is indeed a consistent unit, you look at it more closely and break it up into what appear to be its component parts. Thus the therapist's cigarette lighting, as described by Scheflen, could be analyzed into six components:

1. Taking out a cigarette and bringing it and a pack of matches to the lap
2. Waiting until the patient has finished a story
3. Putting the cigarette in the mouth
4. Waiting until the patient looks away
5. Lighting up
6. Discarding the match

It then becomes necessary to compare other instances of cigarette lighting to see whether, in each case, the components that have been delineated co-occur. What one aims for is the establishment of just those elements that do co-occur, and it is those regularly recurring elements that will constitute a structural unit. For example, if, upon examining the several instances of cigarette lighting available in the transaction being studied, one were to find that the therapist did not always coordinate her sequence of actions with certain aspects of the patient's behavior, as indicated in the list, one would have to exclude steps (2) and (4) as components of the structural unit, even though they sometimes occurred.

But such a unit, having a regular *internal* structure, also has a location within a larger structure. In the cigarette example, for instance, Scheflen found that each time the therapist lit a cigarette, she stopped conversing with the patient and tried to interrupt what he was saying. Scheflen demonstrated, by taking the cigarette lighting in association with other units, which included postural shifting in such a way as to result in the therapist's having a more frontal orientation to the patient and moving closer to him, that the cigarette lighting appeared as part of a complex sequence of moves by which the therapist established a different *kind* of interaction with the patient – shifting from conversation to giving instructions to the patient to act more like a patient. This complex unit, according to Scheflen, appeared to be one of three or four other complex units that, in clinical terms, would be called "working through," "telling anecdotes," and "discussing advice." Further analysis would show that the whole session could be analyzed at a high level as a steplike sequence of units of this sort. Scheflen found that these units have a consistent internal structure, each one *beginning* in a distinctive way – for example, lighting a cigarette, shifting the cigarette to the left hand, shifting to a new posture, and the like.

It will be seen that such units must be regarded as being organized at various levels of complexity. Lower-level units are contained within or framed by units at higher levels of organization. One of Scheflen's best-known proposals, which has an applicability to all conversational situations, not just psychotherapy, is that we may think of behavior in social interaction as being organized on at least three levels. These he has termed in descending order of inclusiveness, the *presentation*, the *position*, and the *point*. Each is marked by some constant feature of behavior serving as an indicator that the unit is in operation. While it is in operation, we may recognize sequences or cycles of behavior that constitute the unit's enactment and that are themselves units at the level of organization below.

The *presentation* refers to the sustained location and orientation maintained by a participant in an interactional event so long as he *is* a participant. Thus, for the duration of such an event as a conversation or a psychotherapy session, the participants maintain a relatively constant spatial and orientational arrangement that disperses once the event is over. While taking part in a presentation, a participant may engage in one or more *positions*. A position is a recurrent configuration of behavior that may be recognized by a distinctive sustained posture; concurrently, the individual engages in a distinctive enactment. For example, Scheflen distinguishes *narrating* and *defending* as positions enacted by one of the participants in the psychotherapy session analyzed in Scheflen (1973); *passive protesting* and *contending* as the positions of another participant; and *listening* and *explaining* as the positions of the therapists (there are nine positions distinguished altogether, but these will suffice here). Each of these different positions is recognizable not only from the kinds of speech acts engaged in, but also from the distinctive sustained posture that is maintained during it. Scheflen's description indicates that participants in an interaction tend to have a limited repertoire of positions. In the psychotherapy session analyzed he shows how the successive phases of the session may be distinguished by the sequencing and cycling of the positions that occur. He suggests that the postural configuration of the position that is held while the position is performed serves as a frame for a stretch of behavior, indicating that a particular theme is informing the participant's activities. Transactions can be analyzed as progressions through several stages, each stage constituting a configuration of positions. The associated postural configuration, thus, can serve to identify for the participants the current stage or phase of the transaction.

Within each position, the participant engages in a number of actions that constitute the performance of the position. For example, within the framework of the position *narrating*, the psychotherapy participant referred to would produce a succession of utterances, addressing first one psychiatrist, then the next. The participant's daughter, as she sat huddled by her mother in the posture that characterized the position of *passive protesting*, would grimace, mutter under her breath, sprawl back on the sofa she was sitting on, and sit forward again. In other words, *within* a position, marked by a total bodily configuration, a series of one or more actions is performed. These Scheflen calls *points*. Points themselves may be further analyzed into components, of course, though Scheflen himself only indicates this additional breakdown. For example, if a point unit is enacted as an utterance, the speech may be analyzed into its component phonemic clauses or tone units, which in turn may be analyzed into their syllabic and intonational components. Any accompanying gestures can be analyzed into gesture phrases and components thereof (Kendon 1972a, 1980). Once again we see that a unit at one level of organization can be viewed as an organization or patterning of units at a lower level of organization.

Several of Scheflen's concepts and findings have been supported by other studies. Thus, Kendon and Ferber (1973), in a study of greetings to be discussed at greater length later, showed how distinct phases of the greeting encounter could be seen as being organized in a hierarchy of frames, matched by bodily spatial location and orientation. Kendon (1977) subsequently generalized these observations in his notion of the F-formation. Erickson (1975) and McDermott, Gospodinoff, and Aron

(1978) have also shown how postural and orientational arrangements can serve to frame distinct phases of interaction, much as Scheflen's original formulations would lead one to expect.

Ethology

One other line of work that has been, and continues to be, influential for the development of the approach here being considered must now be dealt with, and that is ethology. Although it would take us too far from our present purposes to consider the issues ethology has raised for the study of the structure of behavior in any detail, a few general remarks are in order.[20] Ethology is best defined as the biological study of behavior. That is to say, in ethology behavior is studied in the framework of Darwinian evolutionary theory. This means that behavior is viewed from the point of view of its adaptive functioning. In an ethological study, in consequence, one is concerned with the way in which observable behavior serves to relate the animal to its environment and to the other animals it is associated with. The manifest forms of behavior are thus the starting point in any ethological study, and the interest is in working from this manifest form outward, as it were, to see how the behavior functions in sustaining the animal in its world.

In this respect, ethology's emphasis is very different from that of psychology, where behavior is studied for the light it can throw upon inner processes. However, it will be seen that in certain respects the ethological approach to behavior is similar to the approach that is under consideration in this chapter. Like the structural approach, ethology is much interested in the manifest forms of behavior. It lays great emphasis on watching and describing patterns of action. And, like the structural approach, it insists upon examining behavior in the context of its natural setting. In attempting to work out the functioning of behavior patterns, ethology, again like the structural approach to human interaction, seeks to examine how units of behavior are patterned in context. Ethology differs, however, in that it has mostly been concerned with animal rather than human behavior, and it differs importantly in the theoretical context in which its investigations are set. The interest of ethology, as I have said, is ultimately in understanding how behavioral forms can be accounted for by Darwinian evolutionary theory. The interest of the structural approach is in a way more narrow. Its concern is to display the structures into which human behavior is patterned and to consider how these structures function in the construction of interactional events. It sees these structures largely as cultural products and accounts for them, therefore, by reference to cultural processes rather than to the processes of biological evolution (though I should add that this last point is not at all an essential component of the structural perspective).

Other developments

Besides the continuing influence of such workers as Gregory Bateson, Ray Birdwhistell, and E. T. Hall, and the emergence of Scheflen as a major figure, there are at least three further developments since 1956 that should be referred to in any comprehensive treatment of the emergence of the structural approach. First we must mention the work of Erving Goffman, who, ever since the publication, in 1955, of his paper "On Face-Work," has been a powerful exponent of the idea that interactional events have a structure and organization deserving study in their own right. To discuss Goffman's work here would take us too far beyond the bounds of the chapter. But his influence upon the development of interaction studies has been pervasive, not only for the approach being considered here, but on a much broader front.[21] He has been especially influential on the emergence, from the tradition of ethnomethodology, of what is known as *conversation analysis* (Attwell, 1974; Schenkein, 1978; Sudnow, 1972), although this must be considered a separate development. Conversation analysis, which is treated by West and Zimmerman (Chapter 9), had its start more than 10 years ago, but has only begun to have a wider impact since 1974, the year in which Sacks, Schegloff, and Jefferson's work on turn taking in conversation was published in *Language.* That paper proposed a system of rules of great generality, intended to account for one very important aspect of conversational structure, that of taking turns at talk.[22] Once again, to deal at any length with conversational analysis would take us beyond our present purview; for not only is its present efflorescence very recent, as I have said, but it also stems from a very different tradition from those that have been considered in this chapter. It takes its origins in part from the phenomenology of Alfred Schutz (1967), especially as it influenced Garfinkel (1967). It also is indebted to the so-called ordinary language philosophy of J. L. Austin (1962), among others.

The final development that must be mentioned here is that of sociolinguistics, particularly the branch of it known as the ethnography of speaking (Hymes, 1974). Here there is an extremely lively interest in the structure of speech use in everyday social situations, and though a discussion of this work is well beyond our present scope, much that is contained in it is directly relevant for any understanding of interaction.[23]

Brief treatments, intended as introductory surveys of the entire field of interaction studies, have been provided by Kendon (1979b), and a very extensive bibliography (Ciolek, Elzinga, & McHoul, 1979) has been published in association with Kendon's review. This bibliography provides comprehensive coverage through 1978, together with a topical index.

8.3. Investigating greetings: a methodological case study

This section presents an account of the methodological problems and decisions and the theoretical presuppositions involved in undertaking an analysis of the structure of greeting encounters. This study (Kendon & Ferber, 1973) has been chosen for special reference because several important methodological issues were resolved while it was being carried out. The account offered here is of relevance not only to this 1973 study, of course: The conception of behavior structure arrived at and the theoretical background to this conception, in particular, have quite general implications.

The aim of the greetings study was to give an account of the way in which greeting events are organized as behavioral events. It will be recalled that we were working within the framework of an approach in which it was assumed that interaction, to be understood, requires an analysis of all available aspects of behavior, that behavior is organized at multiple levels simultaneously, that the interactive significance of actions can be properly understood only if they are analyzed in context, and that interactants doing things like greetings are making use of familiar behavior patterns. Our interest was in giving an account of these patterns and not in trying to understand the psychology of the individual greeters. Use of such an orientation requires the availability of film specimens, as I have already pointed out. Accordingly, it was arranged to film a social event where many instances of greetings were likely. Our main source of specimens was a film of a child's birthday party, held out of doors, which was attended by many friends of the child's parents and parents of other children.

Details about this film have been published elsewhere (Kendon & Ferber, 1973). Here, however, it is important to point out that the making of the film was not, in fact, the first step in this investigation. The first step was an attempt to frame an initial theory of greetings. This theory of the structure of the greeting, formulated on the basis of reflection on our own experiences of greetings, served to guide the way in which the actual filming was done. I want to stress this point. Although, as I shall remark again later, a film record does indeed allow one to examine what it has recorded, much as one can examine actual specimens, and although it therefore comes as close as we can ever get to a genuine specimen of behavior, in doing the filming one still has to make many decisions about where to point the camera, how to frame the events one wishes to record, what camera angles to employ, and when to begin and when to stop running the camera. These decisions will in fact be made according to some conception of what aspects of the events being recorded are important for subsequent study. Thus one's initial theory about the event one is interested in analyzing is of great importance, because, to a large degree, it will dictate the kinds of specimens of these events that one will acquire. For this reason, our initial theory of the greeting is outlined next, and an attempt is made to indicate how it affected the kind of film record we made.

The initial theory of the structure of greetings

The theory of greeting structure as it was first formulated had two aspects. First, greetings were defined as "those procedures by which focused gatherings are established" (Kendon, 1969). Following Goffman's (1957, 1963) notion of the "focused gathering" as an occasion when participants share a jointly sustained focus of attention, we saw the "greeting" as the means by which such a joint attentional focus was set up. Thus we defined the greeting in functional terms, and we saw it as consequential for subsequent interaction. This point of view already predisposed us to film what happened after the greeting, as well as the greeting itself.

Second, it was proposed that the greeting itself be analyzed "into a number of steps and stages, ordered in time, with each stage setting the conditions for the next stage" (Kendon, 1969). The stages initially proposed were:

1. *Sighting,* in which *P* sights *Q* as the person he wishes to greet and, further, in which he perceives that *Q* is in a greetable condition (for example, that he is not taken up with some other activity that cannot be interrupted). The stage of sighting was recognized as a preinteractional stage.
2. *Mutual recognition,* in which "each party must signal his recognition of the other, and in doing so signal his openness to the other's salutation" (Kendon, 1969). We supposed that, prior to the actual greeting, *P* and *Q* would have to convey to each other that they agreed to be greeted: *P* indicating that he would greet *Q*; *Q* indicating that he knew this and was willing to receive the greeting; *P*, perhaps, in a further step, indicating that he was going to go on with the greeting.

3. *Salutation*, in which each party to the greeting enacts a specific and more or less conspicuous gesture, either kinesic or vocal or both. We had in mind here such things as a handshake, an embrace, and so on.
4. *Setting the scene*, in which it was supposed that there is a transition from the greeting itself to the establishment of the encounter that follows.

It will be seen that this theory of the greeting presupposes that the participants have a plan to greet one another. What the theory attempts to state is the minimum number of steps that would have to be gone through in order to realize this plan. Proposing these steps would provide us, it was thought, with an initial guide about where to look in the material for the overt acts that would be playing a part in the transaction.

The theory with which we started, then, proposed a particular approach to the filming of greetings. Because it recognized a place for greetings in the development of encounters, it encouraged us to film what happened after the salutation itself was completed. As we have seen, we included in the theory the notion of "setting the scene," and this phase, at least, we would attempt to film. We also had formulated the steps that, as we supposed, must lead up to the salutation or greeting, and so we were predisposed to film as much of the behavior that preceded this stage as we could. But we remained open to the possibility that more might be involved than our initial formulation had suggested. For this reason, in filming the occasion on which the greetings took place, we filmed much more than a narrow focus upon greetings might have suggested. As it turned out, this proved to have been a very fortunate decision.

Film records as behavior specimens: properties, limitations, and use

Before I proceed further, a few comments on the nature of film records as behavior specimens, their properties and uses, are perhaps in order. There are two aspects to be discussed here. First is the issue of the nature of the film record, and how it compares with other types of behavior records. As we shall see, the peculiar properties of the film record lead to certain considerations that should be borne in mind by anyone who would acquire behavior specimens by this means. The second matter is the questions that arise when one undertakes a structural analysis of behavior using film specimens, questions concerning the representativeness of such specimens. As we shall see, analyses of behavior structure have so far tended to rely upon relatively few specimens.

There are some important issues that may be raised in connection with the issue of film as a type of record. It will be noted that our resort to film or videotape for the purposes of gathering material to be examined is quite different from the use of some sort of automatic recording device. Such devices – voice-actuated microphones, accelerometers for recording movement, and so on – are highly selective in the aspect of behavior they record, and the choice of one or more of these devices represents a theoretical decision by the investigator about what variables are important, a decision that must be made in advance of any data analysis.

Film or videotape is selective, too, but I think it important to note that it is selective in a different way. Whereas mechanical recording devices record the *effects* of some selected aspects of behavior – giving pointer readings of these aspects, if you will, or traces of them – film or videotape provides us with a means of reproducing the behavior (see Scherer & Ekman, Section 1.3; Rosenfeld, Section 5.4). It obviously is not a complete reproduction, and in using it one must be highly aware of its limitations. The image is two-dimensional. The camera's angle of view is quite restricted, and this angle of view is relatively inflexible. The so-called techniques of film making, using camera movement and editing for the construction of sequences, may be regarded in some respects as techniques for overcoming this limited angle of view. One of the aims of a film maker is to give the viewer a sense of continuity of action and a sense of a coherent world that he feels he inhabits or witnesses. But in making films for the purpose of making behavior specimens we do not have this concern, of course. We should not ever attempt to do things to try to overcome the limits of the field of view of the camera. Rather, we should be fully aware of its limitations and choose, in advance, the size of the frame, the width of view we are to work within. Ideally, of course, we should be in a position to know the relationship between what is included in the frame and what is left out. But within these limitations, we do have a *specimen* – which contains far more information than we ever initially supposed it would (Sandall, 1978). It provides us with a genuine "field" for exploration within which discoveries can be made.

Recognizing, then, the limitations of camera angle, and remembering that the film one is shooting is not intended to structure experience, one must link one's choice of camera position and angle as explicitly as possible to the questions one is asking. One may film at wide angle and with time-lapse devices if one is interested in the long-term fluctuations of groups. One can film with close-ups if one is interested in a detailed analysis of facial expression. In filming greetings, we sought to keep as narrow an angle as was compatible with keeping the full bodies of the participants in the frame at all times. This was because we wanted material that would allow us to understand all the aspects of greeting, from initial sighting to the spatial maneuvering that ensued in the phase we called setting the scene. We were insistent, also, on keeping both participants in view all the time.

Let us return now to the issue of representativeness. Work that attempts to derive the structure of interactional events from the examination of specimens tends to make use of relatively few of them. The reason is partly a practical one: To unpack the various behavioral components in an interactional episode and display their relations to one another is very time-consuming. But also, because one is trying to show how interactional episodes are constructed, it appears appropriate to proceed in a case-by-case fashion and to build up one's argument for a general phenomenon by adducing examples, rather than by demonstrating relationships through the use of large samples and correlational analysis. This is because one is seeking to show how *all* the various components of an interactional event are organized in relation to one another, whereas in undertaking a correlational analysis one must, necessarily, be quite selective about which aspects of behavior one studies. Furthermore, in order to deal with these aspects correlationally, one must reduce them or encode them in some form that will make them amenable to such treatment. In doing this one ceases to deal with them in their manifest form. An analogy might be made with anatomical description: In such description it is necessary to specify the forms of the components of the body being described and to display their arrangements. This is necessarily done on a specimen-by-specimen basis, at least until a general model of the specimen's structure has been formulated. Once this has been done, then of course it is appropriate to make measurements of selected aspects and to undertake quantitative analyses on large samples. Initially, however, one seeks to establish a model for the structure one is trying to describe, and quantitative analyses using large numbers is deemed premature. In the same way, in dealing with interactional events from the viewpoint here being discussed, it is supposed that such events have structures. The first issue is to establish the components and their relationships. Structural studies dealing with selected aspects in a quantitative fashion, on the basis of large numbers of examples, cannot be undertaken until this has been done.

In selecting one's specimens one must be able to assume, of course, that they are typical. One must assume, further, that the behavioral structures observable and the interrelationships that occur are typical of the interactional events of the sort one is studying. One is justified in this assumption to the extent that the participants in the event recorded themselves display no surprise at what is going on, and to the extent that others, oneself included, also recognize the record as showing nothing exceptional. The specimen, then, is used as a vehicle for demonstrating the operation of what one is proposing as general principles of organization. These principles are derived, in the first instance, from reflection upon one's own experience as a participant in interaction. Examination of specimens enables one to see how far these principles may be operating and how far they should be modified in light of what is found in the specimens.

The outcome of this work is twofold. First, one becomes able to propose a more explicit set of principles by which the interactional event one has been looking at is governed. This may be regarded as a hypothesis for guiding future work – and at this point, but not before, one is in a position to propose something general and then to collect instances of behavior and see whether they support the hypothesis. Second, the close examination of behavior may reveal new phenomena that, whether or not they prove to be widespread, have to be accounted for in any general theory one may propose. For example, just two or three well-documented examples of a phenomenon such as interactional synchrony – enough to establish that the phenomenon occurs – are all that is needed to force a revision in one's conceptions of how people may interrelate their behavior.

Strategies for analysis

Given our specimens, then, we may now consider what is involved in working with them. I have tried to show how the initial theory of the event we are interested in influences the way in which this material is gathered. I have emphasized, however, that the material gathered, despite its limitations, remains close to a reproduction of the complete event. We are given by this means a record of a comprehensive range of behavioral aspects, and we are given this in such a way that, within the space–time limitations of the film frame, the structure and organization of these aspects is not prejudged.

So how do we proceed with the analysis? First, in looking through the footage, we have to know what to look at. A conspicuous feature of greeting recognized at the outset is what we have termed the salutation, that is, the point when people shake hands, or bow to one another, or embrace. In locating events for analysis in our study, we relied upon our common understanding as members of the culture to locate instances of salutation. These could be defined, provisionally, as that complex of gesture and spoken utterance that occurred when people came into one another's presence for the first time and that would be recognized by anyone from the culture as a greeting. Of course, such greetings or salutations are not *confined* to the highly conventional forms of behavior just mentioned. What we recognize as a salutation appears to be *any* distinctive behavior that occurs at the time when people are coming together after a period of absence. Thus people can (and do) salute one another by punching, slapping, making their modes of walking into a caricature of the other's mode of walk, turning their backs on the other and standing stock still, loud yells, whistles, or any of a wide range of behaviors. These would, I think, given their location of occurrence in what happens before and what happens afterwards, and given certain features of how they are performed, all be recognized as salutational.

So defined, we could readily enough locate instances of greeting in the footage we had acquired. But having located them, we were confronted with questions: We had to decide where our analysis should begin and where it should end; we had to decide on the kinds of units to be used for describing the structure of the behavior; we had to decide upon the level of detail to which we should take the analysis. Answers to these questions emerged only slowly as the work proceeded. But they are questions one has to keep continually open in this kind of work.

Before outlining the solutions to these and other problems toward which this work led us, I would like to refer to three other methods of approach that could have been followed, methods that indeed have been followed by other investigators. I want to show why we rejected them, for in this way, I think, I can point up even more sharply the features of the procedure that was adopted.

The three kinds of approaches I have in mind are what I shall call the *behavior variables approach*, the *behavior element approach*, and the *complete transcription approach*. Of these, we did make use of the complete transcription approach. This is the second of the five steps of context analysis recommended by Scheflen. As we shall see, however, it did not work and it was abandoned.

The behavior variables approach. In the behavior variables approach one selects in advance what appear to be, on theoretical grounds of one sort or another, the important parameters of behavior, which one then sets out to measure. They are measured and interrelated in some way, either with each other or with other variables (for example, with psychological, sociological, or other characteristics of the participants). This way of proceeding is, of course, widely followed; in fact, I think it would not be inaccurate to say that most of the work in which such aspects of behavior as gaze direction, posture, spacing, and the like are being studied treats these aspects as variables that are measured and interrelated or used as indexes of something, such as "immediacy" or "intimacy."

Had we chosen to follow this approach with the greetings material we would have specified certain features of behavior in advance for measurement. We might have chosen to look at spacing, orientation of gaze, type of facial expression, and amount and kind of touching, and then have measured how these kinds of behaviors varied from instance to instance. We could have measured several such aspects and then intercorrelated them to develop a picture of the covariance of these aspects of behavior. Or we could have compared these behavioral variables with participant variables such as age, sex, or relative social status of the greeters, or with aspects of their social relationship, such as degree of familiarity, liking, and so forth.

Now whatever the value of work of this kind for questions we might ask about greetings, for our purposes it would not do because it takes for granted two of the very questions we were trying to ask. First, in making measurements of behavior at greeting, one must decide when to make them. Although we had, at the outset, some notion of where to look for a greeting, it was one of our goals to try to determine from observable behavior some means of deciding what a greeting is. Setting about making measurements of behavior of the sort suggested here would mean that we had already attained this goal. Secondly, in making measurements, one must be highly selective about what one measures. In making such a selection one is making a decision about what aspects of behavior are significant and why. Once again, because our question was to find out how behavior is organized in greeting, we could not take an approach that already presupposed an answer to the question.

The behavior element approach. One group of workers who have attempted to follow a more descriptivist approach in dealing with human behavior are those who have been trying to apply the methods of ethology. I refer here, in particular, to the work of Blurton Jones (1972) and McGrew (1972), most of which was done with children of nursery school age, which began to appear about nine years ago. In essence, what these workers did was to propose that behavior can be regarded as made up of *elements,* repeatable patterns of behavior that are, as it were, the building blocks whose concatenations and clusterings create the more elaborate sequences and structures.

Both Blurton Jones and McGrew are explicit in acknowledging their debt to the work of the founding fathers of ethology, Lorenz and Tinbergen. Blurton Jones, indeed, before he turned to human behavior, was a student of Tinbergen's and had worked on the English bluetit (*Parus caeruleus*). Both Blurton Jones and McGrew proceeded on the assumption that what one must do is begin by just watching the animal one is interested in – in this case, the child – to see what it does, and then write down all the different behavior patterns it can be observed to produce. Blurton Jones, in the introduction to his book *Ethological Studies of Child Behaviour* (1972), lays great stress upon the need for a "thorough and leisurely descriptive phase of the investigation" (p. 11); he suggests "an emphasis on the use of a large variety of simple observable features of behaviour as the raw data" and an emphasis on "a descriptive and hypothesis generating natural history phase as the starting point of the study" (p. 4). These, he says, are characteristics of the ethological approach. Likewise, McGrew (1972) argues that the ethological method is advantageous because it takes as its starting point descriptions of behavior patterns that are defined objectively, "in terms of body parts and motor patterns . . . Their definitions refer to specific, recurring fixed action patterns, free of motivational pre-judgements" (p. 19).

In accordance with this approach, the first aim of these workers has been to undertake a period of mere watching in order to provide an account of the behavior patterns that can be observed. What emerged from this initially was a series of lists of distinguishable patterns of behavior. Several workers have presented such lists – many running to well over 100 items – as, in McGrew's (1972) terms, "tentative attempt at defining an ethogram for the young *Homo sapiens*" (p. 36; see also Ekman, Section 2.3; Rosenfeld, Section 5.6).

The behavior elements listed as a result of such periods of mere observation then become the basis for further observations. Blurton Jones's subsequent work has consisted in attempts to examine in a quantitative fashion the patterning of such behavior elements in small children. He has tackled a wide range of questions with this method; pertinent for us is his study of greetings and leave takings in nursery school children, done in collaboration with Leach (Blurton Jones & Leach, 1972).

For this study a period of observation at a nursery school was arranged to cover the time when the mother returned and collected her child. The investigators recorded the occurrence of 5 items of mother behavior – whether the mother looked at, smiled at, approached, touched, or talked to the child – and 22 items of child behavior, including such items as *look at mother, smile at mother, avert face from mother, smile at teacher, walk to mother, run to mother, play, suck, arms up, wave, laugh, jump, kiss, cry, tantrum,* and so on. During the period of observation, then, the occurrence of these items was noted and the data were analyzed by intercorrelating their frequency of occurrence; these intercorrelations subsequently received factor analysis.

On the basis of this kind of analysis, Blurton Jones and Leach show that children who cried at separation greeted with a rapid approach to the mother, with their arms up and touching her; children who did not cry on separation greeted by continuing to play and showing or giving objects to the mother. Blurton Jones and Leach discuss their findings in relation to a theory of attachment and the behaviors that might lead one to make use of that concept.

Without going into much further detail on this study, I would like to comment on several of its features.

First, the analysis divides behavior into a repertoire of discrete elements that are regarded as *fixed items* (see McGrew, 1972, p. 19) as quoted earlier in this discussion. In this we can see a direct link to the theoretical notion of the *fixed action pattern.* The interest in Tinbergen's and Lorenz's work was in behavior as a kind of fixed equipment of the animal. For Lorenz, especially, the focus was upon patterns of behavior that are characteristic of the species; he dealt specifically with behavior patterns that always had the same form. This idea has given rise directly, in Blurton Jones's work, to the idea of lists of behavior elements.

One point that may be made is thus that, for all Blurton Jones's claim about "mere watching" and the necessity for a "natural history hypothesis generating phase" of inquiry, in fact he began with a highly theoretical assumption that behavior could be described as a series of repeatable elements. This, of course, is not a criticism. It merely points out that behavioral observation (all observation) is structured by theory of some sort and that the claim that one can begin with "mere observation" cannot be sustained.

Second, a close look at the lists of behavior elements compiled by Blurton Jones and others who have followed his approach shows that there really is no coherent notion of what an element might be. Compare, in the list I quoted from in referring to the study with Leach, *arms up* with *run* or *play, suck* or *smile* with *walk* or *talk.* Some of these items are highly specific, others are very general patterns, recognized not so much by the movement pattern itself as by the immediate goal of the behavior. Thus, even if his assumption about there being repeatable elements is correct, we do not know just *what* he regards as a repeatable element. An *explicit analysis* of what counts as an item in this repertoire has not been presented.

Third, it will be seen that this work assumes not only that there are listable behavior elements, but that it is appropriate to consider their clustering alone. On this view behavior is regarded as a mosaic, the fixed elements constituting the components or tesserae of the mosaic. Their organization is explored by means of intercorrelation and factor analysis, both of which presuppose a very simple view of structure as clustering.

Fourth, as in the behavior variables approach, so here, at least in respect to the study of greetings mentioned, there is no concept of the greeting as a transaction that the participants are aiming to bring off and that therefore requires steps and stages for its accomplishment. As will be recalled from our original formulation of the theory of greetings, we had thought about the successive steps necessary for its accomplishment and had supposed that at each step behaviors would be enacted by which that step would be accomplished and conditions for the next one would be created. In the approach that Blurton Jones and his colleagues have taken, encounters are not thought of in relation to their structuring in time. Analysis deals solely with the clustering of frequencies of behavior elements within the observation period.[24]

Finally, the period of observation in the Blurton Jones and Leach greetings was predefined, and no attempt was made to seek for criteria in the behavior of the participants by which the boundaries of the transaction to be studied could be established.

Our approach to the study of greetings, then, came to differ from the approach followed by Blurton Jones and Leach in several respects. First of all, we began with the notion of the transaction as something that must unfold in time. Second, we supposed that each participant behaves in accordance with an internal plan of action, but under some guidance, nevertheless, from information derived from the other. Third, we did not predefine the outer limits of the greeting transaction. The salutation was defined in advance, but it was thought of as the peak of an episode whose boundaries we did not know. We sought, in the behavior of the participants themselves, for a way of defining the limits of the episode. Fourth, as we came to tackle the problem of behavior units, it also became evident that the notion of "behavior element" as a tessera in a mosaic, the conception held by Blurton Jones and his colleagues, was also inadequate.

The question of transcription. A third approach, and one we did begin to follow, is that which demands the *total transcription* of the specimen prior to any analysis of its structure. This is the approach that follows directly from the methodology suggested by descriptive linguistics, and it is proposed by Scheflen as the second of the five steps of context analysis (see "A. E. Scheflen and context analysis," in Section 8.2). It requires that one attempt to transcribe all aspects of behavior and then, by examining the transcript, derive the way in which the behavior is patterned. Accordingly, in approaching the greetings material, we began with graph paper, establishing a line for every separately articulable body part and a line for speech, and attempting to plot everything that every body part did. We ran into several problems and later abandoned this method. It should be said, however, that the attempt to plot in detail everything that every body part does is a very useful exercise, because it forces one to take a very close look at the behavior, and in consequence one can become very attuned to its detailed structure.

It became apparent that the transcription system one adopts itself embodies a set of hypotheses and assumptions that will thereafter structure one's inquiry. It is of the greatest importance to know what these hypotheses and assumptions are, and whether they are appropriate to the question one is engaged upon, before adopting any system of transcription. It is a mistake to think that there can be a truly neutral transcription system, which, if only we had it, we could then use to produce transcriptions suitable for any kind of investigation.

There are some workers who do use a detailed transcription system as a means of reducing their data. Duncan is one such investigator, and he has stated that in his view the development of structural studies of communicative behavior is hampered by the absence of comprehensive transcriptions of social interactional events that can then be used as references for analysis (Duncan, 1972). For my part, I am inclined to be wary of this approach. The adoption of a transcription system entails a decision about the nature and kinds of units of which behavior is composed. If one uses transcriptions as the basis for all subsequent analysis, as Duncan appears to do, one runs the danger of becoming irrevocably committed to a set of assumptions about the organization of behavior that will almost certainly not be correct. Transcriptions, thus, *embody* hypotheses. The maps one makes of behavioral events should be regarded as a form of *conclusion* to one's investigation, not as a starting point.

The first thing to do, therefore, is not to sit down and make a transcription (unless, of course, one has already reached a set of conclusions to be tested on fresh material; see Scherer & Ekman, Section 1.4). The first thing to do is to sit down and inspect the specimens one has at hand. Usually, one has some previous notion about the structure of the event in question – as we did in our greeting investigation, for instance. If this has not been explicitly formulated and one is merely looking to see what is there, a conception of the structure of the event quite often emerges, simply because one is usually dealing with behavior that is familiar. However, in this stage of preliminary inspection, the aim is to formulate a cognitive or mental map of the structure of the event, and what one then tries to do is to make this map explicit. This one does by making a physical map of the event, typically on paper.

As should be evident from what I have just said, as soon as one puts pencil to paper in making a map, as soon as one begins to make a transcription, one is thereby making a decision, a theoretical decision, about what is important. For no transcription, no matter how fine grained, can ever be complete. One must inevitably make a selection. Thus the map one makes, the transcription one produces, is as much a product of one's investigation as a means of furthering it. But only by laying out on paper a map of the event can one come to perceive its structure; only in this way can one come to "see" one's formulation. The next step, however, is to compare the map with the specimen, to reexamine the specimen in the light of the formulation given in the map. One works, thus, in continual dialogue with the specimen, stopping only at that point where one's current "irritation of doubt" (to adopt an expression from C. S. Pierce) about the issue at hand has been laid to rest.

This is the view of the role of transcription that I now hold, and it appears to me that this is in fact the way in which I have worked in all of the investigations that I have published. That is to say, in each case my first investigatory activity has been to inspect the specimen at hand until I have arrived at a hypothesis about some aspects of its organization. This hypothesis always takes the form of a formulation of pattern.

Formulating behavior structure

We must now deal with the problem of the units into which behavior may be said to be organized. It has just been suggested that one cannot begin mapping the behavior of any specimen until one has some conception of behavioral organization. I will here attempt to give an account of the conception of behavioral organization that emerged in the course of the greetings study. This conception now seems to offer itself as a starting point for other investigations of a similar sort.

In discussing the work of Blurton Jones (1972) and McGrew (1972), under the rubric *behavior element approach,* I suggested that their approach attempts to analyze behavior in terms of elementary units and to understand its complex appearances as concatenations of such units, much as a mosaic can be understood as a clustering of elementary bits of colored stone, or tesserae. However, an examination of specimens of behavior, such as may be acquired through film or videotape recordings, shows that any view of behavior structure dependent upon the idea that it is constructed out of combinations of elementary units is not adequate. Although patterns of action can be recognized and grouped into classifications of various sorts, one cannot find patterns of action that appear to be in any sense elementary. For example, one soon finds that different patterns of action occur simultaneously, overlapping one another in complex ways. Some of these patterns are long lasting, whereas others are relatively short-lived, and such short-lived action patterns may occur while longer-lasting action patterns are in progress. The complexities of behavior thus cannot be understood as constructions built from the clusterings of smaller units. Yet, as any naive observer will attest, behavior is quite certainly organized. Can we find a formulation that will allow us to grasp this organization?

The formulation to be offered here owes much to the proposals of Scheflen (1964, 1966, 1973), of which some account has been provided in Section 8.2. The central point on which this formulation depends is the notion that behavior may be regarded as being organized at multiple levels simultaneously. On this view, higher levels of organization are not seen as reducible to lower levels. They are seen, rather, as including lower levels of organization, and they may themselves be seen as being included in yet higher levels. In a descriptive analysis, then, one does not seek for the ultimate units out of which all behavior is built; one seeks to specify what different levels of organization there may be, and how they are related. The recognition of the different levels at which behavior is organized depends upon the recognition that the flow of action that may be perceived in an individual is produced under the guidance of plans (G. A. Miller, Galanter, & Pribram, 1960), that are themselves hierarchically organized. It is supposed that this hierarchical organization is manifested in the structure of the behavior itself.

An example may help to clarify the point of view here being

suggested. Consider someone delivering a lecture. One has no difficulty in regarding the lecturer as having a plan for the lecture, and seeing that as long as the lecture itself is in progress the lecture plan is in operation, organizing the lecturer's various actions. If we examine the lecture plan, as we may if the lecture has been written out in advance, we may see that it has a hierarchical structure, in the sense that the lecture as a whole may be seen as being divisible into component parts, such as an introduction, a middle, and a conclusion, and that these component parts may themselves be further divisible into subparts. For example, the introduction may contain opening remarks and a synopsis. The middle may contain three main points, each one followed by an example. Each of these components can itself be further analyzed into such units as paragraphs. Paragraphs can be analyzed into sentences, sentences into phrases, phrases into yet further subcomponents, such as words, and so on. These low-level components, however, although they are essential for the carrying out of the lecture plan, do not constitute the plan, either in themselves or in their combinations. The plan is not built up out of combinations of low-level components. The analysis of the lecture plan, therefore, does not proceed from the analysis of the elementary components upward to the larger units. Rather, the larger units are established first and are seen as frames or brackets for the lower-level units. Thus, in analyzing the lecture plan, we seek to specify levels of organization, and each such level can be seen as a unit of the lecture plan. It will be seen that, in such an analysis, we proceed from the larger or more inclusive levels of organization downward.

Now observe the lecturer actually delivering the lecture. We shall see that the kind of hierarchical organization we have observed in the lecture plan is manifested in the observable behavior of the lecturer. Thus, for the duration of the lecture, the lecturer may be observed to be in a particular area of the lecture room in a particular pattern of orientation to the audience. He may be observed to pace up and down, perhaps, but we note that this pacing is done within the confines of a fairly limited space and that although the lecturer thus does not remain in one constant position and orientation, a patterning to his pacings and turnings that lasts for the duration of the lecture can be observed. Thus, insofar as the lecturer maintains a bodily position and orientation throughout, we may see that in this regard he sustains a phrase of behavior that frames or brackets his entire lecture, and therefore he can be seen to manifest, in this aspect of his behavior, an action that refers us to the highest-level unit of organization of the lecture plan. Of course, while the lecturer is sustaining this unit of action, he is also maintaining a complex flow of action, including gesture, and a complex patterning of changes in facial orientation, all of which motions together constitute a configuration of units of action that we recognize as seeming to carry out the lecture plan. But even if the lecturer ceases all of these actions, so long as he still remains within the space he has been employing for his delivery, and so long as he maintains his orientation, we can still see in operation some aspect of behavior that refers us to the highest-level unit of the lecture plan, and we can still say that the lecture plan is in operation, even if some components of its actual execution are suspended. Thus, for the entire duration of the lecture, we can see that there is a complex pattern of action that informs it throughout its manifestation. We may extract, accordingly, one or more behavior phrases that, persisting as they do throughout the lecture, refer us to the highest level of its organization. It is important to bear in mind, it should be added, that such extended behavior phrases may, like bodily position and orientation patterns, be manifested as a single unit or may, like intonation patterns, patterns of head movement, or patterns of gesture, be extracted as single units because of their repetitive character. We may extract extended phases of the performance as being contrastive with other phases, because we see cyclings of action or because we are able to recognize that a succession of actions are bracketed together because they may all be informed by the same theme.

If we then examine the internal structure of the lecture we may observe how the successive main parts – the introduction, middle, and conclusion – are marked in behavior by a variety of devices, including the pauses in speaking that may separate them, differences in voice qualities and in intonation patterns, and differences in the patterns of organization of the words themselves and the content they convey. At even lower levels of organization we may wish to consider specific units of speech, such as locutions or tone units, or specific gestures; and even here we find, not discrete units, but patterns of behavior at multiple levels of organization (Kendon, 1972b, 1980).

For example, at one point in an actual observation, a lecturer was seen partially extending his right arm, with his hand held palm upwards, with the fingers partially spread. This positioning of the right arm was a distinguishable phrase of behavior. While this phrase of behavior was in progress, the right hand and the forearm were observed to move downward vigorously and then to "bounce" upward, twice. This pattern of movement was observed four times. Here we had four behavior phrases, following one upon the other in succession, which were, so to speak, contained within the temporally more extensive phrase of the extended right arm and hand. This complex of behavior phrases was accompanied by a vocal utterance that itself, as we have already noted, may be understood as being analyzable into multiple levels of organization. All this occurred as the lecturer was in that part of his cycle of whole-body maneuverings in which he stood facing the audience at the end of his lateral pacings – a whole-body behavior phrase that was itself contained within the extended one lasting for the whole lecture.

On this view, then, what we seek for and seek to map are units or phrases of behavior at various levels of organization. Rather than look first for elementary units and then attempt to reconstruct the more complex patterns out of their combinations, we try to identify the different levels of organization by which the behavior being analyzed is patterned.

The concept I am here offering for the structure of behavior might be appropriately characterized as closer to a musical concept of structure than to either a tesseral view (which we have rejected) or a strictly constructed hierarchy view.[25] Although it was described in the lecture example as if it were a simple hierarchy of levels, and although such a structure can be found, we usually find structures more complex than this, so that we have to consider not just the possibility of levels of organization that contain lower levels and that are themselves contained by higher levels, but also the possibility of behavioral themes that may bracket aspects of behavior into other organizational units overlapping those that may have been established by other criteria. Just as the description of a piece of music requires us to deal with the many different aspects or modes of organization entailed in the piece – its rhythmical structures, its melodic organization, the roles of the various voices or instruments, its tonal structure, its organization into movements – so also the systematic description of the structure of behavior requires an organizational analysis: We must seek to unravel it by considering its phrasal structure and the structure of relationships between phrases, its rhythmical organization, the parts played in it by the various segments of the body, and its phases and subphases.

Representing a greeting encounter

Let us now consider this approach to the analysis of the structure of behavior in reference to the analysis of greeting encounters we have been using as an illustration. Here I will attempt to show, briefly, how the approach just sketched was arrived at in this investigation.

I have already said that, in viewing the material gathered for the greetings study, it was easy enough to locate occasions that could be recognized as "greetings." A greeting was recognized to have occurred whenever two people not previously in interaction with one another were observed to exchange salutations. A "salutation" was recognized whenever an instance of something that could count as such, like a handshake, an embrace, or a call such as "hi" or "hullo," was observed to have occurred. What was next noticed was that, whenever people exchanged salutations, they always came to a halt when they were close to one another; then, either as they were exchanging salutations or, more often, after they had finished doing so, they would both step away. If they remained in interaction after the salutational exchange, they would adopt a spatial-orientational arrangement that was distinct from the one they had been in during the salutational exchange.

This observation provided us a clue about where we should begin and where we should end our analysis. A little reflection suggested that, in order for two people to carry out a salutation – for example, a handshake – they must arrange themselves in space in a way that allows them to do so. Thus the maneuvering of the bodies of the two participants into an arrangement suitable for the carrying out of the salutation could be regarded as part of the behavior involved in carrying out the greeting; moving away from this spatial-orientational arrangement could be interpreted as constituting a maneuver into a new spatial-orientational arrangement, distinct from the one used for the salutation. Thus, once this second maneuver began, the frame or context suitable for the exchange of salutations was no longer prevailing. Therefore, once this arrangement was dismantled, the unit we were interested in analyzing – the performance of a salutational exchange – was over. By the same token, working backward from the moment at which the salutation was being performed, we could find the place where each participant began upon the maneuver that eventually led him or her to stand in an arrangement with the other within which the salutation could be performed. The spatial-orientational arrangement of the participants' bodies, then, and the maneuver that led to its establishment, provided the outermost limit for the unit we proposed to analyze.

This unit may now be interpreted as follows. What we are suggesting is that, so long as an individual is maintaining his or her body in a location and in an orientation in respect to another suitable for the accomplishment of a close salutation, so long can we say that the salutation plan is in operation. We may say that we can see the beginning of the execution of this plan the moment we see the individual begin upon any action that constitutes the first element of maneuvering that culminates in such an arrangement. Thus, if a man is sitting in a chair with his legs crossed and then gets up and crosses to meet and shake hands with an approaching friend, the moment he begins to uncross his legs can constitute the first moment at which he has embarked upon the maneuver that brings him to the place where he can shake hands. This will count as the earliest point at which we can see the salutation plan being put into operation.

The point I am making here may be stated even more generally. We may note that activity is always *located*. Whatever one may be doing, one must, necessarily, maintain a relationship to one's immediate surroundings, and this relationship is an essential component of whatever it is that one may be doing. The area of the immediate environment that one directly relates to in carrying out whatever one may be doing may be called the *transactional segment* (see Kendon, 1977a). Thus to write or to eat one sits at a table immediately in front of one and there is a space in which the eating or the writing is done. To proceed along a sidewalk, one must have space in front of one into which one may move, and in steering oneself on the sidewalk as one walks one generally makes sure that such a space is available. To watch television, one may sit on a sofa on one side of the room and orient oneself so that one can see the television set clearly on the other side. Once again, one sets up a relationship to the immediate environment that makes possible the carrying out of one's activities; and in doing so one effectively lays claim to a space, or transactional segment, which one uses for the activity. The maintenance of the body in a particular location and in a particular orientation, then, is preserved so long as the relationship that one needs with the immediate surroundings is being maintained. So long as I am to give a lecture, I must set up a spatial relationship with my audience of a certain sort and maintain it. If I am to shake hands with another, I must likewise establish a spatial-orientational relationship with that person in order to make the handshaking possible. Thus major changes in either bodily position or orientation (or, usually, both) provide significant boundary markers in the flow of behavior, for they are undertaken (so I suggest) whenever an individual is shifting into a new relationship with the environment (setting up a new transactional segment), which each person will do whenever he or she is putting into execution a new plan. It will be seen, accordingly, that our decision to make the initial cuts in the flow of behavior at the points where a spatial-orientational arrangement suitable for the salutation were were studying began and ended not only provides us with a highly convenient way of bracketing off the relevant stretch of behavior, but also reflects a theoretical interpretation of the significance of such major changes in spacing and orientation.

Proposing a behavioral segment that begins when the individual begins to move to a new position and orientation and ends when he or she begins the next move provides, I suggest, a way of defining a frame within which we may find behavior that pertains to whatever plan the spatial-orientational segment in question brackets. In the case of greeting sequences, the segment that contains the maneuver to the position used for carrying out the close salutation and the maintenance of the position encloses a number of actions, including the salutation, that constitute several of the steps people go through in effecting a salutational interaction. A specific example will illustrate the way in which a greeting interaction may be represented in this fashion.

Figure 8.1 is an attempt to represent a greeting event in such a way as to show both the successive spatial-orientational segments and the phrases of behavior that are contained within these segments and are, thus, part of the greeting sequence. It will be seen that these phrases, which may be thought of as lower-level components of the greeting sequence and which are produced under the guidance of the overall plan of both participants as they carry off a salutational exchange, are presented in a way that suggests how they are framed by the sustained phrase of the spatial-orientational maneuver.

The converging lines in the center represent the distance separating the two individuals in the course of the greeting encounter. The arrows on either side of the lines indicate the frontal orientations of the two. These lines and arrows show the pattern already described: approach to a stopping point where each faces the other directly, followed by further movement in which they then rearrange themselves in relation to one another. In this particular case, the two individuals came to stand side by side. The boxes above and below the lines represent, for each participant separately, segments of sustained bodily orientation. The outer box in each case represents the total period of time during which the person in question is engaged in sustaining the overall bodily orientation phrase, which includes the salutation. Inside each outer box, two additional boxes are drawn, one outlined with a broken line, another with a double line. These boxes represent, respectively, the period of time during which the person is moving through space and the period of time during which he is stationary, following this maneuver. It will be seen that for each new *stance* the person may have, that is, for each new stable spatial-orientational position his body assumes, there

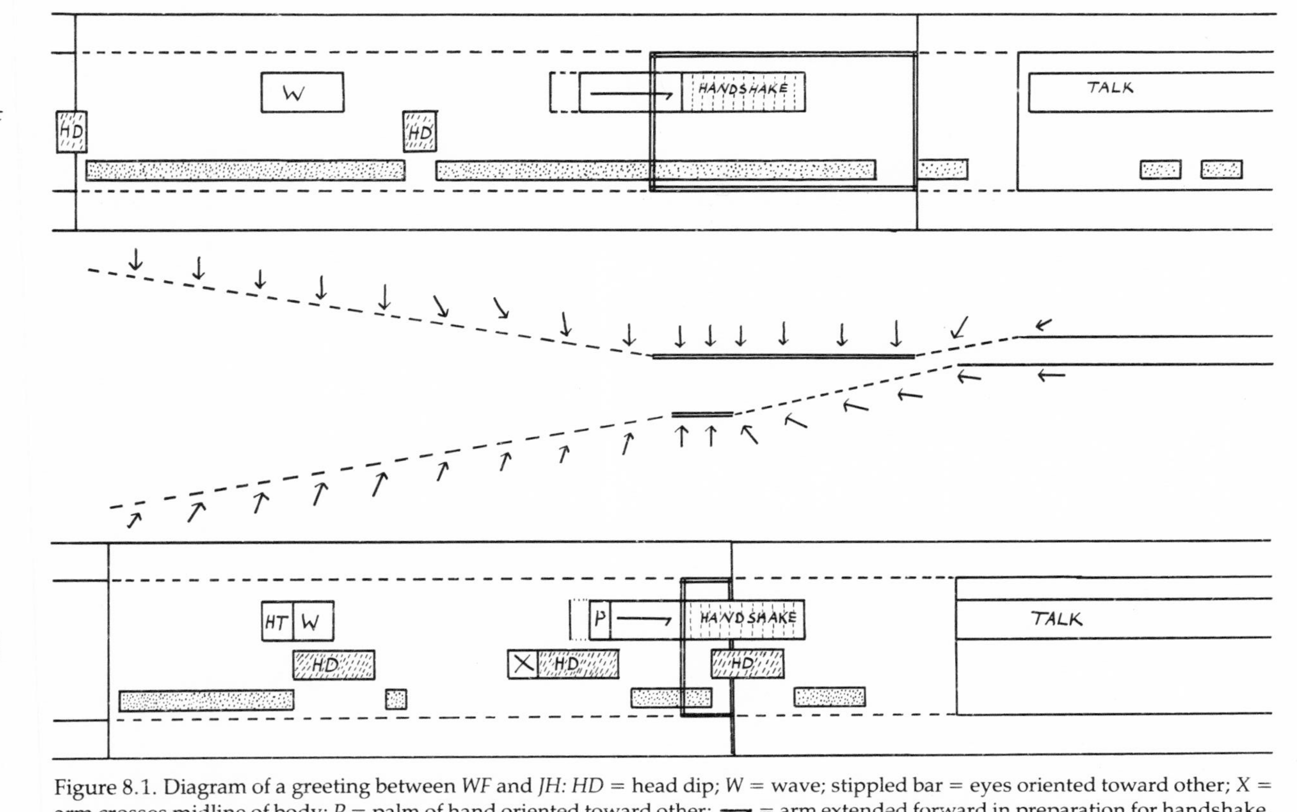

Figure 8.1. Diagram of a greeting between *WF* and *JH*: *HD* = head dip; *W* = wave; stippled bar = eyes oriented toward other; *X* = arm crosses midline of body; *P* = palm of hand oriented toward other; ⟶ = arm extended forward in preparation for handshake. *Source:* Kendon and Ferber, 1973, p. 605 (courtesy, Academic Press, London). Second intervals are indicated at the top of the figure. The numbers are frame numbers of film with a film speed of 24 frames per second.

must be a period of time when he is moving into this stance. This intervening maneuver, together with the period of time during which he remains in a given standing position or stance, is considered as one behavior phrase, at the level of whole-body spatial orientation. Such a phrase may be regarded as having two phases: a *transition phase,* that of moving from one stationary position to another, and a *placement phase,* which lasts as long as the individual remains either stationary or within a confined spatial range (as in the case of the lecturer who paces up and down, or in the case of a conversationalist who makes small oscillatory movements within the framework of the space being used for the conversation).

The narrow boxes drawn on the inside represent various behavior phrases that occurred while the whole-body spatial-orientation behavior phrase was in progress. The stippled bars give changes in orientation of the face – in this instance, only those periods of time when the face was oriented directly at the other are shown. Other small boxes represent other phrases of behavior, depicting only the outer boundaries of these phrases as they occur in time, not their internal structure – which is sometimes quite complex. Furthermore, these phrases are not plotted according to the body parts involved. Thus the phrase in *WF*'s box labeled *W* refers to *WF*'s lifting his forearm above his head and combining this gesture with a forward flap of the hand affected by an extension–flexion of the wrist. Concurrently, *WF*'s mouth opened and closed and a vocalization occurred. This complex of phrases involving several different body parts is here plotted as a single unit: It is a complex of behavior phrases that stands out against the background of the rest of *WF*'s behavior and is recognizable as a unit that could be labeled *wave.* Clearly, should we need to do so, we could adopt a larger scale for the behavior map, and plot out the complex internal structure of such a phrase.

Inside the stance units, then, I have plotted the outer limits of actions or behavior phrase complexes that involve only parts of the body. One of these is labeled *handshake,* and this, it will be noted, occurs within the placement phase of the whole-body locational-orientational behavior phrase. The salutation, that is, as may be seen from the diagram, occurs within the framework of a specific spatial orientation. As this comes to an end, the handshake is over, and with the establishment of a new spatial-orientation frame, we have a new organization of actions – here labeled *talk,* but clearly analyzable into its component phrases of speech and action if one should wish to do so.

Prior to the handshake, both participants engaged in a number of other actions, as is indicated in the diagram. In the study of greeting referred to, approximately 70 greetings were analyzed in this way, and in each case all of the actions that occurred up to and including the close salutation were examined – all of the behavior phrases, that is, that occurred within the frame provided by the whole-body orientation phrase that ends about when the close salutation ends and begins with the end of the previous whole-body behavior phrase, whatever that may have been.

It was found that the part-body behavior phrases that occur within these limits fall into a limited number of classes and occur in a characteristic sequence. Thus, early on, we could distinguish a class of behavior phrases such as waves, calls, and a particular head and face gesture (the "head toss") that functioned as a "distance salutation." This distance salutation is followed by phrases in the head that have the effect of averting one person's gaze from the other. As the two get closer together, certain additional arm phrases may be observed, for example "self-touching" or the "body cross" (an arm placed across the front of the body). A change in orientation of the head then occurs, such that the two greeters "look at" each other (this is often preceded by an exaggerated "looking away" on the part of one, sometimes of both, participants); facial phrases appear – in particular, "smiling" – and also utterances – these again belonging to the class of salutational utterances in most cases. Finally, we see the start of the complex of phrases that constitute the "close salutation" – the handshake, the bow, the embrace, or whatever it consists of.

Such a program of phrases, which is described in detail by Kendon and Ferber (1973), probably functions in part to bring about the coordination of behavior between the two individuals that is necessary if a close salutation can be carried off. Obviously, if two persons are to shake hands or to embrace or otherwise to engage in a salutational exchange, each must be at an appropriate distance from the other and both must be appropriately oriented. Furthermore, each must be ready at the proper moment to perform those patterns of behavior that are to constitute the close salutation, because, as this is a joint performance in most instances, each must be entrained to the other's behavioral rhythm. The behavioral coordination that is necessary has at least the following four components:

1. Each must be apprised of when the other has begun the greeting unit.
2. Each must be able to entrain his behavioral rhythm to the other's.
3. There must be an appropriate degree of motivational calibration between the two, so that, for example, neither should appear too forward in the approach to the other, nor yet be too reserved.

4. An agreement must be reached about the *form* that the close salutation should take.

A detailed consideration of the way in which the organization of behavior on an occasion of salutational exchange subserves these coordinative functions will not be given here, because what we intend by this example is to show how a conception of the behavioral organization of those occasions was attained. A feature of this demonstration has been to show that the method we arrived at for dealing with the behavioral flow depended upon a prior conception of the principles by which that flow was organized. This conception itself derives from a theory of behavioral control that finds its origins in the frame of thinking provided by cybernetics and information theory (see Section 8.2).

If, as in this example, one thinks of greetings as the product of a plan for greeting, one is led to think of all the various actions that can be observed as being organized by such a plan. This train of thought leads to a view of the organization of action that is essentially hierarchical, as we have seen, and accordingly, to an approach to the analysis of observable behavior in terms of such a hierarchical conception. Such a view of action has been widely proposed. Lashley (1951) provides an early exposition. More recent examples are found in Welford (1958), G. A. Miller et al. (1960), and Powers (1974), among others. A view of this sort strongly informs the approach developed by Scheflen, as I have already indicated.

I have suggested here that such a view of the way in which the control of action is organized will have direct implications for the description of the observable flow of behavior. Following this view, one is led to look first for features of the behavior that remain constant throughout the period of time during which a given plan is being carried out and that appear to serve in maintaining the constant conditions needed for carrying out the plan. Once these features have been recognized and mapped, one then proceeds to lower levels of organization, levels that refer to patterns of action by which the various subcomponents of the plan are carried out.

In our study an extended whole-body phrase that could be said to "frame" the sequence of phrases that includes the close salutation was extracted, because it was observed that after the close salutation a new whole-body spatial-orientational phrase was invariably begun. It would seem that the exchange of close salutations, along with the maneuvering and behavioral negotiation that must necessarily precede this exchange, constitutes a functionally distinct package. Accordingly, I propose that a plan serving to coordinate the various behavioral elements that may be observed is in operation while this package is in evidence. These various behavioral elements – the distance salutational actions, the management of gaze, the elements of the close salutation, and the like – constitute the tactics of the plan, to use G. A. Miller et al.'s (1960) expression. These tactics will, naturally, be adjusted according to the circumstances in which the plan is being carried out. However, it would appear that for the period of time during which the plan is in actual execution, each person will of necessity be maintaining an orientation toward a distinct segment of the environment – that segment, in this case, where the other is to be found. The duration of the plan's execution is thus made manifest in the whole-body spatial-orientational phrase by which each person frames the actions that make up the execution of the plan, and by which each differentiates a segment of the immediate environment in relation to which his or her actions will be carried out. What I wish to suggest is that for each package of behavior at the level of a plan such as the greeting plan, each person will adopt a new whole-body spatial-orientational behavior phrase. Once the close salutational exchange is completed, as we have already noted, each adopts a new whole-body orientation, and moves to a new location. Now the two will engage in "talk" – no longer salutational exchange, but a different mode of transaction entirely.

The adoption of a new whole-body orientational phrase and the consequent establishment of a new transactional segment, whatever it entails, as a person shifts from one major mode of engagement with others or with the environment to another, is proposed here as an entirely general phenomenon that is illustrated by the observations made on salutational sequences. Further illustrations have been given elsewhere (Kendon, 1977). It will be noted, of course, that this observation – that a person adopts a new transactional segment whenever embarking upon the execution of a new high-level package of behavior – has implications for the communicative functioning of behavior. This has already been suggested by Scheflen (1964) in his notion of the presentation and position, discussed previously, according to which a person's successive distinct engagements of are marked by changes in his or her physical location, and different units of the person's engagement *within* a given interaction may be marked by gross changes of posture. Scheflen, following Birdwhistell (1956/1970), would agree that the sustained bodily position he is referring to here functions as a "transfix" for a sequence of communicative units, binding them together or cross-referencing them. Such constant or "standing features" of a person's performance (see Argyle & Kendon, 1967) can serve to signal to other participants in the interaction that the person is "in play" in a certain way in the interaction. When the person's posture or transactional segment shifts, other participants can expect a new pattern of behavior. Thus the coordination of the behavior of the various participants is facilitated, insofar as sustainments and changes in posture and orientation function as markers for changes and sustainments of plans.

8.4 Conclusions

I have tried in this chapter to describe one particular approach to the analysis of communication in interaction. This is an approach that attempts to be thoroughly semiotic, for it seeks to treat behavior from a viewpoint that is as far as possible purely communicational. There are two aspects to such an approach. On the one hand, in analyzing behavior from this viewpoint, one may seek to give an account of the code systems into which it appears to be organized. This aspect appears to have been the special concern of R. L. Birdwhistell in his attempt to establish a kinesics to parallel linguistics, an attempt discussed at some length in Section 8.2. On the other hand, one may seek to give an account of the organization of interaction systems, and this, for the most part, has been the aspect stressed here. From this angle an attempt is made to decide how behaviors produced on occasions of interaction serve in the process of behavioral coordination that is the essence of human interaction, considered from this viewpoint. The work of Scheflen (see Section 8.2) and Goffman most fully typifies this aspect. The two aspects are, of course, complementary. One cannot give an account of the organization of interactional events without some knowledge of the code systems of which the participants are making use. On the other hand, one cannot give a full analysis of any of the code systems without being able to understand how they are employed in interaction.

I have sought to show something of the origins of the approach I have outlined. I have sought to show that it represents a genuine synthesis of several different lines of thought stemming from rather different academic disciplines. This illustrates the point that has often been made: that the study of communication must draw upon many different disciplines but that, in doing so, it succeeds in bringing them together into a genuinely new synthesis. We can see in the study of communication a truly unifying field of study.

With respect to the more strictly methodological issues considered in this chapter, it has been my intention to show how theory and methodology are inextricably intertwined, each one implying the other.

Given a particular theoretical outlook, I have argued, a particular strategy of investigation is implied. Given a particular technique of analysis, on the other hand, a particular range of questions is raised and a particular emphasis in examining the phenomena at hand is followed, and this emphasis, in turn, implies a particular theoretical framework. The theoretical frameworks discussed here are indeed best referred to as *frameworks,* or perhaps *orientations* would be a better term, for they are not thoroughgoing theories, fully explicit and articulated. Likewise, the methodology discussed is not fully formalized. It is impossible to lay down a set of rules that, if followed, will lead to fruitful results. There is no substitute for good questions. Once good questions have been formulated, methods emerge in their service. To the extent, then, that I have succeeded in this chapter in showing how the approach here sketched can be source of good questions, to this extent I will be satisfied that it has been successful.

Notes

1. Accounts of the structural approach to the analysis of interaction in which some attempt is made to compare it with other approaches may be found in Sebeok, Hayes, and Bateson (1964), von Cranach and Vine (1973), and Duncan and Fiske (1977). A very thorough treatment may be found in Zabor (1978). For an excellent review of the several different contemporary approaches that all converge on the question of how interactions are entered into and maintained, see McDermott and Roth (1978).
2. As Watzlawick, Beavin, and Jackson (1967) have put it: "Behavior has no opposite . . . [T]here is no such thing as nonbehavior or, to put it even more simply: one cannot *not* behave." They continue: "If it is accepted that all behavior in an interactional situation has message value, i.e., is communication, it follows that no matter how one may try, one cannot *not* communicate" (pp. 48–49).
3. As Bateson (1979) has put it: "Without context, words and actions have no meaning at all. This is true not only of human communication in words but also of all communication whatsoever, of all mental process, of all mind, including that which tells the sea anenome how to grow and the amoeba what he should do next" (p. 15).
4. For Mead's work, see G. H. Mead (1934, 1938) and Strauss (1956). For accounts of Mead's intellectual origins, see Morris (1934), and H. C. A. Mead (1938), and Wallace (1967). Mills (1964) provides a detailed treatment of pragmatism and its relationship to sociology, with special reference to Peirce, James, and Dewey. For a comprehensive bibliography of Mead's works and of works about Mead see Kang (1976).
5. For example, Frieda Fromm-Reichman, Henry Brosin, Jurgen Ruesch, R. E. Pittinger, H. L. Lennard, George Mahl, Peter Ostwald, Hans Strupp, J. S. Matarazzo, Jay Haley, and Don Jackson, among many others.
6. First attempts along these lines include Pittenger, Hockett, and Danehy (1960), Lennard and Bernstein (1960), McQuown (1957), Pittenger (1958),

Pittenger and Smith (1957), and of course, the famous *Natural History of an Interview* (McQuown, 1971b), of which more later (see "*The Natural History of an Interview: the collaboration at Palo Alto,*" later in this section).

7. Freud (1914/1948) set the stage for this scrutiny. The list of psychoanalytically inspired work on such aspects of behavior is extensive. Krout (1935a, 1935b, 1937, 1954), Deutsch (1947, 1949, 1966), and Mahl (1968) are good exemplifications.
8. Concepts of self-regulating systems later formalized by cybernetics were formulated first in physiology by Claude Bernard (1927/1947) and W. B. Cannon (1932). Chapple (see Chapple & Coon, 1942) was one of the first to apply concepts from equilibrium theory in biological systems to patterns of action in face-to-face interaction. Russett (1966) provides a history of the application of the concept of equilibrium in American social thought generally.
9. Numerous formulations for the notion of *interaction* have been put forward, and a formulation in linear, stimulus-response terms was by no means the only one to be offered. It was to remain, however, a very important one, especially because it was the form that tended to be resorted to by those who wished to undertake a quantitative, behavioral analysis of interaction. Thus, Chapple (1940) writes:

   When one or more quanta of action q_1 manifested by Individual A, are followed by one or more quanta of action p_1, manifested by Individual B, the quanta q_1 may be regarded as the stimulus s_1, and the quanta p_{1a} as the response r_1. Such a succession s_1r_1 will be defined as constituting *interaction* between the individuals A and B. [p. 24, original emphasis]

   Homans (1950) says: "When we refer to the fact that some unit of activity follows or, if we like the word better, is stimulated by some unit of activity of another, aside from any question of what these units may be, then we are referring to *interaction*" (p. 36, original emphasis).

   This way of thinking about interaction is fully compatible with a reinforcement learning theory approach to the study of social behavior, an approach that was made quite explicit by Homans in his later work (Homans, 1961). Similar formulations are found in other learning theory treatments, such as those by N. E. Miller and Dollard (1941). Students who did not adhere to a learning theory approach, but were interested in cognitive and perceptual processes in interaction, sometimes offered formulations that were much closer to those which are offered from a cybernetic and information-theoretic perspective (see, for example, Jones & Thibaut, 1958).
10. The most systematic exposition of the methods of structural or descriptive linguistics is to be found in Harris (1951). See also Bloch and Trager (1942).
11. The study of interpersonal spacing has developed extensively and there is now a very large literature. Besides Hall, Robert Sommer has been highly influential. Sommer (1959) early developed an approach to the study of spacing that was influenced by observations in animal behavior. His work differs from that of Hall, insofar as he has not approached spacing as if it can be analyzed as a culturally coded system. Sommer's work is well summarized in Sommer (1969). Reviews of work in interpersonal spacing may be found in Watson (1970), Vine (1975), Evans and Howard (1973), Pederson and Shears (1973), Edney (1974), and Hayduck (1978). For a thoroughgoing structural approach to spacing that differs in many ways from the approaches just cited, see Scheflen and Ashcraft (1976). In this work an attempt is

made to understand the systems of spatial relationships people enter into, rather than to establish spacing as a property of the individual. See also Kendon (1977a).

12. Birdwhistell (1952) did offer the beginnings of a notation system, but this has not proved to be generally usable. Hall (1963) offered a notation for interpersonal spacing, but this is limited because it can be used only for pairs of people. Proxemic notation systems have been reviewed and critically assessed by Ciolek (1977). Much greater progress in the technology of notation for bodily movement has been made by choreographers. Thus, Laban (1956) and Laban and Lawrence (1947) have developed systems for notating both the movements of body parts (see also Hutchinson, 1966) and the dynamics or "efforts" of movement. These systems have been applied by a few students of social behavior (for one example see Lomax, 1968; and see also Davis, 1979), but not as yet in the analysis of interaction. Eshkol and Wachmann (1958) present another system developed initially for choreography. This has been applied in the analysis of social interaction among jackals (Golani, 1976) and also for the notation of manual signs in Israeli sign language (Cohen, Namir, & Schlesinger, 1977). A notation system for the face was proposed by Ex and Kendon (1964/1969; see also Kendon, 1975b). The recent work of Ekman and Friesen on the Facial Action Coding System (Ekman & Friesen, 1978) makes possible detailed analysis of facial behavior in a way that has not been achievable before. Early applications of this may be found in Baker and Padden (1978), Liddell (1978), and Oster (1978).

Systems for the transcription of speech are highly sophisticated. The whole issue of transcription of other aspects, despite the advances mentioned here, remains very poorly developed. It seems likely that no universal system will be developed. Rather, we can expect a number of specialized systems, of which Ekman and Friesen's for the face is one example. Some theoretical issues concerning the nature of transcription are touched on again later (see "Formulating behavior structure," in Section 8.3).
13. A better term than *tacesics* would be *haptics*, as proposed by Wescott (1966)
14. An excellent recent treatment of the eyebrows and the movements they can make is to be found in Ekman (1979). Ekman describes all of the different brow actions that a person can perform and gives some account of the patterns of brow action that are to be observed in emotional expression, and also of those patterns of action that occur in association with vocal utterances in conversation.
15. For an account of the early history of cinematography, see Ceram (n.d.). For a history of its applications in anthropology and psychology, see DeBrigard (1975), Prost (1975), and Michaelis (1955).
16. Recent work on mother–infant interaction using close analysis of specimens of interaction in the form of films or videotape may be found in Hofer (1975), Stern (1977), Schaffer (1977b), Bullowa (1979), and Lock (1978b). It is especially notable that Schaffer (1977a), Newson (1977), Lock (1978a), and Clark (1978) sketch views of the communications process that are very close to those being dealt with in this chapter; yet they make no reference to the particular tradition of inquiry we are here tracing. Clark's (1978) references to G. H. Mead are made as if he had just discovered Mead's relevance for his questions.
17. Bateson and Mead came to use still photographs and films as a method of presenting patterns of behavior in Balinese culture which, they argued, showed similarities of form or theme and thereby displayed the different ways in which the common patterning of Balinese culture was manifested.

Of *Balinese Character* they wrote: "This is not a book about Balinese custom, but about the Balinese – about the way in which they, as living persons, moving, standing, eating, sleeping, dancing and going into trance, embody that abstraction which (after we have abstracted it) we technically call culture" (Bateson & Mead, 1942, p. xii). Bateson, in his book *Naven* (1936), attempted to describe what he referred to as the "ethos" of Iatmul culture, by which he meant "a culturally standardized system of organization of the instincts and emotions of individuals" (p. xi). Such a culturally standardized system, he wanted to show, was an abstraction "that could be applied systematically to all items of behavior" (p. xi). Likewise, Mead, in her earlier works on Samoan and other South Pacific cultures (M. Mead, 1928, 1930, 1935), had sought to show how culture and personality were patterned and had been led to try to characterize the patterning that could be found in daily actions – how mothers treated their children when bathing them or feeding them, for example – or in the ways, times, and places in which feelings and emotions were expressed. Both Bateson and Mead believed, when they came to collaborate in Bali, that to attempt to describe this aspect of culture in words was seriously compromising. By using photographs and films, on the other hand, they believed they could compare the pattern and form of behavior directly. By placing specimens of behavior in juxtaposition they could show how actions as diverse as, say, "a trance dancer being carried in a procession, a man looking up at an aeroplane, a servant greeting his master in a play, the painting of a dream" (Bateson & Mead, 1942, p. xii) all displayed features in common. This interest in showing how all aspects of behavior share a common pattern remains an important component of the work of many engaged in the structural approach to the study of communicative action. It has been stressed many times, by Hall (1959, 1966, 1976) and Birdwhistell (1970), for example, and it is the principal theme of the work of Lomax (1968). McDermott and Roth (1978) have argued strongly that the larger patterns of a culture can be revealed by the ways in which individual members manage their interactions with one another. Thus they say ". . . the institutional constraints which we usually address with broad 'macro' generalities are actually observable at the behavioral level of immediate interaction. The specifics of such socially pervasive facts as gender, ethnicity, status and role are, to use Sapir's (1931) phrase, 'reanimated or creatively confirmed' from one moment to the next . . . participants make the social order observable to each other and to analysts in the fine details of their behavior." [P. 323]. Such views provide a strong theoretical justification for undertaking the kind of detailed analysis of behavior in interaction that the structural approach requires. Notice that such investigations would not be possible without the availability of photographic recording techniques, especially cinematography.

18. See Ruesch (1972) and the very useful review of this work by Bär (1973). Ruesch provides another excellent account of the way in which information theory and cybernetic considerations were brought to bear on the analysis of human interaction. Ruesch and Kess (1956) is another work of historic significance for the tradition we are here considering. It provides an excellent outline of the questions of human communication, and it deals not only with the communicative significance of visible action, but with the environment as well. The book was probably important in drawing the attention of a wide audience to an approach that regards all visible action as of communicative significance. It might also be mentioned that this book was perhaps the first to use the unfortunate term *nonverbal communication* in

its title. On the disadvantages of this term see Sebeok (1976) and, especially, Kendon (1978).

19. *The Natural History of an Interview,* the editorship of which was credited to various members of the Palo Alto group at various times, was for many years listed in bibliographies as "forthcoming" or "in press." It may now be consulted on microfilm in the library of the University of Chicago. See McQuown (1971b).
20. A number of ethologists have tackled the issue of behavior structure and the question how it may be described and into what units it may be analyzed. For important treatments of this issue see, for example, Lorenz (1960) and Barlow (1968, 1977). It is, of course, a central issue in ethology, as it is in the structural approach to human interaction.
21. Works by Goffman of especial relevance to the field of interaction studies include Goffman (1961, 1963, 1967, 1971, 1974, 1976).
22. Turn taking during talk, and the question how it is achieved in a smooth manner, has been the focus of research by Kendon (1967) and, recently, by Beattie (1978, 1979). Their approaches are different from those of the conversational analysts. The major contributor to the study of this issue from something like a structuralist position has been Duncan. See Duncan and Fiske (1977) for a comprehensive summary of this work. Others who have concerned themselves with the subject include De Long (1974), Wiemann and Knapp (1975), and Philips (1976). The analysts of the temporal patterning of utterances in conversation was initiated by Chapple (1939). It has also been the subject of much research by Matarazzo and his colleagues (e.g., Saslow & Matarazzo, 1959) and by Jaffe and Feldstein (1970). For a recent collection of reports on this see Siegman and Feldstein (1979).
23. For a survey of work in sociolinguistics and conversational analysis and of recent British work on discourse analysis, all of which are highly pertinent to our understanding of interaction, see Coulthard (1977). An important work that stands somewhat apart from these other developments is Labov and Fanshel (1977).
24. For a discussion of more recent and more sophisticated quantitative analyses that could be applied in the behavior element approach, and that assume other kinds of underlying structural models, see van Hooff, Chapter 7. The discussion offered here should be read as an account of the way in which the approach we developed in the study of greetings came to be explicitly different from that of Blurton Jones and Leach.
25. A *strictly constructed* hierarchy is one in which units at higher levels in the hierarchy are built out of units at lower levels and in which any level, thus, can be decomposed into such units of construction. In the view offered here, though we speak of a hierarchy, the higher levels in the hierarchy are not strictly constructed but are units in their own right. They are better thought of as providing an organizing or coordinating frame for lower-level units.

References

Argyle, M., & Kendon, A. Experimental analysis of the social performance. In L. Berkowitz (Ed.), *Advances in experimental social psychology* (Vol. 3). New York: Academic Press, 1967.

Attwell, P. Ethnomethodology since Garfinkel. *Theory and Society,* 1974, *1,* 179–210.

Austin, J. L. *How to do things with words.* Oxford: Oxford University Press, Clarendon Press, 1962.

Baker, C., & Padden, C. A. Focusing on nonmanual components of American Sign Language. In P. Siple (Ed.), *Understanding language through sign language research.* New York: Academic Press, 1978.

Bales, R. F. *Interaction process analysis.* Reading, Mass.: Addison-Wesley, 1950.

Bär, E. Semiotic approaches to human behavior. *Semiotica,* 1973, *8,* 132–162.

Bär, E. Context analysis on psychotherapy. *Semiotica,* 1974, *10,* 255–281.

Barlow, G. W. Ethological units of behavior. In D. Ingle (Ed.), *The central nervous system and fish behavior.* Chicago: University of Chicago Press, 1968.

Barlow, G. W. Modal action patterns. In T. A. Sebeok (Ed.), *How animals communicate.* Bloomington: Indiana University Press, 1977.

Bateson, G. *Naven: A survey of the problems suggested by a composite picture of the culture of a New Guinea tribe drawn from three points of view.* Cambridge: Cambridge University Press, 1936.

Bateson, G. *Mind and nature: A necessary unity.* New York: Dutton, 1979.

Bateson, G., & Mead, M. *Balinese character: A photographic analysis.* New York: Special Publications of the New York Academy of Sciences, Vol. 2, 1942.

Beattie, G. W. Floor apportionment in conversational dyads. *British Journal of Clinical and Social Psychology,* 1978, *17,* 7–16.

Beattie, G. W. Contextual constraints on the floor apportionment function of gaze in dyadic conversation. *British Journal of Clinical and Social Psychology,* 1979, *18,* 391–392.

Bernard, C. *[Introduction to experimental medicine]* (H. C. Green, Trans.). New York: Dover Publications, 1947. (1st English ed., 1927.)

Birdwhistell, R. L. *Introduction to kinesics: An annotation system for analysis of body motion and gesture.* Washington, D.C.: Foreign Service Institute, U.S. Department of State, 1952. (Ann Arbor, Mich.: University Microfilms.)

Birdwhistell, R. L. Body motion. In R. L. Birdwhistell, *Kinesics and context: Essays on body motion communication* (chap. 26). Philadelphia: University of Pennsylvania Press, 1970. (Originally prepared as a chapter for N. A. McQuown [Ed.], *The natural history of an interview,* 1956.)

Birdwhistell, R. L. *Kinesics and context: Essays on body motion communication.* Philadelphia: University of Pennsylvania Press, 1970.

Bloch, B., & Trager, G. L. *Outline of linguistic analysis.* Baltimore: Linguistic Society of America, 1942.

Bloomfield, L. *Language.* New York: Holt, Rinehart & Winston, 1933.

Blurton, Jones, N. (Ed.). *Ethological studies of child behaviour.* Cambridge: Cambridge University Press, 1972.

Blurton Jones, N., & Leach, M. Behaviour of children and their mothers at separation and greeting. In N. Blurton Jones (Ed.), *Ethological studies of child behavior.* Cambridge: Cambridge University Press, 1972.

Boas, F. Introduction. In F. Boas (Ed.), *Handbook of American Indian languages* (Bureau of American Ethnology, Bulletin 40). Washington, D.C.: U.S. Government Printing Office, 1911.

Bullowa, M. (Ed.). *Before speech: The beginning of interpersonal communication.* Cambridge: Cambridge University Press, 1979.

Cannon, W. B. *The wisdom of the body.* New York: Norton, 1932.

Ceram, C. W. *The archaeology of the cinema.* New York: Harcourt, Brace & World, n.d.

Chapple, E. D. Quantitative analysis of the interaction of individuals. *Proceedings of the National Academy of Science,* 1939, *25,* 295–307.

Chapple, E. D. Measuring human relations. *Genetic Psychology Monographs*, 1940, 22, 3–147.
Chapple, E. D., & Coon, C. S. *Principles of anthropology*. New York: Henry Holt, 1942.
Cherry, C. *On human communication*. Cambridge, Mass.: MIT Press, 1957.
Ciolek, T. M. *Configuration and context: A study of spatial patterns in social encounters*. Unpublished doctoral dissertation, Australian National University, Canberra, 1977.
Ciolek, T. M., Elzinga, R. H., & McHoul, A. W. (Eds.). Selected references to coenetics. *Sign Language Studies*, 1979, 22, 2–6, 23–72.
Clark, R. A. The transition from action to gesture. In A. Lock (Ed.), *Action, gesture and symbol: The emergence of language*. London: Academic Press, 1978.
Cohen, E., Namir, L., & Schlesinger, I.M. *A new dictionary of sign language*. The Hague: Mouton, 1977.
Coulthard, M. *An introduction to discourse analysis*. London: Longman, 1977.
Davis, Martha. Laban analysis of nonverbal communication. In S. Weitz (Ed.), *Nonverbal communication: Readings with commentary* (2nd ed.). New York: Oxford University Press, 1979.
DeBrigard, Emilie. The history of ethnographic film. In P. Hockings (Ed.), *Principles of visual anthropology*. The Hague: Mouton, 1975.
De Long, A. J. Kinesis signals at utterance boundaries in preschool children. *Semiotica*, 1974, *11*, 43–74.
Deutsch, F. Analysis of postural behavior. *Psychoanalytic Quarterly*, 1947, *16*, 195–213.
Deutsch, F. Thus speaks the body: An analysis of postural behavior. *Transactions of the New York Academy of Science*, 1949, *12*, 58–62.
Deutsch, F. Some principles of correlating verbal and non-verbal communication. In L. A. Gottschalk & A. H. Auerbach (Eds.), *Methods of research in psychotherapy*. New York: Appleton-Century-Crofts, 1966.
Duncan, S., Jr. Nonverbal communication. *Psychological Bulletin*, 1969, *72*, 118–137.
Duncan, S., Jr. Some signals and rules for taking speaking turns in conversations. *Journal of Personality and Social Psychology*, 1972, *23*, 283–292.
Duncan, S., Jr., & Fiske, D. W. *Face-to-face interaction: Research methods and theory*. Hillsdale, N.J.: Erlbaum, 1977.
Edney, J. J. Human territoriality. *Psychological Bulletin*, 1974, *81*, 959–975.
Eibl-Eibesfeldt, I. Similarities and differences between cultures in expressive movements. In R. A. Hinde (Ed.), *Nonverbal communication*. Cambridge: Cambridge University Press, 1972.
Ekman, P. About brows: Emotional and conversational signals. In M. von Cranach, K. Foppa, W. Lepenies, & D. Ploog (Eds.), *Human ethology: Claims and limits of a new discipline*. Cambridge: Cambridge University Press, 1979.
Ekman, P., & Friesen, W. V. *Facial action coding system*. Palo Alto, Calif.: Consulting Psychologists Press, 1978.
Erickson, F. One function of proxemic shifts in face-to-face interaction. In A. Kendon, R. M. Harris, & M. R. Key (Eds.). *Organization of behavior in face-to-face interaction*. The Hague: Mouton, 1975.
Eshkol, Noa, & Wachmann, A. *Movement notation*. London: Weidenfeld & Nicolson, 1958.
Evans, G., & Howard, R. B. Personal space. *Psychological Bulletin*, 1973, *80*, 334–344.
Ex, J., & Kendon, A. A notation for facial positions and bodily postures:

Appendix to Appendix II, progress report to Department of Scientific and Industrial Research, Social Skills Project, Institute of Experimental Psychology, Oxford University, 1964. (Reprinted in M. Argyle, *Social interaction*. New York: Atherton Press, 1969.)

Freud, S. [*The psychopathology of everyday life*] (A. A. Brill, Trans. and intro., 2nd ed.). London: Ernest Benn, 1948. (1st English ed., 1914.)

Garfinkel, H. *Studies in ethnomethodology*. Englewood Cliffs, N.J.: Prentice-Hall, 1967.

Goffman, E. On face-work. *Psychiatry*, 1955, *18*, 213–231.

Goffman, E. Alienation from interaction. *Human Relations*, 1957, *10*, 47–59.

Goffman, E. *Encounters*. Indianapolis: Bobbs-Merrill, 1961.

Goffman, E. *Behavior in public places*. New York: Free Press, 1963.

Goffman, E. *Interaction ritual*. Chicago: Aldine, 1967.

Goffman, E. *Relations in public*. New York: Basic Books, 1971.

Goffman, E. *Frame analysis*. New York: Harper & Row, 1974.

Goffman, E. Replies and response. *Language in Society*, 1976, *5*, 257–313.

Golani, I. Homeostatic motor processes in mammalian interactions: A choreography of display. In P. P. G. Bateson & P. H. Klopfer (Eds.), *Perspectives in ethology* (Vol. 2). New York: Plenum, 1976.

Hall, E. T. *The silent language*. Garden City, N.Y.: Doubleday, 1959.

Hall, E. T. A system for the notation of proxemic behavior. *American Anthropologist*, 1963, *65*, 1003–1026.

Hall, E. T. Silent assumptions in social communication. In *Disorders of communication* (Research Publications of the Association for Research in Nervous and Mental Disease, Vol. 42, pp. 41–55). Baltimore: Williams & Wilkins, 1964.

Hall, E. T. *The hidden dimension*. Garden City, N.Y.: Doubleday, 1966.

Hall, E. T. Proxemics. *Current Anthropology*, 1968, *9*, 83–108.

Hall, E. T. *Beyond culture*. Garden City, N.Y.: Doubleday, Anchor Press, 1976.

Hall, E. T. *Handbook for proxemic research*. Washington, D.C.: Society for the Anthropology of Visual Communication, n.d.

Hare, A. P. *Handbook of small group research*. New York: Free Press, 1962.

Hare, A. P., Borgatta, E., & Bales, R. F. *Small groups: Studies in social interaction*. New York: Knopf, 1955.

Harris, Z. S. *Methods in structural linguistics*. Chicago: University of Chicago Press, 1951.

Hayduck, L. A. Personal space: An evaluative and orienting overview. *Psychological Bulletin*, 1978, *85*, 117–134.

Heims, S. P. Gregory Bateson and the mathematicians: From interdisciplinary interaction to societal functions. *Journal of the History of the Behavioral Sciences*, 1977, *13*, 141–159.

Heyns, R. W., & Lippitt, R. Systematic observational techniques. In G. Lindzey (Ed.), *Handbook of social psychology* (Vol. 1). Reading, Mass.: Addison-Wesley, 1954.

Hofer, M. A. *Parent–infant interaction* (Ciba Foundation Symposium 33, new series). Amsterdam: Associated Scientific Publishers, 1975.

Homans, G. *The human group*. New York: Harcourt, Brace & World, 1950.

Homans, G. *Social behavior: Its elementary forms*. New York: Harcourt, Brace & World, 1961.

Hutchinson, A. *Labanotation: The system for recording movement*. New York: Theatre Arts Books, 1966.

Hymes, D. *Foundations in sociolinguistics: An ethnographic approach*. Philadelphia: University of Pennsylvania Press, 1974.

Jaffe, J., & Feldstein, S. *Rhythms of dialogue*. New York: Academic Press, 1970.

Jones, E. E., & Thibaut, J. W. Interaction goals as bases of inference in interpersonal perception. In R. Tagiuri & L. Petrullo (Eds.), *Person perception and interpersonal behavior.* Stanford: Stanford University Press, 1958.

Kang, W. *G. H. Mead's concept of rationality: A study of the use of symbols and other implements.* The Hague: Mouton, 1976.

Kauffman, L. Tacesics, the study of touch: A model for proxemic analysis. *Semiotica,* 1969, *4,* 149–161.

Kendon, A. Some functions of gaze-direction in social interaction. *Acta Psychologica,* 1967, *26,* 22–63.

Kendon, A. *A proposal for the study of greeting encounters.* Unpublished manuscript, Bronx State Hospital, New York, 1967.

Kendon, A. Movement coordination in social interaction: Some examples described. *Acta Psychologica,* 1970, *32,* 100–125.

Kendon, A. Review of *Kinesics and context* by R. L. Birdwhistell. *American Journal of Psychology,* 1972, *85,* 441–455. (a)

Kendon, A. Some relationships between body motion and speech: An analysis of an example. In A. Siegman & B. Pope (Eds.), *Studies in dyadic communication.* Elmsford, N.Y.: Pergamon Press, 1972. (b)

Kendon, A. The role of visible behavior in the organization of face-to-face interaction. In M. Von Cranach & I. Vine (Eds.), *Social communication and movement in man and chimpanzee.* London: Academic Press, 1973.

Kendon, A. Introduction. In A. Kendon, R. M. Harris, & M. R. Key (Eds.), *Organization of behavior in face-to-face interaction.* The Hague: Mouton, 1975. (a)

Kendon, A. Some functions of the face in a kissing round. *Semiotica,* 1975, *15,* 299–334. (b)

Kendon, A. Spatial organization in social encounters: The F-formation system. In A. Kendon, *Studies in the behavior of social interaction.* Lisse, Holland: Peter DeRidder Press, 1977.

Kendon, A. Review of *Nonverbal communication: A research guide and bibliography* by M. R. Key. *Ars Semeiotica: International Journal of American Semiotic,* 1978, *2,* 90–92.

Kendon, A. Some methodological and theoretical aspects of the use of film in the study of social interaction. In G. P. Ginsburg (Ed.), *Emerging strategies in social psychological research.* New York: Wiley, 1979. (a)

Kendon, A. Some emerging features of face-to-face interaction studies. *Sign Language Studies,* 1979, *22,* 7–22. (b)

Kendon, A. Gesticulation and speech: Two aspects of the process of utterance. In M. R. Key (Ed.), *Nonverbal communication and language.* The Hague: Mouton, 1980.

Kendon, A., & Ferber, A. A description of some human greetings. In R. P. Michael & J. H. Crook (Eds.), *Comparative ecology and behavior of primates.* London: Academic Press, 1973.

Krout, M. H. Autistic gestures: An experimental study in symbolic movement. *Psychological Monographs,* 1935, *46* (Whole No. 208). (a)

Krout, M. H. The social and psychological significance of gestures (a differential analysis). *Journal of Genetic Psychology,* 1935, *47,* 385–412. (b)

Krout, M. H. Further studies on the relation of personality and gesture: A nosological analysis of autistic gestures. *Journal of Experimental Psychology,* 1937, *20,* 279–287.

Krout, M. H. An experimental attempt to determine the significance of unconscious manual symbolic movements. *Journal of Genetic Psychology,* 1954, *51,* 121–152.

Laban, R. *Principles of dance and movement notation*. London: Macdonald & Evans, 1956.

Laban, R., & Lawrence, F. C. *Effort*. London: Macdonald & Evans, 1947.

Labov, W., & Fanshel, D. *Therapeutic discourse: Psychotherapy as conversation*. New York: Academic Press, 1977.

Lashley, K. S. The problem of serial order in behavior. In L. A. Jeffress (Ed.), *Cerebral mechanisms in behavior*. New York: Wiley, 1951.

Lennard, H. L., & Bernstein, A. *The anatomy of psychotherapy: Systems of communication and expectation*. New York: Columbia University Press, 1960.

Liddell, S. K. Nonmanual signs and relative clauses in American Sign Language. In P. Siple (Ed.), *Understanding language through sign language research*. New York: Academic Press, 1978.

Lock, A. The emergence of language. In A. Lock (Ed.), *Action, gesture and symbol: The emergence of language*. London: Academic Press, 1978 (a)

Lock, A. (Ed.). *Action, gesture and symbol: The emergence of language*. London: Academic Press, 1978. (b)

Lomax, A. *Folk song, style and culture*. Washington, D.C.: American Association for the Advancement of Science, 1968.

Lorenz, K. Z. Methods of approach to the problem of behaviour. In *Harvey Lectures, 1958–1959*. Published for The Harvey Society, N.Y. New York & London: Academic Press, 1960.

Mahl, G. Gestures and body movement in interviews. In J. M. Shlien (Ed.), *Research in psychotherapy: Proceedings of the third research conference, Chicago, Illinois, 1966*. Washington, D.C.: American Psychological Association, 1968.

McDermott, R. P., Gospodinoff, K., & Aron, J. Criteria for an ethnographically adequate description of concerted activities and their contexts. *Semiotica*, 1978, *24*, 245–276.

McDermott, R. P., & Roth, D. R. The social organization of behavior: Interactional approaches. *Annual Review of Anthropology*, 1978, *7*, 321–346.

McDermott, R. P., & Wertz, M. Doing the social order: Some ethnographic advances from communicational analyses and ethnomethodology. *Reviews in Anthropology*, 1976, *3*, 160–174.

McGrew, W. C. *An ethological study of children's behavior*. New York: Academic Press, 1972.

McKay, D. M. Formal analysis of communicative processes. In R. A. Hinde (Ed.), *Nonverbal communication*. Cambridge: Cambridge University Press, 1972.

McQuown, N. A. Linguistic transcription and specification of psychiatric interview materials. *Psychiatry*, 1957, *20*, 79–86.

McQuown, N. A. Natural history method: A frontier method. In A. R. Mahrer & L. Pearson (Eds.), *Creative developments in psychotherapy*. Cleveland: Case Western Reserve University Press, 1971. (a)

McQuown, N. A. (Ed.). *The natural history of an interview*. Microfilm Collection of Manuscripts on Cultural Anthropology, 15th Series, University of Chicago, Joseph Regenstein Library, Department of Photoduplication, 1971. (b)

Mead, G. H. *Mind, self and society: From the standpoint of a social behaviorist*. Chicago: University of Chicago Press, 1934.

Mead, G. H. *The philosophy of the act*. Chicago: University of Chicago Press, 1938.

Mead, H. C. A. Biographical notes. In G. H. Mead, *The philosophy of the act*. Chicago: University of Chicago Press, 1938.

Mead, M. *Coming of age in Samoa*. New York: Morrow, 1928.

Mead, M. *Growing up in New Guinea*. New York: Morrow, 1930.

Mead, M. *Sex and temperament in three primitive societies*. New York: Morrow, 1935.
Michaelis, A. R. *Research films in biology, anthropology, psychology and medicine*. New York: Academic Press, 1955.
Miller, G. A., Galanter, E., & Pribram, K. *Plans and the structure of behavior*. New York: Holt, Rinehart & Winston, 1960.
Miller, N. E., & Dollard, J. *Social learning and imitation*. New Haven: Yale University Press, 1941.
Mills, C. W. *Sociology and pragmatism*. New York: Oxford University Press, 1964.
Morris, C. W. Introduction. In G. H. Mead, *Mind, self and society: From the standpoint of a social behaviorist*. Chicago: University of Chicago Press, 1934.
Newson, J. An intersubjective approach to the systematic description of mother–infant interaction. In H. A. Schaffer (Ed.), *Studies in mother–infant interaction*. London: Academic Press, 1977.
Oster, H. Facial expression and affect development. In M. Lewis & L. A. Rosenblum (Eds.), *The development of affect* (Genesis of Behavior, Vol. 1). New York: Plenum, 1978.
Park, R. E., & Burgess, E. W. (Eds.). *Introduction to the science of sociology*. Chicago: University of Chicago Press, 1921.
Pederson, D. M., & Shears, L. M. A review of personal space research in the framework of general systems theory. *Psychological Bulletin*, 1973, *80*, 367–388.
Perry, H. S. Introduction. In H. S. Sullivan, *The fusion of psychiatry and social science*. New York: Norton, 1964.
Philips, S. U. Some sources of cultural variability in the regulation of talk. *Language in Society*, 1976, *5*, 87–95.
Pike, K. L. *Language in relation to a unified theory of the structure of human behavior*. The Hague: Mouton, 1967.
Pittenger, R. E. Linguistic analysis of tone of voice in communication of affect. *Psychiatric Research Reports*, 1958, *8*, 41–54.
Pittenger, R. E., Hockett, C. F., & Danehy, J. J. *The first five minutes*. Ithaca, N.Y.: Martineau, 1960.
Pittenger, R. E., & Smith, H. L. A basis for the contribution of linguistics to psychiatry. *Psychiatry*, 1957, *20*, 61–78.
Powers, W. T. *Behavior: The control of perception*. London: Wildwood House, 1974.
Prost, J. H. Filming body behavior. In P. Hockings (Ed.), *Principles of visual anthropology*. The Hague: Mouton, 1975.
Rosenblueth, A., Wiener, N., & Bigelow, J. Behavior, purpose and teleology. *Philosophy of Science*, 1943, *10*, 18–24.
Ruesch, J. *Semiotic approaches to human relations*. The Hague: Mouton, 1972.
Ruesch, J., & Bateson, G. *Communication: The social matrix of society*. New York: Norton, 1951.
Ruesch, J., & Kees, W. *Nonverbal communication: Notes on the visual perception of human relations*. Berkeley & Los Angeles: University of California Press, 1956.
Russett, C. E. *The concept of equilibrium in American social thought*. New Haven: Yale University Press, 1966.
Sacks, H., Schegloff, E. A., & Jefferson, G. A simplest systematics for the organization of turn taking for conversation. *Language*, 1974, *50*, 696–735.
Sandall, R. Objective graphics: Ways of mapping the physical world. *Art International*, 1978, *22*, 21–25.
Sapir, E. *Language: An introduction to the study of speech*. New York: Harcourt, Brace & World, 1921.

Sapir, E. *Selected writings of Edward Sapir in language, culture and personality* (D. Mandelbaum, Ed.). Berkeley & Los Angeles: University of California Press, 1949.

Saslow, G., & Matarazzo, J. D. A technique for studying changes in interview behavior. In E. A. Rubenstein & M. B. Parloff (Eds.), *Research in psychotherapy*. Washington, D.C.: American Psychological Association, 1959.

Schaffer, H. A. Early interactive development. In H. A. Schaffer (Ed.), *Studies in mother–infant interaction*. London: Academic Press, 1977. (a)

Schaffer, H. A. (Ed.). *Studies in mother–infant interaction*. London: Academic Press, 1977. (b)

Scheflen, A. E. Communication and regulation in psychotherapy. *Psychiatry*, 1963, *26*, 126–136.

Scheflen, A. E. The significance of posture in communication systems. *Psychiatry*, 1964, *27*, 316–331.

Scheflen, A. E. Natural history method in psychotherapy: Communicational research. In L. A. Gottschalk & A. H. Auerbach (Eds.), *Methods of research in psychotherapy*. New York: Appleton-Century-Crofts, 1966.

Scheflen, A. E. *Communicational structure: Analysis of a psychotherapy transaction*. Bloomington: Indiana University Press, 1973.

Scheflen, A. E., & Ashcraft, N. *Human Territories: How we behave in space–time*. Englewood Cliffs, N.J.: Prentice-Hall, 1976.

Schenkein, J. *Studies in the organization of conversational interaction*. New York: Academic Press, 1978.

Schutz, A. *The phenomenology of the social world*. Evanston, Ill.: Northwestern University Press, 1967.

Sebeok, T. A. The semiotic web: A chronicle of prejudices. In T. A. Sebeok, *Contributions to the doctrine of signs*. Lisse, Holland: Peter DeRidder Press, 1976.

Sebeok, T. A., Hayes, D., & Bateson, M. C. (Eds.) *Approaches to semiotics*. The Hague: Mouton, 1964.

Shannon, C. E., & Weaver, W. *A mathematical theory of communication*. Urbana: University of Illinois Press, 1949.

Siegman, A. W., & Feldstein, S. *Of speech and time: Temporal speech patterns in interpersonal contexts*. Hillsdale, N.J.: Erlbaum, 1979.

Simmel, G. *Soziologie*. Leipzig: Duncker & Humblot, 1908.

Simmel, G. The sociology of the senses. In R. E. Park & E. W. Burgess (Eds.), *Introduction to the science of sociology*. Chicago: University of Chicago Press, 1921.

Simmel, G. *The Sociology of Georg Simmel* (K. Wolff, Ed.). Glencoe, Ill.: Free Press, 1950.

Sommer, R. Studies in personal space. *Sociometry*, 1959, *22*, 247–260.

Sommer, R. *Personal space: The behavioral basis of design*. Englewood Cliffs, N.J.: Prentice-Hall, 1969.

Stern, D. N. *The first relationship*. Cambridge, Mass.: Harvard University Press, 1977.

Strauss, A. (Ed.). *The social psychology of George Herbert Mead*. Chicago: University of Chicago Press, 1956.

Sudnow, D. (Ed.). *Studies in social interaction*. New York: Free Press, 1972.

Sullivan, H. S. *The psychiatric interview*. New York: Norton, 1954.

Sullivan, H. S. *Schizophrenia as a human process*. New York: Norton, 1962.

Sullivan, H. S. *Collected Works of Harry Stack Sullivan* (Vols. 1 and 2). New York: Norton, n.d.

Trager, G. L. Paralanguage: A first approximation. *Studies in Linguistics*, 1958, *13*, 1–12.

Trager, G. L., & Smith, H. L. *An outline of English structure*. Norman, Okla.: Battenburg, 1951.

Vine, I. Territoriality and the spatial regulation of interaction. In A. Kendon, R. M. Harris, & M. R. Key (Eds.). *The organization of behavior in face-to-face interaction*. The Hague: Mouton, 1975.

von Cranach, M., & Vine, I. Introduction. In M. von Cranach & I. Vine (Eds.), *Social communication and movement*. London: Academic Press, 1973.

Wallace, D. Reflections on the education of George Herbert Mead. *American Journal of Sociology*, 1967, *72*, 396–408.

Watson, O. M. *Proxemic behavior: A cross-cultural study*. The Hague: Mouton, 1970.

Watzlawick, P., Beavin, J. H., & Jackson, D. *Pragmatics of human communication*. New York: Norton, 1967.

Welford, A. T. *Ageing and human skill*. London: Oxford University Press, 1958.

Wescott, R. W. Introducing coenetics: A biosocial analysis of communication. *American Scholar*, 1966, *35*, 342–356.

Wiemann, J. M., & Knapp, M. L. Turn taking in conversations. *Journal of Communication*, 1975, *25*, 75–92.

Wiener, N. *Cybernetics; or, control and communication in the animal and the machine*. New York: Technology Press, Wiley, 1948.

Zabor, M. R. *Essaying metacommunication: A survey and contextualization of communication research*. Unpublished doctoral dissertation, Indiana University, 1978.

9. Conversation analysis

CANDACE WEST AND DON H. ZIMMERMAN

9.1. Introduction

In 1975, Lewis Coser, then president of the American Sociological Association, gave an address to Association members entitled ". . . Two Methods in Search of a Substance." One "method" critiqued by Coser was path analysis, a statistical technique; the other was ethnomethodology. Among many who were confused (and some who were amused) by this peculiar coupling were those who contended that ethnomethodology was not a method at all, but a particular attitude or perspective, containing several lines of inquiry (see Zimmerman, 1978, for a discussion of many distinct enterprises the term has come to encompass). One such line of inquiry, implying both a method and an attitude toward its data, is conversation analysis.

Conversation analysis is concerned with the social organization of conversational interaction, and conceives of the various situated manifestations of this organization as a set of methodical solutions to locally occurring technical problems that conversationalists must "solve." The orderliness of conversation is thus seen to be an *achieved* orderliness, an accomplishment of conversationalists on actual occasions of their talk. Though it has a distinctive empirical focus of its own, conversation analysis is thus consistent with the tradition of ethnomethodology, which holds that "properties of social life which seem objective, factual, and transformational, are actually managed accomplishments or achievements of local processes" (Zimmerman, 1978, p. 11). In this sense, the task of conversation analysts is similar to that of others engaged in ethnomethodological enterprises, namely, the analysis of those processes or practices through which objective, stable, transsituational features of social environments are continually achieved (see Pollner, 1974, p. 27).

The purpose of this chapter is to provide a systematic account of the approach to the analysis of naturally occurring interaction taken by conversation analysis, and in particular, to make explicit the assumptions that guide its empirical work and constitute its distinctive stance toward the data of social exchange. Such an undertaking poses several tasks. The first of these is to provide a description of the empirical focus of the enterprise, including its relationship to existing research using conversational materials. This discussion, our point of departure, is followed by a description of the theoretical framework, ethnomethodology, which informs the stance of conversation analysis toward the study of natural language practices. Third in our remarks is a sketch of the process of analysis itself, employing actual empirical observations and tracing the procedures conversation analysts use to describe and explicate the organization of social interaction. Our final aim in this chapter is to offer some suggestions regarding the utility of this method for the ongoing study of nonverbal communication. Accordingly, our concluding comments center on the usability of conversation analysis as both a method and a perspective on research of nonverbal exchanges.

9.2. Empirical focus

We begin by noting that the data of conversation analysts have consisted largely – but not exclusively – of conversational materials (see C. Goodwin, 1979a, 1979b; M. Goodwin, 1980; and Ryave & Schenkein, 1974, for notable exceptions). *Materials* generally means audiotapes and transcripts of "naturally occurring interactions" (Schegloff & Sacks, 1973/1974), that is, those exchanges not produced by experimental or interviewing techniques – "chats as well as services contacts, therapy sessions as well as asking for and getting the time of day, press conferences as well as exchanges of 'sweet nothings' " (Schegloff, 1968, p. 1075) – in short, the kind of talk we all do in the process of managing our day-to-day lives.

A focus on conversational interaction as a source of data is, in and of itself, nothing new. For decades, records of verbal interaction have been employed as a resource for the analysis of other social behaviors.[1] Since Bales (1950), for example, various investigations of small groups have applied coding schemes to conversational phenomena to generate indexes of leadership and control (Farina & Holzberg, 1968; Hadley & Jacob, 1973; Mishler & Waxler, 1968; Shaw & Sadler, 1965; Strodtbeck, 1951; Strodtbeck & Mann, 1956). Some studies have focused on patterns of control within families, using the criteria of total talking time (Farina, 1960; Hadley & Jacob, 1973; Strodtbeck, 1951), frequency of interruption (Farina & Holzberg, 1968; Hadley & Jacob, 1973; Lennard & Bernstein,

1969; Mishler & Waxler, 1968), and categorical measures originating in interaction process analysis techniques (Bales, 1950; Caputo, 1963; Murrell & Stachowiak, 1967; Schuman, 1970; Winter & Ferreira, 1967). Others have used speech events as criteria of dominance for studies of sex differences in intimate situations (Shaw & Sadler, 1965; Soskin & John, 1963) and in jury deliberations (Strodtbeck & Mann, 1956).

This research must surely be viewed as a major contribution to the study of social interaction, for it permits the examination of social activities over time, rather than limiting analysis to outcomes of those developments – for example, who finally "won" an argument, or who had the "last word" in making a decision. Yet a careful look at the literature suggests that the evidence provided by such analyses is inconclusive and, at times, contradictory. For example, the use of total talking time as an index of dominance is disputed by Komarovsky's (1962) finding that silence can be influential too, and that the most talkative partner in a marriage is not always the most powerful partner. Brownell and Smith (1973) point to problems arising from variations in the measurement of total talking time (e.g., total number of words, amount of speech in a sentence, temporal duration of total utterances, length of responses, and number of words between pauses).

Multiple measurement techniques have been employed by many (for example, students of family power) in an attempt to avoid such difficulties. But often this "solution" has served only to accentuate the problem. First, as Hadley and Jacob (1973) observe, there have been few systematic evaluations of relationships between measures themselves, and even among the studies that do exist (Alexander, 1970; Bodin, 1966; Hadley & Jacob, 1973), there are methodological disagreements. Second, individual analysts report conflicting results among their own multiple measurements. For example, Shaw and Sadler's (1965) study of interaction between cross-sex conversationalists reports that females are more dominant than males when frequency of interruption is used as the index of dominance. However, males are found to be more dominant than their female partners when dominance is defined by the number of times talk is initiated (Shaw & Sadler, 1965). A possible explanation for this inconsistency is provided by the authors in a methodological caveat: Interruptions were tallied by a voice-actuated chronograph, which made no provision for discrimination among different types of simultaneous speech. Hence, "when the male was actively contributing ideas and task-oriented suggestions, the female might have been 'interrupting' with agreeing, reinforcing comments" (Shaw & Sadler, 1965, p. 350; see also Scherer, Section 4.6). To be sure, some researchers *have* made distinctions among different types of simultaneous speech in describing the relationships of these types to issues of power and control (see Farina & Holzberg, 1968; Hadley & Jacob, 1973; Lennard & Bernstein, 1969; Mishler & Waxler, 1968), but their criteria for doing so are various (e.g., essential "incompleteness" of an idea, "degree of overlap" between speakers, or "dropping out" by the interrupted party).

Interaction process analysts have further compounded these problems by raising initially ambiguous measurement procedures to an even higher level of abstraction. As Simon and Boyer (1968, p. 1) note, interaction analysis systems are explicitly interested in that which "can be categorized or measured." Typically, categorization consists of coding ongoing interaction into prespecified classifications, which, in turn, are organized and interpreted on the basis of the analyst's typifications, for example, as "instrumental" versus "expressive" behavior. Delamont and Hamilton (1976, p. 8) argue that these systems utilize "crude measurement techniques which are characterized by ill-defined boundaries between the categories" (e.g., the distinction between "acceptance" and "encouragement" of another's idea). Still other critics question the applicability of findings of interaction process analysis to interactions occurring outside the context of task-oriented experimental small groups (see Bernard, 1972; Laws, 1971; Slater, 1961). Our point is not that these analyses are examples of poor research. Interaction process analysis has in fact demonstrated very high levels of intercoder reliability. Rather, we suggest that although these systems may, as Flanders (1970) claims, be highly reliable methods of measurement, their validity is not beyond question. In fact, as Delamont and Hamilton (1976, p. 9) propose, they "may assume the truth of what they claim to be explaining." More to the point, social psychological research has generally employed selected features of verbal interaction as indexes of power, leadership, and the like, without providing any systematic basis for doing so, that is, without undertaking an analysis of conversational exchange that would establish that a particular kind of speech event has, for a given interaction and given interactants, the sort of status the analyst claims. Conversation analysis proposes that the linkage of particular classes of verbal behaviors with particular social activities cannot be derived by application of the analyst's prespecified categorizations; rather, it must be extracted from the conversational practices of speakers themselves by approaching the study of conversation as activity or topic in its own right. This proposal (that conversation be studied as a topic rather than employed as a resource) is thoroughly grounded in the stance of ethnomethodology toward naturally occurring interaction. By virtue of the fact that this stance figures centrally in the methods employed in conversation analysis, we turn next to a consideration of the ethnomethodological foundations of the enterprise.

9.3. Ethnomethodology

Coulter (1979, pp. 20–25) provides a succinct description of ethnomethodological inquiry that is particularly pertinent to our purposes here. He proposes that the aim of ethnomethodology is "to work out analyses of the reasoning structures and conventional member-orientations involved in various empirically observed courses of social interaction" (p. 21). The reference to "reasoning structures" centrally implicates the exercise of commonsense knowledge. One interpretation of commonsense knowledge consists of "knowing that" – commonsense knowledge as comprised of differentially distributed, situated and often inconsistent and dubious propositions about the social world; another interpretation consists of "knowing how," and it is this latter view that is crucial. Coulter (1979) writes:

> The aspects of what can be called "commonsense" which interest the ethnomethodologist are those which *enable* anyone possessing it to perform their ordinary activities in ways that are recognizably appropriate, rational, intelligible, proper, correct or reasonable for all *practical* purposes . . . [C]ommonsense amounts to a set of culturally-furnished *abilities*. Such abilities constitute the doing of any mundane activities, such as transmitting information in various contexts, recommending something to someone, persuading someone about something, enumerating, grading, complaining, insulting, warning, apologizing, thanking, promising, ascribing statuses, and countless other practical actions . . . To say of someone that he [or she] is *able to* do such things means that he [or she] *knows how to* do them, and this practical knowledge forms the central core of what is here being descripted as "commonsense knowledge of social structure." [Pp. 21–22, original emphasis]

In short, what one knows how to do is to produce methodically, in concert with others, the varied events and scenes of everyday life. The orderliness of everyday settings is available to us as observers for the very reason that it is available for the "use and appreciation" of members (Schegloff & Sacks, 1973/1974, p. 234), that is, because of the systematic assembly and recognition of social activities made possible by the practices of commonsense reasoning. An important component of this achievement is found in the intimate "tie between [commonsense reasoning] and mastery of natural language" (Coulter, 1979, pp. 21–22; cf. Garfinkel & Sacks, 1970, pp. 341–345). As Coulter (1979) notes:

> An overwhelming number of our ordinary, everyday activities are performed in and through *speaking*, and most of the rest presuppose linguistic abilities . . . The commonsense competence in which the ethnomethodologist has an interest, then, is in large measure *co-extensive* with natural-language competence; the one varies with the other in so far as they are mutually constituted. We learn a language and a common culture together and *pari passu*, and we discover, through speaking with others, where, and to what extent, that common culture of a natural language fragments and where it is substained between us. [p. 22]

The study of natural language involves the investigation of the systematics of producing utterances, sequences of utterances, and other vocal and nonvocal expressions that in turn provide the framework for ascertaining (1) how these conversational "gestures" achieve a particular meaning or delineated range of alternative meanings in some local environment; (2) how they contribute to, establish, negotiate, or expose a definition or definitions of the situation; or (3) how they express and warrant assertions or statements concerning one's or the other's state of mind, motive, feeling, and so on. These activities are seen as situated accomplishments of the use of natural language and are of interest only insofar as they lead to a fuller understanding of how the system that produced them works. Ethnomethodology, then, is not concerned with the interior goings-on of the acting subject, nor merely with rendering a description of the particular meanings attributed to situations by participants' analyses. The concern is instead this: Insofar as *members* recognize and respond to such objects as "state of mind" or "motive" or "the meaning of a situation," then the ethnomethodologist takes it that such objects are methodically produced and appreciated *by members*, an achievement in need of description and analysis in its own right. As Coulter (1979) puts it:

> Nothing in [ethnomethodology's] program commits us to a view of human conduct as beyond the categories of the public, social world; reasoning structures are *cultural* and the abstract categories of ethnomethodology consist in categories alien to psychologism. There are no "egos," no irreduceable "impulses," no "subjective meanings," no "interior states," no individualizing ontology and no interest in "the private domain," whatever that could mean.

> There is no *uncontrolled* intuiting, even though the exercise of commonsense, reasoned intuition forms a necessary first-order step toward getting analysis off the ground. [p. 24, original emphasis]

In sum, the term *methodology* in the compound word *ethnomethodology* refers to the study of the collective use by members of society of systematic procedures for assembling and assessing social activities and events. As Coulter notes, the ethnomethodological concern with the analysis of practical reasoning and the exercise of commonsense knowledge also involves the study of natural language practices. The ethnomethodologically inspired but distinctive tradition of work known as conversation analysis has opened this particular subject matter to sociological inspection.

For example, consider the following brief story told by a young child: "The baby cried. The mommy picked it up" (Sacks, 1972). Sacks suggests that we "hear" this story as saying (in paraphrase), "First the baby cried, and then, because the baby cried, the mother of the baby picked the baby up." That is, we understand the story as reporting a temporally ordered sequence of events (crying, picking up) that also involves an obligatory element (because crying, picking up) as the result of the relationship between the agents of the activities in question (baby, its mother). This understanding far exceeds the explicit information in the two sentences: We cannot, for instance, assert on syntactical grounds whether the mommy in question is in fact the baby's mommy, any more than we can argue the temporal order of the events and their normative linkage from the mere fact that the sentence reporting the crying precedes the sentence reporting the picking up. Something more is implicated here, namely, a culture conceived in procedural terms whose workings must be discovered and described in order to provide an adequate account of our intuitive understanding of the story.

Sacks's analysis of this simple story has a much broader focus than might appear at first glance. He is not, for example, concerned with the interpretation of stories or other accounts as an activity in its own right. In this particular instance he is concerned with the structure of "possible descriptions," that is, with the face validity of a given depiction of social life. This is an important issue for the reason that, in the conduct of everyday life, we all traffic in descriptions, many of which deal with events that cannot be independently verified. Yet, somehow, we are able to distinguish in the descriptions offered us the likely from the unlikely, the credible from the incredible, without the benefit of firsthand knowledge, that is, without knowing whether the description is correct or not. Moreover, it should be noticed that in the very formulation of the description, systematic processes are at work that, for example, transform the "seeing" of "infant human crying" and "adult female picking it up" into "*baby* crying" and "its *mother* picking it up," even in the absence of any sure knowledge that it is indeed the baby's mother (and not, for example, its aunt or babysitter or kidnapper).

A discussion of the cultural (which is to say, natural language) resources Sacks described in his analysis is beyond the scope of this chapter. But an important principle can be discerned in his analysis of "possible description." Sacks (1963) himself formulates this principle explicitly when he proposes "the postulate that what we take as subject must be described" (p. 3); that is, we social scientists cannot leave implicit the matters we know and rely on to manage our everyday affairs, because it is precisely these things that figure into the construction of our subject matter.

Thus it is that Sacks's analysis presses beyond our intuitive understanding of the child's story to identify both the more general issue of "possible descriptions" and the *cultural machinery* by which they are produced and recognized. The analytic interest is therefore shifted from "making sense" of naturally occurring descriptions or accounts, or using cultural competencies to produce our own descriptions of social settings and activities, to an investigation of the very "sense-making" procedures that constitute natural language use.

Of course, the concerns of conversation analysis were extended beyond the issue of sense making, particularly as the attention of Sacks and his associates came to be focused upon the organization of conversational interaction itself. But the principle still obtains, namely, the discovery and description of production apparatuses employed by speaker–hearers to address technical issues in the conduct of conversation, for example, "coordinated entry into conversation" (Schegloff, 1968), "turn-taking" (Sacks, Schegloff, & Jefferson, 1974), "conversational closings" (Schegloff & Sacks, 1973/1974), repair of trouble sources (Schegloff, Jefferson, & Sacks, 1977), and so on. That members of society skillfully employ such "machinery" is a basic assumption of the approach; the social organization of verbal interchange thus topicalized is taken to be native to the field of data, awaiting discovery.

It should be emphasized that the task of bringing natural language practices to description does not evolve from the decision to adopt a subjective point of view (Sacks, 1963, p. 7, n. 7). The notion "point of view of the member" is usually construed in a commonsense way, taken to mean "getting into someone's mind," for example, or incursion into a private sphere of thoughts and intentions; recall the ethnomethodological viewpoint on this matter. Sacks suggests that to adopt the subject's point of view is to undertake to *conceive* of the subject matter in a particular way and, most particularly, as his subsequent work demonstrated, to conceive of the subject matter in terms of a set of methodological constraints on the identification of structures in members' talk or behavior. Not just any regularity detected by analysis will qualify as a feature of the social organization of activities under investigation; the analyst must supply a warrant for the claim that the observed pattern is one produced *by* and *for* the "appreciation and use by co-participants" from the observable data of conversational activities (see Schegloff & Sacks, 1973/1974, p. 234). The distinction between "mere regularity" and "achieved orderliness" will be discussed in more detail later.

We would now like to move toward a more specific examination of what is entailed by the recommendation that we focus close attention on members' methodic construction of social objects, events, and activities, turning to a consideration of techniques and tools of conversation analysis.

9.4. Method and measurement

Consider the seemingly empty proposal that conversation analysis consists of the analysis of conversation. Appearances notwithstanding, we have seen some of the ways in which this statement is profound – for example, in focusing our attention on conversational data as members' *accomplishments*. We would now like to offer some remarks concerning the apparent simplicity of the analytical procedures involved.

Conversation defined

Let us take the question what constitutes naturally occurring interaction (see the preceding section). For example, what might properties of "*un*naturally occurring interaction" be? And are there conditions under which contrived interactions might nonetheless exhibit features of "natural" conversations (see also Scherer & Ekman, Section 1.3)?

The most rigorous definition to assist with such difficulties is offered by Sacks et al.'s (1974) analysis of turn taking in conversation. Observe, these authors suggest, that in any speech exchange system, speaker change recurs and one party talks at a time. Indeed, we can see that both interviews and service contacts are characterized by these features. However, what distinguishes conversation from other speech exchange systems is the variability of the distribution of turns, turn size, and turn content. In a debate, Sacks and his coauthors point out, who speaks first, about what, and for how long is fixed in advance; in a structured interview, topical order and content may be predetermined, too. Even when participants in conversation enter into it with prespecified agendas, to the extent that the occasion is conversational in character, the agendas offer them no guarantee that particular matters will be discussed – a point that will become clear when we discuss the situated character of the management of conversational interchange. Conversations, then, are instances of speech exchange organization with variable turn order, turn size, and turn content peculiar to a given occasion and the participants involved.

Transcribing

Audiotapes (more recently, videotapes) and transcripts furnish the raw materials for conversation analysts. Transcribing talk for the purposes of analyzing that talk requires a great attention to detail from the transcriber. The point is perhaps made best by contrast. Whereas researchers utilizing interview schedules may (and often do) ignore background noise, such as inhalations or exhalations, and gloss over variations in such things as pitch and/or amplitude, conversation analysts, ideally, attempt to include all of these in the transcripts. They do so because transcription itself can properly be considered part of the analysis, rather than a subsidiary chore to be performed by a secretary or untrained assistant. As we shall see, the details of *how* something is said (softly, loudly, with a stutter, with a drawl, in a slur, etc.) may be as important for analytical purposes (see especially Jefferson & Schegloff, 1975) as the content of talk itself, if not more important. Jefferson, who on occasion characterizes herself as "a technician" of this work, describes the goal as follows:

> A task we have undertaken is to provide transcripts that not only serve for current research interests, but are "research generative." This means in its best sense that the transcripts, by capturing events, *illuminate* possible features of the data which are not yet known to be features; and at least that they *preserve* for future investigation, such as-yet-unknown orderly features. [1971, p. 1]

To would-be Jeffersons, striving in desperation to discriminate inhalations from exhalations, or "eh-heh-heh's" from "heh-eh-heh's," the task may seem akin to that of field ethnographers who are impossibly instructed to "capture everything" in their field notes. Insofar as both are involved in discovering organization and organizing principles, their aims are in fact comparable. And the analysis of *how* people achieve orderly conversation – like that of social organization of any other sort – is best achieved through the meticulous examination of their actual behavior in its natural context.

As one illustration of an issue generated by these concerns, consider "normalization" of speakers' utterances. "Normalization," for transcribers of interviews, interrogations, and the like, is commonly seen as the practice of translating what was said into grammatically "proper" language. Thus, "How'd ju," an item heard often in tapes made in the western and southern United States, may appear in transcripts of interviews as "How did you," and might be taken – for the purposes of that research – as a literal transcription of what was uttered. In contrast, the conversation analyst will strive to reproduce such items in their "natural state," without translating them into whatever standard variant of the language is at issue. (Lest this concern seem trivial, recall that one social psychological index of dominance is the number of words uttered by speakers. The translation of "How'd ju" into "How did you" involves fundamentally theoretical as well as technical considerations.)

Not only sounds, but structures of speech events can be obscured by normalization. For example, transcripts of interviews commonly include the notation that one or more participants "(LAUGHS HERE)." However, by actually *transcribing* laughter particles that are heard ("heh-heh," "eh heh heh," etc.), Jefferson (1979b) provides an elegant demonstration of the coordination of laughter invitations with subsequent acceptances or rejections. Another compelling illustration is furnished by Jefferson and Schegloff's (1975) analysis of resolutions of simultaneous speech. There, detailed attention is devoted to transcribing how speakers say what they say when more than one of them speaks simultaneously. Jefferson and Schegloff observe that parties to talk engage in marked competition for a turn space by recycling portions of their talk over the ongoing speech of another party:[2]

Ken: No, they're women who'v devo [ded their l-
Roger: [They're women that hadda=
Roger: = [[bad love [life 'n became nuns.hh [heh hh!
Ken: [[their- [their life- [their life, to uh
(0.6)
Ken: the devotion of the church.

[Jefferson & Schegloff, 1975, p. 11]

Here, we see Ken recycling ("l- their- *their life-*") over Roger's continuing stream of talk, thus preserving a few words ("the devotion of the church") for production in the clear. Obviously, such finely detailed observations and subsequent analyses are completely obscured in transcribed conversations that read like the script for a play.

What this means for transcribers is that every effort must be taken to preserve the sounds that are heard on tape (or seen, in the case of video) in the transcripts themselves, even when those sounds are not immediately intelligible to the listener. Under circumstances of ambiguity (e.g., when sounds are heard that are capable of more than one transcription), then these ambiguities will be indicated in the transcripts themselves. Even at this, cautions Jefferson (see the note on technique and symbols in the appendix at the end of this chapter), there is no guarantee that the transcripts alone will permit doing any unspecified research tasks; they are properly used as an adjunct to the tape-recorded materials.

Although Jefferson is herself credited with production of "readers' transcripts" – written records that attempt to reproduce exactly the sounds that are heard by the ear (Schenkein, 1978a, p. 302 n. 2)[3] – she discourages exclusive reliance on transcripts for the work of *generating* discoveries. This caution is motivated by a concern for "lost" data and "lost" research problems, through *non*verbatim transcription. Consider but one illustration, provided in her overview (Jefferson, 1971, p. 5) of problematics associated with the use of pseudonyms:

Agnes: Thirdy sevin years ago tuhni::ght we were on ar way tuh Ventura.
Guy: Hm. Wuhddiyuh know about that.
Agnes: Sann BARBRA hhh huh//huh
Guy: BARBRA. Uh huh.
Agnes: We gotta MARIAN did'n we.
Guy: Mmyuh.

In this excerpt, the name *Marian* has been used as a pseudonym for *Barbara* the actual name of the couple's daughter. What was actually a skillfully executed nameplay on people and places (going to Santa Barbara and getting Barbara) is "lost" by the substitution of *Marian* for the daughter's name. Jefferson's (1971) point is that names are themselves interactional resources for conversationalists to "do" things with, which the use of a pseudonym completely obscures. Moreover, the pseudonym may obscure for the analyst conversational resources available to speakers themselves: "For example, someone named ANITA reports that she hears that she's been *addressed* when someone has said 'I need a . . .' " (Jefferson, 1971, p. 19). Of course, one proper response to a term of address heard as a summons is an answer, such as "Yes?"

"What?" or something similar (see Schegloff, 1968, on the organization of summons–answers sequences). In this instance, should Anita respond appropriately, she will very probably interrupt the speaker producing "I need a . . ." at the point where *what* is needed comes due. (And recall here that "interruptions" have also been employed as indexes of control in social psychological studies.)

In short, transcribing conversational data for analytical purposes entails strictest attention to what is heard *as it is heard*, in fine detail. The job is time-consuming and painstaking, to be sure (it may very well require 8 to 10 hours of time to transcribe each hour of audiotape; the ratio increases with video). However, as we hope to show next, "the potential rewards of such work are worth the time and effort involved" (Hall, 1974, p. 2).

9.5. Analysis

Supposing, then, one is equipped with a collection of taped conversations and has commanded that transcript technology. Where, formally speaking, does analysis begin? How does it start? Here, again, the task of conversation analysts parallels that of field ethnographers: Begin with the data themselves. It is in this sense that conversation analysis consists of precisely that – seeking first to describe patterns and regularities evidenced in conversations themselves.

Much of Sacks' and his colleagues' work begins with "simple" observations. For example, Schegloff's (1968) analysis of sequencing in conversational openings begins with the observation that, for telephone conversations, the "answerer" speaks first. Jefferson's (1973) investigation of precision timing in ordinary talk starts by noticing that many address terms are overlapped by the speech of recipients for whom they are intended. Schegloff et al.'s (1977) description of the organization of repair in conversation is launched by initial remarks on the extent to which speakers correct their own utterances more often than those of co-conversationalists.

Such observations are "simple" in the sense that "anybody" can make them. That is, not only can Sacks, Schegloff, and Jefferson see these things; on inspecting the materials, we can see them, too. And this is where "simplicity" ends and "systematicity" begins. As Schegloff and Sacks 1973/1974) put it:

> We have proceeded under the assumption (an assumption borne out by our research) that in so far as the materials we worked with exhibited orderliness, they did so not only for us, but for the co-participants who had produced them. If the materials . . . were

> orderly, they were so because they had been methodically produced by members of society for one another, and it was a feature of the conversations that we treated as data that they were produced so as to allow the participants to display to each other their analysis, appreciation and use of that orderliness. [p. 234]

Therefore, the analyst's tasks are documenting, describing, and explicating the ways in which *members* (i.e., conversationalists) produce and display the orderliness extant in naturally occurring interactions.

Schegloff and Sacks (1973/1974) emphasize what was mentioned earlier, the study of conversation "as an activity in its own right," noting that "any actions accomplished in conversation require reference to the properties and organization of conversation for their understanding and analysis, both by participants and by professional investigators" (pp. 233–234). The required "reference to the properties and organization of conversation" points us back to the methodical character of natural language practices discussed earlier. It is in and through the use of these practices that the orderly features of actual conversational interaction are made available, and it is from the particular orderliness they display that their meaning and interactional consequence flow. Moreover, as the quotation highlights, we are able to detect orderliness in such interactional materials "*because* they [have] been methodically produced by members of society *for one another*" (emphasis added). Any orderliness we detect, then, is an orderliness produced by members on which members count and which they use as the grounds for both interpretation and subsequent action.

The purely ethnomethodological interest in conversation does not concern such matters as what gets talked about by what sorts of speakers on what sorts of occasions. The concern is instead with the prior question how a sequence of utterances is organized so as to produce a conversation in which not only is something talked about, but a range of interactional activities is also accomplished. A particularly crucial aspect of the question of conversational organization is, as Goffman (1955) notes, the matter of how turns are allocated, for this is something conversationalists must manage in the course of actually conversing. We offer next a detailed example of what is involved in the study of conversational organization as a topic in its own right, drawing on Sacks et al.'s (1974) analysis of turn taking in conversation.

Turn taking: an example

Turn taking, Sacks and his colleagues note, is a commonplace feature of naturally occurring conversations. We can readily observe, as noted under "Conversation defined," in Section 9.4, that one party speaks at a time and speaker change recurs most of the time in conversation. Once noted, these features might appear obvious, even trivial. But we would remind our reader of a remark by E. A. Ross:

> A condition of order at the junction of crowded city thoroughfares implies primarily an absence of collisions between men or vehicles that interfere with one another. Order cannot be said to prevail among people going in the same direction at the same pace, because there is no interference. It does not exist when persons are constantly colliding with one another. But when all who meet or overtake one another in crowded ways take the time and pains needed to avoid collision, the throng is *orderly*. Now, at the bottom of the notion of social order lies the same idea. The members of an orderly community do not go out of their way to aggress upon one another. Moreover, whenever their pursuits interfere, they make the adjustments necessary to escape collision and make them according to some conventional rule. [Quoted in Goffman, 1971, p. 6]

The moral, then, is that in such apparently unremarkable behaviors (e.g., people on a busy street avoiding collisions with one another, people taking turns when they talk) lies orderliness, and it is the analyst's task to describe that orderliness.

Much earlier (1955), Goffman was viewed as opening up a new approach in proposing that attention should be given to the dynamics as well as the content of social interaction, and particularly the taking of turns.[4] Yet fifteen years later, Yngve (1970, p. 569) could write: "In reviewing the literature on our topic, one is surprised to find that apparently no one has made any kind of a systematic study of how turn changes in dialog." Clearly, this is an overstatement, because some relevant work using stochastic models had appeared earlier (e.g., Brady, 1965, 1968, 1969; Jaffe, Cassotta, & Feldstein, 1964) but the point is well taken: Up to that time, turn allocation per se was not the focus of systematic inquiry. Since then, however, it has received more direct attention from a variety of sources.

The "signaling" approach to turn taking originates in work by Goffman (1955) and Kendon (1967). Following Goffman, Yngve (1970, p. 569), for example, argues that the only way to account for the smooth flow of conversation and the rapid and frequent switching of turns is to suppose that there are conventional signals exchanged during conversation that function to switch the turn variables properly. The signals might be either vocal or gestural or both.

The most prominent body of research pursuing this approach has been developed by Duncan and his co-workers (Duncan, 1972, 1973, 1974; Duncan & Fiske, 1977; Duncan and Niederehe, 1974). Concurring with Kendon's emphasis on the central importance of gestural cues, Duncan (1972, p. 299) contends that turn taking is accomplished through "signals composed of clear-cut behavioral cues [which may be vocal or gestural], conceived to be perceived as discrete." Duncan's primary research focus is identifying these cues and the way they function.

Duncan's basic unit of analysis in what he calls the "turn system" is a phonemic clause (Trager & Smith, 1957) at the end of which speaker change occurs or the current speaker displays one or more of the following cues (Duncan & Fiske, 1977, pp. 169–173):

1. An intonational pattern other than 2 2 | (see also Trager & Smith, 1957)
2. A sociometric sequence (see also Bernstein, 1962)
3. Completion of a grammatical clause
4. Drawl
5. A drop in pitch or loudness during or at the end of a phonemic clause
6. Audible inhalation
7. An unfilled pause
8. A false start
9. Termination of gesticulation or of tensing of the hand
10. Turning the head away from the hearer
11. Relaxation of the foot

At base in the turn system is a mechanism consisting of two signals. The first, a *turn-yielding* signal, is defined as one or more of cues (1)–(4), cue (5) in the context of cue (3), or cue (9) (Duncan & Fiske, 1977, pp. 184–185). The second, a *suppression* signal, is defined as gesticulation or tensing of either hand (Duncan & Fiske, 1977, pp. 188–189). Speakers are thought to give the turn-yielding signal when they are ready to yield their turns to hearers.

Empirical support for Duncan's signaling approach is equivocal (see Dittman, 1973; Duncan & Fiske, 1977; Rutter & Stephenson, 1977; Rutter & Stephenson, 1977; Wiemann and Knapp, 1975, p. 83); accordingly, several questions are raised for those who would attempt to account for the ubiquity of speech exchange under the various conditions in which it occurs. The design of Duncan's turn system limits it in scope to two-party exchanges between persons who are visible to one another. However, as Yngve (1970, p. 569) notes: "One might suppose that gestural cues would be of secondary importance since it is possible to carry on a conversation successfully with someone who is out of sight." Telephone conversations and group discussions are problematic for this model, which relies on the exchange of cues not always available to conversationalists in everyday life.

However, it is not necessary to posit the exchange of conventional signals to provide a systematic account of the ubiquity of speech exchange. Instead, the details of actual conversations may be scrutinized to determine the general organizational mechanisms that shape talk and the activities accomplished through talk. This is the approach taken by Sacks et al. (1974).

The turn-taking mechanism Sacks and his colleagues describe (Sacks et al., 1974, pp. 703–706) can be formulated as a sequence of options available whenever the issue of speaker change arises:

1. The current speaker may select another party as the next speaker.
2. If the current speaker does not elect to do so, then another may self-select as the next speaker.
3. If no other party self-selects as the next speaker, then the current speaker may continue.
4. Finally, if the current speaker does not continue, the option to speak cycles back to (2).

These options were developed and ordered explicitly to "fit" a body of empirical observations about the conversations Sacks et al. (1974) observed.

The analysis of Sacks and his colleagues also describes the properties of the turn-constructional mechanisms for conversation. A *turn* consists not simply of a segment of talk by one person bounded at each end by the speech of others, but rather of a period of time during which one has the right and obligation to speak. Turns are constructed by speakers out of what Sacks et al. (1974) call *unit types*, which, in English, may be single words, phrases, clauses, or sentences. Each speaker, on gaining a turn, has an initial right to produce one such unit, and the terminal boundary of a unit type, for example, the end of a sentence, is a possible *transition relevance place*. At this place, a transfer of the turn from one speaker to another may properly occur, and at this time options (1)–(4) become available in the indicated hierarchical sequence (Sacks et al., 1974, pp. 702–706).

Sacks and his colleagues stipulate that unit types are generally *projective;* that is, they allow the listener to anticipate (or "project") an upcoming transition relevance place so that if turn transition occurs, it can do so with minimum gap (silence) or overlap (simultaneous speech) between turns. In this fashion, their model for turn taking is said to furnish an "intrinsic motivation for listening":

> In its turn-allocational techniques, the model builds in an intrinsic motivation for listening to all utterances . . . independent of other possible motivations, such as interest and politeness. In the variety of techniques for arriving at a next speaker, and in their ordered

> character, it obliges any willing or potentially intending speaker to listen to and analyze each utterance across its delivery. [Sacks et al., 1974, p. 727]

If a party wishes to speak, then she or he will have to be attentive to the occurrence of a transition relevance place where it would be appropriate to initiate an utterance; if selected by another to speak next, the designated speaker must not only have attended to but *understood* the utterance that accomplished the selection. Thus the organization of turn taking also constrains participants to understand what is being done, because the construction of an appropriate response rests on such understanding (see Sacks et al., 1974, p. 728). Sacks et al. (1974) write:

> A participant potentially willing to speak if selected to do so will need to listen to any utterance to find if he is being selected by it to speak next. Since a major class of "current selects next" techniques is constituted by "first-pair parts" – i.e., by type-characterized utterances such as "greeting," "question," "insult," "complaint" etc. – a willing speaker will need to find if an instance of such an utterance-type is being employed, and in a way that possibly selects him as next speaker. And a potentially intending speaker will need to examine any utterance after which he might want to speak, to find whether such a thing was being done to him or some other party. [p. 728]

The turn-taking mechanism is a fundamental organization through which such objects as "indications" and "responses" are managed in the course of building sequences of action. Moreover, because participants are constrained to analyze any current turn at talk for its status as an initial event in a sequence that will then make expectable and thus relevant some next event, the turn-taking system has a built-in "proof procedure." For example, if a current speaker selects a next speaker by employing an initial event – or "first-pair part" – say, a greeting, this procedure also selects the next action by that speaker, namely, a greeting in return. The selected speaker, in seeing that a greeting has been issued and then offering a greeting return, will not only satisfy the constraint engineered by the initiation of the sequence in the first instance, but also thereby display to the first speaker, to others present, and potentially to an analyst *how* the initial remark was understood.

The display of understanding not only is important for conversationalists (furnishing them a checking procedure by which to detect and correct misunderstandings), but also provides, at least in principle, an *analyzed resource* for an investigator who is concerned to respect the "point of view of the member." It is worth noting here that the issue of understanding can be addressed entirely by the use of public materials.

Additional important concepts implicit in the turn-taking model should be considered here. For example, Sacks and his colleagues sought a turn-taking mechanism for conversation that would be both "context-free and capable of extraordinary context-sensitivity" (Sacks et al., 1974, p. 699). *Context-free* means here that (1) the mechanism is formulated to apply *whenever* a transition relevance place occurs in a conversation, and (2) it is usable for conversation by *any* set of participants regardless of the setting, the size of the group, and whatever social categories distinguish the participants (p. 699). *Context-sensitivity* means that (1) what constitutes a transition relevance place is a contextual matter, and (2) the mechanism is usable by participants for managing a wide-ranging set of activities. These activities include such things as changing topics (Maynard, 1980) or insinuating into the local, turn-by-turn development of a conversation exogenous factors like the situated identity of a speaker (e.g., when a subordinate "speaks only when spoken to" or a dominant party interrupts; see West & Zimmerman, 1977; Zimmerman & West, 1975). This point leads to another property of the model.

Sacks et al. (1974) note that "a conversation is constructed or designed in ways which display an orientation and sensitivity . . . to particular . . . participants"; this is the general principle of *recipient design* (p. 727). The context-free, context-sensitive character of the model means that the mechanism by which turns are allocated and regulated is held to be the same in all conversations and invariant to the particular motives, characteristics, and circumstances of the participants. Thus, however unique or variable the features of a conversation may be, and however much a definition of the situation might be negotiated by participants, what remains standard and stable and essentially nonnegotiable is the organization of turn taking. But how that mechanism is used by participants depends on the particular setting, the situated identities of those present, and their purposes at hand; thus it may be pressed into the service of many different interests. It is an abstract and general resource that can be identified in the particulars of everyday talk. Its explication, then, serves as an analytic resource for the further investigation of the nature of social interaction. So the context-free character of the mechanism spans the indefinitely large number of particular conversations, yet, in its context-sensitive aspect, orders "locally idiosyncratic conversational environments" (Schenkein, 1978b, p. 4).

The generality of the model does not reside in its remoteness from interactional exchanges. The shape of a particular conversation – its allocation of turns across participants, its distribution of turn length, silence, simultaneous speech, and content of turns – is generated on a turn-by-turn basis, and hence these are *locally organized* achievements. The turn-by-turn development of a conversation is accomplished through the use of the turn-taking mechanism by actual participants, which is to say that it is *party administered* and its use is fully situated (i.e., subject to the exercise of turn-taking options by parties to conversation). Because parties to conversation must respond to each other's actual or potential use of the options provided, it is said to be *interactionally managed* as well.

The properties of turn taking formulated by Sacks et al. are said to be *oriented to* by the participants of conversation. The term *oriented to* has a different sense here than is found, for example, in Parsons (1951). Here it is not assumed that participants are necessarily able to formulate either the options or the sequence in which they become available. Indeed, the concepts of turn, current speaker, next speaker, and so on, in terms of which the options are formulated, are defined and used by ethnomethodologists. They are not intended to represent or describe participants' *own* analyses of their activities; instead, they refer to features of those activities as they are palpably produced and responded to. That is, the analyst must be able to marshal from the evidence of transcripts, audiotapes, and videotapes the warrant for the organization of interaction she or he claims to have discovered. This warrant, of course, is to be found in the naturally occurring *behavior* of conversationalists – not to be elicited by questionnaire, by interview, or by any means that invites members to formulate their own versions of things as data for further analysis. A key methodological constraint in this kind of naturalistic inquiry is precisely this insistence on evidence internal to the data of actual interaction to support the analytic work of classification and formulation.

Such evidence is provided in the case of *adjacency-pair* organization, for example, in "question–answer" sequences. Given a first-pair part hearable as a question, the event occurring in the immediately adjacent turn is expectably (with certain exceptions, e.g., the case when the first-pair part is "You know what?") an answer; the next turn, in any event, is where one would ordinarily look to find something hearable as an answer, given a prior question. What is the warrant (apart from commonsense wisdom to the effect that questions deserve answers) for claiming such an organization? The sorts of considerations involved in identifying adjacency pairs provide a pointed illustration of the methodological constraints on conversation analysts to furnish evidence that the orderliness they observe is member-produced and member-appreciated. At issue here is the nature of the relationship between serially adjacent items; that is, is adjacency anything more than a contingent proximity of two objects – a mere regularity? Schegloff (1972, pp. 363–364) addresses the issue by introducing the notion of *conditional relevance:* "Given the first, the second is expected; upon its occurrence it can be seen to be a second item to the first; upon its non-occurrence it can be seen to be officially absent – all this provided by the occurrence of the first item." Thus, upon the occurrence of a first-pair part (e.g., a question), a second-pair part (an answer) is relevant and expectable: Should it not be forthcoming, its absence can be noted; if it is present, its nature can testify to the understanding of the first-pair part to which it is addressed.

Conditional relevance provides for our noticing that failure to find an answer in the next turn following a question will, with great regularity, draw a repeat of the question; the repeat, being a form of repair, displaying the orientation of the asker to the absence of an answer (see Sacks et al., 1974, pp. 723–724; Schegloff et al., 1977):

Female: Down by Pierpont and all that, that's where I live.
Male: Is it down by:: California?
(.)
Male: California Stre:et?

[West, 1979]

In this example, the brief pause following initiation of a question is where we might look to find its answer. The absence of an answer in this place is displayed as oriented-to by the asker, who repeats the question in modified form.

To illustrate further, take the case of a violation of the turn-taking rules, for example, when two or more speakers speak simultaneously. The *fact* of violation can be described as oriented-to in that speakers undertake to repair these troubles. They may drop out, for example, ceding the turn-space to another speaker (see Jefferson & Schegloff, 1975):

Female: [Wa-]
Male: [Do] yOU live in Eye Vee:?

[West, 1979]

Here, the abrupt cutoff of speech by one of two simultaneous speakers restores conversation to a state of one party at a time.

Other sources of trouble may be repaired (and thereby identified as troublesome) by, for example, retrieving one's own or the other's talk from overlap through repetition of it "in the clear" (see Jefferson & Schegloff, 1975):

Female: Hm:m (#) Maybe the BELL's not gonna
ring-henh-henh-henh-henh-henh .hh!
hunh- [heh .hh ° .hh-.hh]
Male: [I think they're wai] tin' for us
to finish. °Before they('re) gonna ri:ng
it.
Female: Hm:m?
Male: ((yawning)) I think they're WAITing for
us to fi:nish before they're gonna ring
it.

[West, 1979]

The point to be noted in such cases as "violations," "troubles," "absences," and so on is that these phenomena are warrantably identified, not on the basis of the analyst's unconstrained intuition, but on the basis of the demonstration that speakers are oriented to occurrences that pose problems and address themselves in describable ways to the solutions of those problems. Getting close to an empirical social world and understanding it from the point of view of the member does not require empathetic understanding or access to the subjectivity of actors. The requisite materials are provided by members in the methodical ways they go about the assembly of everyday interactional situations. The orderliness they achieve and their means of achieving it are what observational inquiry could profitably address more closely.

In summary then, we can see that conversation is constructed *within* actual situations by actual participants; it is managed over the course of actual, particular turns at talk. Conversational events thus constituted are securely lodged in a sequential context and thereby display to coparticipants a transparency of meaning (see Wilson & Zimmerman, 1979/1980), except in anomalous instances needing corrective work. (Note here that anomalies and corrective work achieve their statuses as such through the operation of the same procedures.)

By virtue of its context-free property, the turn-taking mechanism is a general and abstract resource, usable by any conversationalist in any conversation. And, *in that usage,* it provides members with a methodical means of producing and recognizing the shape and substance of the social interactions that make up a large part of the round of daily life. In this way, the model decisively takes account of the indexical and reflexive properties of social action.

9.6. Conversation analysis and nonverbal communication

The turn-taking model is one of a family of interrelated conversational mechanisms that includes, for example, the organization of storytelling (Jefferson, 1979a; see also Sacks, 1974); negotiation sequences (Jefferson & Schenkein, 1977; Maynard, 1980; Schenkein, 1978b); agreement–disagreement sequences (Pomeranz, 1975); the opening and closing of conversation (Schegloff, 1968; Schegloff & Sacks, 1973/1974); locational formulations (Schegloff, 1972); and repair systems (Jefferson, 1975; Schegloff et al., 1977). One use of models of this kind in ethnomethodological research is to provide a framework within which investigation of more particular phenomena can proceed (see West, 1979; West & Zimmerman, 1977; Zimmerman & West, 1975). Another use to which they might be put is that of furnishing a basis from which analysis of more general phenomena could depart.

Existing analyses yield several particular parameters of conversational organization that might profitably be examined in the situated context of nonverbal exchanges. In the space remaining, we advance a few of these for the reader's consideration.

Placement

The first set of parameters involves what might be generally referred to as *placement considerations*. Schegloff and Sacks (1973/1974; pp. 241–242) are addressing precisely such matters in their discussion of the "why that now?" issue, an issue that, for conversationalists, turns out to be intimately tied to what "that" is. How do we (as speakers) know, for example, that an answer to a question *is* an answer to a question? Schegloff and Sacks point out that linguistic criteria (semantics, syntax, phonology, etc.), in themselves or in combination with one another, provide no unequivocal way of establishing an utterance as an answer to a question. With variations in paralinguistic features, such items as "yeah," "un huh," and "yep," commonly employed to answer questions, may also be used to acknowledge, agree with, or display understanding of another's utterance. Moreover, some questions (e.g., "Yuh know what?") require further questions (e.g., "No, what?"), rather than statements, as adequate responses. Thus items such as answers achieve their status *as* answers only through placement questions: Their intelligibility is conditionally relevant on the initiation of questions in the first instance. As we have seen, there is a reciprocity involved with sequences such as these; unanswered questions, when left unanswered, are oriented-to as troublesome (e.g., as rhetorical questions, retrospectively, or perhaps as things that were "merely said to be saying something"). The further point, however, is that the meaning of conversational events for conversationalists is in large part a matter of their placement in ongoing talk.

Jefferson's (1973) analysis of speakers' precision placement of overlap initiations also illuminates the matter. For example, speakers are seen to display "independent knowledge" of the content of a current speaker's utterance by beginning to speak simultaneously, with some indication of that knowledge, just as the current speaker produces that speech object. One way this is effected is through overlapping with simultaneous but independent production of the speech object itself:

Joe: So he come [s home one night 'n the sonofa] bitch [bit him.]
Carol: [heh heh heh heh heh heh] [bit hi:m]

[Jefferson & Schegloff, 1975, p. 2]

In this light, the common experience of "saying the same thing at the same time" can be seen as more than a haphazard coincidence; indeed, this phenomenon is a consequence of intensive attention and coorientation among speakers.

It requires no existential leap to imagine that similar production might be effected through nonverbal gestures, operating in compatible – if not comparable – fashion. Such expressions as are regularly employed in demonstrating knowledge, understanding, and the like (e.g., nods, smiles, or the palm turned outward that signifies, "Don't tell me that, I know already") might be reexamined for placement considerations vis-à-vis others' verbal and nonverbal expressions. Surely, if persons are capable of displaying independent knowledge through *saying* the same thing at the same time, they may also be capable of *showing* the same thing simultaneously?

Moreover, the more general question "why that now?" is one that might be put to any number of modes of expression. Rather than routinely observing the generalized phenomenon of synchronization of gestures, a more detailed analysis might attend to precisely *where* in a sequence of activity synchronous expressions emerge, and at what point they dissolve.

Timing

Intimately related to considerations of placement are those of timing. Indeed, the two are often inextricable, insofar as interactional sequences of activity take place over finite periods of time. For example, Jefferson (1973) notes that "displays of recognition" are produced by the precision placement of generalized acknowledgers (e.g., "yeah," "uh huh," etc.) at such a point in the sequence of another's utterance as to indicate both active listenership and recognition of the speech object in the course of production by a current speaker. Her analysis proposes that recognition displays must be inserted in a current speaker's utterance "no later" than just before the completion of a recognizable speech object, and "no sooner" than that point at which the current speaker's utterance projects its conclusion for the listener:

Caller: Fire Department, out at the Fairview [Food] mart there's a-
Desk: [Yes]

Desk: We've already got the uh call on that ma'am.

[Jefferson, 1973, p. 57]

Such items might be viewed as communicating "Yes, I hear you and I know what you're talking about," while they simultaneously *display* "Yes, I know what you're talking about" by producing recognition items precisely at the point at which the "due" items *are* recognizable. Here we see the intersection of placement and timing.

On other occasions, timing considerations may figure more independently of placement ones. For example, active listenership is a basic prerequisite for the production of instances of a particular class of expressions that have not typically been considered as "counting" as words even, and so have not been counted as filling turns (see Duncan, 1974; Kendon, 1967; Yngve, 1970). Such items as "um hmm," "uh huh," and "yeah," when interspersed through a current speaker's ongoing utterance (a matter of placement), are not seen as interrupting the current speaker (see Schegloff, 1972), but instead can serve to display continuing interest and coparticipation in topic development. Along these lines, Fishman (1978) points out the agility with which speakers are able to insert such items; being interjected virtually between breaths, they rarely overlap a current speaker's utterance. Characteristically, the current speaker will continue a turn after insertion of a "yeah" or "um hmm" with little if any discernible pause. Fishman has suggested that these objects serve to do "support work," functioning as indicators that the listener is carefully attending to the stream of talk.

These minimal responses which monitor a speaker's utterance may, of course, be coupled with energetic nonverbal gestures, such as nodding of the head; and expressions like these often replace the verbal comments when conversationalists are face-to-face. It is interesting to note that parties to talk are likely to time these nonverbal gestures to coincide with pauses in a current speaker's utterance, as if some sort of turn-taking principles are invoked here as well (see Dittmann, 1972; Dittmann & Llewellyn, 1967, 1968). Alone or in tandem, the nods and the "um hmms" may be viewed as a kind of affirmation for continued talk, where the provider of such expressions must do active listening work to determine proper placement.

The difference, then, between a monologue and a dialogue is not the number of persons present but the articulation of the roles of speaker and listener. In this view, the promptly issued monitoring response serves to display active listenership (in effect, "I follow what you are saying") with the least intervention in the development of a topic by the other speaker (in effect, "Go on, say more . . ."). That speakers currently holding the floor are oriented to the display of active listenership is sometimes indicated by the use of questionlike forms ("you know?") to elicit response from the putative listener.

Such displays of active listenership can, of course, be simulated, and this is exactly where the matter of timing is an all-important one. Consider the "yes dear" response that husbands are said to utter while their wives talk and they read the newspaper, a kind of minimum hearership sustained by an artfully located standardized response:

B: This thing with uh Sandy 'n Karen 'n Paul is really bugging me
(5.0)
A: Um
(3.0)
B: Well it's really complicating things y'know between Sandy 'n Karen
'n I because I know what's ( ) going on 'n I can see there's
no contradiction to me at all//
A: [Um] hmm
(#)
B: In between Sandy finding (#) I mean in between Paul
finding Sandy attractive (#) 'n Paul finding um uh
Karen attractive
(4.0)
A: Mm hmm
(6.0)
B: Y'know an' sleeping with either of 'em or whatever (2.0) the problem
(x) problem is that when he started finding Karen attractive um (#) it
was at the same time uh as he was finding Sandy unattractive
(10.0)

[Zimmerman & West, 1975, pp. 121–122]

It seems evident that the first speaker introduces a topic in her first utterances (her feelings about the relationship among the three persons mentioned) and attempts to elaborate on it in her subsequent remarks. It is also obvious that the second speaker, in response to the first speaker's attempts, employs several of the minimal responses ("Um hmm," "Um," etc.) just described as types of supportive responses one party gives to another in conversation. The giveaway here is not placement, but timing: With the exception of the overlapping "Um hmm," these minimal responses are all preceded by pauses of up to 10 seconds in length. Rather than being inserted at split-second intervals within the ongoing stream of talk, these minimal responses are considerably delayed.

To be sure, this example offers a rather dramatic illustration, given the duration of silences that occur there. Still, it is the *principle* of timing underlying these matters that permits us to question the attentiveness of such listeners as these:

Patient: They thought I was having a nervous brea:kdown. I- completely lost- I mean- I wuz- had been very well coordinated. .hh An' my hands would shake so much thet when I picked up anything it 'ud drop outta muh ha::n's. Obviously I couldn't drive a ca::r 'r do anything like that. An' they gave me a lot of tranquilizerz until until somebody discovered that I 'ad had (1.0) a hormonal problem so that my hormone level wuz of about a woman twenny years older than I: wuz.
(0.8)
Physician: Uh huh
(0.4)
Patient: An' for seven months they gave me hormones by- injeckshun an' mou:th.
(1.0)
Patient: An' I pulled outta that.=But then lader on yuh know ((begins speaking more quickly still) I've=had=all=these=things=with with u:m uh: oh- (1.0) uh: GYnoCOLogy problems, yuh know, an' I RI:lly think a lotta that wuz goin' on
(2.0)
Physician: Uh huh

[West, 1981]

If we assume that the demonstration of active attention and the invitation to continue a turn support the speaker's developing a topic, then retarding the response may well function to signal a lack of understanding or even absence of interest in and inattention to the current talk. Again, it is not the content of the item, nor its placement in a sequence (i.e., as the next turn after the current speaker's remark), that belies the speaker, but the time that elapses prior to its initiation. It would therefore be reasonable to suppose that the nonverbal accoutrements of minimal responses (especially nods) could also be analyzed in relation to such timing considerations for evidence of spontaneous as opposed to feigned involvement.

Moreover, an analysis motivated by timing considerations might offer an empirically grounded way of clearing up many questions raised by conflicting findings in studies of nonverbal communication, for example, how to discriminate between the "aggressive stare" and the "come-hither look," how to distinguish a "friendly hand" from a "paw," and so on.

Timing, in fact, has already been linked through spatial proximity to the very status of persons' "togetherness" in interaction. Ryave and Schenkein's (1974) examination of the production of "walking together" observes that "participants who have lost some proximity will engage in repair work ranging from hurrying or slowing to calling out or later explaining the separation" (p. 272). Here pacing is found to be a critical factor in production of member-recognizable displays of walking in concert. Elsewhere, Sudnow (1972) provides an overview of the scope of temporal organization in social interaction, employing the pedestrian's problem of negotiating interaction with drivers of automobiles.

Both placement and timing considerations thus figure centrally in the methodical ways in which members of society go about the business of producing for each other – and thereby for the analyst – the orderly structures of social activities.

Implications

Clearly, speech and paralanguage behavior, body movement, setting, and the social and idiosyncratic characteristics of participants combine to form the richness of context in which the mood, intent, and meaning of ongoing communication are understood. For this reason, it is more than reasonable to suppose that an approach to social interaction that uses only verbal and paralanguage information must prove inadequate.[5] Philips (1976), for example, suggests that Sacks et al.'s (1974) mechanism for turn taking in conversation deals

> exclusively with data on the verbal structuring of conversation in the form of transcriptions of tape recordings. The information they

> offer is presented in terms of what one speaker after another does verbally at a given point in time that contributes to the regulation of talk. But of course for every speaker at a given point in time, there is also assumed to be one listener. Tape recordings do not capture the listener's contribution to the regulation of interaction; and a speaker-by-speaker sequence analysis does not allow room, analytically, for considerations of the listener. [p. 83]

Philips's case is perhaps overstated, as Sacks et al.'s analysis does incorporate a significant role for listeners as turn takers. As we have seen, a listener must be engaged in an ongoing analysis of a speaker's talk in order to project the next transition relevance place if she or he is to be able to self-select as next speaker.

However, although gaze direction is acknowledged as a current-selects-next technique, the turn-taking mechanism does not explicitly provide for the listener's nonverbal contribution to interaction. Moreover, some behaviors, including extent and direction of gaze (Argyle & Cook, 1976; Kendon, 1967; Wiemann & Knapp, 1975), head nods (Dittmann & Llewellyn, 1968; Knapp, Hart, Friedrich, & Schulman, 1973), and hand gesticulation (Duncan, 1972, 1974) have been associated with turn transition in various contexts. On this issue, it is important to distinguish between the role of nonlinguistic behaviors as integral elements of turn allocation and their function as a source of information (on the basis of which speakers may choose to select themselves or another party to speak). For example, speakers may recognize in the body posture or tone of voice of co-conversationalists such things as agreement or disagreement, attentiveness or inattentiveness, willingness to listen or impatience to gain the floor (Wilson et al., in preparation). What is not clear, but is the basis of research employing other approaches to these matters (see Duncan, 1972, 1974), is how such behaviors are related to the mechanisms by which speaker change is managed, that is, whether the association of nonvocal behaviors with turn transition is a mere regularity or constitutes the workings of a natural organization of turn taking.

From our overview in this chapter, it might appear that conversation analysts do not "believe in" the importance of head movements, changes in body alignment, shifts in posture, and alterations in eye contact. Such is emphatically not the case. In fact, one could argue that the work of conversation analysis thus far has been to provide a *structure* for analyzing language "neither as abstracted from nor as an abstract correlate of a community, but as situated in the flux and patterns of communicative events" (Hymes, 1974, p. 5). C. Goodwin (1979b), for example, has provided evidence which suggests that speakers' turns are constructed in interaction with a hearer or hearers, and that a key element of this process is the attention of the hearer as manifested by gaze direction. Moreover, the organization of negotiation sequencing (Jefferson & Schenkein, 1977; Maynard, 1980; Schenkein, 1978b), openings and closings of conversation (Schegloff, 1968; Schegloff & Sacks, 1973/1974), and repair systems (Jefferson, 1975; Schegloff et al., 1977) offers fresh approaches to the study of nonverbal interaction (see also Scherer & Ekman, Chapter 1). What Sacks and his colleagues' work implies is that such things as head movement, gaze direction, or alignment are *also* researchable in the same fine detail as conversational events and must *also* be subjected to the same systematic approach if we are to begin to address Hymes's (1974) recommendation seriously in our research agendas.

9.7. Concluding remarks

Although conversation analysis and more generally, ethnomethodology are enterprises in their own right, the analyses they furnish of natural language practices and practical sociological reasoning have profound implications for other scholars whose concerns focus on the investigation of naturally occurring social interaction.

In our view, these approaches furnish a model for investigation and a discipline for analysis not to be found in extant attempts to render naturalistic inquiry "respectable" by bending it to fit conventional methodological precepts. Moreover, they offer a corrective to a kind of radical "situationalism" that denies in practice, if not in principle, that any manner of general formulation can be achieved through the close inspection of social situations. In fact, it appears that through an insistence on the development of abstract and general organizations of interaction, the analysis and illumination of particular settings and social worlds could be materially advanced.

Appendix. Transcribing conventions

The transcript techniques and symbols used here were devised by Gail Jefferson in the course of research undertaken with Harvey Sacks. Techniques are revised, symbols added or dropped as they seem useful to the work. There is no guarantee or suggestion that the symbols of transcripts alone would permit the doing of any unspecified research tasks; they are properly used as an adjunct to the tape-recorded materials.

Mary: I don' [know] John: [You] don't	Brackets indicate that the portions of utterances so encased are simultaneous. The left-hand bracket marks the onset of simultaneity; the right-hand bracket indicates its resolution. Double obliques are also used to mark overlap onset.
A: We:::ll now	Colons indicate that the immediately prior syllable is prolonged.
A: But-	A hyphen represents a cutting off short of the immediately prior syllable.
CAPS or underscoring	Both of these are used to represent heavier emphasis on words so marked.
A: Swat I said= B: =But you didn't	Equal signs used to indicate that no time elapses between the objects "latched" by the marks. Often used as a transcribing convenience, they can also mean that the next speaker starts at precisely the end of a current speaker's utterance.
(1.3)	Numbers encased in parentheses indicate the seconds and tenths of seconds ensuing between speaker turns. They may also be used to indicate the duration of pauses internal to a speaker's turn.
(#)	Score sign indicates a pause of about a second that couldn't be discriminated precisely.
(word)	Single parentheses with words in them indicate that something was heard, but the transcriber is not sure what it was. These can serve as a warning that the transcript may be unreliable.
((coughing))	Double parentheses enclose "descriptions," not transcribed utterances.
A: I (x) I did	Parentheses encasing an *x* indicate a hitch or stutter on the part of the speaker.
A: Oh Yeah?	Punctuation marks are used for intonation, not grammar.
( )	Empty parentheses signify untimed pauses.

°So you did.	The degree symbol represents softness, or decreased amplitude.
.hh hh eh-heh	These are breathing and laughing indicators. A period followed by *hh*'s marks an inhalation. The *hh*'s alone stand for exhalation. The *hehs* and *henhs* are laughter syllables.
(.)	A period enclosed in parentheses indicates a pause of 0.1 sec.

Acknowledgments

This chapter is based in part on a paper by C. West that was presented to the NATO Advanced Study Institute Methods of Research on Nonverbal Communication, Birkbeck College, London, September 1979, and in part on a paper by D. H. Zimmerman that was presented to the Society for the Study of Symbolic Interaction, Boston, 1979. The authors wish to thank Sarah F. Berk, Marilyn Lester, Gilly West, Thomas P. Wilson, and the editors of this volume for comments on earlier drafts.

Notes

1. Another body of research (Duncan, 1972, 1973; Duncan & Fiske, 1977; Duncan & Niederehe, 1974; Kendon, 1967, 1978) *has* developed around particular structural features of conversational exchanges (especially turn taking). Because detailed consideration of that work is provided later in this chapter (see "Turn taking: an example," in Section 9.5), we omit it from our general overview here.
2. The transcribing conventions employed in this chapter are presented in the chapter's Appendix. Here, Jefferson uses underscoring for heavier emphasis, capital letters for loudness, and brackets to indicate the point at which one speaker is overlapped by another.
3. The transcribing conventions Jefferson employs depart in many respects from the principles of the International Phonetic Association (IPA, 1949/1963). Primarily, these departures (e.g., in the use of diacritical marks) are evident in denotations of length, stress, and intonation. Whereas these conventions may pose difficulties for those preferring the International Phonetic Alphabet, their use produces transcripts that are more readily available to a variety of social scientists.
4. The following discussion of the signaling approach for turn taking is adapted from Wilson, Zimmerman, and Wiemann (in preparation).
5. These points are elaborated in Wilson and Zimmerman (1979/1980).

References

Alexander, J. G. Videotaped family interaction: A systems approach. Paper presented at the meeting of the Western Psychological Association, Los Angeles, April 1970.

Argyle, M., & Cook, M. *Gaze and mutual gaze*. Cambridge: Cambridge University Press, 1976.

Bales, R. F. *Interaction process analysis*. Reading, Mass.: Addison-Wesley, 1950.

Bernard, J. *The sex game*. New York: Atheneum, 1972.

Bernstein, B. Linguistic codes, hesitation phenomena and intelligence. *Language and Speech*, 1962, *5*, 31–46.

Bodin, A. *Family interaction, coalition, disagreement in problem, normal and synthetic triads*. Unpublished doctoral dissertation, State University of New York at Buffalo, 1966.

Brady, T. P. A technique for investigating on–off patterns of speech. *Bell System Technical Journal*, 1965, *44*, 1–22.

Brady, T. P. A statistical analysis of on–off patterns in 16 conversations. *Bell System Technical Journal*, 1968, *47*, 73–91.

Brady, T. P. A model for generating on–off speech patterns in two-way communication. *Bell System Technical Journal*, 1969, *48*, 2445–2472.

Brownell, W., & Smith, D. R. Communication patterns, sex and length of verbalization in speech of four-year-old children. *Speech Monographs*, 1973, *40*, 310–316.

Caputo, D. J. The parents of the schizophrenic. *Family Process*, 1963, *2*, 339–356.

Coser, L. A. Presidential address: Two methods in search of a substance. *American Sociological Review*, 1975, *40*, 691–700.

Coulter, J. *The social construction of mind: Studies in ethnomethodology and phenomenology*. Totowa, N.J.: Rowman & Littlefield, 1979.

Delamont, S., & Hamilton, D. Classroom research: A critique and a new approach. In M. Stubbs & S. Delamont (Eds.), *Explorations in classroom observation*. London: Wiley, 1976.

Dittmann, A. T. Developmental factors in conversational behavior. *Journal of Communication*, 1972, *22*, 405–423.

Dittmann, A. T. Style in conversation. *Semiotica*, 1973, *3*, 241–271.

Dittmann, A. T., & Llewellyn, L. G. The phonemic clause as a unit of speech decoding. *Journal of Personality and Social Psychology*, 1967, *6*, 341–349.

Dittmann, A. T., & Llewellyn, L. G. Relationship between vocalizations and head nods as listener responses. *Journal of Personality and Social Psychology*, 1968, *9*, 79–84.

Duncan, S., Jr. Some signals and rules for taking speaking turns in conversation. *Journal of Personality and Social Psychology*, 1972, *23*, 283–292.

Duncan, S., Jr. Toward a grammar for dyadic conversation. *Semiotica*, 1973, *9*, 29–46.

Duncan, S., Jr. On the structure of speaker–auditor interaction during speaking turns. *Language in Society*, 1974, *2*, 161–180.

Duncan, S., Jr., & Fiske, D. W. *Face-to-face interaction*. New York: Halsted, 1977.

Duncan, S., Jr., & Niederehe, G. On signaling that it's your turn to speak. *Journal of Experimental Social Psychology*, 1974, *10*, 234–247.

Farina, A. Patterns of role dominance and conflict in parents of schizophrenic patients. *Journal of Abnormal and Social Psychology*, 1960, *61, 31–38.*

Farina, A., & Holzberg, J. D. Interaction patterns of parents and hospitalized sons diagnosed as schizophrenic. *Journal of Abnormal Psychology*, 1968, *73*, 114–118.

Fishman, P. Interaction: The work women do. *Social Problems*, 1978, *25*, 397–406.

Flanders, N. A. *Analyzing teaching behavior*. Reading, Mass.: Addison-Wesley, 1970.

Garfinkel, H., & Sacks, H. On formal structures of practical actions. In J. C. McKenney & E. A. Teryakian (Eds.), *Theoretical sociology*. New York: Appleton-Century-Crofts, 1970.

Goffman, E. On face work: An analysis of ritual elements in social interaction. *Psychiatry*, 1955, *18*, 213–223.

Goffman, E. *Relations in public*. New York: Harper & Row, Colophon Books, 1971.

Goodwin, C. *Notes on the organization of disengagement: Unilateral departure*. Paper presented at the meeting of the American Sociological Association, Boston, August 1979. (a)

Goodwin, C. The interactive construction of a sentence in natural conversation. In G. Psathas (Ed.), *Everyday language: Studies in ethnomethology*. New York: Irvington, 1979. (b)

Goodwin, M. Processes of mutual monitoring implicated in the production of description sequences. *Sociological Inquiry*, 1980, *50*, 303–317.

Hadley, T., & Jacob, R. Relationship among measures of family power. *Journal of Personality and Social Psychology*, 1973, *27*, 6–12.

Hall, E. T. *Handbook for proxemic research*. Washington, D.C.: Studies in the Anthropology of Visual Communication, 1974.

Hymes, D. *Foundations in sociolinguistics: An ethnographic approach*. Philadelphia: University of Pennsylvania Press, 1974.

International Phonetic Association. *The principles of the International Phonetic Association*. London: Department of Phonetics, University College, 1963. (Originally published, 1949.)

Jaffe, G., Cassotta, L., & Feldstein, S. *Rhythms of dialog*. New York: Academic Press, 1964.

Jefferson, G. *A report on some difficulties encountered when using pseudonyms in research generative transcripts*. Unpublished manuscript, University of California at Irvine, 1971.

Jefferson, G. A case of precision timing in ordinary conversation: Overlapped tag-positioned address terms in closing sequences. *Semiotica*, 1973, *9*, 47–96.

Jefferson, G. Error correction as an interactional resource. *Language in Society*, 1975, *3*, 181–199.

Jefferson, G. Sequential aspects of storytelling in conversation. In G. Schenkein (Ed.), *Studies on the organization of interaction*. New York: Academic Press, 1979. (a)

Jefferson, G. A technique for inviting laughter and its subsequent acceptance/declination. In G. Psathas (Ed.), *Everyday language: Studies in ethnomethodology*. New York: Irvington, 1979. (b)

Jefferson, G., & Schegloff, E. *Sketch: Some orderly aspects of overlap in natural conversation*. Unpublished manuscript, University of California at Los Angeles, 1975.

Jefferson, G., & Schenkein, J. Some sequential negotiations in conversation: Unexpanded and expanded versions of projected action sequences. *Sociology*, 1977, *11*, 87–103.

Kendon, A. Some functions of gaze direction in social interaction. *Acta Psychologica*, 1967, *26*, 22–47.

Kendon, A. Review of *Face-to-face interaction* by S. Duncan, Jr., & D. W. Fiske. *Contemporary Psychology*, 1978, *23*, 5–6.

Knapp, M. L., Hart, R. P., Friedrich, G. W., & Schulman, G. M. The rhetoric of goodbye: Verbal and nonverbal correlates of human leave taking. *Speech Monographs*, 1973, *40*, 182–198.

Komarovsky, M. *Blue-collar marriage.* New York: Random House, 1962.
Laws, J. L. A feminist review of marital adjustment literature: The rape of the Locke. *Journal of Marriage and the Family*, 1971, *33*, 483–516.
Lennard, H. L., & Bernstein, A. *Patterns in human interaction: An introduction to clinical sociology.* San Francisco: Jossey-Bass, 1969.
Maynard, D. Placement of topic changes in conversation. *Semiotica*, 1980, *30*, 263–290.
Mishler, E., & Waxler, N. *Interaction in families: An experimental study of family process and schizophrenia.* New York: Wiley, 1968.
Murrell, S. A., & Stachowiak, J. G. Consistency rigidity and power in the interaction patterns of clinic and nonclinic families. *Journal of Abnormal Psychology*, 1967, *72*, 265–272.
Parsons, T. *The social system.* Glencoe, Ill.: Free Press, 1951.
Philips, S. U. Some sources of cultural variability in the regulation of talk. *Language in Society*, 1976, *5*, 81–95.
Pollner, M. Mundane reasoning. *Philosophy of the Social Sciences*, 1974, *4*, 35–54.
Pomeranz, A. M. *Second assessments: A study of some features of agreements/disagreements.* Unpublished doctoral dissertation, University of California at Irvine, 1975.
Rutter, D. R., & Stephenson, G. M. The role of visual communication in synchronizing conversation. *European Journal of Psychology*, 1977, *7*, 29–37.
Ryave, A. L., & Schenkein, J. Notes on the art of walking. In R. Turner (Ed.), *Ethnomethodology: Selected readings.* Baltimore: Penguin, 1974.
Sacks, H. On sociological description. *Berkeley Journal of Sociology*, 1963, *8*, 1–16.
Sacks, H. On the analyzability of stories by children. In J. Gumperz & D. Hymes (Eds.), *Directions in sociolinguistics: The ethnography of communication.* New York: Holt, Rinehart & Winston, 1972.
Sacks, H. An analysis of a joke's telling in conversation. In R. Bauman & J. Sherzer (Eds.), *Explorations in the ethnography of speaking.* Cambridge: Cambridge University Press, 1974.
Sacks, H., Schegloff, E., & Jefferson, G. A simplest systematics for the organization of turn-taking for conversation. *Language*, 1974, *50*, 696–735.
Schegloff, E. Sequencing in conversational openings. *American Anthropologist*, 1968, *70*, 1075–1095.
Schegloff, E. Notes on a conversational practice: Formulating place. In D. Sudnow (Ed.), *Studies in social interaction.* New York: Free Press, 1972.
Schegloff, E., Jefferson, G., & Sacks, H. The preference for self-correction in the organization of repair in conversation. *Language*, 1977, *53*, 361–382.
Schegloff, E., & Sacks, H. Opening up closings. In R. Turner (Ed.), *Ethnomethodology: Selected readings.* Baltimore: Penguin, 1974. (Originally published in *Semiotica*, 1973, *8*, 289–327.)
Schenkein, J. An introduction to the study of "socialization" through analyses of conversational interaction. *Semiotica*, 1978, *24*, 278–303. (a)
Schenkein, J. Identity negotiations in conversation. In J. Schenkein (Ed.), *Studies in social organization of conversation.* New York: Academic Press, 1978. (b)
Schuman, A. I. Power relations in emotionally disturbed and normal family triads. *Journal of Abnormal Psychology*, 1970, *75*, 30–37.
Shaw, M. E., & Sadler, D. W. Interaction patterns in heterosexual dyads varying in degrees of intimacy. *Journal of Social Psychology*, 1965, *66*, 345–351.
Simon, A., & Boyer, G. E. (Eds.). *Mirrors for behavior: An anthology of classroom observation instruments.* Philadelphia: Research for Better Schools, 1968.
Slater, P. Parental role differentiation. *American Journal of Sociology*, 1961, *67*, 296–311.

Soskin, W. F., & John, V. P. The study of spontaneous talk. In R. Barker (Ed.), *The stream of behavior*. New York: Appleton-Century-Crofts, 1963.

Strodtbeck, F. L. Husband and wife interaction over revealed differences. *American Sociological Review*, 1951, *16*, 468–473.

Strodtbeck, F. L., & Mann, R. D. Sex role differentiation in jury deliberations. *Sociometry*, 1956, *19*, 3–11.

Sudnow, D. Temporal parameters of interpersonal observation. In D. Sudnow (Ed.), *Studies in social interaction*. New York: Free Press, 1972.

Trager, G. L., & Smith, H. L., Jr. *An outline of English structure*. Washington, D.C.: American Council of Learned Societies, 1957.

West, C. Against our will: Male interruptions of females in cross-sex conversation. *Annals of the New York Academy of Sciences*, 1979, *327*, 81–97.

West, C. When the doctor is a "lady": Power, status and gender in physician–patient conversations. Unpublished manuscript, University of California at Santa Cruz, 1981.

West, C., & Zimmerman, D. H. Women's place in everyday talk: Reflections on parent–child interaction. *Social Problems*, 1977, *24*, 521–529.

Wiemann, J. M., & Knapp, M. L. Turn-taking in conversations. *Journal of Communications*, 1975, *25*, 75–92.

Wilson, T. P., & Zimmerman, D. H. Ethnomethodology, sociology and theory. *Humbolt Journal of Social Relations*, 1979/1980, *7*, 52–87.

Wilson, T. P., Zimmerman, D. H., & Wiemann, J. M. *Approaches to the study of turn-taking*. Manuscript in preparation, University of California at Santa Barbara.

Winter, W. D., & Ferreira, A. J. Interaction process analysis of family decision-making. *Family Process*, 1967, *6*, 155–172.

Yngve, V. H. On getting a word in edgewise. In M. A. Campbell et al. (Eds.), *Papers from the sixth regional meeting, Chicago Linguistics Society*. Chicago: University of Chicago, 1970.

Zimmerman, D. H. Ethnomethodology. *American Sociologist*, 1978, *13*, 6–15.

Zimmerman, D. H., & West, C. Sex roles, interruptions and silences in conversation. In B. Thorne & N. Henley (Eds.), *Language and sex: Difference and dominance*. Rowley, Mass.: Newbury House, 1975.

Technical appendix. Audiovisual recording: procedures, equipment, and troubleshooting

HARALD G. WALLBOTT

In recent years the recording of nonverbal behavior using audiotape, videotape, or film has become a major research tool in behavioral research. This appendix deals with selected technical issues concerning audiovisual recording. Owing to space limitations, only aspects considered to be of major importance will be discussed.

After the treatment of general issues in the recording of behavior, procedures used in videotaping, cinematography (here referred to as *cinema*), and audiotaping will be examined in detail,[1] with emphasis on methods of obtaining high-quality recordings. An overview of common technical problems and their potential solutions follows. Finally, special features of recording in the field and ethical concerns will be discussed.

A.1. Basic considerations

Before starting to record, the researcher should decide whether a permanent record of behavior samples is really needed. Some research questions can be answered without using permanent records, and others can be modified in such a way as to make recording unnecessary. In deciding whether to record, the researcher should keep in mind that recording is usually very costly in time, material, and personnel, and often beset by many problems.

Reasons for making a permanent record

There are two major sorts of reasons for making a permanent record, scientific and economic. One scientific reason might be the necessity of repeated viewings or listenings. Another might be the need for slow-motion viewing. Furthermore, permanent records are essential if ratings by observers or judges are to be obtained later or if objective measurement of behavior is planned (e.g., coding of behavioral categories).

Finally, permanent records provide the possibility of selecting and organizing the behavioral samples in specific sequences; for example, editing and splicing techniques can be employed to produce demonstration material or stimulus tapes.

Economic reasons include those entailing future use of the records. The material, for instance, might be used not only in the originally intended manner, but also to study new questions; in this way new experiments or recordings might be rendered unnecessary. Finally, permanent records may be necessary for teaching purposes or for building an archive.

Choice of equipment

A careful consideration of the pros and cons of recording must precede the actual planning of the recording procedures. If a permanent recording is to be made, it is necessary to plan carefully the recording setup and the system to be used. Among other things, the researcher must consider the kind of record that is required, which recording systems and facilities are available, and to what extent interference with the ongoing behavior can be tolerated.

The most important decision concerns the medium on which the record is to be stored. The researcher has to choose between cinema and video, between recording sound and picture separately or on one tape, between cassette recorders or open-reel machines, and finally between different cinema or video systems.

It is quite easy to plan very elaborate recording setups on the drawing board, using five cameras, four microphones, several recorders, and so on. An ideal solution can be rarely attained, however, owing to constraints imposed by the time, equipment, and money available. Usually these elaborate plans have to be changed when reality is faced. In addition, the effects of the recording apparatus on the behavior of the persons studied has to be taken into account. Where, for instance, can the cameras be placed without disturbing the subjects? Will the subjects behave naturally while facing cameras and microphones? The recording actually produced will always be a compromise. The researcher will also do well to keep in mind "Murphy's law," which states simply but concisely, "Whatever can go wrong will go wrong."

Therefore, in planning a recording, the following points have to be considered carefully:

1. Minimal requirements for the recording
2. Availability of technical facilities

3. Obtrusiveness of recordings
4. Costs in time, money, and personnel
5. Anticipated problems

In the following section, the basic choice between cinema and video and, moreover, the choice between different systems within video or cinema recording will be discussed.

A.2. Visual records: comparison of cinema and video

The researcher planning visual recording is confronted with many systems. The situation with regard to cinema is comparatively simple because of the standardized systems of 35-mm film, 16-mm film, Super 8 film, and Single 8 film. Video systems, on the other hand, can be classified (1) according to tape width (i.e., two inch, one inch, three-quarter inch, half inch); (2) according to tape operation (open-reel, cartridge, cassette); and (3) according to the recording principle used (helical scan, quadruplex, longitudinal recording). This is especially confusing in the case of nonprofessional systems, where there are many different systems, such as VHS, SRV, LVR, and Betamax. Furthermore, the video field seems to be characterized not by a trend toward standardization, but rather by one toward the development of additional new systems, which in most cases are incompatible with older ones already on the market. Figure A.1 presents an overview of some of these systems.

In general, the choice between cinema and video is not a simple one. Both systems have advantages and disadvantages. Owing to its ease of operation and the reusability of the tapes, many users currently choose video without considering cinema at all. However, cinema has advantages as well, including superior resolution and picture quality (at least with 16-mm film) and the worldwide standardization. In Table A.1 some of the more important criteria for the choice between systems are listed. The table demonstrates that neither cinema nor video should be preferred as a matter of course.

Some of the respective advantages and disadvantages of cinema and video deserve some further illustration. Roughly, criteria for the choice between the two media may be classified as

1. Problems of compatibility and standardization
2. Issues concerning the recording process (i.e., ease of operation, robustness of equipment, etc.)
3. Problems associated with field recording
4. Quality of the picture, amount of light needed, and so on
5. Playback, editing, copying, and storage considerations
6. Costs and investments

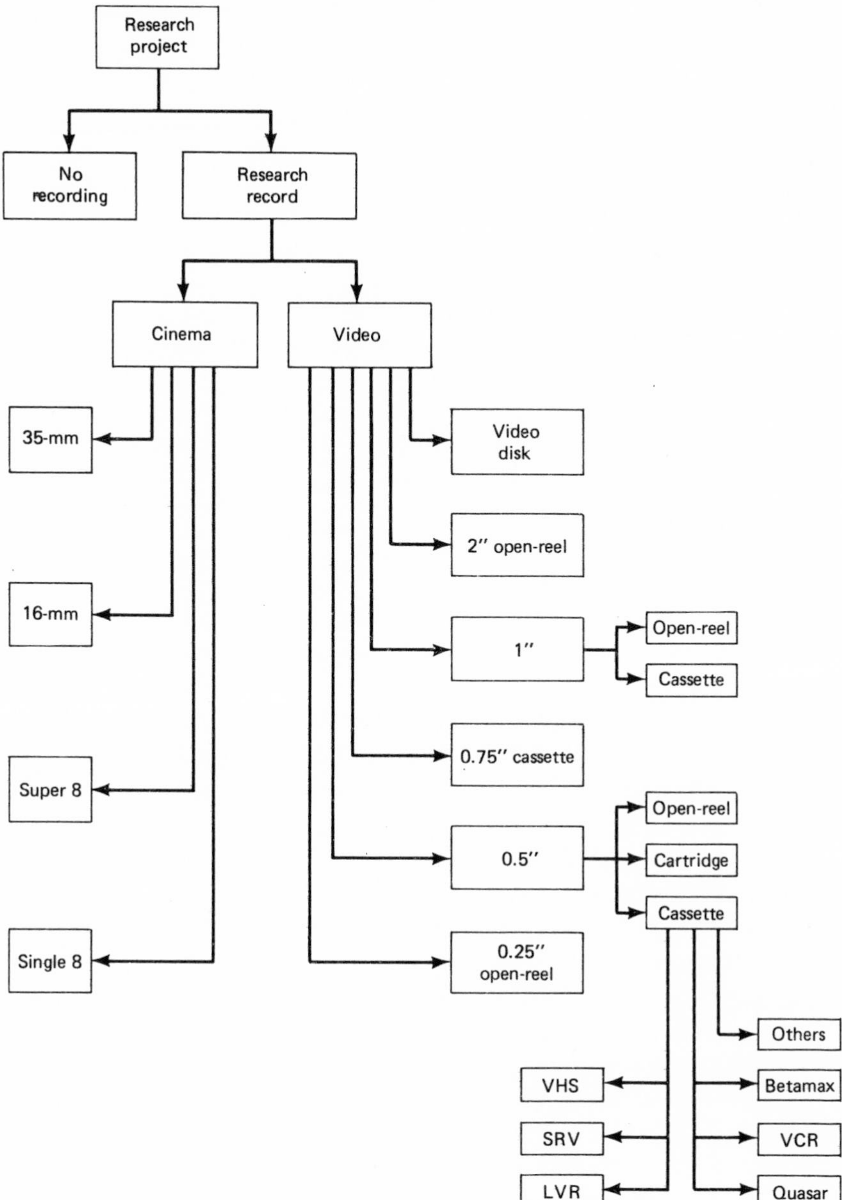

Figure A.1. Film and video recording systems.

Table A.1. *Advantages and disadvantages of cinema and video*

Criterion	Cinema	Video
Recording quality	High quality, good resolution	Resolution and quality depend heavily on the system used
Synchronizing of audio and video	Possible, but not exact when built-in camera sound facilities are used; otherwise expensive	Automatic if sound is recorded on video soundtrack; difficult and expensive if sound is recorded on external recorder
Costs for equipment	Comparatively inexpensive if standard equipment is used; otherwise very expensive	Comparatively expensive; rapid technical development occurring
Instant reviewing	Impossible	Possible (with appropriate equipment)
Sensitivity of cameras or recorders	Sturdy, robust	Sensitive to dust, humidity, and temperature
Technical possibilities	No special cameras or projectors necessary for color recording; slow motion, frame-by-frame recording, and time-lapse recording possible	Different cameras, recorders, and monitors necessary for color recording; fading and mixing possible; effect generators available; frame-by-frame and time-lapse recording possible but expensive
Lighting	Intensive lighting necessary; color temperature may cause problems in color recording	Black-and-white cameras very sensitive to light, especially if special tubes are used; color recording might pose same problems as with cinema

Recording material	Film expensive and not reusable; only relatively brief recordings without interruption possible; otherwise expensive, bulky equipment needed	Tape comparatively inexpensive and reusable; long recording periods without interruption possible
Editing	Mechanical editing possible; editing devices are simple; mechanical damage may occur while editing	Electronic editing often time-consuming and (depending on the quality of the system used) not very precise; two recorders necessary
Duplication	High quality, but expensive	Quality loss, but inexpensive and simple
Storage	Chemical and mechanical characteristics of films may change	Temperature, humidity, dust, or magnetic fields may affect tapes
Playback	Special projector necessary; room has to be darkened or special daylight projection facilities have to be used	Possible with modified TV sets; no special arrangements necessary; scope limited unless a video projection unit (expensive) is used
System compatibility	Automatic, owing to worldwide standards	Problematic, except for some standardized systems (EIAJ, U-MATIC)

Compatibility. The main problems with video seem to be the lack of compatibility and standardization. The diversity of video systems, especially in the frequently used nonprofessional systems (half inch) often prevents tape exchange between users. Tapes recorded with one standard cannot be played back on machines using another standard. Moreover, it is sometimes impossible (at least with older machines) to play tapes recorded on a machine produced by one company on a machine of the same standard manufactured by another company. This is one of the major shortcomings of video technology at the moment, and it is aggravated by the fact that new systems are developed each year and older systems vanish from the market. This constant change poses the additional problem that tapes and spare parts may be no longer available. With cinema, on the other hand, system compatibility is assured.

Recording. The main advantage of video is that laypersons can produce recordings quite easily, because of the immediate replay control and the fact that, if recordings go wrong, they can be easily redone after simply rewinding the tape (if the behavior to be recorded can be reproduced). Furthermore, video allows uninterrupted recording of long duration. Major disadvantages of video are that the electrical and electronic devices are very sensitive to dust, moisture, and temperature and that the equipment is still fairly bulky, whereas cinema recording equipment is generally small and robust.

Field recording. For field recordings it is often easier and less obtrusive to use a small Super 8 camera than video. For video recording, even if portable equipment is employed, one needs a camera, a recorder with batteries and/or an external power supply, and possibly a control monitor. On the other hand, video might be better suited if field recordings of long duration are required and film cassettes cannot be changed every 3 minutes because of the risk of losing important information or because of potential obtrusiveness.

Picture quality. The quality of the video picture (resolution as well as contrast and color fidelity) is usually inferior to that obtained by using comparable cinema equipment. On the other hand, video recordings (at least black-and-white recordings) are possible even under very difficult lighting conditions. Color recording is more difficult when using video because special equipment is required, that is, a special color camera, a color recorder, and for playback a color monitor.

Playback, editing, copying, and storage. With video ordinary TV sets can be used for playback, and instant reviewing at the scene of the recording is possible. Cinema does not allow instant reviewing, and furthermore, special arrangements have to be made for playback (i.e., setting up the projector and the projection screen and darkening the room, unless a special projector with a built-in daylight screen is employed).

If editing and copying become necessary, a major advantage of cinema is that editing is quite easy; copying, however, is expensive and usually can be executed only by special printing laboratories. Video editing is more difficult because manual splicing is virtually impossible and thus special equipment is required, that is, a second recorder with editing facilities or a special hardware video editor. Furthermore, video editing is essentially a copying process, which implies a considerable loss in quality. Finally, the exactness of editing in video is poor. Editing at the level of individual frames, which can be done quite easily and manually with cinema, is entirely impossible with video, unless special and very expensive video editors are employed.

Storage of cinematographic recordings requires attention to temperature and chemical processes that may affect the material. Videotapes are also affected by temperature, dust, and moisture, and additionally by strong magnetic fields. Video cassette recorders and cartridge recorders are better suited than open-reel recorders if the records are to be stored for documentation purposes, because cartridges and cassettes provide better protection against dirt and dust.

Thus the two media have different advantages with regard to playback, editing, storage, and so on. Depending on the reasons for producing a record, factors concerning the ease of playback may be most important in making the choice between cinema and video. Video is better suited if instant replay in needed, for instance, in video feedback or behavior training. Video open-reel recorders (for instance, the Japanese EIAJ standard) are relatively inexpensive and allow manual tape operations, like twisting the reels back and forth to achieve frame-by-frame viewing, to simulate slow motion, or to localize events. Thus these recorders may be preferred for behavior coding. Real slow-motion and frame-by-frame viewing, on the other hand, are either impossible or of poor quality when using open-reel recorders. Though very sophisticated auxiliary equipment for editing and slow motion is available (for instance the U-MATIC system), this equipment requires a large additional investment. The alternative is moving an open-reel tape by hand (which may be both inprecise and tedious!). Thus, for detailed behavior description and coding, which usually require frame-by-frame viewing or at least slow motion, cinema might be preferred; with cinema, frame-by-frame viewing is made easy by the use of such devices as editors or moviolas or special film projectors with a frame-by-frame option (see Kendon, 1979).

Costs. Standard cinematographic equipment is less expensive than video equipment. However, with ordinary film cameras, only brief durations can be recorded without changing the film cassette. Furthermore, this brief recording will contain no sound. If sound is needed, a more expensive sound-film camera or an external tape recorder has to be employed. Considering this factor, cinema is not as inexpensive as it might appear at first glance. High-quality cameras with satisfactory sound-film synchronization are quite expensive, and sometimes an external audiotape recorder will add to the costs. In addition, follow-up costs have to be taken into account. Recording material, processing, and duplicating are more expensive in cinema than in video. Thus, if one compares the costs for a record of 30 minutes' duration without interruptions and with synchronized sound (which poses no problems when using video), video will be less expensive than cinema. To obtain an equivalent cinematographic recording, special cameras capable of handling such long recording durations, as well as synchronizing equipment, an external audiotape recorder, and of course a considerable quantity of expensive film (including costs for processing) and audiotape, are necessary. Cinema might be less expensive than video if only standard equipment is employed and if recording periods are brief.

It is possible to overcome most of the disadvantages of the respective media by spending money on very elaborate systems and techniques. It is quite easy, for example, to achieve as good a resolution and picture quality with video as with cinema, if one is willing to invest a comparatively large amount of money in semiprofessional or professional systems like one-inch or two-inch videotape recorders. Or one may use a video disk (see Ekman, Friesen, & Taussig, 1969) allowing high picture quality and rapid access to each frame. Therefore, the comparisons made here should be understood as based on inexpensive and widely used systems, such as three-quarter-inch cassette machines (like the U-MATIC system); half-inch open-reel recorders (like the Japan EIAJ standard); or half-inch cassette recorders (like Betamax or VHS) on the one hand, and 16 mm film and Super 8 film on the other hand (35-mm and Single 8 film are hardly ever used for scientific research).

A.3. Special issues in obtaining visual records

The use of cinema or video requires careful consideration of some special issues concerning recording techniques. For example, incorrect cable connections, incorrect positions of switches, incorrect tape threading, or dirty recording heads may pose problems (see Section A.5). Bad lighting, however, is one of the major sources of problems and can ruin an entire recording. Two factors are especially important, the placement of the lights and the amount of lighting necessary. Furthermore, the nature of the recording setup, that is, placement of camera(s) and other equipment, camera angle, and so on, will determine the quality and usability of a record. Finally (depending on the reasons for producing the record), the insertion of time codes or time marks has to be considered. This section is devoted to a discussion of these topics.

Placement of the lights

The problem of placing lights is probably well known to everybody who has held a camera – video, cinema, or still photography. Placement of the lights to achieve the proper balance among backlights, frontlights, and sidelights is important, because without such balance important features in the picture may be overshadowed, blurred, or totally invisible. Figure A.2 gives a schematic overview (in a somewhat exaggerated way, to clarify the major problems) of how improper lighting will affect the picture.

Such mistakes in the placement of the lights can seriously limit the usability of a recording. In the analysis of facial expression, for instance, incorrect lighting in closeup shots of the face may result in shadows masking important features of the face. If the frontlights are too strong, there may be no shadows at all; in this case, also, it will be impossible to detect the facial features and movements of interest.

To mention one more problem associated with video, care must be taken not to expose the video tube to very intensive lighting. Video cameras are very light sensitive, and when they are pointed to bright sunlight, reflecting surfaces, or studio lights, damaging of the tube will result. Therefore, the placement of the lights and the camera has to be very carefully planned and arranged. The worst thing that can happen when using cinema with bright light is overexposure of the film; the camera itself will not be damaged.

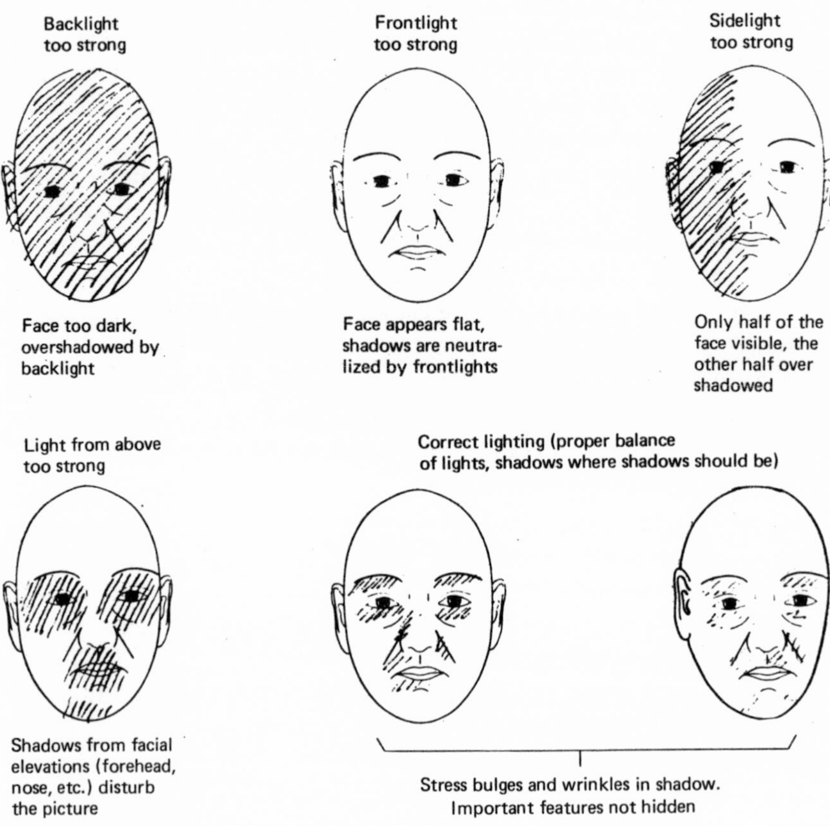
Backlight
too strong
Frontlight
too strong
Sidelight
too strong
Face too dark,
overshadowed by
backlight
Face appears flat,
shadows are neutra-
lized by frontlights
Only half of the
face visible, the
other half over
shadowed
Light from above
too strong
Correct lighting (proper balance
of lights, shadows where shadows should be)
Shadows from facial
elevations (forehead,
nose, etc.) disturb
the picture
Stress bulges and wrinkles in shadow.
Important features not hidden

Figure A.2. Improper placement of the lights.

Amount of light

The second point to consider in connection with lighting, even more important than the first, is the proper amount of lighting, and dependent on that, the proper iris opening of the lenses, often termed *f-stop*. The f-stop determines the amount of light reaching the film or the photoelectric target zone in the video camera tube. The higher the f-stop chosen, the less light falls into the camera within a given time span, and vice versa.

If the lights are dim, a small f-stop should be chosen to allow more light to enter the camera. If the light is very intensive, a large f-stop should be chosen, to produce a smaller iris opening. The problem is that the choice of f-stop not only will affect the amount of light reaching the film or the camera tube, but also will have considerable influence on the depth of field and depth of focus. *Depth of focus* is a measure of the focal distance between the lenses and the target zone (film or camera tube). *Depth of field* refers to the distance between the nearest object recorded in sharp focus and the farthest object in sharp focus. As can be shown mathematically, both parameters are affected by the choice of the f-stop: Choosing a small f-stop to compensate for low light levels will result in a smaller depth of focus and, more important, in a smaller depth of field. This may sound somewhat academic. If, however, an object moves toward and away from the camera while a recording is being made, a small depth of field implies that the moving object, for example, a child at play, has only a small range in which it can move while staying in focus. When it leaves this range, it will be out of focus, and the picture will be blurred. In this case constant adjustments of the focus have to be made. Choosing a larger f-stop, which implies that enough light is available, enlarges the depth of field and allows objects to move toward and away from the camera to a greater extent while staying in focus. To complicate the situation, large f-stops may decrease the contrast of the video picture somewhat (this is not the case in cinema). Hence the final choice of f-stop will always be a compromise among the amount of light available, the depth of field needed, and the contrast desired.

These considerations demonstrate the importance of having a proper amount of light while recording. Of course, the f-stop has to be adjusted until the red exposure control light in the film camera turns to green, until the video control monitor indicates an acceptable picture quality, or until the picture gain control indicator on the video recorder signals appropriate video input. But one should keep in mind that other factors equally essential for high-quality recording, namely, depth of field and depth of focus, are likewise affected by these manipulations. Therefore, it is advisable to provide for proper lighting conditions before starting to record.

Video recording entails some additional lighting problems. Shortcomings in lighting are often not recognizable while a video record is being made. The monitor's contrast knob can compensate for lighting that is too flat or has produced too much contrast between bright and dark areas. Similarly, the brightness knob on the control monitor can compensate for insufficient light or light that is too intensive. The pitfall lies in the fact that these adjustments simply disguise problems that can be corrected only with great difficulty after the recording has been made. As the original record generally should be treated as though it were irreplaceable (as it often really is!), it is usually necessary to produce working copies of the master tape. Copies of poor-quality master tapes, however, will be of even worse quality, and contrast or brightness adjustments can no longer be used to compensate. Especially if automatic gain control was used when light conditions were inadequate, copies will usually be very poor because automatic gain control amplifies light values that are insufficient, in the process decreasing the overall contrast of the picture. (It should be mentioned that under adequate lighting conditions automatic gain control does not have this effect; therefore, if enough light is available, automatic gain control may be used without hesitation.)

Thus, in accordance with the lighting available, the largest possible f-stop should be chosen in order to obtain adequate exposure and large depth of field, and automatic gain control in video recording should be used only in optimal lighting conditions. Obviously, in a recording studio with facilities like variable light sources, dimmers, movable lights, and the like, optimal conditions should not be difficult to achieve. Furthermore, poor lighting can be tolerated if the common Vidicon tubes in the camera are replaced by Newvicon or Plumbicon tubes. Both of these latter types of tubes, although comparatively expensive, are very light sensitive; they are less inert and much more resistant to tube burning than Vidicon tubes. An additional advantage to the use of Newvicon or Plumbicon tubes is that fast movements of objects or the camera will not lead to the ghost images and smearing effects typical of the Vidicon tube.

The situation may be much more complicated when making field recordings. But even here something can be done to improve lighting. For example, small portable and unobtrusive spotlights may be used, or lighting may be improved by replacing the light bulbs in the existing lamps with stronger ones. To sum up, only the proper amount of light, together with the proper placement of the lights, will guarantee high-quality cinema or video recordings.

Setting

Apart from the lighting conditions, the quality of the recording will depend heavily on the kind of equipment used, as well as on the nature of the recording setup. Some points have already been mentioned. If high resolution is required, 16-mm film or one-inch video recorders are essential. If the recording is to be made as unobtrusive as possible, a small Super 8 camera might be better suited than the bulky equipment needed for video recording. As most of these points are especially relevant for field recordings, they will be discussed in Section A.6.

If a studio is available, placement of cameras, microphones, and equipment will not pose major problems, provided that the studio is adequately equipped. But even in the studio careful planning is necessary, especially concerning the location of the camera, the camera angle, and the type of take needed.

The camera should be placed as unobtrusively as possible. Whenever possible, a tripod for the camera should be used to avoid blurring. When recording through a one-way mirror, the loss of light owing to absorption has to be considered. And finally, camera angles and type of take have to be determined. If it is necessary, for comparison purposes, to record all subjects from an identical camera angle, the position of the camera, the camera-to-object distance, the height of the camera, and the camera axis should be kept constant, or the positions should at least be marked. If these precautions are forgotten, later comparisons between recordings might be difficult or even impossible. It is necessary to consider, furthermore, whether constant focal length is to be used for the entire recording, whether it will be necessary to move the camera if the recorded persons move around, and whether a zoom lens should be used in order to accentuate important features of the expression or behavior. All these things should be planned in advance; otherwise, general confusion may result during the recording, and then important, irretrievable information might be lost. Such problems can be avoided by planning carefully and by doing test recordings at the actual site of the recording and under lifelike conditions.

Time codes and time marks

Finally, both in video and in cinema, care has to be taken for proper time marking of the individual pictures or frames. This is especially important if events are to be localized precisely. If, for instance, coding of facial expressions or body movement is planned, it is necessary to localize the exact beginnings and endings of behavioral acts. One possibility would be to use the built-in counter of the video recorder or a film counter. Unfortunately, these devices are quite inaccurate, and the localization of individual frames is entirely impossible.

Both cinema and video provide an exact time base, which is given by the recording speed in cinema (e.g., 18 or 24 pictures per second) and by the impulses on the control track in video (60 *fields* or *half-frames*, i.e., 30 frames, in the USA; or 50 fields, i.e., 25 frames, in Europe). Obviously, counting of pictures or frames is impossible because of their large number, especially if long recordings have been produced. Thus auxiliary equipment that provides a time code has to be employed if the identification of individual frames becomes necessary.

In cinema a time code may be provided by having frame numbers printed on the pictures, a procedure that has to be done in a printing laboratory and is very expensive, or by marking the individual frames on the film's margin, an easier and less expensive process, but one that has a major disadvantage: The numbers are not visible when the film is viewed. Marks on the film's margin may consist of repeated identical impulses or of individually coded marks for each picture or frame. The first technique (impulses) is less expensive, but also less accurate, because the frames are not marked individually and reading errors might occur if the device that reads and counts these impulses misses one or more. Thus individual marks or numbers for each frame are preferable.

When using video, the insertion of time codes or marks is somewhat easier. Again, various techniques may be employed. The simplest systems which for most purposes are sufficient are time-code generators that insert either a consecutive frame number or a digital time display into each video field. These frame numbers or time displays are visible and can easily be used to localize actions or to determine durations of events. For some purposes, time displays might be preferred. Durations of events, for instance, might be easier to obtain from time displays than from frame numbers. More expensive code generators provide additional options, as for instance the possibility of inserting optional codes (for subject identification or other necessary information) in addition to the time-code information.

Other systems are available that insert a digital time code instead of or in addition to the visible code. Such digital codes are necessary if video disks and/or digital computers (see Ekman et al., 1969) are employed for analysis. Still another technical principle is used in generators that write the time-code information on one audio track of the videotape. The advantage here is that the picture is not partly covered by the code information; the disadvantage is that the information is accessible only via expensive auxiliary equipment.

Thus, for most purposes in nonverbal communication research, a time-code generator that produces visible frame numbers or a time display will be sufficient. Only if digital computers or video disks are used is digital information on the video or audio track necessary.

The time-code generator can be used when the actual recording takes place, or the code information can be inserted later while the tape is being copied. Obviously, it is preferable to insert the time marks at the time when the recording is made. If a copy has to be made in order to insert the code, the quality of the picture will deteriorate. Accordingly, this option should be used only if the tape has to be copied anyway. The insertion of time marks during the original recording does, however, require further equipment at the recording site, and thus entails corresponding logistic problems, particularly in the field.

Whether code information is inserted while the recording is being made or afterward, *where* to insert the code information must be carefully considered. One has to make sure that no important features will later be concealed by the code; so the type of take, the camera position, and the scene being recorded must all be considered in choosing an appropriate location for the code. Most time-code generators facilitate this process by permitting the code display to move freely in the horizontal and vertical dimensions. Furthermore, some code generators allow choice between different sizes of display and an adjustment of brightness (which has to be carefully balanced with the brightness of the original picture; if the code is too dim, it may be hardly readable, and if it is too bright, it may render the picture too dark).

Finally, care must be taken not to insert the code information directly at the upper or lower edge of the video frames: Video monitors often do not show the entire recorded video information, because some lines of the picture are usually covered by the facing of the monitor.

A.4. Issues in audio recording

Basic decisions in audio recording

High-quality audio recording is often even more difficult to achieve than good cinema or video recording, because the audio signal is much more easily interfered with than the video signal. Before starting audio recording, one must consider some basic issues. These deal with the nature of the sound source (which affects choice of the microphone type, the direction characteristics of the microphone, the recording setup, etc.) and the degree of audio quality required (which affects choice of the recording system, e.g., the soundtrack on a video recorder, an audio cassette recorder, or an open-reel recorder).

Some of the major decisions to be faced in audio recording are the following:

1. Should the sound be recorded onto the audio track of the videotape and/or separately on an audiotape? If the latter, should a cassette recorder or an open-reel recorder be used?
2. When recording on videotape, should the built-in camera microphone or an external microphone be employed?
3. Should automatic level control or manual level control be used?

The advantages and disadvantages of these possibilities are illustrated in some detail in Figure A.3.

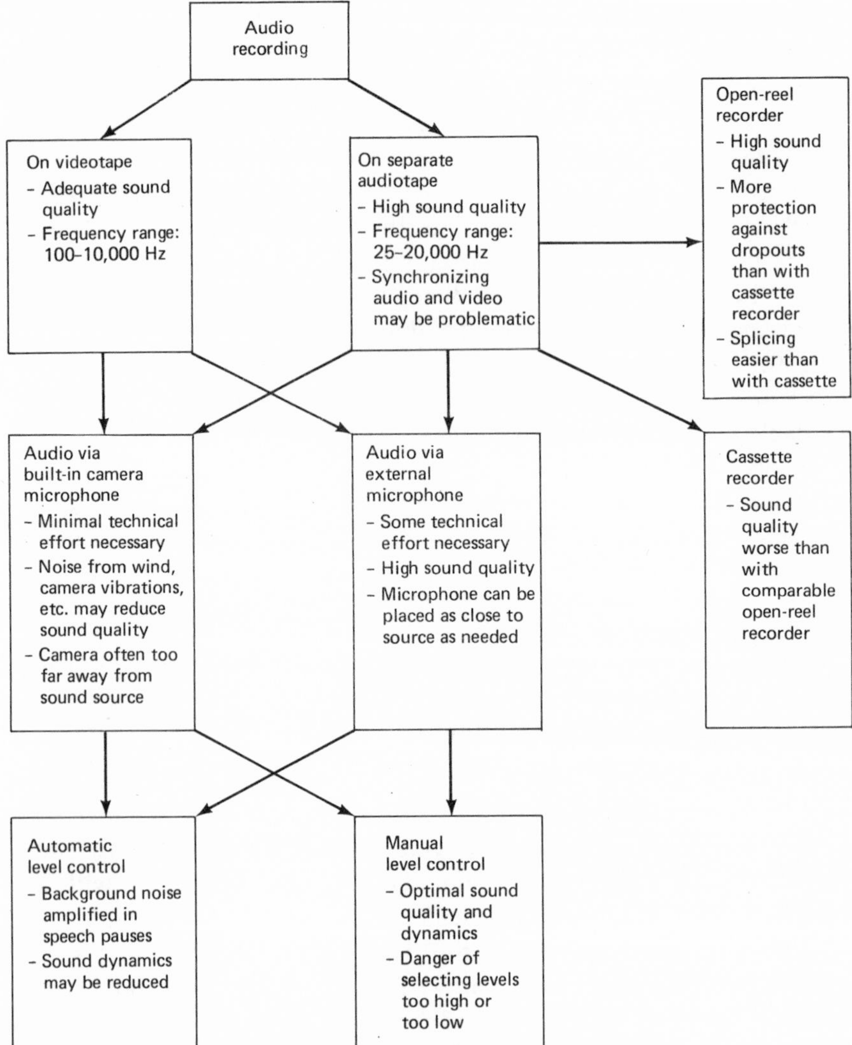

Figure A.3. Alternative procedures for audio recording.

As is evident from this figure, decisions will again be determined by the uses to which the audio recording will be put. If one is interested in the sound only in order to understand what is going on, minimal technical expenditure and minimal sound quality will be sufficient. In most cases this can be attained with, for instance, video sound from the built-in camera microphone or sound recordings on a small cassette recorder. But whereas a minimum of quality may be sufficient, higher quality is often possible with the available equipment. Aside from the researcher's personal satisfaction, superior sound quality is important if transcripts of the verbal interaction have to be made. For more sophisticated speech analysis, particularly for electroacoustic or digital computer analysis (see Scherer, Section 4.6), high-quality sound recordings are an absolute necessity, because poor sound quality may result in artifacts.

It should be stressed that often great improvements in sound quality can be achieved by minor, rather inexpensive changes in the recording setup. When producing field recordings, for instance, sound quality can be improved by replacing the built-in camera microphone with an external microphone that can be placed as close to the sound source as necessary. Another way to ensure high quality is to use manual level control instead of automatic level control. As automatic level control tends to amplify background noise in speech pauses, it should be used very rarely, if at all.

Types of microphones

Figure A.4 gives an overview of various types of microphones and their respective advantages and disadvantages.

Some of the characteristics of the different microphone types may limit their usefulness in some recording settings. If a high-impedance microphone is used, for instance, the final recording may be distorted by a loss of higher frequencies or by hum if the cable is longer than 3 m. Condenser microphones are very sensitive to temperature and humidity; therefore, they cannot be used if recordings are made under extreme conditions. Also, condenser microphones need an external power supply or batteries; not infrequently recordings fail because of a dead, unchecked battery.

One of the major choices is between small lavaliere microphones attached to the speaker and larger stationary microphones. Lavaliere microphones have some definite advantages that encourage their use. They are less obtrusive than stationary microphones placed before the speaker. In addition, they provide a more or less constant speaker-to-microphone distance. This is particularly important if the speaker moves around a great deal, changing the distance to a stationary microphone and requiring constant correction of the gain setting of the tape recorder. However, lavaliere microphones are difficult to use in some conditions. It is sometimes a problem to attach them, either for physical reasons (e.g., if the speaker wears a sweater or a T-shirt) or for psychological

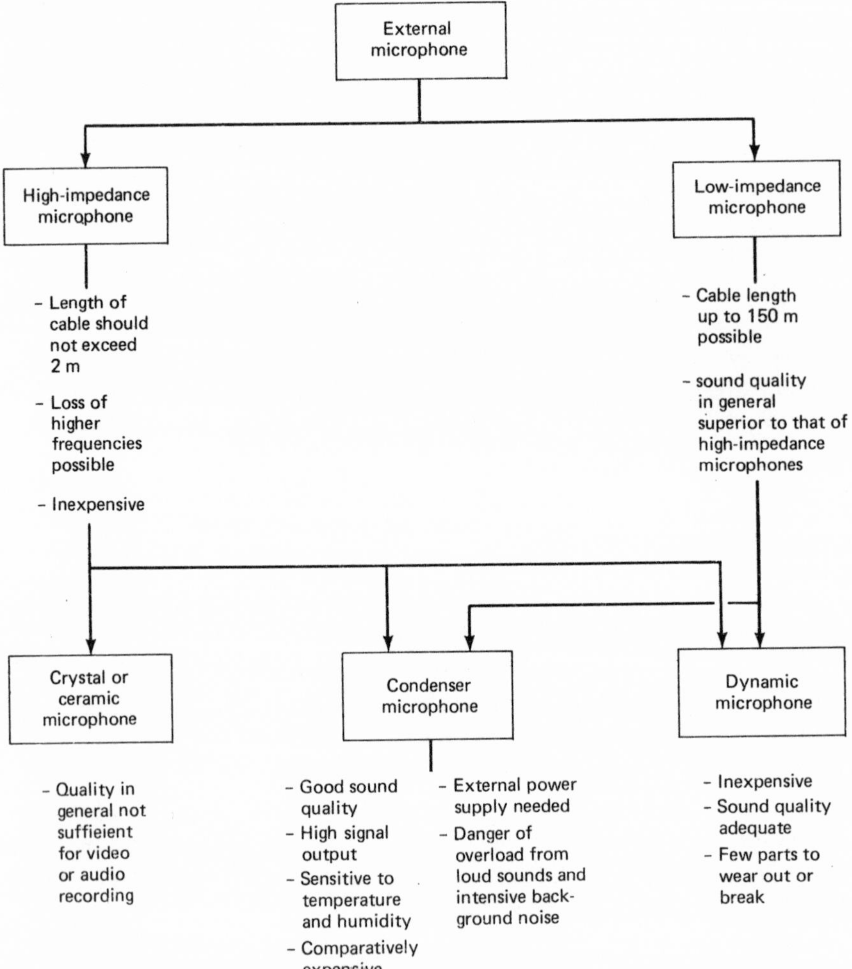

Figure A.4. Advantages and disadvantages of different types of microphones.

reasons (some people, such as psychiatric patients, may be very sensitive to being touched). To make things worse, lavaliere microphones are connected to the recorder via cables, and very often people will handle the cables, thereby producing unwanted noise in the recording. Wireless lavaliere microphones with a transmitter might be used, if the signal is not disturbed on its way from transmitter to receiver, and if a way is found to attach the sender. The advantages of stationary microphones, correspondingly, are that they are easier to set up; they can be hidden, if hiding them seems advisable; and they do not invite handling by speakers. Again, the choice depends on the nature of the situation and the goals of the project.

The same thing may be said of the choice among microphones with various direction characteristics (direction characteristics indicate the sensitivity of a microphone to sounds coming from different directions). This choice is somewhat independent of the choice of the microphone type (i.e., condenser, dynamic, lavaliere, stationary). In Figure A.5 some of the most common direction characteristics are depicted.

The type of direction characteristic one ends up with will be determined by the following factors of the recording situation:

1. Distance between microphone and sound source: The larger the distance the more "directional" the microphone should be, at least if the sound source is not moving.
2. Stationary or moving sound source: Less directional microphones or lavaliere microphones are better suited for a source of sound that constantly changes position. If a fixed unidirectional microphone is employed, one runs the risk of the sound source's leaving the direction of the microphone.
3. Number of sound sources (persons) to be recorded: If a monophonic recording is being made, a unidirectional microphone might be adequate for a single stationary person. A microphone with an "eight" characteristic might be placed between two members of a dyadic interaction. And finally, cardioid or omnidirectional microphones might be used to record a small discussion group.
4. Stereo or mono recording: When recording in stereo, or even on a four-track machine, each person in a dyad or a small group may have his or her own cardioid microphone, connected either to a sound mixer or directly to one track of the tape recorder.
5. Placement of the individuals: No major problems should arise with seated speakers. The situation becomes more difficult, however, if subjects change positions often. In this case, an omnidirectional microphone or the use of lavaliere microphones might be an appropriate solution. Still another possibility consists of employing an assistant whose task involves following the subjects with the microphone as they move around. But this latter procedure is problematic, especially if recordings are to be made as unobtrusively as possible.

Prerequisites for high-quality sound recording

If high-quality recordings are not required, one of the cheap microphones often included in video sets or as an accessory to audio cassette recorders may be used. It should be emphasized, however, that turning on the recorder is really not all there is to audio recording. Producing high-quality sound recordings is a totally different (and difficult) matter. Some of the prerequisites for high-quality sound recording are summarized in Table A.2.

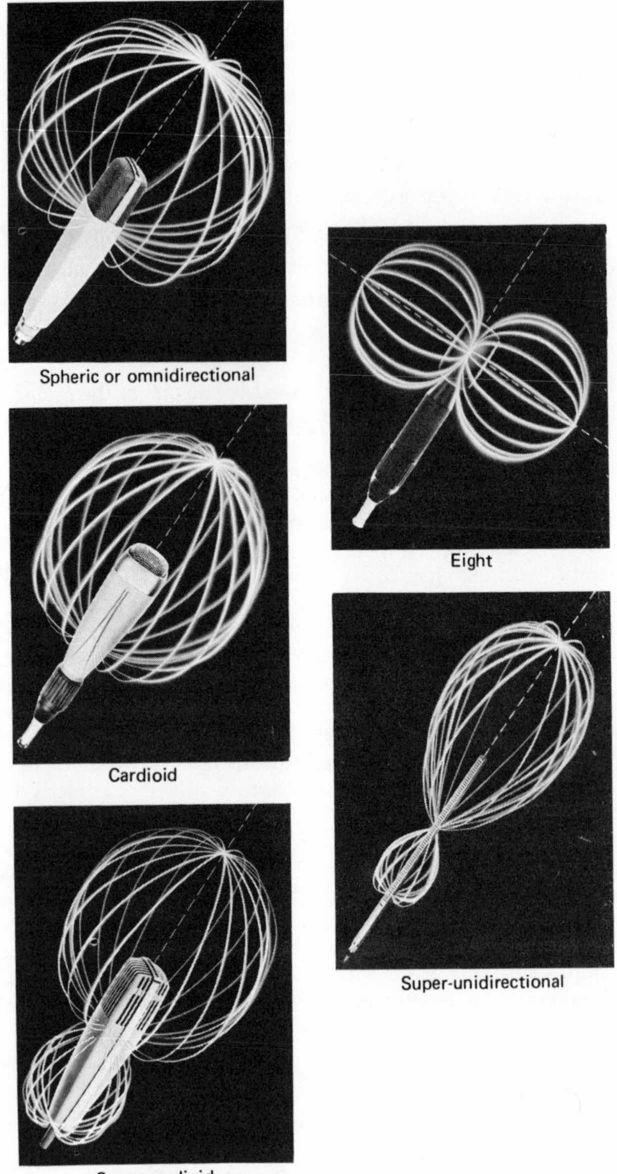

Figure A.5. Direction characteristics of various microphones. (Photographs copyright by Sennheiser Co., West Germany).

Table A.2. *Prerequisites for high-quality sound recording*

Recommended equipment and procedure	Potential trouble
Basic decisions	
Use stereo recording with separate channels when recording two or more speakers whose speech is to be analyzed separately.	With mono recording, analysis of speech of individual speakers may be impossible. It may even be difficult to transcribe the speakers' utterances.
Use open-reel recorder to obtain high-quality sound recording and to allow splicing and other manual tape manipulations like localizing events by manually turning the reels.	Splicing will be difficult if not impossible when using cassettes. Owing to the thin and narrow tapes used in cassettes, the sound quality of the recording is generally not acceptable (low cross-talk attenuation, low signal-to-noise ratio) unless the most advanced systems are used.
Use half-track recording for higher dynamic range and higher cross-talk attenuation, more protection against dropouts.	Quarter-track recording has the same disadvantages as cassettes.
Use the same recorder (or at least the same type) for all recordings in a study.	Different recorders will show differences in recording characteristics (different phase shifting, etc.) that might prohibit comparisons of speech data (the situation will be worse if different types of recorders are used).
Tape	
Use high-quality low-noise tape (standard or double-play).	Cheap tapes will show more dropouts, lower abrasion resistance, and lower signal-to-noise ratio. Super long-playing tapes are very thin and will show a high print-through ratio.
Use high tape speed (19 cm/sec or 38 cm/sec, i.e., 7.5 in./sec or 15 in./sec).	Lower tape speed will reduce frequency range and make it difficult to localize segments when splicing.
Do not copy tapes too often.	Every duplication reduces sound quality, increases noise and hum.
Do not store recorded tapes near strong magnetic fields or under high temperature.	Magnetic fields distort the recorded signal; high temperature raises the print-through ratio.
Level control	
Use manual level control to obtain high sound quality.	Automatic level control will amplify unwanted sounds and background noise, especially in speech pauses. Moreover, sound dynamics will be leveled.

Table A.2 *(cont.)*

Recommended equipment and procedure	Potential trouble
Use fixed level if possible. Mark selected level on level control to be sure.	Variable level will not allow comparisons of intensity, etc., between different speakers.
Test the level before starting the recording and constantly check it while recording.	Otherwise, levels too high or too low may be selected, resulting in distorted or weak speech signals. The appropriate level depends on the loudness range expected. Allow for a margin to comprehend extremely loud sounds.
Video sound	
Use an external microphone for acceptable sound quality on the videotape.	Built-in camera microphones are usually of poor quality. Recordings may be impaired by wind or camera vibrations and sounds. The camera may be too far away from the sound source.
Separate sound recording on a tape recorder.	The frequency range of video sound recordings (100–10,000 Hz) is sufficient for some purposes, but in any case worse than audiotape recording and generally not sufficient for acoustic analysis. Copying sound from videotape reduces quality further.
Microphone characteristics	
Choose appropriate microphone characteristics (i.e., omnidirectional, unidirectional, cardioid, etc.).	Choice of inappropriate characteristics can affect the recording, for instance, if a person moves out of range of a unidirectional microphone.
Choose low-impedance microphones, if the microphone is placed more than 3 m away from the recorder (e.g., if the recorder has to be hidden).	High-impedance microphones may produce a loss of higher frequencies and hum; cable length cannot exceed 3 m.
Use a high-quality dynamic or condenser microphone.	Cheap microphones produce sound distortions and are less sensitive, especially for higher frequencies. Take care when using condenser microphones: They are comparatively fragile, and sound bursts may result in overload.
Use lavaliere microphones for optimal channel separation and constant speaker-to-microphone distance.	With stationary microphones the speaker-to-microphone distance will vary with speaker movements. The speaker may even move out of the range of a fixed microphone. Variable speaker-to-microphone distance will

Table A.2 *(cont.)*

Recommended equipment and procedure	Potential trouble
	result in intensity changes, prohibiting comparisons between speakers with respect to, e.g., loudness of the voice.
Record stationary speakers with a fixed microphone, if recording without the speaker's knowledge.	Fixed microphones (if hidden or partly concealed) are less obtrusive than lavaliere microphones. Moreover, attaching lavaliere microphones may be a problem, and speakers may handle cables, thus producing unwanted noise.
Conditions at recording site	
Try to isolate from outside sound. If impossible, record during quiet periods. Turn off air conditioners and other equipment with constant mechanical noise.	Background noise will impair sound quality.
Use curtains and other sound-absorbing materials to reduce sound reflections.	Reflections will disturb the sound signal.
Place the microphone on a good solid stand, or at least isolate it from floor sounds by placing it on a felt pad.	Otherwise, vibrations, jolts, etc., will impair sound quality.
Check amplifiers, cables, etc. for alternating current hum. If necessary use screens to shut off hum and check connectors for wrong pin wiring.	Otherwise, the 50-Hz (or 60-Hz) hum will disturb the sound signal.
Use a soundproof chamber to obtain perfect sound quality for sophisticated acoustic analysis.	Acoustic chambers can only be used for some types of experiments. Their obtrusiveness may cause speakers to change their speech; some persons may react with fright or feel uncomfortable in such unfamiliar surroundings.

Figure A.6 demonstrates the considerable influence of the type of recording equipment on sound quality. Three power spectra (see Scherer, Section 4.6) for silent portions of a tape recording (i.e., speech pauses) are shown. These spectra show how sound quality deteriorates, owing to the presence of noise in the spectrum, when one is recording with a video recorder or a small portable audio cassette recorder instead of a semiprofessional recorder. The sound quality of video recorders is vastly inferior to that of audio tape recorders and almost never allows acoustic analyses. As Figure A.6 shows, strong noise energy is present

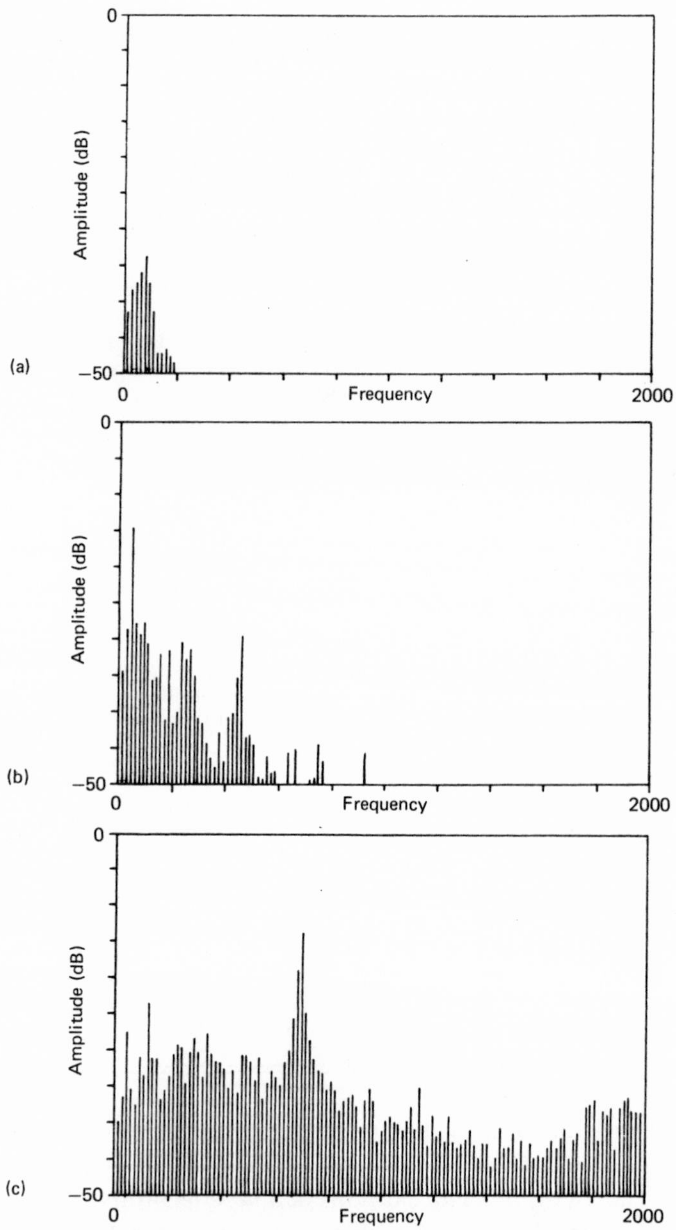

Figure A.6. Noise spectra during silent pauses for (a) high-quality master recording on ReVox A700, (b) Uher 4000 recording copied onto ReVox A700, and (c) SONY AV-3670CE video sound recording copied onto ReVox A77.

in those frequency regions in which one normally finds spectral energy for speech sounds. This may result in serious artifacts if the video soundtrack is subjected to acoustic analysis.

At this point it should be stressed again that the recommendations mentioned are not all applicable to each project and each recording situation. However, at any time when high-quality recordings are to be made, some prerequisites should be met: for example, half-track recording, high recording speed, and use of the appropriate type of microphone as well as high-quality tape.

These matters are especially important when recording in the field. Though good audio recordings are very difficult to obtain in the field, one can often make some minor adjustments, at little additional expenditure, that may greatly improve the quality of the recording. Curtains or other soft materials should be used to cover bare walls or windows to avoid sound reflections. The microphone should be placed on a free-standing tripod or a felt pad to isolate it against jolts and vibrations.

A.5. Troubleshooting

This section is devoted to the difficulties encountered during and after audiovisual recording. The origins of and reasons for various failures and breakdowns described cannot be discussed exhaustively, because many factors may account for defective picture and sound recordings. The diverse distortions of the video or sound signals and other problems discussed here are due to rather common mistakes in operating the equipment; in most cases they can be quite easily detected and corrected.

Video

Figure A.7 lists some of the major distortions one may encounter in video recording, together with the probable causes for the distortions. Often these problems can be solved without consulting a technician.

Basically three things may happen: First, no picture appears at all. This is often the easiest problem to solve. In many cases the reason is that a cable is connected to a wrong socket, a switch is in the wrong position, the recorder or the camera has not been turned to "on," the level control has been turned to "off," or (as silly as it sounds) the lens cap has not been removed. The best thing to do is to check all connections, switch positions, power supplies, and so on once again.

Second, the synchronization of the video picture, that is, the electronic equivalent to film's sprocket holes, does not function properly; as a result, diagonal lines and stripes cross the screen. This problem is often

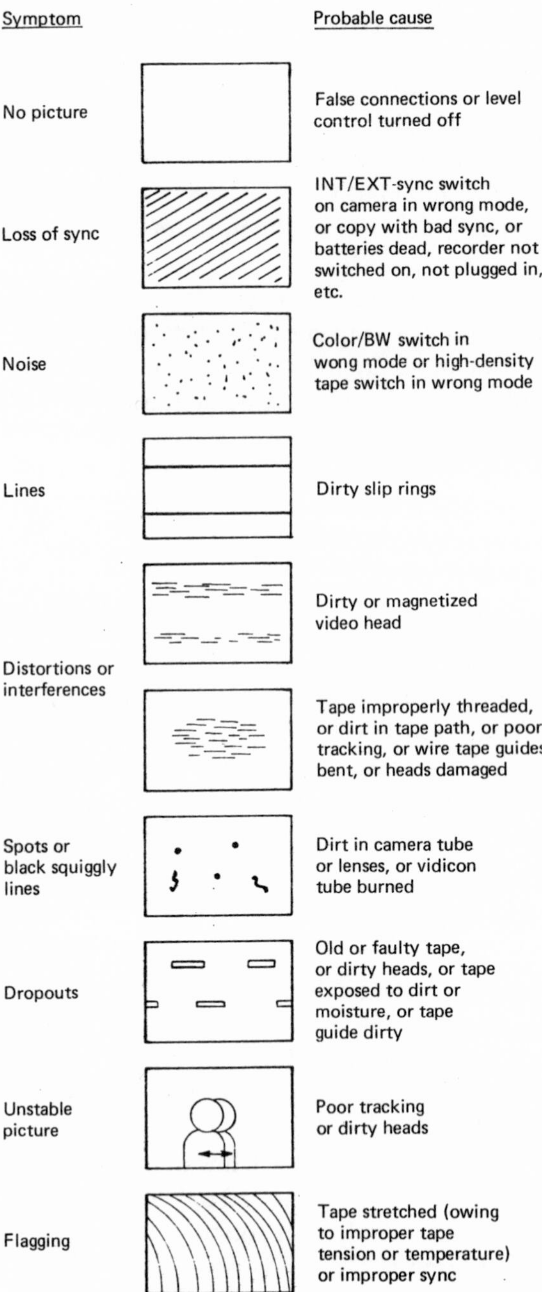

Symptom
Probable cause
No picture
False connections or level control turned off
Loss of sync
INT/EXT-sync switch on camera in wrong mode, or copy with bad sync, or batteries dead, recorder not switched on, not plugged in, etc.
Noise
Color/BW switch in wong mode or high-density tape switch in wrong mode
Lines
Dirty slip rings
Distortions or interferences
Dirty or magnetized video head
Tape improperly threaded, or dirt in tape path, or poor tracking, or wire tape guides bent, or heads damaged
Spots or black squiggly lines
Dirt in camera tube or lenses, or vidicon tube burned
Dropouts
Old or faulty tape, or dirty heads, or tape exposed to dirt or moisture, or tape guide dirty
Unstable picture
Poor tracking or dirty heads
Flagging
Tape stretched (owing to improper tape tension or temperature) or improper sync

Figure A.7. Troubleshooting video: major symptoms and their probable causes.

due to an incorrect position of the sync switch, or in more severe cases to faulty tracking or skewing. Faulty tracking may occur, for instance, if the tape has been exposed to high temperatures (e.g., by being left on a radiator!), because heat causes the entire tape or parts of it to stretch, thus changing the distances between successive sync impulses. This in turn renders an adequate replay of the tape impossible. When these damages have become permanent, there is not much of a chance to repair them, unless a time-base generator can be used to correct the inappropriate sync signal.

The third problem, the one occuring most often when working with video, is that distortions appear in the picture during recording or replay. These may take the form of little dots, black lines, black-and-white stripes, black squiggly lines or dots, or foggy structures. The first thing to do in these cases is to clean the recorder, especially the video recording heads, the slip rings, and the tape path, and see whether the distortions or interferences disappear. Some distortions may be caused by incorrect switch positions (for instance, the color/black-and-white switch or the high-density tape switch may be in the wrong position). Others may be due to a damaged tape. If the tape has been exposed to dirt or moisture, dropouts may occur; it is therefore important to handle a videotape as infrequently as possible and never to leave it on a recorder or exposed to dirt, moisture, or cigarette smoke. Finally, black spots and squiggly lines in the picture may be due either to dirt outside or inside the lenses or within the camera or to burned-in spots in the camera tube. Often these burns are only temporary and will disappear after some time. Others may be permanent, in which case the only practical, although expensive, solution is to exchange the camera tube. The camera should therefore never be directed to very bright surfaces, lamps, or the sun, and it should be covered with the lens cap when not in use. In addition, the iris should be left closed or, if this is not possible, turned to the highest f-stop, that is, the smallest lens opening available.

Most of these problems can usually be solved by such simple procedures as cleaning the heads or checking connections and switches. Of course, some other problems, as for instance burned tubes or damaged recording heads, can be solved only by replacing the respective parts of the camera or the recorder.

Generally, before calling for service, it is worth while to follow some very simple checking and cleaning procedures:

1. Check all connections, switches, and controls.
2. Clean the heads, the slip rings, and the tape path.

3. Check whether the tape is properly threaded.
4. Clean the lenses and check the camera.
5. Try the recording again with a new tape; perhaps only the tape is damaged, because of long usage, dirt, or stretching.

Audio

Troubleshooting procedures for audio recording are basically the same as for video recording. An additional problem is no sound at all, here owing either to faulty connections, to empty batteries in a condenser microphone, or to audio controls turned off. Furthermore, distortions, humming, noise in the sound signal, wow, dropouts, or loss of higher frequencies may appear. Some of these difficulties in audio recording, together with their probable causes, are listed in Table A.3.

Possible solutions and strategies are largely the same as with video recording:

1. Check all connections, switches, and controls.
2. Clean and demagnetize the recording heads.
3. Check whether the tape is properly threaded.
4. Try the recording again with a new tape.
5. Check the level control; perhaps the level is too high (distorted sound) or too low (noise in the signal).
6. Check the microphone, especially batteries in condenser microphones.
7. If alternating current hum or radio noise disturbs the signal, check amplifiers, cables, and connectors (their pin wiring may be faulty), and use screens to shut off the interferences. Often damaged cables, either broken or bent or with faulty isolation, are an important source of malfunction.

Usually, electronic devices such as video or audio recorders are very delicate instruments that can easily be damaged by imprudent actions or lack of care. Cables have to be connected accurately, and switches and controls have to be set to the appropriate positions. This implies that before starting the actual recording one should produce test recordings to detect possible problems. In any case, pretesting should be mandatory, because everything has to work properly during the actual recording.

Finally, reports often indicate that equipment breakdowns and repair expenses increase with the number of people who use audiovisual equipment. People operating the equipment should be well trained: Training and know-how are the best safeguard against failure, breakdown, and trouble caused by technical naiveté, carelessness, or ignorance of the principles of the equipment employed.

A.6. Field recordings

In field recording, each situation confronts the researcher with new problems. It often will not be possible to arrange for optimal lighting; instead, one must make do with the light available, however scanty it

Table A.3. *Troubleshooting audio: major symptoms and their probable causes*

Symptom	Probable cause
Loss of sound	Faulty microphone connections or reversed battery in condenser microphone; audio controls turned off
Distorted sound	Overloading (level too high); recording head or recording amplifier faulty
Hum	Wrong impedance of microphone; pins wired inadequately
Noise	Level too low
Speed variations, wow	Motors, tape guides, or tape tension faulty; tape stretched
Dropouts	Tape faulty
Loss of higher frequencies, muffled hollow sound	Heads dirty or magnetized
Radio noise in audio	Radio station nearby; cables or connectors faulty

may be for recording purposes. It will rarely be possible either to isolate the recording site from background noises or to create all the conditions listed in this appendix as necessary to guarantee high-quality sound recording. Placement of camera(s), microphone(s), and of course recorder(s) and control monitor(s) will also frequently prove to be difficult. These problems often make it impossible to carry out the originally planned recording.

In addition, other difficulties related to either indoor or outdoor recording must be overcome. Indoor shots often pose problems of lighting and camera placement, especially if subjects' attention should not be focused on the camera. Placement of recorders in the room where shooting is to take place may cause additional problems, because of both their visibility and the noise of operation. On the other hand, it may not be possible to take advantage of an adjacent room in order to set up the recorders. Such a room may not be available, and furthermore, the use of long cables required by the distance from cameras and microphones to the recorders creates problems in and of itself.

With respect to audio recording, lighting, and type of shot, outdoor recordings must be planned carefully in advance. The probability of background noises, the occurrence of bright, reflecting surfaces, and the amount of sunshine have to be taken into account. Although it is possible to move as far away as necessary from the subject by employing a zoom lens, for instance, the fact must not be overlooked that the greater the camera-to-object distance, the more people will tend to walk between camera and focal object, thus ruining parts of the recording.

Some steps that might be taken to improve the quality of indoor recording have already been mentioned. One can exchange weak light bulbs in the lamps for stronger ones or add portable spotlights to improve lighting conditions. Or one can select a microphone to fit the special situational demands, use curtains and other materials as sound shields, or place the microphone on a felt pad to prevent vibrations. Placement of camera, microphone, and recorder can be planned to some degree before the actual recording. Test recordings can be made to find the optimal recording setup. Furniture can be rearranged to permit better and possibly less obtrusive camera placement.

When making outdoor recordings, the optimal camera-to-object distance has to be calculated, depending on whether a hidden camera will be used and whether a zoom lens or a fixed-focus lens will be employed. If subjects move around to a large degree, one must take into account that the depth of field is larger when the camera-to-object distance is greater, all other factors held constant. Outdoor audio recording will often pose major problems. An important decision is whether to use the built-in camera microphone, knowing that the recordings will get worse with increasing camera-to-object distance, or to use an external microphone. If it is not possible to place the microphone near the speaker, a unidirectional microphone is necessary, just as a windshield for the microphone may be mandatory in order to reduce noises created by the wind.

Most problems in field and studio recordings are generally easier to solve if the camera or the microphone does not need to be hidden, that is, if unobtrusive recording is not necessary. On the other hand, as soon as camera and microphone need to be hidden so that the recording can be made surreptitiously, various difficulties arise.

It is possible to hide or cover the recording equipment in ingenious ways, for example, behind one-way mirrors, in cupboards, behind bookshelves, in suitcases, and behind parked cars, trees, and so on. The more creative the researcher, the more successful the attempt will be. If it is essential for the success of a study that subjects not discover that they are being recorded, the researcher has to make sure subsequently that indeed they have not done so. Simple questioning after the recording has been completed may not be sufficient, because the demand characteristics of the situation may lead some subjects to deny discovery of the recording instruments. Sophisticated debriefing procedures as described by Orne (1962) may have to be used to assure that the recording went undetected.

Another method might be to expose camera and microphone to subjects, but to give them time to adjust to the uncomfortable situation. In addition, subjects might not be told when recording will take place. Once subjects have become acquainted with the situation, the recording may begin. Finally, technical equipment like the angle lenses used by Eibl-Eibesfeldt (1979), described shortly, or mirrors and other similar devices may be used; or camera and microphone may be placed at such a great distance from the subjects that they do not recognize the situation as one in which recording is taking place (this procedure requires the use of zoom lenses and super-unidirectional microphones).

There are problems inherent in all these solutions, however. For one thing, it is often difficult to find a place to hide equipment. Additionally, it is not yet clear whether subjects can get accustomed to cameras at all, or whether even after a long time of getting accustomed to the recording situation, their behavior will still be affected in an uncontrollable manner. Although little is known about such effects, some recent studies show that behavior indeed changes when subjects are aware of being observed (see Kleck, Vaughan, Cartwright-Smith, Vaughan, Colby, & Lanzetta, 1976).

Angle lenses consist of a dummy lens pointing in a misleading direction and a real lens, through which light reaches the film from the side of the lens system. With such lenses it is possible to record without aiming the camera directly at the object to be recorded. It may be useful to employ these lenses under certain circumstances, but it may look rather ridiculous and be highly obtrusive, making subjects even more suspicious if the camera aims at a place where absolutely nothing is happening. Placing the camera and microphone at a great distance from the subjects may be a solution, but usually problems with sound recording will occur, other people will mask the person or scene to be recorded, or it will prove difficult to follow subjects with the camera or the microphone.

A.7. Ethical concerns

Hiding cameras or recording surreptitiously poses more than technical problems, however. Ethical aspects have to be considered carefully in connection with the research goals. A visible camera or microphone, the knowledge of being recorded, and explicit information about the nature of an experiment may of course change subjects' behavior. It is unknown how behavior is affected by the recording situation or which particular aspects of behavior change to produce artifacts and patterns of behavior resulting only from the recording situation. As a result, experimental manipulation, genuineness of behavior, and factors owing to recording may be hopelessly intermingled, making the record useless for research purposes. As long as the possible effects of the awareness of being recorded are not known to a greater extent, the hidden camera has to be used from time to time.

Subject's consent

Sometimes cameras are hidden, subjects are not informed that they are being recorded, and cover stories are told to deceive them about the goals of the study. The main objection to such procedures is that the researcher takes responsibility for the subjects when making a permanent record of them. This does not imply that recording must necessarily be dangerous for the subject. Obviously, this is not often the case, and most subjects will probably not care much about what is done with their records. Nevertheless, ethical issues as well as legal problems concerning protection of the rights of persons have to be considered (see APA Committee on Ethical Standards in Psychological Research, 1973).

In certain situations, for instance, in the clinical area, this responsibility has to be considered very carefully. Subjects may assume responsibility for themselves when they have known about the recording from the very beginning, when they are given a chance to watch and listen to the tapes, and when they are able to decide on this basis whether to have the tapes erased or whether to give written consent for their usage. This procedure might be problematic with heavily disturbed patients, who are not responsible for their actions and thus are not able to give consent. In these cases, consent should be given by a legal representative of the patient, or the patient should have a chance to watch and listen to the tapes after successful therapy and to give or refuse consent after the event. This written consent should include all information necessary for the subject to be able to evaluate what will be done with the tapes. Such a consent form might include the following points:

1. Who will have access to the records?
2. Will the subject, after having given initial consent, be able to withdraw it later?
3. Does the consent include an agreement for a presentation of the records at congresses, at other institutions, or in publications? If so, which parts of the records may be shown?
4. What masking techniques (effect generators to cover the region around the eyes, black-and-white reversal in video, removal of all names and other recognizable references, electronic voice changes, etc.) are to be used?
5. Will the tapes be erased or destroyed after the research project is finished?

6. Will the subject be able to view and approve any demonstrat educational films, and so on that include his or her records?

Often recording with the subject's full knowledge presents because many records become worthless once subjects are a they are being taped or filmed. Thus the researcher must first consider whether it is essential to record subjects without th knowledge. If it is decided that recording without prior co necessary, subjects must be carefully debriefed after the recording. should view the tapes, decide if they should be erased, and either ag or refuse to sign a written consent. If consent is refused, the tapes hav to be erased immediately.

Another point to consider, especially in clinical settings, is that the recording situation itself might be harmful to subjects. If negative reactions of the patient are to be expected, no recording should be made under any circumstances. Psychiatric patients should never be deceived about being recorded. The therapeutic process runs the risk of being severely disturbed if the patient discovers that he or she has been cheated by a therapist who, after assuring the patient that no recording would take place, proceeded to make recordings.

To sum up, questions dealing with the unobtrusiveness of the recording, ethical issues related to subject, privacy, and the possibility that the mere process of recording may in and of itself be harmful to subjects must be carefully considered before the specifics of the project are decided. A detailed discussion of these topics may be found in Lavender, Davis, and Graber (1979), in the Canada Council *Report on Ethics* (1977), in Rosenbaum (1970), and in Wolstenholme and O'Connor (1966).

Making records accessible to the public

A final problem deserves some attention. Frequently projects last for years. Recordings may have been made, subjects may have signed written consent forms, and then, years later, somebody plans to show some of the material during a congress, to send some of the tapes to a fellow researcher for further analyses, or to use some of the material as illustrations in a publication. Former subjects might not have considered these possibilities when signing consent forms. At this point it might be impossible to contact them to get renewed consent. To prevent such situations, these issues should be included in the original consent document. Obviously, not all things that could possibly be done with the records can be included in such forms; therefore, general agreements between subject and researcher should be included, concerning, for instance, the possibility of the tapes being given to other researchers or their use for demonstration or illustration purposes. The agreement might contain the researcher's assurance that he or she will take full responsibility for what is done with the tapes. This responsibility might include the researcher's insistence that all viewers and listeners who have access to the tapes – including participants at conferences or workshops where records are presented – sign an agreement that they will respect the subject's privacy (i.e., not make use of the information, not talk to other persons about the recordings, etc.). Furthermore, the researcher should take care in preparing demonstration and illustration materials. Some rules can be formulated concerning the accessibility of records to the public:

First, only parts of the record that do not contain any confidential, personal, or incriminating information about the subject should be used. This decision obviously must be made by the researcher, whose responsibility is to protect the subject's privacy.

Second, masking techniques should be used if necessary. They may be especially important when films or videotapes are shown. Pictures are more easily recognized and retained than vocal recordings, and therefore masks might be superimposed on the picture. A black-and-white reversal is easy in video. A speaker's voice, though less recognizable than the face, may be masked, too, by using filters or electronic voice distortion.

In addition, names and all other intimate references may be eliminated from the audio track by replacing them with sounds produced by a sound generator. Finally, written transcripts may be masked by changing names or locations.

Recording imposes a certain responsibility on the researcher, especially when a hidden camera is used. Although audiovisual records are an essential tool for psychological, educational, and psychiatric research, becoming even more valuable as additional areas of application are discovered, it should be stressed that audiovisual records can become a dangerous instrument if used irresponsibly. Records should not be used in a way that could prove harmful, insulting, or discriminating to subjects, even if they will never view the record or find out what has been done with it.

A.8. Selected sources on technical aspects of audiovisual recording

In order to provide the reader with some additional information, a list of selected references dealing with technical aspects of audiovisual recording is provided in this section. Most of these references have been written for laypersons and devote much space to the most popular usages of recording: videotaping friends and relatives, recording TV programs, playing prerecorded tapes, and the like. An advantage of this popular treatment is that the technical aspects are described in a very comprehensible manner. Some of the books listed here provided a great deal of assistance in the preparation of this appendix.

Literature covering the use of audiovisual media in scientific research and the special problems associated with this usage is difficult to find, one important exception being Berger's *Videotape techniques in psychiatric training and treatment*, which is by now almost a classic. Important information can often be found in newsletters distributed by researchers interested in media usage in the social sciences, and some of these newsletters are therefore included.

Books and articles

Bensinger, C. *Petersen's guide to video tape recording*. Los Angeles: Petersen, 1973.

Bensinger, C. *The home video hand book*. Santa Barbara, Calif.: Esselte Video, 1979.

Bensinger, C. *The video guide*. Santa Barbara, Calif.: Esselte Video, 1979.

Berger, M. M. (Ed.). *Videotape techniques in psychiatric training and treatment*. New York: Brunner-Mazel, 1970.

Cary, M. S. Comparing film and videotape. *Environmental Psychology and Nonverbal Behavior*, 1979, *3*, 243–247.

Ekman, P., & Friesen, W. V. A tool for the analysis of motion picture film or videotape. *American Psychologist*, 1969, *44*, 240–243.

Fahry, D., & Palme, K. *VideoTechnik* (2 vols.). Munich: Oldenbourg, 1979.

Fleischer, D. *Praxis der Video-Aufzeichung*. Berlin: Siemens AG, 1974.

Harwood, D. *Video as a second language: How to make a video documentary*. Syosset, N.Y.: VTR Publishing, 1978.

Harwood, D. *Everything you always wanted to know about portable videotape recording*. Syosset, N.Y.: VTR Publishing, 1978.

La Bruzzo, R. The what and how of video hardware and tape. In M. M. Berger (Ed.), *Videotape techniques in psychiatric training and treatment*. New York: Brunner-Mazel, 1970.

Lachenbruch, D. *Videocassette recorders: The complete home guide*. New York: Everest House, 1979.

Lechenauer, G. *Videomachen*. Hamburg: Rowohlt, 1979.

Marsh, K. *Independent video*. San Francisco: Straight Arrow, 1973.

Murray, M. *The videotape book*. New York: Taplinger, 1975.

Oliver, W. *Introduction to video-recording*. London: Foulsham, 1971.

Onder, J. J. *The manual of psychiatric television: Theory, practice, imagination*. Ann Arbor: Maynard House, 1970.

Price, J. *Video visions*. New York: New American Library, 1979.

Robinson, J. F., & Beards, P. H. *Using video tape*. London, 1976.

Robinson, R. *The video primer: Equipment, production, and concepts*. New York: Link Books, 1974.

Scheflen, A. E., Kendon, A., & Schaeffer, J. On the choice of audiovisual media.

In M. M. Berger (Ed.), *Videotape techniques in psychiatric training and treatment*. New York: Brunner-Mazel, 1970.

United Business Publications. *The Video handbook* (3rd ed.). New York: United Business Publications, 1977.

Video CCWG. *Video Handbuch*. Berlin: Büro der Off-Kudamm-Kinos, 1975.

Video Freex. *The Spaghetti City Video Manual*. New York: Praeger, 1973.

Weiner, P. *Making the media revolution*. New York: Macmillan, 1973.

Williams, R. L. *Television production: A vocational approach*. Salt Lake City: Vision Co., 1976.

Wilmer, H. A. Technical and artistic aspects of videotape in psychiatric teaching. *Journal of Nervous and Mental Disease*, 1967, *144*, 207–223.

Zettl, H. *Television production handbook*. Belmont, Calif.: Wadsworth, 1977.

Journals and newsletters

Audiovision: Das Medienmagazin. Monthly journal. Hamburg: Trimedia.

Audiovision in Psychiatrie und Psychotherapie. Newsletter. G. Romahn, Ed., Abt. Psychiatrie–Neurologie des Kindes- und Jugendalters, Planetenallee 33, D-1000 Berlin 19, West Germany.

Human ethology. Newsletter. Cheril Travis, Ed., Dept. of Psychology, University of Tennessee, Knoxville, Tenn. 37916, USA.

Kinesis. Newsletter. Institute for Nonverbal Communication Research, 25 West 86th St., New York, N.Y. 10024, USA.

Nonverbal components of communication. Newsletter. Rosalyn Lindner, Ed., Dept. of Geography/Sociology, State University of New York at Buffalo, 1300 Elmwood Ave., Buffalo, N.Y. 14222, USA.

TV in psychiatry. Newsletter. Dr. L. Thyhurst, Ed., Department of Psychiatry, University of British Columbia, 2075 Westbrook Mall, Vancouver, B.C. V6T 1W5, Canada.

Video. Quarterly journal. Stuttgart: Vereinigte Motor Verlage.

Video for interaction research and training users group (VIRTUG). Newsletter. Angela Summerfield, Ed., Dept. of Psychology, Birkbeck College, Malet Street, London WC1E 7HX, Great Britain.

Videography. Monthly journal. New York: United Business Publications.

Video-Informationen. Newsletter. Dr. Heiner Ellgring, Coeditor, Max-Planck-Institut für Psychiatrie, Kraepelinstr. 10, D-8000 München, West Germany; Harald Wallbott, Coeditor, Justus-Liebig-Universität, Fachbereich 06, Otto-Behaghelstr. 10F, D-6300 Giessen, West Germany.

Acknowledgment

The author wishes to thank the following persons for their valuable comments and suggestions: Paul Ekman, Heiner Ellgring, Wallace Friesen, Klaus Scherer, Robin Shaye, Monika Wallbott, and Harald Zeddies.

Note

1 Drawings (see Efron, 1941/1972) and still photographs (see Ekman, 1972) also have been used frequently in nonverbal communication research. These "static" techniques will not be discussed here.

References

American Psychological Association Ad hoc Committee on Ethical Standards in Psychological Research. *Ethical principles in the condust of research with human participants.* Washington, D.C.: American Psychological Association, 1973.

Canada Council. *Report of the consultative group on ethics.* Ottawa: Canada Council, 1977.

Efron, D. *Gesture and environment.* New York: King's Crown, 1941. (Reprinted as *Gesture, race and culture.* The Hague: Mouton, 1972.)

Eibl-Eibesfeldt, I. Similarities and differences between cultures in expressive movements. In S. Weitz (Ed.), *Nonverbal communication: Readings with commentary* (2nd ed.). New York: Oxford University Press, 1979.

Ekman, P. Universals and cultural differences in facial expression of emotion. In J. Cole (Ed.), *Nebraska Symposium on Motivation* (Vol. 19). Lincoln: University of Nebraska Press, 1972.

Ekman, P., Friesen, W. V., & Taussig, T. G. VID-R and SCAN: Tools and methods for the automated analysis of visual records. In G. Gerbner, D. R. Holsti, K. Krippendorf, W. J. Paisley, & P. J. Stone (Eds.), *The analysis of communication content.* New York: Wiley, 1969.

Kendon, A. Some theoretical and methodological aspects of the use of film in the study of social interaction. In G. P. Ginsburg (Ed.), *Emerging strategies in social psychological research.* Chichester: Wiley, 1979.

Kleck, R. E., Vaughan, R. C., Cartwright-Smith, J., Vaughan, K. B., Colby, C. Z., & Lanzetta, J. T. Effects of being observed on expressive, subjective, and physiological responses to painful stimuli. *Journal of Personality and Social Psychology,* 1976, *34,* 1211–1218.

Lavender, J., Davis, M., & Graber, E. Film/video research recordings: Ethical issues. *Kinesis,* 1979, 1, 9–20.

Orne, M. T. On the social psychology of the psychological experiment. *American Psychologist,* 1962, *17,* 776–783.

Rosenbaum, M. The issues of privacy and priveleged communication. In M. M. Berger (Ed.), *Videotape techniques in psychiatric training and treatment.* New York: Brunner-Mazel, 1970.

Wolstenholme, G., & O'Connor, M. (Eds.). *Ethics in medical progress.* Boston: Little Brown, 1966.

Name index

Subject index

152.384 H191c1 AAL-9019
050101 000
Handbook of methods in nonverb
0 0003 0170433 4
Lyndon State College